CHRIST THE SAVIOR

A Commentary on the Third Part of St. Thomas' Theological Summa

By the

REV. REGINALD GARRIGOU-LAGRANGE, O.P.

Translated by

DOM BEDE ROSE, O.S.B., S.T.D.

B. HERDER BOOK CO.

15 & 17 SOUTH BROADWAY, ST. LOUIS 2, MO.

AND

33 QUEEN SQUARE, LONDON, W. C.

1950

NIHIL OBSTAT

Abbatia Montis Angelorum

P. Albertus Baumann, O.S.B.

Censor Deputatus

IMPRIMI POTEST

✠ *Thomas Meier, O.S.B.*

Abbas

Die 27 Maii, 1949

NIHIL OBSTAT

William M. Drumm

Censor Librorum

IMPRIMATUR

✠ *Joseph E. Ritter*

Archiepiscopus

Sti. Ludovici, die 10a mensis Aprilis, 1950

Vail-Ballou Press, Inc., Binghamton and New York

Contents

Part I

THE INCARNATION

CHAPTER PAGE

Preface 1

Prologue 5

I. The Mystery and Fact of the Incarnation 10

II. The Possibility of the Incarnation 34

III. The Fitness of the Incarnation 44

IV. The Mode of the Union of the Word Incarnate . . 108

V. The Mode of the Union on the Part of the Person Assuming 200

VI. The Mode of the Union on the Part of the Human Nature Assumed 212

VII. The Mode of the Union Concerning the Parts of the Human Nature Assumed 225

VIII. The Order of Assumption 232

IX. The Things Co-assumed. The Grace of Christ . . . 247

X. Christ's Grace as Head of the Church 310

XI. Christ's Knowledge in General and His Power of Contemplation 341

XII. The Beatific Knowledge of Christ's Soul 370

XIII. The Infused Knowledge of Christ's Soul 376

XIV. The Acquired Knowledge of Christ's Soul 385

XV. The Power of Christ's Soul 390

XVI. The Bodily Defects Assumed by the Son of God . . 401

XVII. The Defects of Soul Assumed by Christ 407

XVIII. The Consequences of the Hypostatic Union . . . 420

XIX. What Pertains Commonly to Christ's Unity of Being 427

CHAPTER PAGE

XX. What Pertains to the Unity of Christ as Regards His Will . . . 439
XXI. Christ's Operation and His Merits . . . 472
XXII. Christ's Relation to the Father . . . 487
XXIII. Christ's Prayer . . . 489
XXIV. The Priesthood of Christ . . . 492
XXV. The Adoption of Christ . . . 500
XXVI. The Predestination of Christ . . . 507
XXVII. The Adoration of Christ . . . 516
XXVIII. Christ the Mediator . . . 524

Part II

THE REDEMPTION

XXIX. Prefatory Remarks . . . 531
XXX. Testimony of Sacred Scripture and Tradition . . . 539
XXXI. Christ's Passion . . . 547
XXXII. The Efficient Cause of Christ's Passion . . . 555
XXXIII. The Efficiency of Christ's Passion . . . 562
XXXIV. The Effects of Christ's Passion and the Universality of Redemption . . . 601
XXXV. The Sublime Mystery of Redemption inasmuch as It is a Mystery of Love . . . 608
XXXVI. Christ's Threefold Victory . . . 645
XXXVII. Christ's Death and Descent into Hell . . . 655
XXXVIII. Christ's Resurrection and Ascension . . . 663
XXXIX. Christ the King, Judge, and Head of the Blessed . . . 674
XL. Compendium of Mariology . . . 690

Appendix. The Definability of the Blessed Virgin Mary's Assumption . . . 719

Index . . . 727

PART I

THE INCARNATION

PREFACE

WE have already published treatises on the One God, the Triune God, the Creator, and the Holy Eucharist. These have been presented in the form of a commentary on the teaching of St. Thomas in his *Theological Summa*. It is the purpose of the present treatise on Christ the Savior to explain, in accordance with the more common interpretation of the Thomists, the teaching of St. Thomas on the motive of the Incarnation, the hypostatic union, and its effects. We have discussed at length the more difficult problems, such as the reconciliation of freedom with absolute impeccability in Christ, the intrinsically infinite value of His merits and satisfaction, His predestination with reference to ours, inasmuch as He is the first of the predestined, and the reconciliation, during the Passion, of the presence of extreme sorrow with supreme happiness experienced by our Lord in the summit of His soul.

In all these problems our wish has been to manifest the unity of Christ inasmuch as He is one personal Being, although He has two really distinct and infinitely different natures. Hence the Person of Christ constitutes the one and only principle of all His theandric operations.

In all these questions St. Thomas, according to his custom, wonderfully preserved the principle of economy [1] by reducing all things to the same principles and in the ultimate analysis to the one and only fundamental principle. Similarly, with reference to the Passion everything is reduced to the principle of the plenitude of grace. This plenitude, on the one hand, was the cause in the summit of our Lord's soul of the beatific vision and, on the other hand, it was the cause of His most ardent love as priest and victim, so that He willed to be overwhelmed with grief, and die on the cross a most perfect holocaust.

[1] The principle of economy, as applied to theology, refers to the divine plan in God's external operations. Here it is the relation of the Incarnation to the divine plan. The ultimate principle to which everything is referred is the hypostatic union. (Tr.)

At the end of this treatise we have given merely a compendium on Mariology, since a more complete commentary on this subject has recently been published by us in the French language.

May the reading of these pages be a source of knowledge as well as of spiritual benefit to all students of theology.

THE THIRD PART OF ST. THOMAS' THEOLOGICAL SUMMA

Prologue

IN this prologue St. Thomas shows the place assigned to this treatise in his *Theological Summa,* according to the division made by him at the beginning of this work, in which he had said: "Because the chief aim of sacred doctrine is to teach the knowledge of God, not only as He is in Himself, but also as He is in the beginning of things and their last end, and especially of rational creatures . . . we shall treat:

(1) "Of God (one in nature and triune in persons, and inasmuch as He is the principle of creatures); (2) of the rational advance of creatures toward God (or of God as He is the end of the rational creature); (3) of Christ, who as man is our way to God." [1]

In the present treatise he says: "Because our Savior the Lord Jesus Christ in order to save His people from their sins, as the angel announced, showed unto us in His own person the way of truth, whereby we may attain to the bliss of eternal life by rising again, it is necessary . . . that, after consideration of the last end of human life, and the virtues and vices, there should follow a consideration of the Savior of all and of the benefits bestowed by Him on the human race." [2]

Some theologians prefer another division to that made by St. Thomas, in which the distinction between dogmatic theology and moral theology is more in evidence, so that moral theology is not placed between the treatises on the One God and the Word incarnate. Furthermore, they remark that the treatise on the Word incarnate, because of its dignity justly comes immediately after the treatise on the one and triune God.

[1] *Summa theol.,* Ia, q. 2, introd. to a. 1.
[2] *Ibid.,* IIIa, Prologue.

To this the Thomists reply that, according to St. Thomas, dogmatic theology and moral theology are not two distinct sciences, but two parts of the same science, similar to the science of God of which it is a participation.[3] The unity of this science results from the unity of its formal object both *quod* and *quo.*[4] Its formal object *quod,* or the subject of this science, is God Himself considered in Himself, or as He is the principle and end of creatures. The formal object *quo* is virtual revelation by the light of which are deduced both in dogmatic theology and moral theology the conclusions that are virtually contained in the revealed principles. Therefore dogmatic and moral theology are not two sciences, but two parts of the same science.

They also remark that, although this treatise on the Savior, because of its dignity, precedes the moral part of theology, nevertheless, in the orderly arrangement of knowledge, it is justly placed after the other parts of theology, and this especially for three reasons: (1) because the simpler things come before the composite. In the preceding parts of the *Summa,* however, what pertains to God and to man are discussed separately, whereas the present treatise is concerned with Him who is both God and man.[5] (2) The work of redemption presupposes also that man lived for a long period of time under the law of the Old Testament, as well as it presupposes acts of faith and other virtues necessary in the various states of life. Hence St. Thomas appropriately places this treatise on the Savior at the end of his *Summa.* (3) Moreover, it must be noticed that what is necessary precedes what is contingent. But in the two preceding parts of the *Theological Summa,* what forms the subject of special discussion is the nature of God, and the nature of both angels and man with reference to God; whereas the Third Part of the *Summa* considers the great contingent fact which did not have to be realized, namely, that the *Word was made flesh.* This fact, although it is the greatest of all historical facts in the universe, is a contingent fact; for it is not something absolutely necessary, such as the divine nature for God and also the human nature for man. For this reason, certain philosophers, even certain mystics,

[3] *Ibid.,* q. 1, a. 3, 4.

[4] For a fuller explanation of the *objectum formale quod* and *quo,* see *The One God,* p. 57, footnotes. (Tr.)

[5] Thus a theological knowledge about human nature, habitual grace, the infused virtues is required in advance to discuss such questions as: whether Christ was endowed with habitual grace as well as having the grace of union; whether He had faith, hope, and penance considered as a virtue.

desired to reach union with God, not by way of Christ the universal mediator, although He had said: "I am the way and the truth and the life." [6] These persons did not grasp the practical import of the statement that Christ, or the Word of God incarnate, is the *exemplar and source of all virtues,* without whom nobody can acquire salvation and sanctity.

This deviation from the common method of approach to God is in itself manifestly in opposition to the great truth, namely, that these persons somehow overlooked the fact of the Incarnation, inasmuch as it is not an absolutely necessary fact, and they failed to see that precisely because it is contingent, it becomes, in some aspect, a fact of the greatest importance, inasmuch as it is a transcendent manifestation of God's most free and absolutely gratuitous love for the human race. St. John testifies that: "God so loved the world as to give His only-begotten Son." [7] He also says: "He hath first loved us, and sent His Son to be a propitiation for our sins." [8] In fact, these texts express the fundamental truth of Christianity, which is that God, by a most free act of His love, sent His divine Son to us. Hence the entire third part of the *Theological Summa* of St. Thomas is a detailed narrative of God's gratuitous love for us confirmed by the text: "God so loved the world, as to give His only-begotten Son." [9] It is truly a complete description of this gratuitous love as being the motive of God's mercy, and of the efficacy of this love. It is a canticle of God's gratuitous love for the human race. Thus the contingency of this most prominent fact in the history of the human race does not lessen its importance, but it manifests, on the contrary, the supreme gratuitousness of God's most free love for us.

Indeed, this manifestation of love is of such excellence that, in these days, even the more obnoxious enemies of the Church, such as several idealists, disciples of Hegel and Renan, who deny the existence of a true God really and essentially distinct from the world, say that Christ was the noblest of all men and that nobody was a better type of the evolution of the human race. So wrote Renan.[10] In fact, several communists in these days say the same, and they furthermore remark that this evolution of the human race predicted by Christ can be realized

[6] John 14:6.
[7] *Ibid.,* 3:16.
[8] I John 4:10.
[9] John 3:16.
[10] *Life of Jesus* (about end).

only by communism. Thus, presenting Christ in an entirely false light, whether they wish it or not, they confess that the greatest event in the history of the human race was *the coming of Christ.* But before this statement about Christ can be understood, one must have a correct notion of both God and man. Hence this treatise on the Incarnation is logically placed in the third part of the *Theological Summa.*

From the prologue we see that St. Thomas divides the third part of his *Summa* by considering: (1) the Savior Himself; (2) the sacraments by which we attain to our salvation; (3) the end of immortal life to which we attain by the resurrection.

Thus it is evident that the third part of the *Summa* is a treatise on the Savior, and the benefits He bestowed on us by instituting the sacraments and enabling us to get to heaven, which is our last end.

The treatise on the Savior is divided into two parts.

Part I discusses the mystery itself of the Incarnation (q. 1–26).

Part II discusses the actions and sufferings of our Savior or the mysteries of the life of Christ (q. 27–59).

The first part is often called, in our days, Christology, and the second part is known as soteriology. The mystery of the Incarnation is the principal topic of discussion in the first part, and in the second part St. Thomas considers the mystery of Redemption, in which he discusses especially the passion of Christ (q. 46–52).

The first part of the mystery of the Incarnation contains three sections:

1) The fitness of the Incarnation, in which it is discussed as a historical fact (q. 1).

2) The mode of union of the Word incarnate is considered (q. 2–15). The union itself (q. 2), the union in its relation to the person assuming (q. 3), and then on the part of the nature assumed and its perfections, the grace, knowledge, and powers of Christ are discussed (q. 4–15).

3) The consequences of the union with reference to what belongs to Christ are here discussed: (1) in themselves (q. 16–19); (2) in their relation to the Father, in which the predestination of Christ is considered; (3) with reference to us, in which our adoration of Christ and His office of Mediator are discussed (q. 25–26).

The second part is concerned with the mysteries of the life of Christ, and is divided into four sections: (1) the coming of Christ into the world, which includes Mariology; (2) His life on earth in its gradual development; (3) the end of His life, or His passion and death; (4) His exaltation, or His resurrection and ascension.

This second part which is entitled, *The Mystery of Redemption,* will be a brief treatise on the Passion, as it is the cause of our salvation, the vicarious satisfaction of Christ, its infinite value, Christ's victory, and also Christ as king, judge, and head of the blessed. Finally there will be a compendium on Mariology.

It must be noticed that among the commentators of the *Summa,* John of St. Thomas discusses the satisfaction of Christ at the beginning of His commentary, by considering the fittingness of the Incarnation, inasmuch as the Son of God came down from heaven for our salvation, namely, to redeem the human race. This arrangement is, indeed, appropriate for a complete understanding of the thesis on the motive of the Incarnation. However, in the doctrinal order, so far as operation follows being, St. Thomas is justified in discussing the Incarnation before the Redemption, or before the theandric act of the love of Christ suffering for us. Probably the reason why John of St. Thomas discussed at length the satisfaction of Christ at the beginning of his commentary, is that it ends with the twenty-fourth question in the *Summa* of St. Thomas.

Billuart, however, developed his thesis on the satisfaction of Christ in connection with the merit of Christ, which is question nineteen in the *Summa* of St. Thomas, at the same time discussing the infinite value of the merits of Christ.

Following the arrangement of questions as given by St. Thomas, we shall consider: (1) the mystery of the Incarnation; (2) the mystery of Redemption. This is the method commonly adopted by theologians.

CHAPTER I

THE MYSTERY AND FACT OF THE INCARNATION

PRELIMINARY REMARKS

BEFORE we come to explain the article of St. Thomas, we must set forth what positive theology teaches on the fundamentals of this treatise. Speculative theology, of course, begins with the articles of faith as defined by the Church, and concerning these its method of procedure is twofold. In the first place it gives a philosophical analysis of the terminology employed in these articles of faith. Thus it shows the fittingness of the mysteries, the possibility of which can neither be proved nor disproved. As the Vatican Council says: "Reason enlightened by faith, when it seeks earnestly, piously, and calmly, attains by a gift from God some, and that a very fruitful, understanding of mysteries; partly from the analogy of those things which it naturally knows, partly from the relations which the mysteries bear to one another and to the last end of man." [1]

In the second place, speculative theology deduces from the principles of faith conclusions that are virtually contained in the principles. In this way a body of theological doctrine is established in which there is due subordination of notions and truths, some of these being simply revealed, whereas others are simply deduced from revealed principles. These latter truths do not properly belong to the faith, but to theology as a science.

So does St. Thomas proceed, presupposing in the first article of this third part of his *Summa* the dogma of the divinity of Christ as solemnly defined by the Church. The positive theology of St. Thomas is found especially in his commentaries on the Gospels and on the Epistles of St. Paul.

It is necessary, however, to begin with a chapter on positive theology,

[1] Denz., no. 1796.

First Article

CHRIST'S TESTIMONY OF HIMSELF AND PRIMARILY OF HIS MESSIANIC DIGNITY

State of the question. In our days what claims first attention is the opinion that Modernists and a number of liberal Protestants have about Christ. What they think is known from the propositions condemned in the decree *Lamentabili*.[8] Some of these read: "The divinity of Jesus Christ is not proved from the Gospels, but it is a dogma deduced by the Christian conscience from the notion of the Messias" (prop. 27). "In all the Gospel texts the expression 'Son of God' is equivalent merely to the name 'Messias'; it does not at all, however, signify that Christ is the true and natural Son of God" (prop. 30). "The doctrine of the sacrificial death of Christ is not evangelical, but originated with St. Paul" (prop. 38).

A number of rationalists, such as Renan, B. Weiss, H. Wendt, Harnack, recognize some divine sonship in Christ that is superior to His Messiahship, but they deny that Jesus, in virtue of this sonship, was truly God.[9]

Among conservative Protestants, however, several, such as F. Godet in Switzerland, Stevens and Sanday in England, defended in recent times the divinity of Christ, not only from the Fourth Gospel and the Epistles of St. Paul, but even from the Synoptic Gospels.[10]

Let us first briefly review what the Gospels say about the Messiahship of Christ; a fuller account will be given afterward of His divinity as recorded in the New Testament.

It has already been shown in apologetics by the historical method, that is by considering the Gospels as historical narratives, though not in this connection, as being inspired, that Christ very plainly affirmed Himself to be the Messias announced by the prophets. A few rationalists, such as Wellhausen, deny that Christ said He was the Messias; but very many rationalists, such as Harnack and O. Holzmann, acknowledge that Jesus affirmed His Messiahship, and Loisy admits that Jesus, not at the beginning of His public life but toward its end, taught

[8] Denz., nos. 2027–38.

[9] See Lepin, *Jésus Messie et Fils de Dieu*, p. 228; Lebreton, *La vie et l'enseignement de Jésus*.

[10] Lepin, *op. cit.*, p. 237.

that He was the Messias.[11] The Gospel texts in which the Messiahship is affirmed are quoted in all works on apologetics.[12] The principal texts are given below.

From the beginning of His ministry, Jesus testisfied that He was the ambassador of God, and later on much more explicitly He asserted that He was the Messias and the Savior.

This He affirmed both publicly and privately.

Publicly (1) He declared His mission as teacher and Messias, when the Evangelist says of Him: "He began preaching the Gospel of the kingdom of God. And saying: The time is accomplished, and the kingdom of God is at hand; repent, and believe the Gospel." [13] In choosing His apostles, He said: "Come ye after Me and I will make you to be fishers of men." [14] "And Jesus went about all Galilee, teaching in their synagogues, and preaching the Gospel of the kingdom, and healing all manner of sickness and every infirmity among the people." [15]

In the Sermon on the Mount, Jesus perfects the Mosaic law in His own name, asserting many times: "It was said to them of old. . . . But I say to you." [16] At the end of this Sermon, we read: "For He was teaching them as one having power, and not as the scribes and Pharisees." [17]

2) Jesus replied to the scribes and Pharisees that He is the "Lord of the sabbath," [18] "greater than Jonas and Solomon," [19] greater than David.[20]

3) Likewise, in the synagogue at Nazareth, after Jesus had read the words of Isaias concerning the future Messias: "The spirit of the Lord is upon me. Wherefore He hath anointed me to preach the gospel to the poor, to heal the contrite of heart," we read farther on that "He began to say to them: This day is fulfilled this Scripture in

[11] "Messias" comes from the Hebrew "masiah," which means "anointed," being derived from the Hebrew verb "masah," "to anoint." It corresponds to the Greek χριστός, Μεσσίας (John 1:42; 4:25), and to "Christus" in the Latin Vulgate.

[12] See Garrigou-Lagrange, *De revelatione,* Part II, chap. 3.

[13] Mark 1:14 f.

[14] Matt. 4:19.

[15] *Ibid.,* 4:23.

[16] *Ibid.,* 5:21.

[17] *Ibid.,* 7:29.

[18] *Ibid.,* 12:8.

[19] *Ibid.,* 12:41 f.

[20] Mark 12:35 f.

your ears." [21] When the people did not believe, and said: "Is not this the Son of Joseph?" Jesus replied: "Amen I say to you that no prophet is accepted in his own country." [22]

4) Jesus declared His Messiahship even in plain words, after He cured the paralytic in a certain house at Capharnaum, on the Sabbath. The Jews accused Him of blasphemy, and He replied: "But that you may know that the Son of man hath power on earth to forgive sins, then He said to the man sick of the palsy: Arise, take up thy bed and go into thy house. And he arose and went into his house." [23] Christ claimed for Himself all rights pertaining to the Messiahship, such as the power of doing what His Father does, raising the dead to life, judging all men, and bringing those faithful to Him to eternal life.[24]

Privately. Jesus preferred to make known His Messiahship when speaking more intimately to His apostles.

1) In the beginning, after John the Baptist had given his testimony, and Jesus had spoken to others for the first time, Andrew says to his brother: "We have found the Messias." [25] Philip and Nathanael had similar experiences.[26]

2) Jesus said to His twelve apostles: "And going, preach, saying: The kingdom of heaven is at hand. Heal the sick, raise the dead. . . . He that receiveth you receiveth Me, and he that receiveth Me receiveth Him that sent Me." [27] "He that despiseth Me despiseth Him that sent Me." [28]

3) To the disciples of John the Baptist asking: "Art Thou He that art to come, or look we for another?" Jesus replied: "Go and relate to John what you have heard and seen. The blind see, the lame walk, the lepers are cleansed, the deaf hear, the dead rise again, the poor have the gospel preached to them." [29] This text, however, is manifestly the fulfillment of the prophecy by Isaias, which the Jews understood as referring to the Messias.[30]

[21] Luke 4:18 f.; Mark 2:3; Luke 5:18.
[22] Matt. 13:55; Luke 4:22 f.
[23] *Ibid.*, 9:2–7; Mark 2:3 ff.; Luke 5:24.
[24] John, chap. 5.
[25] *Ibid.*, 1:41.
[26] *Ibid.*, 1:43 f.
[27] Matt. 10:1, 7, 20, 40; Mark 9:36.
[28] Luke 10:16.
[29] Matt. 11:4.
[30] Isa. 35:5.

4) The first time that Jesus came to Jerusalem, He conversed with Nicodemus, one of the rulers of the Jews, and declared to him: "No man hath ascended into heaven, but He that descended from heaven, the Son of man who is in heaven. . . . For God so loved the world, as to give His only-begotten Son; that whosoever believeth in Him, may not perish, but may have life everlasting." [31] It is most evident from this answer that Jesus teaches His Messiahship, in fact, His divine sonship.

5) Jesus spoke similarly to the Samaritan woman, who says to Him: "I know that the Messias cometh (who is called Christ)"; Jesus says to her: "I am He who am speaking with thee." [32] After the Samaritans had heard Jesus, they said: "We ourselves have heard Him, and know that this is indeed the Savior of the world." [33]

All the preceding testimony, however, belongs to the beginning of Jesus' ministry; but toward the end of His life He speaks more explicitly not only to His apostles but also to the people.

THE LAST YEAR OF HIS LIFE

1) As Jesus was approaching the city of Caesarea Philippi, He asks a question, and receives from Peter this answer: "Thou art Christ the Son of the living God." [34] These words at least signify that Jesus is truly the Messias, and they are approved by Christ as being inspired by His heavenly Father.

2) On the festival day of the Jews, Jesus says to them: "My doctrine is not Mine, but His that sent Me." [35] The next day Jesus says to the Jews: "I am the light of the world. . . . I give testimony of Myself . . . and the Father that sent Me giveth testimony of Me." [36]

3) On the occasion of Jesus' triumphal entry into Jerusalem, as the crowd was shouting: "Blessed is He that cometh in the name of the Lord. . . . Hosannah in the highest," [37] Jesus said to the Pharisees: "If these shall hold their peace, the stones will cry out." [38]

4) During the Passion, Jesus affirms before the Sanhedrim that He

[31] John 3:13 f.
[32] *Ibid.*, 4:25.
[33] *Ibid.*, 4:42.
[34] Matt. 16:13 f.; Mark 8:29; Luke 9:20.
[35] John 7:15 f.
[36] *Ibid.*, 8:12 f.
[37] Matt. 21:9.
[38] Luke 19:40.

is the Christ, the Son of God. Thus at least He declared His Messiahship.[39]

5) After the Resurrection, Jesus said to the disciples on their way to Emmaus: "Ought not Christ to have suffered all these things, and so to enter into His glory?" [40] Similarly, Jesus said to the eleven apostles: "As the Father hath sent Me, I also send you." [41]

Conclusion. All this testimony, as Harnack [42] acknowledges against Wellhausen, is so interconnected with the entire Gospel narrative, that without it there would be almost nothing left that is historical in the life of Jesus, and His death could by no means be explained. There was also no time for a gradual idealization of Jesus' life, for the apostles already from the day of Pentecost taught that Jesus is the Messias and the Author of life.[43]

It must be noted that, theologically speaking, it is hard to determine in the Gospel texts when the expression of complete Messianic dignity ceases, and that of the divine sonship of Christ begins. The reason is that Jesus is called the Messias, or Christ, because He is the anointed of God. But the principal source of His anointing comes from the grace of union, by which His humanity is personally united to the Word, and by which He is therefore the Son of God. Hence, among the prophets and apostles, those who were more illuminated concerning the sublimity of the Messianic dignity already had a confused knowledge of the dignity of divine sonship.

Second Article

TESTIMONY OF CHRIST AND THE APOSTLES CONCERNING THE DIVINE SONSHIP

State of the question. Several rationalists, such as Renan, B. Weiss, H. Wendt, and Harnack, recognize some divine sonship in Christ that is superior to His Messiahship, but they deny that Jesus, in virtue of His sonship, is truly God.[44]

[39] *Ibid.,* 26:62 f.; Mark 16:60 f.

[40] Luke 24:26.

[41] John 20:21.

[42] *L'essence du Christianisme* (Fr. tr., p. 140).

[43] Acts 2:36; 3:13 f. Catholics and conservative Protestants agree that the Acts of the Apostles was written by St. Luke about A.D. 70. Harnack says A.D. 78–83, or perhaps 60–70.

[44] Concerning the opinion of these rationalists of modern times, cf. Lepin, *Jésus, Messie et Fils de Dieu,* p. 228.

Several conservative Protestants, such as F. Godet, and in England, Stevens, Gore, Ottley, and Sanday, recently defended the divinity of Christ not only from the Fourth Gospel and the Epistles of St. Paul, but even from the Synoptic Gospels.[45]

Moreover, the Church declared against the Modernists, that the divinity of Christ is proved from the Gospels. Thus several of their propositions were condemned in the decree *Lamentabili.*[46]

Let us see what the Synoptic Gospels, the Gospel of St. John, and the Epistles of St. Paul say about the mystery of the Incarnation.[47]

For the state of the question it must be observed that Jesus is called the Son of God fifty times. The question is: In what sense is this expression to be understood?

In the Scripture, "son" is predicated in two ways. In the strict and literal sense it signifies a living being that proceeds from a living principle in conformity with the laws of nature. In the broad and metaphorical sense it denotes a disciple or an adopted heir. The term, with reference to God, also has two meanings. In the broad sense it is predicated of men who participate in the spirit and life of God, so that Christians are called "sons of God"; [48] in the strict and proper sense, it is predicated of the Second Person of the Trinity, as in the text: "the only-begotten Son who is in the bosom of the Father." [49]

This expression "Son of God" sometimes perhaps in the Gospel means no more that Messias, when it is predicated of Jesus, for instance, by those who do not yet seem to know that He is by nature divine.[50] But from the Synoptic Gospels it is certain that Jesus said He was the Son of God in the proper, strict and most sublime sense of the term, inasmuch as He possesses the divine nature and is not merely a participator or partaker of this nature by grace.[51]

CHRIST TESTIFIES TO HIS DIVINITY IN THE SYNOPTIC GOSPELS [52]

There are two ways by which Jesus in the Synoptic Gospels gradually declares His divine nature. (1) He claims rights or privileges that

[45] About the opinion of these Protestants, cf. *ibid.,* p. 237; see also M. Braun, O.P., *Où en est le problème de Jésus.*

[46] Denz., nos. 2027–38.

[47] *Dict. de la Bible,* art. "Jésus-Christ"; *Dict. de théol. cath.,* col. 1132–1246.

[48] Τέκνα Θεοῦ.

[49] John 1:18; Ὁ υἱός τοῦ Θεοῦ.

[50] Mark 3:11.

[51] Even Christians are said to be "partakers of the divine nature" (II Pet. 1:4).

[52] Cf. Lepin, *Jésus, Messie et Fils de Dieu,* pp. 267–371.

belong only to God. (2) He affirms that He is the Son of God. This gradual development is seen also as regards His Messiahship, which on several occasions is more affirmed as it is more denied or disbelieved by the Pharisees. The divine affirmation of these rights for the salvation of souls is intensified in proportion as the Pharisees increasingly resist these claims.

Moreover, we get a clearer insight into the sublime meaning of these words of Christ in proportion as the gift of infused faith increases within us, just as the validity of the first principles of reason and of being is more fully realized in proportion as the ability of metaphysical argumentation or the power of intellectual penetration increases within us. The scriptural texts that we shall now quote are considered by students of apologetics as it were from without, but in theology they are considered as it were from within, just as there are two ways of viewing the paintings on the windows of churches, either from the outside; or from within the church and thus in their true light, and then they are seen with better effect, and there is a realization of their value.

A. Christ attributed to Himself divine rights. The seven principal ones are these.

1) *Jesus testified of Himself that He is greater than any creature.* He is greater than Jonas and Solomon,[53] greater than David who called Him Lord,[54] greater than Moses and Elias who were present with Him on the day of the Transfiguration.[55] He is greater than John the Baptist, greater than the angels, because "the angels ministered to Him" [56] after His temptation in the desert, and they are His angels, for we read: "The Son of man shall send His angels and they shall gather together His elect." [57]

2) *He speaks as the supreme Legislator,* absolutely equal in authority to the divine author of the Old Law, which He completes and perfects, purging it of the false rabbinical interpretations, repeatedly saying: "It was said to them of old . . . but I say to you." [58] He forbids divorce to the Jews, which Moses permitted because of the hardness of their heart.[59] He says that He is the Lord of the Sabbath.[60]

[53] Matt. 12:41 f.
[54] Mark 12:36; Matt. 22:45.
[55] Matt. 17:3.
[56] *Ibid.,* 11:3, 11; Mark 1:13; Matt. 4:11.
[57] Matt. 16:27; 24:31.
[58] *Ibid.,* 5:21, 48.
[59] *Ibid.,* 5:32; 19:9.
[60] Mark 2:27 f.

3) *He claims the right of forgiving sins,* which the Jews considered a divine privilege. This is evident from the answer Jesus gave to the Jews when He miraculously cured the paralytic, saying: "But that you may know that the Son of man hath power on earth to forgive sins, then He said to the man sick of the palsy: 'Arise, take up thy bed, and go into thy house.' " [61] He even claims the right of communicating to others this power of forgiving sins, saying: "Whatsoever you shall bind upon earth, shall be bound also in heaven." [62]

4) *He performs miracles in His own name,* commanding the paralytic and the dead, saying: "Arise." [63] On the occasion of the storm at sea, He said: "Peace, be still. And the wind ceased." [64] On the contrary, others perform miracles in the name of Jesus, saying: "We have done many miracles in Thy name." [65]

5) *He demands that all believe in, obey, and love Him in preference to all other affections, even at the cost of their life.* "He that loveth father or mother more than Me is not worthy of Me; and he that loveth son or daughter more than Me, is not worthy of Me." [66] These words would express odious and intolerable pride if Jesus were not God. The prophets never spoke in this manner. There are similar texts in the Gospels.[67]

6) *He assigns to Himself the power of judging the living and the dead.* "You shall see the Son of man sitting on the right hand of the power of God and coming with the clouds of heaven." [68] "And He shall send His angels with a trumpet, and a great voice, and they shall gather together His elect from the four winds, from the farthest parts of the heavens to the utmost bounds of them." [69]

7) *He promises to send the Holy Ghost.* "And I send the promise of My Father upon you." [70] Lastly, He accepts adoration from others, whereas, on the contrary, Peter, Paul, Barnabas, and the angels reject this adoration as being unworthy of it.[71]

[61] Matt. 9:6.
[62] *Ibid.,* 18:18.
[63] *Ibid.,* 9:6; Mark 2:9; 5:41; Luke 7:14.
[64] Mark 4:39.
[65] Matt. 7:22; Acts 3:6; 4:10.
[66] Matt. 10:37; Luke 14:26.
[67] Mark 10:29; Matt. 12:30.
[68] Mark 14:62; 8:38; 13:26.
[69] Matt. 24:31.
[70] Luke 24:49.
[71] Acts 10:25 f.; 14:14; Apoc. 19:10; 22:8.

B. In the Synoptic Gospels, Jesus affirms several times that He is the Son of God in the proper and strict sense of the term.[72] There are six principal texts, which shall be set forth in chronological order.

1) "All things are delivered to Me by My Father. And no one knoweth the Son, but the Father; neither doth anyone know the Father, but the Son, and he to whom it shall please the Son to reveal Him." [73]

The authenticity of this text is admitted by the majority of Protestant critics, and it is most ably defended by Catholic authors.[74] This text declares the equality of the Father and the Son both in knowledge and knowability. But this equality implies consubstantiality, as St. Thomas remarks, saying: "The substance of the Father transcends all understanding, since the essence of the Father is said to be unknowable as the substance of the Son is." [75] The Son is known only by the Father; therefore, like the Father, He exceeds all created knowledge, and hence is God. The above-mentioned scriptural text is substantially the same in meaning as when it is said: "No man hath seen God at any time; the only-begotten Son who is in the bosom of the Father, He hath declared Him." [76] These two texts are equally profound and identical in meaning, as several critics admit.

2) *Christ's answer to Peter's confession.* Peter said: "Thou art Christ, the Son of the living God." Jesus answering, said to him: "Blessed art thou, Simon Bar-Jona, because flesh and blood hath not revealed it to thee, but My Father who is in heaven." [77]

Some say that it cannot be historically proved from this confession that Peter affirmed anything more than Christ's Messiahship, since elsewhere he is quoted as saying merely: "Thou art the Christ," [78] "Thou art the Christ of God." [79] Nevertheless, something more than this is clearly enough evident from Jesus' answer. For He says that Peter could not have known His sonship unless it had been revealed to him. The mere knowledge of Christ's Messiahship did not require so great a revelation, for the signs of Messiahship were already made

[72] Cf. P. F. Ceuppens, O.P., *Theologia biblica, De incarn.*, III, 35–51.

[73] Matt. 11:27; Luke 10:21.

[74] Cf. M. J. Lagrange, *Ev. de S. Mathieu*, pp. 226–30; L. de Grandmaison, *Jésus-Christ*, II, 60–62; F. Ceuppens, *Theol., bibl. de SS. Trinitate*, II, 89.

[75] St. Thomas, *In Matt.*, chap. 11.

[76] John 1:18.

[77] Matt. 16:16 f.

[78] Mark 8:29.

[79] Luke 9:20.

manifest to the apostles from the beginning of Jesus' ministry, and several of them acknowledged it.[80]

3) *Parable of the wicked husbandmen.* The authenticity of this parable is admitted by most of the critics, even by very many rationalists. The parable says that the lord of the vineyard sent a servant to the husbandmen at the time of the harvest, then another, and many more, some of whom they beat, and others they killed. "Having yet one son, most dear to him, he also sent him unto them last of all, saying: They will reverence my son. But the husbandmen said to one another: This is the heir; come, let us kill him, and the inheritance shall be ours. And laying hold on him, they killed him and cast him out of the vineyard. What therefore will the lord of the vineyard do? He will come and destroy those husbandmen and will give the vineyard to others. And have you not read this scripture: The stone which the builders rejected, the same is made the head of the corner? By the Lord has this been done, and it is wonderful in our eyes. And they sought to lay hands on Him, but they feared the people. For they knew that He spoke this parable to them. And leaving Him they went their way." [81]

The application of this parable was manifest. The servants sent by the Lord of the vineyard were the prophets, and Jesus stated this more clearly to the Pharisees later on.[82] If, therefore, the servants of the Lord's vineyard are the prophets, His beloved Son is not only more than a prophet, but is truly His Son. Therefore this parable expresses absolutely the same truth as when St. Paul says: "God, who at sundry times and in divers manners spoke in times past to the fathers by the prophets, last of all in these days hath spoken to us by His Son . . . by whom also He made the world." [83]

4) *Jesus questions the Jews about Christ the son of David.* "And the Pharisees being gathered together, Jesus asked them, saying: 'What think you of Christ, whose Son is He.' They say to Him, 'David's.' He saith to them: 'How then doth David call Him Lord, how is He his Son?' And no man was able to answer Him a word." [84]

The authenticity of this text is admitted by the prominent liberal

[80] John 1:41 f.; Matt. 11:4. Cf. M. J. Lagrange, *op. cit.*, p. 322, with whom Lepin, F. Prat, D. Busy, and Ceuppens agree.

[81] Matt. 21:33; Mark 12:1 f.; Luke 20:1 f.

[82] Matt. 23:31.

[83] Heb. 1:1 f.

[84] Matt. 22:42; Luke 20:41 f.; Mark 12:35 f.

critics. But in the Messianic psalm just quoted, David, in calling the Messias "my Lord," acknowledges that this Lord is superior to him and equal to the first Lord, namely, to God the Father.

5) *Jesus answers Caiphas.* When Christ appeared before the Sanhedrim, "the high priest said to Him: 'I adjure Thee by the living God, that Thou tell us if Thou be the Christ the Son of God.' Jesus saith to him: 'Thou hast said it. Nevertheless, I say to you, hereafter you shall see the Son of man sitting on the right hand of the power of God, and coming in the clouds of heaven.' Then the high priest rent his garments, saying: 'He hath blasphemed; what further need have we of witnesses? Behold now you have heard the blasphemy.' " [85] From this answer we see that Jesus is more than the Messias, for divine sonship, sitting at the right hand of the Father, the exercise of supreme power, do not belong to the simple dignity of Messiahship. That is why Caiphas rent his garments, saying: "He hath blasphemed." These texts of the Synoptic Gospels receive further clarification in the Fourth Gospel, in which we read that, after Jesus had cured the paralytic at the Probatic pool, "the Jews sought the more to kill Him, because He did not only break the Sabbath, but also said God was His Father, making Himself equal to God." [86] Similarly, in the history of the Passion we read: "The Jews answered Him: 'We have a law and according to the law He ought to die, because He made Himself the Son of God.' " [87] Hence the question put by Caiphas to Jesus was to get an answer rendering Him guilty of death.[88]

6) *The baptismal formula.* After the Resurrection, we read in the Gospel: "Jesus coming, spoke to them [His apostles], saying: 'All power is given to Me in heaven and in earth. Going therefore teach ye all nations, baptizing them in the name of the Father and of the Son and of the Holy Ghost. Teaching them to observe all things whatsoever I have commanded you. And behold I am with you all days, even to the consummation of the world.' " [89]

Even all liberal Protestants admit this formula,[90] and it was universally accepted in the various Churches at the beginning of the

[85] Matt. 26:63 f.; Mark 14:61 f.; Luke 22:66, 70.

[86] John 5:18.

[87] *Ibid.*, 19:7.

[88] Cf. J. Lebreton, *Histoire du dogme de la Trinité,* I, 311–13.

[89] Matt. 28:18 f.; concerning the authenticity of this formula, cf. Lepin, *Dict. Apol.,* art. "Evangiles canoniques," col. 1621.

[90] This formula is found in *Didache,* VII, 1.

second century. In this baptismal formula the Son is declared equal to the Father and the Holy Spirit.

Conclusion. It must therefore be said, in refutation of the Modernists, that the declarations of Jesus concerning His eminent dignity as recorded by the Synoptics transcend simple Messiahship and express divine sonship that belongs most properly to Christ. Moreover, this divine sonship is not only superior to simple Messiahship, which is conceded, as has been said by several rationalists of our times, such as Harnack, but it establishes Christ above all creatures as equal to, and one in nature with God, the Second Person of the Trinity.

TESTIMONY OF THE ACTS OF THE APOSTLES CONCERNING THE DIVINITY OF CHRIST

The more conservative Catholic and Protestant historians consider it more probable that the Acts of the Apostles was written about A.D. 64 or, at least, before the year 70.[91] The rationalists of the Tubingen school set the date at A.D. 150. But, in our days, historical evidence made the rationalist Harnack assign the date of this work to the years 78–83, or perhaps even to 60–70.[92] From this it is evident that the above mentioned declarations of the Synoptic Gospels were not the result of a certain process of idealization, gradually evolved after Christ's death and ascribed to Him. The time required for this idealization was too short, for it is certain that from the day of Pentecost the apostles taught not only that Jesus was the Messias but also God.

The discourses of St. Peter are recorded in the Acts of the Apostles, in which we read: "The God of Abraham and the God of Isaac and the God of Jacob, the God of our fathers, hath glorified His Son Jesus, whom you indeed delivered up. . . . But the Author of life you killed, whom God hath raised from the dead, of which we are witnesses. And the faith which is by Him, hath given this perfect soundness [the lame man who sat at the gate of the Temple] in the sight of you all." [93]

The Author of life, however, is none other than God Himself. Likewise St. Peter says: "This is the stone which was rejected by you the builders, which is become the head of the corner. Neither is there

[91] Cf. E. Jacquier, *Histoire des Livres du N.T.,* III, 80.
[92] A Harnack, *Die apostelgesch.,* p. 22.
[93] Acts 3:13 f.

salvation in any other."[94] "God hath exalted Him [Jesus] with His right hand to be Prince and Savior, to give repentance to Israel, and remission of sins."[95] But only God is the Savior of souls, forgiving persons their sins.

Similarly St. Peter says: "By the grace of the Lord Jesus Christ, we believe to be saved."[96] Jesus is called by St. Peter "Lord,"[97] "Lord to all,"[98] "He who was appointed by God to be judge of the living and of the dead."[99] Finally, the apostles work miracles in the name of Jesus, confer baptism; and the deacon St. Stephen says, when dying: "Lord Jesus, receive my spirit."[100]

It is no matter of surprise, therefore, that when the Ebionites, who were the first heretics, denied the divinity of Christ, they were immediately condemned by the Church, as is evident from the writings of the Apostolic Fathers.

TESTIMONY OF ST. PAUL ON THE DIVINITY OF CHRIST

The principal epistles of St. Paul[101] were written about A.D. 48–59 or 50–64, as several rationalists admit, among whom are Harnack and Julicher. In these epistles, however, St. Paul, in affirming the divinity of Christ, does not announce it to the Churches as an unheard-of innovation, but he speaks of it as an already accepted dogmatic truth.

It will suffice if we give the principal references of St. Paul to the divinity of Christ.

1) According to St. Paul, Jesus is the Son of God in the strict sense of the term. He says of Him: "Who was predestinated the Son of God in power, according to the spirit of sanctification."[102] And again he writes: "God sending His own Son in the likeness of sinful flesh, . . . spared not even His own Son, but delivered Him up for us all."[103]

[94] *Ibid.*, 4:10 f.
[95] *Ibid.*, 5:31 f.
[96] *Ibid.*, 15:11.
[97] *Ibid.*, 2:36; 11:20.
[98] *Ibid.*, 10:36.
[99] *Ibid.*, 10:42.
[100] *Ibid.*, 7:58. The Word "Lord" (ὁ Κύριος,) in the Acts of the Apostles as in other books of the New Testament, denotes the divinity itself. See A. Lemmonyer, *Théologie du N.T.*, pp. 151–56.
[101] These epistles are I and II Thess., Gal., I and II Cor., Rom., Eph., Col., and Phil. Cf. F. Prat, *Théologie de St. Paul.*
[102] Rom. 1:4.
[103] *Ibid.*, 8:3, 32.

Elsewhere he says: "But when the fullness of the time was come, God sent His Son, made of a woman, made under the law, that He might redeem them who were under the law; that we might receive the adoption of sons." [104]

2) St. Paul affirms that the Son of God existed from all eternity before He became incarnate, and he also states plainly that the Son of God is the Creator. He speaks of "the light of the gospel of the glory of Christ, who is the image of God." [105] He says of Christ: "Who is the image of the invisible God, the first-born of every creature. For in Him were all things created in heaven and on earth, visible and invisible, whether thrones or dominations or principalities or powers; all things were created by Him, and in Him. And He is before all, and by Him all things consist. And He is the head of the body, the Church, who is the beginning, the first-born from the dead; that in all things He may hold the primacy. Because in Him it hath well pleased the Father that all fullness should dwell." [106] In this text the Son of God is clearly declared the Creator, just as elsewhere St. Paul says of God that: "of Him and by Him and in Him are all things." [107] Likewise it is the common belief among Catholics, and even very many non-Catholic critics admit that: "the fullness of the Godhead here signifies "all that is required to constitute Christ as God." [108]

3) St. Paul teaches that Jesus is God and equal to the Father. He says: "But we preach Christ crucified, unto the Jews indeed a stumbling block, and unto the Gentiles foolishness. But unto them that are called, both Jews and Greeks, Christ the power of God and the wisdom of God." [109] And again of Christ he says: "For in Him dwelleth all the fullness of the Godhead corporeally. And you are filled in Him who is the head of all principality and power." [110] In another epistle he writes: "For let this mind be in you, which was also in Christ Jesus: who being in the form of God thought it not robbery to be equal with God; but emptied Himself, taking the form of a servant, being made in the likeness of men, and in habit found as a

[104] Gal. 4:4 f.
[105] II Cor. 4:4.
[106] Col. 1:15.
[107] Rom. 11:36.
[108] Cf. P. F. Ceuppens, *Theol. biblica, De incarn.*, III, 47.
[109] I Cor. 1:23 f.
[110] Col. 2:9 f.

man."[111] There cannot be a clearer affirmation of the divinity of Christ than in this text.

Farther on in this epistle, he writes: "God hath given Him a name which is above all names, that in the name of Jesus every knee should bow."[112]

Likewise he says: "I wished myself to be an anathema from Christ, for my brethren, . . . of whom is Christ, according to the flesh, who is over all things, God blessed forever. Amen."[113] But there is a difficulty concerning the punctuation of this text. Very many even of the liberal critics place merely a comma before the words, "who is over all things, God"; whereas, Tischendorf and Gebhardt put a period, thus making this expression to be only an invocation addressed to God. All the Fathers of the Church and Catholic exegetes saw in this text an affirmation of the divinity of Christ.

Finally, in another epistle, we read: "In these days [God] hath spoken to us by His Son, whom He hath appointed heir of all things, by whom also He made the world. Who being the brightness of His glory, and the figure of His substance, and upholding all things by the word of His power, making purgation of sins, sitteth on the right hand of the majesty on high."[114] According to this teaching, the Son is the Creator, for it is by the Son that God produced all things. With the Jews, however, creation is an act that applies solely to God. The Son is also the preserver of all things, upholding all things by the word of His power. Likewise in this same epistle the angels are called the ministers of Christ, and adore Him.[115] They are therefore inferior to Him.

The preceding texts clearly prove that St. Paul taught the divinity of Christ; and so speaking, he intended to affirm no new doctrine, but to state what was already the universal belief among the early Christians, even among the converted Jews, who adhered most firmly to monotheism.

[111] Phil. 2:5 f. In this utterance the phrase "being in the form of God" (*ὃς ἐν μορφῇ θεοῦ*), the word *μορφῇ* ("form") signifies something that belongs inseparably to the essence of any being. Thus in the present instance it designates the divine essence or nature, and this is confirmed from the words that follow, namely, "to be equal with God."

[112] *Ibid.*, 2:9.

[113] Rom. 9:3 f.

[114] Heb. 1:2 f.

[115] *Ibid.*, 1:6, 7, 13, 14.

ST. JOHN'S TESTIMONY TO THE DIVINITY OF CHRIST

1) *In the prologue* to the Fourth Gospel, we read: "In the beginning was the Word, and the Word was with God, and the Word was God." [116] Three assertions are made: 1. The eternal pre-existence of the Word; 2. The Word is distinct from God the Father; 3. The Word is divine and therefore consubstantial with the Father. Then it is affirmed that all things were made by the Word.[117] Therefore the Word is the Creator, and He is consequently God. That Word or divine person assumed our human flesh, or nature, and lived among men. He is called "the only-begotten Son, who is in the bosom of the Father." [118] Therefore St. John most clearly teaches the divinity of Christ in this prologue, which is a quasi-synthesis of revelation.

2) *In the Fourth Gospel* we find Christ reported as using words by which He declares Himself to be the Son of God and Lord, although He frequently calls Himself the Son of man, thereby showing the humble subjection of Himself as man to His Father.

He says: "Father, the hour is come. Glorify Thy Son . . . that He may give eternal life to all whom Thou hast given Him. . . . And all things are Thine, and Thine are Mine." [119] Again, we read: "The Jews sought the more to kill Him, because He did not only break the Sabbath, but also said God was His Father, making Himself equal to God. Then Jesus answered, and said to them: 'What things soever the Father doth, these the Son also doth in like manner . . . and He giveth life to whom He will. . . . The Father hath given all judgment to the Son, that all men may honor the Son, as they honor the Father. . . . For as the Father hath life in Himself, so He hath given to the Son also to have life in Himself.' " [120] Christ also says: "From God I proceeded and came." [121] And again: "I came forth from the Father and am come into the world. . . . And yet I am not alone, because the Father is with Me." [122]

It is eternal sonship in the strict sense to which Jesus refers, for He

[116] John 1:1.

[117] It is unfortunate that we have not a more accurate translation of the Greek verb ἐγένετο in the Vulgate, which the Douai Version translates "were made." The same applies to the phrase, "The Word was made flesh," which would have no meaning to the Greek mind if used in this sense. (Tr.)

[118] John 1:18.

[119] *Ibid.*, 17:1, 10.

[120] *Ibid.*, 5:20 f.

[121] *Ibid.*, 8:42.

[122] *Ibid.*, 16:28, 32.

says: "Amen, amen, I say to you, before Abraham was made, I am." [123] And again: "Glorify Thou Me, O Father, with Thyself, with the glory which I had before the world was, with Thee." [124]

Moreover, Jesus says: "As the Father knoweth Me and I know the Father." [125] "All things whatsoever the Father hath, are Mine. Therefore I said, that He, the Spirit of truth, shall receive of Mine, and show it to you." [126] Jesus even says: "I and the Father are one." [127] The Jews understood these words in the sense that Jesus was equal in dignity to the Father, for they at once took up stones to stone Him. Similarly He said: "I am the way and the truth and the life"; [128] but only God, who is essential Being, is truth and life; a mere man may have even infallible truth, but is not truth itself, just as he is not self-subsisting being. In this respect there is an immeasurable difference between the two verbs, "to be" and "to have." Hence this last utterance of Jesus would of itself suffice to constitute an explicit expression of His divinity, which is so clearly affirmed in the prologue of St. John's Gospel.

3) *In St. John's First Epistle* we read: "That which was from the beginning, which we have heard . . . and our hands have handled of the Word of life . . . we declare unto you." [129] Farther on he says: "And we know that the Son of God is come, and He hath given us understanding that we may know the true God, and may be in His true Son." [130] These concluding words of St. John's First Epistle most clearly show that the author's intention was to affirm the divinity of Christ just as this was his intention in writing his prologue to the Fourth Gospel.

4) *In the Apocalypse,* that Christ is divine and the Son of God, is clearly evident from the titles assigned to Him; for He is the First and the Last,[131] the beginning of the Creation,[132] the Lord of lords and the King of kings.[133] The divinity of Jesus is also equally manifested from the prerogatives attributed to Him, for He is called the

[123] *Ibid.,* 8:58.
[124] *Ibid.,* 17:5, 24.
[125] *Ibid.,* 10:15.
[126] *Ibid.,* 16:14 f.
[127] *Ibid.,* 10:30; cf. 17:11, 21.
[128] *Ibid.,* 14:6.
[129] I John 1:1 f.
[130] *Ibid.,* 5:20.
[131] Apoc. 1:17; 2:8; 22:13.
[132] *Ibid.,* 3:14.
[133] *Ibid.,* 17:14; 19:6; as God, 6:15 f.; 15:3.

Lord of life and death for all men,[134] the searcher of hearts.[135] He has power to open the book, which no man is able to open,[136] ruling over all things celestial and terrestrial,[137] being omnipotent as God Himself is.[138] The divinity of Christ is also clearly set forth in this book; because of the honors that are rendered to Him from men, the faithful are called servants of Jesus,[139] the faithful both of Jesus and of God.[140] There is reference in these texts to the priests of God and of Christ.[141] The Lamb of God who takes away the sin of the world is adored as God,[142] and adoration is permitted to be given only to God.[143]

From what has been said, it is most clearly apparent that Jesus is God and a divine person distinct from God the Father. This will be more fully explained when we come to discuss the infinite value of the merits and satisfaction of Christ [144] and consider the texts of the New Testament concerning the mystery of Redemption.

Among the principal texts of the Old Testament about the divinity of the Messias, the following must be quoted: "A child is born to us and a son is given to us, and the government is upon his shoulder, and his name shall be called Wonderful, Counselor, God the Mighty, the Father of the world to come, the Prince of Peace." [145] This text forms part of the Introit of the second Mass in honor of the birth of our Lord. The Church sees in this text an affirmation of the divinity of Jesus.

Concerning this text, the Rev. F. Ceuppens, O.P., remarks: "The true meaning of this expression 'God the Mighty,' is very much disputed among Catholics. Following the opinion of such distinguished authors as A. Condamin, E. Tobac, F. Feldmann, and M. J. Lagrange, we think the expression must be accepted in the literal and proper sense, and the reason we give for this is that, in other texts of the Old Testament, the same expression occurs, and it is always predicated

[134] *Ibid.*, 1:18.
[135] *Ibid.*, 2:23; as God, Jer. 17:10.
[136] *Ibid.*, chaps. 5 f.
[137] *Ibid.*, 1:4; 2:26; 4:5.
[138] *Ibid.*, 1:8; 4:8.
[139] *Ibid.*, 1:1.
[140] *Ibid.*, 2:13, 20; 17:14.
[141] *Ibid.*, 20:6.
[142] *Ibid.*, 5:8, 12 f.
[143] *Ibid.*, 19:10; 22:9.
[144] *Summa theol.*, IIIa, q. 19, 48.
[145] Isa. 9:6.

of Yahweh. This being the case, the future Messias is foretold as being truly God, and truly divine by nature. But it is another question whether the Jews, imbued with monotheistic concepts, perfectly understood all these things, and whether the prophet himself fully grasped this doctrine and saw it in all its applications." [146]

Third Article

TESTIMONY OF TRADITION AND THE PRINCIPAL DEFINITIONS OF THE CHURCH

A more detailed account of tradition and the definition of the Church is given in the history of dogmas and in patrology. In this treatise we shall give a brief summary of what everyone is expected to know about these matters.[147] We notice that considerable progress has been made in the development of dogma in the course of combating the various heresies.

1) *In the first three centuries,* the Fathers affirm that Christ is both God and man, because He came to save and redeem us, which He could not have done unless He had been both God, the author of grace, and also man.[148] Hence they reject the errors of the Docetae, who said that Christ's body was imaginary and fantastic, and of the Dualists, who declared that the divine and human natures in Christ were united accidentally.[149] We find Tertullian, in his days, asserting that the union of the two natures in Christ was effected "in one person." [150]

2) *In the fourth century,* whereas the Apollinarists denied a rational soul to Christ, meaning to say that the Word took the place of the mind in Christ, the Fathers clearly affirm that Christ is both perfect God and perfect man; and they also assert that what was not assumed was not healed. If, therefore, the Word did not assume a rational soul, the soul was not healed; and besides, Christ could not have merited and been obedient.[151]

[146] Deut. 10:17; Isa. 10:21; Jer. 32:18; Neh. 9:32; *Theol. biblica, De incarn.,* III, 33.

[147] *Dict. theól. cath.,* art. "Jésus-Christ," col. 1247–62.

[148] St. Clement, I Cor. 32, 2; 36, 2–5; St. Ignatius, *Magn.,* 6, 1; 8:2; *Eph.,* 1, 1; 7, 2; 15, 3; *Pseudo Barnabas,* 5, 11.

[149] St. Irenaeus, *Adv. haeres.,* III, xviii, 1; xxi, 10; v, 18. Tertullian, *adv. Praxeam;* St. Hippolytus, *Philosophumena.*

[150] *Adv. Praxeam, P.L.,* II, 191.

[151] Cf. *Contra Apollinarium,* a work that has been unjustifiably attributed to St.

3) Finally, *in the fifth century,* the Nestorians declared that the union of the two natures in Christ was only accidental, and the Eutychians asserted that there was only one nature in Christ. Against these heresies the Catholic concept of one person in Christ and of the hypostatic union is explicity affirmed, and these points must be fully explained farther on.[152]

Following are the principal definitions of the Church concerning the divinity of Christ.[153]

1) Christ is truly God, He is rightly called the Word, and Son of the Father, consubstantial with the Father, equal to Him, God of God, begotten not made, the only-begotten of the Father by natural and not by adoptive sonship.

2) "I believe in Jesus Christ, our Savior . . . ," which is the most ancient formula.[154]

3) "I believe in Jesus Christ, His only Son [of the Father] our Lord," [155] which is the more ancient formula in the Western Church.

4) The Creed of St. Epiphanius proposed to the catechumens of the Eastern Church: "We believe in one God . . . and in one Lord Jesus Christ the Son of God, begotten of God the Father, the only-begotten, that is, of the substance of the Father, God of God, light of light, true God of true God, begotten not made, consubstantial with the Father by whom all things were made . . . who for us men and for our salvation came down from heaven and was incarnate." [156]

5) The First Council of Nicaea (325) defines, against the Arians: "We believe in one God the Father almighty, Maker of all things visible and invisible. And in our one Lord Jesus Christ, the Son of God, the only-begotten of the Father, that is, of the substance of the Father, God of God, light of light, true God of true God, begotten not made, one in substance with the Father, by whom all things were made, both in heaven and on earth, who for our salvation came down, was incarnate, and was made man, suffered and rose again the third

---

Athanasius. See also St. Gregory of Nazianzus in several of his epistles; St. Epiphanius, *De haeresibus.* Cf. also Denzinger, nos. 65, 85, in which the Apollinarians were condemned by Pope St. Damasus, and by the First Council of Constantinople.

[152] S. Cyrillus Alex., *Epist. I; P.G.,* LXXVII, 27. See Denz., nos. 113 f., Anathematismi Cyrilli contra Nestorium. Also Conc. Chalcedonense, Denz., no. 148.

[153] Denz. (16 ed.), p. 20.

[154] *Ibid.,* no. 1.

[155] *Ibid.,* no. 2.

[156] *Ibid.,* no. 13. This creed is the formula of the Nicene Council: see Denz., no. 54.

day, ascended into heaven, and will come to judge the living and the dead." [157] All these words of the Nicene Council must be seriously considered farther on, when we explain the articles of St. Thomas. The preceding testimony and definitions suffice for establishing the fact of the Incarnation.

[157] *Ibid.*, no. 54.

CHAPTER II

PRELIMINARY QUESTION

The Possibility of the Incarnation

LET us now turn to speculative theology, which, as stated, has two tasks to perform.

1) It must give a philosophical analysis of the terms used in revealed dogma, so that their meaning may be better known, for, as the Vatican Council says in the text already quoted: "Reason enlightened by faith, when it seeks earnestly, piously, and calmly, attains by a gift from God, some, and that a very fruitful, understanding of the mysteries; partly from the analogy of those things which it naturally knows, partly from the relation which the mysteries bear to one another and the last end of man." [1] Thus the mystery of man must be illustrated from analysis of the notions of divine nature, human nature, person, as well as from the connection of this mystery with the mysteries of Redemption and of eternal life. In this part of speculative theology the discussions are either explicative, or subjectively illative.[2]

2) Speculative theology must deduce from revealed truths by a discursive process that is properly and objectively illative, other truths, namely, conclusions that are only virtually contained in the revealed truths. An example would be the following: Christ already had, when on earth, infused knowledge, which was inferior to the beatific vision.

We must begin by discussing the possibility and fittingness of the Incarnation.

St. Thomas starts abruptly by considering the fittingness of the Incarnation, whereas many theologians of later times first speak of its possibility; and this is what St. Thomas had done in the work preced-

[1] Denz., no. 1796.

[2] An example would be to prove that the following proposition: The Word, who is consubstantial with the Father, was made man, is equivalent to this revealed truth: The Word was made flesh.

ing his *Summa.*[3] The reason why the holy Doctor omitted this question of the possibility is probably because he wishes to examine this question afterward, when he discusses the mode of the union (q. 2–15), which is concerned with the principal difficulties against the possibility of this mystery. Moreover, it is not absolutely necessary to begin by treating about the possibility of this mystery, because for the faithful this possibility follows from the fact of the Incarnation, which is of faith. From actuality to possibility, this follows as a logical consequence.

For the general benefit of the doctrine, however, theologians begin by asking whether the possibility of the Incarnation can be proved or known by the natural light of reason. This question has its advantages as regards method.

Incarnation corresponds to the Latin term "inhumanatio," which signifies the act of becoming man, and it is the union or unition of the human nature with the divine in the one person of the Word. This is evident from the traditional explanation of the words of St. John: "The Word was made flesh," [4] in which "flesh" as frequently in Sacred Scripture is concerned with living and human flesh, which is not living and human unless united with a human soul. And it also says that this Word was made flesh to commend the humility of our Savior, who also willed to become man for our salvation.

But can the Incarnation be proved? In the first question of this treatise it will be shown, indeed, that there is no apparent contradiction in the Incarnation, and that it cannot be proved impossible. But the question now is, as posited above, whether this possibility can be proved by reason alone. There does not seem to be any apparent contradiction in the affirmation of a divine quaternity, and yet there lurks a contradiction in this affirmation. There cannot be four persons in God, nor merely two, but three. Is it therefore possible to prove the Incarnation? This question is commonly answered in the negative.[5]

Authoritative proof. St. Paul calls the Incarnation, "the mystery which hath been hidden in God." [6] The Eleventh Council of Toledo says: "If the Incarnation could be shown possible by reason, then it

[3] *Com. in III Sent.,* d. 1, a. 1.

[4] John 1:14.

[5] Cf. St. Thomas, *Com. in III Sent.,* d. 1, a. 2, q. 1.

[6] Eph. 3:9.

would not be an object of admiration; if it were an example, then it would not be unique."[7]

Similarly, against the semi-rationalists, who wish to prove the revealed mysteries, especially against Froschammer, Pius IX wrote: "The author teaches that reason, also in the most secret matters pertaining to God's wisdom and goodness, even too in the mysteries that are dependent on His free will, although granted that they have been revealed, can by itself, not relying on the already established principle of divine authority, but on its own natural principles and powers, acquire a certainty of knowledge. Everyone who has a slight knowledge of the rudiments of Christian doctrine immediately sees and likewise fully realizes how altogether false and erroneous is the author's teaching."[8]

It is true, indeed, that Froschammer wished to prove not only the possibility but also the very fact of the Incarnation. If, however, the possibility of the Incarnation could be apodictically and positively proved, as the possibility of any miracle, for instance, of the Resurrection, then the Incarnation would be only a miracle that is supernatural as regards the mode of its production, but it would not be a mystery in the strict sense, that it is essentially supernatural.

In the condemnation of semi-rationalism, it is stated: "And assuredly, since these dogmas are above nature, therefore they are beyond the scope of reason and natural principles."[9]

The Vatican Council also says: "If anyone shall say that in divine revelation there are no mysteries, truly and properly so called, but that all the doctrines of faith can be understood and demonstrated from natural principles by properly cultivated reason, let him be anathema."[10]

Theological proof.[11] What is essentially supernatural is supernatural as regards its knowability, even for the angels.

But the intrinsic possibility of the Incarnation is the intrinsic possi-

[7] Denz., nos. 282, 284 f.

[8] *Ibid.*, nos. 1669–71. A few lines above in this same document, Frohschammer applied this teaching about reason to the supernatural end of man and the most sacred mystery of the Incarnation. (Tr.)

[9] *Ibid.*, no. 1671.

[10] *Ibid.*, nos. 1671, 1795.

[11] Cf. *Contra Gentes*, Bk. IV, chap. 27; cf. also *Dict. théol. cath.*, art. "Incarnation," col. 1453–63; E. Hugon, *Le mystère de l'Incarnation*, pp. 52 f.

bility of something essentially supernatural, which has no necessary and evident connection with things of the natural order.

Therefore this possibility is supernatural as regards its knowability, even for the angel. Hence it cannot be demonstrated, but only persuasive arguments of fitness can be advanced, and it can be defended against those who deny it.

The major is evident, for truth and being are convertible.

Minor. The Incarnation is not only a miracle that is supernatural as regards the mode of its production, such as the resurrection of the dead, but it is also an essentially supernatural mystery, for it is the intimate union of the human nature with the divine nature as it is in itself, in the person of the Word. But the divine nature as it is in itself, and the person of the Word are essentially supernatural; on the contrary, God as the author of nature has a necessary and evident connection with things of the natural order.

Reason, however, can solve the objections against the possibility of this mystery, by showing them to be either false or unnecessary.[12] Moreover, reason can urge the fitness of this mystery by arguments that are not apodictic but congruent. These arguments are truly profound; in fact, they can always be the result of keen penetration by either the human or angelic intellect, but this penetration can never reach the degree required for demonstration.

Objection. To prove that anything is not contradictory is to prove it possible.

But it is proved that the Incarnation is not contradictory.

Therefore the Incarnation is proved possible.

I distinguish the major. To prove that anything is not contradictory, positively and evidently, this I concede; that it is not so negatively and probably, this I deny. So writes Billuart.[13]

In this kind of argument we do not proceed from some a priori or a posteriori reasoning that is positively demonstrative of this possibility, but our reasoning rests on probable and apparent grounds. Thus it is shown that the possibility of the Incarnation is never disproved; the objections are not impossible of solution, for they can be shown to be either false or at least not cogent.

Another objection. But God is in Himself essentially supernatural,

[12] See St. Thomas *Com. in Boetium de Trinit.*, q. 2, a. 3.

[13] *De incarnatione,* beginning of treatise.

and yet reason alone apodictically proves His existence. Therefore, although the mystery of the Incarnation is essentially supernatural, reason alone apodictically proves at least the possibility, if not the fact of the Incarnation.

Reply. I distinguish the antecedent. That God is in Himself as regards His Deity or intimate life essentially supernatural, this I concede. Nevertheless, as the Author of nature, He has a necessary and evident connection with created effects of the natural order, and so in this inferior aspect the truth of this proposition, God exists, is demonstrated *cum fundamento in re,*[14] although we have not a positive and natural knowledge of God's essence or of His act of essence. On this point St. Thomas says: "To be can mean either of two things. It may mean the act of essence or it may mean the composition of a proposition effected by the mind in joining a predicate to a subject. Taking 'to be' in the first sense, we cannot understand God's existence or His essence; but only in the second sense. We know that this proposition which we form about God when we say 'God is,' is true; and this we know from His effects." [15] But there is nothing similar to this in the Incarnation of the Word, because this mystery, just as the intimate life of the Trinity, has no necessary and evident connection with natural effects; hence neither the fact nor the possibility of this mystery can be demonstrated from natural principles, for this possibility transcends demonstration. These arguments of congruence may always be made more profound, but they will never reach the degree required for an apodictic argument, just as the sides of a polygon inscribed in a circle may be increased indefinitely, yet they will never be identified with the circumference of the circle, because the sides will never be diminished so as to become a point.

But I insist. It is apodictically proved that there is in God a supernatural order of truth and of life.

Reply. We are not positively but only negatively assured of this order by such a proof, which is the case with any order whose mysteries cannot be known in a natural way.

Still Gregory of Valentia insists that at least the angelic intellect can

[14] The expression according to scholastic terminology, means that the truth of this proposition: God exists, understood as the Creator of the universe, has its foundation and objective validity in the subject itself of the proposition, inasmuch as God is externally related to all things He has created, real on the part of creatures to God, though logical on the part of God to creatures. (Tr.)

[15] *Summa theol.,* Ia, q. 3, a. 4, ad 2.

perhaps prove this possibility, because the angel intuitively sees the human nature as distinct from its subsistence or personality, and therefore as assumable by the divine subsistence.

Reply. The angelic intellect cannot know in a natural way whether the divine subsistence, which is essentially supernatural, can, without implying imperfection, take the place of human subsistence.

Corollary. A fortiori the angelic intellect cannot know by its natural powers the fact of the Incarnation.

Gregory of Valentia remarks that the angel, since He sees intuitively that the human nature of Christ is without its own personality, must immediately conclude that this human nature is personally united to some divine person.

Reply. This conclusion is not established, for the angel could conclude: the human personality of this man is hidden from me, because of motives known to God alone. Thus it is certain that the created intellect by its own natural powers cannot know that the Incarnation is possible, much less that it is a fact.

The objections that can be raised, however, against the possibility of the Incarnation are solved in the course of this treatise.[16] It will suffice here at the beginning to take note of the principal objection, by way of a statement of the question. It is one proposed by St. Thomas,[17] and may be stated as follows:

God cannot be subject to any intrinsic change, or be intrinsically otherwise than He is.

But by the Incarnation God would be intrinsically otherwise than He is. Therefore the Incarnation is impossible.

Reply. I distinguish the minor. That God would undergo a change, if by reason of passive potency He were to receive some distinct perfection, this I concede; that God only terminates the human nature, and undergoes a change, this I deny.

God in the Incarnation neither loses nor acquires anything, but merely makes creatures partakers in His perfection. Therefore, as St. Thomas says: "When it is said, 'God was made man,' we understand no change on the part of God, but only on the part of the human nature." [18] Similarly, if we see the sun, it undergoes no change, but is only the object of our vision.

[16] See Chapters 2–16 (passim).

[17] *Summa theol.*, IIIa, q. 16, a. 6, 2nd. obj. Also *III sent.*, d. 1, a. 1, ad 1.

[18] *Summa theol.*, IIa, q. 16, a. 6, ad 2.

As St. Thomas says: "To be man belongs to God by reason of the union, which is a relation. . . . But whatever is predicated relatively can be newly predicated of anything without its change, as a man may be made to be on the right side without being changed, and merely by the change of him who was on his left side." [19] Likewise, anything at first not seen is seen afterward without any change in itself, but inasmuch as it is actually the termination of our vision. It is the visual faculty that is changed, inasmuch as it passes from potentiality to act.

Similarly, as we shall see in the case of the Incarnation, the change is entirely on the part of the nature that is assumed, which is deprived of its own subsistence and acquires the divine. The Word by no means acquires a new and real relation, but the relation is logical; for the real relation is only on the part of the human nature toward the Word, just as the visual faculty is in real relation to the object seen, and not the reverse of this. Hence St. Thomas says: "God is said to be united not by any change in Himself, but in that which is united to Him; similarly, when it is said that He is unitable, this statement does not mean that the union is effected by reason of any passive potency existing in God, but because there is such a potency existing in the creature so as to make this union possible." [20] So also God is said to be visible, and in the next life He is seen by the blessed, not because of any change in Himself, but the change is in the blessed, since He terminates their vision as object seen. Thus a point that already terminates one line, can terminate a second and third line as in the case of the point of a pyramid, and yet the point undergoes no change in itself.

Objection. The Word is the subject of the human nature, and not merely the terminus; for the Word has this human nature, which is truly attributed to Him, as to the subject. Therefore the Word is the recipient of the human nature.

Reply. I distinguish the antecedent. That the Word possesses the human nature in a receptive sense, this I deny; in a terminative sense, this I concede. To possess a form in a receptive sense is to be the subject of this form, just as matter receives its form, or as a substance receives accidental forms; but such is not the case when a subject has some form in a personal or terminative sense. The Word, however, possesses the human nature not in a receptive sense, because He is not in passive potency to receive it; but He possesses it personally and

[19] *Ibid.*, ad 2.
[20] *Com. in III Sent.*, d. 1, q. 1, ad 1.

terminatively, in so far as He is its intrinsic terminus, intrinsically completing it and terminating it, just as the point terminates the line, or the object seen terminates the visual faculty. The difficulty raised by this objection makes it apparent that the possibility of the Incarnation cannot be strictly proved.

Again I insist. What is extrinsic to another cannot become intrinsic to it unless it is received by the other. But the human nature in itself is extrinsic to the Word. Therefore the Word can become intrinsic to the human nature only by becoming the recipient of it.

Reply. I deny the major. For something can become intrinsic to another by the sole fact of being joined to that which receives it by way of intrinsic termination, as a point becomes intrinsic to a line, and so what is received is not received by way of informing act, as if the recipient were in some passive potentiality to be perfected by it. Thus it is shown that the objection is either false or at least unnecessary, and hence of no force.

This point will be made clearer in the course of this treatise, in which it will be shown that God cannot take the place of a created subsistence as informing, but as terminating what is received. The informing form is related to the whole to which it is ordered as the less perfect part, just as the soul is less perfect than the complete man. On the contrary, the terminating perfection is not ordered to the more complete whole, but rather draws the other to Himself. Hence, instead of involving any imperfection, God imparts His perfection to what is assumed. Thus, for example, God's essence without involving any imperfection terminates the vision of the blessed, and the divine essence is not more perfect in being seen by the blessed than if it were not seen by them. Similarly, a beautiful statue is not made more perfect by the fact that it is the object of my admiration, nor is the doctrine of St. Thomas made more perfect by the fact that it is understood by the disciple, but it is the disciple who is made more perfect by the doctrine. Rome is not made more perfect by the fact that any pilgrim, however distinguished, visits it.

Final objection. One substantial being cannot result from the union of several complete beings. But the human and divine natures are complete beings. Therefore one substantial being, such as Christ would be, cannot result from the union of the two natures.

Reply. I distinguish the major. From several beings complete in their natures there cannot result one substantial unity of nature, this

I concede; that there cannot result a substantial unity of suppositum or person, this I deny.

Explanation. From two acts there cannot result something essentially one in nature, and therefore prime matter must be pure potency, so that the human nature is essentially and not accidentally one. But the human nature as such is not complete in the sense that it is a suppositum or person, and thus it is drawn to unity of being with the Word, in the sense that there is one suppositum, which will be more fully explained farther on.[21] Thus in the resurrection the body is united with the soul and constitutes with it one suppositum being.

More briefly, these various objections are solved by saying that the Word is not related to Christ's humanity as recipient subject, for in such case the Word would be in passive potency for His humanity; nor is He related to it as informing form that is received, for in this case He would be less perfect than the whole, which is the complete Christ; but He is related to it as terminating perfection, just as the pre-existing point that already terminates one line again terminates another; or just as the object that terminates the vision of one man, may again terminate the vision of another man. Thus the professor teaches his various students not in a receptive but in a terminative sense. Expressed more briefly, we may say that the Pure Act is unreceived and unreceivable. If He were received in any potency, He would be subjected to participation and limitation; if, however, He were to receive, then He would be in potency for a further act.

"To have terminatively" does not mean to be actuated or to be perfected; rather it means to perfect. Thus the Father, the Son, and the Holy Ghost do not have the Deity receptively, but terminatively. Thus the Son of God has His humanity terminatively, but not receptively. Thus God has His external glory, inasmuch as He is known and praised.

"To have receptively" is to be actuated and perfected. Thus matter receives the form. The created substance receives accidental forms.

"The form terminating" is not a part and involves no imperfection, but perfects and bestows its perfection upon what it terminates. Such is the case with the person of the Word, who unites with Himself and terminates Christ's humanity. So also the doctrine

[21] *Summa theol.,* IIIa, q. 2, a. 6, ad 2.

of St. Thomas unites with himself and terminates the intelligence of a number of students.

"The form informing" is less perfect than the whole, as the soul in man.

The difficulty raised by the foregoing objections against the intrinsic possibility of the Incarnation confirms the thesis, namely, that this possibility cannot be apodictically proved from reason alone, but solely that persuasive reasons can be adduced in defense of this possibility, by showing that the objections of those attacking it are either evidently false or at least unnecessary, and of no force.

We must now treat of the fitness of the Incarnation. Fitness means something more than mere possibility, and it will at once be seen that we are persuaded of this fitness by congruent arguments drawn from reason alone; but the revelation of original sin being presupposed, the Incarnation is proved necessary so that adequate reparation be made to God, if He demands such reparation.

CHAPTER III

QUESTION 1

The Fitness of the Incarnation

THIS question contains six articles that gradually develop the doctrine of the fitness of the Incarnation. St. Thomas begins by discussing: (1) the fitness of the Incarnation; (2) its necessity for the reparation of the human race; (3) its proximate motive, whether, if there had been no sin, God would have become incarnate; (4) whether God became incarnate for the removal of original sin more chiefly than for actual sin; (5) why it was not more fitting that God should become incarnate in the beginning of the human race; (6) why it is not more fitting that the Incarnation should take place at the end of the world.

First Article

WHETHER IT WAS FITTING THAT GOD SHOULD BECOME INCARNATE [1]

State of the question. In this article we are concerned with the mere fitness, not as yet with the proximate motive of the Incarnation. In other words, was the Incarnation not only possible, but was it expedient and fitting, that is, was it in agreement with God's wisdom and goodness? Taken in this sense, the question is whether it was fitting that God should become man; on the other hand, it does not seem fitting that God should become a lion, although this may perhaps be possible. But was it more fitting that the Son of God, rather than the Father or the Holy Ghost, should become incarnate? [2] Likewise, was it more fitting that the Word should assume the human nature rather than the angelic nature? [3]

[1] Cf. *Contra Gentes,* Bk. IV, chaps. 40, 49 f.
[2] See *infra,* chap. 5, art. 8.
[3] See *infra,* chap. 6, art. 1.

This state of the question will be made clearer from the solution of the difficulties posited at the beginning of this article. They constitute, as it were, the nucleus of the difficulties to be solved.

The difficulties are the following. (1) From all eternity God was separated from human nature. Therefore it was not fitting that He should be united to it. (2) It is not fitting for those things to be united that are infinitely distant from each other. This seems to be against the principle of continuity, which states that the highest of the lowest order should reach the lowest of the highest, but not that the very lowest should reach the very highest. Hence it seems to be more fitting that God should have taken the nature of the highest angel, which is perhaps what Lucifer thought. (3) It was not fitting that the supreme uncreated Spirit should assume a body, as indeed He would be assuming what is evil. This objection was raised by the Manichaeans, who held that matter is evil. (4) It is unfitting that the infinite God, the Ruler of the universe, should remain hidden in the tiny body of an infant. So say Volusianus and many philosophers of modern times, who do not see anything unbecoming, however, in pantheism so that the divine nature be confused with the nature even of a stone. Several rationalists of our times say that the Incarnation would be the lapse or descent of the metaphysical absolute into the phenomenal relative, or the lapse of immutable eternity into mutable time. In like manner some go further and say that the Incarnation might perhaps be admitted by those who thought that the earth is the center of the universe, but not by those who hold that the earth is but like an atom among the millions of stars. They also say that the Incarnation is not only derogatory to God's supreme majesty, but also to His mercy, which is more strikingly manifested by simply forgiving the sin without demanding reparation.

Finally, if it were said to be fitting for God to become incarnate, we should also have to conclude that it was unfitting for God not to become incarnate. But this conclusion is false, because God could have willed not to become incarnate, without this being derogatory to Him.[4] All other objections even of modern philosophers are easily reduced to the above-mentioned objections.[5]

Yet the answer is that it was fitting for God to become incarnate.

Authoritative proof. St. Paul and St. Damascene say that it appears

[4] Cf. *Contra Gentes,* Bk. IV, chap. 40, for other objections.

[5] Cf. *Dict. théol. cath.,* art. "Incarnation," col. 1463–73.

to be most fitting that the invisible things of God be made known by the visible things He has created. Thus God created the world in manifestation of His goodness and perfections. But, as Damascene says, the Incarnation shows the goodness, wisdom, justice, and omnipotence of God.

The goodness which Damascene speaks of includes mercy, and already Plato had defined divine goodness as diffusive of itself, it being the love of supreme opulence or perfection for extreme poverty. In a loftier strain, the Evangelist says: "For God so loved the world as to give His only-begotten Son." [6] This thought is developed below.

Theological proof. It starts from a consideration of God's goodness, on which the fitness of the Incarnation has its special foundation, and is a commentary on the words of St. John: "For God so loved the world as to give His only-begotten Son." [7] God's goodness is seen conspicuously in this supreme and most liberal gift, although His wisdom, justice, or omnipotence is also evident.

The argument may be reduced to the following syllogism.

It belongs to the idea of good to communicate itself to others, for good is self-diffusive.[8] But God's nature is essential goodness, or plenitude of being. Therefore it is fitting for God to communicate Himself to others in the highest degree, which finds its complete realization in the Incarnation.

The major is quoted from Dionysius,[9] and is explained by St. Thomas in various places. It contains three principles: Good is self-diffusive, primarily as the end that attracts and perfects. Secondly, inasmuch as the end attracts the agent to act at least immanently. Thirdly, inasmuch as the perfect agent acts to communicate its goodness externally.

Nevertheless, good does not consist essentially in the actual communication of itself, for this would result in pantheistic emanation; but good essentially implies an aptitude or propensity to communicate itself. This means that good is aptitudinally self-diffusive, not of necessity diffusing itself, and, when it does so, this diffusion is sometimes most free and entirely gratuitous; but sometimes this diffusion

[6] John 3:16.
[7] *Ibid.*
[8] *Summa theol.,* Ia, q. 5, a. 4, ad 2.
[9] *Div. nom.,* Bk. IV.

is a necessary act, if the agent is determined to act in only one way, as the primary purpose of the sun is to give light.

These truths have been explained by St. Thomas in various parts of his works. Thus he says: "Goodness is described as self-diffusive, in the sense that an end is said to move," [10] namely, by attracting to itself, as to that which is perfect and perfective. Thus good is more of the nature of a final cause than of an efficient cause. But as stated in the argumentative part of this article just quoted, the end moves the efficient cause to act. Hence St. Thomas says: "The very nature of good is that something flows from it but not that it flows from something else. . . . But, since the First Good diffuses itself according to the intellect, to which it is proper to flow forth into its effects according to a certain fixed form, it follows that there is a certain measure from which all other goods share the power of diffusion." [11]

Thus, this law is verified, namely, that good is self-diffusive throughout the universe, as St. Thomas shows in illustrating the mystery of the Trinity. He says: "The nobler a nature is, the more that which flows from it is more intimate to it." [12] In other words, good is self-diffusive, and the nobler it is, the more fully and more intimately it is self-diffusive. For instance, the sun illumines and heats, or fire generates fire, the plant produces a plant, the grown-up animal or perfect animal generates an animal like itself. Similarly, a celebrated artist or a famous musician conceives and produces wonderful works of art; a prominent scientist or celebrated astronomer discovers and formulates the laws of nature, for instance, the courses of the planets. Great teachers, such as St. Augustine, impart not only their knowledge but also their spirit to their disciples; a virtuous man incites others to lead a virtuous life; great apostles, such as St. Paul, communicate to others their love for God. Hence good is self-diffusive, and the nobler it is, the more fully and intimately it is self-diffusive. We now see how this principle illustrates the mystery of the Trinity, inasmuch as the Father, generating the Son, communicates to Him not only a participation in His nature, His intellect, and His love, but His complete and indivisible nature, so that the Son of God is Light of Light,

[10] *Summa theol.,* Ia, q. 5, a. 4, ad 2.

[11] *Ibid.,* Ia IIae, q. 1, a. 4, ad 1. See also Ia, q. 19, a. 2; *Contra Gentes,* Bk. II, chap. 30, no. 3; chap. 45, no. 1.

[12] *Contra Gentes,* Bk. IV, chap. 11.

God of God, true God of true God. Likewise the Holy Spirit is true God proceeding from the mutual love between the Father and the Son.

There is, however, a difficulty. It is that the principle, good is self-diffusive, proves either too much or not enough. It proves, indeed, too much if we infer from it the moral necessity and a fortiori the physical necessity of the Incarnation. But it does not prove enough if the Incarnation is a most free decree, because then, whether God became incarnate or not seems to be equally fitting.

As a matter of fact, there were extreme views both for and against this principle. Some pantheists, such as the Neoplatonists, in accordance with their emanatory theory, exaggerated this principle, saying that good is essentially and actually self-diffusive and also actually diffusing itself. But God is the highest good. Therefore He is essentially and actually diffusive externally by a process of necessary emanation. This teaching is contrary to the dogma of a free creation, which was explicitly defined by the Vatican Council in these words: "God created both the spiritual and corporeal creature with absolute freedom of counsel," [13] and not from eternity.

Absolute optimists, such as Leibnitz and Malebranche, likewise erred.[14] Hence the principle that good is self-diffusive must be understood in the sense we already noted with the Thomists, as meaning that good does not consist essentially in the actual communication of itself, but that there is essentially in good an aptitude and tendency to be self-diffusive, first as the end proposed, and then as moving the agent to act. But actual diffusion of good is sometimes necessary if the agent is determined in one way, as the sun is to illumine; sometimes this diffusion is a most free and absolutely gratuitous act,[15] because God is not determined in one way in His eternal acts. He is already infinitely good and blessed in Himself, and created good does not increase His perfection; He is not more being after His action.

Thus creation and the Incarnation are absolutely free acts. The freedom of both is confirmed by the revelation of the mystery of the Trinity; for if there had been neither creation nor Incarnation, the

[13] Denz., no. 1783.

[14] They said that God was obliged not by a physical but a moral necessity to create the best possible world, which finds its ultimate perfection in the Incarnation, thus making this latter morally necessary. This is contrary to the gratuity of this greatest gift.

[15] *Summa theol.,* Ia, q. 19, a. 3.

principle that good is self-diffusive would be verified in the case of the internal divine processions.

This sufficiently explains the major of our syllogism, namely, that good is self-diffusive.

Minor. God's nature is essential goodness, for He is the self-subsisting Being and is therefore the very plenitude of being, which means that He is the essential, supreme, and infinite goodness.[16]

Therefore it is fitting for God to communicate Himself to others in the highest degree, and this is, indeed, most effectively accomplished by means of the Incarnation. For by this means God communicates to the creature not only a participation of being, as in the creation of stones, not only a participation in life, as in the creation of plants and animals, not only a participation in the intellectual and moral life of justice and holiness, as in the creation of Adam, the first man, but He communicates Himself in person. St. Thomas quotes St. Augustine in saying: "He so joined created nature to Himself that one person is made up of these three, the Word, a soul, and flesh."[17] Hence it is manifest that it was fitting for God to become incarnate.

This same principle (good is self-diffusive) illustrates the mystery of Redemption, the sacrifice of the Cross, and the institution of the Eucharist.

There is still another difficulty, namely, that this argument does not sufficiently prove. It is that if, in virtue of the principle that good is self-diffusive, the Incarnation is not even morally necessary but absolutely free and gratuitous, then it is equally fitting whether God become incarnate or not. This leaves the question either indifferent or undecided. Therefore, as the nominalists say, it is useless for theology to speak of the fitness of the mysteries that have been accomplished by God's liberality.

Reply. Billuart says: "The incarnation was fitting, not in the sense of its being necessary, but of its being a free act."[18] We say, for instance, the motive for choosing this particular thing is fitting, not as necessitating the will, but it is fitting that this particular thing be a matter of free choice, and not because of any necessity. Thus it is fitting to preserve one's virginity, yet it is equally fitting to make use of matrimony, because each is a free decision. And so incarnation or

[16] *Ibid.*, Ia, q. 6, a. 1, 2.
[17] *Ibid.*, IIIa, q. 1, a. 1, c.
[18] *Com. in IIIam*, q. 1, a. 1.

no incarnation, each was equally fitting. As Cajetan says: "To communicate Himself to others does not denote a new perfection in God but in the creature to whom this perfection is communicated." [19]

Hence theology does not have recourse to useless speculations about the fittingness of the Incarnation, as several nominalists said, and certain philosophers and theologians who wrote that the Incarnation is said to be fitting because it was accomplished; but it would have been likewise and equally fitting for God not to have become incarnate if He had so willed. Therefore the arguments of fitness have no foundation.

This statement would be true if it were not more fitting for God to have chosen to become incarnate than for Him not to have chosen. In the opinion of St. Thomas, before the foreknowledge of merits it is not more fitting for God to choose Peter in preference to Judas; for this choice "depends on the will of God; as from the simple will of the artificer it depends that this stone is in this part of the wall, and that in another; although the plan requires that some stones should be in this place and some in that place." [20] The election of the predestined depends purely on the divine benevolence, which is the culmination of divine liberty.

In the matter we are discussing, it is a certain motive in the divine strategy or in divine providence that makes the Incarnation more fitting than no incarnation,[21] just as creation is preferable to no creation, and just as virginity consecrated to God is better than matrimony. But this reason of fitness does not even morally necessitate the divine will, which is independent of all created good, inasmuch as from all eternity God's goodness is infinite, and is not in need of any created good. Therefore the argument of fitness does not make it necessary for God to become incarnate, but it is advanced as showing the wisdom of such choice.

Difficulty. God would have communicated Himself still more if He had united all created natures with Himself.

Reply. The union is not an absolute impossibility, and it would not have been pantheism, because it would have been accomplished without confusion of the created nature with the uncreated; but then all men and angels would have been impeccable, as Christ is. It is also

[19] *Ibid.,* q. 1, a. 1, no. 6. The author remarks that what Cajetan says here is more forcible than what he said previously on this point. Cf. *in Iam,* q. 19, a. 3.

[20] *Summa theol.,* Ia, q. 23, a. 5, ad 5.

[21] See q. 1, a. 2.

fitting that the Word be united with the human nature, which is the microcosm, the compendium of the universe, inasmuch as it includes corporeity, as also vegetative, sensitive and intellective lives.

It is even more perfect for the Word to be united only with the human nature of Christ, and not with others. The reason is that the whole world demands subordination of beings, and it is fitting that the created nature personally united with the Word be the highest in the order of created beings, as the efficient and final cause of those beings beneath it, as St. Paul says: "For all are yours. And you are Christ's, and Christ is God's." [22]

Concerning this article, Medina asks whether there can be anything more excellent than the humanity of Christ. He replies that there can, indeed, be something more excellent than the humanity of Christ, but not anything more excellent than Christ.

1) God could not make anything that is better than Christ our Lord, because Christ is truly God.

2) God could not elevate human nature to anything better than the hypostatic union.

3) God could have made something more excellent than the humanity of Christ, such as more perfect angels. In fact, as we shall state farther on, God, by His absolute power, could have given to the soul of Christ a higher degree of the light of glory, or one of greater intensity, because the highest possible degree of the created light of glory is inconceivable; for God can produce something still more perfect than anything He has produced. Thus the swiftest possible motion is inconceivable, because such swiftest motion would reach its terminus before it had left its starting point, and would no longer be motion, but immobility.

St. Thomas says: "God can make always something better than each individual thing." [23] Hence in created beings, there is no highest possible, and in this sense there is no highest creatable angel; but nothing can be higher than the hypostatic union of some created nature with some divine person.

What has just been said is the answer to the absolute optimism of Leibnitz and Malebranche.

Reply to first objection. "God was not changed by the Incarnation . . . but He united Himself to the creature in a new way, or rather

[22] I Cor. 3:22 f.

[23] *Summa theol.*, Ia, q. 25, a. 6, ad 1.

united Himself to it," St. Thomas says; "or rather He united it to Himself," because there is a real relation of union of Christ's humanity to the Word, but not of the Word to the assumed humanity. It was fitting for Christ's humanity thus to be assumed.

Reply to the second objection. "To be united to God was not fitting for human flesh according to its natural endowments, but it was fitting by reason of God's infinite goodness that He should unite it for man's salvation."

This distinction is of greatest validity in showing the fitness of the elevation of our nature to the supernatural order, so as to solve the following objection, which is similar to the one raised by Baius: What is eminently fitting must be unconditional, and is opposed to what is gratuitous. But the beatific vision is for us eminently fitting, so that its privation is abject misery. Therefore the beatific vision is unconditionally fitting to our nature, and is not gratuitous.

Reply. I distinguish the major, in accordance with the distinction given in this article. What is eminently fitting according to our natural endowments must be unconditional, this I concede; what is according to God's infinite goodness, this I deny; and I contradistinguish the minor.

Reply to the third objection. It could be fitting for God to assume flesh but not evil, because flesh is from God the author of nature and is ordered to good, whereas evil is not.

Reply to fourth objection. St. Augustine replies to Volusianus that God by the Incarnation at Bethlehem did not lose the government of the world, just as He did not lose His divine nature, but united the human nature to it. "Hence (in the infant) Jesus the greatness of divine power feels no straits in narrow surroundings." God's immensity is not measured by space or by quantity, but it is greatness of power, supporting or preserving all things in being. If a word uttered by a human being in some point of space can be heard by others also even far away, and its meaning has a moral influence upon the whole world, why could not the Word of God, present in the frail body of the child Jesus, still preserve in being and govern all things created? [24]

Finally, what must be said in reply to the objection of modern scientists, who say that the Incarnation perhaps could be admitted if the earth were the center of the universe, which it is not, for it is a

[24] Cf. Monsabré, *Conference 34*.

planet among countless millions of heavenly bodies that are greater, namely, the stars and the nebulae?

Reply. It may be said: 1. Just as the a priori reason why the Savior was sent was not so that the Jewish race be chosen in preference to some other nation, or, among the women of this race, that Mary be chosen as the Mother of our Lord in preference to some other woman, or among the just of this race, there was no a priori reason that Joseph be chosen as the foster father of our Lord; so there is no a priori reason that the earth be chosen in preference to some other heavenly body that may possibly be inhabited, such as Sirius.

We may also say: 2. We do not know whether there are any other heavenly bodies suitable for human habitation, which are inhabited.

On this point both the positive sciences and theology can offer only hypotheses. Therefore it is not on conjectural grounds that the testimony about the Incarnation must be rejected; namely, the testimony of Christ, of the apostles, of so many martyrs, of the Catholic Church must be rejected concerning the Incarnation. This testimony is confirmed, indeed, by miracles and the wonderful life of the Church, which is fruitful both morally and spiritually in all good works.

If some of the other heavenly bodies are inhabited by human beings, God has not deemed it opportune to reveal this fact to us. Some say, if perhaps there are others inhabited, then these human beings are either in the purely natural state, or there was no case of original sin among them, or if there was, then they were regenerated in some other way than by the Incarnation. There is nothing intrinsically repugnant in all these views. It is difficult to say, however, whether these opinions can be reconciled with the free decree of the Incarnation in its relation to the human race. For revelation speaks of the human race as it exists on this earth.

Whatever is the fact about these gratuitous hypotheses, Christ, as the incarnate Word of God, is the culmination of the whole of creation, and, just as He is the head of the angels, at least as regards accidental grace, so He could be such with reference to human beings who might be living on some of the other heavenly bodies. Concerning these things and many others, we have no knowledge, and there is no need for us to stop and discuss them. Some men seem to be of the opinion that on other heavenly bodies perhaps there are rational animals of another species than man. But this seems to be false, for the term "rational animal" seems to be not a genus but the ultimate species, according to the principle of continuity; for the highest in the lowest order, for instance, the sensitive life, touches the lowest in the highest order, namely, the intellective life. Hence there is no conjunction of the highest in the sensitive life with the lowest in the intellective life, except in one species, and this is not susceptible to either increase or decrease.

Finally, it must be noted that even if the world were the mathematical center of the universe, this would be no reason why God should choose it for the Incarnation. Thus Christ was not born in Jerusalem, but in Bethlehem. So also St. Augustine was the greatest theologian of his time, and yet he came into the world and taught not at Rome, which was the center of the world, but in Africa. He was only bishop of Hippo.

The mathematical position of a body is a matter of less importance with reference to a supernatural mystery, which infinitely transcends the spatial order.

What has been said suffices concerning the fitness of the Incarnation.

Second Article

WHETHER IT WAS NECESSARY FOR THE RESTORATION OF THE HUMAN RACE THAT THE WORD OF GOD SHOULD BECOME INCARNATE

State of the question. (1) We assume that the Incarnation was not absolutely necessary, as Wyclif contended, arguing from the false principle that "all things happen because of absolute necessity."[25] Presupposing the fact of creation, the Incarnation was not necessary, whatever absolute optimists, such as Leibnitz and Malebranche, said to the contrary; although the Incarnation may have increased the accidental glory of God, He is absolutely sufficient unto Himself, and is not at all in need of this accidental glory.

2) We assume that after original sin, it was in God's power not to will the reparation of the human race, and in this there would have been no injustice, as St. Augustine says.[26] Therefore we must thank God for having mercifully willed to free the human race from sin.

[25] Denz., no. 607.

[26] *De natura et gratia,* no. 5.

As a matter of fact, indeed, God did not reinstate the fallen angels; and why He permitted their fall was for a greater good, which must be the manifestation of infinite justice. St. Thomas considers the reparation of the human race to be most fitting, for the sin was not in itself irreparable, whereas he considers the devil's sin, which was committed with full knowledge, to be in itself irreparable, just as the sin of final impenitence is for man. He says: "So it is customary to say that man's free will is flexible to the opposite both before and after the choice; but the angel's free will is flexible to either opposite before the choice but not after. So therefore the good angels who adhered to justice were confirmed therein; whereas the wicked ones, sinning, are obstinate in sin," [27] because the angel immediately and intuitively sees whatever must be considered before the choice, with nothing to be considered after the choice.

The question of this article is posited on the understanding that God wills to restore the human race, so far as it is capable of restoration.

A thing is said to be necessary for the end in two ways:

a) simply, when the end cannot be attained in any other way. Thus food is necessary for the preservation of life;

b) in a qualified manner, when the end is attained more conveniently, as a horse is necessary for a journey.

Some thought that St. Anselm in his treatise on the Incarnation [28] taught its absolute necessity after the fall of the human race; but St. Bonaventure and Scotus interpret his statements in a benign sense; in fact, St. Anselm does so himself farther on.[29] Tournely holds that the Incarnation is absolutely necessary after the fall of the human race, if God wills to free the human race from sin.

On the contrary, it is the common teaching among theologians that the Incarnation is not absolutely necessary even after the fall of the human race, even if it is granted that God willed to free the human race from sin, because there were other means of liberation; but it was necessary *secundum quid*. Suarez thinks that it would be rash to deny this common opinion of the theologians; so does Lugo. In fact, Valentia says that the conclusion is most certain, which means that it is a theological conclusion commonly admitted by the theologians,

[27] *Summa,* Ia, q. 64, a. 2.
[28] *Cur Deus homo,* Bk. I, chap. 4.
[29] *Ibid.,* Bk. II, chaps. 5, 17.

one which is supported by many testimonies of the Fathers of the Church.[30]

St. Thomas, who firmly holds this conclusion, begins by positing difficulties that are against even the *secundum quid* necessity of the Incarnation. He argues that the Incarnation does not seem to be necessary even *secundum quid* because: (1) for the reparation of the human race, the non-incarnate Word can do whatever the incarnate Word can do; therefore the Incarnation is not absolutely necessary. (2) God must not demand from man greater satisfaction than man can give. (3) It is better if there had been no Incarnation, because the more men consider God as raised above all creatures and removed from sense perception, the more they reverence Him. But God's dignity seems to be lowered by assuming human flesh.

Yet the answer is:

1) The Incarnation is not indeed absolutely necessary for the reparation of the human race. (2) But it was necessary *secundum quid,* namely, as a better and more convenient means.

First Part: **Authoritative proof.**

A. Billuart holds [31] that this second opinion is the unanimous teaching of the Fathers; he mentions SS. Athanasius, Gregory Nazianzen, Theodoret, Cyril of Alexandria, Gregory the Great, and John Damascene. Likewise St. Augustine in one of his works says: "Foolish people say that the only way by which God in His wisdom could liberate mankind was by becoming man, and by suffering all He did from sinners. To these persons we say that such was absolutely possible for God, but if He had done otherwise, this likewise would have been displeasing to your stupidity." [32]

B. Proof from reason. Concerning this first part of the thesis, St. Thomas says: "God of His omnipotent power could have restored human nature in many other ways." [33] What ways were these?

In the first place, God could have pardoned the offense committed against Him by sin. Tournely denies the possibility of this way by God's ordinary power, because the preservation of justice requires punishment of the offense.

We reply to this objection, according to the mind of St. Thomas,[34]

[30] Cf. *Dict. théol. cath.,* art. "Incarnation," cols. 1474-82.

[31] *Com. in IIIam.,* q. 1, a. 2.

[32] *De agone christiano,* chap. 11. See also *De Trinitate,* Bk. XIII, chap. 10.

[33] *Summa,* IIIa, q. 1, a. 2, § 1.

[34] *Ibid.,* IIIa, q. 46, a. 2, ad 3.

by saying that the supreme judge and legislator can do so, since He is above other judges, and therefore enjoys the prerogative of being able to pardon offenders even without demanding reparation, just as sometimes kings bestow a favor upon or are merciful to those condemned to death.

Or again, God could have accepted some sort of satisfaction from man, or as it pleased Him to accept it; for there is no contradiction implied in these ways of pardoning by Him, and God is absolutely free in His operations *ad extra.*

Or, as we said in the statement of the question, God could even have willed not to restore the human race, although it is extremely fitting for Him to do so.

Proof of thesis (second part). This part states that the Incarnation was *secundum quid* necessary for the reparation of the human race, as being the better way.

First of all, there is the authority of St. Augustine, who holds that the Incarnation was more fitting than any other way for the reparation of the human race.

St. Thomas offers a fine theological proof, in which he shows the fitness of the Incarnation on the part of man, just as in the first article of this question he showed its fitness on the part of God, who, being the supreme good, is in the highest degree self-diffusive. His argument may be reduced to the following syllogism.

That way is better for the reparation of the human race, by which man is better and more easily urged to good and withdrawn from evil. But each of these results is obtained by the Incarnation. Therefore the Incarnation is the better way for the reparation of the human race. The major is evident.

The minor is proved, as regards our furtherance in good, by a consideration of the theological virtues, which are higher than all the other virtues, for God is their immediate object and the ultimate end to whom the sinner must be converted.

Faith is made more certain by the Incarnation, for the very reason that by it we believe God Himself who is speaking.

For the formal motive of faith is the authority of God revealing; but God, who is most exalted, remains hidden from us, even though He speaks to us through the prophets, whose preaching is confirmed by miracles. How much more we are confirmed in the faith, if God Himself comes to us, and speaks to us as a human being, not as the scribes did, but as one having authority, saying: "Amen, amen, I say unto you: he that believeth in Me, hath everlasting life." [35]

This argument seems paradoxical to those who say, as the liberal Protestants do, that Christianity is the most exalted type of religion, provided that the dogma of Christ's divinity be eliminated from it. They say this, since they are imbued with the spirit of rationalism that seeks to judge all things by human reason, and not as God sees them.

On the contrary, if we consider this matter in the spirit of faith, this argument is seen to be most fitting and also most exalted, and not one made up by St. Augustine, who is quoted in this article, but as contained already in the very preaching of Christ and His apostles. Jesus Himself says: "I am one that give testimony of Myself, and the Father that sent Me giveth testimony of Me." [36] No prophet spoke words like these, for only Christ can say such words, because He alone, as He Himself said, "is the truth and the life." [37] He is the First Truth, who gives testimony of Himself, and so He is the formal motive of faith, namely, the authority of God actually revealing, and this authority is confirmed by miracles evident to the senses. Similarly Jesus says: "The words which Thou gavest Me I have given to them. And they have received them and have known in very deed that I came out from Thee; and they have believed that Thou didst send Me." [38] Hence the Evangelist writes: "The Samaritans said to the woman: We now believe not for thy saying, for we ourselves have heard Him, and we know that this is indeed the Savior of the world." [39]

Likewise St. John says in his prologue: "And of His fullness we have all received. . . . No man hath seen God at any time; the only-begotten Son who is in the bosom of the Father, He hath declared Him." [40]

Similarly St. John says: "That which was from the beginning, which we have heard, which we have seen with our eyes, which we have looked upon, and our hands have handled of the World of life. For the life was manifested, and we have seen and do bear witness and declare unto you the life eternal, which was with the Father, and

[35] John 6:47.
[36] *Ibid.,* 8:18.
[37] *Ibid.,* 14:6.
[38] *Ibid.,* 17:8.
[39] *Ibid.,* 4:41 f.
[40] *Ibid.,* 1:16 f.

hath appeared to us." [41] This means that you can believe because what we announce to you we have heard from the Word incarnate, whom we saw by our sense of sight, whom we looked upon, and whom we touched with our hands.

Likewise St. Paul writes: "God who at sundry times and in divers manners spoke in times past to the fathers by the prophets, last of all in these days hath spoken to us by His Son, whom He hath appointed heir of all things, by whom also He hath made the world." [42] And again he says: "For if the word, spoken by angels, became steadfast . . . how shall we escape . . . what has been declared by the Lord, . . . God also bearing them witness by signs and wonders." [43] This means that Christ is a more exalted witness than the angels.

These texts serve to illustrate the argument of St. Thomas, who says that by the Incarnation our faith is reassured since we believe God Himself speaking to us, that is, speaking to us as man in His assumed nature. As St. Augustine says: "In order that man might journey more trustfully toward the truth, the Truth itself, the Son of God, having assumed human nature, established and founded faith." [44]

Certainly in this life we see Christ's divinity neither by the sense of sight nor mentally; but Jesus with so great authority speaks to us, saying: "I give testimony of Myself," [45] making Himself equal to God, so that no man of good will can doubt that Jesus is truly the living God, who is speaking to us. I say: no man of good will in the salutary sense of the Gospel, that is, neither resisting revelation, nor internal inspiration given to one for the purpose of believing.

When Christ says, "Come to Me, all you that labor and are burdened, and I will refresh you . . . he that loveth father or mother more than Me, is not worthy of Me," [46] He means men of good will who do not resist the grace of faith, do not doubt that He is more than a mere man, more than a prophet, because no prophet uttered such words; and they are certain that Christ is the First Truth, who is speaking to us. And it is precisely such great authority as this that proves unbearable to the Pharisees, who therefore turn away from Him.

In other words, what is the greatest light on this earth for men of

[41] I John 1:1 f.
[42] Heb. 1:1 f.
[43] *Ibid.*, 2:2 f.
[44] *De civ. Dei,* Bk. XL, chap. 2.
[45] John 8:14.
[46] Matt. 11:28; 10:37.

good will, becomes obscurity for them. This means that what most of all confirms the faith of men of good will, becomes a source of scandal for them, as Simeon foretold, saying: "Behold this Child is set for the fall and for the resurrection of many in Israel and for a sign that shall be contradicted." [47] For this reason Christ Himself said: "Blessed is he that shall not be scandalized in Me." [48] Our argument was imputed formerly as an objection to our Lord's opponents, and is so too in our days for the rationalists, who, so they say, would be willing to admit the truth of Christianity if it did not include the dogma of Christ's divinity, which means that they would accept Christianity if it were no longer Christianity, but only a higher form of the evolution of natural religion. Thus the greatest light is turned for them into obscurity; but this light is essentially illuminating, and it is only accidentally that it has a blinding effect, that is, on account of the bad disposition of the hearer. As St. Augustine says: "Light is annoying to those of defective eyesight, but it is very welcome to those of good eyesight." [49]

Thus the argument remains most firm, namely, that our faith is made more certain by the Incarnation, since we believe God who speaks to us as man in His assumed human nature. The formal motive of faith is reduced to almost sensible proportions inasmuch it is the supreme authority of Christ speaking. Hence we read in the Gospel that the ministers sent by the Pharisees feared to arrest Jesus, and replied to the chief priests: "Never did man speak like this man." [50] They meant, never did any man utter words so sublime, or in such an exalted and divine manner; for there was a sensible manifestation of something divine in Christ's tone and manner of speech.

St. Thomas says that by the Incarnation we are greatly strengthened in hope. Why is this? It is because hope is a theological virtue that longs for the supreme future and possible good, indeed, but difficult of attainment. Its formal motive is God helping, who has promised us His help not only to keep His commandments that are always possible to observe, but also to save our souls.

Hence hope is trust in God, and this trust increases in us inasmuch as God not only promises His help, but actually bestows it, and mani-

[47] Luke 2:34.
[48] Matt. 11:6.
[49] *Sermon* 53, Vol. 38.
[50] John 7:46.

fests His benevolence even in a way that appeals to our senses. Thus we place our trust especially in friends, because we know their help comes from motives of true and deep love for us.

But by the Incarnation God not only gives us His help, which means not only His grace, but He gives us the Author of grace, who remains present in the Holy Eucharist, which very much increases the virtue of hope in us. It is what St. Augustine says in the passage quoted by St. Thomas in this article.

Thus the virtue of hope is very much strengthened in us since Christ says more reassuringly than any prophet: "Come to Me all you that labor and are burdened, and I will refresh you." [51] I am He who helps, I am the Author of salvation. Similarly, when Jesus says to the paralytic, before healing him: "Thy sins are forgiven thee," [52] that is, your soul is healed, whereas you were demanding only the cure of a bodily ailment. Likewise St. Paul formulated this argument in equivalent words when he wrote: "The mystery which hath been hidden from ages and generations, but now is manifested to His saints, to whom God would make known the riches of the glory of this mystery among the Gentiles, which is Christ in you the hope of glory." [53] Again he writes: "Christ our hope," [54] for Christ Himself, as God, is both the object and the motive of our hope, for God Himself is both helper and helping.

The following special text of St. Paul must here be quoted: "If God be for us, who is against us? He that spared not even His own Son, but delivered Him up for us all, how shall He not also, with Him, give us all things? Who shall accuse against the elect of God? . . . Who is He that shall condemn? Christ Jesus that died, yea that is risen also again, who is at the right hand of God, who also maketh intercession for us. Who then shall separate us from the love of Christ? Shall tribulation or distress or famine . . . or persecution or the sword? . . . But in all these things we overcome because of Him that has loved us." [55] In other words, in all these things we overcome, because of the efficacy of the help of Him who loved us; and in the opinion of St. Augustine and St. Thomas this help is of itself efficacious, and not because our consent was foreseen by God.

[51] Matt. 11:28.
[52] *Ibid.*, 9:6.
[53] Col. 1:26 f.
[54] I Tim. 1:1.
[55] Rom. 8:31 f.

The formal motive of hope is not man's effort cooperating with God's help, but it is God helping, who, by the Incarnation is with us and remains present in the Holy Eucharist. Thus we have the greatest reason for trusting in God.

Thirdly, by the Incarnation "charity is greatly enkindled," says St. Thomas, who quotes here St. Augustine as saying: "What greater cause is there of the Lord's coming than to show God's love for us?" And St. Augustine afterward adds: "If we have been slow to love, at least let us hasten to love in return." [56]

Charity obliges us to love God more than we love ourselves, loving Him as our friend, the formal motive of our love being His goodness, which infinitely surpasses all His favors bestowed upon us. This means that we must will efficaciously the fulfillment of His will, that He may reign truly and profoundly in souls and be glorified forever, since the Scripture says: "Not to us, O Lord, not to us; but to Thy name give glory." [57] What has been said constitutes the definition of charity that surpasses hope, just as the love of benevolence surpasses the love of concupiscence, no matter how much this latter be upright and ordered to its proper end. By the virtue of hope, I desire God for myself, but as my final end, indeed, because He is God. By the virtue of charity, however, I love God efficaciously as my friend, and I love Him more than I love myself, and I will Him all befitting good. This most sublime aspect of charity, more than anything hope can offer, will enable us to cease worrying, too, about the mystery of predestination, notwithstanding its great obscurity. By charity I love God more than myself, and in a general way whatever God has eternally decreed in manifestation of His goodness. Thus God, who is infinitely good, is the eminent source of all goodness being a quasi-ego to myself, and in a certain sense more an ego than I am, for whatever good I possess already is contained in Him in a far more eminent manner. This is that true mysticism which is certainly the normal way to holiness.

But this divine goodness, which is the formal object of charity, is especially made manifest by the supreme act of love in which God gave us His only-begotten Son.[58] It is the fundamental truth of Christianity, because this love is the fountain source of the very gift of the Incarnation. Hence Jesus says: "As the Father hath loved Me, I also

[56] *Summa theol.,* IIIa, q. 1, a. 2, c.
[57] Ps. 113:1.
[58] John 3:16.

have loved you. Abide in My love."[59] And again: "Greater love than this no man hath, that a man lay down his life for his friends."[60] St. John writes: "By this hath the charity of God appeared toward us, because God hath sent His only-begotten Son into the world, that we may live by Him. In this is charity, not as though we had loved God, but because He hath first loved us, and sent His Son to be a propitiation for our sins. My dearest, if God hath so loved us, we also ought to love one another."[61] Farther on he says: "Let us therefore love God, because God first hath loved us."[62]

Likewise St. Paul says: "But God commendeth His charity toward us, because when as yet we were sinners, according to the time, Christ died for us."[63] Writing to Titus, he says: "For the grace of God our Savior hath appeared to all men, instructing us, that denying ungodliness and worldly desires . . . we should live godly in this world, looking for the blessed hope and coming of the glory of the great God and our Savior Jesus Christ."[64]

Thus these three arguments of St. Thomas not only result in a theologically certain conclusion, but they pertain to the faith, and are the sublime object of contemplation. It is also evident that this contemplation, which proceeds from faith illumined by the gifts of the Holy Ghost, is the normal way to holiness of life.

Fourth, the incarnation of the Word sets us an example in the practice of all virtues, whereas Diogenes and several other philosophers said that the search for an exemplar in virtues is a vain quest. It is only Christ who could say to His adversaries: "Which of you shall convince Me of sin?"[65] Hence holiness of life consists in the imitation of Christ.

Fifth. The Incarnation is most appropriate for withdrawing us from evil.

1) Because man by the Incarnation is instructed to despise the devil conquered by Christ even as man, as stated in the legend of St. Christopher.

2) Because by the Incarnation we begin to realize the dignity of our human nature, so that we are urged not to stain our soul by sin.

[59] *Ibid.*, 15:9.
[60] *Ibid.*, 15:13.
[61] I John 4:9 f.
[62] *Ibid.*, 4:19.
[63] Rom. 5:8 f.
[64] Titus 2:11 f. See also 2:4.
[65] John 8:46.

3) Because the Incarnation takes away all presumption from us since God's grace, regardless of any previous merits on our part, is approved in us or bestowed upon us through Jesus Christ, so that St. Paul is able to say: "By the grace of God I am what I am." [66] The sinner, too, who has committed all crimes, can repent by trusting in the infinite merits of Christ.

4) Pride is removed and cured by a consideration of the humiliating conditions of the passion of our Lord.

5) Man is freed from the slavery of the devil and of sin. As St. Thomas says in this article in equivalent words: God, by assuming our human nature, did not lessen His majesty and attracted us more by this means to know Him.[67]

Therefore the Incarnation is a more fitting way of freeing the human race from sin. Nevertheless, God could have chosen not to become man, and this would not have been derogatory to Him, for the Incarnation was a most free act, and an absolutely gratuitous gift.

Hence we must say that it was more fitting for God to become incarnate, but it would not have been inconsistent with God's goodness if He had not become incarnate. Similarly, it was more fitting for God to have created and raised man to the supernatural order, but it would not have been derogatory to His goodness if He had not done so. Thus in human actions, virginity is more perfect than matrimony, but there is nothing unbecoming in matrimony. There is freedom of choice in both cases.

The only remaining difficulty is the one proposed in the second objection of this article, namely, that it does not seem proper for God to demand greater satisfaction than man can give.

St. Thomas replies to this objection by giving a brief summary of the doctrine on satisfaction. He remarks that it would not, indeed, be fitting if God had not given His Son as Redeemer to make the greater satisfaction. But God gave His Son. This difficulty gives us the opportunity to present certain doubts that must be examined in amplification of the doctrine of this article.

First doubt. Was the Incarnation necessary so as to have condign satisfaction for sin?

St. Thomas examines this question in his reply to the second objection of this article.

[66] I Cor. 15:10.
[67] Cf. ad 3.

State of the question. Satisfaction is the compensation or voluntary payment of any debt. It is of various kinds, as may be seen by the following schema.

Satisfaction	perfect	considered as a formal act of justice, it is called rigorous satisfaction; considered on the part of the offense, it is called condign satisfaction.
	imperfect	considered also on the part of the offense, it is called congruent satisfaction.

St. Thomas distinguishes between two kinds of satisfaction.

1) Satisfaction is perfectly sufficient, he says, when it is condign, being in a certain sense adequate in reparation of the fault committed. Thus, if anyone has to pay another a debt of one hundred dollars, and returns the complete sum, then he is said to have made perfect satisfaction in a material sense. Moreover, that the satisfaction be perfect in the formal sense, or as an act of justice, the restitution must be made out of the debtor's own belongings, and must not be owing to the creditor on some other account, nor in any way under his dominion. The last condition is that the creditor is bound to accept the payment as satisfaction.

Perfect satisfaction considered merely materially is called condign satisfaction. Perfect satisfaction in the formal sense is called rigorous or according to the strictest standard of justice.

2) Imperfect satisfaction also in the material sense, or what is not condign, is that which is deemed sufficient, and which a person is contented to accept as satisfactory. Thus, if anyone is bound to pay back one hundred dollars, and returns eighty, the creditor being satisfied with this sum, such satisfaction is often called congruent.

Three certain conclusions follow from these distinctions.

1) Mere man can in the material sense satisfy imperfectly for sin. This conclusion is expressed in equivalent words by St. Thomas toward the end of his reply to the second objection. The expression "mere man" does not mean the exclusion of grace, but only of the divine nature. Thus a just person can satisfy imperfectly for his own mortal sin, or for another's, by a satisfaction which God can accept, if He so wills, and which He could have accepted, if He had not willed to free man from sin by the Incarnation. So also in this life our satis-

factions for our sins, or in reparation for the sins of others, are imperfect even in the material sense. Hence St. Thomas says: "The satisfaction of every mere man has its efficiency from the satisfaction of Christ," [68] even the satisfaction of the Blessed Virgin Mary. Therefore she is not called co-redemptress except in a subordinate sense to Christ, as being quasi subredemptress.

Hence Pope Pius X ratified the common teaching of theologians, when he said: "That which Christ merited for us *de condigno,* the Blessed Virgin Mary merited for us *de congruo."* [69] And likewise she did not satisfy for us *de condigno,* but *de congruo.* Pope Benedict XV declared: "It can truly be said that along with Christ she redeemed the human race," [70] that is, subordinate to Christ with Him, and through Him, the Blessed Virgin Mary's satisfaction was not condign but congruent, or an imperfect satisfaction, which was not of itself (apart from Christ's redemption) perfectly sufficient.

2) Mere man cannot offer complete satisfaction to God for his own sin or for another's. This means that he cannot satisfy according to the strictest standard of justice, because there is nothing either in the natural order or in the supernatural order that he can offer to God which has not been bestowed upon him by God who is His creditor and which God is bound to accept in satisfaction. Thus the Holy See approved the following statement of a provincial council: "No one but the God-man was able to satisfy in strict justice." [71]

3) Mere man could not satisfy *de condigno* for his own or another's mortal sin; and for such condign reparation the Incarnation was necessary.

This conclusion, which is commonly admitted by theologians, is considered certain by St. Thomas, and occurs in the beginning of his reply to the second objection. However, some theologians, following Scotus and Durandus, admitted that some creature, adorned with a very high degree of grace, such as the Blessed Virgin Mary, could satisfy adequately for mortal sin.

There are proofs for this third conclusion.

Authoritative proof. St. Augustine says: "We would not have been liberated through the one mediator between God and man, the man

[68] *Ibid.,* ad 2.
[69] Denz., no. 3034.
[70] *Epistle,* March 22, 1918.
[71] Council of Cologne, 1860.

Jesus Christ, unless He were also God." [72] Likewise, St. Leo says: "If He were not truly God, He could not apply the remedy; if He were not truly man, He could not give us the example." [73]

This traditional and common opinion among theologians was approved recently by Pope Pius XI, who wrote concerning Mary reparatrix: "If the Son of God had not assumed our human nature for the purpose of repairing it, no created power sufficed to expiate the crimes of men." [74]

Thus the traditional thesis is now a ratified pontifical document, and is theologically certain, being an approved theological conclusion.

Theological proof. St. Thomas gives two reasons why adequate satisfaction was impossible. This he does in his reply to the second objection of this article.

a) Condign satisfaction was impossible by mere man "because the whole of human nature has been corrupted by sin," and only a just person can merit *de condigno* and satisfy. But some may say that God could have preserved some man from original sin, or could have sanctified him after the sin was committed and bestowed a high degree of grace upon him so that he could satisfy for it.

The second reason replies to this suggestion.

b) This reason may be presented by the following syllogism. Mortal sin committed against God has a certain infinity considered as an offense. But condign satisfaction must be adequate reparation. Therefore condign satisfaction must have infinite efficacy, as being the satisfactory act of one who is both God and man.

St. Thomas proves the major by saying: "A sin committed against God has a kind of infinity from the infinity of the divine majesty, because the greater the person we offend, the more grievous the offense." [75]

Yet not all Thomists interpret this major in the same sense.[76]

Some theologians say that St. Thomas wrote that "mortal sin has a kind of infinity" [77] as an offense. Therefore its gravity is not absolutely infinite, but only in a qualified sense and objectively; for sin as an act of the will is always finite. Likewise, its malice, since it is a

[72] *Enchir.*, chap. 108.
[73] *Sermo I, De nativitate.*
[74] Encycl., *Miserentissimus Redemptor.*
[75] Cf. ad 2.
[76] Cf. Salmant., *De incar.*, disp. I.
[77] *De veritate*, q. 28, a. 2.

turning to changeable good, is finite; so it does not merit absolutely infinite punishment, for the penalty of damnation consists in the deprivation of the beatific vision, which is something created, although it concerns God objectively. So say certain Thomists such as Soto, Conradus, along with Scotus, Suarez, and Vasquez.

Others say that the gravity of mortal sin is absolutely infinite, not indeed considered as a physical act, nor as a moral act because of its malice and demerit, but because it is an offense. Briefly, a grievous offense against God is absolutely infinite. Such is the view of Capreolus, Cajetan, Gonet, Salmanticenses, and John of St. Thomas.[78]

These theologians say that, more probably mortal sin, because it is an offense, is absolutely infinite in gravity, and this for the reason given by St. Thomas, namely, "because the greater the person we offend, the more grievous the offense." [79] But He who is the supreme good, who is the ultimate end, who is practically denied by mortal sin, is absolutely infinite in dignity; whereas man prefers the creature to God and loves himself more than God. If it were not so, then St. Thomas would be wrong in concluding the necessity of infinite satisfaction.

St. Thomas also says: "Since God infinitely transcends the creature, mortal sin committed against God is an infinite offense, by reason of the dignity of Him to whom somehow harm is done by sin, since God Himself and His precept are despised." [80]

Moreover, the offense is morally in the person offended, inasmuch as the person offended is truly the victim of injustice. Hence the greater is the dignity of the person offended, the greater is the offense. Thus it is a greater offense to insult a general than a soldier, and a king than a general. Hence to insult God is absolutely infinite as a moral act, inasmuch as it practically denies God the infinite dignity owing to Him as the ultimate end or as the infinite good.

Nevertheless, one mortal sin can be more grievous than another in three ways, either because it is committed with greater deliberation and consent; or, objectively considered, because it is more directed against God; or by reason of the circumstances.

Most certainly the gravity of the offense is estimated according to the dignity of the person offended, whereas the value of the reparation

[78] See Billuart, *De peccatis,* dist. VIII, a. 5.
[79] Cf. IIIa, q. 1, a. 2, ad 2.
[80] *De veritate,* q. 28, a. 2. See also *Dict. théol. cath.,* art. "Incarnation," col. 1478–82.

is estimated according to the dignity of the person who makes reparation. The whole force of the argument rests on this statement.

Objection. Some say that although God, who is infinite, is the object of the act of charity, this act is not absolutely infinite in dignity as a moral act. Therefore, although mortal sin offends God who is infinite, considered as an offense in the moral order, it is not absolutely infinite in gravity.

Reply. The difference is that, as regards charity, God is only its object and not its subject; but He is the subject of the moral offense committed against Him. Thus, as stated, the greater the dignity of the person offended, the greater is the gravity of the offense. On the contrary, although God can be the object of venial sin, it does not deny Him the infinite dignity owing to Him as the ultimate end, and thus its offense is not absolutely infinite.

Briefly, a grievous offense against God is absolutely infinite, since it is practically a denial of His absolutely infinite dignity.

This comparison between a mere man's act of charity that is of finite value, and a grave and absolutely infinite offense against God, is founded on the principle that in our negations concerning God there is more of denial than there is of assertion in our affirmations.[81]

A practical denial of the dignity of the ultimate end denies more about it, than its practical affirmation can affirm about it. Hence the general saying that it is easier to destroy than to build. In a moment a man can destroy very precious objects, which only after a long time can be replaced; and it is generally admitted that an inferior can do more against a superior than for him. Matter, by escaping from the domination of its form, can do more against the form of a corporeal thing, such as a plant or an animal, than for it by remaining under it, because without matter this form, for instance, of a lion, totally disappears, but matter alone is not sufficient for the sensitive life of the lion. The mineral kingdom can do more harm to man, for instance, in an earthquake, than good to him; likewise the lack of air necessary for breathing causes death, whereas its presence is not sufficient; for life, food and other things are also required.

Similarly in the human order, a common man can do great harm

[81] As philosophers say: an absolute denial, since it is of a malignant nature, entirely destroys or excludes. For this reason, negative universal propositions are very dangerous, for a single example to the contrary suffices to show their falsity. Such propositions are totally exclusive.

to a king, but he cannot render him all the honors that are due to him. Likewise the common people can be the source of more affliction to men of great ability than joy to them. In like manner, if it is said of a good doctor that he is not so in the medical art, this judgment grieves him more than the opposite judgment could cause him to rejoice.

Generally speaking, the inferior can do more harm to the superior than good to him. Proud Satan is conscious of this; the devil wishes to have power not from grace, but in his own right; and so he wishes to have the power to destroy, which is tantamount to saying: I am preventing the development of the kingdom of God; it is for this reason that I exist and have power.

Hence the truth of the principle: the inferior can do more harm than good to the superior.

Thus it is that the subordination of the inferior helps to some extent the action of the superior, whereas his insubordination sometimes totally impedes it.

The reason is that frequently the inferior is an indispensable condition for the action of the superior, and the lack of this cooperation results in not only a partial but a total frustration of the action of the higher power, as in the case of insanity resulting from a cerebral lesion there follows a total impossibility of judgment. When the brain is in good condition it is of some help to the reasoning faculty, whereas, if seriously damaged, it completely prevents the act of reasoning. Thus many men who enjoy the best of health have not much intellectual ability; but a man of great intellect suddenly becomes insane because of a cerebral lesion.

Likewise, man of himself can do more against God, against the kingdom of God by blaspheming, than he can do for God by honoring Him. Man in the purely natural state suffices for the complete denial of God's ineffable greatness, but he is afterward incapable of completely affirming this greatness, even though restored by grace. Our negations are more absolute in their effect than our affirmations. When the impious person denies God, he denies God completely in his heart; when the just person affirms God, he does not affirm Him completely, but in a finite manner, and, as St. Thomas says, "we cannot know what God is, but rather what He is not." [82] To comprehend is to equate in knowledge the knowable object. God alone has comprehensive knowl-

[82] *Summa theol.,* Ia, q. 3, prologue.

edge of Himself, which attains to the whole of Him and to all that is contained in Him.[83]

In like manner anyone who denies the principle of finality, completely denies it; on the contrary, anyone who affirms the principle of finality, does not completely understand it. This principle, that, "every agent acts for an end," is known better by an angel, and a fortiori by God. Therefore a grievous offense against God is absolutely infinite, since it denies to God absolutely infinite dignity of the ultimate end, or the supreme Good.

Our grave disobedience toward God is graver because of the offense, than our due subjection to Him contributes to His eternal glory. It remains true, therefore, that the gravity of the offense is estimated according to the dignity of the person offended, whereas the value of the reparation is estimated according to the dignity of the person making reparation.

But what is the validity of the minor, that is, that condign satisfaction must be adequate reparation, and hence it must be of infinite value?

Proof of minor. Condign compensation must offer to God what is no less or more pleasing to Him than the offense is displeasing to Him.

St. Thomas says: "He properly atones for an offense who offers something which the offended one loves equally or even more than he detested the offense. But by suffering out of love and obedience, Christ gave more to God than was required to compensate for the offense of the whole human race. First of all because of the exceeding charity from which He suffered; secondly on account of the dignity of His life which He laid down in atonement, for it was the life of one who was God and man; thirdly on account of the extent of the Passion, and the greatness of the grief endured." [84]

The reason why this satisfaction is of infinite value is that it was offered to God from the charity of the Word incarnate, namely, of the divine person whose theandric act is of infinite price, since the estimated value of the satisfaction is derived from a consideration of the person making satisfaction.

On the contrary, an absolutely infinite injury cannot be condignly repaired by a satisfaction of finite value. But the satisfaction of any creature whatever is of finite value; for the value of the satisfaction is

[83] *Ibid.,* Ia, q. 12, a. 8.
[84] *Ibid.,* IIIa, q. 48, a. 2.

derived, as has been said, from a consideration of the person satisfying, inasmuch as this person is the subject who satisfies. Hence the common saying that honor is in the person honoring.

Therefore the greater the dignity of the person satisfying, the greater the estimate of the satisfaction. Hence the satisfaction of Christ is absolutely infinite, because the person satisfying is divine and infinite. On the contrary, the dignity of the creature who satisfies is finite, no matter what may be the number of his supernatural gifts. Therefore a finite creature cannot give adequate satisfaction for an absolutely infinite offense.

This is the reason given by St. Thomas in his reply to the second objection of this article. But on this point, the knowledge acquired through the gifts of the Holy Ghost is of a much higher order and more striking than discursive knowledge.

Second doubt. Would the Incarnation be necessary if the gravity of the offense were only in a qualified manner infinite?

Would the reason given by St. Thomas still be valid if the grievous offense against God were not absolutely infinite, but only in a qualified manner, that is, objectively, as the act of charity is said to be objectively infinite?

Some Thomists, such as Billuart,[85] reply that the reason given by St. Thomas has still some value, in this sense, that the gravity of mortal sin does not consist only in this, that it denies God His dignity as the ultimate end, but that also the depreciation and contempt of the divine majesty comes from a vile creature, who presumes to offend Him. This injury is not compensated by an act of charity of a mere man, because it is more injurious to God to be subjected to a vile creature than the subjection of this creature to Him pays Him honor. Similarly it is more against the king's dignity to be insulted by one of his ministers, than it adds to his honor for him to accept the apology of his minister.

But the reason as proposed is no longer strictly the reason given by St. Thomas, which is derived not from a consideration of the vileness of the person offending, but from the supreme dignity of the person offended. Hence from what St. Thomas says,[86] it is clearly enough evident that he considers a grievous offense against God to be absolutely infinite, inasmuch as it is practically a denial of His absolutely infinite dignity. We have said that such is the conclusion of very many

[85] *De peccatis,* dist. VIII, a. 5.

[86] *Summa theol.,* IIIa, q. 1, a. 2, ad 2.

Thomists, namely, of Capreolus, Cajetan, Salmanticenses, Godoy, Gonet, John of St. Thomas, Billuart.

Third doubt. Can a just man offer condign satisfaction for venial sin?

Reply. The answer is that he can; for a just man can make reparation for venial sin and therefore satisfy for it, because venial sin does not take away from the soul habitual grace, which is the root of the supernatural life, nor does it turn us away from the ultimate end. Moreover, the injury included in venial sin does not deny God His absolutely infinite dignity as the ultimate end. Therefore this injury is not absolutely infinite but finite. Therefore it can be repaired by what remains of the virtue of charity.

Cajetan in his commentary on this article examines other objections raised by Scotus; but these belong more properly to the article on the passion of our Lord, in which St. Thomas asks whether it brought about our savlation by way of atonement.[87]

It must be noted that the thesis of St. Thomas on the necessity of the Incarnation so as to satisfy *de condigno* for mortal sin is absolutely in conformity with tradition. The Fathers frequently have proved, from the dogma of the redemption admitted by heretics, that Christ was truly God.[88]

SOLUTION OF OBJECTIONS AGAINST THE REPLY TO THE FIRST DOUBT

The Incarnation was not necessary to satisfy *de condigno* for sin.

First objection. Condign satisfaction returns to the one offended all that was taken away by mortal sin. But mere man justified by an act of charity returns to God all that was taken away by mortal sin, namely, it returns lovingly what is His due as being the ultimate end. Therefore mere man justified can offer condign satisfaction to God for mortal sin, and so the Incarnation is not necessary.

Reply. I distinguish the major. Condign satisfaction that returns all, and all that is implied by an act that is equal to the gravity of the offense, then I concede the major.

That returns all, but not all that is implied by an act that is not equal to the gravity of the offense, then I deny it.

I contradistinguish the minor in the same way.

[87] *Ibid.*, IIIa, q. 48, a. 2.

[88] Cf. especially St. Irenaeus, *Adversus haereses*, III, vi, 12; also St. Basil, *Com. in Ps. 48*, no. 4. See also Petavius, Bk. II, no. 12 (beginning).

Satisfaction for wrong done requires more than the mere restitution of the object stolen; it also requires that the object taken be returned with due compensation for slighted honor. Thus, if a commoner snatched a king's daughter, it would not suffice for condign satisfaction that the daughter be returned, for in this way reparation for the wrong done to the king would not be made. Similarly, God's dignity is far more offended when the creature despises Him, than honor is paid to Him by the creature's subjection to Him even by an act of charity. Insubordination is not sufficiently repaired by the restitution of subordination that is already due Him.

Mortal sin of any kind offends God's right, His right of being the ultimate end, and therefore every mortal sin is an insult to God, not always explicitly intended as in blasphemy, but resulting as a consequence of the sin. Although man cannot render to God whatever is due Him according to strictest justice, yet he can be strictly unjust to Him by practically denying Him His absolutely infinite dignity to which He is entitled as the ultimate end.

Second objection. He who can merit *de condigno* for others the grace of forgiveness of mortal sin, can likewise satisfy *de condigno* for the mortal sin of others. But a mere man mercifully justified and constituted the head of the human race could merit *de condigno* for others the grace of forgiveness of sin, which is admitted by several Thomists, such as John of St. Thomas. Therefore this mere man could satisfy *de condigno* for the mortal sin of others.

Reply. I deny the major, because there is no parity between merit and satisfaction. Merit is the right to a proportionate reward in accordance with distributive justice, whereas satisfaction concerns the equal compensation of another, in accordance with the standard of commutative justice, by making equivalent reparation for the wrong done. Hence this mere man would give only a modified satisfaction that would fall short of condign satisfaction, and thus God would condone the offense without receiving condign satisfaction, just as the father in family life condones the offense of a younger son on account of the merits of an elder son. Mere man cannot "offer to God offended something He loves equally or even more than He detests the offense." [89]

Another objection. The incarnate Word did not have a higher degree of virtue than the non-incarnate Word. But the incarnate Word

[89] St. Thomas, *loc. cit.*

could satisfy *de condigno.* Therefore the non-incarnate Word could satisfy *de condigno.*

Reply. I distinguish the major. That the Word incarnate had also certain virtues properly His own as man, this I concede. Otherwise I deny the major.

I contradistinguish the minor. That the Word incarnate could satisfy as the Word in the divine nature, this I deny. As the incarnate Word, that is, as man, this I concede.

God could have restored the human race by condoning the offense without demanding satisfaction; but as God, He could not have obeyed, suffered, prayed, offered sacrifice of reparation to God, and merited.

But I insist. The non-incarnate Word also had strictly the power to satisfy. The power to satisfy implies any good without admixture of evil. But the non-incarnate Word has whatever is good without any admixture of evil. Therefore the non-incarnate Word has strictly the power to satisfy.

Reply. I distinguish the major; that it implies any good without admixture of moral evil, this I concede; no admixture of physical perfection on the part of created nature, this I deny.

I contradistinguish the minor. That the non-incarnate Word has all good without admixture of any imperfection whatever, this I concede; otherwise, I deny the minor.

In other words, mixed perfections are not contained formally, but only virtually in the non-incarnate Word.

Still I insist. The non-incarnate Word can have formally, without becoming incarnate, strictly the power to satisfy. The Word can assume the angelic nature. But by assuming this nature the Word can satisfy formally. Therefore the Word can satisfy formally without becoming incarnate.

Reply. I concede the major.

I distinguish the minor. That the Word can satisfy by satisfaction improperly so called that is freely accepted by God, let it pass without comment; by satisfaction in the strict sense, as offered by the Word in the human nature for our redemption, this I deny.

In like manner I distinguish the conclusion.

Final objection. Mere man can satisfy for venial sin. But a slight offense is infinite, if the distance between the offender and the offended is infinite.

Reply. The gravity of the offense is not estimated formally from the distance, but it is estimated from the dignity of the person offended; and the dignity of God as the ultimate end is practically denied only by mortal sin.

Third Article

WHETHER, IF MAN HAD NOT SINNED, GOD WOULD HAVE BECOME INCARNATE

State of the question. We are concerned here not only with the fitness of the Incarnation, which was discussed in the first article, but also with the proximate motive of the efficacious decree of the Incarnation: the motive, namely, not on the part of God willing, but on the part of the thing willed; for God does not will one thing on account of another, but He wills one thing to be as a means for the other.[90] The question precisely is this, whether, in virtue of the present decree, God so willed the Incarnation for the redemption of the human race, that if man had not sinned, the Word would not have become incarnate.

At the time of St. Thomas there was difference of opinion among the doctors on this question. Alexander of Hales and St. Albert held it to be more probable in virtue of the present decree, even if man had not sinned, that God would have become incarnate. This thesis was afterward more tenaciously defended by Scotus and the Scotists.

On the contrary, St. Bonaventure and St. Thomas declare it to be more probable that, if man had not sinned, the Word of God would not have become incarnate. St. Thomas claims only greater probability for his answer.[91] In the present article, he says: "It is more fitting to say."

For a methodical method of procedure in this complex enough question, let us consider:

1) The difficulties of the question as set forth by St. Thomas at the beginning of this article, are arguments in favor of the opposite opinion.

2) The solution of St. Thomas.

3) The stand taken by Scotus.

[90] *Ibid.,* Ia, q. 19, a. 5.

[91] See *III Sent.,* d. 1, q. 1, a. 3. Also *Com. in Tim.,* chap. 1, lect. 4.

4) How Cajetan, John of St. Thomas, and Billuart interpret the teaching of St. Thomas.

5) Godoy, Gonet, and Salmanticenses give another interpretation, Capreolus being quoted for this view.

6) The solution of the objections advanced by Scotus against this second interpretation, which seems to be more probable.[92]

Since the question is complex, we must say right at the beginning, that we wish especially to defend this truth, which seems to us to be admitted by all, namely, God willed the Incarnation for the manifestation of His goodness, to show His mercy toward men to be redeemed, as the Creed says, "for our salvation." We intend and understand nothing else but that: God, by one sole efficacious decree thus willed the Incarnation.

1) The difficulties of the question are evident from the objections posited at the beginning of this article. They are almost the same as those proposed by St. Thomas in one of his earlier works.[93] They reproduce the opinion on this question that was held by Alexander of Hales and St. Albert, an opinion that was afterward developed by Scotus. From these objections it is apparent that St. Thomas had a very good knowledge of the state of the question.

First difficulty. St. Augustine says: "Many other things are to be considered in the incarnation of Christ besides absolution from sin." [94] Hence, even if man had not sinned, God would have become incarnate. In that event, He would not have been the savior and the victim, but the teacher, the mediator, the King of kings for all mankind.

Second difficulty. The purpose of God in creating is to manifest His goodness and omnipotence; but it belongs to God's omnipotence to perfect His works by some infinite effect, namely, by the Incarnation.

Third difficulty. Human nature has not been made more capable of grace by sin. But after sin it is capable of the grace of the hypostatic union. Therefore, if man had not sinned, human nature would have been capable of this greatest grace, nor would God have withheld from it any good of which it was capable.

Fourth difficulty. God's predestination is eternal. But Christ, as

[92] See *Dict. théol. cath.,* art. "Incarnation," col. 1482–1506.

[93] Cf. *Com. in III Sent.,* d. 1, q. 1, a. 3.

[94] *De Trinit.,* Bk. XIII, chap. 17.

man, was predestined to be truly the Son of God. Therefore, in virtue of this predestination, even before sin, the Incarnation was a necessity.

Fifth difficulty. The mystery of the Incarnation was revealed to the first man in his state of innocence without any reference to his future sin for which reparation must be made.

For these reasons, Alexander of Hales, St. Albert, and later on Scotus deemed it more probable that the Word would have become incarnate even if man had not sinned.

This question assumes no less importance if it be proposed as follows: What is the fundamental trait of Christ? Is it to be the Savior and victim, or preferably to be the teacher, King of kings, Lord of all? Is it only of secondary importance that He is the Savior and victim?

St. Thomas' conclusion in the body of this article is the following. "It is more fitting to say that the work of the Incarnation was ordained by God as a remedy for sin, so that, had sin not existed, the Incarnation would not have been. And yet the power of God is not limited to this; even had sin not existed, God could have become incarnate."

St. Thomas in one of his earlier works [95] gives this opinion as probable, in fact, as more probable. Similarly, in another of his commentaries, he says: "We do not know what God would have ordained (by another decree) if He had not foreknown the sin of man. Nevertheless, authoritative writers seem to state expressly that God would not have become incarnate if man had not sinned. I incline more to this view." [96]

Proof. St. Thomas proves his conclusion by one argument, for, as we shall immediately see, there is no distinction between the argument *"sed contra"* and the argument in the body of this article, but he combines them into one argument, which may be presented by the following syllogism.

What depends solely on the will of God, and beyond all to which the creature is entitled, can be made known to us only inasmuch as it is contained in Sacred Scripture.

But everywhere in Sacred Scripture the sin of the first man is assigned as the reason for the Incarnation.

Therefore it is more fitting to say, since it seems to be more in ac-

[95] *Com. in III Sent.,* d. 1, q. 1, a. 3.
[96] *Com. in I Tim.,* chap. 1, lect. 4.

cordance with the meaning of Sacred Scripture, that the sin of the first man is the reason of the Incarnation. This conclusion is both more and less than a theological conclusion. It is more because it appears to be the meaning of Sacred Scripture; it is less because it is not absolutely certain.

The major is evident, because what depends on the most free will of God is known only to Himself, nor is there any other way by which supernatural gifts [97] can be made known except through revelation, which is contained in Sacred Scripture and also in tradition. Hence the Scripture says: "For who among men is he that can know the counsel of God? Or who can think what the will of God is." [98]

Proof of minor. Christ Himself testifies, saying: "They that are whole, need not the physician, but they that are sick. I came not to call the just, but sinners to penance." [99] And again: "For the Son of man is come to seek and to save that which was lost." [100] St. Paul says: "Christ Jesus came into the world to save sinners." [101] Elsewhere he writes: "God sent His Son made of a woman, made under the law, that He might redeem those who were under the law." [102] The beloved Apostle testifies: "God so loved the world, as to send His only-begotten Son, that whosoever believeth in Him may not perish, but may have life everlasting." [103] St. John the Baptist on seeing Jesus, says: "Behold the Lamb of God . . . who taketh away the sin of the world." [104] Likewise the Old Testament assigns the healing of the contrite of heart and the abolition of iniquity from the land, as the only reasons for the promise and expectation of the Messias.[105] Moreover, the name Jesus signifies Savior.[106]

But Sacred Scripture does not say explicitly that this reason for the Incarnation is the only possible one, and it speaks with reference to

[97] If it is a question of things in nature already produced, it is possible for us from things naturally knowable to know that God freely willed to create them.

[98] Wisd. 9:13.

[99] Luke 5:31 f.

[100] *Ibid.*, 19:10.

[101] I Tim. 1:15.

[102] Gal. 4:4 f.

[103] John 3:16.

[104] *Ibid.*, 1:29. See also Rom. 3:22; I John 1:7; 2:12; 3:5; 4:10.

[105] Cf. Isa. 61:1; Dan. 9:24; Zach. 3:9.

[106] Cf. F. Ceuppens, O.P. (*Theol. biblica, De incarnatione,* pp. 6–29) whose conclusion is: "The motive of the Incarnation, according to the teaching of Sacred Scripture, is the redemption of the human race, and no other motive is given in the pages of Sacred Literature."

us men and our salvation. Hence the argument from this point of view is not apodictic.

But this argument drawn from Sacred Scripture is fully confirmed by tradition. The Council of Nicaea, in the symbol which, too, the Church sings, says: "Who for us men, and for our salvation, came down from heaven. And was made flesh by the Holy Ghost, and was made man." [107] Likewise, in the Council of Sens and by Innocent II, Abelard's proposition was condemned, which said: "Christ did not assume our human nature in order to deliver us from the devil's yoke." [108]

The Fathers insist upon the above-quoted passages when speaking about the motive of the Incarnation.

St. Irenaeus says: "If no flesh had to be saved, the Word of God would not at all have become flesh." [109]

St. Cyril of Alexandria remarks: "If we had not sinned, the Son of God would not have become like unto us." [110]

Other Fathers may be quoted. Thus, St. Athanasius writes: "The Word by no means would have become man unless the necessity of mankind had been the cause." [111]

St. Gregory Nazianzen declares: "But what was the reason for God to assume our human nature for our sake? Assuredly that He might prepare the way to heaven for us; for what other reason can there be?" [112]

St. Chrysostom, the head of the Greek Church, likewise says: "He assumed this human nature of ours solely on account of His mercy, that He might have mercy on us; there is no other reason whatever than this alone for dispensing us from our obligation." [113] This means to say that the proximate motive of the efficacious decree of the Incarnation was formally the motive of mercy.

Finally also St. Augustine, the head of the Latin Church, is quoted in

[107] Denz., no. 54. Someone wrote recently: "No Scholastic, as far as we know, would be so imprudent as to quote this text of the Creed on this disputed point." On the contrary, appeal to this text is made by the Salmanticenses, Gonet, Billuart, and many others.

[108] *Ibid.*, no. 371.

[109] Cf. Rouet de Journel, *Enchiridion patristicum,* nos. 406–15. *Adv. haer.,* chap. 14; cf. Rouet de Journel, *op. cit.,* no. 254.

[110] *De Trinitate,* dial. 5 (about middle).

[111] *Adv. Arianos,* Oratio 2, no. 56; Rouet de Journel, *op. cit.,* no. 765.

[112] Oratio 30, no. 2; see also Rouet de Journel, *op. cit.,* no. 991.

[113] Homily 5, *in Epist. ad Hebraeos;* Journel, no. 1218.

the counterargument of this article, who says: "If man had not sinned, the Son of man would not have come." And elsewhere he says: "Since Adam was made, namely, a righteous man, there was no need of a mediator. But when sins had separated the human race far from God, it was necessary for us to be reconciled to God through a mediator." [114] The testimony of the gloss, quoted in the counterargument, must be added to the above quotations, namely: "Take away diseases, take away wounds, and there is no need of medicine." [115]

The Scotists say that these texts from Sacred Scripture and the Fathers prove only that, if Adam had not sinned, Christ would not have come in passible flesh, or as the physician and Savior.

The Thomists reply that in such a case the statements of the Fathers, asserting absolutely, simply, and without restrictions, that Christ would not have come if Adam had not sinned, would be false; or there would certainly be much equivocation concealed in their words. Thus the following affirmation would be false. Christ is not in the Eucharist meaning: He is not in the Eucharist in passible flesh.

But St. Augustine says, as quoted above: "If man had not sinned, the Son of man would not have come," whereas he ought to have said: He would have come indeed but not in passible flesh, as the Redeemer.

The Scotists also appeal to the words of St. Paul, who says of Christ: "Who is the image of the invisible God, the first-born of every creature, for in Him were all things created in heaven and on earth. . . . All things were created by Him and in Him. And He is before all, and by Him all things consist." [116]

Concerning this text the Thomists remark that, even if these words refer not only to the Word before the Incarnation, but also to Christ, yet they do not express the proximate motive of the Incarnation, but that Christ is above every creature, by reason of His personality.

Hence many authors say that the opinion of St. Thomas and of St. Bonaventure has its foundation more in the testimony of the Scripture and the Fathers.[117]

[114] *Enchiridion,* no. 108; Journel, no. 1218.

[115] *Com. in Tim.,* 1:15; cf. *Dict. théol. cath.,* art. "Incarnation," col. 1489–91, in which we find a collection of patristic texts which testify that the Incarnation is for the redemption of the human race. See also Petavius, *De incarnatione,* Bk. II, chap. 9.

[116] Col. 1:15 f.

[117] Cf. Billot, *De incarnatione,* thesis 3; A. Michel, *Dict. théol. cath.,* art. "Incarnation," col. 1500–1506. Father Chrysostom, O.F.M., wrote an article entitled: "Is the redemption the motive of the incarnation?" On page 5 he asserts, and several Scotists

Therefore, because of this fundamental argument, St. Thomas rightly says in his conclusion: "Hence, since everywhere in the Sacred Scripture the sin of the first man is assigned as the reason of the Incarnation, it is more in accordance with this to say that the work of the Incarnation was ordained by God as a remedy for sin; so that, had sin not existed, the Incarnation would not have been," [118] at least in virtue of the present decree; but it could have been regardless of sin in virtue of another decree. This means that the proximate motive of the Incarnation was formally the motive of mercy, namely, to alleviate the misery of the human race.

Confirmation. The Thomists present a second argument which serves as a complete corroboration of the preceding.

Since God's efficacious decrees are not modified by Him, but from eternity include also all the circumstances of the thing to be produced, the present efficacious decree of the Incarnation from eternity includes the passibility of the flesh. But, as the Scotists concede, the incarnation in passible flesh, supposes the fall. Therefore, in virtue of the present decree, the Word incarnate would not have existed if man had not sinned.

Explanation of the major. God's efficacious decree includes all the circumstances of the things to be produced, because it is an act of most perfect prudence, which attends to all the circumstances of the object, inasmuch as it is concerned with all the particulars that can and must be done right at the moment. The difference between God and us consists in this, that we intend many things even as much as these efficaciously be in our power, although we do not attend to all the detailed circumstances, because these do not come under our observation simultaneously but successively, nor can we foresee with certainty the absolutely fortuitous circumstances even of the morrow. On the contrary, God knows all future things from eternity, and nothing happens without either a positive or permissive decree of His will,

---

agree with him, that according to Scotus there is neither a proximate end nor a proximate motive for the Incarnation; for God willed it because of His own excellence, as being the greatest manifestation of His goodness.

We reply to this by saying that, nevertheless, in Sacred Scripture not only the ultimate and most common end of God's works is assigned for the Incarnation, but also its proximate and special end, which is our redemption. At least the texts of Scripture seem to state clearly that the redemption is the principal and proximate motive, and hence the indispensable condition of the Incarnation.

[118] *Summa theol.,* IIIa, q. 1, a. 3.

positive as regards that which is real and good, permissive as regards evil. Hence God's positive efficacious decree, since it is most prudent, includes all the circumstances of the thing to be produced. Hence God, different from us, does not modify His efficacious decrees, and consequently the efficacious decree of the Incarnation in passible flesh, so that *de facto* the Incarnation takes place, is the only one issued by God, and this decree, as the Scotists concede, supposes the fall of the human race. Therefore, in virtue of the present efficacious decree, if man had not sinned, the Word would not have become incarnate.

Therefore the Scotists ought to say that the decree of the Incarnation considered in itself and not in passible flesh is a conditional and inefficacious decree, like God's antecedent will of saving the human race, because it is directed to something considered in itself, abstracting, as it were, from particular circumstances of time and place. But it must be added in virtue of the present inefficacious decree, nothing comes into being, for no being or anything good is produced, because these can be produced only according to conditions right at the moment, and at the moment nothing is realized,[119] for the conditional and inefficacious decree does not refer to the existence of things. Hence, in virtue of this particular, inefficacious decree, the Word *de facto* would not, right in the present circumstances, have become incarnate either in passible or in impassible flesh.

Instance. But perhaps this argument proves only that the reparation of sin was an indispensable condition for the coming of Christ. It does not follow as an immediate consequence that this indispensable condition was the proximate motive of the Incarnation, because not every indispensable condition is the motive of one's action.

Reply. We say that the Scripture assigns this condition as the motive, and no other proximate motive is assigned to this condition, except the common and ultimate motive in all God's works, which is the manifestation of His goodness or His glory.

This argument is most forceful. In fact, it appears to be apodictic, inasmuch as it is equivalent to saying that God, unlike us, does not afterward make a change in what He has efficaciously decreed to bring into being. These decrees are, from the moment of their utterance, most perfect and include future circumstances even to the least detail. Thus, in like manner it was decreed by God that Peter was to attain eternal glory only by way of penance after his threefold denial,

[119] *Ibid.*, Ia, q. 19, a. 6, ad 1.

which was permitted by God. This argument holds good against the opinion of Suarez.[120]

Objection. The election of Peter to heaven is an efficacious decree. But this decree does not include in its object all the circumstances, for instance, whether Peter will reach heaven by means of martyrdom, for this pertains to a subsequent decree. Therefore not every efficacious decree includes all the circumstances.

Reply. I distinguish the major. The election of Peter to heaven is an efficacious decree of the end, this I concede; of the means, this I deny.

I contradistinguish the minor. That the decree does not include all the circumstances of the means, this I concede; of the end, this I deny. Although the decree concerning the end virtually contains the decree concerning the means.

Thus Peter's election to heaven includes a certain degree of glory for this individual person, together with all the associated circumstances. Similarly, therefore, the decree of the Incarnation ought to terminate in the individual Christ, right now to be born of the Virgin Mary, in passible flesh, just as it actually happened.

The Scotists insist saying: I can decree efficaciously that someone must be paid a debt of one hundred dollars, not considering whether this debt is to be paid in gold or silver.

Reply. 1. We mortals can certainly do so, for our decrees are from the beginning imperfect, often vaguely expressed, especially if they concern something to be fulfilled in the future.

[120] Suarez argues that the Incarnation was willed for two ultimate ends, namely, because of its excellence and for the redemption of the human race.

In refutation of Suarez, cf. Gonet (*Clypeus, De incarnatione,* disp. V, par. 3), who says: "The same effect cannot proceed from two causes that are each totally efficient and adequate; otherwise the effect would and would not depend on each cause for the same reason; but there is the same reason for each of the totally final and adequate causes." Hence the two above-mentioned ends are not coordinated, as Suarez would have it, but they are subordinated to each other, in such manner that the redemption of the human race is the proximate reason of the Incarnation.

Moreover, this opinion posits, like that of Scotus, mutability and imperfection in God. God, who foresees everything from all eternity, had foreseen and permitted from all eternity Adam's sin, and therefore does not begin to have another motive for His willing, but He persists immutably in the motive once chosen.

Finally, in the opinions of both Suarez and Scotus, the first decree abstracting from the condition of passible flesh cannot be efficacious, because the efficacious decree is directed to the object right at the moment to be produced, as it truly will be in time. Hence the Thomists, in opposition to Scotus and Suarez, admit only one efficacious decree of the Incarnation, willed by God in manifestation of His goodness by way of mercy for the redemption of man.

2. Moreover, the aforesaid decree concerns the end, namely, the price to be paid, not the means by which it is to be paid.

3. This decree does not concern the production of the thing, but the use of a thing already produced, namely, of a sum of gold or silver. On the contrary, the efficacious decree of the Incarnation concerns a thing to be produced right now, hence in passible flesh, as it actually happened. Therefore this argument rests on very solid grounds, that is, after the Incarnation has become an accomplished fact.

Confirmation of proof. St. Thomas confirms his proof by the solution of the objections which he placed at the beginning of this, his third article.

The first objection was proposed by St. Augustine,[121] who says: "Many other things are to be considered in the Incarnation of Christ besides absolution from sin."

Reply to first objection. "All the other causes which are assigned in the preceding article have to do with a remedy for sin," since, by the Incarnation man is withdrawn from evil and given the greatest of incentives to practice the virtues of faith, hope, and charity.

We must also concede that God, in the decree of the Incarnation, besides the redemption of the human race, had in mind as the ultimate and common end of all His works, the manifestation of His goodness or of His glory; but now it is a question of the proximate motive of the Incarnation, namely, whether it is connected with sin.

The second objection was: It belongs to God's omnipotence to manifest Himself by some infinite effect.

Reply to second objection. "The infinity of divine power is shown in the mode of production of things from nothing. Again, it suffices for the perfection of the universe that the creature be ordained in a natural manner to God as to an end (that is, in the purely natural state). But that a creature should be united to God in person exceeds the limits of the perfection of nature." Therefore, this constitutes the object of a most free decree, the motive of which is made manifest only by revelation.

The third objection was: Human nature has not been made more capable of the grace of the hypostatic union by sin. Therefore, if man had not sinned, God would have willed the Incarnation.

Reply to third objection. St. Thomas concedes the antecedent. He distinguishes the consequent, and concedes that, if man had not

[121] *De Trinitate,* Bk. XIII, chap. 17.

sinned, human nature was capable obedientially of the Incarnation; that it would *de facto* have been raised to the dignity of the hypostatic union in virtue of the present decree, this he denies.

The whole of this beautiful reply to the third objection must be read, because it is of great importance.

There are two things to be noted in this reply.

1) The obediential power concerns a supernatural agent, namely, God whom it obeys; but God, who is absolutely free, does not always complete this obediential power, though He sometimes does so, and gratuitously.

2) "But there is no reason," says St. Thomas, "why human nature should not have been raised to something greater (*de facto*) after sin. God allows evils to happen in order to bring a greater good therefrom. Hence it is written (Rom. 5:20): 'Where sin abounded grace did more abound.' Hence too, in the blessing of the paschal candle, we say: 'O happy fault, that merited such and so great a Redeemer.' "

Thus it is confirmed that the motive of the Incarnation was formally the motive of mercy, and, moreover, it is evident that God permitted original sin for a greater good, which is the redemptive Incarnation. Thus causes are to each other causes, though in a different order. In the order of material cause to be perfected, the merciful uplifting of the fallen human race precedes the redemptive Incarnation; but this latter precedes the fall in the order of final cause or of greater good for which reason sin of the first man is permitted. Thus the body of this particular embryo in the order of material cause to be perfected precedes the creation and infusion of this particular soul, and yet this latter precedes the embryo in the order of final cause, for this soul would not be created unless the embryo were disposed to receive it.

Several Thomists insist on this point, as we shall see, such as Godoi, Gonet, Salmanticenses, whose interpretation is already contained in this reply to the third objection, which was not sufficiently considered by John of St. Thomas and Billuart.

The fourth objection was: Christ as man was eternally predestined to be the natural Son of God.[122] But predestination is always fulfilled. Therefore even before sin, it was necessary for the Son of God to become incarnate.

St. Thomas replies: "Predestination presupposes the foreknowledge

[122] *Summa theol.,* IIIa, q. 24, a. 1.

of future things; and hence, as God predestines the salvation of anyone (for example, of Augustine, to be brought about by the prayers of others, for example, of St. Monica), so also He predestined the work of the Incarnation to be the remedy of human sin."

This reply of St. Thomas to the fourth objection requires a brief explanation. "Predestination," says St. Thomas, "presupposes the foreknowledge of future things," not indeed of all future things. Certainly St. Thomas does not mean that it presupposes the foreknowledge of merits, for then he would contradict himself; [123] but predestination presupposes the foreknowledge of certain future things. Thus, when God predestines Peter, He first wills him eternal life in the order of final cause, but previously in the order of material cause He wills him individuation by means of matter by which he is constituted as Peter. Similarly, when it is a question of the whole human race and of Christ's predestination as the Redeemer of the human race, this predestination presupposes the foreseeing of Adam's sin in the order of material cause only. Likewise a foreseen persecution is the occasion for someone being predestined to the grace of martyrdom. The Thomists consider the person of the predestined, native talents, and other natural gifts, temperament, to be effects postulated by predestination, which follow it in the order of final cause. And as Augustine would not have attained eternal life if St. Monica had not prayed for him, so if man had not sinned, the Word would not have become incarnate.

This reply must be correctly understood, so that it be not interpreted as contrary to a previous conclusion,[124] which stated that the foreknowledge of merits is not the cause of predestination, because the merits of the elect are, on the contrary, the effects of their predestination.

Cajetan explains this point well. He remarks that, when St. Thomas says in his reply to the fourth objection that "predestination presupposes the foreknowledge of future things," he does not mean "of all future things," for Peter's predestination does not presuppose the foreknowledge of Peter's future eternal happiness, but, on the contrary, the foreknowledge of Peter's future eternal happiness presupposes Peter's predestination to eternal happiness, inasmuch as God

[123] *Ibid.*, Ia, q. 23, a. 5.
[124] *Ibid.*

foresees future things in the decrees of His will. But St. Thomas means in this case that "predestination presupposes the foreknowledge of some future things which are presupposed by predestination." [125]

Thus St. Thomas considers that Christ's predestination to natural divine sonship presupposes the foreknowledge of sin, since it was to repair this offense that Christ was predestined; for, as Cajetan observes, the ordering of medicine presupposes knowledge of the disease.[126]

But the difficulty is not solved, for Scotus will argue that this dependence of the Incarnation on sin holds good in the order of execution but not in the order of intention of Christ's predestination.[127] For the orderly way of willing for anyone is to will the end and those things nearer to the end, than other inferior things. Thus God wills for anyone, such as Adam, before He saw either His merits or a fortiori His demerits. Therefore a fortiori God wills divine natural sonship to Christ before having foreseen Adam's demerit.

In answer to this objection it can be said, in accordance with the reply to the third objection, what St. Thomas means is that, even in the order of intention, Christ's predestination is dependent on the foreseeing of Adam's sin, not indeed that it is dependent on this latter as being the final cause, but as being the material cause that is to be perfected.[128]

Thus, when God predestines Peter, He first wills him eternal happiness in the order of final cause, and He first wills him individuation from matter already qualified in the embryo, in the order of material cause; and "to them that love God all things work together unto good." [129] He also wills them their physical temperament.

Likewise, when it is a question of the whole human race, and of Christ's predestination as the Redeemer of the human race, this predestination presupposes the foreseeing of Adam's sin in the order of material cause only.

This distinction is made by Cajetan on this point,[130] and, although not everything that he says here on the ordering of the divine decrees concerning the three orders of nature, grace, and the hypostatic union

[125] *Com. in IIIam,* q. 1, a. 3, no. 6.
[126] *Ibid.;* no. 7.
[127] *Summa theol.,* IIIa, a. 7, q. 3.
[128] See St. Thomas, *Com. in Sent.,* d. 41, q. 1, a. 4.
[129] Rom. 8:28.
[130] *Com. in Summam,* IIIa, q. 1, a. 3, no. 7.

are true perhaps, nevertheless this distinction must be and is upheld by subsequent Thomists.[131]

For Cajetan replies by distinguishing the antecedent as follows: in the order of final cause, one who wills methodically, wills the end before other things, this I concede; that one does so in the order of disposing cause, which reduces itself to material cause, this I deny.

Thus we will first and preferably health to purification in the order of final cause; contrary to this, however, in the order of material or disposing cause, we will purification as a means to health.

This distinction has its foundation in the principle that causes mutually interact, and the application of this principle is afterward developed by the Salmanticenses and Gonet, whose interpretation differs somewhat from Cajetan's, as will be stated farther on.

Cajetan concludes: "It is evident that the Incarnation can be willed by God, without such an occasion (i.e., Adam's sin), but it is not evident that it is *de facto* willed by God independent of such occasion. . . . We must turn to the Scripture if we wish to know that *de facto* God ordained that the Incarnation will come to pass, whether Adam did or did not sin. But because from the Scripture we have knowledge only of a redemptive Incarnation, we say, although God could have willed the Incarnation even without a future redemption, *de facto* He willed it only in the redemption; because by revelation, He did not reveal things otherwise to us, and it is only by revelation that we can know His will. . . . The conclusion is that God willed the greatest good only in conjunction with such less good." [132] Thus, although God could have willed efficaciously the salvation of the whole human race (which to us appears better), it is certain that He willed efficaciously that many be saved, but not all.[133]

Likewise, as Cajetan says: "It is not derogatory to God's wisdom to have disposed things so that He will effect so sublime a good as that (of the Incarnation), sin being only the occasion that urged Him to have mercy. . . . Therefore we must not on this account rejoice at another's fall (that is, Adam's), but at the mercy of God, who causes the foreseen fall of one to redound to another's good." [134] Hence we conclude that the motive of the Incarnation was formally the motive

[131] *Ibid.*, no. 9.
[132] *Ibid.*
[133] *Ibid.*
[134] *Ibid.*, no. 10.

of mercy, since our salvation was the motive, as stated in the Nicene Creed.

Fifth objection. St. Thomas states that the mystery of the Incarnation was revealed to man in a state of innocence without any reference to future sin. Therefore it has no connection with this sin.

Reply to fifth objection. St. Thomas says: "Nothing prevents an effect from being revealed to one to whom the cause is not revealed."

WHAT IS PRECISELY THE VIEW OF SCOTUS? [135]

The question whether Christ was predestined to be the Son of God, affords Scotus the occasion to discuss the problem of the motive of the Incarnation. After replying to the first question in the affirmative, he goes on to show that Christ was predestined as man to the grace of the hypostatic union and to glory independently of the foreseeing of Adam's sin. Scotus proves his point by seven arguments that have been splendidly reproduced by Cajetan.[136] We shall give here the principal arguments with Cajetan's replies.

First argument. The predestination of any person whatever to glory precedes naturally, on the part of the object, the foreknowledge of sin or of the damnation of any man whatever. Therefore with far greater reason this is true concerning the predestination of Christ's soul to supreme glory.

Cajetan replies.[137] He denies the antecedent, because he holds that the foreseeing of sin pertains to the order of general providence, presupposed by the ordering of predestination. But this reply gives rise to many difficulties, since the permission of sin in the life of the predestined, for example, and therefore in the life of Adam himself, is the effect not only of general providence, but also of the predestination of these elect, which itself presupposes the predestination of Christ.[138] Hence theologians in general, and even subsequent Thomists, do not uphold Cajetan in this reply.

But very many Thomists reply as follows. They concede that

[135] See his *Com. in III Sent.*, d. 7, q. 3. Cf. also Father Chrysostom's "Le motif de l'incarnation," in the *Etudes franciscaines,* 1913; also "La Redemption este-elle le motif de l'incarnation," in *La France franciscaine,* 1931, p. 10.

[136] *Com. in Summam,* IIIa, q. 1, a. 3, no. 5.

[137] *Ibid.,* no. 10.

[138] God permits the elect to fall into sin, as in Peter's case, for the sole reason of causing them to be more humble. Thus "to them that love God [unto the end] all things work together unto good" (Rom. 8:28), and Augustine adds "even sins."

Christ's predestination precedes by nature the foreseeing of Adam's sin in the order of final cause; they deny that it precedes in the order of material or disposing cause.

Thus they concede that Peter's predestination to glory precedes by nature the foreseeing of his individuation, in the order of final cause; they deny this precedence in the order of material cause. Likewise, one is predestined to the grace of martyrdom, on the occasion of a foreseen persecution.

Second argument. The orderly way of willing is for one to will first the end, and then those things more immediate to the end. Thus God first wills to give heavenly glory to one before grace, and He first wills this to Christ, and then to the predestined as subordinated to Christ. Moreover, God first wills anyone heavenly glory and grace which He may foresee are in opposition because of sin and its consequences. Therefore God first wills heavenly glory to Christ previous to foreseeing Adam's fall.

Cajetan replies,[139] and this reply is upheld by subsequent Thomists. He distinguishes the major: that the orderly way of willing is for one first to will the end in the order of final cause, this he concedes; in the order of material and disposing cause, this he denies.

By way of example: someone might wish to build the Collegio Angelico in Rome, but has not yet found a suitable place and, having found such a place, his wish of having this college built is realized, or the opportunity offers itself, because he has received the necessary money. Similarly God wills first the soul in the order of final cause, and first the body in the order of material cause, and this particular soul would not be created right at this moment, if this embryonic body were not disposed to receive it. Likewise the Word would not have become incarnate, in virtue of the present decree, unless man had sinned or the human race had to be redeemed.

But you insist. Causes do not mutually interact in the same order. However, this would be the case here in the same order of final cause, if sin is permitted because of this greater good of the Incarnation, and if the Incarnation is willed for our redemption.

Reply. The causes are not in the same order, for sin is permitted because of this greater good of the Incarnation considered as the end for which it is decreed; whereas, on the contrary, the human race to be redeemed stands in relation to the Incarnation in the order of ma-

[139] *Loc. cit.,* nos. 9 and 10.

terial cause to be perfected, or is the subject to whom the redemptive Incarnation is beneficial. Hence the human race is not called the end for whose sake the Incarnation is decreed, but the end to whom it is beneficial. Therefore the causes are not mutually interactive in the same order. And this very redemption of ours as willed by God, presupposes as a prior requisite in the order of material cause the human race to be redeemed.

So also let us take as example one who saves the life of a boy who, because of his imprudence, falls into the river. The rescuer first wills to save the boy's life in the order of final cause, but he would not save the boy's life unless the boy had fallen into the river, and thus had afforded the other the opportunity to come to his rescue. In like manner, the more solemn dogmatic definitions of the Church are always given on the occasion of some error that must be rejected, because it is endangering the freedom of souls.

Third argument. Redemption or the heavenly glory of a soul to be redeemed is not so great a good as the glory of Christ's soul. Therefore the Redemption does not seem to be the sole reason why God predestined Christ's soul to so great glory.

Cajetan replies: [140] God could have willed indeed this great good (of Christ's glory) without its being connected with a less good; but from Sacred Scripture it is evident that He willed this greatest good only as connected with such less good. It is not therefore a question of a possibility, but of a fact. God could have willed efficaciously to save the whole human race, for instance, but from Sacred Scripture it is evident that not all are saved,[141] although, by God's help, the fulfillment of His commands is always possible. Herein lies a mystery that must be believed according to the testimony of Sacred Scripture and not to be determined in human fashion by a priori reasoning.

Fourth argument. It is not very likely that a less good is the only reason for the existence of so supreme a good.

Reply. The Thomists say that the Incarnation is not an incidental good in the strict sense, but it is only improperly so called. For that which the agent does not intend and which happens by chance, is called strictly incidental; such is the case when one digs a grave, and finds a treasure, or when one rescues a boy accidentally who happens to fall into the river. That is improperly said to be occasioned which

[140] *Ibid.*, no. 10.
[141] *Ibid.*, no. 9.

depends on some incident, although it be intended by the agent, as the rescuing of a boy who fell into the river. Thus the Incarnation is an incidental good, and it is fitting that evil be the occasion of eliciting from God so great a good, namely, a good that results from His liberality and mercy, because misery is the reason for commiserating.

Scotus overlooks the fact that many of the finer things in life are improperly incidental, especially many heroic acts, such as saving another's life with danger to one's own, as in the case of shipwreck or of fire. Such are heroic acts performed in defense of one's country, on the occasion of an unjust aggressor; hence the glory acquired by many soldiers is thus incidental. Also incidental are heroic acts in defense of one's faith, such as martyrdom on the occasion of a persecution. The most beautiful dogmatic definitions uttered by the Church on the occasion of the refutation of an error that is threatening to enslave souls, belong to this class. So it was on the occasion of the rise of Pelagianism and Semi-Pelagianism, that St. Augustine wrote his books *On Grace.*

But the difference between God and man is that man could not infallibly foresee the occasion that prompted these heroic acts, and so he does them unforeseen. Other arguments of Scotus presented in different aspects repeat the same objection.

The Scotists insist. They say, with Father Chrysostom,[142] that the material cause is not the end (of the Incarnation), nor is the material element in the Incarnation its motive. Therefore the difficulty remains.

Reply. The material element that enters into the redemptive Incarnation is the reason for the Incarnation, since "the alleviation of misery is the reason for commiseration." [143] Thus in this third article, St. Thomas is able to say: "Redemption is the reason for the Incarnation," [144] although the Incarnation is not subordinated to the redemption.

All these objections can be reduced to the following syllogistic argument: God cannot will that the higher order should be subjected to the lower, for this would be the inversion of order, or perversion.

But our redemption is inferior to the Incarnation.

Therefore God cannot will the Incarnation to be for our redemption.

[142] *La Redemption est-elle le motif de l'Incarnation?,* pp. 24 and 50.

[143] *Summa theol.,* IIa IIae, q. 30, a. 2.

[144] The exact words of St. Thomas in this third article are: "Unde cum in Sacra Scriptura ubique incarnationis ratio ex peccato primi hominis assignetur, convenientius dicitur, incarnationis opus ordinatum esse a Deo in remedium contra peccatum." (Tr.)

Reply. I distinguish the major. That God cannot will the higher order to be subjected to the lower, as being the perfective and ultimate end, this I concede; that God cannot will the higher for the lower, as being the end that must be perfected or repaired from a motive of mercy, this I deny. For the alleviating of misery, is the reason for commiseration. I concede the minor.

I distinguish the conclusion. That God cannot will the higher order to be subjected to the lower on account of this latter being the perfective and especially the ultimate end, this I concede; as being the end that must be perfected or repaired from a motive of mercy, this I deny.

Thus the Thomists say that the redemption of the human race is not the end for the sake of which the Incarnation is decreed, but it is the material element that enters into the motive of the redemptive Incarnation, or the end for which the Incarnation is beneficial. Thus a doctor visits a sick person, or a priest says Mass for the restoration of somebody's health, for the common good and the glory of God.

Therefore the whole teaching of St. Thomas, of St. Bonaventure, and others is summed up in these words: the motive of the Incarnation was formally the motive of mercy. As the Psalmist says: "Have mercy on me, O Lord, for I am weak." [145] "Have mercy on me, for I am poor." [146] "Have mercy on me, O Lord, for I am afflicted." [147]

Cajetan replies most appropriately: "It is not unbefitting God's wisdom that He was disposed to perform so great a good, only because sin was the occasion that urged Him to be merciful." [148] "It is because the alleviation of misery is the reason for commiseration," [149] and divine mercy, alleviating the misery of the human race, is the greatest manifestation of divine goodness and omnipotence. If God's omnipotence is already made manifest in the creation of a grain of sand from nothing, a fortiori it is shown when He brings good out of evil, and so great a good as eternal life of those justified. St. Thomas says: "In itself mercy is the greatest of virtues (and so it is in God, but not in us, because we have someone above us, who must be honored by the practice of virtues); for it belongs to mercy to be bountiful to others, and, what is more, to succor others in their wants. And this pertains

[145] Ps. 6:3.
[146] *Ibid.*, 24:16.
[147] *Ibid.*, 30:10.
[148] *Com. in Summam*, IIa IIae, q. 30, a. 2.
[149] *Summa theol.*, IIa IIae, q. 30, a. 2.

especially to the one who is above others; hence mercy is accounted as being proper to God, and therein His omnipotence is declared to be chiefly manifested." [150] St. Augustine likewise says: "The justification of the sinner is greater than the creation of heaven and earth; for heaven and earth shall pass away, but the justification of the ungodly shall endure." [151] But since misery is the reason for having mercy, the alleviation of misery is more the matter about which mercy is concerned; it is the motive of mercy, not indeed as constituting the perfective end, but as being the end in the order of redemption.

In this there is no inversion of orders. There would indeed be a perversion of orders if the higher were ordained for the lower, as if this latter were the ultimate and perfective end; but not, if by way of mercy, the higher is ordered to the lower end for its perfection or reparation.

Thus it is that the Son of God through His incarnation certainly stoops down to us with sublime mercy, so that the saints are moved to tears at the thought of it. But by thus lowering Himself, He in no way subordinates Himself to us; on the contrary, in alleviating our misery, He restores the original subordination, by making us again subordinate to Himself and God the Father. Thus God, by mercifully lowering Himself, has most splendidly made manifest His goodness and omnipotence, since "to have mercy belongs especially to one who is above others." [152]

In God, inasmuch as He has nobody above Him to whom He would owe allegiance, the greatest of all virtues is mercy, and misery is the reason for being merciful.[153] Thus the beginning of a certain collect reads: "O God, who, more than in all things else, showest forth Thine almighty power by sparing and by having mercy." [154] Therefore Scotus did not destroy the demonstrative middle term of this article.[155]

The preceding doctrine is certainly what St. Thomas taught. On this point, he wrote: "God therefore did not assume human nature because He loved man, absolutely speaking, more than angels; but because the needs of man were greater; just as the master of a house

[150] *Ibid.,* a. 4.

[151] *Com. in Joann.,* 14:12; see also St. Thomas, *op. cit.,* Ia IIae, q. 113, a. 9.

[152] *Summa theol.,* IIa IIae, q. 30. a. 4. See also Ia, q. 21, a. 4.

[153] *Ibid.,* IIa IIae, q. 30, a. 2, 4.

[154] Collect for Tenth Sunday after Pentecost.

[155] This thesis was developed by the author in the periodical *Angelicum,* 1930, pp. 289 f., under the title: "Mercy was the motive of the Incarnation."

may give to a sick servant some costly delicacy that he does not give to his own son in sound health." [156] He also says: "Nor did anything of Christ's excellence diminish when God delivered Him up to death for the salvation of the human race; rather did He become thereby a glorious conqueror" [157] of sin, the devil, and death.

The thesis of St. Thomas, as proposed by him, is most convincing inasmuch as he declares mercy to be the motive of the Incarnation; wherefore Christ was the first of the predestined, but He was predestined as Savior and victim, as the victor of sin, the devil, and death. This title of Savior belongs primarily to Christ, as expressed in the name Jesus, which signifies Savior. This title belongs more fundamentally to Him than do such titles as Doctor, or King of kings, Lord of lords.

Christian faith itself seems to teach this doctrine, although the Scripture does not say that mercy was the indispensable motive of the Incarnation. This doctrine is also most beneficial in the spiritual order, urging us to imitate Christ and show zeal for souls.

Cajetan remarks [158] that, as in the act of hope I desire God for myself, because God is my final end (since God is the ultimate end of this act of hope), so Christ is given to us (for our sake or as our end), for the glorification of God (who is the ultimate end for which God performs all His works). Thus the Incarnation is not subordinated to our redemption,[159] but is its eminent cause. Thus contemplation is not subordinated to apostolic action, which must result from the fullness of contemplation, this being its higher source, as St. Thomas points out.[160] Therefore, no matter what the Scotists may say, the words of St. Paul still apply, who says: "For all are yours. And you are Christ's. And Christ is God's." [161] In this Thomistic thesis, Christ is not subordinated to us, but we are subordinated to Him.

Agreement and disagreement between Thomists. They all agree upon the principal conclusion as explicitly formulated by St. Thomas,

[156] *Summa theol.,* Ia, q. 20, a. 4, ad 2.

[157] *Ibid.,* ad 1.

[158] *Com. in IIa IIae,* q. 17, a. 5, no. 6.

[159] If certain Thomists of more recent times say that the Incarnation is subordinated to the redemption, they use the word subordination in a broad sense; for the eminent cause cannot be subordinated to its effect in the strict sense, but in some way it is ordained to produce it; otherwise divine omnipotence would be subordinated to creatures which it produced.

[160] *Summa theol.,* IIa IIae, q. 188, a. 6.

[161] I Cor. 3:23.

which is: If Adam had not sinned, the Word would not have become incarnate.

But they are not altogether in agreement concerning a secondary issue.

Several Thomists, adopting the views of Cajetan, such as John of St. Thomas and Billuart, refuse to answer the question, why God permitted Adam's sin and original sin. Moreover, they multiply divine conditional decrees. According to their views: (1) God willed the natural order; (2) the elevation of the human race to the supernatural order; (3) He permitted the sin of the first man; (4) He decreed the redemptive Incarnation in passible flesh.

Other Thomists, such as the Salmanticenses, Godoy, Gonet, and very many of more recent times, insisting on what St. Thomas remarks in this article, and elsewhere, say: [162] Certainly God permits evil only because of a greater good. This doctrine is certain and *de fide,* otherwise God's permission of sin would not be a holy act. It cannot indeed be said a priori that God permitted original sin because of some greater good, but, after the fact of the Incarnation, it appears that God permitted original sin because of the redemptive Incarnation, so that the redemption of the fallen human race is prior in the order of material cause to be perfected, and the redemptive Incarnation is prior in the order of final cause. This distinction is made by Cajetan in his commentary on this article, but much of its force is lost inasmuch as he multiplies exceedingly the divine decrees, so different from what he wrote earlier in his commentary.[163]

Moreover, these Thomists say that divine conditional decrees must not be multiplied, for this multiplication results from the weakness of our intellect, and we must do our best to overcome this defect. Hence God, previous to any decree, saw by His knowledge of simple intelligence all possible worlds with all their contents, just as the architect has in mind various possible houses and all their component parts. Thus God had in mind a sinless world not in need of redemption, but brought to perfection by the example of the Word incarnate; also another possible world, in which man sinned, and which was perfected by the redemptive Incarnation. God chose *de facto,* by a single decree, this latter, in which, therefore, the redemptive Incarnation is prior in the order of final causality (as the soul is prior to the

[162] Cf. ad 3; also Ia, q. 20, a. 4, ad 1.

[163] *Com. in Iam,* q. 22, a. 2, ad 2 and a. 4.

body), and the reparation of the fallen human race is prior in the order of material causality to be perfected, as the body is prior to the soul.[164]

This second interpretation is entirely in conformity with the reply given by St. Thomas to the third objection of this article, and also with a previous statement in his *Summa,* in which he says: "God loves Christ not only more than He loves the whole human race, but more than He loves the entire created universe, because He willed for Him the greater good in giving Him a name that is above all names, so far as He was true God. Nor did anything of His excellence diminish when God delivered Him up to death for the salvation of the human race; rather did He become thereby a glorious conqueror," [165] namely, of sin, the devil, and death.

This reply of these Thomists is also precisely what St. Thomas says in his reply to the third objection of this article, in which he quotes the words of St. Paul: "Where sin abounded, grace did more abound," [166] and of the liturgy: "O happy fault, that merited such and so great a Redeemer!" [167]

And St. Augustine says in his commentary on the forty-seventh psalm: "Therefore Adam fell for our resurrection," [168] which means that God permitted Adam's sin for this greater good of the redemptive Incarnation.

Moreover, the divine decrees must not be multiplied without necessity; for this frequency of recourse to divine decrees has its foundation in the imperfection of our manner of understanding the divine decrees. In fact, it is evident that various events of the natural order,

[164] These two possible worlds, the second of which God chose by one sole efficacious decree in all its component parts, may be illustrated by the following schema.

Innocent world to be preserved in its innocence

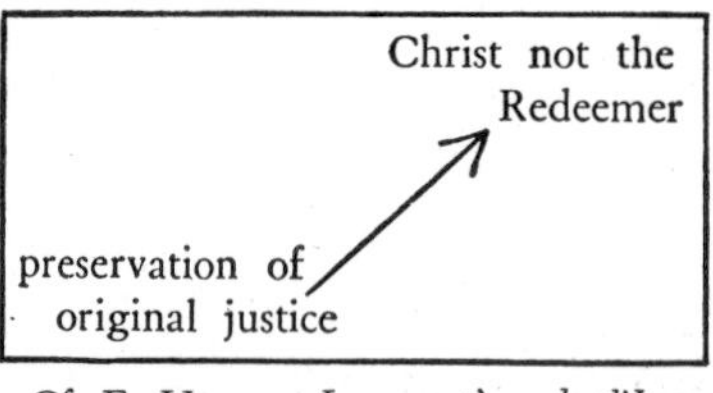

Sinful world to be redeemed

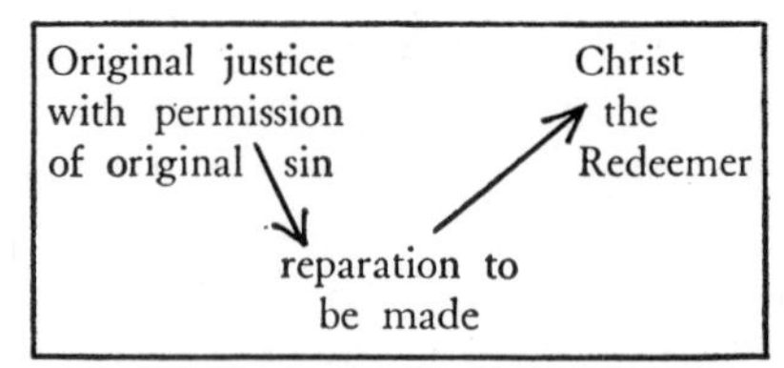

Cf. E. Hugon, *Le mystère de l'Incarnation,* p. 75; also *Dict. théol. cath.,* art. "Incarnation," col. 1504.

[165] *Summa theol.,* Ia, q. 20, a. 4, ad 1.

[166] Rom. 5:20.

[167] Blessing of paschal candle.

[168] *P.L.,* XXXVI, 539.

such as the death of a good person from some disease, which at first sight seems to depend solely on natural causes and the general provisions of Providence, are to be attributed to the supernatural operation of predestination.[169] Therefore it is apparent that God, by a single decree, willed this present world with its three orders of nature, grace, and the hypostatic union.

THE LIBERTY OF THE DECREE CONCERNING THE INCARNATION

A COMPARISON BETWEEN THE DOCTRINE OF ST. THOMAS AND THAT OF SCOTUS

On first consideration, it is surprising that St. Thomas, who is an intellectualist, should say: Since the Incarnation is a most free and absolutely gratuitous gift of God, its motive can be known only by revelation; whereas Scotus, who is a voluntarist inclined to liberalism, wishes to establish this motive of the Incarnation by arguments or quasi a priori reasonings, as the extreme intellectualists do, such as Leibnitz and Malebranche, who say that the Incarnation is morally necessary so that the world may be the best of all possible worlds.

The reason for this difference of opinion between St. Thomas and Scotus seems to consist in this, that St. Thomas, because of his moderate intellectualism, distinguished exactly between the order of nature and the order of grace, by establishing the proper object of the created intellect, whether human or angelic.[170] Hence St. Thomas fully acknowledges God's perfect liberty in elevating the human nature (or the angelic) to the order of grace, and a fortiori to the hypostatic union. Thus his moderate intellectualism most correctly acknowledges the rights of divine liberty.

On the contrary, Scotus, in virtue of his voluntarism does not succeed in distinguishing so exactly between the orders of nature and of grace; he says that there is in our nature an innate appetite and not merely one that is elicited for the beatific vision, and he adds that,

[169] For example, that a certain man die, indeed, from a disease right at the moment when in the state of grace, and that he should have the grace of final perseverance, this depends on supernatural predestination; similarly, the end of the world, in the material sense, will come when the number of the elect is completed. Therefore it cannot be said that God willed the natural order and its events independent of the order of grace, and this latter independently of the order of the hypostatic union; but by one decree He willed this present world and its three orders.

[170] See *God, His existence,* II, 54.

if God had so willed, the beatific vision would be natural for us.

Hence he is inclined to regard the supernatural order as the complement of the natural order, and the hypostatic order as the complement and quasi-normal consummation of the supernatural order. Thus he does not acknowledge sufficiently the rights of divine liberty as regards this twofold elevation; and he speaks finally, almost like the absolute intellectualists of the Leibnitz type, who think that the Incarnation is morally necessary for the world to be the best of all possible worlds. Thus extremes meet.

Absolute intellectualism reduces to an ideal right the accomplished fact. Absolute libertism reduces the right itself to an accomplished fact.

These two systems are in the inverse order, but practically they meet, because both admit that the accomplished fact is the same as the ideal right, and success is identical with morality; yet the followers of the former system insist on the right, whereas the followers of the latter system insist on the accomplished fact. But moderate intellectualism lies between these two extremes, because it safeguards both the validity of the first principles of reason and true liberty, which latter is denied by absolute intellectualism.

Thus in Thomism the Incarnation is seen to be the supreme fact of the entire universe, but it is a contingent fact in which God's most free and gratuitous love for us is made manifest by way of mercy. "For God so loved the world as to give His only-begotten Son." [171]

Thus this thesis of St. Thomas, if we compare it with his other theses on moderate intellectualism and liberty, has a deep significance, for it means that, in the supernatural order, inasmuch as this order is gratuitous, divine liberty reigns supreme and its predilection is most free, the motive of which can be known only by revelation. But the discarding of this principle results in the incomplete understanding of several fundamental utterances in the supernatural order, such as the following words of St. Paul: "But the foolish things of the world hath God chosen that He may confound the wise; . . . and things that are not, that He might bring to nought things that are." [172]

[171] John 3:16.

[172] I Cor. 1:27 f. For this same reason, frequently in the supernatural order God by an inequality of graces compensates for the inequality of natural conditions; for this is what is meant when it is said in the beatitudes, as recorded in the Gospels: "Blessed are the pure in spirit, for theirs is the kingdom of heaven; blessed are the meek; blessed are they that mourn; blessed are they that suffer persecution for justice'

But these questions are most profound, and their solution has caused great intellects to take opposite views.

Spiritual corollaries. These corollaries are developed in another book,[173] in which the doctrine of St. Thomas on the motive of the Incarnation is explained not so much scholastically as spiritually. These corollaries are as follows:

1) It follows from this doctrine that it is not something accidental that Christ is the Savior, both priest and victim. This is the dominant trait of Jesus, as the name indicates. Jesus is not especially King of kings and sublime Doctor who happened to become the Savior of humanity and victim on account of the fall of the human race. No, but in virtue of the present decree He came principally and primarily as the Savior of men. His entire life was directed to this final end, namely, the sacrifice on the cross.

2) Christ thus appears nobler, and the unity of His life is better made manifest, since it is the unity of the Savior's life, who is merciful and also victorious over sin, the devil, and death.[174]

3) Wherefore Christ calls the hour of the Passion "My hour" as if it were pre-eminently this.

4) Therefore in the present economy of salvation, it is not something accidental in the sanctification of souls, that they must carry their cross daily in union with our Savior, as He Himself says.[175]

5) Hence for sanctity, even great sanctity, learning is not necessary, nor the performance of many external works; it suffices for a person to be conformed to the image of Christ crucified, as in the case of St. Benedict Joseph Labre of the seventeenth century, who showed himself a living image of Christ in his poverty and love of the cross.[176]

6) Finally it follows, as St. Thomas explains in his treatise on the effects of baptism,[177] that sanctifying grace in the redeemed is strictly the grace of Christ, for it is not only a participation of the divine

sake" (Matt. 5:3 f.; Luke 6:20 f.). Therefore we must not say: (1) God willed the natural order with its events; (2) the supernatural order; (3) the hypostatic union. But He first had in mind the present world as possible with all its subordinated parts, and by a single decree chose it in preference to other equally possible worlds.

173 *Le Sauveur et son amour pour nous,* p. 136 f.

174 *Summa theol.,* Ia, q. 20, a. 4, ad 1.

175 Luke 9:23.

176 But this view of the Christian life completely harmonizes with that held by St. Francis of Assisi and St. Bonaventure. Scotus seems to take a somewhat different view of the Christian life, however, in his thesis on the motive of the Incarnation.

177 *Summa theol.,* IIIa, q. 62, a. 2.

nature as in Adam and the angels before the Fall, but it makes us conformable to Christ the Redeemer, and by it we are made living members of His mystical body. Wherefore this grace, inasmuch as it is the grace of Christ, disposes us to live in Christ the Redeemer by a love of the cross, for it disposes us to make reparation for our own sins and the sins of others, inasmuch as the living members of Christ must help one another in the attainment of salvation.

Therefore, it is only after a period of painful probation that any Christian ideal and any Christian society produces true fruits of salvation, for our Lord says: "Unless the grain of wheat falling into the ground die, itself remaineth alone. But if it die, it bringeth forth much fruit." [178]

Thus Christians are made conformable to Christ, who said of Himself to the disciples on the way to Emmaus: "Ought not Christ to have suffered these things, and so to enter into His glory?" [179] Hence St. Paul says: "We are heirs indeed of God and joint heirs with Christ; yet so, if we suffer with Him that we may be also glorified with Him." [180]

These spiritual corollaries are deduced from this teaching.

A certain special opinion. It has been held by some in recent times [181] that so far the question is always presented unfavorably since it always appears in a hypothetical form, namely, "Whether, if man had not sinned, God would have become incarnate." "For," as they say, "if man had not sinned (or in this supposition), there would be another order absolutely different from the present order, and what would have happened in such an order God alone can know." The proper way of positing the question, according to these theologians, must be by presenting it in the form of a positive and universal proposition, that is, "What is the adequate universal reason for the Incarnation in the present order?" Father Roschini [182] replies to this question as follows: "The primary reason of the Incarnation is God's free election from all eternity of the present order with all that is included in it; inasmuch as only the present order exactly corresponds to the measure and mode likewise freely prearranged by God, by which He willed to bestow His goodness *ad extra* and hence procure extrinsic glory."

[178] John 12:24 f.
[179] Luke 24:26.
[180] Rom. 8:17.
[181] Cf. P. Roschini, *Mariologia,* II, 40 f.
[182] *Ibid.*

An answer to Father Roschini's view appeared in the *Angelicum;* [183] its gist is as follows: The question posited by the Scholastics concerns the present order, and a new way of presenting the question is outside the scope of the present problem, and brings us only to the common truth that is admitted by all schools of thought. It is most certain to all theologians that the Incarnation depends on God's free choice of the present order, and what He has ordained for the manifestation of His goodness. This is God's supreme reason, but, now the question is, what is His proximate reason?

Evidently the hypothetical question put by the great Scholastics concerns the present order; namely, in virtue of the present decree, if we make abstraction of the sin of the first man, would the Word have become incarnate? This abstraction is not a lie, nor does it change the order of the thing considered. It is the same as asking: Would the soul of this particular man have been created if his body in his mother's womb was not sufficiently developed to be informed by it? Or we might ask: Will this temple remain intact if this particular column is removed? The truth of a conditional proposition, as logic teaches, depends solely on the connection between the condition and the conditioned.

Hence in replying to the objection, we say: If man had not sinned, the present order of things would be changed, I distinguish: if it meant there would be a change in virtue of another decree, this I concede; in virtue of the present decree, this I deny.

As stated in the above-mentioned reply to Father Roschini: "The reasoning of the Scholastics is not, and cannot be, other than this, otherwise how are we to explain the fact that those doctors are so eager in their futile search, concerning which nothing for certain can ever be known? . . . Without saying, then, what to attribute to those ponderous and so circumspect theologians, with St. Thomas as their leader, a general view of the case would justify us in considering them at least as scholars."

St. Thomas would have improperly stated the question, or would not have corrected the question improperly stated, a question that is even useless, and of course quite irrelevant.

But it is true to say, with the holy Doctor, that in speaking of another order of things, "We do not know what (God) would have ordained,

[183] See *Angelicum,* January, 1942, pp. 97–103: "Ancora intorno alla ragione primaria dell'esistenza di Cristo."

if He had not had previous knowledge of sin." [184] St. Thomas says the same in the present article, for he writes: "And yet the power of God is not limited to this; even had sin not existed, God could have become incarnate, namely, in another order of things."

Final Conclusion

THE MOTIVE OF THE INCARNATION

Therefore it must simply be said that God willed the Incarnation for the manifestation of His goodness by way of mercy for the redemption of the human race, or "for our salvation," as stated in the Creed.

Those who admit, as the Thomists do, one efficacious decree concerning the redemptive Incarnation in passible flesh, by this very fact must say with St. Thomas that, in virtue of the present decree, "if Adam had not sinned, the Word would not have become incarnate," or, expressed affirmatively, it must be said that, in the present decree, the redemptive Incarnation supposes the fall of the human race to be redeemed, although this fall was permitted for a greater good, which is the redemptive Incarnation. Thus the creation of the soul presupposes that the embryonic body is sufficiently disposed, and this sufficient predisposition was willed and produced by God for the soul. Causes mutually interact though in a different order, without implying a vicious circle. It would be a vicious circle if we were to say that the permission of Adam's sin was on account of the Incarnation, and that the Incarnation took place because of the permission of Adam's sin. The truth is that the Incarnation took place, not on account of the permission of sin, but for its reparation.

It would likewise be a vicious circle to say that men are for the sake of Christ, and in the same way Christ is for the sake of men. But it is true to say that Christ is the destined end of men, and men are the end to whom the redemptive Incarnation is beneficial.

Hence the truth of the assertion is established, that God willed the Incarnation as a manifestation of His goodness by showing His mercy toward men for their redemption, or "for our salvation," as stated in the Creed.[185]

[184] *Com. in Ep. ad Tim.* They are two very different questions, just as these two are: (1) Would this building remain intact if this column were removed? (2) If the architect had not willed this particular column in the building, what would he have ordered in its place for the permanence of the structure?

[185] For a complete examination of this problem in answer to recent objections, cf.

Fourth Article

WHETHER GOD BECAME INCARNATE IN ORDER TO TAKE AWAY ACTUAL SIN, RATHER THAN TO TAKE AWAY ORIGINAL SIN

The reply is in the affirmative.

Scriptural proof. We read in the Gospel: "Behold the Lamb of God who taketh away the sin of the world," [186] that is, as St. Bede says, the sin that is common to the whole human race. St. John wrote "the sin of the world." [187]

But the principal text is quoted in the body of the article, in which we read: "For judgment indeed was by one [i.e., by Adam] unto condemnation . . . as by the offense of one, unto all men to condemnation: so also by the justice of one [i.e., of Christ], unto all men to justification of life." [188]

This purpose of the Incarnation of the Son of God is likewise expressly affirmed in a provincial council and also to some extent in the Council of Trent.[189]

Theological proof. It includes two conclusions.

1) Christ came to take away all sins, because He came to save men, and all sins are an obstacle to salvation.

2) St. Thomas proves that Christ came first of all to take away original sin, since this sin is absolutely greater extensively, inasmuch as it extends to the whole human race, by which the race is infected; although actual sin is greater intensively, because it has more of the nature of voluntary.

Hence in virtue of the present decree, it is probable that Christ came also only to take away original sin, but not solely for the taking away of actual sins; because, if there had been no original sin, this would eliminate the more important reason for the Incarnation. Moreover, in virtue of the present decree, Christ came in passible and mortal

---

the article "De motivo incarnationis," pp. 7–45, in the *Acta Acad. Romanae S. Thomae,* 1945.

[186] John 1:29.

[187] Nestle's critical edition of St. John's Greek text has *τὴν ἁμαρτίαν τοῦ κόσμου.*

[188] Rom. 5:15 f. These words are quoted from the Vulgate, which differs somewhat from the text as given by St. Thomas in this article.

[189] Cf. the Sixth Council of Toledo, and the Council of Trent, Sess. VI, chap. 2; Denz., no. 794.

flesh; but, if there had been no original sin, His flesh would have been neither passible nor mortal.[190]

Fifth Article

WHETHER IT WAS FITTING THAT GOD SHOULD BECOME INCARNATE IN THE BEGINNING OF THE HUMAN RACE

The answer is in the negative. But He came "in the fullness of time" as St. Paul says.[191]

For it was not fitting that God become incarnate before sin, since the Incarnation is for the redemption of the human race; nor was the Incarnation fitting immediately after sin, and this for three reasons.

1) That man, being humbled, would more readily acknowledge the seriousness of the disease and the necessity of Redemption, and so would cry out for it.

2) That the human race might gradually be led from imperfection to perfection by means of the natural law, the Mosaic law, and the Gospel.

3) Because it befitted the dignity of the Word incarnate that His coming be announced by the prophets.

Sixth Article

WHETHER THE INCARNATION OUGHT TO HAVE BEEN PUT OFF TILL THE END OF THE WORLD

St. Thomas denies this, but says it was fitting for the Incarnation to take place "in the fullness of time," as stated by St. Paul,[192] or morally speaking "in the midst of the years." [193]

Three reasons are given.

[190] If there had been no original sin, then a number of persons would not have needed redemption, because they would have remained in the state of grace, in fact, of innocence; but in the others there would have been actual or personal sin, which is not transmitted except by example or by a sort of heredity. It must be noted that St. Thomas says in this fourth article: "It is certain that Christ came into this world . . . also to take away all sins that are subsequently added to original sin; not that all are taken away, and this is from men's fault, inasmuch as they do not adhere to Christ . . . , but because He offered what was sufficient for blotting out all sins."

[191] Gal. 4:4.

[192] *Ibid.*

[193] Hab. 3:2. This text is quoted by St. Thomas in the counterargument of this article.

1) Because it is not fitting that the efficient cause of perfection be put off so long a time.

2) Because at the end of the world there would have been almost no knowledge of God among men.

3) Because it was fitting that the salvation of the human race be effected by faith in the Savior, not only by faith in some future thing but also by faith in something present and past.

Thus the question of the fitness of the Incarnation has been sufficiently examined both as to its relative necessity for the reparation of the human race, and its absolute necessity as regards condign reparation. The proximate motive of the Incarnation has also been considered, which was formally the motive of mercy, namely, the alleviation of the human race from its misery, or "for our salvation," as the Nicene Creed says.

Having discussed the fact of the Incarnation, we now come to consider its nature.

CHAPTER IV

QUESTION 2

Prologue

THE MODE OF THE UNION OF THE WORD INCARNATE

ST. THOMAS has the following considerations about this mode of union.

1) The union itself (q. 2).

2) The person assuming the human nature (q. 3).

3) The nature assumed and the perfections or defects of this assumed nature (q. 4–15).

Then the consequences of this union will be discussed, namely, as regards being, volition, and operation.

Hence this second question is about the essence of the Incarnation, or about the hypostatic union.

This second question contains twelve articles, and is divided into three parts.

The first part (a. 1–6) discusses what is and what is not the nature of this union. It inquires 1. whether the union took place in the nature; 2. or in the person; 3. or in the suppositum; 4. whether the person of Christ is composite; 5. what is the union of body and soul in Christ?

Thus the question is gradually solved, and the sixth article, which is of great importance, unites the preceding articles, by asking whether the human nature was united to the Word accidentally.

The second part considers the union with reference to the divine actions, which are creation and assumption (a. 7, 8).

The third part considers the union with reference to grace: Is it the greatest of unions (a. 9)? Did it come about by grace (a. 10)? Was it the result of merit? Was the grace of union natural to the man Christ (a. 12)?

This second question virtually contains the whole treatise on the Incarnation, just as the third question of the first part of the *Summa,* in which God is defined as the self-subsisting Being, virtually contains the whole treatise on the One God.

As regards the order of the questions, it must be noted that in the *Summa theologica* St. Thomas follows the logical order rather than the historical, whereas in the *Contra Gentes* (Book IV, q. 27 f.) he follows primarily the historical order by refuting the various heresies that arose concerning the Incarnation.

Heresies concerning the Incarnation. For an understanding of the articles of this question, a brief explanation must be given of the principal heresies condemned by the Church: Arianism, Apollinarianism, Nestorianism, Monophysitism, and Eutychianism.[1]

A threefold division is made in these heresies, inasmuch as some erred concerning the divinity of Christ, others denied His humanity, and finally some erred about the union of the two natures.

God permits errors so that by opposing them the truth may be presented in clearer light.

- Errors
  - divinity of Christ
    - This was denied by the Ebionites, Cerinthians, Arians, and others. The Arians and Apollinarians denied that Christ had a soul.
  - humanity of Christ
    - The Docetae and Valentinus denied that Christ had a real body.
  - the union of natures
    - The Nestorians denied that the union was personal.
    - The Eutychians and Monophysites denied that there were two natures in Christ.

Thus it was that already in the first four or five centuries of Christianity almost all the errors possible against the Incarnation were proposed.

[1] See Tixeront, *History of Dogmas,* for an account of these heresies in their historical aspect.

1) *The divinity of Christ* was denied.

In the first century, by the Ebionites and Cerinthians. In the second and third centuries by the Adoptionists and Gnostics.

In the fourth century, by the Arians. They declared that Christ is not the Son of God consubstantial with the Father but is a creature; that the Word (Logos) pre-existed, but was created, and is a mediator, who assumed in the womb of the Blessed Virgin Mary only a body and not a soul. Thus the Arians concluded that Christ is neither truly God nor truly man. Hence St. Athanasius replied [2] that such a conception of Christ made it impossible for Him to satisfy for the human race or free it from sin. This means that the denial of the mystery of the Incarnation includes the denial of the mystery of Redemption, and thus there is left but the semblance of Christianity.[3]

Later on, in the sixteenth century, the Socinians denied the divinity of Christ, and the same must be said in our times of the Unitarians, who deny the Trinity, and also liberal Protestants and Modernists of the present day.

2) *The humanity of Christ.* Some denied that Christ's body was real, others that He had a soul. The Docetae, such as Marcion and the Manichaeans, said that Christ merely appeared to have a body.

Appelles and Valentinus in the third century said that Christ's body was real but celestial, sidereal or aerial, and therefore He did not derive His human nature from the Virgin Mary.

The Arians and Anomoeans taught that the Word did not assume a soul. In the fourth century the Apollinarians held that Christ had only a sensitive soul, and that the Word performed the functions of the rational soul, though they admitted, contrary to the Arians, that the Word was not created.[4]

3) Some denied the unity of person in Christ, others the twofold nature. In the third century, the unity of person was denied by Paul of Samosata. In the fourth century, Diodorus of Tarsus said that the Word was only accidentally united to Christ. So also Theodore of Mopsuestia and the Nestorians, teaching a sort of personal union, rejected it really, however, inasmuch as they posited merely a moral union between the two natures. In this way they sought to refute

[2] *Contra Arianos,* II, 7.

[3] Denz., nos. 54, 61, 705, concerning the definitions of the Church against the Arians. Cf. *Dict, théol. cath.,* art. "Arianisme."

[4] Denz., nos. 85, 206, 223, 227, 271; definitions of the Church against Apollinaris.

Apollinarianism. The consequence of these errors was the view that Mary is not the Mother of God.

The prominent opponent of the Nestorians was St. Cyril of Alexandria who, in refuting them, availed himself of the principal argument used by St. Athanasius against the Arians, namely, that, if Christ is not God, but only morally united to Him, as a saint is, then how could He satisfy for us or free the human race from sin? [5]

In our times, too, the disciples of Gunther denied the unity of person in Christ, since they defined a person as a self-conscious nature, for in Christ there are two self-conscious natures.

So also, Rosmini acknowledges between the Word and the human will in Christ merely an accidental union, inasmuch as the human will, since it was completely dominated by the Word, ceased to be personal. Rosmini says: "Hence the human will ceased to be personal in Christ as man, and, since it is personal in other men, in Christ there remained but the human nature." [6] Thus the union in Christ between the Word and the human will would be merely accidental and moral. The error of Rosmini and Gunther is that both do not seek to define person ontologically by reason of subsistence, but only psychologically through self-consciousness, or by reason of liberty. This error is the result of the nineteenth-century psychologism.

The Modernists say about the same, since they reduce the hypostatic union, if they give it any thought, to God's influence upon the human conscience of the historic Christ, or to the subconscious self in Christ by which He perceived that He was loved by God above all others.

Finally, the Eutychians or Monophysites denied that there were two natures in Christ. Eutyches posed as the adversary of Nestorius and the defender of the theology of St. Cyril of Alexandria, which he did not understand. He was a man of little learning, and obstinate, and so he went to the other extreme of Nestorianism. He was so insistent in affirming the unity of person in Christ against the Nestorians that he ended in denying His twofold nature. He said: "I confess that our Lord was of two natures before the union; but after the union I acknowledge one nature," [7] either because the human

[5] *Ibid.*, nos. 113, 168. Cf. also P. Jugie, *Nestorius et la controverse Nestorienne;* also *Dict. théol. cath.*, art. "Union hypostatique," col. 471, and art. "Nestorius."

[6] Denz., no. 1917.

[7] Cf. *Dict. théol. cath.*, art. "Eutyches."

nature was absorbed by the divine nature, or because each nature commingled to form a third nature, distinct from each before the union, or because the human nature and the Word were absolutely united as the soul and the body are. Hence Eutyches by this method succeeded in proclaiming something that the Nestorians denied, since they denied that the Blessed Virgin Mary is the Mother of God.

In the fourth century, however, the Monothelites, professing that Christ had but one will, by this very fact rejected the doctrine that there were two natures in Him. The followers of the modern heresy that declares the Word really emptied Himself, also deny a twofold nature in Christ, since they hold that the Word, at least partly and for a time, set aside His divine attributes.[8]

Thus several heresies made their appearance as excessive reactions against the preceding ones; so also not infrequently it happens that the human mind in its aberrations passes from one extreme to the other.

1) Arius says that Christ is the created Word united to a human body, without a soul. St. Athanasius says correctly: then Christ could not have satisfied for us.

2) But Apollinaris says that Christ is the uncreated Word united to a human body, without a rational soul, since this latter was capable of sinning, and consequently could not satisfy for us.

3) Then Nestorius, in a reactionary spirit, says that Christ has a rational soul which is morally united to the Word. Thus the union of the natures is no longer personal.

4) Finally, Eutyches goes to the other extreme and asserts that the union of the natures is not only moral but also physical, meaning that after the union there is only one nature. This doctrine is Monophysitism.

These last three mentioned heresies deny that the Blessed Virgin Mary is the Mother of God, and they do so for various reasons. Apollinaris says that Jesus is not a man, Eutyches says that His body is not of the same nature as ours, whereas the Nestorians assert that Jesus is not God, but morally united to Him.

The dogma strikes a medium between Nestorianism and Monophysitism, transcending both of them, inasmuch as it states that both natures in Christ are united in one person.

[8] *Ibid.,* art. "Kenose." This heresy is also known as the kenotic theory, from the Greek *κενώσις*, which means "an emptying."

Teaching of the Church. It is evident from the Gospels, the Apostles' Creed, and the condemnation of the above-mentioned heresies.

1) Already even in the Apostles' Creed it is stated that Jesus Christ is truly God and truly man, inasmuch as it says: "I believe . . . in Jesus Christ His only Son, who was conceived by the Holy Ghost, born of the Virgin Mary." [9]

2) In the First Council of Nicaea (325) and the First of Constantinople (381), the consubstantiality of the Word with the Father is explicitly declared. The First Council of Nicaea says: "God of God, light of light, true God of true God, born not made, *of one substance* with the Father, which the Greeks call homoousion." [10] It is likewise declared against the Docetae, Gnostics, and Apollinarians that "Christ had a complete human nature." [11]

3) In the fifth century, the Athanasian Creed declares all that is of faith on this point, in these few words: "Jesus Christ the Son of God is God and man. God, of the substance of the Father, begotten of the Father from all eternity; and man, of the substance of His Mother, born in time. . . . Who, although He be God and man, yet He is not two, but one Christ; one, not by conversion of the Godhead into the flesh, but by the assumption of the manhood into God; one altogether, not by confusion of substance, but by unity of person." [12]

The Council of Ephesus (431) proclaims against Nestorius that there is one person in Christ, and two natures hypostatically united,[13] and also proclaims "that this same Christ is both God and man." [14]

Likewise, not long afterward (451), the Council of Chalcedon defines against Eutyches and the Monophysites that "One and the same Christ, Son, Lord, Only-begotten, must be acknowledged to be in two natures, without confusion, change, division, separation; the distinction of natures being by no means destroyed by their union; but rather the distinction of each nature being preserved and concurring in one person and one hypostasis; [15] not in something that is parted or divided into two persons, but in one and the same and only-begotten

[9] Denz., no. 6.

[10] The Greek text reads: *'Ομοούσιον τῷ πατρί,'* "of one and the same nature with the Father."

[11] Denz., nos. 85, 86.

[12] *Ibid.*, no. 40.

[13] *Ibid.*, no. 114.

[14] *Ibid.*, no. 118.

[15] The Greek text reads: *καὶ εἰς ἐν πρόσωπον καὶ μίαν ὑπίστασιν.*

Son of God the Word, the Lord Jesus Christ." [16] This text is quoted almost verbatim in various subsequent councils, the Council of Florence being the last to refer to it (1441).

Finally Pope Pius X condemned the following proposition of the Modernists: "The Christological teaching of SS. Paul and John, and of the Councils of Nicaea, Ephesus, and Chalcedon is not Christ's own teaching, but that which the Christian conscience conceived concerning Jesus." [17]

Let us now undertake the philosophical analysis of these definitions of the Church.

First Article

WHETHER THE UNION OF THE INCARNATE WORD TOOK PLACE IN THE NATURE

State of the question. The meaning is: Does this union, referred to in the heading of this article, result in only one nature, as Eutyches and Dioscorus taught? In this article we have the refutation of Monophysitism.

The reason why St. Thomas refutes Eutyches before Nestorius is that he is following the logical order and not the historical order. It is in accordance with logical procedure to state first in what this union does not consist, and afterward what constitutes it.

The difficulties presented at the beginning of this article are arguments of Eutyches, who sought to defend the teaching of St. Cyril of Alexandria against the Nestorians, but Eutyches had a wrong conception of St. Cyril's teaching.

First difficulty. The text quoted by St. Thomas in this first objection is not St. Cyril's, as found in the acts of the Council of Chalcedon, but is to be attributed to the heretic Dioscorus. However, since the words can be interpreted in a good sense and are attributed to St. Cyril, they are examined by St. Thomas here. The text reads: "We must understand not two natures, but one incarnate nature of the Word of God." It does not say simply "one nature," but "one incarnate nature"; and this is true, since only the divine nature became incarnate, as explained afterward in the Second Council of Constantinople,[18] and the words

[16] *Ibid.,* no. 148.
[17] *Ibid.,* no. 2031; proposition 31.
[18] *Ibid.,* no. 220.

of the council on this point are quoted by St. Thomas in his reply to the first objection.

St. Cyril had said that this union was not moral but physical.[19] By calling the union physical, St. Cyril by no means meant that it signified a commingling of the two natures, but that the union was more than moral and accidental, and as used by St. Cyril the expression came to be commonly accepted as equivalent to hypostatic union.[20]

In the Latin Church, the terms "person" and "nature" have a distinct meaning already from the time of Tertullian, who admits in Christ one person but two natures, almost as clearly as St. Hilary and St. Augustine declared after him.[21]

Second difficulty. It is taken from the Athanasian Creed, in which it is said of Christ: "As the rational soul and the flesh together are one man, so God and man together are one Christ." But the soul and the body unite in constituting one nature. Eutyches applied this remote analogy in the literal sense.

Third difficulty. St. Gregory Nazianzen says: "The human nature [in Christ] is deified," just as St. Cyril had said, "the divine nature is incarnate." But some could understand the expression to mean a certain transmutation and blending of the natures.

Eutyches understood the expression in the following sense: "That our Lord was of two natures before the union; but after the union there was one nature." Eutyches said: "Christ is of two natures, not in two natures, nor is He consubstantial with us according to the flesh; the deity suffered and was buried."

The reply of St. Thomas, notwithstanding these difficulties, is as follows: The union of the Word incarnate did not take place in the nature or essence, such that in Christ there is only one nature. In fact, this is absolutely impossible; but there are in Christ two distinct natures.

This conclusion is a dogma of our faith defined as such against Eutyches in the Council of Chalcedon in these words: "We teach that Christ . . . is perfect as God and that He is perfect as man, true God

[19] *Ibid.,* no. 115. St. Cyril's expression is: ἕνωσις φυσιχή.

[20] *Ibid.,* no. 114; καθ' ὑπόστασιν.

[21] The exact signification of the terms οὐσία, φύσις, ὑπόστασις, πρόσωπον in the Greek Church, however, was the result of a gradual process of determination. In the Greek language πρόσωπον signifies a theatrical mask or face, a figure used by actors to represent heroes, and therefore it often designates a dramatic person on the stage.

and true man . . . and that He is in two natures,[22] without confusion, . . . the properties of each nature being preserved, and that He is in one person and one subsistence." [23] The Second Council of Constantinople defines similarly.[24] Likewise the Athanasian Creed declares: "One altogether, not by confusion of substance, but by unity of person." [25] Subsequent councils and professions of faith give similar definitions.

Scriptural proof. From the many passages already quoted, it is evident that Christ is truly God and truly man. It suffices here to give the following text from the Old Testament: "A child is born to us . . . and His name shall be called . . . God the Mighty." [26] Thus also in the New Testament, the greater and especially more sublime prophets were already illumined to perceive the divine nature of the promised Messias.

From the New Testament we have the following texts: "I am the way and the truth and the life." [27] "Who being in the form of God, thought it not robbery to be equal with God, but emptied Himself, taking the form of a servant." [28] Here we have the twofold form or nature, namely, of God and the servant, each distinct, without confusion (of natures). Again we read: "That which was from the beginning, which we have heard, which we have seen with our eyes, which we have looked upon, and our hands have handled, of the Word of life." [29] Here again we have the two natures distinctly mentioned, namely, the one divine in the words "of the Word of life," the other the human nature, in the words "which we have looked upon and our hands have handled."

Proof from reason. It is given in the body of the article, in which, from an analysis of the notion of nature, the absurdity of Monophysitism is shown, which is just as absurd as pantheism. There are two parts to this article. The first part considers what is meant by the word "nature." The second part shows the impossibility of the union taking place in the nature.

First part. It determines, by the way of invention, following Aris-

[22] The Greek text reads: *'εν δύο φύσεσιν ἀσυγχύτως.*

[23] Denz., no. 148. The concluding words of this quotation in the Greek read: *εἰς ἓν πρόσωπον καὶ μίαν ὑπόστασιν.*

[24] *Ibid.*, nos. 219 f.

[25] *Ibid.*, no. 40.

[26] Isa. 9:6.

[27] John 14:6.

[28] Phil. 2:6.

[29] I John 1:1.

totle[30] and Boethius, the various acceptations of the term "nature."

This noun signifies: 1. birth or begetting of living beings; 2. the principle of this begetting; 3. whatever intrinsic principle of motion essentially belongs to the subject in which it is, such as the principle of the vegetative life, or of the sensitive life, in each and every subject; 4. The substantial form, which is this radical principle of natural operations, for instance, in the plant; 5. matter, which is the principle of natural passivity; thus it is said that the animal is naturally mortal; 6. the essence also of spiritual things and of God Himself, inasmuch as this essence is the radical principle of their operations. So says Boethius, who is quoted in this article, and St. Thomas concludes: "But we are now speaking of nature as it signifies the essence."

Second part. It is shown to be impossible for the union to take place in the nature. The argument of St. Thomas may be reduced to the following syllogism. There are only three possible ways for the union to take place in the nature, namely: 1. by the composition of things that are perfect in themselves and that remain perfect; 2. by the mixture of things perfect in themselves that have undergone a change; 3. by the union of things imperfect in themselves that have been neither mixed nor changed.

But these ways are incompatible. Therefore it is impossible for the union to take place in the nature.

Union	of two perfect things	1. that remains such, as a heap of stones or a house: called composition. One nature does not result from this union.
		2. that have been changed, as a combination of elements resulting in a mixture; but the divine nature is absolutely unchangeable; for Christ would be neither truly man nor truly God.
	of imperfect things	that have been neither changed nor mixed, as man is composed of soul and body. But both the divine and the human natures are in themselves perfect. But the divine nature cannot be even a part of the compound as form, for then it would be less than the whole.

[30] Cf. *II Phys.*, chap. 1.

The whole article must be read.

More briefly: This union does not take place in the nature, so that there results from it but one nature:

1) Because Christ would not be truly man and truly God, but a sort of chimera.

2) Because the divine nature is unchangeable and cannot constitute a part of any whole, not even as form, for thus it would be less perfect than the whole.[31]

Objection. Some have said that there can be a transubstantiation of the human nature into the divine, just as there is a transubstantiation of the bread into the body of Christ, without any corruption in the process.

Reply. Even if this transubstantiation were not incompatible, the result of this would be that after the Incarnation the human nature would cease to exist, and thus Christ would not be truly man, which is against the faith. Christ is truly man, for He was born, suffered, and died.

The reply of St. Thomas is confirmed from the solution of the difficulties presented at the beginning of the article.

Reply to first objection. This difficulty is taken from the text attributed to St. Cyril and explained by the Second Council of Constantinople,[32] in the sense that the physical union,[33] which St. Cyril spoke of when arguing against the Nestorians, who admitted only a moral union, was meant by St. Cyril as referring not to a union in the nature, but in the person, or to a subsistential union, as the words themselves denote.[34]

Reply to second objection. When the Athanasian Creed says, "As the rational soul and flesh together are one man, so God and man together are one Christ," the analogy has its foundation in the similarity between the parts, namely, inasmuch as soul and body constitute one person, but not in the dissimilarity, namely, inasmuch as the soul and the body constitute one nature.

[31] Similarly pantheism, since it confuses the divine nature with created natures, involves a contradiction, and *de facto* this theory means either that the world is absorbed in God, and then we have acosmism as taught by Parmenides, or pantheism; or else it means that God is absorbed in the world, as in the case of absolute evolutionism, a theory that maintains God is in a process of becoming in the world and never will be a reality.

[32] Denz., no. 220.

[33] The Greek text is: ἕνωσις φυσική.

[34] Denz., no. 114. The Greek words are: ἕνωσις καθ' ὑπόστασιν.

Reply to third objection. Damascene explains correctly the words attributed to St. Cyril, who says: "The divine nature is incarnate," inasmuch as it is united personally to flesh. He gives a similar interpretation to the words of St. Gregory Nazianzen, who says that "the human nature is deified"; namely, not by change, but by being united with the Word, the properties of each nature remaining intact.

Second Article

WHETHER THE UNION OF THE INCARNATE WORD TOOK PLACE IN THE PERSON

State of the question. The meaning is: whether this union took place in such manner that there is only one person.

In this article we have the refutation of Nestorianism, a heresy that denied there was only one person in Christ, and that admitted only a moral union such as found in saints united by love with God.

The first two difficulties posited at the beginning of this article, are arguments raised by the Nestorians.

First difficulty. In God there is no real distinction between person and nature. If, therefore, this union did not take place in the nature, as the Nestorians say, then it did not take place in the person.

Second difficulty. Personality is a dignity that belongs to us as human beings. Hence it is not attributed to irrational animals or to other beings of a lower order, for these have individuality, but not personality. But Christ's human nature has no less dignity than ours. Therefore it was much more reasonable that Christ's human nature should have its own personality.

This difficulty is still proposed in our days by many theologians who disagree with Cajetan's interpretation of St. Thomas' teaching. These theologians, as we shall see, in advancing this difficulty against Cajetan, seem to be unaware of the reply to the second objection of this present article.

Third difficulty. It is taken from the definition of person as given by Boethius, who says: "a person is an individual substance of a rational nature." But the Word of God assumed an individual human nature, namely, this humanity belonging to Christ. Therefore this humanity belonging to Christ has its own personality.

This difficulty of necessity calls for the making of a profound distinction between individuality, or individuation, and personality. St.

Thomas most fittingly makes this kind of distinction in his reply to the third objection, which is thoroughly explained by Cajetan. Nevertheless, even many Scholastics seem to have only a superficial knowledge of this reply to the third objection, perhaps because they did not begin by examining with sufficient care the state and difficulty of the question, as St. Thomas did in his presentation of these difficulties, which constitute, so to speak, the very problem to be solved in this article.

The reply, in spite of these difficulties, is: The union of the Word incarnate took place in the person of the Word, such that there is only one person in Christ. This declaration is a dogma of our faith.

This reply was defined against the Nestorians in the Council of Ephesus, in which the union was declared to be hypostatic, or personal,[35] and it condemned the assertion of two persons morally united in Christ. It likewise condemned the Nestorian expression, Christ the man is theophoron, that is, God bearer.[36] Likewise it declared that, "if anyone does not confess that the Word of God suffered and died in the flesh, let him be anathema." [37] It also defined that the Blessed Virgin Mary is the Mother of God,[38] since she is the mother of this man Jesus who is God, constituting one person.[39]

These definitions are confirmed in the Council of Chalcedon, which says: "One and the same Christ . . . acknowledged to be in two natures, without confusion . . . and concurring in one person and one hypostasis, not in something that is parted or divided." [40]

Similarly the Apostles' Creed confesses that one and the same person is the Son of God and of man; particularly the Creed of St. Athanasius, which says of the union, "absolutely one, not in confusion of substance, but in unity of person." [41]

Sacred Scripture. This doctrine of the faith is already clearly expressed in the New Testament; for it attributes the properties of both the divine and the human natures to one and the same Christ, since it is the same Christ who is conceived, born, baptized in the Jordan, who fears, is sad, hungry and tired on His journey, who suffers and

[35] *Ibid.,* nos. 114–18; ἕνωσις καθ' ὑπόστασιν.
[36] *Ibid.,* no. 117.
[37] *Ibid.,* no. 124.
[38] Θεοτόκον.
[39] Denz., no. 113.
[40] *Ibid.,* no. 148.
[41] *Ibid.,* no. 40.

dies on the cross. This same person is called the Son of God, God above all, the Author of life, for He Himself says: "I am the truth and the life." [42] Hence we see that the properties of each nature are attributed in Sacred Scripture to the same intelligent and incommunicable subject, that is, to the same person. But this person is the eternal person of the Word, as expressed by the Evangelist in these words: "The Word was made flesh," [43] that is, the Son of God became man. Therefore the Son of God and man are not two persons, but one person.

The common notion of person suffices for an understanding of the preceding statements, namely, that a person is an intelligent and *sui juris* [44] or free agent. This subject can be merely a man, an angel, God, or any divine person.

Nestorius objected that a moral union was sufficient.

Reply. A moral union is established by means of affection. But, however intimate is the friendship between two persons, one friend is not said to have become the other friend, neither is a saint who is united with God by a bond of most fervent love said to have become God, nor is God said to have become either Peter or Paul, although there is a moral union between them and God.

In fact, Christ could not have said truthfully: "I am the way, the truth, and the life." [45] In other words, speaking of Himself, He could not have attributed truly to Himself divine attributes and also those that belong to the human nature. The pronoun "I" denotes the person speaking, and there is only one person; for if there are two persons, it cannot be said that one is the other. In affirmative judgments, the verb "is" expresses real identity between subject and predicate. Thus: I am the truth, signifies: I, who by my mouth, am speaking, am the same person who am the truth. Otherwise the judgment is absolutely false, and it is as if Paul were to say: I, who am Paul, am Peter.

[42] John 14:6.

[43] *Ibid.*, 1:14.

[44] The expression *sui juris* as applied to the definition of person implies a subject to whom ultimately all the actions are attributed. It also means a subject that has a complete nature that is individualized, and consequently incommunicable as such to any other. Just what constitutes a subject *sui juris* is very much disputed in the schools of Catholic theology. When a subject is intelligent and *sui juris* it follows that it must be endowed with freedom, though it may not always be able to exercise this power. On this point, cf. Garrigou-Lagrange, *God, His Existence and His Nature,* II, 306.

[45] John 14:6.

Testimony of the Fathers.[46] Tertullian, Origen, St. Ephrem, St. Athanasius, St. Gregory Nazianzen, St. Jerome, St. Cyril of Alexandria, St. Leo I, and St. John Damascene quoted by St. Thomas in the counterargument of this third article have all affirmed clearly and most explicitly that there is one person in Christ.

It must be noted that in the liturgy of the Church the termination of the orations frequently is, "Through our Lord Jesus Christ who liveth and reigneth with Thee in the unity of the Holy Ghost, forever and ever."

Body of the article. It contains two parts. In the first part a distinction is made between person and nature. The second part proves that the union of the Word incarnate took place in the person.

First of all the article must be explained, and then we shall consider the erroneous system of several modern philosophers concerning personality, and also the systems freely discussed among Catholic theologians.

In the first part of this article, as regards the distinction that is made between person and nature, by a gradual process the argument proceeds from common sense or natural reasoning, to the establishment of a philosophical proof that acknowledges and defends the real validity of natural reasoning against either empiric or idealistic phenomenalism.

The first part of this article must be read. It is divided into three parts: 1. the conclusion; 2. definition of suppositum; 3. definition of person, which is completed in the reply to the third objection.

First conclusion. It may be expressed briefly as follows: There is a real difference between suppositum and nature in every creature, just as there is a real difference between the whole and its parts.

The reason is that the nominal definition of suppositum or the subject of predication signifies the whole, and in every creature existence and accidents are not included in its essence. Such is the case in the angels, for Michael is not his existence nor his action.[47] Moreover, in corporeal things, in addition to the essence of the species, each has individuating principles that are derived from quantified matter, such as these bones, this flesh.

Hence this real distinction between the created nature and the sup-

[46] Cf. Rouet de Journel, *Enchiridion patristicum,* Index theol., nos. 384 f.

[47] *Summa theol.,* Ia, q. 54, a. 1.

positum that contains it, is not a distinction between two separate things, but it is a distinction that prevails between a real and actual whole, and its real, formal, and perfective part.

Contrary to what has been said, there is a real distinction in God between suppositum and nature.

The real definition of suppositum is given in the following words. The suppositum is taken to be a whole which has the nature as its formal part to perfect it; and as stated in the reply to the third objection, the suppositum is the whole that exists and acts separately by itself. This point must be carefully considered, because it constitutes the philosophical foundation of the whole treatise.

Thus the suppositum is *that which is*, namely, the real subject of attribution, so that the suppositum is not attributed to any other subject; whereas nature is that by which a thing is such as it is, in such a species. Similarly, existence is that by which a thing is placed outside of nothing and its causes; a faculty is that by which the subject can operate, and operation is that by which it actually operates.

All the above-mentioned are attributed to the suppositum, and this latter is not attributed to any other subject. Moreover, it must be noted that the following divers affirmative judgments: Peter is a man, Peter exists, Peter can act, Peter does act, all these affirmative judgments assert real identity between subject and predicate by the word "is." They are equivalent in meaning to: Peter is the same real subject that is the man that exists, that can act, that does act. For these judgments to be true, this real identity between subject and predicate must be verified outside the soul, although Peter's essence is not his existence, nor the faculty by which he acts, nor his action. Hence there must be something by which the subject is the same real subject, or that by which something is "that which by itself (separately) exists and acts," [48] as stated in the reply to the third objection.

Farther on we shall see how *that by which* a thing is a *quod* (or subject of attribution) [49] is subsistence, for which reason the suppositum is that which is competent to exist by itself separately. This truth

[48] Concerning the correlation prevailing between abstract terms and concrete terms, it must be said: just as humanity is that by which a man is a man, so personality is that by which a person is a person, and subsistence is that by which a suppositum is a suppositum; more briefly, subsistence or even personality is that by which a thing is a what or subject of attribution.

[49] The words in parentheses are the translator's explanation.

constitutes the philosophical foundation of this entire treatise.[50]

Person is defined as an intelligent and *sui juris* or free subject, namely, a suppositum having a rational, or intellectual, nature.

This definition is given at the end of the first part of this article in the following equivalent words: "And what is said of a suppositum is to be applied to a person in rational, or intelligent, creatures; for a person is nothing else than an individual substance of a rational nature, according to Boethius."

In addition to this it must be said that a person is an intelligent *sui juris* subject by itself separately existing and by itself operating, such as Peter, Paul. St. Thomas says similarly: "Person is a subsistent individual of a rational nature." [51]

This definition is explained at the end of the third objection. The

[50] This fundamental doctrine concerning the suppositum is found in the writings of Aristotle. In his *Perihermeneias* (On Judgment), Bk. I, lect. 3, 5, 8, the significance of the verb "is" in affirmative judgments is explained. In the *Metaphysics,* Bk. V, chap. 6, lect. 7, it is shown that every verb is resolved into the following parts of the verb "to be": "am, art, is," and its participle.

The source of judgment is the verb "is." Thus, "Peter walks" signifies "Peter is walking," or that Peter is the same real subject that is walking.

See also *Met.,* chap. 7, lect. 9 of St. Thomas, no. 893, where we read: "Any verb whatever can be reduced to a form that includes the verb 'is.' Hence it is evident that there are as many modes of predication as there are modes of being, such as substantive, or quantitative, qualitative, active, passive, relative, and so forth. Thus the predicaments or categories of being are like different adornments of the verb 'is,' as when we say: "Peter is substantially a man, quantitatively great, qualitatively wise," and so forth.

Similarly, in Aristotle's *Post. Analytics,* Bk. II, lect. 10 of St. Thomas, *on the third mode of per se predication,* it is stated that first substance, or anything that subsists by itself (Peter, for instance), is not in another as in its subject, whereas second substance, as in the case of humanity, is attributed to Peter, as also are his accidents, although in another manner. The first mode of per se predication is the definition, the second is the necessary property, the third is first substance, the fourth is the proper cause which is of itself and immediately as such required for the production of its proper effect, as singing is required for a singer, or killing for a killer. On this point cf. *God, His existence,* I, 379 f. (Tr.)

St. Thomas says (Ia, q. 13, a. 12): "In every true affirmative proposition the predicate and the subjects signify in some way the same thing in reality, and different things in idea." Other citations on this point from St. Thomas are: Ia, q. 14, a. 14; q. 85, a. 5; IIIa, q. 2, a. 2, 6; q. 4, a. 2 (Cajetan's *Comment.*); q. 16, a. 1; q. 17, a. 2. *Contra Gentes,* Bk. I, chap. 57.

Cf. also the *Tabula aurea* of the works of St. Thomas, under the word *verbum,* nos. 77 f.

We have treated this question at length in *Le sens commun et la philosophie de l'être.* pp. 50, 320–58.

[51] *Summa theol.,* Ia, q. 29, a. 3.

objection states that according to Boethius, person is an individual substance of a rational nature; but Christ assumed an individual human nature; therefore He assumed a human person, and so there are two persons in Christ, namely, the person assuming and the person assumed.

In the solution of this objection, St. Thomas in his reply most splendidly illustrates the definition of Boethius, by distinguishing accurately between individuality, or individuation, and personality.

This reply to the third objection must be read.

Not every individual in the genus of substance, even in rational nature, is a person, but that alone which exists by itself, and not that which exists in some more perfect thing. Hence the hand of Socrates, although it is a kind of individual, is not a person, but the part of a person, the part of a person and the part of a substance.

On the other hand, we know that according to St. Thomas [52] quantified matter *is the principle of individuation,* that is, as Cajetan explains: "Matter capable of this particular quantity so that it is not susceptible of that other quantity; for it is in this way that we distinguish between two drops of water that are most alike: not having the same quantified matter, they are thus in different parts of space. Hence individuation, which is derived from matter, is of the lowest order in man, whereas personality, as stated in the reply to the second objection, pertains to the dignity of a thing and to its perfection, so far as it pertains to the dignity and perfection of that thing to exist by itself." [53]

In Christ, as we shall see, individuation, as in our case, is effected by matter, whereas His personality is uncreated and thus there is an infinite difference between the two. St. Thomas discusses this point in his reply to the third objection, and elsewhere he says: "Person signifies what is most perfect in all nature, that is, a subsistent individual of a rational nature." [54]

Therefore we must not confuse the individual nature, individuated or singular, with suppositum and person. For even the individuated nature is not *that which is,* but that by which anything is constituted in a certain species that is limited or contracted to an individual grade of being, for example, an individuated nature is this humanity. Simi-

[52] *Ibid.,* Ia, q. 13, a. 9; IIIa, q. 77, a. 2.
[53] *De ente et essentia.*
[54] *Summa theol.,* Ia, q. 29, a. 3.

larly matter is that by which anything is material.[55] On the contrary, by suppositum or person is meant this person separately existing by himself and acting, to whom this humanity is attributed, as constituting a part of him; hence we do not say that this man is his humanity, for the verb "is" expresses by a logical distinction real identity between the whole and its parts. We truly say that this man is not his humanity, but has humanity, or has his nature. Thus the common sense or natural reason of all men, by so speaking, distinguishes in a confused manner between person and nature, or between *that which is,* and *that by which* something is constituted in a certain species.

Hence St. Thomas [56] and the Thomists, in explaining the definition of person as given by Boethius, make some addition and say that a person is an entirely incommunicable individual substance of a rational nature, inasmuch as a person is the first subject of attribution, which is predicated of no other subject, and to whom is attributed whatever pertains to person, such as nature, existence, properties and actions. But communicability is threefold.[57]

Communicability	of the part to the whole	to this whole that is the suppositum: e.g., of the humanity to the Word.
		to this essential or quantitative whole: e.g., of the soul to man; e.g., of the arm to the body.
	of the universal to the inferior	e.g., of the humanity to all individuals of the species.

Hence, when it is said that a person is incommunicable, what is especially meant is that such person is incommunicable to another

[55] If matter were that which is, and not that by which stones, plants, and animals are something material, materialism would be true: for then all bodies, even the human body, and man himself would be accidental modifications of this particular matter that exists by itself, which was the view of Thales, Anaximenes, and Heraclitus.

[56] *Summa theol.,* Ia, q. 29, a. 3 et ad 4.

[57] *Ibid.*

suppositum, although even both to inferiors and to the quantitative whole.

St. Thomas discusses this incommunicability of person in various parts of his works.[58]

Thus the transition is made gradually from the common or popular notion of person to the philosophical notion of the term. It is not necessary here by way of conclusion to this article to explain the various systems freely disputed among Catholic theologians concerning personality, or what formally constitutes a person.[59]

Second conclusion. Toward the end of the argumentative part of this article, what St. Thomas intends to prove concerning the formal constituent of person may be expressed by the following syllogism.

Everything that adheres to a person, whether it does or does not pertain to the nature, is united to it in the person, which is the whole by itself separately existing.

But our Catholic faith teaches us that the humanity of Christ adheres to the person of the Son of God.

Therefore it is united to the person of Christ, but not to His nature.

The major follows from the definition of person, since it is the whole or the subject by itself separately existing and acting to whom are attributed as to the ultimate subject of attribution all those things that pertain to a person, such as nature, existence, accidents, and other notes.

The minor is evident from revelation, inasmuch as the human nature as also its parts and properties, such as the soul, the body, passibility, and other qualities are attributed to the Son of God.[60]

First confirmation. There are only two possible unions; either the union of the Word was with the nature, or with the person. For union by affection or by reason of the extraordinary grace bestowed upon the person loved, such as Nestorius imagined in the case of Christ, does not belong solely to the Word, but is common to the three persons of the Trinity operating together *ad extra,* and this union is already found in varying degrees in all the just.

Second confirmation. If there are two persons in Christ, then we

[58] *Ibid.,* Ia, q. 3, a. 3, ad 3; q. 19, a. 3, ad 4.; q. 29, a. 3, ad 4. *De potentia,* q. 9, a. 2, ad 2; *Summa theol.,* IIIa, q. 72, a. 2. Cf. *Tabula aurea,* under the heading *"Incommunicable."* This question has been given considerable attention in the book entitled *Le sens commun,* pp. 320–58.

[59] See the appendix to this article, concerning the various theories about personality.

[60] See *Cajetan's commentary,* nos. 6 f.

are not redeemed; for neither of these two persons could have redeemed us from sin: not the divine person, because He could neither suffer nor satisfy for sin nor merit for us; not the human person, because he could not confer infinite value upon his satisfactory and meritorious works, such as was required for our redemption, so that the redemption be adequate.

It remains for us to reply to the first two difficulties proposed at the beginning of this article.

The first objection was: The person of God is not distinct from His nature. But the union of the Word incarnate did not take place in the nature. Therefore it did not take place in the person.

Reply to first objection. I distinguish the major: that there is no real distinction between nature and person in God, this I concede; that they do not differ in meaning, this I deny. I concede the minor.

I distinguish the conclusion. Therefore the union did not take place in the person, if by this is meant that the divine person is not even distinct in meaning from nature, then I concede the conclusion; otherwise I deny it. The reply to the first objection must be read.

Therefore this union of the humanity with God took place, not in the divine nature, but in the person of the Son.

Thus the mental distinction between God's mercy and justice is the foundation for the truth of these propositions: God punishes not by His mercy, but by His justice, although these two attributes are not distinct. Thus God understands by His intellect and not by His will. Likewise the Word is united to the humanity not in the nature but in the person.

As Cajetan says: "The reply is confirmed by reason of the fact . . . that the union of the human nature in the mystery of the Incarnation does not add anything to the meaning of nature, but it does indeed add something to the notion of person, because it adds the notion of *subsisting in the human nature.*" [61]

Moreover, it must be noted that St. Thomas in this reply to the first objection and often afterward, says: "The Word subsists in the human nature." So does Cajetan,[62] whereas many modern theologians say less correctly: The humanity subsists in the Word. In truth, that which subsists is not the humanity, which is that *by which* the Word is man; that which subsists is the very Word incarnate.

[61] *Ibid.*, no. 8.
[62] *Ibid.*

Second objection. It is still proposed in these days by many theologians who object to Cajetan's interpretation of St. Thomas' teaching. It reads as follows: Christ's human nature has no less dignity than ours. But personality belongs to dignity. Hence, since our human nature has its proper personality, there is much more reason for Christ's to have its proper personality.

Several theologians in our times revive this argument against Cajetan, saying: Personality cannot be a substantial mode that terminates the nature, rendering it immediately capable of existence, as constituting it that which by itself separately exists.

The reply of St. Thomas is quoted by Pius XI in his encyclical commemorating the decrees of the Council of Ephesus against Nestorius. The following statement summarizes the reply of St. Thomas: Personality pertains to dignity inasmuch as it is that by reason of which a person exists separately by oneself. But it is a greater dignity to exist in something nobler than oneself than to exist by oneself. The complete reply to the second objection should be read.

Thus it is more perfect for the sensitive life to be united to the intellective, and for every inferior to be united to the superior. Just as it is more perfect for the deacon to be made a priest, so it is more perfect for the human nature to exist in the person of the Word, than to have its own personality; because whatever perfection there is in its own personality, is found infinitely and more eminently in the Word, so that there is intrinsic independence not only from inferior material things, as in the case of every rational soul, but from every creature, for Christ, indeed, is not a creature, but above every creature.

And what St. Thomas says in this reply concerning one's own personality can be said of the substantial mode by which, as Cajetan remarks, it is that by which it exists separately.

Cajetan gives a good explanation of St. Thomas' reply to the second objection, saying: "Just as it is nobler for the sensitive life to have its complete specific nature by a form of a nobler order, namely, by the rational soul, so a greater dignity was bestowed upon the human nature of Christ from the fact that it was assumed by the divine personality." [63]

Later Thomists, such as Billuart, make this additional comment: Subsistence or personality is the perfection and completion of the nature, perfecting it not in its notion of nature or essence, but in its no-

[63] *Ibid.*, no. 9.

tion of suppositum or person, inasmuch as it pertains to the dignity of a thing that it exist by itself; as St. Thomas says: "It is a greater dignity to exist in something nobler than oneself than to exist by oneself. Hence, from this very fact, Christ's human nature is not less noble but more noble than ours." [64]

It must be noted that the above definition of person, namely, an intelligent and free subject, easily finds its verification both in the human person, the angelic person, and the divine person. In all of them the subject is incommunicable, which cannot be attributed to another, and all of them enjoy intelligence and free will. But it is evident that person is not predicated univocally of God and man; it is predicated analogically, though not metaphorically, but properly; for the formal signification of person is properly retained in God proportionally, just as the proper signification of intelligence and liberty, of the real subject.[65]

Difficulty proposed by more modern critics. The final difficulty is thus proposed by many modern philosophers of the Guntherian and Rosminian trend of thought. They say that the mystery of the Incarnation is absolutely unintelligible from the mere abstract and metaphysical notion of either suppositum or subsistence or personality. For it is not only the metaphysical or ontological concept of personality that must be considered; it must be viewed in its psychological and moral aspects likewise, which come under experience. But psychologically, personality seems to consist in consciousness of oneself, and in personal judgment. Hence Locke, and after him Gunther, defined person as "a nature conscious of itself." [66] But in the moral order, personality seems to consist in this, that every one is *sui juris,* or is master of himself, or is free to act as he wishes, and Rosmini insists on this point.[67]

In the days of Modernism (1905) several students of dogmatic theology attending this course in a certain university did not even listen to the professor who was explaining the treatise on the Incarnation. They wrote letters or read books not pertaining to dogmatic theology, because, as they said, the conception of personality as proposed by scholastic theology is unintelligible.

[64] *Summa theol.,* IIIa., q. 2, a. 2, ad 2; see also IIIa, q. 4, a. 2, ad 2 et ad 3.
[65] Cf. *God, His Existence.* I, 216, no. 19.
[66] Denz., nos. 1655 f.
[67] *Ibid.,* no. 1917.

I then said to one of these students: "Therefore, in your opinion in what does personality consist so as to give us a better understanding of the mystery of the Incarnation?" He replied: "Personality consists in a consciousness of oneself, and this is enough." I asked him how many consciousnesses and intelligences there are in Christ? This student had not even considered the fact that there are two intelligences and consequently two consciousnesses in Christ. Therefore there ought to be two personalities in Christ, if personality formally consisted in consciousness of oneself.

Another of these students replied to me: "Personality consists in freedom or dominion over oneself." But neither had he considered that in Christ there are two freedoms, and so there ought to be two personalities and hence two persons, which is the heresy of Nestorianism.

Hence it is manifest that, for assuming a more profound notion of personality, it must be considered in its ontological aspect, and not merely in its psychological and moral aspects.

For the solution of this difficulty, which is very widespread in these days, it will be useful at the beginning of this treatise, for its clarification, to start with a certain introduction or ascent from the psychological and moral notion of personality, especially as found in the saints, ending in the ontological notion of the most exalted personality of Christ. The notion of personality will thus be present in a less abstract, but more vivid and concrete manner, as befitting this mystery, when speaking not only with modern philosophers, but also with the faithful who are not accustomed to the language of philosophy, and who must, nevertheless, live by faith in the Incarnation, and who aspire to the contemplation of this mystery.

INTRODUCTION OR ASCENT TOWARD A CERTAIN UNDERSTANDING OF THE INCARNATION

There are three articles of St. Thomas that enable us to make this ascent.[68] But what pertains to the psychological and moral aspects of person must be added.

This introduction must begin by a definition of person considered under this threefold aspect, namely, ontological, psychological, and

[68] *Summa theol.,* Ia., q. 29, a. 1, which gives the definition of person; a. 3, which asks whether the name "person" should be applied to God; also IIIa, q. 2, which inquires whether the union took place in the person.

moral, and in accordance with the law of true progress from the psychological and moral aspects of personality.

Person under this threefold aspect is defined as an intelligent and free subject, or a substance of a rational nature, by itself separately existing and operating, conscious of and responsible for itself, such as Peter and Paul.

Human personality is that by which a man is thus by himself separately existing, and hence conscious of and responsible for his actions, which means that he is master of his actions. What must especially be noted about personality is that, besides its common independence from every suppositum, inasmuch as it exists separately by itself, it enjoys a threefold special independence, for a person is a suppositum by itself separately existing, whose specific existence and operation, namely, understanding and willing, does not intrinsically depend upon matter.

Therefore a person enjoys the following threefold independence:

1. Its existence does not intrinsically depend upon matter, and thus the soul separated from the body remains immortal.

2. In like manner its understanding does not intrinsically depend upon matter, and thus it transcends actually existing individual things and extends to the universal.

3. It will also remain independent of particular goods that are mingled with evil, for these do not infallibly attract the will, which is specified by universal good. Thus personality far surpasses individuation by means of matter.

What, then, is the law of true and complete progress concerning psychological and moral personality?

Some think that this law consists simply in progress of the aforesaid independence, which would finally be in every respect absolute, or it would consist in complete autonomy of spirit and will, as Kant says. In accordance with this tendency, however, the complete evolution of man's personality would mean that he recognizes nobody his superior. Once this personality is fully developed, there would no longer be any place for virtues that are called passive, such as humility, obedience, patience, meekness, even for the theological virtues; and hence this superior personality would not differ much from the perfect insubordination of him who said: "I will not serve." This absolute autonomy, which is the doctrine of Kant, was condemned by the Vatican Council in these words: "If anyone shall say that human reason is so independent that faith cannot be enjoined upon it by God; let him be anathema." [69]

It is manifest that the law of true and complete progress of personality does not consist merely in progress of the above-mentioned independence; for the true and legitimate independence of the human person toward things inferior to it has its foundation in the strict dependence toward realities that are superior to it. Thus our reason transcends sensible things, space and time, because it is ordered to universal truth, and so to the knowledge of Him who is supreme Truth, at least so far as He is naturally knowable.

Likewise, as our will is free and independent with reference to the attraction of particular good, this is because it is ordered to universal good, and so to the supreme Good, which means to God the author of nature, who is to be loved above all things.

True personality has this characteristic, that its legitimate independence or relative autonomy toward things inferior to itself has its foundation in immediate dependence on truth and goodness, on supreme Truth and supreme Goodness, that is, God.

What follows from this characteristic as regards the law of true and complete progress of psychological and moral personality? It follows that the more personality dominates inferior things and the more intimately it is dependent on God, then the more perfect it is.

This is the true law of its progress, which is easily illustrated by examples, ascending gradually from the lowest grade of human personality until we reach the personality of Christ.

Thus the lowest grade of psychological and moral personality is verified in the man who is addicted to inordinate passions. Yet this man is a person or a substance of an intellectual nature, but insufficiently conscious of his dignity and dominion. Such a man is not ruled by right reason, but by his senses, imagination, and inordinate passions as in the case of irrational animals. He has not dominion over himself, nor independence as regards those things inferior to him, acting as if invincibly attracted by the lowest kind of good, by pleasure and every concupiscible object, living according to the prejudices of the world, rather its slave than its master; he is the slave of sin. What is developed in him is not personality but the lowest type of individuality, which manifests itself as individualism or egoism. He wishes to be the center of all things, and truly becomes the slave of all things,

[69] Denz., no. 1810.

the slave of his passions that are in open rebellion against one another, inasmuch as they are not controlled; he becomes the slave of men and events that can in the twinkling of an eye definitely take away from him the least happiness he enjoys.

Moral personality is far nobler in the virtuous man, who is conscious of his human dignity and succeeds in controlling his passions, in proportion as he increases in the love of truth and justice, that is, in proportion as he increasingly makes his life dependent on God who is to be loved above all things.

This was, in a certain manner, understood by the great philosophers of antiquity, such as Socrates, Plato, Aristotle, and to some extent by the Stoics.[70]

Likewise, in the intellectual order, to what shall we attribute that superiority of intellectual personality in men of great genius compared with those of ordinary intellectual ability? It must be attributed to the fact that a man of great genius depends less on the help to be obtained from men of his age and country, and this because he receives a higher inspiration from God, and is more dependent on God. Aristotle said about these great men, who are called divine, such as the divine Plato: "They follow an interior instinct, and it is not expedient for them to be given advice, because they are moved by a better principle," [71] that is, they depend more immediately on God, and their lives are dominated by this higher inspiration, which sometimes is most impelling. Thus genius is defined as a certain special nearness to God, a relationship with the absolute.

But how far superior are the saints to men of ordinary virtue and to men of great genius! The saints alone fully understood the law of true and complete progress of human personality, that human personality is the more perfect in proportion as it is more dependent on God, and united with Him, dominating inferior things. This aspect of personality is something that belongs most especially to the saints, being found only in them, since they exemplify in their lives these words of Christ: "He that loveth his life shall lose it; and he that hateth his life in this world keepeth it unto life eternal." [72] The saints, thoroughly understanding these words of our Lord, engaged in a real

[70] See Aristotle's *Ethics,* definition of virtue.

[71] *Magnae moralis,* Bk. VII, *De bona fortuna.*

[72] John 12:25.

conflict with their own ego, fought against a personality that is the result of egoism or self-love, and reached such a superior degree of psychological and moral personality that it is truly supernatural, and even distinguished in the order of grace.

The saints in dying to themselves, submerge themselves, their personality in God's personality, so that they become truly and most profoundly servants of God, as the Church says: for the servant is not free, is not master of himself. God's servant, however, participates in His supreme independence; hence it is commonly said that to *serve God is to reign,* and this is the culmination of created personality, which bears a certain remote resemblance to Christ's uncreated personality.

How did the saints acquire this eminent personality? In dying to themselves, they are guided in their intellect not by their own more or less inordinate judgment, but by the most correct judgment of God received in them by means of faith and the gifts of the Holy Ghost. Thus it is said that the just man lives not by his own inspiration but by faith, and considers all things, so to speak, as God sees them, in the mist of faith.

Likewise, in the case of the will, the saint gradually substitutes God's will for his own will, in accordance with our Lord's words: "My meat is to do the will of Him that sent Me that I may perfect His work." [73] They live continually faithful to the divine will of expression, and they completely abandon themselves to the divine will of good pleasure not yet made manifest, so that they become in the profoundest sense the servants of God, just as our hand is the servant of our will; they become in some manner something of God, or a creature of God, always in the hand of his Creator. As St. Thomas says, "They live not for themselves, but for God," [74] in that charity of friendship with God, and God is to them another ego.

In fact, the saints keenly perceive that God is to them another ego that is much more intimate to them than their own ego, and infinitely more perfect, inasmuch as what perfection there is in their own ego is found most eminently in God, and inasmuch as God is the radical principle of their intimate life. Thus the saints, giving up entirely, as it were, their own will and independence in their relation to God to

[73] *Ibid.,* 4:34.

[74] *Summa theol.,* IIa IIae, q. 17, a. 6, ad 3.

be loved above all things, finally come to say with St. Paul: "I live, now not I, but Christ liveth in me," [75] or "For to me, to live is Christ, and to die is gain." [76] As St. Thomas remarks: "As the hunter is preoccupied with hunting, and the student with study, and as the sick person is preoccupied in regaining health, so with the saints to live is Christ, because He is the principle and end of their lives." [77]

Thus the psychological and moral personality of the saints in the supernatural order exceedingly transcends the type of personality found in wise pagans, just as grace transcends nature. The personality of the saints transcends not only sensible things, space and time, but in a certain manner all created things inasmuch as the saints live not for themselves but for God.

This supernatural transcendence is the extraordinary secret of St. Paul's personality, so that after twenty centuries a vast number of Christians daily model their lives according to his epistles, as if these had been written yesterday; whereas only a few of the learned read once in their lives the epistles of Seneca. It is also the secret of the personality of all the saints, for example, of St. Francis of Assisi, of St. Catherine of Siena, of St. Vincent de Paul, who, in a certain manner die to their own personality, so that they might live to God, so that their supernatural influence is felt not only in their own times and countries, but practically throughout the Church and for many centuries.

Pascal excellently pointed this out in one of his works, saying: "The saints have their realm, their glory, their victory, their luster, and have no need of temporal or spiritual (intellectual) aggrandizement, which in no way affects them, neither increasing nor decreasing their greatness. The saints are seen by God and the angels, not by bodies or curious minds. God suffices for them." [78]

This is strictly speaking to live not for oneself but for God, as St. Thomas remarks.[79] This means, so to speak, to lose one's own personality in God by denial of oneself, acquiring perfect mastery over one's passions and all inferior things. Yet there is an infinite distance between God and the saints, inasmuch as their ontological personality is created, even though they may say with St. Paul: "I live, now not

[75] Gal. 2:20.

[76] Phil. 1:21.

[77] *Com. in Epist. ad Phil.,* 1:21.

[78] *Les Pensées,* p. 267.

[79] *Summa theol.,* IIa IIae, q. 17, a. 6, ad 3

I but Christ liveth in me." [80] They are intimately united with Him in the moral order.

The error of Nestorius, and afterward of Rosmini, consisted in reducing the union of the Word incarnate to God's union with the saints, so that the difference between them was only one of degree, and the union itself was accidental. Hence the following proposition of Rosmini was condemned: "In Christ's humanity the human will was so rapt by the Holy Spirit to adhere to the objective entity of the Word, that it gave up completely its human control to the Word, and the Word personally assumed this control, thus uniting the human nature to Himself. Hence the human will ceased to be personal in Christ as man, and, although it constitutes a person in other human beings, in Christ as man it remained a nature," [81] This means the confusion of the psychological and moral manifestation of the ontological personality with its personality.

Truly the uncreated personality of Christ is the inaccessible culmination of the true and complete progress of personality that can be conceived by us. For not only in Christ's intellect is God's judgment substituted for His own human judgment, not only in His will is God's will substituted for His own volition, but radically in these faculties, in fact, radically in the very soul of Christ, there is no human personality, but in its place there is the uncreated personality of the Word that assumed Christ's humanity in an ineffable manner. And whereas the saints almost never speak in their own person except to accuse themselves of their sins, Christ speaks of His uncreated and adorable person saying: "I am the resurrection and the life." [82] "I and the Father are one." [83] "I" designates the uncreated personality of the Word, in whom the human nature of Christ exists.

Thus the fitness of the Incarnation is in a certain way made manifest, and a certain knowledge of this mystery is acquired by considering, on the one hand, that it belongs to the notion of the supreme Good, namely, God, that He communicate Himself in the highest manner to the creature, which means in person, as already stated.[84] On the other hand, the more intimately personality is dependent on God and is united with Him, dominating things that are inferior,

[80] Gal. 2:20.
[81] Denz., no. 1917.
[82] John 11:25.
[83] *Ibid.,* 10:30.
[84] *Summa theol.,* IIIa, q. 1, a. 1.

the more perfect it is. The saints are, in a way, one in judgment and will with God, since theirs is in complete conformity with His. The ideal union would be if our human nature were united, without any commingling, with the divine nature in the same divine person, and in the same divine existence. But this wonderful union, which absolutely transcends our natural desire, is verified in the Incarnation of the Word, in which supreme personality is made manifest according to the greatest possible intimacy with God, and its domination over inferior things.

All these notes are implicitly contained in the true definition of person, which is an intelligent and free subject. To say that a person is a subject or person is to declare its ontological personality; to say that it is intelligent and therefore conscious of itself is to declare its psychological personality; to say that it is free and is master of itself is to declare its moral personality, or to consider it in its moral aspect. From what has been said, it is clearly evident that ontological personality is the root or foundation of psychological and moral personality. Therefore they must not be separated, but must be considered as one person.

Thus it is easy to see that in accordance with revelation, Christ is but one person, namely, just one intelligent and free subject, although He has two intellects and two wills. In Christ it is not merely the ontological union of two natures in one person, for it also follows that there is a wonderful union in Him in the psychological, moral, and spiritual orders. This union is a kind of compenetration of Christ's two intellects, inasmuch as His most holy soul, from the moment of its creation, enjoys the beatific vision, as will be stated farther on.[85] Thus His human intellect sees immediately, without any impressed and expressed species, God's essence and intellection, and by this supreme intellection is comprehensively seen, and by it is continually reinforced by the light of glory, which is preserved in it and measured by participated eternity. Likewise there is in Christ's most holy soul from the beginning of its existence a kind of interpenetration of the two wills, for Christ as man, by reason of His infused charity intensely loves God's good pleasure as regards everything, and is in the highest degree loved by God.[86]

Thus Christ's ontological personality results in a union not only of

[85] *Ibid.*, IIIa, q. 9, a. 2.
[86] *Ibid.*, q. 18, a. 5.

natures in the order of being, but also in a union of activities in accordance with the most perfect and intimate subordination of the two intellects and wills in the order of operation, or in the psychological, moral, and spiritual orders.

TWO THEORIES ABOUT THE HYPOSTATIC UNION

It is of faith, as we have said, that the union of the two natures in Christ was personal or subsistential,[87] as the Council of Ephesus stated,[88] and for this reason the union is called hypostatic. But theologians dispute about what formally constitutes a person, or what is meant properly by personality or subsistence.

Hence, after a brief examination of the theories condemned by the Church, we must explain those freely disputed among theologians.

Theories condemned by the Church. There are two, namely, Gunther's system that reduces personality to consciousness of oneself, and Rosmini's that would have personality to consist in freedom of will or in dominion over oneself.

Gunther's theory.[89] According to Gunther the fundamental question in philosophy is the theory of knowledge, which, he said, has its foundation in the consciousness of oneself, which is what Descartes taught. Gunther rejects pantheism, of course, but he admits a substantial unity of all created beings, considering these to be manifestations of the same substance, which he calls nature. This nature that is unconscious of itself, becomes conscious in man.

Hence Gunther holds that personality properly consists in a consciousness of oneself, and this note belongs to the rational soul.

From the notion of personality Gunther seeks to explain the mysteries of the Trinity and the Incarnation. He is unwilling to admit that God is conscious of Himself by His essence, for then there would be only one person in God. If, therefore, says Gunther, God knows Himself, it is because in Him subject and object are in opposition, and he affirms the equality of each. The subject conscious of itself is the Father, the object conscious of itself is the Son; finally, the consciousness of equality between each results in the Holy Spirit. Thus Gunther seeks to demonstrate the Trinity, and reduce it to the order

[87] *καθ' ὑπόστασιν.*

[88] Denz., no. 114.

[89] *Ibid.*, nos. 1665 f.; see also Vacant, *Etudes sur le Concile du Vatican,* I, 130. Gunther was a German priest born in 1873, who sought to put new life into theology by means of a Kantian inspired philosophy.

of philosophical truth. In this we have the essence of semi-rationalism, which does not deny supernatural revelation, but seeks to reduce all revealed mysteries to truths of the natural order, as if revelation were supernatural only as to the manner of its production, not substantially or essentially, namely, on the part of the object revealed.

Gunther also denies the freedom of creation, admitting the absolute optimism of Leibnitz. Just as the elevation of the human race to the supernatural order was necessary, as Baius contends, so also was the Incarnation.

Finally, Gunther explains the union of the Word incarnate. His theory that personality consists in a consciousness of oneself leads to Nestorianism, for there are in Christ two consciousnesses, just as there are two intellectual natures. Gunther, however, in order to avoid the heresy of Nestorianism, devises a theory that scarcely differs from it, inasmuch as he makes the human nature in Christ conscious of its subordination and dependence on the divine nature. But this condition is already verified in all the saints, and is not something special that is found in Christ alone.

This theory, as also Gunther's semi-rationalism, was condemned by Pius IX in his papal brief to Cardinal de Geissel, archbishop of Cologne.[90]

This theory is refuted philosophically and theologically.

Philosophically. Consciousness of oneself testifies to or asserts the identity of our person, but does not constitute it. This means that we know and remember from our past lives that we are the same persons, and consciousness of ourselves tells us that we are today the same persons we were in the past. Therefore both memory and consciousness imply or presuppose an already constituted person; they merely announce the presence of or are attributed to person. They constitute only the psychological aspect of personality.

Hence the saying: I am conscious of myself or of my personality; if consciousness constituted personality, we should have to say: I am conscious of my consciousness. Person is a substance, whereas consciousness is an act.

Confirmation of the preceding. If consciousness together with memory constituted personal identity, this identity would be lessened, in fact would be destroyed, as often as the exercise of memory or consciousness is lessened or suspended.[91]

[90] Denz., no. 1655.

[91] Cf. Zigliara's *Ontologia,* chap. 29.

Expressed briefly, a person is a subject conscious of itself, but it must be first constituted as a subject in order that it be conscious of itself.

Theologically. Gunther's theory is refuted by the very fact that it posits in Christ two persons regardless of his wishes; for Christ's humanity is conscious of itself, and so is the Godhead. Nor does he avoid the error of Nestorianism by saying that Christ's humanity is conscious of the subordination to and dependence on the Godhead; for this union, which is already realized in the saints, is nothing else but a moral and accidental union with God's judgment and will. Pius IX was right in condemning this theory. Modernists express themselves in almost the same terms as Gunther.

Rosmini's theory. Rosmini (1797–1855) did not start, as Gunther did, with the *"cogito"* of Descartes, being more of an ontologist than Gunther. St. Thomas says: "The first thing conceived by the intellect is being. Hence being is the object of the intellect." [92] But Rosmini teaches [93] that what is first conceived by the intellect is the beginning of being, which is something divine, belonging to the divine nature; it is something divine not by participation, but in the strict sense it "is an actuality that is not distinct from the remainder of the divine actuality"; [94] "it is something of the Word." [95]

All Rosmini's theories are deduced from this principle.

1) He seeks to prove the Trinity about the same way Gunther did, by distinguishing in God between subjectivity, objectivity, and sanctity, or between reality, ideality, and morality, inasmuch as these are three supreme forms of the being, namely, subjective being, objective being, and their union by love.[96]

2) He denies the freedom of creation, as Gunther did.[97] He admits generationism or traducianism, saying: "The human soul, by coming in contact solely with its intuitive sentient principle, becomes a being, and by this union that principle, which before was only sentient, becomes intelligent, subsistent, and immortal." [98] Rosmini held that the will constitutes human personality, by which everyone is responsible for and master of himself. Hence Rosmini teaches: "In Christ's humanity, the human will was so rapt by the Holy Spirit to adhere to

[92] *Summa theol.,* Ia, q. 5, a. 2, c.
[93] Denz., no. 1891.
[94] *Ibid.,* no. 1893.
[95] *Ibid.,* no. 1897.
[96] *Ibid.,* nos. 1915 f.
[97] *Ibid.,* no. 1908.
[98] *Ibid.,* no. 1911.

the objective entity of the Word, that it gave up completely to the Word its human control. . . . Hence the human will ceased to be personal in Christ as man, and, although it is a person in other human beings, in Christ as man it remained a nature." [99]

This theory is refuted both philosophically and theologically about the same way as Gunther's.

Philosophically. It is false to say that the will constitutes the person in human beings, for the will is attributed to an already ontologically established person, such as Peter or Paul, and the will is this will, since in that it is the will of this particular subject, by itself separately existing. Person is a substance, whereas will is its accident, an inseparable accident, indeed, but a predicamental accident, although it is not a predicable, which means that it is not contingent.

Theologically. Rosmini's theory leads to Nestorianism, for the union it admits is only a union of wills or a moral union, such as we find in the saints, who would differ from Christ only according to the degree of their love for Him.

What results from the condemnation of these two theories?

It follows that merely phenomenalist or dynamistic notions of personality cannot be reconciled with the Catholic doctrine of the Incarnation, as we showed in another work.[100]

According to the empiric phenomenalism of Hume, Stuart Mill, and Taine, we have knowledge only of phenomena or states of consciousness, but not of the "ego" itself as substance. But conscious facts are united according to the laws of association, and then personality is established by a dominating state of consciousness. But if there be a psychological disturbance, as in madness, some think that there are two personalities, for at times a person considers himself a king, and at other times a servant.

The rational phenomenalism of Renouvier considers personality to be an *a priori* form of our mind, which unites all that belongs to us. Our existence is merely so far as it is represented.[101]

As for the dynamic evolutionism or philosophy of becoming (of such philosophers as H. Bergson), person is neither an association of phenomena nor a certain category of the mind, but it is a vital and

[99] *Ibid.*, no. 1917. This philosophical system about person was condemned by the Holy Office, December 14, 1887.

[100] *Le sens commun*, pp. 320–23.

[101] Renouvier, *Logique*, II, 493.

free impulse, which manifests itself in an unbroken series of divers states of consciousness.

It is evident, however, that the person of the Word incarnate, as conceived by the Catholic Church, cannot be either a certain association of phenomena or a certain category of the mind, or a vital and free impulse; all these pertain to the finite and hence created order, and cannot constitute the uncreated personality of the Word incarnate.

But in contrast to either empiric or rational phenomenalism, or the philosophy of becoming, traditional philosophy may be called the philosophy of being, inasmuch as the formal object of our intellect is neither an internal nor an external phenomenon, nor a category of the mind, but it is the intelligible being of sensible things. This is, as H. Bergson avows, the natural metaphysics of human intelligence, or the conception of natural reason, or the *sensus communis,* which develops by a gradual process from the confused state of rudimentary knowledge to the clearly defined state of philosophic knowledge. Gradually our intellect ascends from the knowledge of the being of sensible things to the knowledge of the soul and of God, who is conceived as the First Being or as the self-subsisting Being.

According to this philosophy of being, however, person is something more profound than phenomena and their laws, either empiric or *a priori,* something of even deeper significance than the becoming of being that underlies phenomena, for it is a substance of a rational nature by itself separately existing, or an intelligent and free individual subject, permanent in itself, by itself operating, and hence conscious of itself and because of free will responsible for its actions. Briefly, person is an intelligent and free subject. Hence the aforesaid theories consider only the psychological or moral aspects of personality, but not ontological personality, on which these aspects depend. This ontological personality is that by which a person is a subject or a whole by itself separately existing, intelligent and free.

As we said, a person enjoys a threefold independence, inasmuch as its being, its understanding, and its will are not intrinsically dependent on matter. Thus it is evident that ontological personality is the foundation of psychological personality and of moral personality.

It is also apparent that those notes which constitute personality, namely, a subject subsisting in itself, endowed with intelligence and freedom, are absolutely simple perfections, which can be attributed analogically and in the proper sense to God, whereas, on the contrary, merely phenomenal personality cannot be attributed even analogically to Him, since God is absolutely above the phenomenal order.

VARIOUS SCHOLASTIC VIEWS ABOUT PERSONALITY

There are different views about ontological personality among the Scholastics. They are radically divided: some admit and others do not admit a real distinction between what is and its existence, a distinction that is declared among the greater in the philosophy of St. Thomas, and which forms one of the twenty-four theses approved by the Sacred Congregation of Studies in 1916.

Some say, in these days, that the first of these twenty-four propositions on which the others depend, is not found in the works of St. Thomas, who admitted, so they say, only logical composition of potentiality and act, but not real composition in every created being.[102]

On the contrary, St. Thomas said explicitly: "Everything that is in the genus of substance is a real composite . . . ; and its existence must be different from itself. . . . Therefore everything that is directly in the predicament of substance is composed at least of existence and that which exists." [103] This means that there is a real distinction in the created suppositum between that which exists and its existence. The suppositum is the whole, and its existence is a contingent predicate.

Again he writes: "The act that is measured by aeviternity, the aeviternal existence, differs indeed really from that whose act it is"; [104] which means that an angel's essence differs really from his existence. On this point Father Norbert del Prado, O.P., has collected many similar texts from St. Thomas in the famous book he wrote on this subject.[105] In this work, he shows that the first truth by way of doctrinal judgment though the highest of causes is that in God alone essence and existence are the same; He alone can say: I am who am.

These truths presupposed, however, among Scholastics who deny a real distinction between what is and its existence, and between essence and existence, Scotus says that personality is something negative, namely, the negation of the hypostatic union in a singular nature.[106] Suarez considers personality to be a substantial mode that

[102] *Revue de philosophie,* December, 1938.

[103] *De veritate,* q. 27, a. 1, ad 8. See also *Contra Gentes,* Bk. II, chap. 52.

[104] Cf. *I Sent.,* d. 19, q. 2, a. 2.

[105] *De veritate fundamentali philosophiae Christianae,* pp. 23 f.

[106] Cf. *III Sent.,* d. 1, q. 1, nos. 5 f. According to Scotus, person and personality are negative notions, since not being assumed by a higher principle constitutes the formal

presupposes the existence of a singular nature, and that renders it incommunicable.[107]

Among those Scholastics who admit a real distinction between existence and what exists, there are especially three opinions. Cajetan and very many Thomists say that personality is that by which a singular nature becomes immediately capable of existence.[108]

Others, following Capreolus, say less clearly that personality is a singular nature as constituted before it exists.[109] Lastly, Father Billot reduces personality to existence that actuates the singular nature.[110]

- Personality
  - (real distinction admitted)
    - It is that by which a singular nature becomes what it is, or becomes immediately capable of existence. (View of Cajetan and very many Thomists).
    - It is a singular nature as constituted before it exists. (Capreolus.)
    - It is existence that actuates a singular nature. (Billot.)
  - (real distinction denied)
    - It is a substantial mode that presupposes the existence of the substance. (Suarez.)
    - It is something negative, the negation of the hypostatic union. (Scotus.)

---

notion of person or personality in human beings. Since the human nature of Christ was actually and aptitudinally such that it was assumed by the person of the Word, it did not have its own person or personality. As Garrigou-Lagrange points out, therefore the hypostatic union for Scotus consisted in something negative in this respect. The term "singular" is applied to anything that cannot be multiplied numerically. (Tr.)

[107] *Disp. Met.,* disp. 34, sects. 1, 2, 4; *De incarn.,* disp. 11, sect. 3.

[108] Cajetan, *Com. in IIIam,* q. 4, a. 2, no. 8.

[109] Cf. Capreolus, *Com. in IV Sent.,* d. 5, q. 3, a. 3, pp. 109–19.

[110] *De Verbo incarnato,* q. 2, pp. 75, 84, 140. See also *Dict. théol. cath.,* art. "Hypostase," cols. 411 f.

CRITERION TO BE FOLLOWED IN THE EXAMINATION OF THESE OPINIONS

All these theologians wish to retain the ontological validity of the common notion of person, namely, an intelligent and free subject, and they wish to pass methodically, although they do not all do so, by the light of revelation, from this common notion of person to the more philosophical notion of person, which is like the guiding star.

We said, however, that according to natural reason, a person is an intelligent subject by itself separately existing, and this absolutely must be maintained.

Moreover, it must be observed that there are assertions of natural reason confirmed by revelation, and these must likewise be preserved intact. First of all, there are affirmative judgments, in which those things that pertain to a person are predicated of the person as a real subject of predication, such as: Peter is a man, Peter is existing, Peter is acting. In these affirmative propositions, however, the verb "is" affirms real identity between subject and predicate, and postulates the same real subject underlying nature, existence, and operation.

Lastly, the following truth must be retained. God alone is His existence, He alone can say: "I am who am." [111] Peter is not his existence. This statement means that the act of existence even when in act is included only in God's essence, which is related to existence as A is to A, for God's essence is the self-subsisting Being.[112] On the other hand, no created essence is its existence, no created essence contains existence as an essential predicate, for in such a case it would be self-existent and would not be created; but existence befits it as a contingent predicate, inasmuch as it is possible for this essence not to exist. Hence it is said of Michael the archangel, that he is not his existence, just as a grain of sand is not its existence. These propositions are commonly admitted by theologians as true, which means that they correspond to a reality, and hence we must say, as the Thomists assert, that before the consideration of our mind, Michael's essence or man's essence is not his existence, which means that it is really distinct from its existence.[113]

Nevertheless we say that Michael is existing, Peter is existing. Thus the verb "is" signifies real identity between subject and predicate

[111] Exod. 3:14.
[112] *Summa theol.,* Ia, q. 3, a. 4.
[113] *Ibid.*

notwithstanding the real distinction between created essence and existence.

This principle is the criterion in the judgment of the above-mentioned opinions, and it is manifest that it makes a considerable difference in the notion of person, to whom essence and existence are attributed, according as a real distinction between essence and existence is or is not admitted. The true teaching about person has its foundation in this, that it is a requisite for the verification of the following judgments: Peter is existing, but is not his existence, whereas Christ is existing, and is His existence, just as "He is truth and life." [114]

1) Opinion of Scotus. Scotus holds that a twofold negation is added to the notion of person as applied to a singular human nature, namely, actual dependence on the divine person, and aptitudinal dependence on this same divine person.[115] Thus this humanity of ours is a person, because it is neither naturally apt to be terminated, nor actually terminated by the divine personality.

Scotus gives the following reasons for this conclusion: [116]

1) Because then there would be some positive entity in the human nature that would be incapable of assumption by the Word. (2) Because it would follow that the human nature assumed by the Word would be wanting in some positive entity . . . and thus Christ would not be universally a man.

Criticism. Cajetan [117] reproduces exactly these arguments of Scotus, and examines them.[118] Capreolus had already examined them.[119] Later on John of St. Thomas,[120] Zigliara,[121] and Billot [122] had discussed these arguments. The Thomists show that this opinion of Scotus is contrary to the teaching of St. Thomas, and that it does not preserve the common notion of person.

Fundamental argument. The constitutive element of that which is not perfect in nature cannot be assigned to something negative. But

[114] John 14:6.
[115] *Com. in III Sent.*, d. 5, q. 3, par. 2, p. 105.
[116] *Ibid.*
[117] *Ibid.*, q. 4, a. 2, nos. 3, 13.
[118] *Ibid.*, nos. 15 f.
[119] *Ibid.*, d. 5, q. 3, par. 2, p. 105.
[120] *Cursus phil., phil. nat.*, q. 7, a. 1.
[121] *Ont.*, chap. 29.
[122] *De Verbo incarn.*, q. 2, par. 1, p. 125.

as St. Thomas says, "Person signifies what is most perfect in all nature, that is, a subsistent individual of a rational nature." [123] Therefore its constitutive element or its personality cannot be assigned to something negative. John of St. Thomas explains this point well.

1) "Subsistence," he says, "is not the negation of dependence. It is impossible for the independent not to be more perfect than the dependent. But dependence is something positive. Therefore, a fortiori, independence in that genus, cannot be a pure negation, although it is explained negatively, just as simplicity is explained by indivision." [124]

Thus infinity in substance; although it is explained negatively, yet it is something positive. Hence God's independence in being constitutes His greatest perfection.[125] Therefore that by which anything is a subject by itself, separately existing, cannot be a mere negation, for it is that which constitutes a subject as the first subject of attribution. Likewise every negation has its foundation in something positive, as Father Billot says against Scotus.

2) "Moreover," adds John of St. Thomas, "natural and proper subsistence is not only opposed to the hypostatic union, but it is also opposed to the existential mode of accident, or even of a part. And if the inherence of accident is something positive and not a negative notion, a fortiori the subsistence of first substance, to which second substance is attributed, must be something positive." [126]

3) Then again, proper subsistence is something *primo* and *per se* natural, because it constitutes something of the natural order. Therefore it cannot *primo* and *per se* consist in the negation of the hypostatic union, which is supernatural, although the negation may also include this latter, just as in anything of the natural order we have the negation of the supernatural, although things of the natural order are not *primo* and *per se* constituted as such by this negation. Thus, according to the opinion of Scotus, either Heraclitus or Thales would

[123] *Summa theol.*, Ia, q. 29, a. 3.

[124] *Cursus phil., phil. nat.*, q. 7, a. 1.

[125] Our conception of God's independence is negative, because our first knowledge is of creatures that are dependent on God. So also we conceive spiritual beings negatively, as immaterial, because our first knowledge is of material things. On the contrary, God and the angels, whose first knowledge is of spiritual beings, must conceive material beings negatively, as non-spiritual. See *The One God,* p. 161, in which Garrigou-Lagrange points out that self-subsisting Being is the supreme truth from which all God's attributes are derived. (Tr.)

[126] *The One God, loc. cit.*

have been persons, because their nature was not hypostatically united to any divine person.

4) Finally, in the case of the divine persons, there are in the strictest sense of the terms, three subsistences and three personalities, which, inasmuch as they are subsistences, denote positive realities, and not three negations. And the subsistence of the Word substituting Its subsistence for that of the human nature; but this union did not consist in anything negative, but in something positive.

But there must be analogy between the divine personality and created personality. "Nor is there something unbefitting resulting from this, as Scotus would have, for the Word assumed whatever pertains to the human nature, as a nature, although not whatever pertains to man as a suppositum." As St. Thomas says, "It is a greater dignity to exist in something nobler than oneself than to exist by oneself." [127]

5) Furthermore, it must be said against Scotus that this theory does not make it clear how the following affirmative judgments can be true: Peter is a man, Peter is existing; for the verb "is" expresses real identity between subject and predicate. But this real identity cannot be established by something negative. In other words: that by which anything is a *who* or a *what,* or a first subject of attribution, cannot be something negative.

Some Scotists say that a subject is a singular nature.

Reply. The nature itself is not this subject, for as St. Thomas often says: "nature, i.e., humanity, is that by which anything is such, i.e., a man; it is not that which is." [128] Individuation alone is not that by which anything is a *who* or a *what,* for matter constitutes this individuation in Christ, namely, this humanity; yet it does not constitute a subject distinct from the Word. Individuation is also found in the parts of a nature, for example, in this flesh, these bones, but these parts do not have the incommunicability that belongs properly to the suppositum.

Moreover, as we said, individuation derived from matter is something very low in dignity, but subsistence and especially personality is something far nobler, for it is that by which anything is a subject by itself separately existing and operating. On the contrary, matter is not that which is, but that by which anything is material.

6) Finally, Scotus denies a real distinction between created essence

[127] *Summa theol.,* IIIa, q. 2, a. 2, ad 2.
[128] *Ibid.,* q. 17, a. 2.

and existence, and so we should have to say: Peter is his existence, just as we say: God is His existence. But before the consideration of our mind it is true to say: God is His existence, and there is no real distinction between the Deity and His existence. Whereas, on the contrary, before any consideration of the mind, it is true that Peter is not his existence, but has existence, just as Peter cannot say: "I am the truth and the life," but only "I have truth and life." Hence, before any consideration of the mind, there is a certain distinction, not indeed spatial, but real or ontological between Peter's essence and his existence. More briefly, that which truly is not its existence, before any consideration of the mind is distinct from its existence, in some way just as matter is not form, but is related to it as potency is to act, as potency limiting to act determining. Act of itself is not limited, but is limited by the potency in which it is received; so also existence is in various ways limited in the essence of stones, plants, animals, and other things in which it is received.

Wherefore we said that the true doctrine of person has its foundation in this, that it postulates the truth of the following judgments: Peter is existing, but is not existence; whereas Christ is existing and is His existence.

7) It follows from the thesis of Scotus that there are two existences in Christ, which is contrary to the teaching of St. Thomas,[129] and then this means that the humanity of Christ has its own ultimate actuality, namely, its own existence. Thus, before its union with the Word, it is absolutely complete, both substantially and subsistentially. Hence there is danger of Nestorianism in this opinion, since the human nature in Christ appears to be a suppositum distinct from the Word, with whom it can be united only accidentally. Scotus does not wish to affirm this, but his principles ought to lead him to this conclusion. There would be two supposita whose union would not have its foundation in anything positive.[130]

[129] *Ibid.*

[130] Billot, *De Verbo incarn.,* q. 2, p. 125; also Zigliara, *Summa phil., Ontologia,* chap. 29, par. 4.

Father Billot says that Scotus and Father Tiphanus, S.J., hold almost similar views on this question. The latter, in his work entitled *De hypostasi et persona,* chaps. 10–24, holds that there is merely a logical distinction between nature and suppositum, inasmuch as a complete and singular nature is a person by the very fact that it is a whole in itself, or because it is not either actually or aptitudinally united with another suppositum. According to Father Billot the arguments against Scotus are equally valid against Tiphanus on this point, concerning the concept of person.

2) Opinion of Suarez.[131] This opinion of Suarez is examined after that of Scotus, since the two views are much alike, although Suarez departs from Scotus inasmuch as he holds personality to consist in something positive, namely, in a substantial mode, which in his opinion presupposes existence for the essence. How does Suarez reach this conclusion?

Often in his eclecticism, Suarez searches for a via media between St. Thomas and Scotus. In the present question, he sees, as the Thomists say, that personality must consist in something positive, and then he says: this positive element cannot be an accident, since person is a first substance. Therefore it must be a substantial mode by which a singular nature is rendered incommunicable, which is what Cajetan said. In Christ, he says, the human nature is not a person, because the mode of personality is wanting to it, the mode of the union taking its place.

But, on the other hand, Suarez holds, as Scotus does, that there is no real distinction between created essence and existence. Hence, in his opinion, the substantial mode which constitutes ontological personality, presupposes not only essence or nature, but also existence.

Thus Suarez frequently in accordance with his eclecticism, as in this question, refutes Scotus by St. Thomas, and St. Thomas by Scotus. But this via media is most difficult to follow, since it is very difficult to maintain the proper equilibrium or stability by this method, so that Suarez in the development of his theses not infrequently fluctuates or oscillates between St. Thomas and Scotus, not taking a firm stand for either view.

Criticism. The Thomists reply:

1) This opinion does not preserve what is fundamental in the truth

---

This seems true, as also Father Hugon observes in his *De Verbo incarnato,* q. 2, a. 2. But Tiphanus, *op. cit.,* chap. 7, differs from Scotus in that he holds a real distinction between essence and existence, which he says is fundamental and clearly taught by St. Thomas.

Opinions similar to that of Scotus are held by Franzelin, *De Verbo incarnato,* props. 7–9; Galtier, *De incarnatione et redemptione,* thesis 15.

Hugon, *De Verbo incarnato,* q. 2, a. 2, par. 5, sums up all the arguments against the aforesaid opinion of Scotus as follows: "The constituent of that which is most perfect in nature cannot consist in something negative. But person, as St. Thomas says (Ia, q. 29, a. 3), is that which is most perfect in nature. Therefore the constituent of person cannot consist in something negative."

[131] *Disp. Metaph.,* disp. 34, sects., 1, 2, 4, nos. 9 f.; *De incarn.,* disp. 11, sect. 3. Almost similar views are held by De Lugo, *De incarn.,* disp. 12, sect. 1, nos. 1–4; Vasquez, *Com. in Summam theol.,* IIIa, q. 4, a. 2, disp. 31, chap. 6.

of the following proposition: Peter is not his own existence, for only God is His existence. He alone can say: "I am who am," [132] "I am the truth and the life," [133] and not merely "I have being, truth, and life." But these judgments, acknowledged to be true by all theologians, demand a real distinction between created essence and existence; for, that these propositions be true even before any consideration of our mind, there must be a real distinction between Peter and his existence, whereas, on the contrary, God is really His existence, without even the least of real distinctions.

Hence the Sacred Congregation of Studies (1916), among the twenty-four propositions of St. Thomas that it declared to be the greater, posited a real distinction between created essence and existence. It is the third proposition which reads: "All other beings (except God) which participate in being, have a nature which is limited by existence, and consist of essence and existence, as really distinct principles." [134]

Furthermore, the Thomists with John of St. Thomas [135] say that the substantial mode, which is subsistence, does not presuppose existence, for it is by subsistence that the suppositum is formally constituted as either a suppositum or a person. But, as St. Thomas says: "Being is consequent upon nature, not as upon that which has being, but upon that whereby a thing is such; whereas it is consequent upon person or hypostasis, as upon that which has being. Hence it has unity from the unity of the hypostasis, rather than duality from the duality of the nature." [136] Peter is that which is, and first comes the concept of person and personality before existence that is attributed to the person when we say: Peter is existing, but is not his existence.

Hence personality terminates the nature and ultimately comes existence as primarily befitting the suppositum, and through the intermediary of the suppositum the nature. This is the constant teaching of St. Thomas.[137] There is no existing subject unless the whole being is terminated and incommunicable (e.g., Peter), to whom existence is applicable as a contingent predicate. Being and becoming befit the

[132] Exod. 3:14.
[133] John 14:6.
[134] *Acta Apost. Sedis,* VI, 383.
[135] *Cursus philosophicus, loc. cit.*
[136] *Summa theol.,* IIIa, q. 17, a. 2, ad 1.
[137] *Ibid.,* q. 2, a. 5, ad 1.

suppositum, as St. Thomas shows,[138] for the terminus of creation, or even of generation, is that which is, not that by which anything is such as it is.

Therefore very many Thomists say with Cajetan that the substantial mode is the terminus that causes the singular nature to be incommunicable and terminated, just as the point terminates the line and does not continue it,[139] nor is subsistence an unexplainable entity. But it must be something real that constitutes this mode, not nature alone, however, nor existence. Therefore it must be by what terminates the mode. Thus John of St. Thomas, following Cajetan.[140]

3) The Thomists and Father Billot also say against Suarez:

Since the existence of substance is its ultimate actuality, as St. Thomas often says, whatever accrues to substance already complete in its existence accrues to it accidentally. But this mode consisting in personality or subsistence, according to Suarez, accrues to substance after existence. Therefore the mode is not substantial as he would have it, but accidental.

Hence, as already stated against the opinion of Scotus, the union of the Word incarnate would thus be merely accidental, since each nature would have its own existence, or its ultimate actuality.

3) **Opinion of Father Billot.** Father Billot, S.J.,[141] insists especially on this, that St. Thomas maintains there is only one existence in Christ.[142] Father Billot vigorously asserts this against Scotus and Suarez, because he firmly defends against them the opinion of a real distinction between essence and existence. On this point he is truly in agreement with St. Thomas and the Thomists.

But on the other hand, Father Billot, always attacking Suarez, will not admit a substantial mode even in Cajetan's sense, for he says: "There is nothing positive about the terminus itself except what it terminates, for all that the point does which terminates a line is to deny its further extension, adding absolutely nothing to it." [143]

[138] *Ibid.,* Ia, q. 45, a. 4.

[139] Similarly the period serves a useful purpose in terminating a proposition, such as: This is My body. For if the period is not inserted at the end, the proposition is not considered complete, and someone could add an adjective, such as figurative, which would completely change the meaning of the proposition, because then the body of Christ would be in the Eucharist only figuratively and not really.

[140] *Cursus phil., phil. nat.,* q. 7, a. 1.

[141] *De Verbo incarnato,* q. 2, pp. 75–84, 137 f.

[142] *Summa theol.,* IIIa, q. 17, a. 2, and similar passages.

[143] *De Verbo incarnato,* p. 88.

Cajetan would reply by saying that the terminus itself is not indeed a new thing or reality, but is a real mode, really and modally distinct from the thing itself. Thus a line is made up of divisible parts and of indivisible points; a point that terminates a line, or two lines that converge in it, is neither a nonentity nor a part; [144] so the roundness of a metallic sphere is not nothing; it is something really and modally distinct from substance, even from the metallic quantity that it terminates; the quantity of this metal is not its roundness, and it could have another shape.[145]

But since Father Billot refuses to admit this substantial mode as terminating the nature, so that it is immediately capable of existing, he says that person is a singular nature under its own existence, and he identifies subsistence or personality with the existence of the substance.[146]

He quotes for his opinion especially the passage [147] in which St. Thomas asserts, and in similar passages, that there is one being in Christ. This assertion is indeed valid against Scotus and Suarez, but not against Cajetan, for he also maintains that there is one being in Christ.

Father Billot,[148] who quotes Capreolus for his view, interprets him as saying that person is a singular nature with its existence. Cajetan's answer would be: Yes, it is a singular nature (terminated) with its existence, but it must be declared terminated, for nature in itself is only that by which anything is such as it is, it is not that which is.

The exact words of Capreolus on this point are: "1. The name suppositum is affirmed of that individual which subsists by itself. 2. Understood formally, as a mode, and then by suppositum is meant the composite that consists of the individual with its suchness and its own subsistence." [149] It cannot be inferred from this text that a person and the singular nature are identical, for a person is *what* is, and the nature *that by which* something is; nor can it be said that personality is exist-

[144] It was Euclid who gave us the postulate, that a point is that which has position but not magnitude. (Tr.)

[145] Roundness is indeed a mode that is really distinct from quantity, for the same quantity could have another shape. But there could be no roundness without quantity, whereas in the Eucharist the quantity of the bread is without substance.

[146] *De verbo incarnato,* pp. 89, 140.

[147] *Summa theol., IIIa,* q. 17, a. 2.

[148] *De verbo incarnato,* p. 69.

[149] *Com. in IIIam,* d. 5, q. 3 (toward the end).

ence, for personality is attributed to a person already formally constituted as a person.

Criticism of Father Billot's opinion. It may be reduced to the following arguments.

1) This opinion is not in harmony with the teaching of St. Thomas, who says: "Being is consequent upon nature not as that which has being, but upon that whereby a thing is; whereas it is consequent upon person or hypostasis as upon that which has being." [150] Hence being or existence does not formally constitute personality, because it is consequent upon a person already formally constituted as such by personality. St. Thomas speaks similarly in the body of the article just quoted.

2) Moreover, St. Thomas takes up this disputed point in discussing Christ's unity of being,[151] by considering, as he himself says in the prologue to the previous question,[152] the consequences of the union. Therefore he first established his teaching on the hypostatic union,[153] and from this that there is only one person in Christ. Then he goes on to deduce that there is one being in Christ, inasmuch as being is immediately consequent not upon nature, but upon person, which alone is *what is*.

Hence if Father Billot's opinion were the true teaching of St. Thomas, the holy Doctor ought to have shown at the beginning of this treatise [154] that there is one being in Christ, so as to make it clear that there is only one person and only one personality in Christ. But he considers this point only farther on,[155] which presupposes the solution of the problem concerning what constitutes the hypostatic union.

3) The Complutenses Abbreviati [156] note that St. Thomas teaches that "the angel is composed of existence and what is." [157] Thus Michael is existing but is not his existence. Hence the holy Doctor teaches that existence enters into composition not only with essence, but also with the suppositum. It would not be so, however, if existence were the same as subsistence or personality. Likewise, the *principium quod* of the theandric operations in Christ is not common to the three

[150] *Summa theol.,* IIIa, q. 17, a. 2, ad 1.
[151] *Ibid.,* q. 17 (*in toto*).
[152] *Ibid.,* q. 16.
[153] *Ibid.,* q. 2.
[154] *Ibid.*
[155] *Ibid.,* q. 17.
[156] *De generatione,* disp. 15, q. 3.
[157] *Summa theol.,* Ia, q. 50, a. 2, ad 3.

divine persons.[158] But existence is common to the three divine persons. Therefore the *principium quod* in Christ is not formally constituted by existence.

4) St. Thomas says: "Existence does not pertain to the notion of a created suppositum," [159] which means that Peter is not his existence. But subsistence pertains to the notion of suppositum, and personality to the notion of person. Therefore they are not really the same as being or existence, at least for St. Thomas.

Finally, St. Thomas [160] treats as distinct the following two questions, namely, whether essence and existence are the same, and whether essence and suppositum are the same. This would be superfluous if there were no real distinction between existence and subsistence. Such is the excellent observation of the Complutenses Abbreviati.

Moreover, it must be observed so as to avoid ambiguity, that subsistence does not mean existence of substance, but subsistence is the abstract name that is the correlative of the concrete name suppositum. Hence subsistence is to suppositum as personality is to person, as existence is to exist, and as running is to run.

Hence subsistence is not an abstract name that would correspond to the concrete to subsist, but to the concrete that is called suppositum. But to avoid this ambiguity, it is better to use the word personality than subsistence, because it is evident that personality corresponds in the concrete to person, and not as such to the word "subsist." Hence subsistence is to suppositum as personality is to person, and as existence is to exist or to being.

5) Father Billot's opinion leads to the denial of a real distinction between essence and existence, a distinction that he firmly maintains nevertheless against Scotus and Suarez. For it must be said that being which is not its existence, is, before the consideration of the mind, really distinct from its existence. But Peter's person, even his personality, is not his existence. Therefore Peter's person, even his personality, is really distinct from his existence.

The major of this argument is the principle from which we deduce that there is a real distinction between essence and existence, and this Father Billot accepts. But the minor is most certain, namely, that

[158] By the *principium quod* is meant the suppositum or person that performs the act. (Tr.)

[159] *Quodlibet* 2, q. 2, a. 4.

[160] *Ibid.*

Peter's person is not his existence, and therefore it differs from the person of the Word; moreover Peter's personality is not his existence, because it formally constitutes Peter's person, which is not his existence.

In other words, the denial of a real distinction between a created person, constituted as such by his own personality and existence, means that a real distinction between created essence and existence is without any foundation; for a being that is not its own existence is, before the consideration of the mind, really distinct from its existence. But Peter's person, formally constituted as such by his personality, just as his essence, is really distinct from his existence. Only God is His existence, and the truth of this assertion will be most clearly seen in the beatific vision.

This point was more fully explained by quoting several texts of St. Thomas,[161] and in the examination of the recent work of Father Charles Giacon, S.J.[162]

Certain disciples of Father Billot advance the following objection. Peter is not his nature. Yet there is no real distinction between him and his nature. Therefore between him and his existence there is no real distinction.

Reply. I concede the major. I deny the minor and parity of agreement. For Peter is not his nature, because his nature is an essential part of himself, and even an essential part is not identified with the whole.

Thus I concede the major: Peter is not his nature. I deny the minor, for there is a real distinction between Peter and his nature, just as there is a real distinction between the real whole and its real part, and I deny also the parity of argument, because Peter's nature is an essential part of himself, but his existence is not. Thus when we say, "Peter is a man," man is an essential predicate; on the contrary, when we say, "Peter is existing," existing is a contingent predicate.

Father G. Mattiussi replies to this as follows: "St. Thomas says that existence is not included in the notion of suppositum, inasmuch as existence is not essential to any finite thing; but the suppositum can be considered in the order of possible things, without its actually existing."[163]

[161] Cf. *Angelicum,* June, 1945, pp. 83–85.
[162] *I grandi commentatori di S. Tomasso.*
[163] *De Verbo incarnato,* p. 116.

To this it must be said: When I say that Peter is not his existence, I am not concerned with Peter's possible existence, but with his actual existence; just as when we say that the essence of a created thing really differs from its existence, it is not a question of a possible essence, but of a real essence that underlies the existence which it limits. For as Father Mattiussi himself admits, the act of existing is multiplied and limited only by the real essence and not the possible, in which it is received. Similarly, existence is a contingent predicate of existing Peter, and not of possible Peter. Of existing Peter we say that Peter is existing, but is not his existence; whereas of God, we say that God exists and is His existence.

That being which is not its existence is really distinct from its existence. But Peter's person, even his personality, is not his existence, which is a contingent predicate. Therefore Peter's person, even his personality, is really distinct from his existence, which is really distinct from his personality.

Father Mattiussi [164] quotes three texts of St. Thomas in proof that he, too, was of the same opinion, namely, that subsistence is the existence of substance. On the contrary, in these texts we read: "Subsistence is said of that whose act is to subsist, just as essence is said of that whose act is to exist." [165] On the contrary, these texts do not in any way contradict Cajetan's opinion. Father Mattiussi does not search for that by which anything is a what, or for that in which the concrete, this man differs from this humanity. This man is what is, humanity that by which he is. They differ however by that which constitutes man the first subject of attribution, for it is the concrete that is constituted, whereas the form is in the subject. The Complutenses Abbreviati present this argument in various forms and excellently, showing that otherwise the proposition, man is existing, would be an eternally true proposition, just as this proposition, man is a substance of a rational nature. They insist on this, that subsistence or personality is intrinsic to the notion of a created person, whereas existence accrues

[164] *Ibid.*, pp. 118 f.

[165] *Summa theol.*, Ia, q. 29, a. 2; *De potentia*, q. 9, a. 1; *I Sent.*, d. 23, q. 1, a. 1. In the above-quoted text it is manifest that subsistence or personality is distinct from existential substance or from subsisting; for St. Thomas says in this text: "Subsistence or personality is said of that whose act is to subsist"; therefore it is not identified with the act that is received in it. In other words, subsistence is an abstract term that does not correspond to this concrete that is said to subsist, but to this concrete that is the suppositum.

to it and is completely outside the notion of person.[166] Hence Father Billot's opinion denies the truth of the following proposition: Peter is not his existence.

6) Moreover, Father Billot's opinion denies the truth of another proposition, namely, that Peter is existing. For in every affirmative proposition, the word "is" expresses real identity between subject and predicate. This real identity, however, must have its foundation in some real positive thing, in that by which anything is a what. But that by which anything is a what, is neither even a singular nature nor existence. For nature is that by which anything is such, for example, a man; existence is that by which anything is established beyond nothing and its causes. And two elements related to each other as *by which,* do not constitute a *one that is a what,* that is, a subject of itself separately existing.[167]

7) Moreover, Father Billot overlooks the fact that in God there are three personalities and one existence, not three relative existences but one *esse in* that is substantial. St. Thomas says: "There is only one being in God and three subsistencies." [168] Therefore personality is not being. [169]

8) Capreolus does not say that personality is formally constituted by existence, but he says, supported by Cajetan on this point: "The being of actual existence is called the act of the essence as whereby of the suppositum, and the act of the suppositum as what exists. . . . Existence thus pertains to the notion of suppositum, not forming a part of the suppositum, nor is it included in the essence of this latter, but is related to it by way of connotation and is implied indirectly, which is about the equivalent of saying that the suppositum is identical with the individual substance having existence. Such was the opinion of St. Thomas, so I think." [170] Cajetan admits this. There is, indeed, a

[166] *De generatione,* disp. 15, q. 3.

[167] Objection. But subsistence or personality also is related to the subject as that by which. Therefore the difficulty remains.

Reply. Personality is that by which a person is formally a what, or a subject of itself separately existing. But essence is that which constitutes the being in a certain species, and existence places it outside nothing. Hence there is no parity of argument, for personality is *that by which* most formally anything is constituted a *what,* but it differs from a person as the abstract term does from the concrete term.

[168] *Summa theol.,* IIIa, q. 17, a. 2, ad 3.

[169] Cf. Penido, *Le rôle de l'analogie en théologie dogmatique,* Part II, chap. 1, *La Trinité.*

[170] *Com. in IIIam Sent.,* d. 5, q. 3, a. 3, no. 2.

more recent opinion that maintains person is the singular nature itself underlying its existence.

Criticism. This does not explain whereby anything is properly what is, or the first subject of attribution subsisting of itself, first substance. For the singular nature, for example, this humanity, is not what is, but whereby anyone, namely, Peter or Paul, is a man. Hence we say: Peter is not his humanity, because the whole is not its part, it is not identical with its part, but includes other things besides; thus Peter includes his nature, existence, and accidents. Hence we seek that whereby a person is formally constituted the first subject of attribution, not attributable to another subject; whereas, on the contrary, this humanity is attributed to each human being.

Moreover, this humanity immediately is not capable of the act of existing, for it is not what exists. We are seeking the subject of this singular nature, of its existence and accidents.[171]

Common opinion among Thomists. It is Cajetan's opinion, which he explains,[172] and very many Thomists follow.

Cajetan passes methodically from the commonly accepted definition of person, namely, a subject of a rational nature, to the definition of personality. He notes that the name personality signifies that whereby a person is constituted the first subject that is of itself separately, so that it cannot be attributed to another subject.

But that whereby anything is a subjective what, cannot be anything accidental, or a permanent accident, such as the intellectual faculty, or the free will, or a transitory accident, such as an act of conscience or even a free act. It must be something substantial, as constituting the subject of attribution.

But this substantial can be neither a singular nature that is an essential part of this subject but not the subject itself, nor existence, which is a contingent predicate of whatsoever created person, and hence does not formally constitute it. Therefore personality is a substantial mode that terminates the singular nature, so that it may become the immediate subject of existence, for the subject is *what is,* and not the nature.

This substantial mode terminates the singular nature in some way as the point terminates the line and makes of the line a complete whole; thus, when a line is divided by a point into two lines, whichever of these, that before was in potentia to be continued, now becomes

[171] Cf. no. 5, the refutation of Scotus' opinion.

[172] *Com. in IIIam,* q. 4, a. 2.

a line in act, becomes some whole in act, by the very fact that it is terminated. Similarly, the line itself, for instance, a circular line terminates the surface of a scroll. This is also the case in the order of substances, for, when an animal of the lower order, a worm, for instance, is divided in two, then we have two worms, two supposita; before the division they were potentially two, now they are actually two.

Thus this humanity, which is in Christ, could be terminated in its own right, and thus it would be a distinct suppositum, a human person. *De facto,* however, it is terminated by the pre-existing personality of the Word, just as a line is extended so that it remains one line and not two lines; or, better still, just as two lines terminate in the same point at the apex of an angle.[173]

[173] Cajetan, *loc. cit.,* nos. 6–11, gives the following interpretation of St. Thomas' doctrine on this point: "We must say that there is some real difference between this humanity and this man, so that man includes something real . . . whereby this man is susceptible of both the act of existing, as of real filiation. . . . For this difference between this man and this humanity belongs to the nature of things . . . and for this reason cannot be reduced to a difference in the various ways of understanding the terms, or to a difference according as it is outside the scope of connotated things, whatever these may be; for this difference precedes all extrinsic things and modes of understanding and signifying. The difference does not come within the scope of negations, for a negation does not constitute the real entity of the subject. . . . Hence there must be something positive included in this man that is not included in this humanity, by which this man becomes primarily and directly susceptible of this thing (existence) of which humanity is not capable."

But this positive element must be that whereby first substance is what exists separately of itself. Therefore it must be something substantial, like a terminus, as the point is the terminus of the line. Cajetan says (*loc. cit.,* no. 11): "Just by dividing a line each part acquires a new terminus in the genus of quantity . . . for each part becomes actually a whole (something)." Likewise, as Aristotle teaches (*De anima,* Bk. II, chap. 2, lect. 4 of St. Thomas): "just by dividing an imperfect animal, such as a worm, we get two actual substances, two animals." St. Thomas considers that this analogy applies to the Incarnation, for he says (*III Sent.,* d. 5, q. 3, a. 3): "What is assumed, is drawn to something more complete, existing incomplete before its assumption; and this is contrary to the notion of person, which has the maximum of completion."

And St. Thomas concedes (*ibid.,* ad 3): "If Christ were separated from His assumed humanity, solely by such separation this humanity would become this man." To the objection that, from the thing separated nothing is acquired by the thing separated, St. Thomas replies: "Separation gives to each of the parts totality, and in things of continued quantity it also gives to each of the parts actual existence. Hence, in the supposition that Christ were to cease as man, that man would subsist of himself in the rational nature, and by this very fact would be entitled to be called a person," just as in things of continued quantity, by the fact that the part separated from the whole is terminated, and has actual existence, so in the substantial order, a singular nature by the fact that it is terminated receives actual existence.

Cajetan's fundamental argument. It may be reduced to the following syllogism.

Something real and positive is required by which the created subject is what is, which is against Scotus. But this cannot be either the singular nature, which is related to the subject as whereby, or existence, which is a contingent predicate of the created subject, which is against other opinions. Therefore something else positive is required, namely, personality, which ultimately disposes the singular nature for existence. It would indeed be repugnant if a substantial mode accrued to substance already existing, for then it would be an accident, which is against Suarez; but it would not be so if it accrued to substance before it existed.

Cajetan's opinion is admitted by Francis Sylvester (Ferrariensis),[174] by Bannez,[175] by John of St. Thomas, Gonet, Goudin, by Billuart,[176] by the Salmanticenses, and by very many Thomists.

There are two proofs for this opinion. 1. It is proved on the authority of St. Thomas; 2. it is proved from reason; 3. it explains satisfactorily the dogma of the Incarnation; 4. it is defended against those who attack the opinion.

Proof from St. Thomas. Cajetan quotes four texts,[177]

a) "Being is consequent upon nature, not as upon that which has being, but as upon that whereby a thing is; whereas it is consequent upon person or hypostasis, as upon that which has being." [178] Therefore being does not constitute personality but presupposes it, and as that which is really distinct from the singular nature, which is not the what or suppositum, as is evident in ourselves who have this flesh, these bones, and also in Christ who has this humanity.

b) "Temporal nativity would cause a real temporal filiation in Christ if there were in Him a subject capable of such filiation." [179] The subject would be a human person, not a nature. On the contrary, the Word cannot acquire a new relation, or an accident that is superadded to Him.

c) "If the human nature had not been assumed by a divine person, the human nature would have had its own personality. . . . The

[174] *Contra Gentes,* Bk. IV, chap. 43.
[175] *Com. in Iam,* q. 3, a. 5.
[176] *Com. in IIIam,* d. 4, a. 1.
[177] *Ibid.,* a. 2.
[178] *Summa theol.,* IIIa, q. 17, a. 2, ad 1.
[179] *Ibid.,* q. 35, a. 5, ad 1.

divine person by His union hindered the human nature from having its personality." [180]

d) "If the human personality had existed prior to the union . . . then it would have ceased to exist by corruption." [181] And again: "I say that essence is predicated of that whose act is to exist, subsistence of that whose act is to subsist." [182] Therefore subsistence is not identical with subsist. Finally St. Thomas says: "The form signified by the word 'person' is not essence or nature, but personality." [183] But in God there are three personalities and only one essence and one existence. Therefore personality is not existence. St. Thomas likewise says: "The name 'person' is imposed by the form personality, which means the reason for subsisting in such a nature." [184]

Proof from reason. Cajetan's opinion has its foundation in the principle that on the part of the object it is required that the commonly accepted definition of person, namely, an intelligent and free subject, be true, and that these two judgments are true: Peter is existing, but is not his existence.

Cajetan says: "If we all acknowledge this principle, in examining the quiddity of the thing signified, why turn away from what is commonly admitted?" [185] In other words, in the transition from the nominal definition to the real definition, why depart from the nominal definition of person, which is, what exists separately of itself in a rational nature? The quiddity of the name contains confusedly the quiddity of the thing, and the explicit definition must not be the negation of the implicit or nominal definition, but must be in conformity with it, otherwise philosophical reason disagrees with the findings of natural reason.

Moreover, for the verification of the two above-mentioned judgments (Peter is existing, but is not his existence), there must be a foundation for the real identity between subject and predicate, which is affirmed in the first judgment, yet such that there is not identity, which is rightly so denied in the second judgment. But this foundation, must be something positive, real, which is substantial and not

[180] *Ibid.*, q. 4, a. 2, ad 3; see also q. 4, a. 1, c. et ad 3; q. 2, a. 3, ad 2.

[181] *Contra Gentes,* Bk. IV, chap. 43.

[182] *Com. in I Sent.*, d. 23, q. 1, ad. 1. See also *De potentia,* q. 9, a. 1; *Summa theol.,* Ia, q. 29, a. 2; *III Sent.*, d. 5, q. 3, a. 3, c. et ad 3.

[183] *Summa theol.*, Ia, q. 39, a. 3, ad 4.

[184] *Com. in I Sent.*, d. 23, q. 1, a. 4, ad 4. See also *I Sent.*, d. 4, q. 2, a. 2, ad 4.

[185] *Com. in IIIam,* q. 4, a. 2, no. 8.

accidental, which is not existence, however, for this is a contingent predicate of Peter, or nature, which is related as whereby and as an essential part of this subject. It must formally be that whereby anything is a what or a real subject of these divers predications.

Therefore a terminus is required or a mode that is substantial and not accidental. This argument, namely, that on the part of the object there is required real identity between subject and predicate in the affirmative judgment, Peter is existing, is confirmed by several theologians.[186]

The search or hunt for the definition of personality can be more briefly set forth, by beginning with the nominal definition, and by comparing personality with those things unlike it, namely, with negations and accidents, and with those things like it and related to it, such as with the singular nature and with existing substance, as also by separating in this way those things that do not pertain to the genus of substance to which person belongs.

1) Personality is not anything negative, but is something positive, because it formally constitutes person, which is something positive.

2) Personality is not anything positive that is accidental, because person is a substance. Thus consciousness of self, liberty, or dominion of oneself cannot constitute ontological personality.

3) Personality is not the singular nature itself, because the singular nature is not what is, but that whereby anything is constituted in a certain species. If personality were the singular nature itself, then in Christ there would be two personalities, and in God there would be only one person.

4) Personality is not existence itself that actuates the nature, because existence is a contingent predicate of a created person, and it comes to the person already formally constituted as having existence. Peter is not his existence, but only has existence. Peter exists contingently, whereas Peter necessarily is Peter, and, by virtue of the principle of identity, can be only Peter.

5) Personality is therefore that whereby the singular nature becomes immediately capable of existence, and thus the subjective what is really constituted.

[186] Cf. Billuart, Index, the word "person"; also his *Dialectica,* Bk. II, chap. 1, art. 2(19); III, chap. 2; *ibid.,* 21, nos. 5, 6; *ibid.,* 22, no. 7. Also Zigliara, *Della luce intellectuale,* II, Bk. III, no. 374. Gonzales, *Logica,* p. 51; St. Bonaventure says something similar in his *Com. in IIIam Sent.,* d. 4, a. 1, q. 3, and *IV Sent.,* d. 8, q. 1.

This is the commonly accepted opinion among Thomists, and this real definition of personality corresponds to the nominal definition, that personality is that whereby any intelligent subject is a person, just as existence is that whereby a subject exists. This latter assertion is almost frankly admitted by all, and in a confused manner implies that personality is not the same as a person's existence.

3) Finally, **Cajetan's opinion** very well explains the dogma of the Incarnation.

1) It explains that there is one person in Christ, because it posits in Him two natures, indeed, but only one subsistence or personality, and only one existence, which follows the one and only person in Christ.

2) It explains why the councils call this union subsistential or hypostatic, and not existential or natural. It is not called an existential union, but a hypostatic union, which means a union that is according to subsistence or personality, which means that whereby anything is a what, or a terminated whole, of itself separately existing.

Moreover, as St. Thomas says, "the three persons in God have only one being." [187] Therefore St. Thomas is of the opinion that personality or subsistence is not being or existence, nor is it the singular nature, which is related to the suppositum as whereby and as an essential part. Therefore personality is a substantial mode by which a singular nature is made immediately possible of receiving existence.

The truth of this doctrine is to be seen in the instinct of self-preservation. Now, for instance, every suppositum whether mineral, vegetable, or animal seeks to retain what it possesses. Similarly the human person seeks to retain his nature, body and soul, his existence, his faculties, his integral parts, his operations; he seeks to retain all he possesses. It is not his individualized nature that possesses all these things, but his very person considered as the first subject of attribution, his very "ego."

What has been said also clearly shows the sublimity of Christ's personality; for He has not a human personality, and therefore all that pertains to His human nature is under the dominion of the Word incarnate. It is the person of the Son of God who possesses all these things, and therefore nowhere in creation has there been such a perfect illustration of God's supreme dominion both in the past and in present times, as in the case of Christ's most holy humanity.

The Complutenses Abbreviati give a good explanation of this doc-

[187] *Summa theol.*, IIIa, q. 17, a. 2, ad 3.

trine in their philosophical works. It is fitting here to quote their proofs. They remark: "It must be said that there is a real distinction between subsistence and existence. Such is the teaching of St. Thomas, for he says: 'Being is consequent upon nature, not as upon that which has being, but upon that whereby a thing is; whereas it is consequent upon person or hypostasis, as upon that which has being.' [188] But that which is consequent upon another is really distinct from it. . . . He also says: 'An angel is composed of existence and what is,' [189] and he expounds this doctrine here remarkably well by saying that existence forms a composite not only with the essence of a thing, but also with its suppositum; but if it were really identical with the subsistence of a thing, it could not enter into composition with the suppositum, but we should have to say that it formally constitutes the suppositum. Then in another work, he says: 'Existence does not pertain to the notion of suppositum,' [190] but subsistence belongs to the notion of suppositum, and even formally constitutes it as such. . . .

"Finally, the holy Doctor, in discussing various questions, asks whether essence and existence are identical in created things, and also whether the essence and suppositum are the same.[191] This would be superfluous if existence and subsistence are not really distinct. . . .

"The second proof for this thesis is founded on an argument taken from St. Thomas,[192] which may be presented as follows: Act is really distinct from the real subject in which it is received; but the suppositum is the real susceptive subject of existence. Therefore the suppositum is really distinct from its existence. This second consequence is a legitimate inference from the first consequence; for it is by subsistence that the suppositum is formally constituted. Hence if existence really differs from the suppositum, and is received in this latter, it must presuppose subsistence as a reality, and be really distinct from this latter. The minor is clarified: because that receives as what existence, which comes into being as what and operates as what; for becoming is ordered to being, and being to operation; but to come into being as what, and to operate as what belongs properly to the suppositum, which is the common teaching of scholastic theologians and

[188] *Ibid.*, ad 1.
[189] *Ibid.*, Ia, q. 50, ad 3.
[190] *Quodl.*, II, q. 2, a. 4.
[191] *Ibid.*, II, a. 3, 4; *Com. in II Sent.*, d. 3, a. 1, 2.
[192] *Summa theol.*, IIIa, q. 17, a. 2, ad 1.

philosophers. Therefore the suppositum really is the recipient as what of existence.

"The third proof for this assertion made above is taken from the previously quoted argument of St. Thomas,[193] and is substantially as follows: That which belongs intrinsically to the notion of suppositum is really distinct from that which accrues to it and is completely superfluous to the proper notion of suppositum; but subsistence belongs intrinsically to the notion of suppositum, whereas existence accrues to it and is not at all included in its proper notion. Therefore existence is really distinct from subsistence. The major and the consequence are evident. But the first part of the minor is sufficiently clear, . . . and the Complutenses give a brief proof and conclude that this is an eternal verity, namely, the suppositum is a subsisting substance and incapable of being attributed to another. . . . The second part of the minor is expounded as follows: Existence does not apply necessarily and essentially to the suppositum, otherwise this proposition, the suppositum exists, would be an eternal truth, which is absurd. Therefore existence is an accidental attribute of the suppositum, and is not included in its proper notion.

"The first confirmation of these proofs is that the suppositum is identical with the first substance that is directly assignable among the predicamentals; but the aforesaid substance is not constituted a reality by existence, inasmuch as all things placed among the predicamentals prescind from the notion of existence. . . .

"The second confirmation is that existence and subsistence are lacking in every principle of identity. Therefore they are not really the same. The antecedent is proved first of all because existence does not pertain to the notion of subsistence; otherwise anything of which subsistence is predicated would also require existence to be predicated of it. Consequently, just as this proposition, man is subsisting, is eternally true, so also this proposition, man is existing, would be eternally true, which nobody would concede. Again, existence does not enter into the concept of any third object by which it would be identified with subsistence: for no third object can be thought of, except the suppositum, whose concept, however, does not include the notion of existence, as we have just seen. Finally, existence and subsistence do not originate from the same form." [194] Such are the splendid com-

[193] *Quodl.,* II, a. 3, 4.
[194] *De generatione,* disp. 15, q. 3.

ments of the Complutenses, who preserve absolutely intact, therefore, the interpretation of St. Thomas offered by Cajetan.

SOLUTION OF OBJECTIONS AGAINST CAJETAN'S OPINION

First objection. In a certain work we read: "The necessity of this substantial mode is freely affirmed, namely, that an individualized substance be immediately capable of existing separately; it is of the very notion of an individualized and complete substance that it exist in itself and of itself." [195]

Reply. Substance or individualized nature is not what exists, but whereby any subject is such as it is, constituted in a certain species with its individualizing conditions. What exists is not this humanity of Peter. Otherwise this humanity of Christ would already be what is, and thus there would be two supposita in Christ, or two persons. On the contrary, there is only one suppositum in Christ, to whom the two natures are attributed.

Such is the common teaching of theologians in discussing the theandric acts of Christ, and the infinite value of His merits and satisfaction. They say these meritorious and satisfactory acts are of infinite value not because of the principle from which they are elicited, namely, the human nature, its faculties and infused virtues, but because of the subjective principle that elicits these acts, that is, the divine suppositum or divine person.

Personality must therefore be a real, positive, and substantial thing, distinct from the individualized nature and also from existence that is a contingent predicate of the created person. This means that personality is properly that whereby any intelligent and free subject is *what is*. Thus the common teaching of St. Thomas is that, in any creature whatever, there is a difference between *what is* and *being*.[196]

Second objection. On the part of substance, to subsist is to exist. But the relation between subsistence and to subsist is the same as between existence and to exist, with which latter it is identified. Therefore subsistence is the same as existence.

Reply. I concede the major, inasmuch as subsistence is the fact of existence attributed to the person, but not constituting the person, for the person is the thing that *de facto* exists. Hence we concede the major, or let it pass without comment.

[195] Cf. *Dict. théol. cath.*, art. "hypostase," col. 418.

[196] *Contra Gentes,* Bk. II, chap. 52.

I deny the minor; for the relation is not between subsistence and to subsist, but between subsistence and the suppositum, which is the same as between existence and to be or to exist; which means that it is a relation between the abstract and the concrete, as between a race and running. This becomes clearer if we substitute "personality" for "subsistence"; for the relation is not between personality and subsistence, but between personality and person, which is a relation between the abstract and the concrete. Hence the relation is the same as that between existence and to exist, and between a race and running. And thus there is a real distinction between personality or subsistence and existence, or between to exist and to subsist, which *de facto* is attributed to the suppositum as a contingent predicate.

St. Thomas admits this distinction; for he writes: "The relation between life and to live is not the same as that between essence and to exist; but rather as that between a race and to run, one of which signifies the act in the abstract, and the other in the concrete." [197]

Thus there is a threefold order in the signification of both the abstract and the concrete:

abstract:	essence: humanity	personality or subsistence	existence
concrete:	being: man	person (Peter)	to exist

As St. Thomas says: "The three persons in God have only one being," [198] and this latter is identified with the divine essence, which is not really distinct from the divine persons, although there is a real distinction between the persons.

Against Cajetan's argument other objections have been proposed in our times, such as the following.

Objection. St. Thomas says: "Being and operation belong to the person by reason of the nature, yet in a different manner. For being belongs to the very constitution of the person, and in this respect it has the nature of a term, that is, as ultimate actuality; consequently unity of person requires unity of the complete and personal being. But operation is an effect of the person by reason of the former nature. Hence plurality of operations is not incompatible with personal unity." [199]

[197] *Summa theol.,* Ia, q. 54, a. 1, ad 2.
[198] *Ibid.,* IIIa, q. 17, a. 2, ad 3.
[199] *Ibid.,* q. 19, a. 1, ad 4.

Reply. In this text St. Thomas is not inquiring into the formal constituent of person, which has already been determined; [200] but why there are two operations just as there are two natures, whereas there is one being. He replies that "being belongs to the very constitution of the person," [201] namely, to the person constituted as a person, as to that which has being, as St. Thomas said. For it is the person that immediately is, whereas operation, which follows personal being, belongs to the person through the intermediary of the nature and its faculties. Thus in Christ there are one being and two operations, just as there are two natures. In this text St. Thomas is not inquiring about the formal constituent of person, since this he had already done,[202] and had no need to postpone the determination of this formal constituent of person, when confronted by the doubt, which he proposed to himself, namely, whether there is only one operation in Christ; [203] for operation follows being, and what belongs to being must be considered before what concerns operation.

Father Mattiussi, S.J.,[204] presents three texts from the works of St. Thomas in proof that he taught the identity between subsistence and existence. But the true gist of these texts is: "Subsistence is said of that whose act is to subsist, as essence is said of that whose act is to exist." [205] Therefore, as existence is really distinct from essence in which it is received, so suppositum and subsistence that formally constitutes suppositum, is distinct from existence.

Another objection. From two acts there does not result per se unity; wherefore prime matter must be pure potency. But essence, subsistence, and existence are three acts.[206] Therefore these three acts cannot result in per se unity.

Reply. I distinguish the major. That there cannot result from two acts a nature one per se, this I concede; that there cannot result a suppositum one per se, this I deny. I concede the minor. Essence, subsistence, and existence are three acts, yet so ordered that one is the terminus of the other. I distinguish the conclusion. Therefore from these three acts there does not result a third per se nature, this I con-

[200] *Ibid.*, Ia, q. 29, a. 1, 2; also IIIa, q. 2, a. 2.

[201] *Ibid.*, IIIa, q. 17, a. 2, ad 3.

[202] *Ibid.*, q. 17, a. 2.

[203] *Ibid.*, q. 19.

[204] *De Verbo incarnato*, p. 118.

[205] Cf. *I Sent.*, d. 23, q. 1, a. 1; *De pot.*, q. 9, a. 1. *Summa theol.*, Ia, q. 29, a. 2.

[206] One per se, or unity per se, is said of a being that is specifically one, such as man, lion, and not a combination of several specific essences. (Tr.)

cede; that there does not result a one per se suppositum, this I deny. For when the rational nature is completed by personality, it is constituted a person, to whom existence applies accidentally or contingently. Aristotle distinguished between four modes of per se predication: [207] (1) definition which shows that the nature is one per se; (2) per se predicate that denotes a necessary property; (3) per se predication that declares something is of itself subsisting or a suppositum, which means that it is one per se as a subject, although it may be an essential part and have accidental parts; (4) predication that denotes a cause that is per se, and not per accidens. It must be noted that in a certain article of a Carmelite periodical, personality is something relative and is only reduced to the category of substance.[208] In reply to this, we say that the divine personalities are indeed relative entities, that is, they are subsisting relations, paternity, filiation, passive spiration, whose *esse in* (or inexistence) is substantial. But either human personality or angelic personality is not a relative entity, but an absolute entity; for it does not imply reference to another person, as paternity does. It is predicated as belonging indirectly to the category of substance, as a substantial mode, whereby an individual nature becomes immediately capable of existence.

Conclusion. Thus in the opinion held by Cajetan there is a legitimate transition from the commonly accepted definition of person, namely, that person is the first subject of attribution in a rational nature, to the philosophical notion of personality. Cajetan so very well says: "If all acknowledge this, then why in scrutinizing the quiddity of the thing signified, do we turn away from the common admission?" [209]

According to this common admission, person is that which exists separately of itself in a rational nature, and personality is that whereby person is formally constituted as a what of itself separately existing, to whom existence is attributed contingently.

Hence the entire opinion of Cajetan reduces itself to what is required on the part of the object, which is the verification of these two judgments admitted by all theologians, namely, the person of Peter exists, but he is not his existence. And just as no created essence is its existence, so no created person, formally constituted as such, by its own personality, is his own existence. Only God is His existence.

[207] *Post. Anal.*, Bk. I, lect. 10.
[208] *Etudes carmélitaines,* April, 1936, pp. 125 f., art. "Recherche de la personne."
[209] *Com. in IIIam,* q. 4, a. 2, no. 8.

Doubt. Does Cajetan consider subsistence or personality to be the intrinsic terminus of substance?

Reply. He certainly does, inasmuch as subsistence is the formal constituent of first substance, or the suppositum, although it does not belong to the notion of nature. Thus subsistence pertains to the substantial order. Father Hugon correctly says: "The metaphysical foundation for this opinion is the radical difference prevailing between what belongs to the existential order and what belongs to the substantial order. This means that no created person is his existence. Likewise the end of motion is what properly terminates it, but it is no longer motion, which has ceased; so also it is subsistence that terminates the nature, but is not the nature; however, it constitutes the first substance, or suppositum. No created person, whether understood denominatively as a singular nature, or formally, that is, with personality, is its existence. The second article of St. Thomas may now be read again, so that this doctrine may be more clearly understood." [210]

Recapitulation. The principal argument in this opinion that is held by very many Thomists is reduced to the following conclusion, as stated above. Something real and positive is required whereby a created and existing subject is what is, which is against Scotus. But this something cannot be either the singular nature, which is related to the subject as constituting it in its species, or existence, which is a contingent predicate of the created subject, which is against other opinions. Therefore some other positive entity is required, namely, personality, which is the ultimate disposition of a singular nature for existence. A substantial mode that would accrue to substance already existing would, indeed, be a contradiction in terms, for it would thus be an accident, which is against Suarez; but there would be no contradiction if it came to substance before it existed.

Third Article

WHETHER THE UNION OF THE WORD INCARNATE TOOK PLACE IN THE SUPPOSITUM OR HYPOSTASIS

The meaning of the title is: whether the union of the Word incarnate so took place that in Christ there is one suppositum, only one hypostasis.

[210] *De Verbo incarnato,* p. 351.

The answer is in the affirmative, and it is of faith. The Council of Ephesus declares that "the union is subsistential." [211] But some heretics said that there is one person but two supposita.

St. Thomas refutes this heresy by three arguments.

1) He points out that, by the addition of the note of person to the hypostasis, the nature becomes determinate and rational.

2) If it be said that "what person adds to the hypostasis is a dignity," then the union would be according to a certain dignity, or it would be a moral union, as Nestorius contended.

3) If there were two supposita in Christ, then to one of these what pertains to God would be attributed, and to the other what pertains to man. This would result in the severance of the subsistential union.[212]

Fourth Article

WHETHER AFTER THE INCARNATION THE PERSON OR HYPOSTASIS IS COMPOSITE

State of the question. Some deny that the person of Christ is composite, such as St. Bonaventure, Durandus, Scotus; and this for reasons posited by St. Thomas in his objections at the beginning of this article. He points out: (1) that the person of Christ is the very person of the Word, who is in Himself most simple, and in no way composite. (2) Moreover, the divine nature cannot be a part in Christ, because the part is always less perfect than the whole. (3) It cannot be said that Christ is composed of two natures, because thus there would be a composite nature, just as the human nature is composed of soul and body, and then the Deity would be to the composite as form, and therefore as part. This would be Monophysitism.

Reply. The person of Christ is one, but is composed of two natures.

First proof. It rests on the authority of St. Damascene, who is quoted in the counterargument of this article. Moreover, the Second Council of Constantinople corroborates the conclusion stated above, saying: "The Holy Church of God . . . confesses that the union of the Word of God with the flesh was by way of composition, which means that it was subsistential." [213]

[211] *Denz.,* no. 114.

[212] *Summa theol.,* IIIa, q. 2, a. 3, ad. 2., for a more complete explanation of the notion of person.

[213] Denz., no. 216.

Second proof. The argument is from reason, and there are two parts to it.

a) The person of Christ in itself is an absolutely simple uncreated being, even as the nature of the Word is, and therefore in itself is in no way composite. Thus Christ is one subsisting being.

b) Nevertheless, this person of Christ subsists in two natures, and thus He can and must be said to be a composite of two natures.

First objection. The reply is evident from the argumentative part of the article.

Reply to second objection. The divine nature, however, is not to be considered as a part of this composite. For "this composition of a person from natures is not so called on account of parts, but by reason of number, even as that in which two things concur may be said to be composed of them." Hence Christ is not a composite of parts, but of extremes that are united. St. Thomas explains this point more fully elsewhere,[214] remarking that composition may be viewed in two ways.

1) It may be considered as the union of parts which causes and results in the totality of the being, and this union implies imperfection, inasmuch as the part is an incomplete being, not so perfect as the whole, and inasmuch as the being of the whole is dependent on its parts and thus is caused.

2) Composition may be viewed as the union of extremes in some third entity that communicates being to the extremes. The extreme, however, prescinds from the notion whether it be a complete or incomplete being. Thus, for example, seeing terminates in the thing seen without resulting in any imperfection on the part of the object seen, on which the seeing depends, but which does not depend on the seeing. Thus the intellect of the blessed is united to God who is clearly seen, without involving any imperfection on the part of God. There is something similar to this in the hypostatic union, but in the order of being and not merely of operation, since the human nature is terminated by the absolutely simple person of the divine Word, without involving any imperfection on the part of the divine person. The person of the Word is related to the human nature not as informing act, but as terminating act.

First corollary. Christ is also a composite of the person of the Word and the human nature, because He consists of these really distinct and united. Yet it cannot be said that Christ is a creature, because created

[214] Cf. *Com. in III Sent.,* d. 6, q. 2, a. 3.

being applies to the person, who is what is. The person of Christ, however, is uncreated, but in Him the human nature is something created.

Second corollary. Although Christ is thus composite, He is not more perfect than the Word not made flesh in this composition, because the Word is the infinite extreme eminently containing the perfection of the human nature.

In contrast to this, God is not said to be a composite of persons and nature, because the divine persons, although united in the same nature, are not united among one another, but are rather in opposition, not being united with the nature, because They are simply identical with the nature. Thus They are not really distinct from the nature, but They are really distinct from one another by a relation of opposition.

Fifth Article

WHETHER IN CHRIST THERE IS ANY UNION OF SOUL AND BODY

State of the question. If so, then it seems that there would be in Christ a human person, for the human person is the result of the union of the soul with the body.

Reply. The answer is in the affirmative and it is of faith.[215] But the human nature thus being a composite has not its own personality.

Sixth Article

WHETHER THE HUMAN NATURE WAS UNITED TO THE WORD OF GOD ACCIDENTALLY

This article is both a recapitulation of the preceding articles and the completion of their definition of the hypostatic union.

State of the question. It seems that this union is accidental, for whatever accrues to a being after it is complete as an entity, accrues to it accidentally. Whatever does not pertain to the essence of anything, is its accident. But the human nature does not pertain to the divine nature of the Son of God. Therefore the union of the human nature with the divine nature is accidental.

Reply. It is given about the end of the argumentative part of the article. St. Thomas says: "The Catholic faith, holding an intermediate position between Monophysitism and Nestorianism, does not affirm that the union of God and man took place in the essence or nature, nor

[215] Cf. ad 1, ad 2, ad 3.

yet in something accidental, but midway, in a subsistence or hypostasis." [216]

1) *Indirect proof.* It is drawn from the counterargument, and is expressed by the following argument. Whatever is predicated accidentally, is not predicated substantially, but quantitatively or qualitatively. But the humanity of Christ is not predicated quantitatively or qualitatively. Therefore it is not predicated accidentally.

2) *Direct proof.* It is founded on the arguments defining the faith on this point, which declare that the union is not natural, which is against Eutyches, nor accidental, which is against Nestorius, but is subsistential. The two opinions quoted by the Master of the Sentences in this article may be included in the error of Nestorius. The argument may be reduced to the following syllogism.

The union of substantial things that form the composite of one person is not accidental. But such is the union of the Word incarnate. Therefore the union is in no way accidental, but substantial, which means that it is subsistential.

This implies more than the expression "in the person," for even accidents are in the person to whom they are attributed.[217] To understand this article it must be noted that there are four modes of *per se* predication, and that personal union means more than union in the person, as Cajetan observes.[218]

There are four modes of *per se* and not *per accidens* predication, as Aristotle explains.[219] St. Thomas says in his commentary on Aristotle: In the first mode of *per se* predication, definition is predicated of the subject, for instance, man is *per se* or essentially a rational animal.

In the second mode of *per se* predication a property is predicated of the subject, for instance, man is risible, or has the power of laughing, which manifests itself on his countenance as an indication of intelligence, and this power does not belong either to the angel or to the irrational animal.

The third mode of *per se* predication is more the mode that pertains to existence, and not to predication, since it signifies something that exists in itself and not in another as in a subject. Thus first substance,

[216] Denz., no. 114.
[217] See replies to objections in this article, especially ad 2 and ad 3.
[218] See his commentary on this article, no. 10.
[219] Cf. *Post. Anal.,* Bk. 1, chap. 4 (lect. 10 of St. Thomas).

for example, Peter, is *per se* or in himself existing, in opposition to accident, and to second substance, for example to humanity, which is predicated of Peter and is in him.

The fourth mode of *per se* predication is according to the notion of causality, when the proper effect is attributed to its proper cause. Thus the doctor restores to health, that is, he does this inasmuch as he is a doctor; strangling kills, light illumines. Contrary to this, it is accidental that the doctor sings.

It is evident that the humanity is united with the Word neither in the first mode, nor in the second mode, nor in the fourth mode, but in the third mode, inasmuch as it exists in the Word not *per accidens,* but *per se,*[220] and as Cajetan says,[221] it is united with the Word not only as in the person or in the hypostasis, as accidents are so united with substance, but it is united with the Word hypostatically, which means substantially, according to the third mode of predication.

Solution of difficulties. Durandus holds that this union is not predicamentally or physically accidental, because humanity belongs to the predicamental substance, and not to any of the others. But the union is predicably or logically accidental, because the predicable accident is defined as that which can be either present or absent from its subject of predication, without the corruption of this latter. But the humanity can be either present or absent from the Word, which remains unchanged.

The principal objections in scholastic form are the following.

First objection. What accrues to anything after the completion of its being, accrues to it accidentally. But the human nature accrues to the Word after the completion of the former as a being. Therefore the human nature is united with the Word accidentally.

Reply. I distinguish the major: if it is not drawn into the same personal being, I concede the major; otherwise I deny it. I contradistinguish the minor: that the human nature is drawn into the personal being of the Word,[222] this I concede; that it is not, this I deny.

But I insist. Even though it is drawn into the same personal being, it is united accidentally. The accident that accrues to any subject is drawn into the same being of the subject. But the accident is united

[220] The expression *per se,* as used here, means that the humanity is in the Word as a substance, and not as in a subject of inhesion, in that the Word has given to the humanity, not only individualization, but also subsistence and existence. (Tr.)

[221] *Com. in IIIam,* q. 2, a. 6, no. 9.

[222] See reply to the second objection of this article.

with this subject. Therefore the human nature is united with the Word accidentally.

Reply. I distinguish the major: that it is drawn into the same being of the suppositum, this I deny; improperly so, I concede; for it has its own being, but inheres in a subject. It belongs to the being of accident to inhere. I concede the minor. I distinguish the conclusion: if the human nature were an accident inhering in the Word, then I concede the conclusion; otherwise I deny it.

The human nature is truly united with the Word not only in the person as accidents are, but also substantially inasmuch as it is terminated by the personality of the Word, and has one personal being or one existence with it, just as body and soul are so united.

Again I insist. Nevertheless the union is accidental at least predicably, if not predicamentally as Durandus says.

What is not predicated of a subject *per se* is a predicable accident.

But the human nature is not predicated *per se* of the Word.

Therefore the human nature is united with the Word as a predicable accident.

Reply. I distinguish the major; what is in no way predicated *per se,* I concede; what is at least predicated *per se* in the third mode or *per se* as subsisting, I deny. I contradistinguish the minor, and I deny the consequent and consequence. The humanity of Christ does not indeed belong to the definition of the Word or of the Second Person of the Trinity, nor is it a property of the Word, but the Word subsists in the human nature, and the human nature in the Word.

Finally I insist. Nevertheless, what can be either absent or present, the subject remaining intact, is united with the subject accidentally. But the human nature can be absent from the Word, which remains intact. Therefore the human nature is united with the Word accidentally.

Reply. I distinguish the major: the subject remaining intact considered as a composite, this I concede; the subject considered as a mere subsisting form, I deny. I contradistinguish the minor: the human nature can be absent, the Word remaining intact considered in Himself, as the eternal person, I concede; considered as the Word incarnate, I deny.

Thus the body is not united accidentally with the soul, and yet the body can be separated from the soul, this latter continuing to exist, though the composite ceases as such. In other words, there can be no separation of the body from the soul unless there is a cessation of the composite, and so the union is *per se* and not *per accidens*. Similarly the humanity is united with the Word, although the union between the two is not essential.

Corollary. Hence the hypostatic union differs from an essential union that would result in one sole composite nature, such as the union between body and soul. It also differs from an accidental union. It is, however, an absolutely unique union of its kind, one that is subsistential or hypostatic, or a formally personal union, and not only a material union in the person, for even accidents, which accrue to man, are united to him materially in the person, but not formally as constituting the person.

Therefore Christ's human nature in the Word is neither a predicamental accident, as, for example, the intellectual faculty is in the rational soul or in the angel, nor a predicable or contingent accident as, for example, a certain person may be sitting instead of standing.

Thus is determined the exact meaning of this conciliar expression, namely, "hypostatic union." We are not concerned here with a theological conclusion deduced from the dogma, but with a metaphysical explanation of the dogma. The hypostatic union is not a new truth concerning the Incarnation, but it is a metaphysical explanation of this revealed truth.

Seventh Article

WHETHER THE UNION OF THE DIVINE NATURE AND THE HUMAN IS SOMETHING CREATED

State of the question. It seems that the union is not anything created, and this for the following reasons.

1) Because this union is in God, for it is God united to the human nature, and there can be nothing created in God.

2) The terminus of the union is the uncreated person of the Word. Therefore the union itself is not anything created.

This question presents considerable difficulty, because there are three possible meanings to the word "union." It may be understood: (1) as unitive action; (2) as rather the passive union of some things into one; (3) as a relation that follows from this union.

1) If we consider the union as meaning the act of uniting the human nature with the Word, then certainly the action is uncreated, and

it is common to the whole Trinity, for the Father and the Holy Ghost united Christ's human nature with the Word, although they did not assume it.[223] This action common to the whole Trinity, inasmuch as it is dependent on the omnipotence that is common to the three Persons, is formally immanent, but virtually transitive, and hence is certainly uncreated.

2) If we consider the union as implying a real relation of dependence on the part of Christ's human nature on the Word, St. Thomas clearly shows it to be something created, and so it presents no difficulty.

3) But if we consider the union rather as denoting a passive combination of Christ's humanity with the Word, then theologians dispute whether it is something real and created that is distinct from the human nature. Scotus, Suarez, Vasquez, and certain Thomists, such as the Salmanticenses and Godoy, as also Father de la Taille in recent times, affirm this view.[224] But Scotus would have it to be something relative that is an extrinsic adjunct, whereas others say it is a substantial mode and the foundation of the real relation of which St. Thomas speaks.

On the contrary, Cajetan and several other Thomists, such as Billuart and Father Billot, deny that the union is something created, remarking that there is no substantial mode in this case, one that is a quasi-intermediate connection formally uniting the human nature with the Word, so that it is impossible to detect any other formal union distinct from the extremes united, except the relation itself that follows from the passive change effected in the human nature by the action of the Word uniting to Himself. So says Billuart. Thus passive creation is merely a real relation of dependence, nothing else, and it has its foundation in the being of a creature, inasmuch as a creature is not its own existence. This seems to be the true solution of the difficulty.[225] Let us see what St. Thomas says.

In the counterargument he observes that this union began in time, therefore it is something created. In the body of the article, however, he determines what this something created formally is. St. Thomas

[223] See a. 8 of this question.

[224] In fact, Father de la Taille says that the grace of union may be called created, whereas St. Thomas and the majority of theologians say that this grace is uncreated. See *infra,* q. 6, a. 6; *De veritate,* q. 29, a. 2 (about end); also the *Tabula aurea* of the works of St. Thomas, under the word "Christ," nos. 68 f.

[225] Cf. *Dict, théol. cath.,* art. "Incarnation," cols. 1525 f.

speaks only of relation here. His argument is reduced to the following syllogism.

Every relation between God and the creature is real in the creature and logical in God. But the relation about which we speak is a certain relation of Christ's humanity to the Word. Therefore this union is in Christ's humanity as something real, and created, namely, a real relation of dependence on the Word assuming this nature, just as creation is a real relation of dependence of the creature on the Creator.[226]

But what is the foundation for this relation? St. Thomas says in the body of this article: "By the change effected in the creature such a relation is brought into being," that is, this foundation is passion that corresponds to the unitive action. Whether this passion is really distinct from the human nature passively assumed, is a disputed point among the above-mentioned theologians.

Let us see whether the replies to the objections define more clearly the nature of this union.

Reply to first objection. It declares that this union is not anything real in God.

Reply to second objection. It states that this union is something real and created in the human nature. It is not apparent from this reply that the union is anything more than a real relation.

Did St. Thomas speak more explicitly on this point elsewhere? He certainly did; for in another of his commentaries he says: "We must know that in the union of the human nature with the divine there can be nothing intervening that is the formal cause of the union with which the human nature is joined before it is united with the person. For, just as there can be no intervening entity between matter and form that would be in the matter prior to the substantial form, otherwise accidental existence would be prior to substantial existence, which is impossible; so also between the nature and the suppositum there can be nothing intervening in the above said mode." [227] Thus there is nothing intervening between the Word and the humanity. Hence union in the passive sense or created is nothing else but a real relation of the human nature that is dependent on the Word as a person, just as creation in the passive sense is nothing else but a real relation of dependence of the creature on the Creator.

[226] Cf. *Summa theol.,* Ia, q. 45, a. 3.
[227] Cf. *Com. in III Sent.,* d. 2, q. 2, a. 2, quaestiuncula prima.

Which is the more probable opinion? An intervening substantial mode between the Word and the human nature, as Cajetan, Billuart and others show, appears to be inadmissible.

Proof. The Word is united with the human nature by that whereby the Word terminates and maintains it. But the Word by Himself or solely by his personality, every formal connection excluded, terminates and sustains the human nature. Therefore the Word Himself or His personality is united with the human nature.

The union of the Word with the human nature means nothing else but the termination of this latter; thus analogically, in the order of operation, God clearly seen immediately terminates the beatific vision.

First confirmation. Created subsistence is by itself immediately united with created nature. Therefore a fortiori uncreated subsistence is so united, as it is most actual in the notion of terminating.

Second confirmation. Likewise existence, as the ultimate actuality, by itself immediately actuates the created suppositum; similarly personality by itself immediately is united with created nature, or terminates it; so also one and the same point immediately terminates two lines that meet in it, which is a very faint image of the union of the two natures in the Word.

Doubt. Was the human nature changed in being assumed by the Word?

Reply. In the strictest sense of the term, it was not, because it did not exist before it was assumed, inasmuch as it did not have its own personality, but was assumed by another personality. A nature must be first produced before it can be assumed.

Thus St. Thomas shows [228] that creation is not a change except as we conceive it, for he says: "Change means that the same something should be different now from what it was previously." [229] But this cannot be either in creation, or even in the assumption of Christ's humanity, which did not exist before its assumption. And St. Thomas says: "When motion is removed from action and passion, only relation remains." [230] Hence creation in the passive sense is nothing but a real relation of dependence that has its foundation in created sub-

[228] *Summa theol.,* Ia, q. 45, a. 3.

[229] *Ibid.,* a. 2, ad 2.

[230] *Ibid.,* a. 3, c. Transitive action is motion as it is coming from the agent, and passion is motion as it is in the patient. Therefore, when motion is removed from action and passion, nothing remains but a relation of dependence on the agent, which operates by an action that is not formally transitive.

stantial being. Similarly, in the hypostatic union, the soul of Christ is created as dependent on the Word as a person. If other authors wish to affirm that it is something else, namely, a special substantial mode, let them prove its existence. St. Thomas never spoke about this special mode.

What is therefore the foundation of the relation in the hypostatic union? It is Christ's humanity, inasmuch as it is not terminated by its own created personality, and so it can be terminated and possessed by the Word.

Eighth Article

WHETHER UNION IS THE SAME AS ASSUMPTION

First conclusion. There is a distinction between union as implying a relation, and assumption that implies an action; for this relation is in Christ's humanity and follows the active assumption, which is the foundation for this relation, just as passive generation is the foundation of the relation of filiation.

Second conclusion. Hence assumption implies becoming, whereas union implies having become. Thus we say of what took place, that the Word assumed the human nature, and even now that it is united with the Word.

Third conclusion. Whereas union implies a relation of quasi-equivalence, and both the divine nature and the human nature are declared united; but assumption, which is the action of the one assuming, does not designate the divine nature, but the agent assuming and the human nature that is assumed.

Fourth conclusion. Who unites and who assumes are not the same absolutely, for only the Son of God assumed the human nature, but the Father and the Holy Spirit are said to unite, but not to assume. For union as an action implies only the conjunction of extremes, whereas assumption as an action means the same as the *taking to oneself,* inasmuch as He who assumes unites to Himself personally, and is the end of the terminating action and not merely its beginning. Every external action of God is common to the three persons, just as omnipotence is, from which action derives its power; but one person, such as the person of the Word, can be separately the terminus of some real relation.[231]

[231] See reply to the second objection of this article.

Ninth Article

WHETHER THE UNION OF THE TWO NATURES IN CHRIST IS THE GREATEST OF UNIONS

State of the question. St. Thomas, as Cajetan remarks, considers union here not so much as a relation, but as it is a substantial and immediate conjunction of the two natures in the person of the Word. And the conjunction is the foundation of the above-mentioned relation. There are difficulties, as stated in the beginning of this article.

1) Unity that is the principle of number, seems to be a greater unity than Christ.

2) It seems that this union is not the greatest, because the divine and human natures are infinitely apart, and the greater the distance between the extremes that are united, the less is the union.

3) It seems that the union between body and soul is greater, because from it there results what is one not only in person, but also in nature.

The counterargument presents a contrary objection, as if the union of the Incarnation were greater than the unity of the divine essence.

Reply. The hypostatic union is the greatest of unions, not on the part of the things united, but on the part of the person in whom they are united.

First part. It is proved in the body of this article, and in the reply to the second objection as follows: The greater the distance between the extremes united, the less is the union in this respect. But the divine and human natures, which are the extremes of this union, are infinitely apart. Therefore the union of the divine and the human natures is the least in this respect.

Second part. It is proved as follows: On the part of the medium in which the extremes are united, so much the greater is the union as this medium is more one and simple, and more intimately united with the extremes. But the medium in this union, namely, the person of the Word, is most simple in Himself, and really identical with the divine nature, and substantially united with the human nature, so that the person of the Word imparts to the human nature both subsistence and existence.[232] Therefore this union, on the part of the medium in which it took place, is the greatest of created unions.

This same principle serves as the means of illustrating the mystical body of Christ. Although the members of His mystical body live far

[232] Cf. IIIa, q. 17, a. 2, for a clearer explanation of this truth.

apart from one another in most distant climes, yet they are most closely united both in Christ and in the Holy Spirit.

Thus it is that sometimes two saintly persons living far apart according to their nationality, are more intimately united in Christ than with their fellow citizens. The principle on which the unity of the mystical body of Christ depends is, indeed, far more productive of this spirit of unity than that of any family or nation on this earth.

It is the formal unitive principle that is of greater consideration in union than the actual distance, however great this may be, which separates the members. Thus it is apparent that the greatest intimacy is to be found in the hypostatic union, which evidently far transcends the unity of the mystical body of Christ. Nevertheless the hypostatic union is not so great as the unity of the Trinity; [233] for the unity of the Trinity is a unity of an absolutely simple nature, which is numerically one in the three divine persons and identical with each of them.

St. Bernard has given us three conclusions in equivalent words in one of his works, saying: "Among all things that are properly called one, the unity of the Trinity holds the first place, in which the three persons are one in substance or nature; conversely, that union holds the second place by which three substances are present in the one person of Christ," [234] namely, the Deity, the soul, and the body.

Reply to first objection. The unity of the divine person in Christ is greater than numerical unity, which is the principle of number; for the unity of a divine person is an uncreated and self-subsisting unity, and is incompatible with the nature of a part.

This union is sublime; for what is extraordinary in the order of the beautiful is sublime. Beauty is splendor of unity in variety, and the more distant are the extremes that are united and the more intimately they are united, the more beautiful is their union. This union of which we are speaking is unique, and is both a miracle and an essentially supernatural mystery. Its real possibility is not apodictically proved by reason alone, but it is persuaded and defended against those denying it.

There remains, however, the principal difficulty.[235] It may be expressed by the following syllogism.

That union is greater from which results not only one person, but

[233] See reply to the fourth objection of this article.
[234] *De consideratione,* Bk. V, chap. 8.
[235] Cf. IIIa, q. 2, a. 9, obj. 3.

also one nature. But such is the union between soul and body. Therefore it is greater than the hypostatic union.

Reply to third objection. On the part of the medium in which it takes place, the hypostatic union is nobler, for "the unity of the divine person is greater than the unity of person and nature in us."[236] This is evident, for the divine person of the Word is absolutely simple, whereas the human person and the human nature are composite. Thus the human composite is corruptible, whereas the hypostatic union is incorruptible.

How shall we reply, therefore, to the major of this objection, namely, that union is greater from which results not only one person but also one nature? I distinguish: that the union is greater on the part of the extremes, this I concede; on the part of the medium, this I deny.

Thus the union in the Incarnation is intensively more perfect than the union between soul and body, and therefore is indissoluble; whereas soul and body are separated by death, and as long as the soul is separated it is not properly a person.

This article is most sublime in doctrine. It can be developed so as to elevate the mind to spiritual things, combining this article with the above-mentioned principle, namely, "It is a greater dignity to exist in something nobler than oneself than to exist by oneself."[237] This principle is very rich in possibilities if closely examined, first as found in Christ, and then as it applies in a certain extended sense to us in the operational order. Thus it is better for us to be passive in our relations with God, by a perfect conformity of our will with the divine will, than following our own will to rule the world, which is contrary to Satan's doctrine, who, in seeking to tempt Christ, said: "All these things will I give Thee, if falling down Thou wilt adore me."[238] Thereupon Jesus says to him: "Begone, Satan! For it is written: The Lord thy God shalt thou adore, and Him only shalt thou serve."[239] It is a greater dignity for one to exist in someone nobler than oneself than to exist by oneself, and to act in conformity with God's will than to perform great acts by one's own choice. As Cajetan says: "It is better to obey the king, than to rule over one's house-

[236] *Ibid.*, ad 3.
[237] *Ibid.*, q. 2, a. 2, ad 2.
[238] Matt. 4:9.
[239] *Ibid.*, 4:10.

hold,"[240] or it is better to be in a passive frame of mind as regards those superior to us, than to assume an active role as regards those inferior to us; and although it is better to give than to receive, it is better to receive from someone superior to us, than to give to someone inferior to us. Thus the true way of passivity in the spiritual life is nobler than to act, relying on one's own ability, as Dionysius says of Hierotheus that he was "passive to the divine operations (*patiens divina*)"[241]

Tenth Article

WHETHER THE UNION OF THE TWO NATURES IN CHRIST TOOK PLACE BY GRACE

State of the question. The difficulties at the beginning of this article show clearly the purpose of this question. It seems that the union did not take place by grace, because grace is an accident inhering in the soul of everyone in the state of grace; whereas the hypostatic union is substantial, as stated above, and belongs exclusively to Christ.

Reply. This union did not take place by created grace, which is an accident, and an habitual gift inhering in the soul, but it took place by uncreated grace, which is the gratuitous will of God doing something without any preceding merits on the part of the beneficiary of the gift.

First part. It is evident, because this union is substantial, and not accidental.

Second part. It is also evident, because this union infinitely transcends the faculty and exigencies of created nature, even the angelic.[242]

In this article St. Thomas does not speak of a substantial mode that would be present between the Word that assumes and the humanity that is assumed.

Eleventh Article

WHETHER ANY MERITS PRECEDED THE UNION OF THE INCARNATION

State of the question. In a certain sense it seems the Incarnation was merited, for the just of the Old Testament merited eternal life, to

[240] *Com. in IIIam,* q. 2, a. 9.
[241] *Ibid.*
[242] Cf. argumentative part of this article, and ad 1.

which they could attain only through the Incarnation. Therefore it seems that they likewise merited the Incarnation. Also the Church chants of the Blessed Virgin that "she merited to bear the Lord of all." [243]

On the contrary, St. Augustine teaches that no merits preceded our regeneration,[244] and he gives St. Paul as his authority.[245] Therefore no merits preceded the generation of Christ. Moreover, in the above-mentioned work, St. Augustine shows in his own beautiful way that the predestination of Christ as man to divine natural sonship, could not have been because of Christ's foreseen merits, for these merits presuppose His person already constituted. From this St. Augustine concludes that likewise our predestination, of which Christ's predestination is the exemplar, is not because of our foreseen merits, which are the effects of our predestination, as explained by St. Thomas.[246]

Reply. There are three conclusions in the body of the article.

First conclusion. Christ could not merit His incarnation, because every operation of Christ followed the hypostatic union; for Christ was not first a mere man, and afterward united to the Word, but at the very moment His human nature was created, it was personally united to the Word. This conclusion is *de fide* against Photinus.[247]

Second conclusion. The patriarchs of the Old Testament and the Blessed Virgin Mary did not merit and could not merit *de condigno* the Incarnation, and this for three reasons.

1) Because the Incarnation transcends the beatitude of eternal life, to which the merits of the just are ordained as their ultimate reward. The Incarnation establishes the hypostatic order above the order of grace and glory.

2) Because the principle of grace cannot fall under merit, for it would be its own cause. Thus the state of grace does not fall under merit, and a fortiori this applies to the Incarnation, which is the principle of grace, for the Gospel says: "Grace and truth came by Jesus Christ." [248]

[243] Little Office of B.V.M., Ant. at Benedictus.
[244] *De praed. sanct.,* chap. 15.
[245] Titus 3:5.
[246] *Summa theol.,* Ia, q. 23, a. 5.
[247] Denz., nos. 65, 85, 88, 233.
[248] John 1:17.

3) Because the incarnation of Christ is for the reformation of the entire human nature, and therefore it is not on account of the merit of any particular man. St. John says: "Of His fullness we have all received." [249]

Third conclusion. Yet the patriarchs of the Old Testament merited the Incarnation congruously or in a broad sense by desiring and beseeching, for it was becoming that God should hearken to those who obeyed Him. "The Blessed Virgin," says St. Thomas, "is said to have merited to bear the Lord of all; not that she merited His incarnation, but because by the grace bestowed upon her she merited that grade of purity and holiness which fitted her to be the Mother of God." [250] These are golden words, and in the strictest sense express what the Blessed Virgin Mary truly merited, for she did not merit the Incarnation, which is the principle of that plenitude of grace which she received so as to merit, but she merited an increase of grace by which she became worthy to be the Mother of God.[251]

There are some doubts that arise concerning this article.

For the solution of these doubts we must recall the division of merit as set forth in the treatise on grace. Merit is a work performed that is deserving of a reward, or, more correctly, there is a right to a reward in this work performed. Hence the foundation for this division is according to the excellence of the work performed, inasmuch as there is or is not equality of proportion between the work performed and the reward. There is this proportion in condign merit, but not in congruous merit.

[249] *Ibid.,* 1:16.

[250] Cf. IIIa, q. 2, a. 2, ad 3.

[251] St. Thomas seems to say something more (*III Sent.,* d. 4, q. 3, a. 1, ad 6.), for he writes: "The Blessed Virgin did not merit the Incarnation, but, presupposing the Incarnation as an established fact, she merited that it should take place through her not by condign merit, but by congruous merit, inasmuch as it was becoming for the Mother of God to be most pure and most perfect." On careful consideration, however, this way of presenting the case does not make any addition to the previous statement. It merely asserts that the Blessed Virgin merited that the Incarnation should take place through her, inasmuch as she merited that degree of purity and holiness, which befitted the Mother of God, and no other virgin could merit this, because no other virgin received from her conception this original plentitude of grace. So the Blessed Virgin Mary in the order of execution could have prepared herself for the divine maternity, but she could not have merited it, for, such being the case, she would have merited the Incarnation.

- Merit
  - condign: which has its foundation at least in distributive justice, inasmuch as there is condignity or equality of proportion between the work and the reward.
  - congruous
    - in the strict sense: is founded on friendship, or a friendly right between persons, inasmuch as friendship is a potential part of justice.
    - in the broad sense: is founded on God's pure mercy, without implying any right or obligation to reward because of the work performed.

First doubt. Could Christ have merited His incarnation by works that followed from it? [252]

Some theologians, such as Suarez, Ruiz, Coninck, are of this opinion, inasmuch as God had decreed the execution and continuance of the Incarnation in future times because of the foreseen future merits of Christ.

The Thomists deny this view. They defend this first conclusion of St. Thomas by saying that Christ neither merited nor could have absolutely merited His incarnation either *de condigno* or *de congruo,* not even by works that followed from it.

The reason for this is that the principle of merit neither falls nor can fall under merit, for it would be its own cause, as explained in the treatise on grace.[253]

More briefly, Christ did not merit His own self. Merit is the morally efficient cause of reward, inasmuch as it is a right to a reward; if, therefore, the principle of merit were to fall under merit as a reward, then merit would be its moral cause; and thus it would be its own cause; it would be both cause and effect in the same genus and in the same aspect, which is absurd.

But the Incarnation is the principle of the whole of Christ's merit

[252] Cf. Gonet, disp. 7, a. 3.

[253] *Summa theol.,* Ia IIae, q. 114, a. 9; *De veritate,* q. 29, a. 6.

because it is impossible to conceive of any of Christ's operations that does not proceed from His person as the efficient principle that operates, since actions belong to the supposita, and operation follows being, and the person of the Word gives an infinite value to Christ's merits, which will be more clearly explained farther on.

Hence not even Christ's good works following from the Incarnation could have merited it either *de condigno* or *de congruo,* for these works would have been the cause of Christ Himself. Similarly the Incarnation would have been both cause and effect in the same aspect; it would have been both principle and principled, prior and posterior to itself, all of which are contrary to the principle of contradiction, that must be preserved in these mysteries, otherwise mysteries would be nothing but absurdities, not above reason, but contrary to reason.

Confirmation. The Incarnation was decreed even as regards its execution before the merits of Christ were foreseen. For just as being precedes operation, so the being of Christ was decreed before His operation.[254] Hence Christ could not have merited His incarnation at least in its essentials.

Second doubt. Did Christ merit the circumstances of His incarnation?

The Thomists answer by distinguishing between circumstances either preceding or accompanying the Incarnation, and others that follow from it. They also subdistinguish the preceding circumstances so far as they either are or are not necessarily connected with the Incarnation.[255] They say:

1) Christ did not merit the preceding or concomitant circumstances of the Incarnation that essentially belong to His being or were its necessary accompaniments.[256]

The reason is that Christ's merits presuppose His incarnation as their principle, and likewise the aforesaid circumstances that belong to His essence and individuation in the Incarnation.

Moreover, God cannot infallibly foresee Christ's future merits, unless He previously foresees that Christ will exist in some moment of time.

Hence Christ did not merit to be conceived of the Holy Ghost, to

[254] See solution of objections in Gonet, disp. 7, a. 3; Billuart, diss. 5, a. 1.

[255] Cf. *Salmanticenses,* disp., 7, dub. 2, par. 7.

[256] We are here concerned with circumstances that are necessarily connected according to a hypothetical necessity with the Incarnation in the concrete, as it is willed by God, such as the conception and birth of Jesus.

be born of the Blessed Virgin Mary, of the Jewish race, in a certain place, at a certain time, and in a certain manner.

2) Christ merited those circumstances of His incarnation that neither essentially belong to His being nor were its necessary accompaniments, or those that did not pertain to His essence and individuation in the Incarnation.

These circumstances are not the cause or principle of merit, nor does Christ's merit depend on them. Christ merited all that fittingly can be called merit. Thus He merited what the prophets foretold about Him, what the angel announced,[257] and more probably the virginity of Mary, for Mary's virginity does not essentially belong to the Incarnation, any more than that a mother be of the white race; nor does it seem necessarily connected with the Incarnation. Likewise Christ merited the Immaculate Conception of the Blessed Virgin Mary.

3) Christ merited the circumstances that followed from the Incartion; because these are not connected with the principle of merit, but follow from it. Thus He merited the multitude of angels singing after His birth, the adoration of the Magi, the appearance of the star, the care given to Him by the Blessed Virgin Mary and St. Joseph, to be the judge of the world, the institutor of the sacraments, His resurrection.[258]

More briefly, as the Salmanticenses say: "Concerning all the circumstances of the Incarnation, it may be said that Christ did not merit those that belong to the essence and individuation of the Incarnation, such as to be conceived of the Holy Ghost, to be born of the Virgin, and so He did not merit the maternity of the Blessed Virgin Mary; but He merited all the circumstances that do not belong to the essence of the mystery.

"The reason is, as regards the first conditions, that the principle of merit, the Incarnation, does not fall under merit; concerning the other circumstances, the reason is that these are not connected with the principle of merit." [259] Briefly, Christ did not merit His own self.

[257] That Christ merited what preceded His conception presents no difficulty, and so He merited the redemption of the just of the Old Testament. The reason is that merit is not a physical but a moral cause; a physical cause exerts no influence before it exists, whereas God, foreseeing and willing the future merits of Christ, gave grace to those who were justified before the coming of Christ.

[258] Cf. IIIa, q. 19, a. 3.

[259] *Com. in IIIam,* disp. 7, dub. 2, par. 7, no. 53.

<table>
<tr><td rowspan="3">Circumstances of the Incarnation</td><td rowspan="2">preceding and accompanying it</td><td>those pertaining to essence and individuation of Incarnation</td><td>e.g., conceived of the Holy Ghost, born of the Virgin Mary; i.e., Christ did not merit her virginal maternity (so the Salmanticenses).</td><td>Christ did not merit these</td></tr>
<tr><td>what does not pertain to essence of Incarnation</td><td>what the prophets foretold about Him, what the angel announced, and other such things</td><td rowspan="2">Christ merited these</td></tr>
<tr><td>following from it</td><td colspan="2">adoration of Magi, care given to Him by Blessed Virgin and St. Joseph, to institute sacraments, to rise from dead</td></tr>
</table>

Third doubt. Did Christ merit the continuation of His incarnation? Suarez and certain other theologians affirm that He did.

The majority of the theologians, especially among the Thomists, say that He did not. They give as their reason, that the continuation does not differ from the Incarnation itself, which cannot be the object of merit. The Incarnation is not a continuation after the manner of successive and divisible things by some addition, namely, by way of part, degree or help, but it is simultaneously whole and is measured by an absolutely indivisible duration, which transcends the continuity of solar time, and also the discrete time in the succession of thoughts of angels. This duration, that measures the Incarnation, is participated eternity, participated indeed inasmuch as the Incarnation had a beginning. The reason is that the hypostatic union is unchangeable, and more permanent than the beatific vision, which is really measured by participated eternity on the part of the object, inasmuch as there is neither change nor succession in it.

Confirmation. Now the continuation of the state of grace until death no more falls under merit than the beginning of this state, which is the principle of merit; a fortiori, therefore, the continuation of the Incarnation, which is the radical principle of all merits of both Christ and baptized persons, does not fall under merit.

Fourth doubt. This concerns the merits of the patriarchs of the Old Testament and of the Blessed Virgin Mary.

St. Thomas clearly shows indeed that they could not have merited *de condigno* the Incarnation, which is the radical principle of the merits of all men after the Fall and their regeneration, and which transcends our beatitude or the ultimate end of our merit. This is the commonly accepted and certain opinion among theologians, which is expressed in passages of Holy Scripture where it is stated that the Incarnation is a work of mercy. The canticle that is called the *Benedictus,* says: "Through the bowels of the mercy of our God, in which the Orient from on high hath visited us." [260] St. Paul says: "But when the goodness and kindness of God our Savior appeared; not by the works of justice which we have done, but according to His mercy He saved us." [261]

Hence neither the Blessed Virgin Mary could merit *de condigno* the Incarnation; but it was the radical principle of all the merits of the Blessed Virgin Mary, who received the grace of the Immaculate Conception because of the future merits of Christ, as Pius IX declared.[262]

Therefore the only difficulty that remains is that which concerns congruous merit. In other words, what does St. Thomas mean by saying toward the end of the body of this eleventh article: "Yet the holy fathers of the Old Testament merited the Incarnation congru-

[260] Luke 1:78.
[261] Titus 3:4 f.
[262] Denz., no. 1641. Bull *Ineffabilis Deus.*

ously by desiring and beseeching; for it was becoming that God should hearken to those who obeyed Him"?

Is it here a case of congruous merit in the strict sense, a merit that is founded on friendship, or on an amicable right; or is it merely congruous merit in the broad sense, which has its foundation in God's pure mercy who hears our prayers even without their being meritorious either *de condigno* or *de congruo,* as when He hears the prayers of sinners who cannot merit to be heard, since they are in a state of sin?

Several theologians, even some Thomists, say that congruous merit is here meant. But they are incapable of solving the objection that immediately presents itself, namely, that the incarnation of Christ is the principle of the whole merit acquired by the Blessed Virgin Mary, and by the fathers of both the Old Testament and of the New.[263] The principle of merit does not fall under merit, not even under congruous merit in the strict sense, for this merit has its foundation in friendship or in charity that comes from Christ. St. Thomas says: "Christ is the Savior of the whole human race,"[264] as the angel said: "He shall save His people from their sins."[265]

Some theologians reply that in the intentional order the Incarnation is the principle of merit concerning the fathers of the Old Testament, and in the order of execution the merits of the fathers prepare for the Incarnation. In other words, the Incarnation and these merits are mutually causes, though in a different order; the Incarnation is the final cause, but merits constitute the moral efficient cause.

This reply is of no value. It would perhaps apply to the merits of Adam in the state of innocence, but here it is valueless; for the merits of the fathers are dependent on the future merits of Christ, not only as final cause, but as moral efficient cause. These causes are mutually causes, though in a different order. Hence St. Thomas says: "The mystery of the Incarnation is the principle of merit, because of His fullness we all have received,"[266] even all the just of the Old Testament. The same must be said of the merits of the Blessed Virgin

[263] Because of this principle, St. Thomas at times feared to affirm the privilege of the Immaculate Conception of the Blessed Virgin Mary, when, for instance, he did not have in mind her preservative redemption.

[264] *Summa theol.,* IIIa, q. 27, a. 2, ad 2.

[265] Matt. 1:21.

[266] *Summa theol.,* IIIa, q. 2, ad 2.

Mary. In the present state of man after the Fall, there is no merit, nor is it possible to conceive of any, which does not derive its value and power of meriting from the merits of Christ. Merits in Christ are not conceived as morally efficient cause of our merits, except so far as Christ is considered as existing, or absolutely will exist in some moment of time, and consequently actually existing and not merely intending to exist; for actions belong to supposita that exist, and operation follows being. Hence the principle "causes mutually interact" does not apply here, for they would be causes in the same genus of causality, which constitutes a vicious circle.[267]

Hence neither the fathers of the Old Testament nor the Blessed Virgin could merit strictly *de congruo* the accomplishment of the Incarnation as foreseen and decreed by God, nor therefore as taking place in time. If we merit the attainment of glory in the order of execution, it is because God so willed this by His eternal and effective decree. This means, as it is commonly said, that in the intentional order God *freely wills* to give glory to His elect, but He does not will to *give it freely* to the adult elect in the order of execution. This means that the adult must merit glory to which they have been freely predestined.[268]

Solution of the doubt. Several Thomists, such as Sylvius and Gotti, say that the problem concerns congruous merit in the broad sense of the term, which has its foundation in God's pure mercy hearing our prayers even though they are not strictly meritorious, such as the prayers of sinners.[269] And this seems to be the meaning of the following text of St. Thomas: "It was becoming that God should hear the prayers of those who obey Him." [270] Therefore congruous merit in the broad sense is the same as impetration.

Otherwise 1. the Fathers would have merited something better than Christ Himself merited; 2. Christ would be indebted to the fathers for His incarnation; 3. The Incarnation would not be a work of pure mercy.

Thus the principle enunciated by St. Thomas in the body of this

[267] Cf. Billuart and Gotti on this difficulty, who discuss the problem better than Gonet and the Salmanticenses.

[268] By the word "adult" the Catholic Church understands those who have come to the use of reason. (Tr.)

[269] Whereas merit refers to divine justice, at least according to an amicable right, prayer as such not necessarily meritorious, refers to divine mercy.

[270] *Summa theol.,* IIIa, q. 2, a. 11, c (end).

eleventh article, namely, "the principle of merit does not fall under merit," remains intact. This principle applies equally to strictly congruous merit, which is the result of God's love obtained for us by Christ, as to condign merit. Sacrosanct also is the principle that Christ is the source of the merits of the regenerated both in the Old Testament and in the New, even of the merits of the Blessed Virgin Mary.

This interpretation is confirmed by the fact that St. Thomas denies that the Blessed Virgin Mary merited the Incarnation, for he writes: "The Blessed Virgin is said to have merited to bear the Lord of all, not that she merited His incarnation, but because by the grace bestowed upon her she merited that grade of purity and holiness which fitted her to be the Mother of God." [271]

St. Thomas said practically the same in another of His works, in which he wrote: "The Blessed Virgin did not merit the Incarnation, but after its accomplishments she merited to be instrumental in bringing it about, not by condign merit, but by congruous merit, inasmuch as it was becoming that the Mother of God should be most pure and most perfect." [272]

Objection. Strictly congruous merit has its foundation in the mutual friendship prevailing between the one who merits and the one who rewards. But the holy fathers who desired the Incarnation were God's friends, and a fortiori the Blessed Virgin was. Therefore the Blessed Virgin and the holy fathers *de congruo* merited the Incarnation.

Reply. I distinguish the major; when nothing militates against the notion of merit, I concede the major; otherwise I deny it. But the obstacle here is that the Incarnation is the principle of merit for the fathers, and cannot be merited. Moreover, as already stated, the Incarnation constitutes a special hypostatic order, which is beyond the scope of merit; for the only purpose of merit is for the attainment of eternal happiness, and "the union of the Incarnation transcends the union of the beatified mind with God, and therefore it cannot fall under merit," [273] as St. Thomas says.

[271] *Ibid.,* ad 3.

[272] *Com. in III Sent.,* d. 4, q. 3, a. 1, ad 6.

[273] *Summa theol.,* IIIa, q. 2, a. 11 c (middle).

Twelfth Article

WHETHER THE GRACE OF UNION WAS NATURAL TO THE MAN CHRIST

Cajetan remarks that this question concerns Christ, not as God, but as man. Is the grace of union natural to Him?

Reply. The grace of union is not natural to Christ, if this would mean that it is caused by the principle of the human nature; but it may be called natural inasmuch as it was bestowed upon Him together with the human nature, and moreover, inasmuch as it comes from the divine nature of Christ. Infused habitual grace in the soul of Christ is also natural in this sense.

The reason is that both graces are substantially supernatural and were given to Christ at the moment of His conception.

Doubt. Was the Blessed Virgin Mary the instrumental cause of the union of the human nature with the Word at the very moment of Christ's conception?

Reply. Most certainly no creature was or could be the principal efficient cause of the Incarnation, for the Incarnation is not only a work that belongs properly to God, such as creation, but it is His greatest work; for it is a miracle of the first order surpassing in substance all created and creatable powers and all exigencies of whatsoever created nature. It is also a mystery that transcends the mysteries of grace and that constitutes a special order, known as the hypostatic order.

The Incarnation was a work of the Trinity, by reason of omnipotence, which is a common attribute of the three persons. Thus, as we stated, the Father and the Holy Ghost joined in the act of uniting the human nature with the Word, but only the Son assumes or takes this nature to Himself.

But a doubt arises. Was the Blessed Virgin the instrumental cause of the Incarnation?

The question is disputed. St. Thomas says that Mary was not, for he writes: "In the conception of Christ, the Blessed Virgin took no active part, but was merely the material cause." [274] But the instrumental cause takes an active part through the power of the principal agent.

[274] *Ibid.*, q. 31, a. 5; q. 32, a. 4, c.

Likewise St. Thomas maintains that there is no instrumental cause in creation,[275] not even in the creation of the souls of infants, which occurs every day. The parents are not the efficient cause, but merely furnish the matter or dispose the body for the reception of the soul; a fortiori there is no instrumental cause in the Incarnation.

The principle on which this a fortiori argument rests may be illustrated by the following syllogism.

An instrument must dispose the subject for the effect of the principal agent. But, as in creation, there is no subject from which is produced that which is created from nothing; so in the Incarnation there is no pre-existing subject to be disposed, for the Incarnation is the communication of the personality of the Word to the human nature of Christ. The Word, however, is beyond the scope of created action, and is not the subject on which created action operates. Matter cannot be disposed for something uncreated, namely, for the Word that assumes. Therefore there is no instrumental cause in the Incarnation.[276]

Hence, if the Blessed Virgin is said at times to be the instrumental cause of the creation of Christ's soul and even of the Incarnation, this must be understood in a broad sense, inasmuch as she provided the matter which was formed by the Holy Ghost into the human nature and united with the Word.

[275] *Ibid.,* Ia, q. 45, a. 5.

[276] Cf. *Dict théol. cath.,* art. "Incarnation," cols. 1509 f. Also art. "Marie," col. 2362. Cf. also John of St. Thomas, Gonet, Salmanticenses, Contenson.

CHAPTER V

QUESTION 3

The Mode of the Union on the Part of the Person Assuming

AFTER the consideration of the hypostatic union in itself, we must now discuss the nature of this union on the part of the person assuming.

John of St. Thomas observes in the beginning of his commentary on this third question that St. Thomas divides it into two parts: 1. the person assuming (a. 1–5); 2. the manner of the assumption (a. 6–8).

First Article

WHETHER IT IS FITTING FOR A DIVINE PERSON TO ASSUME

Cajetan says the purport of this title is to show that the question of this article concerns the divine person as such, so far as we introduce a mental distinction between person and the divine nature.[1]

State of the question. It is apparent from the first two difficulties presented at the beginning of the article, namely, that there is no possibility of any addition to a divine person because this person is in Himself infinitely perfect. Also incommunicability belongs to the concept of person.

Conclusion. To assume a nature is most properly befitting to a person.

Authoritative proof. St. Augustine, who is quoting St. Fulgentius, says: "This God, that is, the Only-begotten One, took the form, that is, the nature of a servant to His own person."

Proof from reason. It may be expressed in syllogistic form as fol-

[1] For a fuller explanation of this distinction, which is called a virtual minor distinction, see *The One God,* pp. 168 f.; also *God, His Existence,* II, 203–46. (Tr.)

lows: The word "assume," which practically means to take to oneself, is both the principle and the term of an act. But only a person can be both the principle and term of an act. Therefore only a person can assume.

The other articles of this question will bring out more clearly the meaning of the adverb *"most properly."*

Proof of minor. It belongs to a person to act, for actions are attributed to supposita, and a person is that which by itself separately exists and acts. Moreover a person is the term of this assumption, because the union took place in the person and not in the nature.

Assumption is properly an action by which the human nature is drawn into the subsistence of the Son, so that it may subsist by this subsistence. Hence this action not only produces in the human nature of Christ a relation of dependence on the Word, but communicates to it the personality of the Word.

Reply to first objection. No addition is made to the divine person, who is infinite. But what is divine is united to man. Hence not God, but man is perfected.

Reply to second objection. "A divine person is said to be incommunicable inasmuch as it cannot be predicated of several supposita, but nothing prevents several things being predicated of the person. . . . But this is proper to a divine person, on account of its infinity, that there should be a concourse of natures in it, in subsistence." [2]

Doubt. Does the termination of another nature belong exclusively to a divine person, so that it would be repugnant to every created or creatable personality? Can an angel, for example, or a devil assume the human nature? Some thought that St. John the Baptist was an angel incarnate, and that Antichrist will be a devil incarnate.

Reply. It is the common teaching among theologians that no created person can assume a nature into union with its suppositum. So say Cajetan, Soto, Alvarez, Medina, Suarez, Vasquez, Billuart. The reason is that finite personality derives its limitation and species from the nature whose complement and term it is. Although subsistence is the mode and term of the nature, it does not specify the nature, but is specified by it. Thus we speak of the human personality, or of the angelic personality; hence it implies a contradiction for the same personality of one nature to terminate another. On the contrary, the

[2] Cf. IIIa, q. 3, a. 1, ad 2, quaestiuncula 3a.

divine personality because of its infinity, as St. Thomas says,[3] is above both genus and species and contains formally and eminently the power of all possible personalities.

Second Article

WHETHER IT IS BEFITTING TO THE DIVINE NATURE TO ASSUME

State of the question. The meaning of the title is, as Cajetan remarks, whether *de facto* it is true that the Deity, or rather God, assumed the human nature.[4]

It seems not to be true, because the union did not take place in the nature, but in the person; also because to assume in this manner could be said of the three persons.

Nevertheless, St. Augustine or rather St. Fulgentius, who is quoted in the counterargument, says that the divine nature took our nature.

Conclusion. In the strictest sense a person is said to assume inasmuch as it is both principle and term of the assumption. In a secondary sense, however, it can be said that the Deity or God assumed the human nature inasmuch as the Deity was the principle of the assumptive act but not its term. The whole article must be read.[5]

All the other articles of this question, on the supposition of the real possibility, even of the very fact of the incarnation of the Word, examine what else was either possible or impossible. I say: "on the supposition of the real possibility of the incarnation of the Word," which, as already stated, is neither demonstrated by reason alone, nor can be disproved, but is persuaded and defended against those denying it, and is firmly held by faith.

Third Article

WHETHER THE NATURE ABSTRACTED FROM THE PERSONALITY CAN ASSUME

State of the question. The meaning of the title is: Can the divine nature assume a nature different from its own, if by God we understand, in the way the pagans and Jews imagine Him to exist, without personal relations and without persons, as our Catholic faith acknowledges to be in Him?

[3] *Ibid.,* ad 1.
[4] *Ibid.,* ad 3.
[5] *Ibid.,* ad 1, ad 2, ad 3.

It seems that the divine nature cannot so assume; because, as stated above, it befits the nature to assume because of the person, and because the union took place not in the nature, but in the person.

Reply. It is affirmed, nevertheless, that the divine nature can assume our nature.

Proof. It is taken from the counterargument of this article, from the argumentative part and from the reply to the second objection. The reasons given are: 1. In this hypothesis, God's omnipotence, by which the Incarnation took place, would remain. 2. There would also remain the one personality of God as the Jews understand, which could be the term of the assumption.[6]

In God, the Deity and God are identical, or in God whereby it is and what is are the same; for God's essence is His self-existing being.[7]

First doubt. Is it something absolute or something relative that immediately terminates the human nature of Christ?

Reply. It is something relative that immediately and proximately terminates Christ's human nature, namely, the personality of the Word, which is constituted by relative subsistence, or by the subsisting relation of sonship, as explained in the treatise on the Trinity. The divine relations are subsisting relations, inasmuch as their *inexistence* (*esse in*) is substantial and not accidental as in created predicamental relations, for example, in created paternity and created sonship.[8]

Proof. The Eleventh Council of Toledo in its profession of faith says: "Neither the Holy Spirit nor God the Father, but only the person of the Son took flesh." [9] But if the Word were to terminate the human nature formally and proximately by a common and absolute subsistence, then the Father and the Holy Spirit equally with the Son, would have been incarnate.

Second doubt. Could the triune God assume the human nature primarily on account of absolute subsistence, and only secondarily on account of relative subsistences?

Reply. The triune God could have assumed absolutely our human nature, because this absolute subsistence "could be the principle and term of this assumption," as stated by St. Thomas in this article.[10] For the reason why God subsists in His own nature, can be the reason

[6] Cf. ad 2.

[7] Cf. Ia, q. 3, a. 3.

[8] Cf. IIIa, q. 3, a. 2, 4.

[9] Denz., no. 285.

[10] Cf. IIIa, q. 3, a. 3, ad 1, ad 2.

why He subsists in a different nature. But absolute and common subsistence could be the reason for His subsistence in a different nature.

Third doubt. What is the difference between the incommunicability of absolute subsistence and of relative subsistence?

Reply. The first incommunicability is not within the Trinity, but only external to it. The second incommunicability is both internal and external to the Trinity. Common and absolute subsistence does not formally attribute incommunicability internally to the Deity, for the Deity is communicated to the Son and to the Holy Ghost. On the contrary, the personality of the Father is not communicated to the Son. But God by reason of His common and absolute subsistence is incommunicable externally, in this sense that He is by Himself separately existing, really and essentially distinct from the world. St. Thomas says: "A person is said to be incommunicable inasmuch as it cannot be predicated of several supposita." [11]

What the philosopher means by saying that God is personal, is that He is the separately existing being, distinct from every creature, intelligent and free and so is externally incommunicable. When theologians speak of the three divine persons, what they first of all have in mind is internal incommunicability. Thus the Father communicates the whole divine nature to the Son, but not His personality, which is the subsistent relation of paternity in opposition to filiation.[12]

Objection. The Fathers and councils never mention this absolute subsistence, which seems to have been discovered by Cajetan.

Reply. They never referred to it because there was no occasion of doing so to refute errors against it such as Nestorianism and Monophysitism, which had not yet arisen. It sufficed to exclude union in the nature and affirm the union in the person of the Word, as recorded in revelation. Absolute subsistence was not discovered by Cajetan, for St. Thomas explicitly refers to it in this third article.

[11] *Ibid.,* a. 1, ad 2. See also Penido, *Le rôle de l'analogie en théologie dogmatique,* pp. 337 f.

[12] The Deity is not communicated internally inasmuch as it is terminated by paternity. Thus in the figure that represents the Holy Trinity, in the equilateral triangle, the first angle that is formed communicates indeed to the second and third angles its superficies, but not itself, nor its superficies so far as this latter is terminated by itself. Thus it is that this same superficies is terminated by the three angles that are really distinct from one another and are not really distinct from their common superficies.

Fourth Article

WHETHER ONE PERSON WITHOUT ANOTHER CAN ASSUME A CREATED NATURE

State of the question. The difficulty, as presented by the first objection, is that assumption, being a certain external operation, pertains to all three persons, who operate externally by a common omnipotence. Thus it has been shown [13] that the Trinity of persons cannot be known from creatures by natural reason; for "the creative power of God is common to the whole Trinity." [14]

Reply. Nevertheless it is of faith that only the Son of God became incarnate, neither the Father nor the Holy Spirit. The Eleventh Council of Toledo says: "We believe that of these three persons, only the person of the Son . . . true man . . . assumed [our nature]." [15]

The body of the article contains the solution of the difficulty arising from the definition of assumption, or to assume.

Assumption implies two things: the act of assuming and the term of the assumption. But revelation says that only the person of the Son is the term of the assumption. Therefore assumption, considered as the term, applies only to the person of the Son, although considered as an act, it is common to the three persons.

Thus we said that the Father and the Holy Ghost united the human nature with the Word, but They did not assume it in the sense of term.

Fifth Article

WHETHER EACH OF THE DIVINE PERSONS COULD HAVE ASSUMED HUMAN NATURE

State of the question. The difficulty is, as stated in the second objection, that by the divine Incarnation, men acquired the adoption of sons, which is a participated likeness of natural sonship, which applies only to the Son. Therefore it seems that only the Son could be incarnate. Moreover, to be incarnate is to be sent, which cannot apply to the Father, who cannot be sent by any person, since the other two persons proceed from Him.

Reply. Nevertheless it is affirmed, that each of the persons could

[13] *Summa theol.,* Ia, q. 32, a. 2.
[14] *Ibid.,* a. 1.
[15] Denz., no. 282. See also no. 422, profession of faith enjoined upon the Waldensians.

have assumed human nature. For to assume another nature is befitting to God because of His omnipotence, as the principle of the assumption, and because of His person, as the term of the assumption. But each of the divine persons is omnipotent and has His own personality. Therefore each of the divine persons could have assumed human nature.

Reply to first objection. It was fitting, if the Father became incarnate, for Him as man to have been the Son of man, for example, the son of David; for this would be according to difference of natures, and would not result in confusion of realities, but at most of names.

Reply to second objection. It contains a beautiful scriptural text concerning adoptive sonship, which is a certain participated likeness of natural sonship. But if the Father became incarnate, we would have received this adoptive sonship from Him, as coming from the principle of natural sonship;[16] but farther on in this question, it is shown that it was more fitting for the Son to have become incarnate.[17]

Reply to third objection. The Father, who is innascible as to eternal birth, could have been born temporally as man if He had become incarnate. In such case the Incarnation would not have been a mission. Thus the Father dwells in the just, as the Son and the Holy Ghost do, but He is not sent, and so He comes without being sent; whereas the other two persons are sent by Him. So the pope sends His legate, but he himself is not sent, but comes.

Sixth Article

WHETHER SEVERAL DIVINE PERSONS CAN ASSUME ONE AND THE SAME INDIVIDUAL NATURE

State of the question. The meaning is: Can the three persons assume this human nature, terminating it proximately and immediately by their own relations?

The difficulty is that it could not then be said the human nature is assumed by one man or by several men, because there would be one human nature and three divine persons who possess it.

Reply. Yet St. Thomas affirms the possibility of the three persons assuming one and the same human nature. It is the commonly accepted teaching, but it was attacked by Scotus.

[16] The entire reply should be read.
[17] Cf. ad 8.

Indirect proof. It is taken from the counterargument of this article, and proceeds by way of analogy; for just as the divine nature is common to the three persons, so likewise the human individualized nature can be common to Them.

A more direct and proper proof is found in the argumentative part of this article. It may be expressed by the following syllogism.

The divine persons do not exclude one another from communicating in the same nature, since they terminate together the same divine nature.

But in the mystery of the Incarnation, the whole reason of the deed is the power of the doer, as Augustine says.

Therefore in passing judgment on the act, we must take into special consideration the condition of the person assuming, who does not exclude the other two persons from communicating in the same nature.

There is no repugnance on the part of the human nature, because it can be assumed, not by reason of its natural limited power, but because of its obediential power, which extends to all that is not essentially repugnant.

What is truly impossible is for a divine person to assume a human person, for then there would be two persons in one person.

Reply to first objection. It contains the solution of the difficulty proposed in the objection, namely, that, granting the hypothesis, it would be true to say that the three divine persons were one man, because of the one human nature, just as we say that they are one God, because of the one divine nature, which is one numerically, without any multiplication and division.[18]

Seventh Article

WHETHER ONE DIVINE PERSON CAN ASSUME TWO HUMAN NATURES

State of the question. This question is posited, as the preceding questions are, so as to make it known more clearly in what the mystery of the Incarnation consists on the part of the person assuming.

The difficulty is that there would be one suppositum for two natures of the same species, for example, the same divine person would be Peter and John. Another difficulty is that it could not then be said

[18] Consult the Thomist theologians for the solution of the objections raised by Scotus.

that the person incarnate is one man, because He would have two human natures; nor several men, because several men have distinct supposita. It is not apparent how these two human natures could be united to each other, one of these natures being perhaps in one part of the world, and the other in another part.

Reply. St. Thomas affirms, however, the possibility of such an assumption.

Indirect proof. It is taken from the counterargument of this article, and may be expressed by the following syllogism.

Whatever the Father can do externally, the Son also can do. But after the Incarnation, the Father can assume a human nature distinct from that assumed by the Son. Therefore the Son can assume a human nature distinct from the one He assumed.

Direct proof. This same principle is again invoked, as in the following syllogism.

The power of a divine person, both as regards the principle in the assumption and as regards the term of the assumption, is infinite; nor can it be restricted to what has been created. But a divine person would be restricted in power if He could assume only one human nature. Therefore a divine person can assume more than one human nature.

Some have objected that such two human natures would interpenetrate.

Reply. To establish the truth of this conclusion, it is not necessary for the divine person to assume these two natures in the same place; for divine immensity makes it possible for any of the divine persons to assume one of the human natures in Rome, and the other in some place far away from this city. Such action involves no absurdity.[19]

Reply to first objection. "There can be a numerical multitude on the part of the nature, on account of the division of matter, without distinction of supposita."

Reply to second objection. There would still be one man, and not several, because there is only one suppositum. In fact, one divine person could assume many individual human natures, and there would be no pantheism in this for there would be no confusion of the divine nature with the human nature; but all these natures would be impeccable. Toletus gave us a good rule to follow, one that is taken from the teaching of St. Thomas. He says: "For the multiplication of con-

[19] Cf. ad 3, which should read: "It would not be necessary (*non oporteret*)," according to the Leonine edition.

crete substantive names both kinds of multitude are required, namely, of supposita and of forms; the absence of one results in unity."[20]

Eighth Article

WHETHER IT WAS MORE FITTING THAT THE PERSON OF THE SON RATHER THAN ANY OTHER DIVINE PERSON SHOULD ASSUME HUMAN NATURE

State of the question. It seems that it is not, because the effect of the Incarnation is a kind of second creation, which befits the Father, inasmuch as creative power is appropriated to Him. Besides, the Incarnation is ordained to the remission of sins, which is attributed to the Holy Ghost.

Conclusion. Yet it was most fitting that the person of the Son should become incarnate, and this for three reasons.

1) Because of the principle of the union. All things were made by the Word, as by the exemplary cause. Therefore it was fitting that all things be restored by the Word. Thus the craftsman, by the intelligible form or concept of his art, whereby he fashioned his handiwork, restores it when it has fallen into ruin.

2) The end of the union. It was fitting that He who is the natural Son of God, should make us adoptive sons.[21] He received by eternal generation the whole divine nature without its being multiplied or divided; but we receive a participation of the divine nature, or the radical principle of strictly divine operations, and finally a participation of the beatific vision.[22]

3) Reparation for sin. An inordinate desire for knowledge had resulted in the sin and spiritual death of man. Hence it was fitting that reparation be made by Him to whom wisdom is attributed.

St. Paul says: "[God] predestinated [us] to be made conformable to the image of His Son, that He might be the first-born among many brethren."[23] St. Thomas in commenting on this text[24] shows clearly

[20] Cf. *Summa theol.,* Ia, q. 36, a. 4, ad 2; q. 39, a. 3; IIIa, q. 3, a. 6, ad 1; a. 7, ad 2.

[21] This analogy enables us to see more clearly that adoptive sonship is a certain participated likeness of eternal natural sonship. See a. 5, ad 2, of this question. St. Paul expresses the same analogy in the following text: "God predestinated us to be made conformable to the image of His Son, that He might be the first-born among many brethren" (Rom. 8:29).

[22] Read the text of St. Thomas, the second reason.

[23] Rom. 8:29.

[24] *Com. in Ep. ad Rom.*

that adoptive sonship is a participated likeness of natural and eternal sonship. Adoption is generally known as the legal acceptance of an unrelated person as son.[25] To adopt is to admit someone freely as heir to one's estate.[26] It befits the whole Trinity to adopt men, "although in God, to beget belongs to the person of the Father, yet to produce any effect in creatures is common to the whole Trinity, by reason of the oneness of Their nature; because, where there is one nature, there must be one power and one operation." [27] The adopted son of God is not strictly begotten, but made; yet sometimes it may be said that he is begotten, by reason of spiritual regeneration, which is gratuitous and not natural. Hence it befits the whole Trinity to adopt men as sons.

Nevertheless St. Thomas says: "Adoptive sonship is a certain likeness of the eternal sonship. . . . Now man is likened to the splendor of the eternal Son by reason of the light of grace which is attributed to the Holy Ghost. Therefore adoption, though common to the whole Trinity, is appropriated to the Father as its author; to the Son as its exemplar, to the Holy Ghost as imprinting on us the likeness of this exemplar." [28] It is easy to assign similarities and differences between the divine, natural, eternal sonship and adoptive sonship; for the Son of God is by nature begotten, not made; He is light of light, true God of true God; possesses the whole Deity that can neither be divided nor multiplied. The adopted son is made, not begotten, but he is spiritually born of God by grace, which is a participation of the divine nature, and this radically disposes him for strictly divine acts, namely, to see God face to face and love Him for all eternity.

Recapitulation. What has been discussed in this third question will enable us to acquire a better understanding of the hypostatic union in all its aspects so far considered.

Therefore it has been established that in the strictest sense it befits a divine person to assume a created nature, that is, take it to Himself (a. 1 and 2). Nevertheless, God as conceived by Jews and Monotheists, not consisting of three persons who are related to one another, could assume a created nature, because He is omnipotent, and He could

[25] Cf. *supra,* a. 5, ad 2.
[26] *Ibid.,* IIIa, q. 23, a. 1.
[27] *Ibid.,* a. 2.
[28] *Ibid.,* ad 3. Cf. Ia, q. 93, a. 4, ad 2; IIa IIae, q. 45, a. 6; IIIa, q. 3, a. 5, ad 2; a. 8; q. 39, a. 8, ad 3; q. 45, a. 4.

terminate this nature by absolute subsistence, which is common to the three divine persons.

It follows from this, as has been stated, that anyone of the divine persons could assume the human nature. In fact, the three divine persons could assume one and the same human nature, just as they have one and the same divine nature.

Finally, one divine person could assume two human natures, because the power of the person on the part of the principle and the term of the assumption is infinite. But although these divers hypotheses are possible, it was more fitting that the Son of God rather than the Father or the Holy Ghost should assume the human nature of Christ.

CHAPTER VI

QUESTION 4

The Mode of the Union on the Part of the Human Nature Assumed

WE must now discuss the mode of the union not on the part of the person assuming, but on the part of what was assumed; and here two things must be considered.

1) What the Word assumed:

a) The human nature itself (q. 4).

b) Of the parts of the human nature, which refutes Docetism and Apollinarianism (q. 5).

c) Of the order of this assumption, for example, whether the soul was assumed before the flesh (q. 6).

2) What things were co-assumed; (a) of perfections, where the habitual grace of Christ, His knowledge and power are discussed; (b) of defects, or of those defects which Christ voluntarily accepted for our satisfaction, such as passibility of the body, death, in which Christ's impeccability is discussed, as also His propassions. (q. 7–15)

Thus the treatise on the hypostatic union is complete, since we find discussed: (a) the union itself (q. 2); (b) the person assuming (q. 3); (c) the nature assumed, both as to its parts and those things co-assumed (q. 4–15). Afterward there will be a discussion of the consequences of the union, in themselves and in their relations both to the Father and to us.

The fourth question contains six articles, treating of the human nature in itself, both in its relation to human personality, which Christ did not have, and in its relation to individuals of the human nature.

First Article

WHETHER HUMAN NATURE WAS MORE ASSUMABLE BY THE SON OF GOD THAN ANY OTHER NATURE

State of the question. The inquiry concerns human nature as assumable, not according to its natural passive power nor according to its obediential power,[1] but according to its fitness.[2] The more common opinion among theologians affirms with St. Thomas [3] that according to God's absolute power any other nature is assumable. The discussion here concerns only its fitness.

This question is of some importance in determining whether besides the obediential power there is a fitness attached to the nature, but not necessarily so, for example, a fitness of assumption in the human nature rather than in the angelic.

First objection. The difficulty is that God's absolute power is not limited to one nature; for just as there is no such thing actually as the best of all possible worlds, so there is no created nature that is more fitted for the hypostatic union.

Second objection. The difficulty is that also in irrational creatures there is a trace of God's image.

Third objection. In the angelic nature we find a more perfect likeness of God than in the human nature, and there is need of redemption for angels that are sinners.

Fourth objection. Finally the whole universe is more capable of assumption than the human nature.

Conclusion. It was more fitting, says St. Thomas, for the human nature to be assumed by the Word, than any other nature.

Authoritative proof. This fittingness is intimated in various passages

[1] Cf. IIIa, q. 1, a. 3, ad 3.

[2] The obediential power in itself implies only a non-repugnance to elevation, because God's power to elevate is limited only by repugnance. Thus in every individualized human nature, such as in Peter and Paul, there is an obediential power for the hypostatic union, and this applies even to the angelic nature; but besides the obediential power there can be a certain fitness in the nature. But besides the obediential power in our intellect to be raised to the supernatural order and hence to the beatific vision, there is a certain fitness in the intellect, which is not absolutely the same as the obediential power or capacity of being raised to this order. This point is not sufficiently taken note of by some theologians, when they read in the works of St. Thomas (Ia q. 12, a. 1) of the natural desire of seeing God in His essence.

[3] *Com. in III Sent.*, d. 2, q. 1, a. 1.

of Scripture. Thus the Wisdom of God is represented as saying: "My delights were to be with the children of men." [4] Similarly St. Paul writes: "For it became Him, for whom are all things, and by whom are all things, who had brought many children into glory, to perfect the author of their salvation, by His passion. . . . For nowhere doth He take hold of the angels, but of the seed of Abraham He taketh hold. Wherefore it behooved Him in all things to be made like unto His brethren, that He might become a merciful and faithful high priest before God, that He might be a propitiation for the sins of the people." [5] Christ had to be both priest and victim because no other victim was worthy of fulfilling this role.

Theological proof. It may be reduced to the following syllogism.

This greater fitness may be viewed both according to the dignity and the necessity or need of the assumable nature.

But the human is more worthy than the irrational nature since it can attain to union with the Word by knowledge and love.[6] Moreover, it needed reparation, since it was subjected to original sin, which is not true of the angels, for all did not sin, and those who did are already confirmed in their sin and incapable of redemption. Therefore it was more fitting for the human nature than any other nature to be assumed by the Word. This conclusion must be understood in the sense given by St. Thomas at the end of the argumentative part of this article, where he says: "Hence it follows that only human nature was assumable."

Moreover, as St. Thomas remarks in another of his works,[7] the human nature is a quasi-compendium of the universe, a microcosm, inasmuch as it contains within itself being, as in minerals, life as in the lower forms of living animals, intelligence as in the angels, although in not so perfect a way.

The solution of the difficulties raised in the objections confirms this last observation of St. Thomas.

Reply to first objection. Here it is shown that besides the obediential power, which includes everything that is not in itself repugnant to

[4] Prov. 8:31.

[5] Heb. 2:10, 16 f.

[6] Wherefore only a rational nature or intellectual nature is capable of the merit and satisfaction that are required in offering the sacrifice of redemption, and this sacrifice had to be offered by one whose nature is specifically the same as the human race that had to be redeemed.

[7] *Com. in III Sent.,* d. 2, q. 1, a. 1.

reason, there can be a certain fitness or congruity in the human nature for its being assumed by the Word in the hypostatic union, a fitness that is not found either in stones, plants, a lamb, or a dove. Hence St. Thomas says in this reply: "Therefore a creature is said to be not assumable, not as if we withdrew anything from the power of God, but in order to show the condition of the creature which has no capability for this." Therefore this capability, which is in neither stone nor dove, is not this obediential power for assumption, which is in either a stone or in any animal, for example, in the most spotless lamb.

As Cajetan remarks, St. Thomas did not ask whether the Word can assume the nature of a stone. There is nothing intrinsically impossible in this according to God's purely absolute power, but there would be no end or purpose in doing this. Thus God can by His purely absolute power annihilate the Blessed Virgin Mary, but there is no reason for doing so on the part of the end in view. Therefore this is repugnant, if not by God's purely absolute power, at least by His ordained power, either ordinary or extraordinary.

Yet there is truly in the nature of either a stone, a lamb, or a dove a non-repugnance or obediential power for the hypostatic union, although there is no capability in the sense of congruity.

From this reply to the first objection, it seems to follow that the capability or fitness of our nature to be elevated to the beatific vision is not this obediential power, which of itself requires nothing else but a non-repugnance to this elevation, inasmuch as God can do whatever is not repugnant. In fact, as will be stated farther on, there is in the most holy soul of Christ the obediential power for a greater degree of the light of glory.[8] The obediential power of our intellect is in itself unrestricted, because our intellect by God's absolute power, can always be raised to a higher degree of the light of glory, and our will to a higher degree of charity.

There remains this obediential power in the nature of the damned for being raised to the beatific vision, but it is no longer any fittingness in them.

Reply to second objection. "The irrational creature which falls short of the union with God by operation has no fitness to be united with Him in personal being."

Reply to third objection. Concerning the reply to this third objec-

[8] Cf. IIIa, q. 10, a. 4, ad 3.

tion, which must be real, Cajetan observes against Scotus, that for St. Thomas personality is something positive and real that is distinct from the individualized nature, for instance, from Michaelness, because St. Thomas says: "In this way, nothing pre-existing would be corrupted in it," [9] if God, by producing a new angelic nature, were to unite it to Himself.

In this same reply, it is pointed out that the bad angels fell irreparably, though not indeed absolutely, but according to the way that is consistent with divine providence, as already explained by St. Thomas, for, when asking whether the will of the demons is confirmed in evil, he says: "The angel's free will is flexible to either opposite before the choice, but not after." [10] This means that the angel's choice elicited by means of intuitive and simultaneous knowledge of those things that must be considered in the object, is irrevocable, and thus it participates in the immutability of the divine choice, which is both most free and absolutely immutable. On the contrary, our choice is elicited by means of abstractive and discursive knowledge, which only gradually acquires the knowledge of all those things that must be considered. Hence it is revocable, inasmuch as after the choice we can consider certain new things not previously considered.[11]

Hence man is capable of redemption, but not the angel. Moreover, the first man was tempted by the devil and fell, whereas the devil fell solely by his own will. Hence the human nature is more worthy of compassion than the nature of the fallen angel.

First doubt. Can an irrational nature, such as that of a lamb or dove, be united befittingly with the person of the Word?

Reply. Several theologians give an affirmative answer, just as it was not unbecoming for the Word incarnate to be scourged, spit upon, and to die. In fact, during the three days of death, the Word remained hypostatically united to the corpse, not personally, but subsistentially. But these reasons do not rest on solid grounds, for the Word was united to the corpse of Christ, only because it was previously united to His human nature, and, if the Word was scourged and crucified, this was meritorious for our redemption. Whereas there is no com-

[9] Cf. ad 3.

[10] Cf. Ia, q. 64, a. 2.

[11] But the devil, after his confirmation in sin, cannot consider anything previously not considered about the sin. There is only one way for him to return to God, which is by humility and obedience, and pride makes him unwilling to accept this way, even though it were offered to him.

parison in the above-mentioned hypothesis, because the dove and the lamb are incapable of meriting and satisfying.

Second doubt. St. Thomas says in various passages that suppositum and nature are the same in the angels; [12] yet in his reply here [13] he holds that the angelic nature is assumable, which cannot be unless it is distinct from the suppositum.

Reply. Cajetan, Medina, Alvarez, Gonet, and Billuart say that St. Thomas in the passage cited above [14] means that the angelic nature is not distinct from its individualizing notes; but he holds that the angel has its own subsistence or personality that is distinct from its nature, which it would lose if the angelic nature were united with the Word. On several occasions St. Thomas says that there is a difference between what is (suppositum), and being (existence).[15] For it is manifest that Michael has not only his nature or Michaelness, but also his being and accidents, such as successive intellections and volitions.

Second Article

WHETHER THE SON OF GOD ASSUMED A PERSON

State of the question. The difficulty is that the Son of God assumed an individualized nature and thus it appears that He assumed this particular man or person.

Reply. Nevertheless, the answer is that He did not assume a person, which is of faith against Nestorius,[16] inasmuch as the Church defined the union to be subsistential, so that there is only one person in Christ. the counterargument gives a quotation from St. Fulgentius, under the name of St. Augustine.

The theological explanation is given in the body of the article, which may be explained by the following syllogism. What is assumed must be presupposed to the assumption. But a person in human nature is not presupposed to assumption, but is rather the term of the assumption. Therefore the human person is not assumed; but the person of the Word assumed to Himself the human nature.

Indirect proof of minor. If the person were presupposed, then it

[12] *Summa theol.,* Ia, q. 3, a. 3.
[13] *Ibid.,* IIIa, q. 4, a. 1, ad 3.
[14] Cf. Ia, q. 3, a. 3.
[15] *Contra Gentes,* Bk. II, chap. 52.
[16] Denz., no. 217.

was either corrupted, in which case its assumption was to no purpose; or it remained after the union, and then there were two persons in Christ, which is contrary to revelation, and then the union would not be personal, but accidental, as Nestorius contended.

Reply to first objection. The Son of God assumed an individualized human nature, or a singular human nature, namely, this human nature of Christ.

Reply to second objection. It is pointed out that "the nature assumed did not have its own personality through the loss of anything pertaining to the perfection of the human nature, but through the addition of something which is above human nature, which is union with a divine person." Concerning this difficulty, St. Thomas had said: "It is a greater dignity to exist in something nobler than oneself than to exist by oneself." [17]

Reply to third objection. St. Thomas says: "The divine person by His union hindered the human nature from having its own personality." Therefore St. Thomas considers personality to be something positive, real, and distinct from the nature. It is not identical with existence, because existence is a contingent predicate of any created person, whose formal constituent is personality. No created person, even created personality, is his or its existence. Thus St. Thomas often says that in every creature there is a difference between *quod est* and *esse,* namely, between suppositum and existence.[18]

Concerning Cajetan's great commentary, it suffices to note that he shows there is a distinction even between the individualized nature and subsistence. He says: "The whole force of the argument consists in this, that the constituent of a thing, in this respect, is that a being intrinsically and primarily susceptive of real entity, must be some reality. But this man, in this respect, differs from this humanity, because he includes in himself something by which he is primarily and intrinsically susceptive of some real entity that is repugnant to this human nature. Therefore he includes in himself a reality that constitutes him in being, by which he differs from this human nature.

[17] *Summa theol.,* IIIa, q. 2, a. 2, ad 2. Cf. Cajetan, who in his famous commentary on this article gave his interpretation of St. Thomas' teaching on personality. We have already (*supra,* q. 2, a. 2) expounded the doctrine of St. Thomas on personality, and there is no need of again referring to it.

[18] *Contra Gentes,* Bk. II, chap. 2: "In intellectual substances (and in every creature), there is a difference between existence and what is."

But he differs only in personal being, whereby this man is a hypostasis or person, which this human nature is not. Therefore the person of this man adds some reality that intrinsically constitutes him a human person, which this human nature is not."[19] This man is what is, whereas his individualized humanity is that whereby he is constituted in a certain species.

Wherefore St. Thomas says in the present article: "If created personality were presupposed to assumption, then it must either have been corrupted . . . or there would be two persons." And also in his reply to the third objection, he also says: "The divine person by His union hindered the human nature from having its personality." Hence Cajetan's interpretation, by which he shows that created personality is a substantial mode, truly has its foundation in this text quoted from St. Thomas.

More briefly, Cajetan's whole argument may be reduced to the following syllogism. The created suppositum differs from the nature inasmuch as it is what is, namely, the real subject of existence, which is attributed to it contingently. But that whereby anything is a real and not merely a logical subject of existence is something real, distinct from this nature and from existence, which is predicated contingently of a created person already formally constituted as a person. Therefore the created suppositum is something real that differs both from the individual nature and from existence.

Hence the whole of Cajetan's interpretation has its foundation in the legitimate transition from the common sense notion of personality to its philosophical notion, namely, from its nominal definition to its real definition, or from the Christian acceptation to its theological notion, as Cajetan himself remarks.[20]

Cajetan's opinion asserts only what is required for the verification of the following three arguments of common sense.

1) This man, Peter, is not his human nature, which is attributed to him as an essential part, and the part is not predicated of the whole; for the whole is not the part, but has the part.

2) This man, Peter, is not his existence, which is attributed to him contingently and not essentially. This means that it constitutes neither the essence nor personality of Peter, but is really distinct from them.

[19] *Com. in IIIam,* q. 4, a. 2, no. 7.
[20] *Ibid.,* no. 8.

Thus in every creature there is a real difference between suppositum and existence.[21]

3) This man, Peter, is existing, namely, it is the same suppositum that is existing. In this judgment the word "is" affirms real identity between subject and predicate, which means that the predicate is identical with the suppositum. Therefore subsistence is that whereby anything is what; and as a substantial mode, it is distinct both from nature, whereby anything is constituted in a certain species, and from existence, whereby anything is established outside nothing and its causes.[22]

Likewise, applying this doctrine to Christ, in accordance with revelation, we say: "This man Jesus is God,"[23] meaning that this man is the same suppositum that is God, or is the same person. But the divine personality of Christ is distinct from the human nature He assumed.

Doubt. Could the Word have assumed a nature terminated by its own subsistence, this latter remaining.

Reply. The answer is in the negative. The reason is that it implies a contradiction for the same nature to subsist and not to subsist in a suppositum different from its own.

Objection. The divine nature is terminated simultaneously by the three personalities. Therefore, in like manner, the human nature could be terminated simultaneously by two personalities.

Reply. The comparison does not apply, for the three divine personalities are not foreign to but belong properly to the divine nature,[24] and from several subsistences that belong properly to the divine nature there follows one effect which is to subsist and be terminated in itself, although in divers ways. On the contrary, from a subsistence proper to a person and one foreign to it there follows a double effect that

[21] *Contra Gentes,* Bk. II, chap. 52.

[22] Objection. But Peter is not his personality.

Reply. I concede the statement. But personality is a most formal part of Peter, formally constituting Peter as a person, thus enabling him to receive existence.

[23] Matt. 1:21 f. Cf. *infra,* q. 16, a. 1.

[24] These personalities or subsistent relations are only virtually distinct from the divine nature or essence. See *God, His Existence,* II, 7 f. Also *The One God,* pp. 303–5. There is also a virtual distinction between God's absolute subsistence and the relative subsistences of the divine persons. The human nature was united with the relative subsistence of the Word, for, as the absolute subsistence of God cannot denote incommunicability of perseity to the other persons, all three persons would have assumed the human nature, which is contrary to revelation. (Tr.)

is repugnant, inasmuch as the person subsists in itself and not in another, and also subsists in another and not in itself.

Third Article

WHETHER THE DIVINE PERSON ASSUMED A MAN

Is it strictly true to say that God assumed a man?

Reply. It is not, because man is the name of a person that signifies the human nature as subsisting. But God did not assume a created person. Hence, in the strict sense, it is not true to say that the Word assumed a man. After the Incarnation, however, it is true to say that the Word is man.[25] Similarly, the proposition, "God is man," and also the proposition, "man is God," are true, because of the unity of the person.[26] The word "is" expresses real identity between subject and predicate, and this identity is identity of suppositum or person, which means that this man Jesus is the same being or suppositum that is God.

Reply to first objection. If the Fathers at times said that the Word assumed a man, this word "man" must not be taken in the strict sense of the term.

Fourth Article

WHETHER THE SON OF GOD OUGHT TO HAVE ASSUMED HUMAN NATURE ABSTRACTED FROM ALL INDIVIDUALS

This article is inserted here to refute the error of certain Platonists, who admitted that the Son of God ought to have assumed such a nature.

It is denied that the Son of God assumed a nature abstracted from individuals, because such a nature has only mental existence,[27] and also because by the very fact that the nature is assumed by some person, it belongs properly to this person. Moreover, only common and

[25] Cf. *infra,* q. 16, a. 1.

[26] *Ibid.*

[27] The human nature can be considered apart from its individualizing notes, but it cannot exist separated from them; for it implies common matter, that is, bones and flesh, which can exist only if they are these particular bones and this particular flesh. (Cf. *Met.,* Bk. VII, chap. 15, no. 2.) On the contrary, being, one, true, good, do not claim in their definition common matter, and can exist apart from singular sensible things.

universal operations can be attributed to the common nature, by which a person does not merit, because merit pertains to a particular circumstance and time. Finally, even though the human nature were to exist apart from sensible things, as Plato contended, the assumption of this kind of separated human nature would not be fitting, because the Son of God assumed the human nature so that He could be seen by men.

Reply to first objection. Nevertheless, it remains true that Christ is "the universal cause of human salvation," for this universality is not of predication, but of causation.

Fifth Article

WHETHER THE SON OF GOD OUGHT TO HAVE ASSUMED HUMAN NATURE IN ALL INDIVIDUALS

Reply. It is denied that the human nature should be assumed by the Word in all individuals: 1. because the multitude of supposita which are natural to human nature, would thus be taken away; 2. because this would be derogatory to the divinity of the incarnate Son of God since He is the first-born of many brethren according to the human nature, even as He is the first-born of every creature according to the divine nature. Finally, divine wisdom demands this subordination, for St. Paul says: "For all are yours, and you are Christ's, and Christ is God's."[28] It must be noted that, if the Son of God had assumed the individualized nature of all human beings, then all human beings would have been impeccable.

Sixth Article

WHETHER IT WAS FITTING FOR THE SON OF GOD TO ASSUME HUMAN NATURE OF THE STOCK OF ADAM

The Son of God could, indeed, have assumed the human nature created anew, just as Adam was created.

Reply. The answer is, nevertheless, that it was fitting for the Son of God to assume the human nature of the stock of Adam, and this for three reasons: 1. so that He might satisfy for the race that had sinned; 2. because the conqueror of the devil should come from the race conquered by the devil; 3. to manifest God's omnipotence that

[28] I Cor. 3:22.

raised a weakened and corrupt nature to such virtue and dignity. God permits evil only for a greater good.

Hence in the Roman Breviary, the Church recites: "That flesh hath purged, what flesh hath stained." [29] The Scripture says: "Who can make him clean that is conceived of unclean seed. Is it not Thou who only art?" [30] Thus there are sinners in Christ's genealogy, although He is separated from sinners in this respect.

Reply to first objection. Christ's innocence is the more wonderful in this, that, although He assumed His nature from a mass tainted by sin, it was endowed with such purity.

Reply to second objection. It was not fitting for the Word to assume the particular nature of Adam, who was a sinner; because Christ, who had come to cleanse all sinners, had to be separated from all who sinned.

Third objection. The difficulty is this: "If the Son of God wished to assume human nature from sinners, He ought rather to have assumed it from the Gentiles than from the stock of Abraham, who was just."

Reply to third objection. Christ, indeed, had to be like sinners in His assumed nature, but He also had to be separated from them as regards sin. Hence it was fitting that between the first sinner and Christ, some just men should intervene, who were to be in certain respects conspicuous types of Christ's future holiness, and these began in Abraham.

But why the Jewish race was chosen in preference to any of the Gentile nations depends on God's absolute free choice, just as the predestination of Christ, of His Blessed Mother, of Abraham, Isaac, Jacob, and the prophets are so dependent. The mystery of predestination is apparent in the whole course of Jewish history, since one is chosen in preference to another, for instance, Abel to Cain, Noe to those who died in the flood, Isaac to another son of Abraham, Jacob to Esau; and so it is with other descendants. It must be noted that the merits of the elect are not the cause of their predestination, because they are its effects. This is especially evident both as regards Christ's predestination to divine natural sonship, and the predestination of the Blessed Virgin Mary to divine maternity.

[29] Feast of Ascension, Hymn for Matins.

[30] Job 14:4.

SUPPLEMENTARY QUESTIONS

First doubt. Does the human nature united with the Word still have an innate desire for its own subsistence?

Reply. The common opinion of the Thomists, especially of Cajetan and John of St. Thomas, is that it has no such desire as a reflected act (*actus secundus*), because it is perfected by a more perfect subsistence, which contains formally and eminently absolutely whatever there would be in its own subsistence. Therefore the natural desire of the assumed human nature rests satisfied in the higher subsistence.[31]

Second doubt. Can incomplete substances and accidents be assumed immediately by the Word, such as prime matter, non-subsistent forms, for instance, the substantial form of bread, or of another body?

Reply. The query is denied, because these incomplete realities are intrinsically incapable of having their own subsistences. Thus prime matter, the substantial form of bread, and accidents cannot be assumed except mediately, that is, through the mediation of substance, whose parts they are, or in which they inhere. But the rational soul separated from the body, which is capable of having its own subsistence and existence, is assumable.

Corollary. Integral parts of the human body, such as the hand, the head, feet, so long as they are united to the whole, cannot be assumed unless the whole is assumed. But if these parts are separated by death, they can remain united with the Word, because these parts separated from the whole are capable of having their own subsistence and existence, distinct from the subsistence and existence of the whole.

[31] *Summa theol.,* IIIa, q. 2, a. 2, ad. 2.

CHAPTER VII

QUESTION 5

The Mode of the Union Concerning the Parts of the Human Nature Assumed

SINCE these parts are the body and soul, Docetism and Apollinarianism are here refuted.

First Article

WHETHER THE SON OF GOD OUGHT TO HAVE ASSUMED A HUMAN BODY

It is of faith that the Word assumed a real body, and not a phantom or shadow. This truth has been frequently defined in such councils as Nicaea, Ephesus, Constantinople, Chalcedon, and others,[1] against the Marcionites and Manichaeans, who attribute to Christ the semblance of a body, because they thought every body comes from the principle of evil, and is evil. Simon Magus, Saturninus, and Basilides are likewise condemned. This latter heresiarch, says St. Irenaeus,[2] maintained that Simon of Cyrene was crucified instead of Jesus, who exchanged external figure and countenance with Simon of Cyrene.

Scriptural proof. In the New Testament we read: "The Word was made flesh." [3] And again: "Every spirit which confesseth that Jesus Christ is come in the flesh, is of God. And every spirit that dissolveth Jesus, is not of God." [4] St. Paul says: "Concerning His Son, who was made to Him of the seed of David, according to the flesh." [5] Christ

[1] Denz., nos. 20, 216, 255, 344, 393, 462.
[2] *Adversus haereses,* Bk. I, chap. 24.
[3] John 1:14.
[4] I John 4:2.
[5] Rom. 1:3.

speaking of Himself, says: "Behold we go up to Jerusalem, and the Son of man shall be betrayed . . . , and crucified, and the third day He shall rise again." [6] Finally, after the Resurrection, Jesus said: "Handle and see; for a spirit hath not flesh and bones, as you see Me to have." [7]

Theological proof. It is taken especially from the arguments proposed by the Fathers, especially from Tertullian,[8] and from St. Irenaeus.[9]

Three reasons are given in the body of the article. 1. Christ would not be a true man if He did not have a true body. 2. If Christ is not truly man, then He did not truly die, as narrated in the Gospels. 3. Jesus did not speak the truth when He said: "Handle and see; for a spirit hath not flesh and bones, as you see Me to have." [10]

Second Article

WHETHER THE SON OF GOD OUGHT TO HAVE ASSUMED AN EARTHLY BODY

This means: Ought Christ to have assumed flesh and blood, rather than a heavenly body?

Reply. The answer is in the affirmative, and it is of faith against the Valentinians, who said that Christ assumed a celestial body and passed through the Blessed Virgin, as water flows through a channel.[11]

Scriptural proof. In the New Testament we read: "A spirit hath not flesh and bones, as you see Me to have." [12] St. Paul says of Jesus: "He was made to Him [Father] of the seed of David, according to the flesh." [13] And again: "God sent His Son, made of a woman." [14] In Christ's genealogy, it is said of Him: "Son of David, son of Abraham." [15] The angel says to Mary: "Behold thou shalt conceive in thy womb and shalt bring forth a son, and thou shalt call His name

[6] Matt. 20:18 f.
[7] Luke 24:39.
[8] *Contra Marcionem,* Bk. III, chap. 8.
[9] *Adversus haereses,* Bk. V, chap. 20.
[10] Luke 24:39.
[11] Denz., no. 710. This heresy is recalled in the decree for the Jacobites.
[12] Luke 24:39.
[13] Rom. 1:3.
[14] Gal. 4:4.
[15] Matt. 1:1.

Jesus."[16] St. Joseph is also declared to be "the husband of Mary, of whom was born Jesus."[17]

All these texts would not be true if Christ had come down from heaven with a celestial body, and had merely passed through the Blessed Virgin, as through a channel.

Theological proof. 1. If Christ had not assumed our nature, then He would not be truly man, since flesh and bones are required for a nature to be truly human. 2. Also Christ would not have been really hungry, or have suffered and died, as recorded in the Gospels. 3. He would have told a lie in presenting Himself to men as having a body of flesh. If St. Paul says that "the first man was of the earth, earthly: the second man from heaven, heavenly,"[18] this means that Christ's body was formed from the womb of the Blessed Virgin Mary by a heavenly power, namely, by the Holy Ghost.[19]

Reply to second objection. Christ came in passible flesh, "that He might carry through the work of our redemption." Hence Christ's death was not the result of original sin, but the consequence of a nature conceived in passible flesh, and this consequence He offered in submission for our redemption.[20] He submitted to the penalty of death not for Himself, but for our sake.

That the Word came, however, in passible and mortal flesh, rather than in impassible flesh, presupposes Adam's sin, although in Christ death was not the result of original sin, which He did not contract. The same must be said of the Blessed Virgin, who was preserved from original sin.

Reply to third objection. It pertains to the greatest glory of God that He raised a most weak and earthly body to such sublimity. It was mercy that moved God to unite the highest with the lowest for our salvation. St. Thomas has treated this question more fully in another work.[21]

Doubt. Was Christ's blood hypostatically united with the Word? This question is of no slight importance, because it concerns the precious blood of Jesus Christ that was shed in His passion and that is offered daily in the Mass.

[16] Luke 1:31.
[17] Matt. 1:16.
[18] I Cor. 15:47.
[19] Cf. ad 1.
[20] Cf. IIIa, q. 50, a. 1. The entire article ought to be read.
[21] *Contra Gentes,* Bk. IV, chap. 30.

This doubt was formerly the subject of much dispute. Durandus denied that the Word hypostatically united with Himself the natural blood. Alphonsus Tostatus (Abulensis),[22] Richard,[23] and several Franciscan theologians were of the same opinion. St. Thomas took the affirmative view both here and in his commentary on the resurrection of Christ.[24] The Thomists, Cajetan and Capreolus, and almost all theologians are in agreement with St. Thomas on this point. Since this question gave rise to bitter contention between the Franciscans and Dominicans, the latter defending the doctrine of St. Thomas, Pius II (1464) issued a decree [25] putting an end to these disputes, until it was defined what must be believed. Later on, however, as Suarez observes, the Franciscan view was eliminated from their schools of theology, as being neither pious nor safe teaching.

There are three proofs for this affirmative view, which is the one most commonly held.[26]

Scriptural proof. St. Paul says: "Therefore because the children [i.e., men] are partakers of flesh and blood [i.e., are composed of flesh and blood], He Himself [Christ] in like manner hath been partaker of the same." [27]

This same teaching is confirmed in other passages of Sacred Scripture, in which our redemption is attributed to the blood of Christ, His Son, as in the following text: "The blood of Christ, His Son, cleanseth us from all sin." [28]

Authoritative proof. The Council of Trent, in its discussion on the Holy Eucharist, affirms the natural union of the body and blood of Christ in these words: "The body itself is under the species of bread, and the blood is under the species of wine, and the soul under both, by the force of that natural connection and concomitance, whereby the parts of Christ our Lord . . . are united together." [29] Therefore the blood is a part of Christ.

Similarly Clement VI affirmed that the blood of Christ was united

[22] He was so called because of his having been appointed bishop of Avila. (Tr.)

[23] The Catholic Encyclopedia says of him that he was a Franciscan whose origin and nationality are unknown. (Tr.)

[24] Cf. IIIa, q. 54, a. 2.

[25] Denz., no. 718.

[26] Billuart, *De Verbo incarnato.*

[27] Rom. 2:14.

[28] I John 1:7. See also I Pet. 1:2.

[29] Denz., no. 876.

with the Word, saying: "The innocent and immaculate lamb is known to have shed His blood, a single drop of which, on account of its union with the Word, would have sufficed [for our redemption]." [30]

Theological proof. Blood is a necessary part of the human body because it is required for its life and for the nutrition of its various parts, as also for the natural process of combustion by which natural heat is generated.

Hence theologians maintain that there will be blood in glorified bodies, inasmuch as this pertains to the integrity of the body.[31]

Confirmation of proof. From the definition of the Church on the Holy Eucharist.

If the Word did not assume hypostatically the blood, then the Word is not by concomitance under the species of wine. For that is by concomitance in the sacrament which is united really and substantially with the primary term of the consecration and conversion. But, if the Word did not assume hypostatically the blood, the Word is not really and substantially united with the blood, which is the primary term in the consecration of the chalice. Therefore, in this case, the Word would not be by concomitance present under the species of wine, which is contrary to the teaching of the Council of Trent.

Objection. Those holding the opposite opinion have said that blood is not animated, and is not actually a part of the body. The Thomists contradict this assertion, remarking that the blood is a fluid that contributes to the nutrition of the other parts of the body.

Again the opponents object, saying: What the Word once assumed, remained always united with Him. But He severed His union with the blood.

Reply. In answer to this, we say with St. Thomas: [32] I deny the minor; for the blood of Christ, just as His corpse, although it was no longer animated, remained hypostatically united with the Word during the triduum of death because it had to be reassumed.[33] And if, during the triduum of death, there had been the consecration of the

[30] *Ibid.,* no. 550.

[31] Cf. IIIa, q. 54, a. 2, especially the argumentative part, and the replies to the second and third objections.

[32] *Ibid.,* a. 3, ad 3.

[33] The author means only that amount of blood that was required for reassumption. (Tr.)

wine in the chalice, the divinity would have been present by concomitance under the species of wine, as the Council of Trent declares.[34] This cannot be said of Christ's blood that was shed at the circumcision, because it was not intended to be reassumed.

It must be observed that when St. Thomas says: "All the blood which flowed from Christ's body, belonging as it does to the integrity of human nature, rose again with His body," [35] this must be understood of all the blood shed in a moral sense, but not of absolutely all the blood in a physical sense. As Pius II says, it is not contrary to faith for one to assert that a portion of the blood that was shed by Christ on the cross, or at the crowning of thorns, was not reassumed; but then this portion of blood, if it was not reassumed, was not hypostatically united with the Word, because, just as in the case of the blood shed at the circumcision, this blood was not indeed intended to be reassumed in the resurrection for the integrity of Christ's body. What has been said suffices, in our days, for the solution of this doubt that was formerly disputed.

Third Article

WHETHER THE SON OF GOD ASSUMED A SOUL

State of the question. The next two articles are written in refutation of Apollinaris and Arius, who first of all denied that Christ had a soul; then, retracting this former opinion, they granted that He had a soul, but it was not an intellectual soul, saying that the Word took the place of the intellect.

The Council of Ephesus defined against these heretics that the Word assumed an intellectual soul.[36]

Scriptural proof. Our Lord says of Himself: "My soul is sorrowful even unto death." [37] And again: "Father, into Thy hands I commend My spirit." [38]

St. Thomas explains in the body of the article that these words cannot be taken metaphorically, especially because the Gospel says that Jesus wondered, was angry, and hungry. These acts belong to a soul that is both intellectual and sensitive.

[34] Denz., no. 876.
[35] *Summa theol.,* IIIa, q. 5, a. 3, ad 3.
[36] Denz., nos. 216, 223, 227, 271, 710.
[37] Matt. 26:38.
[38] Luke 23:46.

Theological proof. The principal reason given in the theological proof is that Christ would be neither truly man nor the Son of man as declared in the Gospel, unless He had a soul; and thus there would be no more any truth to the Incarnation.

Reply to first objection. If St. John says in his prologue, "And the Word was made flesh," flesh is taken for the whole man, just as sometimes in Sacred Scripture we read such assertions as, "All flesh shall see that the mouth of the Lord hath spoken." [39]

Reply to second objection. The Word is the effective cause of Christ's human life, the soul is its formal cause, and hence it is not useless. Moreover, the Word cannot be the formal cause of the human body, because the formal cause is the intrinsic cause and therefore is a part of the composite, not so perfect as the composite. But this cannot be said of the uncreated Word.

Fourth Article

WHETHER THE SON OF GOD ASSUMED A HUMAN MIND OR INTELLECT

Reply. That the Son of God assumed an intellect has been defined against the Arians and Apollinarians as belonging to the faith.

Scriptural proof. Jesus says: "Learn of Me because I am meek and and humble of heart." [40] Christ was also obedient and merited, which was possible only if He had a human intellect and a human will; for the divine intellect and the divine will cannot be the principle of an act of obedience as regards a higher will.

Theological proof. The principal reason in this proof is that, if Christ did not have a human intellect, then He was not truly man, which is contrary both to what He Himself said and to Scripture.

[39] Isa. 40:5.
[40] Matt. 11:29.

CHAPTER VIII

QUESTION 6

The Order of Assumption

State of the question. This question is inserted here especially because of Origen's error that was condemned by Pope Vigilius in the following canon: "If anyone says or thinks that our Lord's soul existed and was united with God, the Word, prior to His incarnation and birth from the Virgin, let him be anathema." [1]

Origen said that Christ's soul was created at the beginning of the world, and by the performance of good works merited to be united hypostatically with the Word, and was *de facto* united with the Word, before it was united with the body in the womb of the Blessed Virgin. Hence Vigilius declared: "If anyone says or thinks that the body of our Lord Jesus Christ was first formed in the womb of the Blessed Virgin, and that afterward God the Word and the soul were united with it, as if He had already existed, let him be anathema." [2]

Hence the teaching of the Church as defined against Origen is that Christ's soul and body, or His entire humanity, was at the same moment assumed by the Word. St. Thomas explains this teaching of the Church especially in the third article of this question. In the other articles, however, especially in the fifth, he considers what was assumed by priority of nature, both on the part of the agent assuming and according to his intention, and thus the entire human nature of Christ was first assumed; and also he considers what was first assumed on the part of the subject assumed in the order of execution, and thus the parts were assumed before the whole, and so the soul was first assumed, and the body through the soul as intermediary, and finally the whole as resulting from each, or the complete human nature.

[1] Denz., no. 204.
[2] *Ibid.*, no. 205.

Thus this distinction being established between priority of time and priority of nature together with the aforesaid subdistinction, the whole of this question will be understood.

First Article

WHETHER THE SON OF GOD ASSUMED FLESH THROUGH THE MEDIUM OF THE SOUL

State of the question. In this article soul and body are compared in accordance with the natural order, and thus this article is distinct from the third, although for the benefit of the doctrine St. Thomas begins by distinguishing between the temporal order and the natural order.

There are two conclusions.

First conclusion. In the order of time the Word united the whole human nature of Christ to Himself simultaneously, at the very moment of the creation of Christ's soul.[3]

This conclusion is defined to be of faith against Origen.[4] It will be explained more fully farther on,[5] when St. Thomas, discussing

[3] Cf. *infra,* IIIa, q. 33, a. 2, in which St. Thomas asks whether Christ's body was animated at the first moment of its conception. He answers in the affirmative, giving as his reason that for the conception to be attributed to the Son of God, as we say in the Apostles' Creed, "who was conceived by the Holy Ghost," we must say that the body itself of Christ, when it was conceived, was assumed by the Word of God. But now in this first article it is shown that the Word assumed the body through the intermediary of the soul without which the body would not have been a human body.

St. Thomas also says (*loc. cit.*): "In the generation of other men, he is first of all a living thing, and afterward an animal, and after that a man (so that animation or passive conception is completed after the inceptive passive conception of the embryonic body), because the body is successively formed and disposed for the soul . . . ; but Christ's body, on account of the infinite power of the agent was perfectly disposed instantaneously. Wherefore, at once and in the first instant it received a perfect form, that is, the rational soul." Nevertheless the period of gestation was not shortened. Even in accordance with the present condition of medical science, the hypothesis can very safely be admitted which teaches that the ordinary process is for the spiritual soul not to be created and united with the embryonic body until one month after the conception of the embryonic body. The dogmatic definition of the Immaculate Conception affirms nothing that is contrary to this hypothesis, for it is concerned solely with the preservation of the person of the Blessed Virgin Mary from original sin; but the person does not exist prior to the existence of the spiritual soul. The dogmatic definition is not concerned with the question of the first moment of the conception of the body as distinct from its animation.

[4] Denz., no. 204.

[5] Cf. IIIa, q. 33, a. 3.

Christ's conception, shows that it is contrary to the faith to say that Christ's flesh was first conceived and afterward was assumed by the Word of God. This assertion is against Photinus who said that Christ was first a mere man and afterward by the sanctity of His life came to be considered the Son of God.[6] In such a case, the Blessed Virgin would not be the Mother of God.

St. Thomas gives us the reason for this conclusion in these words: "If Christ's flesh had been conceived before being assumed by the Word, it would have been at some time a hypostasis other than that of the Word of God," [7] and so there would have been two hypostases in the Word incarnate, or one would have been destroyed, which is not fitting. Hence Christ's entire humanity was simultaneously assumed.

Second conclusion. In the natural order, however, the Word instantaneously united the flesh with Himself, through the intermediary of the soul, since the soul is mediating link by reason of its dignity and causality. There is clearly here a distinction between priority of time, which is denied, and priority of nature which is affirmed, inasmuch as the very moment that Christ's soul was created, the Word assumed the flesh through the mediation of the soul; otherwise the flesh would not be human.

Third objection. It must be noted that St. Thomas says that, if the medium is taken away, then the extremes are separated. But the soul is taken away by death, though the union of the Word with the flesh still remains; for "what is bestowed through God's grace is never withdrawn except through fault." [8] Therefore the Word was not united with the flesh through the mediation of the soul.

Reply to third objection. The soul, before its separation from the body, rendered the latter apt for assumption, though it did not sever the union of the Word with the flesh; just as the loss of a woman's beauty, though this beauty contributed to her fittingness for marriage, does not sever the marriage bond.

[6] Denz., nos. 63, 85, 88, 233.

[7] *Summa theol.,* IIIa, q. 33, a. 3.

[8] Cf. IIIa, q. 50, a. 2, 3, where this statement is made clearer.

Second Article

WHETHER THE SON OF GOD ASSUMED A SOUL THROUGH THE MEDIUM OF THE SPIRIT OR MIND

The purpose of this article is to explain the following text of St. Augustine, quoted in the counterargument: "The invisible and unchangeable Truth took a soul by means of the spirit, and a body by means of the soul."

Conclusion. The Word assumed by means of the mind the other parts of the soul, just as He assumed the body by means of the soul, on account of the dignity of the order and the congruity of the assumption; for mind is the highest part of the soul in its relation to the sensitive soul.[9] What is meant by mind is the essence of the spiritual soul from which the higher faculties are derived, those that are purely spiritual, namely, the intellect and will.

Third Article

WHETHER THE SOUL WAS ASSUMED BEFORE THE FLESH BY THE SON OF GOD

This article is strictly concerned with priority of time, for the purpose of denying such priority against Origen, and thus it differs from the first article. Origen not only maintained that all immortal souls were created in the beginning along with the angels, before they were united to bodies, but he also said this especially of Christ's soul, inasmuch as it is nobler than the angels.

Reply. The answer is that Christ's soul was not created prior to its union with the Word, and it is of faith, as evident from the condemnation of Origen by Pope Vigilius.[10]

In the counterargument St. Thomas quotes the authority of St. John Damascene, who most clearly is against Origen's opinion.

Theological proof. It shows the unfittingness of Origen's view. It is derogatory to Christ's dignity to suppose that His soul was created before its assumption, because then it would have had its own subsistence, and hence there would be two subsistences in Christ, and two supposita, or else one subsistence would have been destroyed,

[9] The Greek word νοῦς corresponds to "intellect," whereas ψυχή refers to the sensitive soul.

[10] Denz., no. 204.

which is unbecoming to Christ, as well as being a mere assertion without any foundation.

Likewise it is derogatory to Christ's dignity to suppose that His soul was created and simultaneously assumed before His body was formed, because then this soul of Christ would not seem to be of the same nature as our souls, which are created at the same time that they are infused into our bodies, inasmuch as it is the very nature of the soul to be the form of the body, and thus it differs from the angels.

As St. Thomas says in this article, quoting St. Leo: "Christ's soul excels our soul not by diversity of genus, but by sublimity of power." [11]

Doubt. Is St. Thomas speaking only of sublimity of supernatural power, that is, of plenitude of grace, whereby Christ's most holy soul excels the sanctity even of the first and second highest among the choirs of angels, namely, the seraphim and cherubim; or has he in mind the natural and individual nobility of the soul, whereby Christ's soul excels in nobility the soul of any human being?

Reply. The holy Doctor admits inequality of power among human souls in the same species.[12]

Since matter and form are mutually causes, and "since the form is not for the matter, but rather the matter for the form," [13] Providence made Christ's body more apt for its union with the nobler part, which is the soul, just as He made the body of the Blessed Virgin Mary more fitting so that she might be worthy of becoming the Mother of God.

St. Thomas says: "It is plain that the better the disposition of a body, the better the soul alloted to it. This clearly appears in things of different species, and the reason thereof is that act and form are received into matter according to the capacity of matter. Thus, because some men have bodies of better disposition, their souls have a greater power of understanding, wherefore it is said that it is to be observed that 'those who have soft flesh are of apt mind.' [14] Secondly, this occurs in regard to the lower powers of which the intellect has need in its operations; for those in whom the imaginative, cogitative, and memorative powers are of better disposition, are better disposed to understand." [15]

[11] Cf. ad 2.

[12] Cf. Ia, q. 85, a. 7; IIIa, q. 31, a. 5. Also *Tabula aurea,* under the word "anima," nos. 69, 72, 73.

[13] Cf. Ia, q. 76, a. 5.

[14] Aristotle, *De anima,* Bk. II, chap. 9.

[15] *Summa theol.,* Ia, q. 85, a. 7.

St. Thomas applies this teaching to Christ, showing that the body was miraculously formed from the most pure blood of the Blessed Virgin Mary.[16]

On the one hand, the soul, although it is created and not educed from matter, thus depends materially, but not intrinsically, on the body, and therefore it can continue to exist after its separation from the body.

On the other hand, the body is better disposed, inasmuch as it depends finally and formally and in some way in the evolution of the embryo efficiently on the better disposed soul. Hence St. Thomas says: "What is received in anything can be considered both being and perfection. According to its being it is in the one in which it is received, after the manner of the recipient; nevertheless, the one that received it is drawn to its perfection." [17] Thus heat is received in water, light in the air, the soul in the body, grace in the soul, and the subject that receives is made conformable to the perfection received.

So there is a mutual transcendental relation between matter and form, body and soul, which therefore remains individuated after its separation from the body by reason of this transcendental relation to the body, which will be again informed by the soul on the day of the resurrection of the dead.

Father Gredt correctly remarks that "one human soul differs from another in perfection substantially, of course, though not essentially but accidentally, taking the word 'accidentally' as a predicable accident," [18] but not as a predicamental accident, which is an operative faculty that is really distinct from substance. Thus the soul of Christ, even as a substance, is individually, although not specifically, nobler than the soul of any other human being, just as His body, which was miraculously formed in the womb of the Blessed Virgin Mary, was better disposed than any other human body whatever. It is also evident that the souls of great doctors of the Church, in which there are signs of great genius, are individually nobler than many other souls.

Thus we have a beautiful verification of the principle that causes mutually interact, but in a different genus; for the form determines the matter, and the latter is ordained for the form, as also the agent attains the end which attracts it.

[16] *Ibid.*, IIIa, q. 31, a. 5.
[17] *De veritate*, q. 24, a. 8, ad 6.
[18] *Elementa philosophiae*, I, no. 461.

Fourth Article

WHETHER THE FLESH OF CHRIST WAS ASSUMED BY THE WORD BEFORE BEING UNITED WITH THE SOUL

State of the question. This article concerns priority of time. The purpose of this article, as stated in the first and second difficulties, is that, according to the teaching of the ancient philosophers, in the conception of other men, living flesh is found in possession of vegetative life, and already of the sensitive life, before the rational soul, which is created by God, comes to it. Thus in the first two objections of this article, disposition of the matter precedes the coming of the form, and in human beings, the body is conceived before the rational soul comes to it.

But, on the other hand, as we stated in the first article, it is evident, concerning the condemnation of Origen's teaching, that the Word assumed simultaneously the flesh and soul of Christ, for flesh is not human before the soul comes to it.

This question presupposes another, namely, whether Christ's flesh was conceived or formed, at least in accordance with its remote natural dispositions, before it was united with the rational soul. The solution of the present article depends on this query, but this point concerns the question of Christ's conception, and is therefore explained farther on.[19]

In the passage quoted above, St. Thomas shows that it is against the faith to say that Christ's flesh was first conceived, and afterward was animated and assumed by the Word. This is evident from what the Church has declared against Origen and against Photinus.[20]

Reply. Christ's flesh ought not to have been assumed before the soul.

Authoritative proof. St. John Damascene says: "At the same time the Word of God was made flesh, and flesh was united to a rational and intellectual soul." [21] This means to say that Christ's flesh was conceived, animated, and assumed simultaneously. This is what the Church declares against Origen and against Photinus.[22]

[19] *Summa theol.,* IIIa, q. 33, a. 2, 3.

[20] Denz., nos. 204, 205; also nos. 63, 85, 88, 233.

[21] *De fide orthod.,* Bk. III, chap. 2 (about the end); see also IIIa, q. 33, a. 2, *sed contra.*

[22] Denz., no. 205: "If anyone says or thinks that the body of our Lord Jesus Christ was first formed in the womb of the Blessed Virgin Mary, and that afterward God,

Theological proof. It is expressed briefly in the last line of the argumentative part of the article. Flesh is not strictly human before it receives the rational soul. But the Word assumed only strictly human flesh. Therefore flesh ought not to have been assumed before the soul.

This is well explained in the body of the article. For human flesh is assumable by the Word according to the order it has to the rational soul. But it has not (at least this immediate) order, before the rational soul comes to it; because the moment that the matter is ultimately disposed for the form, it also receives the form. The whole article must be read.[23]

But how is the difficulty that is presented in the first objection to be solved. It states that our bodies are conceived before they are animated by the rational soul. St. Thomas admits this statement as at least probable in fact, inasmuch as the body first has the vegetative life, then the sensitive life, before it is ultimately disposed for the rational soul, which is created by God instantaneously from nothing, and is not educed from matter.

St. Thomas replies to the first objection of this article, saying that it is certainly so with us, remarking that "before the coming of the human soul, there is no human flesh," but there is in the body a previous but not ultimate disposition for human flesh. He goes on to say: "In the conception of Christ, the Holy Ghost, who is an agent of infinite might, disposed the matter and brought it to its perfection at the same time." Likewise, he says farther on: "Christ's body, on account of the infinite power of the agent, was perfectly disposed in-

---

the Word, and the soul were united with it, as if it had already existed, let him be anathema." Thus St. Gregory says (*Moral.,* Bk. XVIII, chap. 27): "As soon as the angel announced it, as soon as the Spirit came down, the Word was in the womb, within the womb the Word was made flesh." St. Thomas says: "For the conception to be attributed to the very Son of God, as we confess in the Creed, when we say, Who was conceived by the Holy Ghost, we must say that the body itself, in being conceived, was assumed by the Word of God. Now it has been shown above (q. 6, a. 1, 2) that the Word of God assumed the body by means of the soul, and the soul by means of the spirit" (IIIa, q. 33, a. 2), because it is only by means of the rational soul that the flesh is human (cf. *ibid.,* ad 3). If the divine maternity were to terminate in the conception of the flesh that is not united with the Word, the Blessed Virgin would not be the Mother of God, but the mother of a man, who in losing afterward His own personality, would have received the divine personality.

[23] Cajetan says (*Com. in IIIam,* q. 6, a. 4, no. 3): "The proper matter of any form is said to be either in the process of becoming, and so it is prior even in time to the reception of the form; or else it is actually in being, and thus it is proper only at the very moment that it receives the form."

stantaneously. Wherefore at once and in the first instant it received a perfect form, that is, the rational soul." [24] Farther on he says: "Christ's conception must be said to be entirely miraculous (on the part of the active power), and in a qualified manner natural (on the part of the matter contributed by the mother)." [25]

Thus in the miraculous conversion of water into wine at Cana, the matter of water (without any previous dispositions) is disposed to receive the form of wine. So also, in the operational order, the conversion of St. Paul was instantaneous; similarly the sanctification of the Blessed Virgin Mary took place at the very moment of her conception, inasmuch as, when her soul was created, it instantaneously received a plenitude of grace, and was preserved from original sin through the merits of Christ. So too, in the natural order, men of great genius solve problems, but, at times, they do not sufficiently prepare their pupils to understand their teaching, which is then understood in a wrong sense, and thus these pupils fall into error.

Different from Christ's conception, St. Thomas does not admit that the rational soul of the Blessed Virgin Mary was created at the moment of her conception, for he distinguishes between this moment and the moment after the animation of her flesh. In this he distinguishes between the virginal conception of Christ and that of the Blessed Virgin Mary, which was not miraculous, inasmuch as her conception was not virginal, but natural; for she was born in a natural way from a father and mother. St. Thomas asks whether the Blessed Virgin Mary was sanctified before animation, which is distinct from the passive conception of the body. But complete passive conception of the body, inasmuch as it is distinct from the beginning of this conception, took place in the Blessed Virgin at the same time as animation, which is the usual procedure in human beings.[26]

Reply to third objection. The conception, animation, and assumption of Christ's body were instantaneous. But by priority of nature the body was preserved by the Word as a being, before its animation, because the body is first a being, and then a body.

Nevertheless, as regards the personal union, Christ's body was, in accordance with nature, first united with the soul, before it was united with the Word, because it is from its union with the soul that it is

[24] *Summa theol.,* IIIa, q. 33, a. 2, ad 3.
[25] *Ibid.,* a. 4.
[26] *Ibid.,* q. 27, a. 2.

capable of being united with the Word in person; especially since a person, as such, is found only in the rational nature. So it was that during the three days in which our Lord's body was separated from the soul, the Word was not united personally but only subsistentially with Christ's corpse. The entire reply to the third objection should be read.

A question that deserves special attention is: When is the rational soul created? Does this take place at the moment of conception or afterward? Father Gredt says: "The ancient philosophers taught that, first of all, . . . the merely vegetative soul that is imperfect and transitory would be educed, and this soul by a process of evolution would become corrupt and would be substituted by another that is imperfect, the sensitive soul, which also becomes corrupt, and forty days after conception the rational soul would finally be created and infused into the body." "Nevertheless," says Father Gredt, "it is better to say with modern philosophers that from the very beginning the germinal cells are united, and there is present a special organization and proximate disposition for the infusion of the rational soul, which is therefore created and infused by God, without the intervention of any other soul."[27]

On the contrary, Father Barbado, O.P., says: "It is not our purpose to decide this question that is so much disputed among Scholastics. However, we must point out that experience shows the foundation for this traditional view, which the ancient philosophers took from embryology, is strongly supported by present-day investigations. . . . For the egg, in the segmentation process and the follicles in the blastodermic process do not possess actually but only potentially the future organization, and it is only much later that the organs come to perfection."[28]

Moreover, after death or the separation of the rational soul from the body, facts seem to attest that for some time the vegetative soul remains, since the hair and nails still grow. If such be the case after the separation of the rational soul from the body, why not before the creation of the soul?

[27] *Elementa philosophiae,* no. 536.

[28] *Propedeutica ad psychologiam,* p. 461 (Mss.).

Fifth Article

WHETHER THE WHOLE HUMAN NATURE WAS ASSUMED THROUGH THE MEDIUM OF THE PARTS

This title is not concerned with the order of time, but with that of nature.

State of the question. The purpose of the article is to explain what St. Augustine means when he says, as quoted in the first objection: "The invisible and unchangeable Truth assumed the soul through the medium of the spirit, and the body through the medium of the soul, and in this way the whole man." We stated in the first article that the Word assumed flesh through the medium of the soul. But the whole human nature results from the union of the parts.

Conclusion. The Word of God assumed the human nature through the medium of the whole. This means the body and the soul, because of their relation to the whole. Evidently the article is concerned only with the order of nature and not with that of time.

Authoritative proof. It is taken from St. John Damascene, who is quoted in the counterargument.

Theological proof. The order of nature, which concerns us here, is of two kinds. It may be considered either on the part of the agent assuming, or on the part of the subject assumed. In the Incarnation, however, our attention must be given especially to the first kind, because the whole idea of the deed is estimated from the omnipotence of the agent.

But on the part of the agent, that is absolutely first which is first in intention, which is to assume the entire human nature. Therefore the Word of God assumed the parts of the human nature through the medium of the whole, or on account of the whole that was first intended.[29]

Sixth Article

WHETHER THE HUMAN NATURE WAS ASSUMED THROUGH THE MEDIUM OF GRACE

This article is inserted here because of the necessity of explaining the threefold meaning of the word "grace."

[29] Cf. ad 1 (end).

1) There is a certain grace that is the uncreated will of God freely doing or donating something. In this sense, it is called effective grace, but not formal grace.

2) In Christ there is the grace of union which is formally in Him, and it is the very personal being of the Word, which terminates, possesses, and sanctifies the human nature of Christ.

3) Habitual grace is also formally in Christ, inhering in His soul as an accident, which will be more clearly explained in the following question.

Two conclusions follow from this distinction.

1) The hypostatic union did not take place through the medium of the grace of union or through the medium of habitual grace. For the grace of union is the very personal being of Christ, which is the term of the assumption. Habitual grace, which inheres in the soul of Christ, is the consequent effect of the hypostatic union, and this will be made clearer in the following question.

2) The hypostatic union took place by grace that is God's uncreated will, not as a medium, but as efficient cause.

Thus St. Thomas, speaking of the grace that predestines the elect, inquires whether predestination places anything in the predestined, and he replies: "Predestination is not anything in the predestined, but only in the person who predestines. . . . But the execution of predestination, which is the calling, the justification, the magnification, is in the predestined." [30]

Doubt. Is there a created actuation produced by the uncreated act in the hypostatic union by the very fact that Christ's human nature began to be actuated terminatively by the Word, as Father de la Taille contends? Is the grace of union in Christ anything created, as St. Thomas maintains?

This question is about the same as that concerning the substantial mode whereby Christ's humanity is united with the Word.[31]

Reply. Both parts of the question are denied. St. Thomas says in the present article: "The grace of union is the personal being that is given gratis from above to the human nature in the person of the Word," and therefore it cannot be understood in the sense of a created medium, a created actuation that is produced by the uncreated act.

[30] Cf. Ia, q. 23, a. 2. The whole of this article should be read, as also the replies to the first and second objections.

[31] Cf. IIIa, q. 2, a. 7.

The grace of union is not something created, but it is the very Word that terminates the human nature, both possessing and sanctifying it.

Likewise, when St. Thomas inquires about the union of the two natures in Christ, as to whether it was effected by grace, he replies: "If grace be understood as the will of God gratuitously doing something, . . . then the union of the Incarnation took place by grace, . . . but not as though there were a habitual grace by means of which the union took place." [32] It would have been so, however, if there were a created and indeed supernatural actuation produced by the uncreated act.

St. Thomas says, too, in the present article: "Grace is an accidental perfection of the soul, and therefore it cannot ordain the soul to personal union, which is not accidental." [33]

We have already quoted the passage in which St. Thomas says: "It must be known that in the union of the divine nature and the human nature, there can be no medium that formally causes the union, to which the human nature is previously joined before it is united with the divine person; just as there can be no mediating being between matter and form, which would be previously in the matter before the substantial form, otherwise accidental being would be prior to substantial being, which is impossible. So also, between nature and suppositum there can be no medium in the above-mentioned manner, since each conjunction is for substantial union." [34] But it is shown that the union, as a real relation of the human nature with the Word, is the consequent or resulting effect; for St. Thomas says: "This relation follows, which is called union; hence union is the medium, not as causing the assumption, but as following it." [35]

St. Thomas also shows elsewhere that the union is declared to be something created since it is a real relation of Christ's human nature to the Word, but it is only a logical relation of the Word to the human nature. Thus creation in the passive sense is a real relation of the creature to the Creator.[36]

As we remarked above,[37] it cannot properly be said that the human nature undergoes a change in its assumption by the Word, and that

[32] *Ibid.*, q. 2, a. 10.
[33] *Ibid.*, q. 6, ad 2.
[34] *Com. in III Sent.*, d. 2, q. 2., quaestiuncula 1a.
[35] *Ibid.*, q. 3.
[36] *Summa theol.*, Ia, q. 45, a. 3; IIIa, q. 2, a. 7.
[37] *Ibid.*, IIIa, q. 2, a. 7.

this change is the finite actuation produced by the uncreated act.

St. Thomas shows that we look upon creation as a change, whereas in reality it is not a change, saying: "Change means that the same something should be different now from what it was previously." [38] But this is impossible in the case of creation, and even in the assumption of Christ's humanity, because the subject that is to undergo the change is not as yet in existence. As Thomas says, "When motion is removed from action and passion, only relation remains." [39] Hence passive creation is simply a relation of dependence, which is likewise the case with Christ's hypostatic union. This means that Christ's human nature is dependent on the Word.

Likewise the formal effect is not distinct from the form that is received in the subject. Thus the formal effect of whiteness is to make a thing white, and it is only by this whiteness that anything is white. Similarly man is made pleasing to God by habitual grace.

Matter is also actuated by form, and there is no distinction between this actuation and its substantial form, otherwise, as St. Thomas stated above, "accidental being would be prior to substantial being, which is impossible." [40]

But if the actuation of prime matter is the same as the formal act that it receives, so also the actuation produced by the uncreated act cannot be anything created, because then there would be a real and infinite distinction between it and the uncreated act.

Thus we terminate the metaphysical questions concerning the mode of the union of the human nature with the Word, first in itself, and then on the part of the person assuming, and of the human nature that is assumed together with its parts, as also the order in which these parts are assumed. Let us pass on now to consider questions that are not so much metaphysical as psychological and spiritual, and that concern the co-assumed parts, such as Christ's grace, knowledge, power, His sensitive nature or His propassions. But metaphysical questions will again arise, when we consider the consequences of the hypostatic union,[41] namely, the truth of the propositions because of the personal unity in Christ, and when we come to inquire whether

[38] *Ibid.*, Ia, q. 45, a. 2.

[39] *Ibid.*, a. 3. Transitive action is motion as coming from the agent, and passion is motion that is in the patient. Hence with the removal of action and passion, there is nothing left but a relation of real dependence.

[40] *Com. in III Sent.*, d. 2, q. 2, *quaestiuncula* Ia.

[41] Cf. IIIa, q. 16, 17.

there is unity of being in Christ, just as there is unity of person in Him.[42]

It is already to some extent apparent that the answer will be in the affirmative.

[42] *Ibid.*, q. 17, a. 2.

CHAPTER IX

QUESTION 7

The Things Co-assumed

THE GRACE OF CHRIST

HAVING considered the nature that was assumed, we pass on to treat of what pertains to the perfection of Christ's human nature, namely, His grace, knowledge, and power; then we shall discuss His passibility together with His sensitive nature. The thirteenth question is concerned with Christ's human will, namely, with those things that pertain to the conformity of the two wills in Christ. There are two questions on Christ's grace, namely: (1) Christ's grace as an individual man (q. 7); (2) Christ's grace as the head of the Church (q. 8).

Theologians generally distinguish between two graces in Christ: (1) the grace of union, that is, His personal being that is gratuitously given by God to His human nature; (2) His habitual grace, as an individual man and as head of the Church.

In the seventh question St. Thomas, in discussing Christ's habitual grace as an individual man, includes the whole organism of the supernatural life in Christ's most holy soul, namely, the grace that is called "the grace of the virtues and of the gifts"; in that the virtues and the gifts belong properly to this grace. He also treats of the graces *gratis datae* and of the plenitude of Christ's grace. Some might object to the order followed in these questions, and say that the present problem, just as the question concerning the union of wills in Christ, ought to be relegated to the latter part of this treatise, when the consequences of the union are discussed.

The answer must be, in all probability, that the proper place to discuss the things co-assumed on the part of the human nature is here; whereas, on the contrary, from the sixteenth to the twenty-sixth questions inclusive, those things consequent to the union of the two natures are discussed, namely, Christ's unity as regards being, will, and operation, as also His relation to the Father, and to us, for example, that Christ must be worshiped as God.[1]

Hence the proper place to discuss the things co-assumed is here, this being the truly logical order, after the consideration of the nature that was assumed.

Hence, after consideration of the nature that was assumed, the truly logical order is to discuss the things that were co-assumed, from the seventh question to the fifteenth question.

There are three parts to this seventh question.

First part. It discusses habitual grace, the virtues and gifts in Christ (a. 1–6).

Second part. It treats of the graces freely bestowed upon Christ by His heavenly Father.

Third part. It is concerned with the plenitude of Christ's grace (a. 9–13).

All these articles pertain to Christ's sanctity. But after the time of St. Thomas, Christ's sanctity was discussed more in detail by way of a preliminary question, which is usually inserted here by way of a preliminary by the Thomists. The precise purport of this question is to settle the doubt whether the substantial grace of union sanctifies formally or merely radically Christ's human nature.

This question must be examined here since it serves as an introduction to the articles of the seventh question, enabling us to understand them better, for the substantial grace and uncreated grace of union is, so to speak, the radical cause of habitual grace, or the grace of the virtues and gifts in Christ.

Preliminary Question

Christ's Substantial Grace of Union as the Source of His Sanctification

State of the question. Gonet observes: "It is a question of three kinds of grace, to which St. John briefly and indirectly alludes. For concerning the substantial grace of union, he says: 'The Word was made flesh.' [2] Concerning Christ's habitual grace as an individual person,

[1] Cf. L. B. Gillon, O.P., *Angelicum:* "La notion de consequence de l'union hypostatique dans le cadre de la IIIe pars. q. 2–26."

[2] John 1:14.

he adds: 'We saw His glory full of grace and truth.' Finally, there is indirect allusion to Christ's grace as head of the Church when, farther on he says: 'And of His fullness we have all received.' "[3]

Cajetan observes in his commentary at the beginning of this seventh question that St. Thomas already discussed the grace of union, not under the name of grace, however, but inasmuch as it is the hypostatic union of Christ's human nature with the Word. But when the question arose, whether Christ's human nature is formally sanctified by the substantial and uncreated grace of union, then Durandus[4] and the Scotists said that Christ's human nature is not formally but only radically sanctified by the grace of union. The affirmative opinion prevails as the more general one among Thomist theologians and those of other schools, which is the conclusion we come to from the teaching of the councils and the Fathers of the Church, and there is more than an indirect reference to this opinion in the passages we shall quote from St. Thomas. Of this opinion are John of St. Thomas, Godoy, Soto, Salmanticenses, Gonet, Billuart, and more recent Thomists, as also Suarez, de Lugo, Valentia, Vasquez, Franzelin, Billot, Hurter, and Pesch. It is the common and certain doctrine.[5]

Thesis. Christ's human nature is not only radically, but also formally sanctified by the substantial and uncreated union of the Word with the human nature.

In other words, Christ's sanctity is not accidental, but it is also substantial and uncreated, because it began at the very moment of His virginal conception. To understand this doctrine we must recall what sanctity is. St. Thomas says that sanctity is steadfast union with God, which implies "stainless purity."[6]

This steadfast union is unchangeable in heaven or among the blessed. The just have not as yet in this life attained to this unchangeableness, but, as St. Thomas says,[7] the holiness of the wayfarer causes him to direct his thoughts and actions toward God or is firmly turned to Him.

[3] *Clypeus theol. thom., de incarn.,* disp. 11.

[4] *Com. in IIIam,* d. 13, q. 1, no. 7.

[5] *Dict. théol. cath.,* art. "Jésus-Christ," cols. 1274–85. See also E. Hugon, *Le mystère dé l'incarnation,* part 4, chap. 1; also Garrigou-Lagrange, *Le Sauveur;* Monsabré, *Exposé du dogme catholique,* conference 40.

[6] *Summa theol.,* IIa IIae, q. 81, a. 8. The Greek word for holy is ἅγιος, as though meaning earthless.

[7] *Ibid.*

There is a twofold acceptation of sanctity as thus defined.

1) It may mean the proximately operative virtue of good, and in this sense there is no difference between it and the virtue of religion that is commanded by the theological virtues and that firmly directs all our actions to the worship of God.

2) It may be regarded as the foundation for this union with God, and thus in us it is habitual grace, which for this reason is called sanctifying grace, or the grace that unites us with God and makes us pleasing to Him.

All admit that Christ, as God, possesses essential and uncreated sanctity. But the question is whether the uncreated and substantial grace of union sanctifies Christ's human nature radically, namely, in that it is the source of habitual grace, or whether it sanctifies His human nature formally, that is, in the true and strict sense of the word, independently even of habitual grace. Likewise, farther on there will be a question of whether the grace of union suffices for the negative effect of sanctity, namely, impeccability; and the answer will be in the affirmative.

1) Teaching of the Fathers on Christ's sanctity. The passages commonly quoted are as follows:

St. Cyril: "Christ was anointed not as other saints and kings are; but because the Word is flesh," [8] that is, because the Word was made flesh.

St. Gregory Nazianzen: "Christ is so called because of His divine nature; for that is the unction of His human nature, which is not effected by operation, as in others that are anointed, but Christ is sanctified by the presence of the whole divine unction." [9]

St. John Damascene: "He [Christ] anointed Himself, which means that as God, He anointed His body by His divine nature; He was anointed, however, as man. . . . Moreover, the divinity is the unction of His humanity." [10]

St. Augustine, commenting on this scriptural text, "that they also may be sanctified in truth," [11] says: "The Son of man was sanctified from the beginning of His creation, when the Word was made flesh; because one person became Word and man. Therefore He was sancti-

[8] *Com. in Joan.,* Bk. IV, chap. 29.

[9] *Oratio* 30, no. 31 (cf. Rouet de Journel, no. 995).

[10] *De fide orthod.,* Bk. III, chap. 3 (Rouet de Journel, no. 1842).

[11] John 17:19.

fied by Himself in Himself; because the one Christ, who is Word and man, sanctifies the man in the Word." [12]

In another work St. Augustine says likewise: "Christ . . . was known to be anointed by that mystic and invisible union, at the time when the Word was made flesh, namely, when the human nature, without any previous merits because of good works, was united with the Word of God in the womb of the Virgin so as to become one person with the Word." [13]

2) St. Thomas says in a similar manner: "The grace of union is the personal being that is given gratis from above to the human nature in the person of the Word, and it is the term of the assumption, whereas the habitual grace pertaining to the spiritual holiness of the man is an effect following the union." [14] But the effect, inasmuch as it is a consequent accident, presupposes substantial sanctity.

Likewise St. Thomas,[15] in proving the necessity of habitual grace in Christ, does not seek the reason for it in His already established sanctity by the grace of union, but he explains it: (1) because of the union of His soul with the Word; (2) because it had to be the connatural principle of knowledge and love in the supernatural order; (3) on account of Christ's relation to the human race, since He is its head.

Hence St. Thomas does not say that Christ's habitual grace is sanctifying grace. In fact, he says farther on that Christ's human nature during the Passion had "the actual holiness of a victim, from the charity which it had from the beginning, and from the grace of union sanctifying it absolutely." [16] St. Thomas speaks in similar terms when discussing the plenitude of Christ's grace. After having said that by habitual grace man is united to God by love, he adds: "There is another kind of union of man with God, which is not only accomplished by love or the indwelling of the Holy Spirit, but also by the unity of the hypostasis. . . . And this belongs properly to Jesus Christ . . .

[12] *Com. in Joan.,* tract. 108, no. 5.

[13] *De Trinitate,* Bk. XV, chap. 26, no. 46 (Rouet de Journel, no. 1680). See also Council of Frankfort (Denz., no. 311). This council says: "Christ is by nature anointed, but we are by grace; because in Him was the fullness of the divinity." Otherwise there would be only an accidental difference in accordance with the degree of grace between Christ's sanctification and ours.

[14] *Summa theol.,* IIIa, q. 6, a. 6.

[15] *Ibid.,* q. 7, a. 1.

[16] *Ibid.,* q. 22, a. 2, ad 3.

and makes Him most pleasing to God, so that it may be said of Him as an individual: This is my beloved Son in whom I am well pleased." [17]

Again, when St. Thomas asks whether Christ can be called the adopted Son of God, he replies: "The sonship of adoption is a participated likeness of natural sonship; nor can a thing be said to participate in what it has essentially. Therefore Christ, who is the natural Son of God, can nowise be called an adopted Son." [18]

He also shows that Christ, as man, was predestined primarily and principally for natural and divine sonship, or for the grace of union, and secondarily and consequently for habitual grace and glory, as the effects of the grace of union.[19] St. Thomas, in his comment on the scriptural text, "Whom the Father hath sanctified and sent into the world," [20] referring to St. Hilary, likewise says: "He precedes the rest by this, that He was sanctified as the Son." [21] Hence St. Thomas taught even explicitly the doctrine of the present thesis, and, though he did not use the same terminology as nowadays, yet he expressed himself in equivalent terms.

Theological proof. This proof from reason that is proposed in various ways by the Thomists, may be clearly expressed by the following syllogism.

Formal sanctity which the just possess by reason of sanctifying grace, includes but four requisite conditions. But these four requisite conditions are found in Christ solely because of the grace of union, even independently of habitual grace. Therefore the substantial grace of union is what formally constitutes sanctity in Christ. Therefore His sanctity is innate, substantial, and increate. Accidental sanctity, which results from habitual grace is derived from this grace of union.

Proof of major. Formal sanctity about which we are concerned, is not a proximately operative virtue that is really distinct from the virtue of religion, but it is that union with God which the just have by reason of habitual or sanctifying grace. This formal sanctity, however, includes but four necessary conditions, so that the just person be formally holy. These conditions are the following.

[17] *Comp. theol.,* chap. 214; Matt. 3:17. Even though Christ's soul were not adorned with habitual grace, these words of God the Father would still be true.

[18] *Summa theol.,* IIIa, q. 23, a. 4.

[19] *Ibid.,* q. 24, a. 1, 2.

[20] John 10:36. *Catena aurea., Com. in Joan.* 10:36.

[21] *Catena aurea, loc. cit.*

1) That the person be united with God and somehow drawn into union with the divine being.

2) That the person be constituted the son of God, heir of His kingdom, pleasing to Him and loved by Him.

3) That the person be radically disposed to perform supernaturally good works.

4) That the principle of life is in such a person, which principle is incompatible with mortal sin.

All these four conditions are fully explained in that part of the treatise in which habitual or sanctifying grace is discussed, or that grace which makes us pleasing to God.

Minor. But Christ possesses these four conditions in a much higher degree by reason of His substantial and increate grace of union, even independently of habitual grace. For 1) by the grace of union, Christ's human nature is more perfectly drawn to and united with the divine nature than by habitual grace. For Christ's human nature is drawn to the divine nature as it is in Itself, and not merely to a participation in the divine nature. It is also united with the divine nature not merely accidentally and lovingly, but substantially and personally.

2) By the grace of union, Christ as man becomes the natural Son and heir of God, most pleasing to Him and loved by Him, whereas by habitual grace man becomes merely the adopted son of God. St. Thomas shows that love on God's part is the diffusion of good, and He could not confer a greater good on the human nature than to give Himself substantially to it.[22]

3) The grace of union makes Christ the *principium quod* [23] of theandric operations that are infinitely meritorious, whereas Christ has need of habitual grace only so that these supernatural operations be elicited connaturally by His human faculties.

4) Finally, the hypostatic union implies greater incompatibility with sin than habitual grace does, for, as will be stated farther on, not only is this union incompatible with mortal sin, but even with the slightest sin, and it makes such a man not only sinless, but absolutely impeccable.[24]

[22] *Summa theol.,* IIIa, q. 1, a. 1, 2.

[23] It is almost impossible to give the concise equivalent in English of *"principium quod."* By this expression the Scholastics meant the suppositum or person that performs the act, in accordance with the axiom that actions are attributed either to the suppositum or to the person. (Tr.)

[24] Cf. IIIa, q. 15, a. 1.

Therefore the conclusion follows that the substantial grace of union is what makes Christ formally holy, and this holiness is not accidental, but substantial, increate, and also innate.

Confirmation. By the grace of union, Christ is the natural Son of God. To be the natural Son of God means the maximum of sanctity, or the greatest of union with God and of supernatural union with Him, in accordance with what the Father said: "This is My beloved Son, in whom I am well pleased." [25]

Objection. The grace of union cannot make a man formally blessed. Therefore it cannot make him formally holy.

Reply. I deny the consequent. The difference between the two is that formal blessedness is a vital act consisting in the vision and love of God; formal holiness, however, with which we are here concerned, consists in habitual union with God, which is ordered to right action; and just as habitual grace gives one a right to eternal happiness, provided this grace be not lost by mortal sin, so a fortiori does the grace of union.

Again I insist. But if the Word were to assume an irrational nature, for example, a dove or a lamb, such a creature would not be sanctified by the Word.

Reply. The reason for this lack of sanctification would be that such subject or nature that is assumed is incapable of it; in fact, the Word would not give personality but only subsistence to such a nature. Likewise during the three days of Christ's death, the Word remained united with Christ's corpse, not because it was a person, but because it was a suppositum.

Another objection. The divine nature can formally sanctify Christ's human nature only by intrinsically perfecting it and really changing it as its intrinsic form. But the divine nature cannot be in relation to Christ's human nature as its intrinsic form. Therefore the divine nature cannot formally sanctify Christ's human nature. This means that Christ's human nature would be holy only by extrinsic denomination.

Reply. I distinguish the major: unless the divine nature intrinsically perfected the human nature as the intrinsic form that terminates it, or rather as the act that intrinsically terminates it, this I concede; that the divine nature could formally sanctify it only as its intrinsic form that informs it, this I deny. And I contradistinguish the minor.

For just as Christ's human nature is really and intrinsically per-

[25] Matt. 17:5.

fected, not because it is a nature, but because it is a suppositum, inasmuch as it is terminated by the Word, so it is really and intrinsically sanctified by its personal union with the Word.

But I insist. There can be no holiness without the intrinsic form that excludes sin. But this intrinsic form must inform, just as sin is an inherent privation; so also blindness is removed only by the inherent power to see, and not as proposed by reason of the terminating object.

Reply. I concede the major. I deny the minor, for sin is absolutely impossible in Christ's human nature solely because this human nature is assumed by the Word. The reason is that sin is a privation that introduces disorder in the entire suppositum, and the divine suppositum cannot be subjected to disorder. On the contrary, blindness is only the privation of some particular accident, namely, the power to see, and hence this blindness is removed only by the restoration of the inherent visual faculty.

Final objection. But in such a case, Christ's human nature is sanctified by the increate sanctity and consequently would be God or the Godhead. Confusion of the nature would follow the form.

Reply. I distinguish the consequent as in the previous objection. That Christ's human nature would be God or the Godhead, if it were sanctified by the divine nature, as the informing form, this I concede; as the act that properly terminates the nature, this I deny. Therefore Christ's sanctity is substantial, increate, and also innate.

Doubt. Is Christ's human nature formally and substantially sanctified by the divine nature that is included in the personality of the Word, or is it sanctified by His relative personality, because of what this adds to the absolute perfections, or even by the very mode of the union?

Reply. Gonet, Billuart, and several other Thomists say that Christ's humanity is substantially sanctified by the divine nature that is included in the personality of the Word, but not in the other two ways. There is authoritative proof for this affirmation from the quotations of the above-mentioned Fathers, especially St. Gregory, who says: "Christ [anointed] is so called because of His divine nature, for that is the unction of the human nature." [26] But what anoints the human nature is formally what sanctifies it. Therefore the human nature is formally sanctified by the divine nature.

Theological proof. Christ's human nature is formally sanctified by

[26] *Oratio* 30, no. 21.

the divine sanctity. The divine sanctity, however, is the divine nature as such, which is included in the personality of the Word, and therefore the three divine persons are holy by the same essential holiness.[27]

Confirmation. Habitual grace formally sanctifies inasmuch as it is a participation of the divine nature, and thus it is the source of strictly divine operations and ultimately of the beatific vision. Therefore, in like manner, what formally sanctifies Christ's human nature is precisely the divine nature that is included in the personality of the Word.

Hence the other two modes are rejected. First of all, it is clearly evident that Christ's human nature is not formally sanctified by the mode itself of the union, because, in our opinion, there is no such mode of union; and if there were, it would not formally sanctify the nature, because it would not be the sanctifying form, but merely the application of the nature to the form. Thus the just person is not said to be sanctified by the mode of union with habitual grace, but by habitual grace itself.

Finally, Christ's human nature is not formally sanctified by the relative personality of the Word because of what this personality adds to the absolute perfections of the divine persons, for, according to the more probable opinion of several Thomists as explained in the treatise on the Trinity, the divine personalities considered as such or because of the notion of reference to the opposite correlative in the order of divine relations (*esse ad*), which they add to the divine essence, do not declare a new perfection, and therefore sanctity, but rather they abstract, as the free act of God does, from both perfection and imperfection. Otherwise we should have to say that the Father is lacking in a certain perfection since He does not have sonship, or that subsistent relation which constitutes the person of the Son. Hence the subsistent, divine relations, that are opposed to one another and God's free act, are not absolutely simple perfections at least in the strict sense; for an absolutely simple perfection is defined as a perfection the concept of which implies no imperfection, and which is better to have than not to have. Thus the Father has all absolutely simple perfections, otherwise He would not be God, but He does not have the correlative opposite relation of sonship. It is also not better

[27] In other words, the person of the Word sanctifies the human nature of Christ, because the person is divine.

for Him to have the free act of creating than not to have it. For God is not better because He created the universe.

Objection. Some say that Christ's nature is formally sanctified by that with which it is immediately united. But it is more immediately united with the subsistence of the Word than with the divine nature. Therefore Christ's nature is formally sanctified by the subsistence of the Word.

Reply. I distinguish the major. If this to which the human nature is immediately united is the sanctifying form, then I concede the major; otherwise I deny it.

It is not unbefitting Christ's human nature to be united with the divine nature through the medium of the personality of the Word, because this union cannot be effected in the nature, but only in the person. Likewise it is only through the medium of the person of the Word that the human nature is united with the one and only divine nature.[28] Similarly habitual grace sanctifies the whole being of man, although it is not united immediately with the whole of his being.

Thus it remains true that Christ's human nature is formally sanctified by the substantial and increate grace of union, but with a union not by participation with the divine nature, but with the divine nature itself, in the person of the Word. Thus, as already stated, Christ's sanctity is not only a transport of joy experienced in His intellect and will, but it is also the transport of joy that is felt in His whole being.

This preliminary article does not give the complete teaching of St. Thomas on this question, but it covers a particular phase of it, for this is what he had already said in equivalent words.

Having discussed Christ's substantial sanctity, we must now consider the question of His accidental sanctity, which consists in habitual grace that was infused into His soul at the moment of His conception. St. Thomas treats of this grace throughout the whole of this seventh question.

First Article

WHETHER IN THE SOUL OF CHRIST THERE WAS ANY HABITUAL GRACE

State of the question. Paludanus asserts [29] that some theologians were of the opinion that there was no habitual grace in Christ, be-

[28] *Summa theol.,* IIIa, q. 17, a. 2.
[29] *Com. in IIIam,* d. 13, q. 2.

cause they thought it to be entirely superfluous in Him. Their reasons are given by St. Thomas in the objections placed at the beginning of this article, and are as follows:

1. Grace is a certain participation of the divine nature; but Christ is God not by participation, but in truth.

2. By the mere fact that Christ was the natural Son of God, He had the power of doing all things well in the supernatural order, and eternal life was His by right.

What is true about these arguments, as will at once be evident, is that, absolutely speaking, Christ could have acted freely, and, by way of transient help that functions instead of habitual grace, be elevated to elicit supernatural and even meritorious acts, but these would not have been connatural to Him.[30] It is difficult to deny this statement, which is admitted by several Thomists, such as Gonet, Godoy, Billuart, and others.

Let us suppose that Christ or the Word incarnate had not received habitual grace and, nevertheless, had offered Himself for us on the cross; this oblation would not only be salutary, as our acts are that precede justification and dispose us for it, but by virtue of the grace of union this oblation would also be meritorious, in fact, of infinite value.[31] Nevertheless, as we shall immediately show, this oblation would not have been connatural, as it must be, nor would it have been connatural merit *de condigno.*

Conclusion. We must say that Christ's soul was endowed with habitual grace.

It is the common opinion among theologians, which the Scholastics hold along with the Master of the Book of Sentences [32] and the commentators of St. Thomas on this article. This conclusion is at least

[30] Gonet, *De incarnatione,* disp. 12, a. 2, nos. 35, 44–53.

[31] Cf. Salmanticenses, *De incarnatione,* disp. XIII, dub. 4, nos. 60, 62, 90. Nevertheless the Salmanticenses (*ibid.,* nos. 66, 70) say: "Christ could not merit *de condigno* supernatural rewards without habitual grace," because in their opinion, as given in the places cited above: "Condign merit of any reward has a connatural tendency for this reward."

On this point, the Salmanticenses differ from Godoy, Gonet, Billuart, and a fortiori from Suarez, who unjustifiably holds that Christ could have merited *de condigno* the supernatural rewards without the assistance, by way of transient help, of supernatural and elevating grace (cf. *ibid.,* no. 92). Suarez says this because he admits against the Thomists, that there is in our nature an obediential potentiality that is not only passive and elevational, but also active.

[32] *Com. in IIIam,* d. 13.

theologically certain which is correctly deduced and commonly admitted, so that it belongs at least to "the science of theology," which is subordinate to faith and above theological systems.

For the purpose of reconciling the various theologians who do not attach the same note of censure to the opposite opinion, Francis Sylvius made the following distinctions.

In his opinion: (1) It is certainly of faith that Christ even in His human nature was holy and pleasing to God.

2) It is probably of faith that Christ was sanctified by habitual grace that was infused into His soul, especially because, as Sacred Scripture attests, Christ had charity and the other infused virtues, which presuppose habitual grace.

3) Christ in His human nature was sanctified in two ways: first by the grace of union; secondly by habitual grace. The first sanctity is substantial, the second is accidental. Hence the opinion of those who said that Christ's habitual grace must be denied as superfluous, because He was sanctified by the grace of union, must be rejected, as at least temerarious.

Scriptural proof. St. Thomas quotes in the counterargument, the following text: "The Spirit of the Lord shall rest upon Him [i.e., Christ, or the Messias]: the spirit of wisdom and of understanding, the spirit of counsel and of fortitude, the spirit of knowledge and of godliness, and He shall be filled with the spirit of the fear of the Lord." [33]

This text from Isaias proves directly the presence of the gifts of the Holy Ghost in the soul of Christ and consequently the presence of created habitual grace, from which the gifts proceed as explained in the treatises on grace and the gifts. Thus grace is called by theologians the grace of the virtues and gifts, because these are derived from it.

The Evangelist explains these words of Isaias as referring to Christ,[34] and the interpretation of St. Thomas on these words is the one generally followed.

There is another text that must be quoted concerning this grace. The Evangelist writes: "And the Word was made flesh . . . and we saw His glory as it were of the only-begotten of the Father [which is the grace of union or natural divine sonship], full of grace and truth" [35] [where the fullness of habitual grace is implied]. The

[33] Isa. 11:2 f.
[34] Luke 4:1.
[35] John 1:14.

Evangelist likewise says: "And of His fullness we have all received, and grace for grace." [36] We have confirmation of this grace from those texts of Scripture attributing to Christ virtues that presuppose habitual grace, such as charity, humility, and other virtues.

The meaning of these texts of Sacred Scripture is made clearer by the testimony of tradition, which is the living commentary of Scripture.

Patristic proof.[37] St. John Chrysostom says: "The full measure of grace has been poured out over that Temple [Christ]: for the Spirit does not measure this grace out to Him. . . . We have received of His fullness, but that Temple has received the complete measure of grace. . . . In Him is all grace, in men but a small measure, a drop of that grace." [38]

St. Cyril of Alexandria says: "Christ sanctifies Himself, since as God He is holy by nature; but according to His human nature He is sanctified together with us." [39]

St. Augustine says: "The Lord Jesus Christ Himself not only gave the Holy Spirit as God; but also received it as man, and therefore He is said to be full of grace [40] and of the Holy Spirit.[41] And it is still more plainly written of Him, 'Because God anointed Him with the Holy Spirit.' [42] Certainly, not with visible oil, but with the gift of grace, which is signified by the visible ointment wherewith the Church anoints the baptized." [43]

St. Bernard, commenting on these words of the Evangelist, "And therefore also the Holy that shall be born of thee," [44] says: "He [Christ] was undoubtedly and particularly holy through the sanctification by the Spirit and assumption by the Word." [45] These last words contain two distinct assertions. Evidently, the words "and through the assumption by the Word" signify the increate grace of union; hence the preceding words, "through the sanctification by the Spirit," imply created or habitual grace.

[36] *Ibid.*, 1:16.
[37] Rouet de Journel, *Enchiridion patristicum,* Index theol., no. 394.
[38] *Com. in Ps. 44.* (Journel, *op. cit.,* no. 1208.)
[39] *Dial. de SS. Trinitate* (*op. cit.,* no. 2088). *P.G.,* LXXV, 1018.
[40] John 1:14.
[41] Luke 4:1.
[42] Acts 10:38.
[43] *De Trinit.,* Bk. XV, chap. 26, no. 46 (*op. cit.,* no. 1680).
[44] Luke 1:35.
[45] *Hom. 4* super *Missus est,* no. 5.

We do not find, however, that the Fathers distinguish so clearly between the increate grace of union and created habitual grace as the Scholastics do and especially as St. Thomas does. Yet the Fathers distinguish more explicitly between the Word and charity that is infused into Christ's soul, because the Gospels and epistles frequently refer to Christ's charity and His other virtues that always presuppose habitual grace. The Fathers spoke more in the concrete, that is, they spoke of Christ's acts and were not so much concerned with the abstract question of habitual grace. Such is always the case, inasmuch as our intellect gradually makes the transition from the concrete to the abstract and then returns to the concrete for a better understanding of the question. We find this to be the method of procedure in all treatises.

Theological proof. Three proofs from theological reasoning are given in the body of this article.

1) On account of the principle which is the hypostatic union.

2) In view of the end, or the purpose of the supernatural operations in Christ's soul.

3) Because of Christ's relation to the human race.

The article must be read.

1) The reason on the part of the principle, which is the hypostatic union, is reduced to the following syllogism.

The nearer any recipient is to an inflowing cause, the more does it partake of its influence. But Christ's soul is most closely associated with the Word of God, the Author of grace, since it is united with the Word in the person, and there cannot be a closer union. Therefore Christ's soul receives the maximum influx of grace from God.

It follows from this that Christ's habitual grace, though it is not a physical property, is at least a moral property of the hypostatic union, inasmuch as the Word incarnate was connaturally entitled to it. It is not, however, a physical property, for the Word does not constitute with Christ's human nature one nature, but only one person.

A similar reason, all due proportions being observed, prevails for the fullness of grace in the Blessed Virgin Mary.

2) The reason, because of the end of Christ's operation in His soul, may thus be expressed: That the operations of the soul, namely, knowledge and love, may attain to God the Author of grace, who is to be loved above all things, the soul and its faculties must be elevated by habitual grace as by a second nature. But it was necessary that

operations of Christ's soul should *most closely* and therefore connaturally attain to God the Author of grace, by knowledge and love. Therefore Christ's soul and its faculties had to be elevated by habitual grace.

The major is evident, inasmuch as habitual grace is necessary so that these operations be elicited connaturally. For the agent operates connaturally when it has in itself the nature or permanent form by which it is inclined to its act. But Christ's soul could be inclined intrinsically and permanently to vital supernatural acts only by habitual grace. Therefore, that Christ's soul be inclined intrinsically and permanently to vital supernatural acts, it had to have habitual grace.[46]

The nature itself of the soul did not suffice nor did the grace of union.

For the soul by nature is entitatively natural and hence it is intrinsically incapable of eliciting vital supernatural acts; but with merely actual grace it could indeed elicit such acts, just as a sinner elicits a salutary act before justification; but such an act is not connatural to the soul, as it is generally admitted to be in the case of a just person.[47]

The grace of union likewise did not suffice, because this grace is, as already stated by St. Thomas: "the personal being that is given gratis from above to the human nature in the person of the Word." [48] Thus this grace was the *principium quod* of the operations, but not the *principium quo*. That by which Christ's soul is intrinsically, permanently, and connaturally inclined to supernatural acts, must be in the soul by way of a second nature, as the radical *principium quo* of operations, just as the infused virtues are the *proximate principium quo*.

It is evident from this that habitual grace in Christ was not superfluous, but it was necessary for the eliciting of connatural supernatural and meritorious acts.[49]

We must insist upon the word "connatural" because, absolutely speaking, Christ, in virtue of the grace of union, and with a transient help, could have elicited supernatural and even meritorious acts. But that He should elicit these acts connaturally, His soul had to be

[46] *Summa theol.*, IIIa, q. 7, a. 1, ad 3.
[47] *Ibid.*, ad 1.
[48] *Ibid.*, q. 6, a. 6.
[49] *Ibid.*, q. 7, a. 1, ad 2.

endowed with habitual grace as a second nature, which is a participation of the divine nature. Otherwise His soul would be imperfect, which is absolutely unbefitting Him.

3) The reason of Christ's relation to us confirms the preceding proofs, and may be expressed by the following syllogism.

The mediator between God and man must have grace overflowing upon others. But Christ, as man, is the mediator between God and man, for the Scripture says: "Of His fullness, we have all received, and grace for grace." [50]

We shall see farther on that Christ's grace as head of the Church is not precisely the grace of union, but it is habitual grace as presupposing and connoting the grace of union. For St. Thomas says: "Everything acts inasmuch as it is a being in act . . . , hence the agent is nobler than the patient. . . . And therefore from this pre-eminence of grace which Christ received, it is befitting to Him that this grace is bestowed on others." [51]

Truly Christ is the head of the human race inasmuch as He merited and satisfied for us, and He could not connaturally elicit these meritorious and satisfactory acts without habitual grace, as already stated. But the grace of union is presupposed so that these acts may be of infinite value on the part of the *principium quod* of these operations.

For a more complete understanding of this article, the following three conclusions taken from Gonet, with whom several other Thomists such as Godoy and Billuart agree, must be noted. However, the Salmanticenses differ from the others concerning the third conclusion.

1) Habitual grace was required in Christ's soul for the completion and perfection of His sanctity. Such is the opinion of all theologians except Vasquez.

2) Habitual grace was required in Christ's soul for His supernatural acts to be connatural.

3) It was necessary for Christ to have habitual grace so that He could merit connaturally a supernatural reward. By Christ's absolute power, however, without this grace He could have merited a supernatural reward with intrinsically supernatural help by way of a transient light of glory.

So say several Thomists, such as Godoy and Billuart.

[50] John 1:16.

[51] *Summa theol.,* IIIa, q. 8, a. 5.

Objection. The argument raised against this third conclusion is that St. Thomas says: "Although there is a certain note of infinity in Christ's merit because of the dignity of the person, yet His actions are meritorious because of habitual grace, without which merit is impossible." [52]

Gonet replies as follows: "I answer that the purpose of St. Thomas in the passage just quoted is to point out that without habitual grace there can be no question of connatural merit. It does not follow from this, absolutely speaking, and according to God's absolute power, that Christ's soul solely with the grace of union and an actual help in the supernatural order could not merit a supernatural reward, but only that He could not do so connaturally." [53]

John of St. Thomas is of about the same opinion, saying: "Habitual grace is not absolutely necessary for the validity of Christ's merit and satisfaction that transcends the former and that is derived from the value of the person." [54]

The conclusion of St. Thomas is confirmed from the solution of the objections in this article.

Reply to first objection. "The soul of Christ is not essentially divine. Hence it behooves it to be divine by participation, which is by grace."

Reply to second objection. In Christ's soul "the beatific act and its fruition could not be without grace."

Reply to third objection. "Christ's humanity is the instrument of the Godhead, not indeed an inanimate instrument, which nowise acts, but is merely acted upon, but an instrument animated by a rational soul, which is so acted upon as to act." For Christ's soul to act supernaturally by the love of charity, it was at least the normal requisite for His soul to have habitual grace. It would have been something absolutely abnormal for Christ not to have this habitual grace.

Another objection. If Christ had habitual grace, He would be the adoptive son of God, for adoptive sonship is the formal effect of habitual grace. We shall see further on that Christ cannot be called the adopted son of God, because He is already the natural Son of God in His own right.

Reply. I deny the consequence, for adoptive sonship is not the

[52] *De veritate,* q. 29, a. 5, ad 4.
[53] *De incarnatione,* disp. 12, a. 2, no. 45.
[54] *De incarnatione,* disp. 8, a. 2, no. 2.

primary effect of habitual grace, but only its secondary effect, and even if it were the primary effect, it would not be communicated to Christ, because He is already the natural Son of God and hence is incapable of being an adopted son of God. Adopted sonship applies to anyone by reason of the suppositum, or person, and hence the person who is the natural Son of God, cannot be called the adopted son. Hence the Blessed Virgin Mary is the first of the adopted children of God.

First doubt. When did Christ receive habitual grace?

Reply. He received this grace at the moment of His conception, because habitual grace is the connatural consequence of the hypostatic union.[55]

Second doubt. Did Christ at the first moment of His conception dispose Himself by an act of free will for the habitual grace that was then infused?

St. Thomas answers this question in the affirmative, because this mode of sanctification by one's own disposing act, as in adults, is more perfect than to be sanctified by the disposing act of another as an infant.[56]

St. Thomas holds that "Christ's intellect in regard to His infused knowledge, could understand at the first moment of His conception, without turning to phantasms." [57] Many doctors admit this truth as applicable to the Blessed Virgin Mary. So also the angels; Adam and Eve, who were created as fully grown, by receiving habitual grace at the moment of their creation disposed themselves for it by actual grace.

Objection. Some say that this act of free will comes from habitual grace and therefore cannot dispose one for it.

Reply. Several Thomists, such as Gonet and Serra rightly maintain in their treatises on grace, when discussing the justification of adults, that the free act that ultimately disposes in the order of material cause for habitual grace follows it in the order of formal cause and hence is the effect of habitual grace, in accordance with the principle: causes mutually interact, though in a different order.

Likewise the due organization of the human body disposes it for

[55] Cf. IIIa, q. 34, a. 1.
[56] *Ibid.*, q. 34, a. 3.
[57] *Ibid.*, a. 2, ad 3.

the reception of the human soul; however, the body has this ultimate disposition only from the soul, as St. Thomas teaches.[58]

Other Thomists, such as Goudin, say that the free act which is the ultimate disposition for habitual grace in adults proceeds effectively from the virtue of charity that is not as yet permanently communicated as a habit but is of the nature of a transient actual help. The former answer seems the more profound.

St. Thomas solves this question, saying: "Because the infusion of grace and the remission of sin regard God who justifies, hence in the order of nature, [instantaneously] the infusion of grace is prior to the freeing from sin. But if we look at what takes place on the part of the man justified, it is the other way about, since in the order of nature, the being freed from sin, is prior to the obtaining of justifying grace." [59] But the being freed from sin is the ultimate disposition for the attainment of habitual grace, and this takes place in the adult only by an act of free will (as stated in the body of the article); this movement of the free will to God proceeds from the actual infusion of habitual grace and follows it in the orders of formal, efficient, and final causes, although it precedes this grace in the order of material cause, as the ultimate disposition in the body in its relation to the soul.

Second Article

WHETHER IN CHRIST THERE WERE VIRTUES

State of the question. We are concerned with virtues that are so called in the strict sense, such as the theological and cardinal virtues. Afterward, in discussing Christ's knowledge, we shall devote a question exclusively (q. 9) to the consideration of the intellectual virtues, which are not virtues in the strict sense inasmuch as they do not make a person absolutely good, but only in a qualified manner, such as when we say a person is good in metaphysics or mathematics.

We are concerned not only with directly infused moral virtues, but also with moral virtues of the natural order, which are acquired by our individual acts.

Conclusion. Christ had all the virtues. This means that He had all virtues that do not in their notion imply any defect in the soul of Christ, who was both wayfarer and comprehensor, as will be pointed

[58] *Ibid.*, Ia, q. 76, a. 4, ad 1.
[59] *Ibid.*, Ia IIae, q. 113, a. 8, ad 1.

out farther on. Thus in the following articles we shall have occasion to remark that Christ did not have either faith or hope or penance.

Scriptural proof. The Gospels authoritatively represent Christ as the exemplar of all virtues. Rationalists, such as Renan, acknowledge this to be true. We must insist upon this truth for the better manifestation of Christ's sanctity, which is the motive of credibility that leads to faith in Him.

There is negative evidence of this truth inasmuch as Christ was sinless, so that He could say to the Jews who sought to kill Him: "Which of you shall convince Me of sin?" [60] And nobody dared to contradict Him. Truly, indeed, as the Gospel narrates: "The chief priests and the whole council sought false witness against Jesus that they might put Him to death, and they found not." [61] But it was only because Jesus confessed that He is Christ, the Son of God, that "the high priest rent His garments, saying: 'He hath blasphemed.' " [62] Even Judas confessed, saying: "I have sinned in betraying innocent blood"; [63] and Pilate said: "I am innocent of the blood of this just man, look you to it." [64]

Moreover, Christ had all virtues and even most different kinds of them which He practiced in a heroic degree. Love and dutiful submission to God are especially evident in the life of Jesus, His love and mercy for men, perfect self-denial, humility and utmost magnanimity, most perfect meekness as also fortitude and patience on the cross, as when He prayed for those who tortured Him. We find wonderfully reconciled in Christ that holy rigor of justice toward the impenitent Pharisees and that immensity of mercy toward those sinners who do not resist God's grace.

In fact, as shown in apologetics, this harmony and perseverance that prevails between such vastly different virtues practiced in a heroic degree is a moral miracle. For this sublime and profound harmony between the virtues or holiness of life is impossible without God's special intervention, for it consists in an inseparable union with God which can come only from God, inasmuch as the order of agents must correspond to the order of ends. Apologetical arguments founded not on revelation but on reason make this already evident.

[60] John 8:46.
[61] Matt. 26:59.
[62] *Ibid.*, 26:65.
[63] *Ibid.*, 27:4.
[64] *Ibid.*, 27:24.

In fact, Christ's sanctity is not only eminent, but is manifestly extraordinary in that it unites in itself vastly different heroic virtues. We have seen indeed that a person is at times naturally disposed or is by force of habit ready to perform acts requiring fortitude of soul, who, nevertheless, is not ready to perform acts that call for meekness of soul, for by nature such a person is determined one particular way. But that anyone may have all the virtues and also excel in them, even those so vastly different, such as supreme fortitude and supreme meekness, perfect love of truth and justice and also the greatest of mercy toward those that err and fall into sin, this is impossible without God's special help, who alone in the simplicity of His nature contains formally and eminently vastly different perfections, and who can unite these in the human soul, so as to make it a perfect image of God. Thus the soul of Christ is that most sublime image in which it is possible to contemplate the Deity.

Theological proof. It can be proved by theological reasoning that Christ had all the virtues. This reasoning of St. Thomas is valid for the infused virtues, and may be expressed as follows:

As the faculties of the soul stem from its essence, so the infused virtues stem from habitual grace, and in a proportionate degree. But Christ's soul was endowed with habitual grace from the moment of His conception, and indeed in the highest degree of perfection, as will be more clearly explained farther on.[65] Therefore Christ had all the infused virtues and in the highest degree.[66]

[65] Cf. IIIa, q. 7, a. 9 f.

[66] This argument presupposes that created habitual grace is in Christ's soul. But we can invert the process of argumentation by appealing to Sacred Scripture where it is asserted that infused virtues, such as charity and humility, were and are in Christ's most holy soul so as to prove likewise that this created habitual grace, which is the root of the infused virtues and the gifts, and which, for this reason, is called "the grace of the virtues and the gifts," was and still is in the soul of Christ (cf. IIIa, q. 62, a. 2).

This argument in reverse now makes it clear that it would have been most unbefitting for Christ's most holy soul not to have had created habitual grace, for then the infused virtues would have been in His soul without their proximate and normal foundation, or rather instead of the infused virtues there would have been in His soul only a transient supernatural help, functioning like a transient light of glory.

Hence, although the created habitual grace is not absolutely necessary, presupposing the actual presence of the increate grace of union (by which Christ's soul is already most holy), but only most fitting; nevertheless this fitness is such that its absence would be most unfitting; for it would mean that Christ's soul would then be imperfect, in fact, a sort of monstrosity in the supernatural order. On the contrary, when it is said that "it was fitting for God to create, rather than not to create,

We are concerned with virtues which, in what they mean, imply no defect in the soul of Christ, who was both wayfarer and comprehensor. Thus faith, hope, and repentance must be excluded.[67] The reason given by St. Thomas holds good for charity and all the infused moral virtues.

Reply to first objection. Habitual grace performs supernatural acts only through the medium of the virtues.

Reply to second objection. Christ had the virtues most perfectly, beyond the common mode. In this sense Plotinus gave to a certain sublime degree of virtue the name of virtue of the purified soul, as Macrobius says.[68]

Reply to third objection. "Christ showed the highest kind of liberality and magnificence by despising all riches." For these virtues, just as wittiness which has to do with joking, can be either made use of or despised for the sake of a higher end. But Christ had no evil desires whatever, as will be shown farther on.[69] Thus Christ had perfect temperance, but not continence, which St. Augustine says is not a virtue but something less than the virtue of chastity, for the continent person, strictly speaking, has evil tendencies, but resists them by will power. Cajetan [70] remarks, taking the name "continence" in the more common acceptation of the word, that there is nothing that prevents us from calling Christ continent.

First doubt. Did Christ have all moral virtues that of themselves can be acquired? Theologians generally give an affirmative answer to this question.

The reason is that the sensitive appetite in Christ was no different from ours, which is an inclination to sensible delectable good; that it may completely and perfectly tend to its natural and fitting good, it requires a superadded form, that can be nothing else but a moral vir-

---

to raise us to the supernatural order, and will the Incarnation . . . rather than not to will such things," then the absence of such would have meant no unfitness.

In this we see how very fitting it was for Christ to have habitual grace. Thus all due proportion preserved, it is fitting for the just to have the seven sacred gifts of the Holy Ghost. Otherwise their life of grace would be imperfect, which would be unbefitting as regards Providence that disposes all things sweetly and firmly. (Cf. Ia IIae, q. 68, a. 2.)

[67] Cf. *infra,* q. 15, a. 1, ad 5. Although Christ's detestation of sin was perfect, yet there could be no repentance in Him, simply because He could not sin.

[68] *In somno Scipionis,* Bk. I, chap. 8.

[69] Cf. IIIa, q. 15, a. 1, 2.

[70] *Com. in IIIam,* q. 7, a. 2, ad 3.

tue that is directly acquirable. Infused moral virtues did not suffice, because the direct purpose of these is to incline the will to supernatural acts. The correlative moral and acquirable virtues, although they are in themselves in their own order truly virtues, are related to the virtues as dispositions from which there arises an extrinsic facility for the practice of the infused virtues, for they exclude inordinate inclinations resulting from repetition of acts.[71] The acquired moral virtues are in their relation to the infused virtues somewhat like dexterity in manipulating the harp is to the art that is in the practical intellect of the musician. Hence it is certain that Christ had moral virtues that are of themselves acquirable; otherwise He would have been morally imperfect, just as beginners in the Christian life who, by the very fact that they are in the state of grace, have infused prudence, which scarcely manifests itself, however, because they lack the virtue of acquired prudence, without which it is difficult to practice the virtue of infused prudence.

Confirmation. Christ's will must be perfected as regards good, just as much as His intellect is as regards truth. But there was acquired knowledge in Christ's intellect, as will be made clear farther on.[72] Therefore, likewise in His will and sensitive appetite there was the possibility of acquiring moral virtues.

First objection. To perform a most perfect act is to act from a supernatural motive. But Christ always had to perform most perfect acts. Therefore He always acted from a supernatural motive or by acts of the infused virtues and not by acts of virtues that of themselves were acquirable.

Reply. I distinguish the major: to perform a most perfect act is to act from a supernatural motive, when this motive is the end in view of the person acting, this I concede; that the deed performed must always be in itself supernatural, this I deny. Hence, just as Christ performed not only acts of charity, but also acts of the infused virtues, so also He performed natural acts that as regards the object and end of these acts were good and fitting, though they were subordinated to the supernatural end of charity as being the end in view of the person acting. Thus Christ said: "Render to Caesar the things that are

[71] The infused virtue of itself does indeed give intrinsic facility for its acts, but there may be an extrinsic difficulty because of inordinate passions, if the acquired correlative virtue is lacking, as in the case of the repentant drunkard in whom the acquired virtue of sobriety is wanting.

[72] Cf. IIIa, q. 9, a. 4.

Caesar's. . . ."[73] These are natural obligations, just as even pagans know that commutative justice requires the payment of debts.

As grace does not destroy nature but perfects it, so also the infused virtues neither destroy nor render the acquired virtues useless, but perfect them, directing them to be performed for the love of God, not that the acts themselves are supernatural, but that the end in view of the agent is supernatural. Thus the act of the acquired virtue of temperance is modally supernatural, whereas the act of the infused virtue of temperance is substantially supernatural. Thus the acquired moral virtues are subordinated to the infused moral virtues in some way just as the imagination and sensitive memory are subordinated to knowledge, philosophy to theology, and theology to the doctrine of faith that transcends the science of theology. There is a normal hierarchy of functions in this subordination.

Second objection. But the acquired virtues are required to restrain the immoderate tendencies of the passions, which Christ did not have, for, as will be mentioned farther on,[74] Christ was free from concupiscence. Therefore He had no need of the acquired virtues.

Reply. I distinguish the antecedent: that the acquired virtues are necessary in a secondary sense so as to check the immoderate tendencies of the passions, this I concede; that they are primarily necessary, this I deny. For the primary and special purpose of these virtues is to enable the faculties to act properly, promptly, and with facility in the natural order. It is in this way that chastity operates, for example, even when there are no temptations to be overcome or passions to be curbed. Thus humility in Christ did not check the first movements of pride, but it completely subjected His will to the divine majesty.

Thus Adam in the state of innocence had those virtues that are of themselves capable of attainment, and they remain in the blessed, as St. Thomas teaches.[75]

Second doubt. Did Christ have these moral virtues that can be acquired of themselves by infusion, or did He acquire them by His own acts?

It is difficult to give a definite answer to this question.[76] The more probable opinion of several Thomists is that they were infused, just as

[73] Matt. 22:21.

[74] Cf. IIIa, q. 15, a. 2.

[75] *Ibid.,* Ia IIae, q. 67, a. 1.

[76] So say Gonet, Billuart, as also Suarez and Vasquez, but the latter on different grounds.

Adam in the state of innocence had them from the moment of his creation. However, Adam was created in the adult state, whereas Christ as man gradually grew up to manhood.

The principal reason for this answer is that Christ was never without these virtues, for to be deprived of them for any time is in itself something evil, and no defect is admissible in God, except those that are not contrary to the end of the Incarnation, such as the privation of the glorification of His body for a time. But such is not the case with the temporary privation of these virtues. It would be more derogatory to Christ's dignity that He should be for a time without these virtues, than increase in perfection by acquiring them, which cannot be instantaneous, but only a progressive process. Moreover, the Church declared in the Second Council of Constantinople: "Christ was not subjected to passions, nor did He become better by the repetition of virtuous acts." [77]

Objection. But the Gospel says: "Jesus advanced in wisdom and age, and grace with God and men." [78]

Reply. The answer of St. Thomas is: "Christ advanced in wisdom and grace as also in age (not by an actual increase of the habits but), because as He advanced in age He performed more perfect works." [79]

Another objection. St. Thomas says farther on [80] that Christ advanced in acquired knowledge. Therefore He also advanced in moral virtues that of themselves can be acquired.

Reply. There is not parity of argument. (1) The natural sciences do not make man absolutely good, such as the moral virtues do, but good only in a qualified sense, such as good in mathematics or in physics. (2) If the natural sciences were infused in Christ, then His active intellect would be in a state of continual idleness as regards its first function, which is to abstract intelligible species from the senses. Therefore it is more probable that Christ had moral virtues that of themselves can be acquired from the time of His conception.

Third Article

WHETHER IN CHRIST THERE WAS FAITH

The general opinion of theologians is that Christ did not have faith. Such is the opinion of St. Thomas.

[77] Denz., no. 224.
[78] Luke 2:52.
[79] Cf. IIIa, q. 7, a. 12, ad 3.
[80] *Ibid.,* q. 9, a. 4, and especially q. 12, a. 2, c; also ad 3.

The reason given in the counterargument does not absolutely prove this assertion, for the words of Peter quoted here, namely, "Thou knowest all things," [81] were spoken after Christ's resurrection. Hence these words prove to some extent that at least after the resurrection Jesus did not have faith concerning mysteries in the strict sense, but the beatific vision.

The body of the article presupposes what must be proved farther on,[82] namely, that Christ from the first moment of His conception completely saw God in His essence. But the clear vision of God excludes the notion of faith, which is of things not seen.

In other words, a virtue cannot be in a subject to whom its primary act is derogatory. But the primary act of faith refers to God not seen. Therefore Christ could not have had faith, since from the moment of His conception He clearly saw God in His essence. This is the common opinion among theologians. No theologian holds that an act of faith is simultaneously compatible with the beatific vision, because the scriptural text of St. Paul is clear on this point: "Faith [83] . . . is the evidence of things that appear not." Durandus thinks that the habit of faith, however, if not its act, can remain in the blessed. Scotus holds this to be possible, but useless. St. Thomas and St. Bonaventure are of the opinion that the habit of faith cannot co-exist with the beatific vision. Thus St. Thomas says: "The object of faith is a divine thing not seen. But the habit of virtue . . . takes its species from the object. Hence, if we deny that the divine thing was not seen, we exclude the very essence of faith." [84]

At least the permanence of the beatific vision excludes both act and habit of faith. The beatific vision as a transient act, which St. Augustine and St. Thomas think St. Paul had on this earth, excludes the act of faith concerning this object, but not the habit of faith.

Reply to first objection. The moral virtues, although they are inferior to faith, were and are always in Christ because they imply no defect as regards their subject matter.[85]

Reply to second objection. St. Thomas does not teach that Christ had the merit of faith, but He had what constitutes the reward of our faith, which is perfect obedience to the loving commands of God.

[81] John 21:17.
[82] Cf. IIIa, q. 34, a. 4.
[83] Heb. 11:1.
[84] Cf. IIIa, q. 7, a. 4.
[85] However, in the case of the infused moral virtues, the imperfection of the discursive method of prudence enters in, and for this reason they are inferior to the gifts.

But Christ was faithful to His promises, and this is sometimes called faith in Sacred Scripture.[86] Thus the prophet says of the Messias: "Faith shall be the girdle of His loins." [87]

Therefore the maximum of faith that any intellectual creature had was the theological faith of the Blessed Virgin Mary, for her faith was proportionate to her plenitude of grace. From this we conclude how sublime must have been the acts of faith and hope made by the Blessed Virgin Mary, especially on Mount Calvary, not in the least doubting that her Son, who seemed to be conquered, was the Son of God, the conqueror of the devil and sin, and the proximate victor of death.

Fourth Article

WHETHER IN CHRIST THERE WAS HOPE

State of the question. There is some difficulty, for the Psalmist, speaking in the person of Christ, says: "In Thee, O Lord, have I hoped." [88] Moreover, Christ awaited or hoped for the glorification of His body and the building up of His mystical body.

Conclusion. St. Thomas, with whom the majority of theologians agree, maintains that Christ did not have the virtue of hope but had a certain act of hope or rather of desire concerning things He did not yet possess.

Scriptural proof. St. Paul says: "What a man seeth, why doth he hope for?" [89] But Christ did not have faith, as was said above,[90] because from the beginning (of the hypostatic union) He enjoyed the vision of the divine essence. Therefore, too, He did not have the virtue of hope.

Theological proof. The reason for this proof is taken from the formal or primary object of hope, for hope, considered as a theological virtue, has God Himself as its primary object, whose fruition is expected. But Christ from the beginning of His conception had the complete fruition of the divine essence, as will be stated farther on.[91] Therefore He did not have the theological virtue of hope.

[86] Osee 2:20.
[87] Isa. 11:5.
[88] Ps. 30:1.
[89] Rom. 8:24.
[90] Cf. a. 1.
[91] Cf. IIIa, q. 34, a. 4.

The principle of the preceding article applies equally here, namely, a virtue cannot be in a subject to whom its primary act is derogatory.

However, at the end of the argumentative part of this article, St. Thomas admits that Christ had a certain act of hope or rather of desire as regards some things, so that He could expect the glorification of His body and the building up of the Church. Thus the Psalmist, speaking in the person of Christ, says: "In Thee, O Lord, have I hoped." [92] But these things do not constitute the primary object of the theological virtue of hope, and thus it remains true that Christ did not have this theological virtue of hope.

Therefore of all intellectual creatures, the hope of the Blessed Virgin Mary was the most sublime especially on Mount Calvary, when all the apostles, with the exception of St. John, did not have the courage to witness the death of Christ. Hence it is said of her: "Grant that I may carry the cross of Christ." [93]

First doubt. To what virtue must we attribute this act of desire in Christ for the glorification of His body and the building up of the Church?

Reply. This act must be attributed to the virtue of charity, as its secondary act, whereby Christ loved Himself and the Church, for God's sake, as the Evangelist says: "Greater love than this no man hath, that a man lay down his life for his friends." [94]

Thus the love of concupiscence by which we desire eternal life for the glory of God, is attributed to us as a secondary act of charity.

Second doubt. Was there penance as a virtue in Christ?

Reply. There was no penance, as a virtue, in Christ, because it implies in the strict sense sorrow for one's own sins. But Christ was impeccable, as will be explained farther on. The Sacred Congregation of the Holy Office forbade such invocations as: "Heart of Jesus, penitent for us, Jesus penitent, Jesus penitent for us." [95]

The truth of this reply is clearly established since it agrees with the

[92] Ps. 30:1.

[93] *Stabat Mater.* After Christ's death, the Blessed Virgin Mary, during her life on earth, made more sublime acts of faith and hope subjectively, but not objectively. Thus it is said that all Christ's acts were personally of infinite value subjectively, but His act of love on the cross was nobler objectively. Thus to teach the subject matter of theology is more meritorious than to be engaged in any other material pursuit, even though done under obedience; but to teach theology subjectively and personally is less meritorious when one is not actuated so much by charity.

[94] John 15:13.

[95] A.S.S., XXXVI, 319.

generally accepted teaching of St. Thomas, which declares that penance is a special virtue that is distinct not only from the virtue of religion, but also from the virtue of vindictive justice and of all the other virtues.[96]

Thus the primary and specific act of penance is sorrow for one's own sins with the motive of amendment, and the intention of performing salutary acts in satisfaction for one's past offenses.

But a virtue cannot be in a subject to whom its primary act is intrinsically repugnant. But the act of penance is intrinsically repugnant to Christ's human nature, because it was united to the Word.[97] But Christ had a perfect detestation for sin inasmuch as it is an offense against God, arising from the intensity of His love for God offended and for souls that are dead to God through mortal sin.

Fifth Article

WHETHER IN CHRIST THERE WERE THE GIFTS

State of the question. The difficulty is that gifts are given to help the virtues. But the virtues were most perfect in Christ. Therefore He did not need this help.

Moreover, Christ had already on this earth the contemplation of heaven as explained farther on. But the gifts of wisdom, knowledge, and understanding seem to belong to contemplation in this life, and apparently these are useless in a soul that already enjoys the beatific vision.

Conclusion. It is commonly admitted, however, that the soul of Christ had these gifts in a pre-eminent degree.

Gonet maintains that this conclusion is a certainty of the faith, because of the text of Isaias quoted in the proof.

Scriptural proof. The prophet says: "The Spirit of the Lord shall rest upon Him: the spirit of wisdom and of understanding, the spirit of counsel and of fortitude, the spirit of knowledge and of godliness. And He shall be filled with the spirit of the fear of the Lord." [98]

Instead of the words, "the spirit of knowledge and of godliness," the Hebrew text reads, "the spirit of knowledge and of fear." Thus fear is mentioned twice. The Greek version and the Vulgate give

[96] Cf. IIIa, q. 80, a. 2.
[97] *Ibid.*, q. 15.
[98] Isa. 11:2. See also q. 7, a. 1.

"godliness," which is about the same in meaning as reverential godliness. The Old Testament does not distinguish so clearly between godliness and fear as the New Testament does, which is not the law of fear, but of love.[99]

The Fathers and Scholastics are generally agreed that this text concerns Christ's human nature.

Theological proof. Although it has been revealed that Christ had gifts and still has them, this assertion can also be proved from higher revealed principles, namely, from the definition of gifts. St. Thomas says in this article: "The gifts, properly, are certain perfections of the soul's powers, inasmuch as they have a natural aptitude to be moved by the Holy Ghost," according to St. Luke, who says: "And Jesus being full of the Holy Ghost returned from the Jordan and was led by the Spirit into the desert." Hence it is manifest that the gifts were in Christ in a pre-eminent degree.

The thesis is confirmed by the fact that the gifts of the Holy Ghost follow from habitual grace and are connected with charity, as St. Thomas teaches.[100] But Christ had habitual grace in the most perfect manner and the highest degree of charity. Therefore He also had pre-eminently the gifts.

The thesis is also confirmed from the solution of the objections.

Reply to first objection. It points out that as a man, however perfect he may be, needs to be helped by God, so also, no matter how perfect the virtues are, they need to be helped by the gifts, which perfect the powers of the soul, inasmuch as these are not controlled by reason illumined by faith, but by the Holy Spirit. This reply confirms the teaching of St. Thomas as set forth in a previous passage [101] where he shows that the infused virtues, even the highest degree, are specifically distinct from the gifts as regards their formal object *quo* or their rule or motive; [102] for to be ruled by right reason even though illumined by the light of faith differs from being ruled by the Holy Spirit, which means to be ruled by His special inspiration, which transcends the discursive process of reasoning. Thus there is a mani-

[99] Although in this text of Isaias there is no mention made of the gift of godliness, yet St. Paul refers to it when he says: "You have received the spirit of adoption of sons, whereby we cry: Abba (Father)" (Rom. 8:15). The liturgy of Pentecost attests that the doctrine of the sacred sevenfold gifts is the constant tradition of the Church.

[100] *Summa theol.,* Ia IIae, q. 68, a. 5.

[101] *Ibid.*

[102] See *God, His Existence,* II, 57.

fest difference between being ruled by infused prudence, which proceeds from living faith, and being ruled by the gift of counsel.

Reply to third objection. It states that the gifts were not useless in Christ, for He also had earthly knowledge, as will be stated farther on; [103] for Christ was both wayfarer and comprehensor. He was comprehensor as regards the higher part of the soul, and wayfarer inasmuch as His soul still was passible and His body passible and mortal, so that He looked forward to beatitude in all those things which were wanting to Him of beatitude. Moreover, as explained elsewhere,[104] the gifts remain in heaven.

As stated in this last citation, this doctrine of the permanence of the gifts in heaven is affirmed by St. Ambrose,[105] and the reason is that the gifts of the Holy Spirit perfect the human mind to follow the prompting of the Holy Spirit, which is especially the case in heaven. But in heaven, evil and temptation being no more, by the gifts of the Holy Spirit we are perfected in good, not entirely as regards the same material object but the gifts will preserve in us intact the same formal objects both *quo* and *quod* of the virtues by which latter they are specified; for as theologians in heaven will see the object of theology, either in the Word if in this life they studied it out of love for God, or outside the Word; so also all the blessed in heaven will receive special inspirations from the Holy Spirit to know something special by means of experimental knowledge, according as it is connaturally related to divine things, for instance, to know for what wayfarers they must especially pray. The beatific vision precedes beatific love, whereas the knowledge obtained by the gifts follows this love. Finally, there is neither succession in knowledge nor acquisition of anything new, whereas by the gifts it is possible for the blessed to acquire additional knowledge.

But obscurity and similar imperfections that now actually belong to the gifts, either of wisdom or counsel, or of other such gifts, do not belong to the state of glory, nor were these defects in Christ.

Thus the gift of wisdom disposed Christ so as to be moved with facility by the Holy Spirit to pass certain judgment on divine things by the highest of causes, in accordance with a connaturalness that is founded on charity for things.

[103] Cf. IIIa, q. 15, a. 10.
[104] *Ibid.*, Ia IIae, q. 68, a. 6.
[105] *De Spiritu Sancto,* Bk. I, chap. 1.

But the gift of understanding attributed to Him correct and immediate penetration of those things that pertain to the kingdom of God.

The gift of counsel likewise attributed to Christ the power of immediately finding out the motive for action.

The gift of knowledge so that even in the consideration of inferior motives, He might judge with absolute certainty about things that happened.

The gift of fortitude expelled from Him the fear of death and its attendant tortures.

Gonet says these conclusions are admitted by all theologians as being certain and beyond dispute.

Sixth Article

WHETHER IN CHRIST THERE WAS THE GIFT OF FEAR

State of the question. There are two difficulties: (1) It seems that hope is stronger than fear, for the object of hope is good, whereas the object of fear is evil. If, therefore, Christ did not have the virtue of hope, a fortiori He did not have the gift of fear. (2) The gift of fear makes one afraid either of being separated from God, or of being punished by Him. But these two were impossible for Christ, because He was impeccable.

Reply. Christ had the gift of fear.

Scriptural proof. The testimony of the prophet, quoted in the preceding article, is: "He shall be filled with the spirit of the fear of the Lord," [106] which also in the Hebrew text refers to the spirit of fear. Moreover, the Church condemned the following proposition of Abelard: "The spirit of the fear of the Lord was not in Christ." [107]

Theological proof. This assertion of Sacred Scripture is not so much proved as explained by the following syllogism.

God is feared by an act of reverential fear, not only inasmuch as He can inflict punishment but on account of His pre-eminence, who cannot with impunity be resisted. But the soul of Christ was moved by the Holy Spirit toward God by certain reverential affection. Therefore Scripture attributes to Him the fullness of the gift of fear, not indeed of the fear of punishment, or sin, but of reverential fear.

[106] Isa. 11:3.
[107] Denz., no. 378.

Confirmation. This gift of fear, understood as reverential fear, remains in the blessed, for the Psalmist exclaims: "The fear of the Lord is holy, enduring forever and ever." [108] It is said of the angels, especially of those called Powers: "The Powers tremble." [109] For every creature that is not self-existent trembles in the sight of Him who alone is and can be the self-subsisting Being. But Christ's human nature is not His being, although it exists by the very being of the Word, inasmuch as there is one being in Christ, just as there is one person.[110]

Doubt. What is the primary object of the gift of fear?

It is God's pre-eminence, who cannot with impunity be resisted; and its primary act is reverence for this divine pre-eminence, and so this gift can be both in Christ and the blessed. The secondary object of the gift of fear, or of filial fear, is the evil of sin that must be avoided.

In contrast to this, the primary object of fear, considered as a passion, is terrifying sensible evil, and the primary act of this fear is flight from this evil. Finally, the primary object of servile fear is the evil of punishment to be inflicted on account of the offense committed.

Thus it remains true that the habits of the virtues and the gifts properly and directly refer to good, but to evil as a consequence.

Seventh Article

WHETHER THE GRACES GRATIS DATAE WERE IN CHRIST

State of the question. By placing the article about the graces gratis datae here, it is evident that St. Thomas draws a complete distinction between them and the gifts as he has already shown.[111] The seven gifts, which are connected with charity, belong to the organism of the supernatural life, but the graces gratis datae do not.

The difficulty is that the graces gratis datae are freely given by way of a transient act. But Christ had permanently the fullness of grace. Hence He did not need these secondary graces. The Gospel does not say that He had the gift of tongues.

Reply. Nevertheless the answer is that all the graces gratis datae were pre-eminently in Christ as the first and chief teacher of the faith.

[108] Ps. 18:10.
[109] Preface of Mass.
[110] *Summa theol.,* IIIa, q. 17, a. 2.
[111] *Ibid.,* Ia IIae, q. 111. a. 4; IIa IIae, q. 171.

Authoritative proof. St. Augustine says: "As in the head are all the senses, so in Christ were all the graces." [112] St. Augustine is also expressly referring here to the graces gratis datae in Christ.

The Master of the Book of the Sentences is precisely of the same opinion,[113] and it is commonly admitted by the scholastic theologians.

Theological proof. Graces gratis datae are ordained for the manifestation of faith and spiritual doctrine, because the manner of their enumeration makes this evident,[114] and also the explanation of St. Thomas.[115] But Christ is the first and chief teacher of the faith and of spiritual doctrine. Therefore the graces gratis datae were in Christ.

This means that the graces gratis datae were most excellently in Christ, being ordained for the benefit of others. They may be expressed by the following schema.

- Graces gratis datae that are ordained for the instruction of others in divine things
  - to acquire complete knowledge of divine things
    - faith concerning principles.[116]
    - word of wisdom concerning the principal conclusions.
    - word of knowledge concerning the examples and effects.
  - to confirm the divine revelation
    - by doing
      - grace of healing.
      - working of miracles.
    - by knowing
      - prophecy.
      - discerning of spirits.
  - to convey fittingly to the hearers the divine message
    - kinds of tongues.
    - interpretation of speeches.

Christ had to have in the most perfect degree all these graces that were bestowed on others; for they denote no imperfection that is re-

[112] *Ep. ad Dardan.*, no. 287.
[113] *Com. in IIIam,* d. 13.
[114] I Cor. 12:7 f.
[115] Cf. Ia IIae, q. 111, a. 4; IIa IIae, q. 171.
[116] This faith is not the theological virtue, but a gift whereby those who instruct others in the principles of the faith are endowed with certainty.

pugnant either to the beatific vision or to the hypostatic union. They are also becoming to the dignity of the head of the mystical body, as St. Augustine says in the counterargument of this article.

Reply to first objection. St. Thomas points out that these graces are called "diversities of graces," [117] inasmuch as in the saints these graces are divided; but Christ had these graces all at once and in their plenitude just as He had and always has the plenitude of habitual grace.

Reply to second objection. It was fitting for Christ to have habitual grace, not according to His divine nature, but according to His human nature.

Reply to third objection. It is pointed out that, although we do not read of Christ having had the gift of tongues, because He preached only to the Jews, "yet a knowledge of all languages was not wanting to Him, since even the secrets of hearts, of which all words are signs, were not hidden from Him." [118]

Christ likewise had the grace gratis datae of faith. This grace is a certain pre-eminence of knowledge concerning the revealed mysteries whether such knowledge be clear or obscure; [119] it is also a facility given by the Holy Spirit of proposing the things of faith simply and in a way adapted to all, so that they can be understood even by the ignorant, as explained by St. Thomas.[120] It is evident from the Gospel that Christ had both kinds of excellence.

There is no doubt about Christ's powers concerning either the grace of healing or the discernment of spirits, for the Evangelist says: "And Jesus seeing their thoughts [of the Pharisees], said: 'Why do you think evil in your hearts?' " [121] Again he says: "Jesus knowing their thoughts." [122]

Finally, Christ had pre-eminently the grace of interpretation of speech for explaining the Scriptures in the true and most exalted sense. Hence the Evangelist relates that the disciples going to the town called Emmaus said: "Was not our heart burning within us, whilst He spoke in the way, and opened to us the Scriptures?" [123]

[117] I Cor. 12:4.
[118] *Summa theol.,* IIIa, q. 12, a. 1; q. 20, a. 2.
[119] Cf. *ibid.,* Ia IIae, q. 111, a. 4.
[120] *Com. in I Cor.,* XII, lect 2.
[121] Matt. 9:4.
[122] *Ibid.,* 12:25.
[123] Luke 24:32.

Eighth Article

WHETHER IN CHRIST THERE WAS THE GIFT OF PROPHECY

State of the question. St. Thomas posited this special article about prophecy, because this grace gratis data presents a particular difficulty. For the first objection of this article remarks that prophecy implies a certain obscurity. But Christ already enjoyed on this earth the beatific vision. Also prophecy concerns distant things or those that are far off, and seems to imply an essential imperfection, as faith and hope do. Moreover, the Apostle says that in heaven, "prophecies shall be made void." [124]

Reply. The answer is in the affirmative.

Scriptural proof. Moses announced to the Israelites: "The Lord thy God will raise up to thee a Prophet . . . of thy brethren . . . Him thou shalt hear." [125] Jesus applied to Himself what Moses foretold of Him, saying: "He wrote of Me." [126] Likewise Jesus said of Himself in the synagogue at Nazareth: "A prophet is not without honor, save in his own country." [127]

Theological proof. He is a prophet who knows and announces what is distant both from himself according to his state and from his hearers. But Christ, who was not only comprehensor but also wayfarer, knew and announced very many things which were distant from Him according to His state as wayfarer, such as His betrayal, death, and resurrection,[128] as also the destruction of Jerusalem, the signs preceding the end of the world, the denial of Peter, and several other events. Therefore Christ was a prophet.

Reply to first objection. Prophecy, as usually communicated, is obscure and enigmatic not in itself, but because of the imperfection of the hearer. Its clarity or obscurity, that it be communicated transiently, or permanently, are of themselves a matter of indifference. But in Christ prophecy was clear and permanent because of the union of His human nature with the Word.

But if the Apostle says that in heaven "prophecies shall be made

[124] I Cor. 13:8.
[125] Deut. 18:15.
[126] John 5:46.
[127] Matt. 13:57.
[128] *Ibid.*, chaps. 15, 20.

void," [129] he has in mind complete beatitude, which is incompatible with the state of wayfarer.

Ninth Article

WHETHER IN CHRIST THERE WAS THE FULLNESS OF GRACE

State of the question. The third part of this question begins here. After the consideration of the grace of the virtues and of the gifts and of the graces gratis datae in Christ, St. Thomas treats of the fullness of grace. He asks whether Christ was simply full of grace, both intensively and extensively.

This article and those that follow are therefore concerned with the perfection of Christ's grace.

Conclusion. Christ had fullness of grace, both intensively, that is, as regards its perfection, and extensively, that is, as regards the various effects it can produce.

Scriptural proof. The Evangelist says: "We saw His glory . . . full of grace and truth. . . . And of His fullness we have all received, and grace for grace." [130] Likewise St. John the Baptist testified concerning Christ, and the Evangelist says; "He whom God hath sent, speaketh the words of God; for God does not give to Him the spirit by measure. The Father loveth the Son, and He hath given all things into His hand." [131]

The Fathers of the Church have often explained these texts by showing that Christ, who is most full of grace, had every kind of holiness.[132]

Theological proof. It is simply discursive and explanatory, explaining the above quoted text.[133]

This proof may be reduced to the following syllogism.

Fullness of grace is of two kinds, namely, intensive and extensive.

[129] I Cor. 13:8.

[130] John 1:14 f.

[131] This text is clarified from what St. Paul says in one of his epistles: "The charity of God is poured forth in our hearts by the Holy Ghost, who is given to us" (Rom. 5:5). St. Thomas explains (Ia, q. 43, a. 3) that the mission of the Holy Ghost takes place in that the Holy Ghost becomes present in the soul in a new way by sanctifying grace, and by an increase of this grace. Hence Christ, inasmuch as He received the fullness of grace, is said not to have been limited in His reception of the Spirit.

[132] Cf. Rouet de Journel, *Enchiridion patristicum,* no. 394. See also St. Augustine's *Com. in Joan., loc. cit.*

[133] John 1:14.

But Christ had each kind. Therefore Christ had absolutely or completely fullness of grace.

Major. It is thus explained. There is intensive fullness of any quality in a being, for instance, of whiteness, when the being has as much of this quality as it can naturally have. Thus it appears that a lily has the highest possible degree of whiteness; so also snow.

Hence intensive fullness is estimated from the degree and radication of any quality in the subject. But extensive fullness of any quality is estimated from the relation to the various effects that any operative principle is capable of producing; for example, the irrational animal has not extensive fullness of life, because it has not intellectual life, but only the vegetative life and sensitive life.

Minor. Its parts are proved. Christ had intensive fullness of grace, that is, in the highest degree that it can be had, for two reasons.

1) Because His soul, which was united to God by the most exalted of all possible unions, which is the hypostatic union, received the greatest influx of grace, just as the air that is nearer to the fire is warmer and more luminous.

2) Because grace was given to Christ, as the head, from which it was to be poured out upon all others; just as in this world nothing is brighter than the sun, which illumines all other things. Hence the Evangelist quotes Jesus as saying: "I am come to cast fire on the earth, and what will I but that it be kindled?" [134] The reference is to fire that purifies, illumines, and kindles spiritually.

From these proofs it is apparent that intensive fullness of any quality is estimated from its intrinsic perfection inasmuch as it is pure and free from all imperfection. Thus snow is perfectly white; it has whiteness in all its intensity or purity, containing no element that is not white.

If there is reference to some operative habit, since this habit determines the faculty to operate, it is all the more perfect intensively, the more it determines the faculty with reference to the formal object of the operation to be elicited, that is, it actuates the faculty and is radicated in it. There is something similar in the case of habitual grace, which is an entitative habit, which is received in the essence of the soul, and is radically operative, inasmuch as the virtues are derived from it, just as the faculties are derived from the essence of the soul. Thus intensive fullness of habitual grace is estimated from

[134] Luke 12:49.

its intrinsic perfection free from all imperfection, and its radication in the soul, which it especially determines radically to operate most holily free from all imperfection. This intensive fullness of grace would apply to Christ even if His soul were ordered solely to the performance of acts of the love of God.

Likewise Christ had extensive fullness of grace, which is estimated from its relation to the various effects it can produce.

The reason is that, as St. Thomas says: "Christ had grace for all its operations and effects, and this because it was bestowed on Him, as upon a universal principle in the genus of such as have grace . . . just as the sun is the universal cause of generation." [135]

This twofold fullness, intensive and extensive, is called absolute on the part of the grace itself, which by God's ordinary power cannot be received in a more perfect manner. It is not merely relatively perfect or according to the exigencies of the state or dignity of the subject. In fact, this most exalted dignity of head and redeemer of the human race demands absolute fullness of grace.

Doubt. Is this plenitude of grace more perfect intensively than extensively?

Reply. It is the common opinion among theologians that intensive plenitude is the more perfect, just as quality is to be preferred to quantity, although positivism is inclined to the contrary view; for indeed intensive plenitude is immediately estimated from the intrinsic perfection of the quality, and is the foundation of extensive plenitude. This is especially evident in knowledge, for its intensive plenitude results from the deeper penetration of its first notions and principles, whereas its extensive plenitude, both habitual and actual, is estimated according to the number of conclusions that are deduced from the principles. There are certain physicists who know all the conclusions of their own science in its actual state of development, and who have read all the books of any importance belonging to this science. This does not mean, however, that they have penetrated more deeply into the principles of this science; for the scientific habit is not yet, perhaps, established in their intellect as a sort of second nature. On the contrary, another physicist knows more from on high the principles of this particular science, and their subordination to the other sciences, even though he may have forgotten certain conclusions. The perfection of a science is not estimated according to the

[135] Cf. IIIa, q. 7, a. 9, c.

number of its conclusions, for although science may make use of many subordinated ideas, it is a simple quality that perfects the intellect in its relation to some formal object and to certain first principles, which virtually contain all the conclusions of this particular science.

Thus there is a great difference between Aristotle and the author of a textbook on peripatetic philosophy. Although the author of such a textbook may perhaps succeed in giving to this science new conclusions, yet he has not the genius of Aristotle, nor could he be the author of such works as the *Organon, Physics, Metaphysics,* and *Ethics* of the Stagirite. There is also a similar difference between St. Thomas and his commentators, although the latter may succeed in giving to the science new conclusions.

Likewise those historians who write a critical estimate of the life of Napoleon have a more extensive knowledge perhaps than the ambassadors and soldiers of his time, but they generally do not penetrate so intensively and vividly into the mind of such a genius as Napoleon.

Similarly those historians who insist on giving us a critical evaluation of the Gospels, certainly have a less intensive knowledge of Christ's preaching than the apostles had who heard Him. Thus St. John the Evangelist had a better knowledge of Christ's teaching than a theologian would have who would know all the condemned propositions contained in Denzinger's *Enchiridion.*

Therefore, a fortiori, there was in Christ intensive plenitude of habitual grace and hence of the virtues and gifts.

TENTH ARTICLE

WHETHER THE FULLNESS OF GRACE IS PROPER TO CHRIST

State of the question. The reason for inserting this article is that Sacred Scripture attributes at least a certain fullness of grace to some others. Thus the angel says to the Blessed Virgin Mary: "Hail, full of grace."[136] The Scripture also says: "Stephen, full of grace and fortitude."[137] In fact, St. Paul writing to the Ephesians, thus expresses his desire to them: "That you may be filled unto all the fullness of

[136] Luke 1:28.
[137] Acts 6:8.

God."[138] Moreover, for all the blessed in heaven, beatitude is the fullness of all good, which presupposes a certain fullness of grace in this life. What is therefore the fullness of grace that is proper to Christ?

First conclusion. Absolute fullness of grace, but not relative fullness, belongs to Christ alone.

Scriptural proof. The Evangelist says: "We saw His glory, the glory as it were of the only-begotten of the Father, full of grace and truth."[139] But to be the only-begotten of the Father, belongs to Christ alone. Therefore, too, does fullness of grace.

Theological proof. Absolute fullness of grace is attained when there is as much grace as can be had, at least according to God's ordinary power. But Christ alone had grace in the highest possible degree of excellence and intensity that can be had, at least according to God's ordinary power. Therefore Christ alone had absolute fullness of grace, both in its intensity and extent, as was stated in the preceding article.

Second conclusion. Relative fullness of grace does not belong to Christ alone, but is communicated to others through Him.

There is, indeed, relative fullness of grace when it is of such a nature and extent as demanded by the condition and office of the person to whom it is attributed.

But several saints, especially the Blessed Virgin Mary, had grace that was perfectly proportioned to the state and duty assigned to them. Thus the Blessed Virgin is declared to be "full of grace."[140] Therefore relative fullness of grace does not belong to Christ alone.[141]

Corollary.[142] Christ's habitual grace, from the very moment of His conception, excelled in both intensity and extent all grace, even the ultimate grace of angels and men combined. The reason is that the grace in Christ is in proportion to the hypostatic union, and is in Him as the source from which it flows even to the angels; for, as will be stated farther on, Christ is the head of the angels at least as regards accidental grace and glory, inasmuch as the angels are His ministers in the kingdom of God. Jesus said, "The Son of man shall send His angels, and they shall gather out of His kingdom all scandals, and

[138] Eph. 3:19.
[139] John 1:14.
[140] Luke 1:28.
[141] Cf. ad 1. The whole of this article should be read.
[142] Cf. *infra*, q. 35, a. 5.

all them that work iniquity, and shall cast them into the furnace of fire." [143] He likewise said: "He shall send His angels and shall gather together His elect." [144]

From these texts it is evident that Christ has a higher degree of grace than all angels and men combined, including the blessed, just as in a way the sun is brighter in its intensity than any lesser light whatever, and iron is of more value than a huge pile of common stones. Moreover, it is also said of the Blessed Virgin Mary that her first fullness of grace excelled in intensity the final degree of grace, though not the glory of angels and men combined, and so it is said: "The holy Mother of God has been raised above the choirs of angels to the heavenly kingdom." [145]

It even appears to be true that the grace received by the founders of religious orders excels, as regards the founding of the order, the grace of their combined associates, in this sense, that these associates, unless their founder had been especially inspired by God, would not have started this order, whereas, contrary to this, the founder, deputed by God for this work, could have done it with other companions. Thus the grace, either of St. Benedict or of St. Dominic or of St. Francis, seems to excel the grace of his companions. Likewise, the degree of grace in St. Thomas is greater than that of all his commentators combined. This is more readily understood in that grace is a quality and hence its perfection is qualitative but not quantitative. Consequently, grace that is equivalent for ten talents is of a higher degree than ten graces each of which is equivalent to one talent. Thus a saint, such as the saintly parish priest of Ars, has a greater degree of grace and accomplishes more than many of the faithful and even priests whose charity is of a less degree.

Thus St. Thomas shows [146] that charity—and he says that the same applies to habitual grace—is not increased in intensity by the addition of charity to charity; for this would be a multiplication of charity, but not an increase of it. It is increased, however, by becoming more firmly rooted in the recipient or, not using metaphysical language, by a greater actuation or determination of, and inherence in the recipient; for it is the nature of an accident to inhere.

[143] Matt. 12:41.
[144] Mark 13:27.
[145] Versicle and response for Second Vespers of Assumption.
[146] *Summa theol.,* IIa IIae, q. 24, a. 5.

All these statements are but one and the same way of expressing the intensification of qualities. A new degree of charity, and a more perfect actuation of this charity and of its inherence in the recipient, mean the same thing.

If, then, a higher degree of grace is taken in a qualitative sense and not in its quantitative sense, it is easy to see that Christ's habitual grace excels in intensity even every ultimate grace of men and angels combined. From the moment of His conception it excelled their glory.

St. Thomas teaches that this fullness of grace is of three kinds. He says: "There is sufficient fullness by which anyone has sufficient grace to perform meritorious and excellent acts, as St. Stephen did. There is likewise redundant fullness by which the Blessed Virgin excelled all the saints on account of the eminence and abundance of her merits. There is also efficient and affluent fullness, which applies to Christ alone as man, as to the quasi-author of grace. Thus there was an outpouring of grace on us by the Blessed Virgin, yet she was by no means the author of grace. . . . Christ's fullness of grace is the cause of all the graces in all intellectual creatures." [147]

St. Thomas says in this text, "of all graces" in general; he does not, however, determine the kind, and he does not say "even of essential grace and glory" in the angels, which elsewhere he denies.[148]

Objection. There would be great disproportion in the natural body if the head were larger than the rest of the body. Therefore, for a similar reason, there would be disproportion in the mystical body if the grace of Christ as its head were in intensity to exceed or equal all the grace of those that constitute His mystical body.

Reply. Gonet answers this objection by conceding the antecedent and denying the consequence, because, as he points out, a distinction must be made between quality and quantity, and there is by no means parity of argument between the mystical body and the natural body. There is indeed similarity of comparison between the two bodies as regards the influx of the head in the members and its pre-eminence over them. But in the natural body the substantial form demands a determinate quantity, both in the head and in the members, that the body may be able to perform its vital operations: and so it is necessary that our head be smaller than our body. Moreover, since habitual grace is the form that vivifies the mystical body of the Church, it

[147] *Com. in Joan.,* Bk. XVI, lect. 10.
[148] *Summa theol.,* IIIa, q. 59, a. 6.

does not demand a determinate intensity, but can be increased indefinitely.[149] Hence in the head of the mystical body there can be a greater intensification of grace than in all other persons, and this even pertains to the dignity of the head. Finally, there is in no way any vital dependence of the mystical body on the members, whereas, on the contrary, the head of the physical body depends on the heart, lungs, and other parts.

Eleventh Article

WHETHER THE GRACE OF CHRIST IS INFINITE

State of the question. This article is evidently not strictly concerned with the increate grace of union, for St. Thomas said: "The grace of union is the personal being that is given gratis from above to the human nature in the person of the Word." [150] This increate grace of union is infinite inasmuch as it is identical with the very Word of God that terminates the human nature. But it is strictly a question here of habitual grace which is "an effect following the union." [151]

Theologians are not all agreed on this point. Major [152] asserts that Christ's grace is absolutely infinite in intensity. Maldonatus [153] and Hurtado [154] afterward said the same. St. Bonaventure, Durandus, Scotus, Ricardus, and the Thomists Cajetan and Nazarius are of the same opinion, since they taught that Christ's grace could not be increased by God's absolute power. But the opposite opinion seems far more probable and more in conformity with the teaching of St. Thomas, and it is commonly held by theologians, not only of the Thomist school of thought, but also of other schools.

St. Thomas splendidly presents the difficulty of the question at the beginning of this article, where he remarks that Christ's grace appears to be infinite, because the Gospel declares it to be measureless or immense, saying: "God doth not give His Spirit by measure"; [155] whereas, contrary to this, St. Paul says of others: "To every one of us is given grace, according to the measure of the giving of Christ." [156]

[149] *Ibid.*, q. 7, a. 12.
[150] *Ibid.*, q. 6, a. 6.
[151] *Ibid.*
[152] *Com. in III Sent.*, d. 13, q. 3.
[153] *Com. in Lucam*, 2:40.
[154] *Phys.*, disp. 13, par. 47.
[155] John 3:34.
[156] Eph. 4:7.

Moreover, Christ's grace extends to the whole human race. Finally, if Christ's grace were finite, then some other person's grace might increase so much as to equal Christ's grace. These objections consider in habitual grace, not only the being of grace, but also the nature of grace.

Nevertheless it is evidently true to say that Christ's habitual grace, inasmuch as it is distinct from His grace of union, is something created. But everything created is finite, as stated in the counterargument of this article. Therefore Christ's habitual grace must be finite.

How is this question to be solved? The article must be read.

First conclusion. The grace of union is infinite, because it is the very person of the Word, who terminates Christ's human nature, as stated above.[157]

Second conclusion. Christ's habitual grace, inasmuch as it is a being, or considered as an entity, is not physically infinite, because it is in Christ's soul, as an accident is in its subject. But Christ's soul is a certain creature having finite capacity. It will be made clear in the following article that grace can always be increased, but considered as a being, since it is something created, it can never be physically and actually infinite.

Third conclusion. Christ's habitual grace, not considered as a being, but according to what strictly pertains to the notion of grace, can be termed infinite.[158] Almost all Thomists understand this conclusion in this sense, namely, that Christ's grace is in its notion of grace morally infinite, though not physically so.[159] For St. Thomas says: "As stated above (q. 7, a. 12) there cannot be a greater grace than the grace of Christ with respect to the union with the Word; and the same is to be said of the perfection of the divine vision; although,

[157] Cf. q. 6, a. 6.

[158] Thus a distinction can be made in our intellect, first in that it is a being and accident of the soul; secondly in that it is an intellect that is intentionally infinite, inasmuch as it regards universal truth. The same distinction must be made for the will, and even for habitual grace, which, as a grace, is a participation of the divine nature.

[159] When it is said that this habitual grace is morally infinite, this means that it is not physically infinite, since it is a formal participation of the divine nature; but it means that it implies a dignity to merit and satisfy for us, a participated dignity from its personal union with the Word of God. But there is such a great difference between each kind of grace; for grace considered in the first sense is actually finite, although taken in the second or moral sense it is absolutely infinite, as when we say that Christ's merit is absolutely infinite in value.

absolutely speaking, there could be a higher and more sublime degree by the infinity of the divine power." [160] He says the same in the reply to the second objection of the next article of this question.[161] Neither does St. Thomas say, concerning this third conclusion of ours: "We must say that Christ's grace, considered as grace, is infinite," but he says "it can be termed infinite," which means, if interpreted in some good sense.

Hence this third conclusion thus understood of grace that is morally infinite viewed in its specific nature of grace, is easily proved.

Two proofs are given in the body of this article, inasmuch as this grace is considered both intensively and extensively.

Intensive proof. Christ's habitual grace is intensively infinite because it has whatever can pertain to the nature of grace, and it is not bestowed "in a fixed measure," just as we may say that the light of the sun is infinite, not indeed in being, but in the nature of light, inasmuch as it has whatever can pertain to the nature of light.

This means that Christ's habitual grace is according to its intensity in the highest degree of its excellence capable of being bestowed on others, at least according to God's ordination and His ordinary power.[162]

We shall see that it can be increased by God's absolute power.[163] Moreover, it must be noticed that the three objections placed at the beginning of the present article conclude that Christ's grace, considered in its specific nature, is also infinite, and that this is denied in the counterargument.

Something of very great importance must be added here which is implied in the present article,[164] namely, that this habitual grace of Christ, by reason of its union with the Word, is the principle by which Christ performs meritorious and satisfactory acts that are intrinsically and absolutely infinite in value. This infinity, although it comes from the divine person as the principle that operates, nevertheless redounds

[160] *De veritate,* q. 29, a. 3, ad 3. See also IIa IIae, q. 29, a. 3, ad 3.

[161] In this passage St. Thomas says: "Although the divine power can make something greater than the habitual grace of Christ, yet it could not make it to be ordained to anything greater than the personal union with the only begotten Son of the Father; and to this union, by the purpose of the divine wisdom, the measure of grace is sufficient."

[162] Cf. q. 7, a. 12, ad 1, where it is said that "Christ's grace is finite in its essence."

[163] *Ibid.,* ad 2.

[164] *Ibid.,* a. 11, ad 2.

in moral value and worth on the habitual grace that is the principle by which Christ perfoms meritorious acts that are strictly and intrinsically infinite in value. Farther on we discuss the commonly accepted thesis of Thomists and almost all theologians, with the exception of Scotists, namely, that Christ's operations were not only extrinsically accepted by God, but they were also intrinsically "absolutely infinite in value both for meriting and for satisfying." [165]

All these things considered, it is no wonder that St. Thomas says in this article, concerning Christ's habitual grace taken in its intensity, that it can be termed infinite, viewed in its specific nature of grace, though he afterward adds that it can be increased by God's absolute power.[166]

Extensive proof. Christ's habitual grace is at least morally infinite because, as St. Thomas says in this article, it is bestowed on Christ's soul, as on a universal principle for bestowing grace on human nature. St. Paul says: "He hath graced us in His beloved Son." [167] This means that Christ's habitual grace extends to all effects that pertain to the nature of grace, even to those that are syncategorematically infinite. Thus we shall see that this habitual grace is called the grace of headship, inasmuch as by it there flows from Christ upon the members of the Church (through the influx of His merits) grace and glory; but glory is without end, since it is eternal life.[168]

But if Christ's grace does not extend so far as to merit the essential grace of Adam in the state of innocence and of the angels, this is not because it did not have the power, but because these were not included in the divine ordering. Hence Christ's grace viewed in its specific nature of grace is morally infinite, both in intensity and extent.

The answer of St. Thomas, as understood in the sense stated above, receives its confirmation in the solution of the objections.

First objection. The Gospel declares: "God doth not give the Spirit by measure [to the Son]." [169] Therefore Christ's grace is infinite.

St. Thomas replies that the words of the Baptist as recorded by St. John can refer: (1) either to the eternal and infinite gift, namely, to the divine nature which the Father from all eternity communicated

[165] *Ibid.,* q. 19, a. 4.
[166] *Ibid.,* a. 12, ad 2; q. 10, a. 4, ad 3.
[167] Eph. 1:5 f.
[168] Cf. IIIa, q. 8, a. 5.
[169] John 3:34.

to the Son; (2) or to the grace of union that is infinite inasmuch as the Word terminates the human nature; (3) or to habitual grace inasmuch as it extends to all that pertains to grace, namely, to the word of wisdom or to the word of knowledge, or to other such gifts.

Hence St. Thomas does not concede the conclusion of the objection, that Christ's habitual grace is absolutely and physically infinite, so that it cannot be greater by God's absolute power.

Reply to second objection. "The grace of Christ has an infinite effect," which means that it includes the salvation of the whole human race "both because of the aforesaid infinity of grace," which for this reason is called the grace of headship, and because of the unity [170] of the divine person, to whom Christ's soul is united. Thus, as we said, Christ's habitual grace, because of its union with the Word, is the principle by which His meritorious and satisfactory acts for us were intrinsically of absolutely infinite validity, and He could have merited eternal life for an ever greater and vast number of human beings, even though, for example, the generations of human beings were to continue even after the end of the world.

By this reply St. Thomas shows that he does not concede the conclusion of this second objection, which is that Christ's habitual grace viewed in this sense is absolutely and physically infinite, so that it cannot by God's absolute power be increased.

Third objection. It states that, "if Christ's grace were finite, then the grace of any other man could increase to such an extent as to reach to an equality with Christ's grace." The Beghards were condemned for saying: "If one could always advance in perfection, then someone more perfect than Christ could be found." [171]

Reply. St. Thomas does not say that Christ's habitual grace is physically and absolutely infinite viewed in its specific nature of grace, but he says: "The grace of any man is compared to the grace of Christ as a particular to a universal power." By way of illustration, the light of the moon, no matter how much it may increase in intensity, cannot equal in intensity the light of the sun from which it receives its light. For the moon does not have its own light, but transmits the light it has received from the sun. St. Thomas, in accordance with the physics of ancient times, made use of another example because he thought the

[170] An editorial footnote to this article in the English Dominican translation remarks that perhaps we should read "infinity" instead of "unity." (Tr.)

[171] Denz., no. 471.

stars were incorruptible, and the light and heat of the sun were of a kind different from the heat of terrestrial fire. Spectral analysis, however, has established the fact that the stars are not incorruptible, but that the same chemical combinations take place in these as on this earth.

Therefore Christ's habitual grace is a finite being, and viewed in its specific nature of grace, if it is not physically infinite, is at least morally infinite, both in its intensity and in its extent, inasmuch as it concurs with the grace of union to produce merit that is intrinsically of infinite validity.

Cajetan, in his commentary on this article, adverting to the fact of his recent elevation to the cardinalate, considers this all the more a reason why the mysteries of Christ should be examined and made known to all. His purpose is to show that Christ's habitual grace is in Him in all the perfection that grace as such can have. In other words, this grace is in Christ "as in the whole that is equivalent to it as such," just as heat is not in the air but in the fire; just as a line could be infinite in length, viewed as a line, although finite as a being, just as whiteness, which is finite indeed, as a being, since it is an accident, is intensively infinite in its nature of whiteness, since there could not be a more perfect whiteness.

Nevertheless Cajetan maintains [172] that Christ's habitual grace, as well as that of others, is of the same most particular species, as regards its essence; the difference is only as regards the mode of its being, just as heat differs in its mode of being as found in terrestrial fire and in the air.[173]

Let us see in what Cajetan agrees and disagrees with other Thomists.

Cajetan [174] maintains, indeed, with other Thomists, that charity can always be increased in this life, and that charity in itself has no ultimately possible degree, because it is a participation of infinite charity and so it differs from heat and from whiteness. But Cajetan is not in agreement with other Thomists when he says that charity

[172] *Com. in IIIam,* q. 7, a. 11, no. 5.

[173] This last example supposes that fire, according to the physics of the ancients, is a substance, namely, one of the four elements: earth, air, fire and water. Nowadays physicists look upon fire as an incandescent body, for example, like coal or vapor, resulting from the combustion of certain bodies. Thus they consider a flame to be a burning, lucent vapor, of greater or less intensity.

[174] *Com. in IIam IIae,* q. 24, a. 7.

in itself does not exclude the highest possible degree of this virtue, especially so if it is ordered to the greatest possible union, namely, the hypostatic union, for then it has, as proportionate to this union, the highest possible degree of this virtue, as heat in fire, and whiteness in snow.

Other Thomists justly reply to him by saying that there is a greater difference between habitual grace or charity and natural qualities, such as heat in fire and whiteness in snow.

First difference. These natural qualities have their own intrinsic and finite specification, and are not defined with reference to something else; whereas habitual grace is defined as a formal and physical participation in the divine nature, the possibility of this participation being infinite. Thus of itself there is no limit to it, but it even excludes this, which means that it seeks intrinsically to have syncategorematically no limitation, which means that the highest possible degree of habitual grace, or of charity or of the light of glory, is intrinsically repugnant, just as the absolutely swiftest motion is a contradiction in terms, for it is always possible to conceive a swifter motion, accomplished in a shorter time, that is however distinct from the indivisible instant of time.

Second difference. Natural qualities, such as heat in fire—a better illustration is whiteness in snow—are natural properties of some natural and finite substance; whereas habitual grace is not a natural property of the created intellectual substance, not even of Christ's soul as united with the Word, because it flows in a certain measure not necessarily, but freely from the Word, a point that will be more clearly explained in the following article.[175]

Third difference. Natural qualities, such as heat and whiteness, are received in the subject according to its passive and finite natural power, whereas habitual grace is received in the subject not according to its natural power, but its obediential power. And St. Thomas says: "The obediential power, inasmuch as it can receive something from God, is not limited in this respect because, whatever God does in the creature, there still remains in it the power to accept something from God." [176]

Finally, grace is something freely given that is dependent in its measure on the divine good pleasure.

[175] Cf. IIIa, q. 7, a. 12, ad 2.
[176] *De veritate,* q. 29, a. 3, ad 3.

Cajetan seeks to defend his opinion and says: "It is possible for one to have a higher degree of the vision of God (than the degree granted to the soul of Christ) from a more sublime intellect equally illumined," [177] in other words, if to an equal degree of the light of glory an angel were assumed by the Word of God into unity of person.

Other Thomists reply that then the degree of the beatific vision would not be formally more sublime but only materially; in fact, not even materially, because this angel would not have a clearer vision of the divine essence, which is an essentially supernatural object that absolutely transcends the power of whatsoever created intellect, as Alvarez remarks.[178]

Cajetan likewise sets forth his same view in his treatise on charity.[179] He maintains especially in his great commentary, that charity in this life can always be increased and in itself this virtue is not found in the highest possible degree, though it does not exclude this degree, as it excludes mortal sin. In fact, for it to be proportionate to this union, then charity must be in the highest possible degree.

Cajetan, seeking to magnify Christ's habitual grace, minimizes the sublimity of absolutely assumed grace, as we shall see in the explanation of the following article.

So far, Cajetan asserts but he does not prove that Christ's habitual grace is not in the highest possible degree. We shall see in the explanation of the following article what he adds in confirmation of his special opinion.

Twelfth Article

WHETHER THE GRACE OF CHRIST COULD INCREASE

State of the question. St. Thomas clearly sets forth the difficulty of this problem, for he says:

1) To every finite thing addition can be made. But Christ's habitual grace, as we said, considered as a being, is finite. Therefore it can be increased.

2) Also considered as grace, it seems that it can be increased, for increase of grace is effected by divine power; and since this power is absolutely infinite, there are no limits to it.

[177] *Com. in IIIam,* q. 10, a. 4, ad 3.
[178] *Com. in IIIam,* q. 10, a. 4, ad 3.
[179] *Com. in IIam IIae,* q. 24, a. 7.

3) The Evangelist says that "Jesus advanced in wisdom and age, and grace with God and men." [180]

Conclusion. Christ's habitual grace could not be increased after the first moment of His conception, either on the part of the grace itself, or on the part of the recipient of this grace. Thus Christ differs from all others, even from the Blessed Virgin and the angels, who were wayfarers and not comprehensors.

Let us first of all examine the proofs of this article; afterward we shall consider Cajetan's interpretation; finally we shall discuss the interpretation of other Thomists.

Scriptural proof. The Evangelist says: "We saw His glory, the glory as it were of the only-begotten of the Father, full of grace and truth." [181] "But nothing can be or can be thought greater than that anyone should be the begotten of the Father. Therefore no greater grace can be or can be thought than that of which Christ was full." [182] Thus we said in the preceding article that Christ's grace is at least morally infinite inasmuch as it is the principle by means of which He performed meritorious and satisfactory acts that are of absolutely infinite value. Thus Christ's habitual grace absolutely excels the grace of all men and angels combined.

Moreover, the Second Council of Constantinople defined: "If anyone defends the assertion that Christ . . . as He advanced in the performance of good works became better . . . let him be declared anathema." [183] This means that Christ did not either become more perfect, or was subjected to passions, or offered sacrifice for Himself.[184] In this Christ differs from all the just, even from the angels in heaven, who became more perfect in the second instant of their creation, since they were wayfarers and merited, and after this they were only comprehensors. But if St. Luke says that "Jesus advanced in wisdom and age, and grace with God and men," [185] St. Thomas replies in this article, along with the whole of ecclesiastical tradition: "Christ did not increase inasmuch as the very habits of wisdom and grace were increased in Him . . . , but as regards the effects, . . . since in the course of time He did more perfect works, to prove Him-

[180] Luke 2:52.
[181] John 1:14.
[182] Counterargument of St. Thomas.
[183] Denz., no. 224.
[184] *Ibid.*, no. 122.
[185] Luke 2:55.

self true man, both in the things of God and in the things of man."[186] The Greek and Latin Fathers generally take this view when they speak of the fullness of Christ's grace.[187]

Theological proof. There are two subdivisions to this proof.

a) On the part of the recipient of this grace, Christ's grace could not be increased from the beginning, because as man He was from the first moment of His conception truly and completely comprehensor, as will be made clear farther on.[188] But in comprehensors, or in the blessed, there can be no increase of grace, subjectively speaking, for they have already reached their final end to which they were eternally predestined. Therefore, subjectively speaking, there can be no increase in Christ's grace.

b) On the part of grace. Christ's grace from the beginning could not be increased, because Christ as man was from the beginning personally united with the Word, and He already received, as St. Thomas says in this article, "the highest measure of grace."

This consequence is proved by one syllogism on which Cajetan very much insists.

It is in reference to the end that a measure is prefixed to each form; for example, in accordance with the physics of the ancients, there is no greater gravity than that of the earth because there is no lower place than that of the earth. Or, as we now can say, in our solar world there is no greater light and heat than the light and heat of the sun, which is the center of attraction of this solar world.

But the end of grace is the union of the rational creature with God, and there cannot be a greater union than the hypostatic union of Christ's human nature with the Word.

Therefore, from the moment of His conception, Christ's grace attained its highest degree of grace, and there was no possibility of its future increase; whereas, on the contrary, the first fullness of grace in the Blessed Virgin always received an increase of this grace until it acquired its consummate fullness when she entered heaven.

St. Thomas determines more clearly the force of this conclusion in his replies to the objections placed at the beginning of this article.

[186] Cf. IIIa, q. 7, a. 12, ad 3.

[187] *Enchiridion patristicum,* nos. 394, 399, 404, 405. See also IIIa, q. 10, on the beatific knowledge of Christ.

[188] Cf. *infra,* q. 10.

Reply to first objection. To the proposed difficulty that "to every finite thing addition can be made," St. Thomas replies by making the following distinction: that addition can be made to every finite mathematical quantity, namely, to every line, to every number, I concede; that addition can be made to every natural quantity I deny, for example, the quantity or height of a dog or a horse, or an elephant, or a man cannot always be increased. St. Thomas concludes at the end of his reply by saying: "Hence it is not necessary that addition should be capable of being made to Christ's grace," although it is finite in its essence, which means that it is finite as having reached "the highest measure of grace" as stated toward the end of the argumentative part of this article.

Second objection. "It is by divine power that grace is increased and, since this power is infinite, it is confined by no limits."

Reply. St. Thomas answers by saying: "Although the divine power can make something greater and better than the habitual grace of Christ, yet it could not make it to be ordained to anything greater than the personal union with the only-begotten Son of the Father; and the measure of grace corresponds sufficiently (not adequately) to this union, in accordance with the definition of divine wisdom." This text is of great importance. Similarly farther on it is stated that, "absolutely speaking, there could be a higher and more sublime degree [of the beatific vision] by the infinity of the divine power." [189]

Concerning the interpretation of this second reply and of what is said in the body of this article, Cajetan and Nazarius differ from the rest of the Thomists, both ancient and modern. Let us consider each interpretation.

Cajetan's interpretation.

Cajetan gives the following interpretation to this article. He himself says: "What is substantially for the end must be commensurate with the end (as the shape of the saw for the cutting of wood), . . . wherefore, since the tendency of a heavy object is to fall down, . . . the lowest point to which an object can fall must be governed and measured only by the maximum influence exerted on it by the law of gravitation. Thus the greatest union of the rational creature with God must be measured only by the greatest grace." [190] Farther on

[189] *Ibid.,* q. 10, a. 4, ad 3.
[190] *Com. in IIIam,* q. 7, a. 11, no. 2.

Cajeton remarks: "Therefore Christ's grace is finite and at the same time it excludes addition." [191]

In the reply to the second objection, when St. Thomas says that "God can make something greater and better than the habitual grace of Christ," Cajetan introduces the following distinction: that God can make something greater and better inasmuch as it is a being, this I concede; inasmuch as it is ordained to its proper end, which is the hypostatic union, this I deny.[192]

Criticism. Cajetan does not sufficiently explain the words of St. Thomas in his reply to the second objection, when he says: "To this [hypostatic] union such measure of grace is correspondingly sufficient, according to the definition of divine wisdom" or the divine ordination. He also does not explain the similar and clearer text of St. Thomas concerning the higher degree of the light of glory that is possible by God's absolute power.[193]

It is of no avail to say that God can produce something better than Christ's grace because this is an accident, and God can produce substance or even give to an angel the same degree of the light of glory.

In these considerations Cajetan, who almost always views problems in their formal aspect, seems to understand the reply to the second objection of this article in a material sense, as well as the other reply similar to this.[194]

He seems to stress too much the quasi-material aspect in the subject of grace and the fact that grace is an accident, and not a substance.

Now indeed, as St. Thomas says: "The good of grace in one is greater than the good of nature in the whole universe," [195] that is, than all created and creatable creatures. Hence, when St. Thomas says, "The divine power can make something greater and better than the habitual grace of Christ," [196] his purpose is not to speak of substance God can produce. Nor does it seem true, as stated above, that an angel, who would have the same degree of the light of glory as the soul of Christ, would have a clearer vision of the divine essence, because the divine essence is an essentially supernatural object, which

[191] *Ibid.*, no. 5 (the end).
[192] *Ibid.*, no. 6.
[193] *Ibid.*, q. 10, a. 4, ad 2.
[194] *Ibid.*, ad 3.
[195] *Ibid.*, Ia IIae, q. 113, a. 9, ad 2.
[196] *Ibid.*, IIIa, q. 7, a. 12, ad 2.

does not seem to be seen more clearly because of the keener penetration of a material and created intellect.

Common interpretation of Thomists. Such are Capreolus, Bannez, John of St. Thomas, Salmanticenses, Gonet, Billuart, and others.

To understand this interpretation, we must bear in mind the division commonly admitted by the Thomists about the divine power. It may be expressed by the following schema.[197]

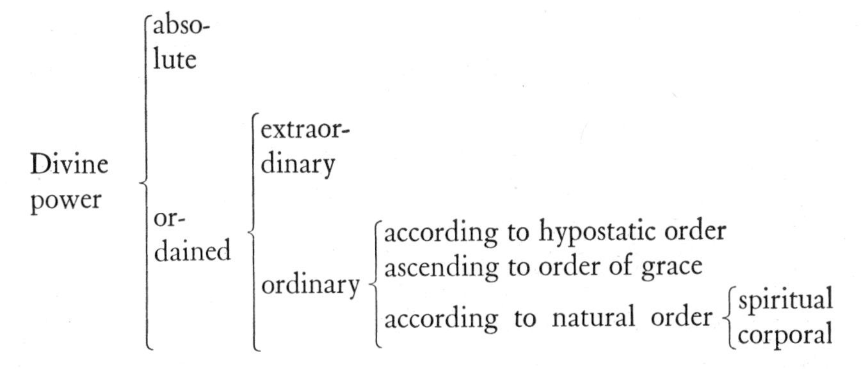

The merely absolute divine power is the divine power considered apart from the ordination of divine wisdom, and so considered it refers to all things not intrinsically repugnant even though they may be extrinsically repugnant on the part of the end.[198]

Thus God, by His merely absolute power, could annihilate all the blessed in heaven, even the Blessed Virgin and Christ's human nature, since He freely preserves these in being. This annihilation is not intrinsically repugnant but extrinsically repugnant on the part of the end, for on the part of the end there can be no purpose in this annihilation. Hence this annihilation is repugnant to God's power as regulated by divine wisdom.

The ordained divine power is that which refers to the ordaining of divine wisdom, and it concerns everything that is neither intrinsi-

[197] *Ibid.,* Ia, q. 25.

[198] Some think that such a consideration of God's merely absolute power is useless, because truly God can act only by His power as regulated by His wisdom.

Reply. This consideration is not useless; it must be properly understood, namely, on the part of possible effects. This explains why certain effects are intrinsically possible, such as the annihilation of all creatures, both material and spiritual, although such effects may not be extrinsically possible on the part of the end and the agent, because God can have neither motive nor end in annihilating spiritual creatures.

cally repugnant, nor extrinsically repugnant on the part of the end.

It is divided into ordinary and extraordinary. The ordinary ordained divine power is that which operates in accordance with the laws as established by God, either in the natural order, or in the supernatural order, or even in the order of the hypostatic union.

It is called extraordinary, when it is called into action and reaches beyond the above-mentioned laws either of the natural order (as when miracles of the physical order are performed) or of the supernatural order (such as a sudden and miraculous conversion as in the case of the conversion of St. Paul) or of those that pertain to the hypostatic union. Thus the question is put, whether Christ's habitual grace could have been greater by God's absolute power, and also by His ordained power and His extraordinary power, so that the Incarnation could have taken place without Christ suffering. There seems to be no doubt that the fullness of even the grace acquired by the Blessed Virgin Mary at the time of her death could have been intensively greater not only by God's absolute power but even by His ordained power and also His extraordinary power.

These principles established, Thomists almost unanimously hold that by God's absolute power Christ's habitual grace could have been increased in intensity, although He actually had the highest possible degree of such grace by God's ordained and ordinary power. So say Capreolus,[199] Bannez, Medina, John of St. Thomas, Alvarez, Suarez, Vasquez, and others, against the Scotists and Cajetan.

John of St. Thomas says that this opinion is more probable and undoubtedly more according to the mind of St. Thomas. This seems to be proved when he says: "As stated above, there cannot be a greater grace than the grace of Christ with respect to the union with the Word; and the same is to be said of the perfection of the divine vision; although, absolutely speaking, there could be a higher and more sublime degree by the infinity of the divine power." [200] So says St. Thomas in this passage, and he is plainly speaking of God's absolute power and he cites and explains what he had said previously about Christ's grace.[201]

To be sure, Cajetan says that Christ's beatific vision could increase, not because of a greater light of glory but because of a greater natural

[199] *Com. in IIIam,* d. 13.
[200] *Summa theol.,* IIIa, q. 10, a. 4, ad 3.
[201] *Ibid.,* q. 7, a. 12, ad 2.

power, for example, if the Word were to assume an angelic nature.

Reply. The beatific vision is regulated and measured only according to the elevating power which is the light of glory; for the vision itself is an essentially supernatural act, specified by an essentially supernatural object, which infinitely transcends the natural vigor of any created or creatable intellect whatever.

Doubt. Is it possible to conceive a grace and light of glory of a higher species, and can Christ's grace be of a higher species than ours?

Reply. The answer is, No, for the following reasons. (1) Because grace, as in the just and in Christ is already a formal and physical participation in the Deity, having in each case the same definition, and there cannot be anything capable of participation that is higher than the divine nature or the Deity as it is in Itself, or in other words, God's intimate life; this view is against a certain thesis of Father Billot.[202]

2) Because otherwise Christ would not contain in Himself all the effects of grace if He did not have a certain species of grace. Therefore the only possible conception of a higher beatific vision is that resulting from a greater penetration of the divine essence and from an increase in the intensity of habitual grace and of the light of glory in the same species.

This same interpretation is also proved from the previous reply of St. Thomas to his query about the possibility of charity being increased infinitely. He says: "In no way, either on the part of the form or of the agent or of the subject is a limit to be set to the increase of charity in this life. For there is no limit to the increase of charity in what properly belongs to it in its species, for it is a certain participation of infinite charity, which is the Holy Spirit. Similarly also the causal agent of charity is infinite in power, for it is God. Similarly, too, on the part of the subject, there can be no pre-assigned terminus

[202] *De Verbo incarnato,* thesis 17, p. 208. Father Billot asks why God, as the author of grace, cannot be participated in various species of grace, since there is such participation of God as the author of nature. Against this thesis of Father Billot, it must be said that there is, indeed, a participation of God as the author of nature in divers natural species, through the intermediary of the divine ideas, but habitual grace is the immediate participation of the divine nature, or of the Deity as It is in Itself, that is, of God's intimate life. Hence for there to be two species of habitual grace is impossible. Moreover, if Christ's grace were of a higher species than ours, then His beatific vision would be of a higher species, because it is immediately specified by God Himself clearly seen, by the very Deity as It is in Itself. Therefore only different degrees of this vision are possible, and only God's uncreated and comprehensive vision of Himself transcends all other visions.

set to this increase since the greater the increase, the greater the aptitude for further increase,"[203] because as St. Thomas also says here, "by it [charity] the heart expands."[204] As we already remarked, St. Thomas says: "The obediental power, inasmuch as it can receive something from God, is not limited in this respect, because whatever God does in the creature, there still remains in it the power to receive something from God";[205] for the obediental power in the creature has immediate reference not to some object that must be known or loved, or to some act that must be elicited, but it has reference to the absolutely free agent, who is infinite in power, whom it obeys and from whom it can always receive something.

Hence we must conclude, as St. Thomas says in this article: "By the purpose of divine wisdom, the measure of grace is sufficient for this [hypostatic] union."[206]

John of St. Thomas remarks: "Clearly St. Thomas signifies that the end in view of that grace is union with the Word, not in the absolute sense, but as it serves the purpose of divine Wisdom, who assigned such measure of grace to Christ. Hence we conclude that by another purpose of divine Wisdom, there is nothing repugnant in a different measure and increase of grace being given to Christ."[207]

Solution of objections.

Objection. St. Thomas says in his counterargument to this twelfth article: "Therefore no greater grace can be or can be thought than that of which Christ was full."

Reply. That St. Thomas says this about Christ's grace with reference to its extrinsic end, which is the hypostatic union, of which he speaks in the preceding article of this question, and as it serves the purpose of divine Wisdom, with which his reply to the second objection of this article is concerned, this I concede; that he says this about Christ's grace taken in the absolute sense of the term and independently of the purpose of divine Wisdom, this I deny.

Thus Christ's grace on account of the union of His human nature with the person of the Word, was the greatest in this order in which it is produced; that is, it is connaturally the greatest, for the purpose or ordination of divine Wisdom that pre-assigned the connatural

[203] *Summa theol.,* IIa IIae, q. 24, a. 7.

[204] *Ibid.,* ad 2.

[205] *De veritate,* q. 29, a. 3, ad 3.

[206] Cf. ad 2.

[207] *Com. in IIIam,* q. 7, a. 12, no. 24.

limits to all forms, according to the connatural order in which these were established by this Wisdom. As God, who gave to St. Peter, to St. John, and to St. Paul, also to St. Augustine, and to St. Thomas a fitting degree of wisdom and charity, could have given them a higher degree, so He gave Christ a higher degree of grace, but on absolute consideration He could have given Christ a higher degree, because the highest possible degree cannot be conceived. Thus the final argument fittingly terminates the best sermon, although, absolutely speaking, there could still be another exhortation.

Another objection. St. Thomas said in the preceding article: "Christ's grace has whatsoever can pertain to the nature of grace."

Reply. This must be understood from the immediate context and from other texts of St. Thomas in this same question, because we cannot suppose that He contradicted himself. In other words, he meant that Christ's grace has whatever pertains to the nature of grace, considered in its moral aspect and with reference to its union with the Word.

Finally, God's power would be exhausted if He could produce nothing more perfect by His absolute power, and even by His extraordinary ordained power.

Final objection. If a higher degree of grace were possible, then Christ would have merited this grace, for His merits were of infinite value.

Reply. That Christ would have merited a higher degree of grace if He had not already been a comprehensor and beyond the condition of wayfarer, let this pass without comment; but although the comprehensor, by means of grace performs many good works, this neither increases grace nor merits an increase of it in the comprehensor, as is evident in the blessed, who in this respect are like to God, inasmuch as God's works can in no way increase His perfection. God did not become better by the fact that He created the universe or sent His Son into the world for our salvation.

If Christ merited the glorification of His body, the reason is that the temporary lack of this glorification of the body was conducive to the end of redemption; whereas, on the contrary, He had from the beginning grace in the highest degree according to His connatural state both as comprehensor and as wayfarer, and thus He absolutely transcended all the just, both angels and men. The Second Council of Constantinople declared that Christ was not made better by advancing in the performance of good works.[208] On the contrary, the Blessed Virgin, by her continuous and uninterrupted performance of meritorious acts until death, was made better.

Corollary. Hence Christ adored God's supreme good pleasure by which He simultaneously freely willed the Incarnation and determined the degree of habitual grace befitting the Word incarnate. In this also Christ could say: "I confess to Thee, O Father, Lord of heaven and earth . . . for so hath it seemed good in Thy sight." [209] God's most free decrees must be adored and they are infinitely good, since they are decrees that are the result of infinite wisdom and of infinite love. From this the sublimity of the Deity and of grace taken in the absolute sense, which by God's absolute power can always be increased, is more clearly seen since it is a participation of the divine nature, which is always capable of participation in a more sublime way.

Thirteenth Article

WHETHER THE HABITUAL GRACE OF CHRIST FOLLOWED AFTER THE UNION

Reply. The grace of union precedes the habitual grace of Christ, not in order of time but by nature and in thought, and this for three reasons.

1) Because of the principles of both graces. For the mission of the Son by the Incarnation precedes by nature the mission of the Holy Spirit by habitual grace and charity, just as in the order of nature the Holy Spirit proceeds from the Son.

2) Because of the relation of grace to its cause. For Christ's habitual grace is caused by God's presence in Him through His personal union with the Word just as the brightness of the sun comes from the sun.

3) Because of the end of grace. For the purpose of grace is good action, and actions belong to the suppositum and presuppose the suppositum constituted in being. Therefore Christ's habitual grace, since the purpose of it is good action, presupposes the union of the human nature with the Word.

Reply to second objection. "Habitual grace is not understood to have preceded the union but to have followed it, as a natural property";

[208] Denz., no. 224.
[209] Matt. 11:25 f.

however, as already stated, the degree of this habitual grace does not flow of necessity from the Word, but "the measure of grace is sufficient to this union by the purpose of divine Wisdom." [210]

This terminates the question of Christ's grace inasmuch as He is a certain individual man. This question presents to us a sublime illustration of the definition of grace, inasmuch as now we see more clearly that there cannot be a nobler species of habitual grace than ours, or a more exalted species of the beatific vision than that which the blessed possess.

[210] Cf. q. 7, a. 12, ad 2.

CHAPTER X

QUESTION 8

Christ's Grace as Head of the Church

THERE are two parts to this question.

First part. It treats of grace which befits Christ as head of the Church (a. 1–6).

The first article considers the meaning of the expression, head of the Church. Then there is a discussion of the grace of headship as it extends to men and angels (a. 2–4).

Finally whether to be head of the Church is proper to Christ.

Second part. It concerns the devil and Antichrist. Is the devil the head of all the wicked? (a. 7.) Can Antichrist be called the head of all the wicked? (a. 8.)

It must first of all be noted that this whole doctrine has its foundation in the epistles of St. Paul, in which Christ is often spoken of as the head of the Church. Christ indeed had already said, as reported by the Evangelist: "I am the true vine, and My Father is the husbandman. Every branch in Me that beareth not fruit He will take away; and everyone that beareth fruit He will purge it that it may bring forth more fruit. . . . I am the vine, you the branches; He that abideth in Me, and I in Him, the same beareth much fruit; for without Me you can do nothing. If anyone abide not in Me, he shall be cast forth as a branch, and shall wither, and they shall gather him up and cast him into the fire, and he burneth." [1]

This same doctrine is developed under another analogy, namely, of the head and mystical body of Christ, in whom the faithful must gradually be incorporated, by participating in the hidden life of Christ, His public life, His sorrowful life, and finally His glorious life. As St. Paul often says in the following text and in others: "He

[1] John 11:1 f. See also *Com.* of St. Thomas on St. John's Gospel.

[God] . . . hath made Him [Christ] head over all the Church, which is His body, and the fullness of Him who is filled all in all." [2]

First Article

WHETHER CHRIST IS THE HEAD OF THE CHURCH

State of the question. We are concerned with the Church, though the title of the article does not as yet determine whether we are concerned only with the Church militant, or also with the Church triumphant, for this will be determined farther on. We are also concerned with Christ as man.

The difficulties are these: (1) The head imparts sense and motion to the members, and it seems, as St. Augustine says, that Christ as man does not give the Holy Spirit, and hence He does not impart spiritual sense and motion to those men who are the faithful of His Church. (2) Furthermore, the head of man receives an inflow of blood from the heart, for just as it could not live without receiving this influx of blood from the heart, and its re-oxygenation in the lungs, so the head of man is dependent on the heart, the lungs, and also on other organs; whereas, on the contrary, Christ does not depend either formally or efficiently, or finally on the faithful, but they depend on Him. Thus this article is most appropriate for the discernment of the dissimilarities and similarities in this analogy.

Reply. Christ as man is head of the Church. The expression "as man" must not be understood absolutely in its reduplicative sense, as if it meant solely by reason of Christ's human nature, but it must be taken in its special sense, namely, as man subsisting by the divine personality, which will be more clearly explained farther on.

Scriptural proof. The following text is especially cogent: "God . . . raising Him up from the dead, and setting Him on His right hand in the heavenly places . . . hath made Him head over all the Church." [3] It is manifest, however, that St. Paul is here speaking of Christ as man, for he says that He was raised from the dead.

St. Paul has developed this doctrine at considerable length in his epistles, from which he proceeds to establish four conclusions.

1) Christ is the head of the regenerated human race raised to the

[2] Eph. 1:22 f. Cf. Rom. 12:4 f.; I Cor. 12:13 f.; Eph. 4:15 f.; 6:5; Col. 4:18 f. Cf. also Father Vosté, O.P., *Com. in Ep. ad Eph.*, p. 289.

[3] Eph. 1:20 f.

supernatural and fallen from it. St. Paul says: "For if by the offense of one many died, much more the grace of God, and the gift, by the grace of one man, Jesus Christ, hath abounded unto many. . . . For if by the offense of one many died, much more the grace of God, and the gift, by the grace of one man, Jesus Christ, hath abounded unto many. . . . For if by one man's offense death reigned through one, much more they who receive abundance of grace, and of the gift, and of justice, shall reign in life through one, Jesus Christ. Therefore, as by the offense of one, unto all men to condemnation, so also by the justice of one unto all men to justification of life." [4]

For God permits evil only for a greater good, and He permitted Adam's sin only for the greater good of the redemptive Incarnation, as we showed above, when discussing the motive of the Incarnation.[5]

St. Paul likewise says: "For as in one body we have many members, but all the members have not the same office, so we being many, are one body in Christ, and everyone members one of another." [6]

2) St. Paul teaches that the influx of Christ as head over all men, even the angels as His ministers, presupposes the great pre-eminence of Christ. Most striking is the following text: "You are filled in Him [Christ], who is the head of all principality and power." [7]

3) St. Paul says that this influx of Christ as head makes itself felt on various persons throughout the course of the centuries. Thus he writes: "The whole body . . . groweth unto the increase of God." [8]

4) St. Paul insists on the unity of this mystical body, both as regards the head, source of this influence, and as regards the end of this unity. In many texts he speaks of our common participation in the blood of Christ.[9]

This doctrine of Christ's headship is *de fide,* not only as contained in Scripture and the ordinary teaching authority of the Church, but it is also the teaching of the Council of Trent, which says: "For whereas Jesus Christ Himself continually infuses His virtue into the said justified, as the head into the members and the vine into the branches, and this virtue always precedes and accompanies and fol-

[4] Rom. 5:15 f.
[5] Cf. IIIa, q. 1, a. 3, ad 3.
[6] Rom. 12:4.
[7] Col. 2:10; Eph. 1:20; Col. 1:18.
[8] Col. 2:19. See also Eph. 4:11 f.; 5:23.
[9] I Cor. 12:12 f.; 10:16 f.; also I Cor. 15:21 f.

lows their good works, which without it could not in any wise be pleasing and meritorious before God. . . ." [10] The Council likewise says: "If anyone denies that Christ whole and entire, the fountain and author of all graces, is received under the one species of bread, because, as some falsely assert, He is not received, according to the institution of Christ Himself, under both species; let him be anathema." [11]

In the body of the article, St. Thomas gives three reasons why Christ is fittingly called the head of the Church, according to a metaphorical analogy in which there is similarity of proportionality and also dissimilarity.

1) Argument from order. The head is the first part of man, that is, the superior part. But Christ as man, on account of His nearness to God, by grace is higher than all, for St. Paul says: "For whom He foreknew, He also predestinated to be made conformable to the image of His Son, that He might be the first-born among many brethren." [12]

2) Argument from perfection. In the head flourish all the senses, both interior and exterior. But Christ has the fullness of all graces, for the Evangelist says: "We saw Him full of grace and truth." [13]

3) Argument from power. From the head proceeds the motion and direction of the members, by reason of the sensitive and motive power that resides in the head. But Christ has the power of bestowing grace on all members of the Church, for the Evangelist says: "Of His fullness we have all received." [14]

Reply to first objection. Christ as God is the principal physical cause of grace, and as man He is the meritorious or moral cause of grace for us, and furthermore its physical instrumental or efficient cause, on which more must be said farther on.[15]

Therefore this analogy of proportionality is extremely appropriate,

[10] Denz., no. 809.

[11] *Ibid.,* no. 936. Cf. also St. Augustine's *Book of 83 questions,* chap. 9, no. 69; *De civitate Dei,* Bk. X, chap. 20.

[12] Rom. 8:29.

[13] John 1:14.

[14] *Ibid.,* 1:16.

[15] Cf. ad 1, and also IIIa, q. 13, a. 2, where we shall engage in a long discussion on the question of the physical and instrumental causality of Christ's soul. Likewise q. 43, a. 2: Whether Christ worked miracles by divine power. Also see IIIa., q. 48, a. 6: Whether Christ's passion brought about our salvation efficiently. And q. 49, a. 1: Whether we were delivered from sin through Christ's passion

though it is not analogy of proper proportionality, because, according to the strict meaning of head, it designates the higher part of the animal; but the metaphor is appropriate because of the above-mentioned similarities. There are also dissimilarities, as in all analogies, especially in those that are metaphorical.

Reply to second objection. "A natural head depends on the other members or organs, from which it receives nourishment; but the father of a family is subject to the civil governor, and Christ as man is subject to God, so that there is no reason why God cannot be the head of Christ."

In a general reply to the third objection it may be observed that the natural head is dependent on other members and organs for its nutrition and life, and it is therefore a member. Contrariwise, the moral head of the Church, Christ, is in no way dependent on the members and the body for His spiritual life. Thus Christ cannot be called a member of the Church; although St. Thomas in other passages conceded that Christ can be called, though not in the strict sense of the term, a member of the Church, since He is united with the Church as His mystical body, and receives an influx from God as the principal head of the whole Church.[16]

Third objection. Why cannot Christ be called the heart of the Church, since the metaphor would be even more fitting, because the heart influences the head and other members?

Reply to third objection. The head has a manifest pre-eminence over the other members; but the heart has a certain hidden influence. And hence the Holy Ghost is likened to the heart, since He invisibly quickens and unites the Church; but Christ is likened to the head in His visible nature in which man is set over man.

Second Article

WHETHER CHRIST IS HEAD OF MEN AS TO THEIR BODIES OR ONLY AS TO THEIR SOULS

State of the question. The meaning of the title to this article is clear from the tenor of the third objection, in which it is doubted whether Christ, even as regards His body, is head over other men even as regards their bodies.

[16] Cf. St. Thomas' *Com. in Ep. ad Cor.,* chap. 12; also *De veritate,* q. 29, a. 4, ad 6.

head is this, that the former not only can preserve and direct those members it already has, but it can also unite others to itself, and with reference to these it is called a potential head.

Reply to second objection. The Church that has neither spot nor wrinkle is the Church triumphant in heaven. But the Church militant actually consists both of the just and the faithful in the state of mortal sin, and these are imperfect members, being only in a qualified sense united with Christ.

This needs some explanation, because of what Quesnel maintained. For those among the faithful who are in a state of mortal sin actually receive from Christ an influx, which consists in a certain permanent bond, namely, in infused faith, and by this bond they are permanently united with the other members of the Church in one belief. Perfect union with Christ, indeed, requires charity. But it is already something of great importance to preserve the gift of infused faith.

This doctrine that was denied by John Hus and Quesnel, is manifestly in agreement with what Sacred Scripture says. The Gospel compares the Church to a threshing floor in which along with the wheat there is chaff that must be burnt, or to a net cast into the sea that contains good and bad fishes; [21] or it is compared to ten virgins, five of whom were foolish, not having provided themselves with the oil of charity.[22] Thus the Fourth Council of the Lateran defined the Church as a "congregation of the faithful," saying: "There is but one universal Church of the faithful outside which absolutely nobody is saved." [23]

But if certain Fathers of the Church said that the wicked do not belong to the Church, this must be understood as meaning that they are not perfect members of the Church; they are, nevertheless, imperfect members if they have faith.

Those among the faithful who are in the state of mortal sin are called members of the devil, or of the Babylonian city, inasmuch as they are turned away from God; but they are called members of the Church, so far as they keep the faith. So also in our bodies, a member that no longer has the sensitive life is an imperfect member. Thus the hair and nails are still parts of the body.

Corollary. All who have faith are members of the Church, even if

[21] Matt. 3:12; 13:29, 47.
[22] *Ibid.*, 35:2.
[23] Denz., no. 430.

they are only catechumens or schismatics, although it is true to say that schism easily drifts into heresy, and there is scarcely any formal schismatic who was not a heretic.

Reply to third objection. The ancient fathers of the Old Testament, "by observing the legal sacraments, which were types of future things, were born to Christ by the faith and love of charity," and so "they belonged to the same body of the Church as we do." However, Christ, who merited for them the grace of salvation, did not physically influence them, for a physical influence presupposes the existence of the influencing cause. On the contrary, the moral meritorious cause can be as yet non-existent and future, because it moves not as actually existing, but as known as pertaining either to the future or the past. Thus, on account of Christ's future merits, God bestowed grace on the just of the Old Testament. They received medicinal grace and redemption dependent on Christ's future merits, just as we receive such grace and redemption dependent on Christ's past merits. But Christ always living now exerts a physical influence on us, as the instrumental cause of grace.

First doubt. Is Christ actually the head of baptized and occult heretics, because of the baptismal character that remains in them? The query is concerned with formal heretics.

Reply. The answer is in the negative, against Cajetan's view, because in their case not even infused faith remains, which means that they do not belong to the third class. St. Thomas has in mind in the body of the article, those who are united with Christ neither by glory nor by charity in this life, but by faith. The Church is defined as "the congregation of the faithful," inasmuch as faith is the foundation and beginning of the supernatural life.

Christ, to be sure, influences these heretics by actual graces, but these graces only dispose them for the life of grace, and are not anything permanent in them, which means that they do not constitute a permanent bond uniting the member with Christ. Thus nobody is said to be a member of a family, merely because he visits it occasionally. Christ also bestows actual graces on infidels, of whom certainly He is actually the head.

Cajetan's objection. Christ bestows on baptized infidels something spiritual and permanent, namely, a baptismal character.

Reply. It is not enough for Christ to bestow on them something spiritual and permanent, for this something spiritual and permanent must be both vital and uniting the baptized with the one who is believed or loved. Otherwise Christ would be the head of the baptized who are damned. Cajetan concedes this last conclusion, but St. Thomas clearly denies it at the end of the argumentative part of this article.

It would be an error in the other extreme opposed to that of John Hus and Quesnel.

Hence the baptized formal heretic is not an actual member of the Church, and yet the Church has the right of punishing him, inasmuch as he does not maintain what he promised to believe, just as a king has the right to punish fugitive soldiers.

St. Robert Bellarmine's objection. The pope who becomes a secret heretic is still an actual member of the Church, for he is still the head of the Church, as Cajetan, Cano, Suarez, and others teach.

Reply. This condition is quite abnormal, hence no wonder that something abnormal results from it, namely, that the pope becoming secretly a heretic would no longer be an actual member of the Church, according to the teaching as explained in the body of the article, but would still retain his jurisdiction by which he would influence the Church in ruling it. Thus he would still be nominally the head of the Church, which he would still rule as head, though he would no longer be a member of Christ, because he would not receive that vital influx of faith from Christ, the invisible and primary head. Thus in quite an abnormal manner he would be in point of jurisdiction the head of the Church, though he would not be a member of it.

This condition could not apply to the natural head in its relation to the body, but such a condition is not repugnant in the case of the moral and secondary head. The reason is that, whereas the natural head must receive a vital influx from the soul before it can influence the members of its body, the moral head, such as the pope is, can exercise his jurisdiction over the Church, although he receives no influx of interior faith and charity from the soul of the Church. More briefly, as Billuart says, the pope is constituted a member of the Church by his personal faith, which he can lose, and his headship of the visible Church by jurisdiction and power is compatible with private heresy. The Church will always consist in the visible union of its members with its visible head, namely, the pope of Rome, although some, who externally seem to be members of the Church, may be private heretics. Thus the conclusion we must come to is, that occult heretics are only apparent members of the Church, which they externally and visibly profess to be the true Church.

Second doubt. Was Christ the head of our first parents in the state of innocence?

This is a difficult question, and the answer depends on the way we solve the problem concerning the motive of the Incarnation.

The Scotists and Suarez answer this question in the affirmative, for they maintain that Christ as man was the head of Adam in the state of innocence, even as regards essential grace, because Christ is the first of all the predestined.

Many Thomists deny this assertion of the Scotists and Suarez, for they say that the primary and principal reason of Christ's coming was to redeem the human race, and Adam in the state of innocence did not need redemption. Nevertheless, among Thomists, Godoy and Gonet maintain that Christ as man was truly and in the strict sense the head of our first parents in the state of innocence about as in the case of the angels, as regards the accidental grace of faith in Christ to come not as redeemer, but as consummator of glory.[24]

Let us now see how the more common opinion of the Thomists is explained by those who hold, as the Salmanticenses do, that God permitted Adam's sins for a greater good, namely, the redemptive Incarnation, so that the Incarnation is prior in the genus of final cause, and the fall of the human race is prior in the genus of material cause to be perfected or repaired, as we explained above in discussing the motive of the Incarnation.

Thesis. Christ as man was not the head of our first parents in the state of innocence as regards essential grace.

Authoritative proof. St. Augustine says: "He [Adam] was not in need of those graces resulting from Christ's death; the blood of the lamb absolved fallen men from both hereditary sin and personal sins." [25] He calls the grace of the state of innocence, God's grace, and the grace bestowed on man after the Fall, Christ's grace.[26]

St. Thomas likewise says: "Granted as true the opinion that Christ would not have become incarnate if man had not sinned, Christ before sin would have been the head of the Church only as God, but after sin He must be the head of the Church as man." [27]

[24] Cf. Gonet, *De incarnatione,* disp. 14, nos. 64, 104.

[25] *De correptione et gratia,* chap. 11.

[26] *Ibid.,* chap. 12.

[27] *De veritate,* q. 29, a. 4, ad 3.

Fundamental theological proof. The more common opinion of the Thomists is proved by the following syllogistic reasoning.

Christ was willed by God first and principally as the Redeemer, and so the grace bestowed by Christ is a medicinal and healing grace. But Adam had no grace in the state of innocence that was a medicinal and healing grace. Therefore Adam had no grace in the state of innocence that was bestowed on Him by Christ.

In other words, according to the present decree, Christ was willed as a remedy for the human race because of original sin. Thus the redemptive Incarnation depends on Adam's sin not indeed in the genus of final cause or of efficient cause or of formal cause, but in the genus of material cause that must be perfected or repaired, inasmuch as the alleviation of misery is the reason for being merciful. Hence every grace coming from Christ as head comes from Him by reason of His redemption and death for the human race.

SOLUTION OF OBJECTIONS

First objection. The principal reason for the opposite Scotist opinion is this. Christ is the first of all the predestined, as St. Thomas himself says.[28] But the first of all the predestined is the cause of all the graces the other predestined receive, among whom are the first parents. Therefore Christ was the cause of all the graces received by the first parents, even their essential grace, and so He was their head.

Reply. I distinguish the major: that Christ is the first of all the predestined by a priority of dignity as regards all, even the angels, this I concede, because He is predestined to divine and natural sonship, and not to adoptive sonship; that He is the first of all predestined by a priority of meritorious causality of all, this I deny; for He is only thus first of all as regards the redeemed, since He came as redeemer for us men. I contradistinguish the minor; the first of all the predestined is the meritorious cause of all the graces of the predestined to be redeemed, as redeemed, this I concede; that He is the meritorious cause of the essential grace of the others, that is, of the angels and Adam, not as to be redeemed, but as innocent, this I deny. And I deny the consequent and consequence, for the notion of head requires causality by way of merit. Thus farther on we shall state that Christ as man is truly the head of the angels inasmuch as, if He did not merit for them the essential grace of justification and glory, at least He merited accidental graces for them to be ministers in the kingdom of God. Adam

[28] Cf. IIIa, q. 24.

in the state of innocence, however, was not Christ's minister in the kingdom of God.

Third doubt. Was Christ, as man, the end of the essential grace bestowed on our first parents in the state of innocence? It is not here strictly a question of Christ's merits, but of Christ as He is the end of creatures.

The Thomists, as also the Salmanticenses, generally agree in saying that Christ was the end of this essential grace, not in its production but in its reparation. For Christ was first intended as the Redeemer of the human race, and therefore this presupposes the destruction of original justice through Adam's sin.

According to the interpretation of the Salmanticenses and Gonet concerning the teaching of St. Thomas on the motive of the Incarnation, which we admitted, the end to which Christ was appointed is the permission of original sin by which original justice is destroyed, and not the production of this original justice. Hence Christ is not appointed for the production of this original justice, but for its reparation. So say the Salmanticenses [29] and Billuart.[30]

As regards the essential grace and glory of the good angels, we shall discuss this farther on. Although this grace is not the result of Christ's merits, yet it is ordained to Christ as to its end. For this grace was neither destroyed nor to be repaired, and the decree of the Incarnation did not therefore presuppose its destruction by some sin permitted by God.

All these statements are consistent with what we previously said about the motive of the Incarnation,[31] namely, that God among innumerable possible worlds saw by His knowledge of simple intelligence the world free from sin, perfect and glorious not redeemed by the Incarnation, and the world of sin made perfect and glorious by the redemptive Incarnation, and by one simple and efficacious decree for the manifestation of His glory chose this second world, that is, He permitted both Adam's sin destroying original justice and willed the redemptive Incarnation, as a greater good without which He would not have permitted the aforesaid sin. Hence the permission of original sin and the restoration of original justice are ordained to Christ, as to their end; in fact, as will be stated farther on, the angels

[29] Cf. *De incarnatione,* disp. XVI, dub. 4, par. 1, nos. 52 f.
[30] Cf. *De incarnatione,* disp. IX, a. 2, par. 3, solv. obj. 4.
[31] See pp. 32–71.

themselves and their essential grace and glory not destined to be destroyed are likewise ordained to Christ, as to their end, because there is only one decree for all parts of the universe, so that they may pass from the state of possibility to that of futurity.[32]

Second objection. Adam's essential grace in the state of innocence is the effect of his predestination. But Adam's predestination, like ours, is the effect of Christ's merits. Therefore Adam's essential grace in the state of innocence is the effect of Christ's merits, who was therefore in the strict sense his head.

Reply. I distinguish the antecedent: that the grace as first given in the state of innocence was the effect of Adam's predestination, I deny; that it was so as destined to be repaired, I concede. For this grace as first given was not ordained efficaciously to glory, but only as it was repaired after its loss. Hence in the state of innocence, this grace did not depend either on Adam's predestination or on Christ's predestination, but on God's general providence in the supernatural order, just like the sufficient graces that were given, for example, to the angels who were not predestined.

I insist. But God's general providence is subordinated to the providence of the hypostatic union as end. Hence there is no solution of the difficulty.

Reply. The Salmanticenses [33] answer by making the following distinction: that this subordination to the hypostatic union prevails as regards the reparation of this original justice, I concede; as regards the state itself of original justice, I deny. "Although," as they say, "the providence of the hypostatic union, to which Christ's predestination belongs, which is the cause of ours, on behalf of the dignity of its object, namely, of Christ, was sufficient to subordinate to Himself and to that providence the state of original justice, and God could fittingly

[32] Thus by the diagrams given below we may again represent these two possible worlds, the second of which was chosen by God by one sole efficacious decree together with all its parts.

World before the fall to be preserved in this state.

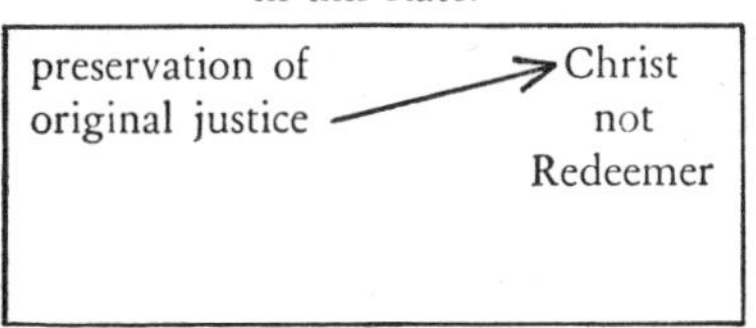

World after the fall to be redeemed

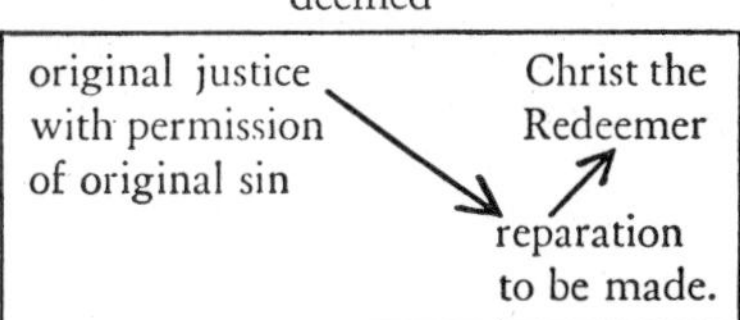

[33] *De incarnatione,* disp. XVI, nos. 69 f.

enough so decree; yet, on the present supposition that *de facto* God intended Christ as a remedy for original sin, He could by His consequent power extend His decree to the above-mentioned subordination. The reason is that He could not look upon that first state of innocence except through the medium of original sin, which is the formal destruction and non-existence of this state; and therefore He could exert no influence on this being, as stated above. Consequently the influx of providence in the hypostatic union *de facto* consists precisely in those things that concern or connote original sin; it does not extend to other things, although in another series of things, considering the sufficiency of this providence, it could be extended to include them." [34]

Yet it remains true, as the Salmanticenses furthermore say, that "all things which God decreed in reparation after the Fall, were directed to Christ as to their end." [35] Thus original justice was only mediately and indirectly the material cause of the Incarnation, since this latter was decreed in reparation after sin.

Still I insist. But in the other predestined, such as in St. Peter, even the first of the series of graces interrupted by sin, is the effect of the person's predestination, according to the Thomist doctrine.[36] Therefore the same must be said of Adam's first grace, though the series of graces was interrupted by sin.

Reply. There is not parity of argument in each case, for in the person predestined and redeemed, as in St. Peter, the first grace bestowed is given with the intention of leading him to glory by the recovery of this grace. On the contrary, grace was not bestowed on Adam in the state of innocence with the efficacious intention of leading him to glory in that state, but it came from God's general providence. That state of innocence had to be admitted and the decree of Christ's coming and His predestination depended on its loss, and through Christ's merits we are all redeemed. Hence Adam's first grace was the effect of his predestination, only as recovered, not as first bestowed.

Another difficulty. Is Christ as man Adam's head in the state of innocence as regards accidental graces, just as, as we shall immediately say, He is of the angels? Essential grace is habitual grace or sanctify-

[34] *Ibid.*, no. 61.
[35] *Ibid.*
[36] Billuart, *De praedest.*

ing grace, and accidental grace is illuminating grace of the intellect, which is not absolutely necessary for justification.

It is a disputed question among Thomists. Some deny that Christ is Adam's head, because, so they say, the angels are Christ's ministers in the kingdom of God, but Adam in the state of innocence was not Christ's minister. So says Billuart.

Nevertheless Gonet's teaching is probable. He writes: "Christ as man was head of our first parents even in the state of innocence, for a moral influence came from Christ on our first parents still in the state of innocence, just as it was given to the angels, namely, some accidental grace, such as faith in Christ to come, not indeed as the redeemer, but as the consummator of glory." [37]

Other Thomists, such as Billuart, reply with the following distinction: that Adam in the state of innocence believed in Christ, that is, in Christ objectively considered, I concede; that he had this belief through Christ, I deny. But if it is insisted that Adam believed in Christ as the consummator of glory, and therefore as the head, they reply: as the future head as being the consummator of glory, let this pass without comment; as the head actually exerting His influx in the state of innocence, this I deny.

At least it must be granted that Adam's belief in Christ to come as the consummator of glory was directed to Christ as to the end; and Adam continued in this belief, since it was not lost as the grace of original justice was, because Adam, strictly speaking, did not sin against faith, and so he did not lose it.

Final doubt. If we admit the teaching of St. Thomas on the motive of the Incarnation, is it probable that Adam's essential grace in the state of innocence rests on a twofold title: namely, (1) on God elevating him to this grace, independently of Christ; (2) dependent on Christ's merits.

Reply. Certain Thomists, such as Godoy, O.P., and Cipullus, O.P., maintain this for the angels and also, so it seems, for Adam in the state of innocence. Their reason is that this contributes to Christ's glory, just as the glorification of His physical body rests on a twofold title: namely, (1) as being connatural, since it is the overflow of glory from the soul, and (2) on the title of merit. Likewise, so they say, the essential grace of the angels and Adam rested on a twofold title.

[37] *De incarn.*, disp. XIV, a. 3, par. 3, no. 52. See also IIIa, q. 1, a. 3, ad 5; and for the angels: Ia, q. 64, a. 1, ad 4.

This opinion of Godoy and Cipullus is attacked by Billuart and by Gonet, and to these last-mentioned theologians Contenson replies by saying: "According to this opinion, God the Father by the first expression of His will freely gave His grace, and afterward also willed to confer it because of Christ's merits; so that, if at first He had not decided to give it, by virtue of this second will it would be bestowed efficaciously. Certainly this way of presenting the case claims for itself probability, since it by all means safeguards Christ's dignity." [38]

Contenson says that this conclusion is only probable, because we do not know what is positively contained in God's free decree on this point. It has not been sufficiently revealed.

However, even though this opinion were probable concerning the essential grace of the angels, it is not so probable as regards the essential grace of Adam in the state of innocence, because Christ came as the Redeemer on the supposition that Adam's sin was permitted, by which the grace in the state of innocence was lost, whereas the first grace of the predestined angels was not lost.

Fourth Article

WHETHER CHRIST IS THE HEAD OF THE ANGELS

State of the question. It concerns Christ as man, for there is not indeed any doubt that Christ, as God, is the head of the angels even as regards essential grace and glory, which is a participation of the divine nature.

There are three difficulties presented at the beginning of this article. (1) It seems that Christ is not the head of the angels, because the head and members are of the same nature; but Christ, as man, is not of the same nature with the angels. (2) The angels do not belong to the Church, which is the congregation of the faithful who are wayfarers exiled from the Lord. (3) Christ as man gives life to the souls of men, but in this respect He does not give life to the angels.

Reply. Christ is the head of the angels.

Scriptural proof. St. Paul says: "In Him [Christ] dwelleth all the fullness of the Godhead corporeally, and you are filled in Him, who is the head of all principality and power." [39] There is a similar text from St. Paul quoted in the body of this article.[40] In fact, the words

[38] *De incarn.*, disp. IV, chap. 2, no. 54.
[39] Col. 2:9 f.
[40] Eph. 1:20.

of Jesus, as quoted by the Evangelist, are evidence of this truth, for He says: "The Son of man shall send His angels." [41] And again: "He shall send His angels, and shall gather together His elect." [42] "He shall send His angels with a trumpet, and a great voice." [43] "All power is given to Me in heaven and in earth." [44] Likewise St. Paul declares that Christ has inherited "a more excellent name than the angels," [45] and this for three reasons, because He is the only Son of God, because He is the Lord of God's kingdom, whereas the angels are His ministers, and because He is full of grace, this fullness being absolute and superabundant.

Theological proof. It is proved by two syllogistic reasonings, as follows:

There must be one head to one body. But there is one mystical body of the Church, which consists of men and angels, who are ordained to the same glory. Therefore this particular body, which is one because of the unity of its end, has one head.

But this one and only head is Christ, because He is nearer to God. Therefore not only men, but angels share in Christ's influence.

The first syllogism has its foundation in the one end of the entire mystical body, inasmuch as men and angels are ordained to the same ultimate supernatural end. The source of their spiritual life is derived from the same divine truth and from the same supreme divine good.

The second syllogism has its foundation in this principle: that Christ is nearer God by the hypostatic union and more perfectly shares in God's gifts, according to the absolute fullness of grace.[46]

Thus the conclusion is that Christ is truly and in the strict sense the head of the angels, as attested by St. Paul.[47]

The solution of the difficulties confirms this conclusion.

Reply to first objection. Christ as man is not in agreement with the angels in their specific nature, but in their generic nature, or in the generic grade of intellectuality. And though this does not suffice for natural headship, at least it does so for moral headship, otherwise

[41] Matt. 13:41.

[42] Mark 13:27.

[43] Matt. 24:31.

[44] *Ibid.,* 28:18. This text is commonly quoted in our times to show that Christ even as man, because of His grace of union and fullness of habitual grace, is king of all creatures, even of angels.

[45] Heb. 1:4; 2:1-4; I Cor. 15:25 f.

[46] Cf. a. 4, c.

[47] Col. 2:10.

God Himself would not be the head of the angels. Moreover, Christ has the same specific nature as the angels in the supernatural order, namely, the same and only species of habitual grace, which is the participation of the divine nature.

Reply to second objection. "The church in heaven is the congregation of comprehensors." But Christ already in this life was both wayfarer and comprehensor, having grace and glory to the fullest extent.

Reply to third objection. "Christ's humanity, by virtue of the divine nature, can cause something in the spirits of angels on account of its close conjunction with God, that is, by personal union."

Several doubts must be examined.

First doubt. Is Christ, as man, truly and strictly speaking, the head of the angels as regards their external government?

Theologians generally agree that Christ is the head in this sense, and to deny it would be an error on account of the very clear texts of Sacred Scripture, as quoted above. Also, just as the pope is called the head of the Church as regards its eternal government, so Christ as man, by reason of the hypostatic union, is the prince and lord of the entire Church triumphant, which consists of men and angels. Manifestly this is so from the very fact that Jesus said: "The Son of man . . . shall send His angels," [48] and "All power is given to Me in heaven and in earth." [49]

Hence St. Thomas shows that Christ ascended above every spiritual creature,[50] and that Christ's judiciary power, as man, extends to the angels, who are His ministers concerning men.

Second doubt. What grace does Christ as man bestow on the angels?

Reply. There is no doubt that He bestows on them accidental grace, which consists in the illumination of their intellect concerning those things that pertain to our redemption, especially the mystery of the redemptive Incarnation, that they may cooperate with Christ as His ministers in the business of man's salvation. Thus the archangel Gabriel was sent to the Blessed Virgin Mary, St. Joseph was enlightened by the angel concerning those things that pertain to Christ and His defense, and Christ sends His angels to be guardians of men.

Thus Christ, as man, bestows on the angels by a physically instrumental influx, accidental graces that they minister to us, and so He

[48] Mark 13:26 f.

[49] Matt. 28:18. See also Heb., chaps. 1 and 2.

[50] Cf. IIIa, q. 57, a. 5.

purges them from error in this ministry, illumines and perfects them. Similarly Christ as man bestows accidental reward or accidental glory on the angels, on account of this ministry, and accidental joy in the objective and indirect reparation made for those seats lost by the fallen angels, through the justification and glorification of the saints. Thus the angels rejoice in the fact that, because of Christ's merits, the Blessed Virgin Mary has been exalted above their choirs and that the soul of St. Joseph is among them.

But Christ formerly merited the accidental graces, which by His physical instrumentality He bestows on the angels; for He merited whatever He afterward confers. This is clearly enough expressed by St. Paul in the following text: "Are they not all ministering spirits, sent to minister for them, who shall receive the inheritance of salvation?" [51]

Now indeed, since Christ as man rules over the angels, and merited the accidental grace and glory He now bestows on them, He is truly and properly called their head, more than the pope is as regards the faithful; for the pope only governs the faithful and does not either merit or bestow such accidental grace and glory on them. In fact, Christ is more the head of the angels than of infidels, who are not actually subjected to Him as their head; for He does not impart actual graces to infidels as to actual living members of the Church, but only to dispose them to receive the life of faith.

It is not necessary for the moral head of the angels to bestow on them essential grace, for it is not the primary function of the natural head to give essential life to the members of the body, for this comes from the soul as the substantial form of the body; but it imparts only some vital motion as its secondary act. A fortiori, it suffices that the moral head exert its influence by ruling, as the pope does in the Church and the king in his kingdom.

Third doubt. Does Christ as man bestow on the angels also essential grace and glory, these being a participation of the divine nature? It is certain that as God He bestows this grace on them; but the question is whether He bestows this grace in His human nature, inasmuch as it is personally united with the Word and because of the fullness of grace possessed by Christ in His human nature.

It is a disputed question among theologians. Some absolutely affirm that He does, such as Scotus, the Scotists, Suarez, Valentia, and Godoy,

[51] Heb. 1:14.

among the Thomists. They give as their principal reason that Christ is the first of all the predestined, and therefore He is the cause of all graces for others.

On the contrary, some absolutely deny that Christ as man gives this grace to the angels. Many of these are Thomists, such as Medina, Alvarez, John of St. Thomas, Gonet, Billuart, and others; outside the school of St. Thomas, we have Vasquez and de Lugo.

The principal reason advanced by these Thomists is that Christ came as the Redeemer, to redeem us men, and He did not die for the angels who were not in need of redemption.

But others try to reconcile the two above-mentioned opinions. Among the Thomists are Vincent of Asturia and Cipullus, who maintain that the essential grace of the angels rests on a twofold title: (1) on God's liberality, and (2) on Christ's merits, just as there were two reasons for the glorification of Christ's body, namely, the connatural overflow of this glory from His soul, and the merit He acquired.

Finally, the Salmanticenses seem to solve the question better by saying: "Christ bestowed this essential grace on the angels, not indeed as physically efficient cause or as morally meritorious cause or as redemptive cause, but by way of objective end," [52] inasmuch as Christ was first intended by God above the angels.

Let us first consider the more common opinion among the Thomists, namely, that Christ as man does not bestow essential grace and glory on the angels.[53]

Scriptural proof. In the Gospel we read: "The angel said to them [the shepherds], 'I bring you good tidings of great joy . . . for this day is born to you a Savior.' " [54] The angel says: "to you," not "to us." Similarly St. Bernard in one of his homilies, quoting the scriptural text, "A child is born to us, and a Son is given to us," [55] says: "He was not given also to the angels, who having the great, did not need the very little. Therefore He was born for us, given to us, because He is necessary to us." [56]

But if St. Gregory the Great says, "No man or angel is holy except through Christ," [57] this can be understood of Christ as God.

[52] *De incarn.*, disp. XVI, dub. 5, no. 76.
[53] Cf. Gonet, Salmanticenses, *De incarnatione.*
[54] Luke 2:10.
[55] Isa. 9:6.
[56] Hom. 3 super *Missus est.*
[57] *Com. in I Reg.*, Bk. I, chap. 2.

Moreover, the Church says of the Son of God: "Who for us men and for our salvation came down from heaven and became incarnate," [58] not for the angels.

Proof from various texts of St. Thomas. Thus he says: "The angels are not wayfarers as regards their essential reward and therefore in this sense Christ did not merit anything for them. But they are in some manner wayfarers as regards their accidental reward; inasmuch as they minister to us, and this is what Christ merited for them." [59]

Again he says: "He [Christ] does not exert His influence on the angels by removing the obstacle either by meriting grace for them or praying for them, because they are already in a state of bliss; but He exerts His influence in those things that pertain to hierarchic acts, inasmuch as one angel illumines, purges, and purifies another." [60]

St. Thomas likewise says, concerning the extent of Christ's judiciary power as regards the angels: "They are submitted to Christ's judgment: (1) as regards the dispensation of those things which are done through them . . . whereas they minister to Christ as man; (2) as to other accidental rewards . . . ; (3) as to the essential reward of the good angels, which is everlasting bliss; and as to the essential punishment of the wicked angels, which is everlasting damnation. But this was done by Christ from the beginning of the world inasmuch as He is the Word of God." [61]

The principal theological proof for this more common opinion among the Thomists is about the same as for Adam's essential grace in the state of innocence and may be expressed by the following syllogistic reasoning.

Christ was willed by God primarily and principally as the Redeemer; and the grace that comes from Him is medicinal or healing, derived from His death. But the essential grace of the angels is not at all medicinal or healing, nor did Christ die for them.

Therefore the essential grace of the angels is not the result of Christ's merits.

Confirmation. In fact, God's efficacious decree of the Incarnation in passible flesh presupposes, even for the Scotists, that He permitted and foresaw Adam's sin; and this permission presupposes that He

[58] Nicene Creed.

[59] *De veritate,* q. 29, a. 7, ad 5.

[60] *Com. in III Sent.,* d. 13, q. 2, a. 3, *quaestiuncula,* 1.

[61] Cf. IIIa, q. 59, a. 6.

permitted the devil's sin, inasmuch as *de facto* Adam's sin came about from the temptation by the devil, who was the first to fall. Therefore the Word incarnate, as incarnate, was not the cause of essential grace in the angels, which had been lost through the devil's sin.

Solution of objections. The principal reason advanced by the Scotists in opposition to the Thomist opinion is as follows:

Christ as man is the first of all the predestined. But the first of all the predestined is the cause of all graces for the others, among whom are the good angels. Therefore Christ as man was the cause of the essential grace and glory of the angels.

Reply. As in the case of essential grace for Adam in the state of innocence, the answer is made by distinguishing the major: that Christ is the first of all the predestined by a *priority of dignity,* this I concede, because He was predestined to natural divine sonship which far transcends adoptive sonship of the angels;[62] that He is the first of all the predestined by a priority of meritorious causality, this I deny, because He is such only as regards those to be redeemed, since He came as Redeemer for us men and not for the angels. I contradistinguish the minor: the first of all the predestined is the meritorious cause of all the graces of the predestined to be redeemed, this I concede; of the others, namely, of the angels, this I deny. And I deny the consequent and consequence.

But I insist. The Scotists in confirmation of their thesis add: For Christ to be truly and in the strict sense the head of the angels, it is not enough for Him to bestow upon them accidental grace and glory. For Christ is the head only of those on whom He bestows those gifts by which they are constituted members either of the Church militant, suffering, or triumphant, and which are grace, charity, faith, and in heaven the light of glory and the beatific vision.

Reply. The Thomists distinguish the antecedent. That the bestowal of accidental grace and glory is not enough for Christ to be considered in the absolutely strict sense the head of the angels just as He is the head of the just, this I concede; that such is not enough for Him to be truly their head, this I deny. Indeed, it is not the primary function even of the natural head and a fortiori of the moral head to bestow essential life on the members. It is not the primary function of the head to make the members living members, for this pertains to the soul as the substantial form of the whole body; but the head

[62] Cf. *infra,* q. 24.

imparts to the members a vital motion, which is life in its secondary act. A fortiori the moral head, such as the pope in the Church or the king in his kingdom, each exerts influence on the members by external government, and yet each is truly called the head. But Christ as man, not only governs the angels by sending them on this or that ministry, but He also bestows on them accidental graces or illuminations for the correct and devout fulfillment of their ministry; and because of their having fulfilled their ministry in this way, He bestows on them an accidental reward. Thus Christ as man is truly and in the strict sense the head of the angels, although in a way not so perfect as He is the head of the just, though He is more the head of the angels than the pope is the head of the faithful.

Finally, the Scotists quote in their favor the following scriptural texts: "No man cometh to the Father, but by Me," [63] and "For if by the offense of one, many died, much more . . . the grace of one man, Jesus Christ, hath abounded unto many." [64]

The Thomists point out that the scriptural texts and statements of the Fathers to which the Scotists refer on this subject, either do not certainly concern the angels but only the just, or if the angels are included, it is not evident from these texts that Christ as man bestows on them essential grace. Thus, when St. John quotes our Lord as saying: "No man cometh to the Father but by Me," [65] the meaning is: No one, either angel or man, comes to the Father, except through the Son, but in a different way; for man comes to the Father through the Son veiled in the flesh, but the angel through the Son inasmuch as He is God.

Fourth doubt. If the doctrine of St. Thomas on the motive of the Incarnation be admitted, is it probable that there are two reasons why the angels have their essential grace and glory, namely: (1) because of God's liberality independently of Christ; (2) dependent on Christ's merits?

Reply. Among Thomists, Godoy O.P. and Cipullus O.P., are of this opinion. Although Gonet and Billuart are against them, yet their opinion, as Contenson shows,[66] does not lack probability. Their principal reason for this opinion is that it contributes to Christ's glory for

[63] John 14:6.
[64] Rom. 5:15.
[65] *Ibid.*
[66] *De incarn.,* disp. IV, chap. 2.

Him to be the source of all graces; and in truth, Christ Himself obtained the glorification of His body by a twofold right: (1) in that it was connatural to Him, as being the overflow of glory from the soul; (2) by having merited this right.

As Contenson remarks,[67] this opinion is probable. But if against this opinion the objection is raised that Christ, however, did not die for the angels, and therefore He did not merit for them, then the answer is that neither did Christ die for Himself, and yet He merited for Himself the glorification of His body, and this by a twofold right.

But this opinion cannot be demonstrated because, if it is an established fact, then this opinion depends on God's most free decree that has not been sufficiently revealed; nor can it be deduced with theological certainty from revealed principles. Hence St. Thomas observes a prudent silence concerning these things known to God alone. As the Apostle says, it behooves us "to be wise unto sobriety." [68]

Fifth doubt. Is Christ as man the final cause of essential grace and glory in the angels?

Reply. That Christ is the final cause, we affirm along with the Salmanticenses, who say: "We add that Christ bestowed substantial grace and first justification on the angels, not indeed that He was either the efficient physical cause or the moral, meritorious, or redemptive cause, but He was the cause by way of objective end." [69] This can most probably be declared in two ways.[70]

The first reason, indeed, is that Christ was intended by God as the end of all things, to whom God ordained all things He decreed to

[67] *Ibid.*

[68] Rom. 12:3.

[69] *De incarn.,* disp. XVI, dub. 5, par. 1, no. 76. This view is also affirmed by several other Thomists, though more or less incidentally, whereas the Salmanticenses insist on this, and rightly so, inasmuch as it can clearly be seen from their interpretation of St. Thomas' teaching on the motive of the Incarnation.

[70] This opinion becomes increasingly evident from what we said concerning the motive of the Incarnation (*Com. in IIIam,* q. 1, a. 3), in explaining the reply to the third objection of this article. See also what we shall say further on (IIIa, q. 24, a. 3, 4) concerning Christ's predestination as He is the exemplary cause of our predestination.

This view presupposes that God by one decree chose all parts of this possible world, which includes angels and men to be redeemed by Christ. In this possible world Christ is the end of all, although He is not either the meritorious cause or the efficient cause of essential grace in the angels; for everything in such a world is subordinated to Him inasmuch as He is the God-man, for St. Paul says: "All things are yours . . . and you [even the angels] are Christ's, and Christ is God's" (I Cor. 3:21).

make, as we explicitly showed.[71] Now it suffices to say of this particular disposition on God's part that on the one hand there is nothing derogatory to God, and on the other that it is most befitting the excellence of Christ, our Lord, who, as He was the first of the predestined and the exemplary cause of all the predestined, thus it was becoming for Him to be the quasi-intermediate end for whose sake all things were created, and to whom God referred and subjected all things, so that they should serve Him and increase His glory.[72] Hence, whatever grace and perfection they had and the angels have, they all participate in Christ's bestowal of this in the genus of final cause.

The second reason, however, is that the angels in the state of probation, and also our first parents in the state of innocence, believed in Christ as the consummator of glory. Thus Christ bestowed faith on the angels, and on our first parents in the state of innocence objectively.

Hence Christ is the end of essential grace in the angels, but He does not appear to be the meritorious cause of this grace, unless their grace rests on a twofold title, which is conjectural but cannot be proved; because, if it is so, this depends on God's decree that is not sufficiently made manifest.

Conclusion. Therefore Christ is truly and in the strict sense the head of the angels, although not so completely as He is of the just, whom He redeemed and on whom He certainly bestows not only accidental grace, but also essential grace and glory.[73] The unanimous teaching of theologians is that Christ did not redeem the angels, and it is the more common opinion among Thomists that He probably did not merit for them essential grace.

Fifth Article

WHETHER THE GRACE OF CHRIST AS HEAD OF CHURCH IS THE SAME AS HIS HABITUAL GRACE, INASMUCH AS HE IS MAN

State of the question. Is Christ's grace as head of the Church really distinct from His personal habitual grace, or are the two graces identical?

[71] *De incarn.*, disp. II, dub. 1, nos. 4, 26.
[72] Heb. 2:10; Col. 1:15.
[73] *De veritate*, q. 29, a. 4, ad 5.

It seems that they are not the same, for the following reasons.

1) The actual or personal sin of Adam differs from original sin which He transmitted to posterity. Therefore the personal grace of Christ the new Adam is not the same as His grace of headship.

2) These graces are distinct inasmuch as they are ordained to different acts, for Christ's personal grace is ordained for His sanctification, whereas His capital grace is for the sanctification of others.

3) Theologians usually distinguish between three kinds of graces in Christ: the grace of union, the individual grace of the man, and the capital grace.

Conclusion. Christ's personal habitual grace and His capital grace are essentially the same, though there is a mental distinction between them.

Very many theologians accept this conclusion, though Vasquez and certain others teach that Christ's capital grace and His grace of union are really the same.

Scriptural proof. The Evangelist says: "of His fullness we all have received." [74] Hence Christ is our head inasmuch as He had the fullness of personal habitual grace. Hence there is no real distinction between Christ's habitual grace and His capital grace; at least, the text quoted above implies that these two graces are really identical.

Theological proof. There is no difference between the act whereby anything is in act and whereby it acts, and the agent must be nobler than the patient. But Christ as man is constituted supernaturally in act by the personal habitual grace which He received in the highest degree. Therefore Christ as man bestowed this same grace on others, namely, on those members whose head He is.

The major is evident, for it is founded on the principle that everything acts inasmuch as it is a being in act. Thus what is hot heats according to the heat whereby it is hot. For the agent acts, inasmuch as it determines, and the manner of its determination is in accordance with its own determination.

The minor was explained above: for personal habitual grace intrinsically and physically informs Christ, as man. Thus this grace is the operative principle whereby He radically operates supernaturally, performing acts that are infinitely meritorious and satisfactory. The *principium quo* of these operations is habitual grace as it connotes the grace of union, or as it connotes the *principium quod,* or the person

[74] John 1:6.

of the Word, from whom these works derive their infinite value.[75]

Therefore this same habitual grace is called capital, inasmuch as by it Christ can bestow on the members of the Church grace and justification, that is, by exerting a moral influence on them by means of His infinitely meritorious and satisfactory works. It is precisely this influence that constitutes Him their head, although He also exerts a physically instrumental influence on them. Christ, the head of the faithful of the Old Testament, could not exert a physically instrumental influence on them, but only a moral influence by His merit and satisfaction, since they lived before His coming.

St. Thomas often speaks of this physically instrumental causality of Christ's human nature, inasmuch as it is the instrument united with the divine nature, whereas the sacraments are separate instruments.[76] As one who blows a trumpet emits the sound by this instrument, so God can cause grace by Christ's human nature; so also our soul makes use of vocal chords as the instrument of speech. Moreover, it must be observed that, although Christ's body, inasmuch as it is in heaven as in a place, is locally distant from ours, the higher part of Christ's soul and of our soul are not of themselves localized, nor is Christ's mind locally distant from our mind, which is influenced by His mind, inasmuch as it is the instrument of His divine nature.[77]

As regards moral causality by way of merit, it is not necessary that the moral cause already exist for it to exert its influence, since the moral cause operates inasmuch as it is known, and can be known as coming into existence. Thus God conferred grace on the faithful of the Old Testament because of Christ's future merits.

The solution of the objections confirms the conclusion.

Reply to first objection. We must distinguish in Adam between his personal sin and original sin that had its origin in him, which is a sin of the nature, "because in him the person, by turning away from God, corrupted the nature; and by means of this corruption the sin of the first man is transmitted to posterity. . . . Now grace is not vouchsafed us by means of human nature, but solely by the personal action of Christ Himself. Hence we must not distinguish a twofold grace in Christ, one corresponding to the nature, the other to the per-

[75] Cf. *infra,* q. 19, a. 3, on Christs merits.

[76] Cf. IIIa, q. 43, a. 2; q. 48, a. 6; q. 62, a. 4.

[77] Cf. *infra,* q. 13, a. 2: the power of Christ's soul; its physical and instrumental causality.

son." This means, as Cajetan observes, that "grace is not communicated to us by the action of the nature, or by communicating the nature as Adam would have communicated it, not corrupted, to his children, if he had not sinned, but by Christ's personal action, by which He merited for us and of His own will bestowed grace on us." [78]

Reply to second objection. The eminence of Christ's personal habitual grace is the reason for the justification of others.

Reply to third objection. "The personal and the capital grace agree in the essence of the habit"; they are the same habit inasmuch as their more proximate purpose is for the performance of some meritorious act. On the contrary, the direct purpose of the grace of union is not for the eliciting of a meritorious act, and it is not a habit but, as stated above, "the grace of union is the personal being that is given gratis by God to the human nature in the person of the Word." [79]

Objection. But for Vasquez the capital grace and the grace of union are identical because, so he says, the infinite value of Christ's merits is derived from this grace of union.

Reply. That the value of Christ's merits is derived remotely from the grace of union as from the *principium quod* [80] that is connotated, this I concede; that it is derived proximately as from the operative *principium quo,* this I deny, although charity is the immediate principle of merit. It pertains to the notion of capital grace, however, for it to be the root, instrumentally, of those merits because the head of the Church as such exerts at least a moral influence on the members by His meritorious works.

But I insist. If Christ did not have habitual grace, He would, nevertheless, still be our head; for habitual grace is not absolutely necessary so as to enable Him to elicit meritorious acts. Therefore Christ is not the head because of habitual grace.

Reply. I distinguish the antecedent: If Christ did not have habitual grace, He would still be our head because of His divine personality, this I deny, for His personality does not constitute Him the operative principle of merit; because of the transient help given by it, this I concede. But then Christ would not be the connatural operative principle of merit.

[78] *Com. in IIIam,* q. 8, a. 5, no. 5.

[79] Cf. IIIa, q. 6, a. 6. See Cajetan's comment on the reply to this third objection.

[80] See note 75.

Again I insist. Grace that is ordained for the sanctification of others is not grace gratum faciens, but grace gratis data. Therefore Christ's capital grace that is ordained for our sanctification is not identical with His personal habitual grace.

Reply. I distinguish the antecedent: Grace that is primarily ordained for the sanctification of others is not gratia gratum faciens, this I concede; grace that is only secondarily so ordained is not such, this I deny. Thus the gift of wisdom is included in sanctifying grace, although its secondary purpose is for the direction of souls, which means that it is for the benefit of others. Such was Christ's habitual grace.

Sixth Article

WHETHER IT IS PROPER TO CHRIST TO BE THE HEAD OF THE CHURCH

In this article, as in the remaining ones of this question, St. Thomas shows that it is proper for Christ to be the head of the Church by a certain intrinsic influence of grace and justification, because He has this power from habitual grace, inasmuch as it presupposes the grace of union, to which is attributed the infinite value of His merits.[81] But to be the head of the Church in its external government for a time befits the pope as regards the Church militant during the time of his pontificate. In this way, he is the vicar of Christ.

Seventh Article

WHETHER THE DEVIL IS THE HEAD OF ALL THE WICKED

Lucifer, the prince of devils, is the head of all the wicked not by interiorly influencing their wills, for God alone can interiorly move the will; but he is their head by inducing them to commit sin by means of suggestions and temptations, it being easier to destroy than to build.

[81] However, according to the common teaching of theologians, what Christ merited for us *de condigno,* the Blessed Virgin merited for us strictly *de congruo,* namely, by merit that had its foundation not in justice, but in charity which united her to God and to us, or by an amicable right. Wherefore Mary is the universal Mediatrix and Mother of all men, and is like the neck that joins the head to the body. She is also called the aqueduct of all graces.

Eighth Article

WHETHER ANTICHRIST MAY BE CALLED THE HEAD OF ALL THE WICKED

Antichrist is neither the head of all the wicked as regards those that lived before his time, since he will come only about the end of the world, nor as regards his power of influencing them, since he cannot have any influence on those sinners who lived before his coming; but he is their head only by reason of the perfection of his wickedness, so that all the wicked who preceded him are, so to speak, signs of Antichrist.[82]

[82] In recapitulation of those things that pertain to Christ's capital grace, read carefully the encyclical of Pius XII on "The Mystical Body of Christ" (1944).

CHAPTER XI

QUESTION 9

Christ's Knowledge in General and His Power of Contemplation

AFTER the consideration of Christ's grace, both personal and capital, we must discuss the question of His knowledge: (1) What knowledge indeed or what kinds of knowledge did He have? (2) Then we shall inquire into each particular kind of knowledge, namely, His beatific knowledge (q. 10), His imprinted or infused knowledge (q. 11), His acquired knowledge (q. 13), that is, Christ's intellectual life, even His most sublime contemplation.

It is therefore evident that, as St. Thomas says, "We are here taking knowledge for any cognition of the human intellect," [1] even that which is not discursive. The most important article of this ninth question is the second, which inquires whether Christ had already in this life the knowledge that the blessed or comprehensors have, namely, the beatific vision. The first article, however, may be considered an introduction to the inquiries about Christ's created knowledge.

Notice must be taken of the fact that Sacred Scripture, which is a manifestation of divine truth for the purpose of salvation, insists more on the moral and religious than on the intellectual aspects of our Lord's life as Savior. But the idea of Christ as man is not of one who had the most sublime conception of moral and religious perfection to the exclusion of a proportionate knowledge of God, the soul, the world, the kingdom of God. It is in this way that the theologian is induced to treat of Christ's knowledge, and he inquires what can be known of Him from Sacred Scripture, tradition, and theological reasoning.[2]

[1] Cf. IIIa, q. 9, a. 1 (about end).

[2] *Dict. théol. cath.,* art. "Jésus-Christ," cols. 1273 f. See also "Science du Christ."

First Article

WHETHER CHRIST HAD ANY KNOWLEDGE BESIDES THE DIVINE

State of the question. The meaning of the title is whether Christ had any other knowledge besides the uncreated knowledge. Why is it that any other knowledge is not superfluous since the uncreated knowledge already includes all other kinds of knowledge?

Reply. The answer is in the affirmative, namely, that Christ had created knowledge as well as uncreated knowledge. The conclusion is *de fide*.

Scriptural proof. That Christ had created knowledge is, indeed, quite clear, for He says of Himself: "I know Him [My Father] and do keep his Word"; [3] but He kept his Father's word by created actions as man. Therefore He likewise knew His Father by created knowledge. Moreover, Christ prayed, merited, obeyed, and performed many other human acts, and it is only by acts of the created intellect and of the created will that these can be performed. It was not, indeed, as God that He prayed, merited, and obeyed; for these acts presuppose the subordination of the created will under the guidance of the created intellect to the uncreated will.

Hence the Monothelites were condemned by the Third Council of Constantinople for refusing to admit two wills in Christ, namely, the uncreated will and the created will. This Council defined that Christ "is perfect both in His divine nature and in His human nature, truly God and truly man, of rational soul and body . . . and has two natural wills not contrary to each other . . . , and His human nature is in every respect human, sin absolutely excepted." [4]

Medina maintains that it is manifestly heretical to deny that Christ's soul had created knowledge, at least in act.

As John of St. Thomas observes, concerning the last sentence in the body of this article, it was not indeed defined by the Council that Christ has two kinds of knowledge, but two wills and operations, and that He had a human nature, and all that belongs to it, except sin. From these definitions, by closer attention to the meaning than to the words, it follows that the Council condemned the view of those who deny two kinds of knowledge in Christ.

[3] John 8:55.
[4] Denz., nos. 290 f.

Theological proof. It is taken from the argumentative part of this article, and may be expressed in the following syllogistic form.

The human nature is imperfect without its connatural and proper act of knowledge. But the Son of God assumed a perfect human nature. Therefore the Son of God had the connatural and proper created act of intellective knowledge.

Major. Three reasons are given for its proof.

1) That the intellective soul is imperfect unless it be reduced to its act of understanding, for which it is ordained.

2) That everything is on account of its operation, or as Cajetan explains, operating on account of itself, not that the knowledge is innate, but inasmuch as, when the terms of the principles have been proposed, the intellect naturally adheres to them.

Minor. It is revealed, but it is also clearly stated in the previously quoted canons of the Third Council of Constantinople.[5] Hence human intelligence would be for no purpose in Christ unless He could make use of it, and in this respect His soul would be more imperfect than the souls of the rest of mankind.

Doubt. Could Christ, as man, understand by communication from the uncreated act of understanding, as the Master of Good Hope thought? [6]

Reply. This possibility is generally denied by theologians. For the act of understanding in the soul is a vital act, since it proceeds from an intrinsic principle, from the soul and its faculty. But the Deity cannot function as the soul, or a faculty, or a habit, for example, as the light of glory. In such a case it would not be the form as terminating but as confirming, and hence would be less perfect than the whole composite of which it is a part. Therefore Christ's soul could not understand by communication from the uncreated intellect.

Second Article

WHETHER CHRIST HAD KNOWLEDGE WHICH THE BLESSED OR COMPREHENSORS HAVE

State of the question. This article must be fully explained. First of all, it must be noted that Catholic theologians consider as theologically certain the doctrine that Christ's soul was free from all ignorance, that

[5] *Ibid.*
[6] He is so called from the monastery of Good Hope in which he lived. (Tr.)

even from His conception He knew all things in the Word, which God knows by the knowledge of vision. This was formerly denied by several heretics and in our times especially by liberal Protestants and by Modernists.

Let us first consider these denials and their foundation.

The Nestorians, who said there were two persons in Christ, considered Christ as man to have been subject to ignorance and error. The Apollinarians and Anomoeans, who maintained that the Word functions as the mind in the Savior, denied all human knowledge to Christ. Likewise the Monophysites and Monothelites, who taught that there is only one operation in Christ, denied Him human knowledge. Finally, in the sixth century, the Agnoetae, under the leadership of Themistius, deacon of Alexandria, contended that Christ, as other men, was subject to the corruption of the flesh and was, as a human being, ignorant.[7] They quoted two Gospel texts in their defense: (1) "But of that day or hour [of the judgment], no man knoweth, neither the angels of heaven, nor the Son." [8] (2) But of that day and hour no one knoweth, "not the angels of heaven, but the Father alone." [9]

In our times, particularly the liberal Protestants hold that Christ was ignorant of many things from the beginning, and it was only gradually that He acquired a knowledge of His mission. The disciples of Gunther [10] and others, as more recently Dr. Schell, said that Christ's knowledge was subject to the laws of human progress, and that in the beginning He did not have the beatific vision, but acquired it by His merits. Finally, the Modernists [11] boldly asserted that Christ neither knew all things, nor was always conscious of His Messianic dignity, and even in some things He erred, for example, concerning the end of the world.

Against these errors, it is *de fide* that Christ never erred, that He even could not err, or in other words, that He was already infallible in this life. It is at least the commonly accepted and theologically certain doctrine that Christ's soul was free from ignorance. What follows makes this clear.

It is *de fide* that Christ, as man, was free from all error in His

[7] *Dict. théol. cath.*, art. "Agnoetes."

[8] Mark 13:32.

[9] Matt. 24:36.

[10] Denz., nos. 1665 f.

[11] *Ibid.*, nos. 2032-35.

knowledge, that Christ, in fact, the founder of the Church, even in this life was infallible, just as He was impeccable.

1) Sacred Scripture is evidence of this, inasmuch as Christ says of Himself: "I am the way and the truth and the life." [12] As God, He is truth and life; as man He is the way to essential truth, inasmuch as His human nature and His whole human intellectual life is personally united with essential truth. Thus, as man, He is presented to us as the master of truth, whom we must hear. "Neither be ye called masters, for one is your master, Christ," [13] and as the leader, following whom we never walk in darkness; [14] who, in establishing His Church, made her infallible in her teaching, saying: "Thou art Peter, and upon this rock I will build My Church, and the gates of hell shall not prevail against it." [15] But if it had been possible for Christ to err, a fortiori the Church He established could err in her teaching.

2) Christ was not only infallible in the doctrine He delivered to His apostles, but also in His acts, as is evident from the Gospel narrative, for it says that Christ, already in this life, saw and knew the thoughts of men, and had complete knowledge of the free future, foretelling the events long before the time. Thus He foretold the circumstances of His passion, the destruction of Jerusalem, the continuance of His Church until the end of time.[16]

Finally and especially in the Gospel it is recorded that Christ is the Word of God made flesh, "full of grace and truth." [17] That Christ was infallible, as we have seen, not only in the doctrine He delivered, and the events affirmed by Him, but this also follows as universally established by reason of the hypostatic union. The Word, indeed, assumed the complete human nature, but free from error and sin, for as sin is evil of the will, error is evil of the intellect; and as it is absolutely repugnant, as will be stated farther on, that the Word incarnate sinned or even was able to sin, so it was repugnant that He erred or even was able to err. For error would reflect on the very person of the Word in accordance with the adage: actions are attributed to the supposita. Hence error and sin cannot be attributed to the Word of God, who is essentially truth and holiness. Thus it is com-

[12] John 14:6.
[13] Matt. 23:10; John 3:11; 9:16; 19:37.
[14] John 8:12.
[15] Matt. 16:18.
[16] *Ibid.,* 20:18 f.; 26:21 f.; 24:5 f.; 16:18 f.; 28:19 f.
[17] John 1:14.

monly said to be *de fide* that Christ, as man, the founder of the infallible Church, was infallible. To show the truth of this discursion by the explanatory method suffices, namely, an explanation of the terms of revelation, for an objectively illative method of reasoning is not necessary, namely, one by which a new truth is acquired that is not in itself revealed.

It is at least commonly accepted and theologically certain doctrine, that Christ's knowledge was absolutely exempt from all ignorance and not only from error.

St. Thomas proves this, presupposing that Christ had both beatific knowledge and infused knowledge.[18] But it is first fitting to manifest the truth of this assertion from Sacred Scripture and tradition, so that by a quasi a posterori method it may afterward be clearly seen how it befitted Him to have this beatific knowledge even in this life.

Sacred Scripture. The texts already quoted state clearly that Christ's knowledge was absolutely exempt from all ignorance. Thus Christ is declared "full of grace and truth." [19] He also knew the secrets of hearts,[20] as also distant objects and the free future.[21] These texts, however, do not refer to His uncreated knowledge, but to His human knowledge, which governed His human operation. Therefore Christ as man was exempt from all ignorance. Thus as man He was, as He Himself said, the way that leads to the truth and life.

Tradition likewise establishes more clearly that Christ's knowledge was immune from ignorance, especially from the declaration of St. Gregory the Great to the patriarch of Alexandria against the Agnoetae. The Pope says: "[But] concerning what is written: 'of that day or hour no man knoweth, neither the angels of heaven, nor the Son,' [22] this has been most correctly understood by your beatitude, since this text most certainly refers not to the Son, inasmuch as He is the head [of the Church], but to His body which we are. [St. Augustine] also says . . . that it can be understood of the Son, because the omnipotent God does speak at times in a human way, as when He said to Abraham: 'Now I know that thou fearest God.' [23] It is not because then God Himself knew that He was feared but because then He

[18] Cf. IIIa, q. 10, a. 2; q. 11, a. 1.
[19] John 1:14.
[20] Matt. 16:8; Mark 7:17; John 2:24 f.
[21] John 1:48; 11:14; Matt. 20:15 f.
[22] Mark 13:32.
[23] Gen. 22:12.

made Abraham acknowledge that he feared God. For just as we declare a day joyful, not that the day itself is joyful, but because it makes us joyful, so the omnipotent Son says that He does not know the day which He causes to be unknown, not because He does not know it, but because He does not at all permit it to be known. . . . And so the knowledge He did not have according to His human nature, which made Him, like the angels, a creature, this knowledge along with the angels who are creatures He said He did not have. Therefore He who is God and man knows the day and the hour of judgment; but the reason for this is because God is man. But the issue is most manifest, for whoever is not a Nestorian can nowise be an Agnoete. For anyone who confesses the very incarnate wisdom of God, how can he say there is anything that the wisdom of God does not know? It is also written: 'Jesus knowing that the Father had given Him all things into His hands.' [24] If He knows all things, assuredly He knows the day and the hour of the judgment; therefore who is so foolish as to say that the Son received into His hands what He was ignorant of?" [25]

In accordance with this doctrine thus explicitly formulated by Pope St. Gregory the Great, the common teaching of theologians will always be that Christ knew the day of judgment in His human nature, but not by reason of His human nature, which means that He did not know it by the natural light of the created intellect. Thus the angels, too, know this day only if they are supernaturally enlightened.[26]

Before the time of St. Gregory several Fathers spoke in a similar manner, namely, that Christ knows all things, even the day and hour of the judgment; but He is silent about this latter event, or He says He does not know because He does not permit it to be known, and because it is not expedient that men be informed about it.[27] St. Augustine teaches that ignorance can in no way be attributed to that Infant in whom the Word was made flesh.[28]

Sophronius [29] is of the same opinion, and St. John Damascene says: "If the flesh from the moment of conception was immediately united

[24] John 13:3.
[25] Denz., no. 248.
[26] Cf. IIIa, q. 10, a. 2, ad 1.
[27] Such are the comments of St. Basil, *Adv. Eunom.*, Bk. IV, chap. 3.
[28] *De peccatorum meritis et remissione,* Bk. II, chap. 48.
[29] *Ep. ad Sergium,* Rouet de Journel, no. 2290.

with God . . . and the two constituted one identical suppositum, then how can it be that it was not endowed with absolutely all the gifts of wisdom and grace?" [30] It is in this sense that the Fathers interpreted the words "full of grace and truth," [31] concerning the Word incarnate.

In our times there are several Modernist propositions that have been condemned by the Church concerning Christ's knowledge.[32] Among these are: "The natural sense of the Gospel texts cannot be reconciled with what our theologians teach about the consciousness and infallible knowledge of Jesus Christ." [33] "Christ was not always conscious of His Messianic dignity." [34]

Also later on the Holy Office declared that the following propositions cannot be safely taught: (1) "There is no evidence that Christ's soul in this life possessed that knowledge which the blessed or comprehensors have; (2) That opinion cannot be called certain that concludes Christ's soul was exempt from ignorance, but knew everything in the Word, past, present, and future, from the moment of His conception, or that He knew everything God knows by His knowledge of vision; (3) The opinion of certain more recent theologians about Christ's limited knowledge is equally to be accepted in Catholic schools, as the opinion of the ancient theologians concerning Christ's universal knowledge." [35]

We shall see later on, in the explanation of the article, the theological reasons given by St. Thomas for maintaining the universality of Christ's knowledge.

Modernist objections. On the one hand, the Modernists assert that Christ erred in announcing that the end of the world was near; on the other hand, He said that He did not know the judgment day. These two objections are contradictory.

First objection. It has been examined at length by us in our work on apologetics,[36] and there is no need to dwell upon it here. The difficulty arises from two Gospel texts. After foretelling the destruction of Jerusalem and the day of judgment, Jesus says: "This genera-

[30] *De fide orthod.,* Bk. III, chap. 22. Cf. Journel, no. 2368.
[31] John 1:14.
[32] Denz., nos. 2032–35. Decree *Lamentabili.*
[33] Proposition 32.
[34] *Ibid.,* 35.
[35] Denz., nos. 2183–85.
[36] *De revelatione,* Bk. II, chap. 4, a. 4; chap. 11, a. 1.

tion shall not pass till all these things be done." [37] In the other text it is recorded that before the transfiguration of Jesus, He said: "There are some of them that stand here, that shall not taste death, till they see the Son of man coming in His kingdom." [38]

Reply. This last text more probably alludes to the future and proximate resurrection of Christ.[39] But other texts quoted from Sacred Scripture on this subject are indeed difficult to reconcile, for in this same discourse Christ spoke of both the end of Jerusalem and the end of the world, and although the first event is a figure of the second, it is difficult to detect what belongs to the first event, and what to the second. But what any particularly learned author has to say on this topic must be understood, if possible, as showing that there is no contradiction between the texts. However, as Catholic exegetes show,[40] and several conservative Protestants, such as Godet and Sanday, the rationalist and Modernist interpretation is not founded on the Gospel texts, but is very much in contradiction to it.

1) Christ not only sent His apostles to the people of Israel, but He said to them: "Go ye into the whole world, and preach the gospel to every creature," [41] and "Going therefore teach ye all nations." [42] He expressly says: "And unto all nations the gospel must first be preached," [43] before the second coming. Also: "And . . . many shall come from the east and the west. . . ." [44] But Christ did not announce these events as taking place in the immediate future.

2) He even distinguished in point of time between the destruction of Jerusalem and the end of the world, saying: "Jerusalem shall be trodden down by the Gentiles, till the times of the nations be fulfilled," [45] and *de facto* it is trodden down. Christ especially refused to state precisely when the end of the world would be, but He said: "It is not for you to know the times or moments which the Father hath put in His own power." [46]

[37] Matt. 24:34.
[38] *Ibid.*, 16:28.
[39] For already Christ gloriously risen from the dead, by divers aparitions, came forth as victor over the devil, sin, and death in His kingdom.
[40] Cf. Lepin, *Jésus Messie et Fils de Dieu,* pp. 385–99.
[41] Mark 16:15.
[42] Matt. 28:19; Luke 24:47.
[43] Mark 13:10.
[44] Matt. 8:24; Luke 13:29; Rom. 11:25 f.
[45] Luke 21:24.
[46] Acts 1:7.

Second objection. Some of the earlier Fathers, such as St. Athanasius, St. Gregory Nazianzen, St. Cyril of Alexandria, say that Christ was ignorant of the Judgment Day.[47]

Reply. These earlier Fathers were refuting the Arians and their only purpose was to bring out clearly the divinity of Christ in these texts, exempting it of every defect attributed to it, especially ignorance. Hence they said: If Christ was ignorant of the Judgment Day, He was ignorant of it not as the Word, but as man. The question of the perfection of Christ's human knowledge had not as yet been agitated. Hence no wonder that these earlier Fathers spoke somewhat inexactly on this subject.

Moreover, we shall see that also the more recent doctors and even Scholastics say that Christ knew the Judgment Day not from His human nature, that is, not by the natural light of the created intellect, but only by supernatural enlightenment.

Third objection. Some, too, have proposed the difficulty that the Gospel records that Christ often asked questions of men, such as, what they thought of Him, where the body of Lazarus was laid, and other such questions. They say that He even expressed amazement, for example, at the faith of the centurion and the incredulity of the people.

Reply. It is evident from the Gospel narrative that Christ asked questions in a human way, and likewise expressed admiration, but this was not from lack of knowledge, for the Evangelist says: "He needed not that any should give testimony of men; for He knew what was in man." [48]

It is therefore clearly established from all these texts that Christ was exempt from all error, which is *de fide,* and from all ignornace, which is at least theologically certain. Thus we gain a clearer understanding why the question is put about whether Christ already in this life enjoyed the beatific vision.

Did Christ, during His mortal life, enjoy the beatific vision?

Reply. The answer is that Christ did, and ever since the twelfth century it has been the traditional teaching of all theologians, so that it is at least a theologically certain truth.[49]

[47] Cf. Rouet de Journel, nos. 774, 925, 2072.

[48] John 2:25.

[49] Cf. Salmanticenses, *De incarn.,* disp. 17, dub. 4, nos. 42, 44; Melchior Cano, *Loc. theol.,* Bk. XII, chap. 14; S. R. Bellarminus, *De anima Christi,* Bk. I, chaps. 1, 8; Suarez, *De incarn.,* disp. 25.

Hence the Sacred Congregation of the Holy Office declared (June 7, 1918) that the following proposition cannot be safely taught: "There is no evidence that Christ, living among men, had in His soul the knoweldge the blessed or comprehensors have." [50]

Scriptural proof. There are, indeed, several texts in the New Testament from which it is evident that the Son of God, as God, sees the Father. Thus Jesus says of Himself: "As the Father knoweth Me, and I know the Father," [51] and "No one knoweth the Son but the Father; neither doth anyone know the Father, but the Son." [52]

It is considerably difficult to show from these texts that Christ even as man, already in this life, saw God immediately in His essence. But there are texts in the Fourth Gospel which make it sufficiently clear that Christ as man, already in this life, saw the Father.

For in this Gospel we read: "No man hath seen God at any time; the only-begotten Son who is in the bosom of the Father, He hath declared Him." [53] And again: "He that cometh from above is above all. . . . And what He hath seen and heard, that He testifieth." [54] Also: "I speak that which I have seen with My Father." [55] Hence the common method of argumentation among theologians may be expressed in the following syllogistic form.

What Christ preached as man, He knew as man, for human speech is the result of human intellectual knowledge; otherwise the Word would take the place of the rational soul in Christ, which was the contention of Appollinaris. But as man, Christ declared what He saw with the Father and in the bosom of the Father. Therefore Christ saw those things in the bosom of the Father, as man, and it is also said that He heard them, which properly belongs not to God inasmuch as He is God, but to man.

Moreover, all knowledge of divine things, exclusive of the beatific vision, pertains to the order of faith. Hence, if Christ did not see those truths that are in God, we should have to say He believed them, and thus as man He would not have known many and most sublime truths. It would have to be said of Him that concerning God He had known what He is not, instead of what He is. But we have already

[50] Denz., no. 2183.
[51] John 10:15.
[52] Matt. 11:27.
[53] John 1:18.
[54] *Ibid.*, 3:31 f.
[55] *Ibid.*, 8:38.

seen that Christ, as man, was exempt from ignorance. Nevertheless there is truly a difference between nescience and ignorance, and it would be possible for one to say that Christ did not know the secret of God's intimate life, but not that He was ignorant of it, simply because it was not as yet fitting for Him to know it. On the contrary, this fittingness will be clarified farther on in the theological proof from reason.

This argument is confirmed by the following Gospel text: "Not that any man hath seen the Father, but He who is of God, He hath seen the Father." [56]

This means that He not only saw the secrets of the Father in His hidden life, but He also saw the Father Himself. The word *"Vidit"* is written as a quasi-preterite so as to make it clear that this vision transcends time, or, as the theologians say, it is measured by participated eternity.

There are two other texts from the Gospel which make it manifest that Christ had consciousness of and not merely faith in His divine nature and personality. For the Evangelist records Jesus as saying: "Although I give testimony of Myself, My testimony is true, for I know whence I came and whither I go"; [57] I know and not only believe. And again He says: "I came out from God. I came forth from the Father and am come into the world." [58] When Christ says, "I know whence I came," He was conscious not only of His mission, but also of His divine nature and personality. But this clear consciousness of His divine nature transcends the supernatural knowledge of faith, for faith is of things not seen, and above the supernatural knowledge of faith there is only the beatific vision, as will be more clearly seen farther on.

Finally, there is another Gospel text in which Christ speaks more clearly as man when He says: "No man hath ascended into heaven, but He that descended from heaven, the Son of man who is in heaven." [59] The Son of man is Christ as man, and it is said of Him that He has already ascended into heaven, and that He is now in heaven, which means in paradise or in the beatific state. It cannot be said that He is already in heaven solely by means of the hypostatic union, for

[56] *Ibid.,* 6:46.
[57] *Ibid.,* 8:14.
[58] *Ibid.,* 16:27 f.
[59] *Ibid.,* 3:13.

the whole context is concerned with ascent in the order of knowledge; for in the text that immediately precedes, Jesus had said: "If I have spoken to you earthly things, and you do not believe; how will you believe if I shall speak to you of heavenly things." [60] Christ, in calling others to the faith, never says that He Himself believes, but that He sees, and knows whence He came, namely, by the knowledge of vision, and that already "He is in heaven." This text is confirmed by another, in which Jesus says: "Father, I will that where I am, they also whom Thou hast given Me may be with Me; that they may see My glory, which Thou hast given Me." [61]

Proof from tradition. The above-mentioned texts of Sacred Scripture are furthermore declared and explained by tradition. The Second Council of Constantinople implicitly affirms Christ's beatific vision in this life, when it says that "He did not increase in holiness as He advanced in the performance of good works." [62] If He did not have the beatific vision from the beginning of His existence, He would have very much increased in holiness, by passing from the state of faith and of wayfarer to that of vision, and to the final state of glory in heaven. The Fathers likewise in various ways affirming that Christ did not increase in holiness, implicitly teach that He was from the beginning of His existence both comprehensor and wayfarer, which we find afterward is the common teaching, especially since the twelfth century.

Rouet de Journel [63] quotes several patristic texts that explicitly affirm Christ's beatific vision in this life. Thus Eusebius of Caesarea says: "Then, too, when [Christ] was living among men, He nevertheless accomplished everything, in the meantime being with the Father and in the Father, and at the same time He likewise took care of all things, both celestial and terrestrial, nowhere without that presence, which is in all things, our way excluded, nor hindered by the divine presence from acting in His accustomed way." [64] St. Basil clearly enough affirms that Christ, our Savior, already had the beatific knowledge in the highest degree.[65]

This is more clearly asserted by St. Fulgentius, who writes: "How

[60] *Ibid.*, 3:12.
[61] *Ibid.*, 17:24.
[62] Denz., no. 224.
[63] *Enchiridion patristicum,* nos. 670, 2238, 2239.
[64] *Ibid.*, no. 670.
[65] *Ibid.*, no. 913.

harsh it is and entirely incompatible with sound faith to say that Christ's soul, even in this life, did not have complete knowledge of His divine nature, with which we believe that He naturally constituted one person." [66] And he adds: "That soul knew His divine nature completely, yet the soul is not the divine nature. Therefore that very divine nature is naturally known to it, but that soul received from the divine nature, which it knew, the power to know It." [67]

Finally, St. Augustine maintains that Paul, who was rapt to the third heaven, saw the divine essence and not merely a certain refulgence of this brightness.[68] But if, as St. Augustine says, St. Paul had the beatific vision transiently, already in this life, then a fortiori Christ Himself must have had it, and not merely in a transient way.

Theological proof. The first argument is taken from the end of the Incarnation. It is one of fitness and from this point is most convincing. It may be expressed by the following syllogism.

What is in potentiality is reduced to act by what is in act. But men are in potentiality to see God to which they are ordained by God, and to which they must be brought by Christ's human nature. Therefore Christ as man most fittingly had the beatific vision.

Major. It is evident, for it enunciates the very principle of causality. Thus nothing becomes hot except by what is actually hot; and the cause must always be more efficacious than its effect.[69]

It is, of course, true that Christ's soul is only the instrumental cause of glory in the blessed, not by its own power, but by the power of the principal agent, namely, the Deity. Nevertheless it is a most excellent instrument, which is capable of being instrumental in producing the form which is beatitude. Therefore it is fitting for the soul actually to have this beatitude. Hence St. Thomas does not infer that this was strictly necessary but that it was proper because it was becoming.[70]

We thus have from this application of the major to Christ's humanity an argument of fitness. It must also be said, however, that what is more fitting and more excellent must be granted to Christ, unless it be incompatible with the end of the Incarnation, and especially if

[66] *Ibid.*, nos. 2238 f.

[67] *Ibid.*

[68] *Epist.* 147, chap. 13; also *Super Gen. ad litt.*, Bk. XII, chap. 27, which is quoted by St. Thomas in IIa IIae, q. 175, a. 3.

[69] Cf. IIIa, q. 9, a. 2, c. (end).

[70] The Dominicans have translated *"oportuit"* by "necessary," but perhaps they mean "necessary" in a broad sense. (Tr.)

it manifestly contributes to this end, as will be explained in the minor. Christ is, of course, the most perfect Redeemer.

Minor. It is *de fide,* both as to the ordaining of men to the beatific vision, and as to Christ's influence as Savior on them, in bringing them to eternal life. Christ said; "I am the way and the truth and the life." [71] He is the way as man, and as God He is the truth and the life. Similarly a text from St. Paul is quoted in this article, which says: "It became Him, for whom are all things, and by whom are all things, who had brought many children into glory, to perfect the author of their salvation, by His passion." [72] For Him to bring men into glory, He most fittingly had it already in this life.

The force of this argument of fitness is more clearly seen when Christ as man is compared with the apostles, the great doctors of later times, and the higher contemplatives. The Savior of all, as we said, the head of the Church, both militant, suffering, and triumphant; He was the supreme doctor in divine matters, the Master of all masters and contemplatives, from whom we have received the fullness of the revelation of life. In other words, already on earth, He was, as man, the supreme witness of divine truth, already transcending the beatified angels,[73] so that St. Paul speaking in Christ's name, could say: "But though we or an angel from heaven preach a gospel to you besides that which we have preached to you, let him be anathema." [74] Thus Christ as the Master of all masters and higher contemplatives is the most perfect leader to beatitude even to the end of time, which means that He will be surpassed by no master. Therefore it was most becoming to him, as man, that He should give testimony as an ocular witness concerning the beatific vision, and that He should have complete knowledge of the ultimate end to which He must bring all wayfarers of all times in this life.[75]

[71] John 14:6.

[72] Heb. 2:10.

[73] *Ibid.,* chaps. 1, 2.

[74] Gal. 1:8.

[75] Plato, speaking of the ideal teacher, says (in his *Banquet,* chap. 29): "Do we not think it would be a fortunate sight, if man had eyes to see the true beauty, the divine beauty, I mean, pure and clear and unalloyed, not clogged with the pollutions of mortality and all the colors and vanities of human life? Do you not think such a man would produce not the semblances of virtues, since He attains not to the image but to the reality, and since he begets and feeds upon true virtue, will be made the friend of God and of all other men, he will be immortal in the highest degree?" But this finds its verification in Christ already in this life.

Confirmation. This argument of fitness is all the more convincing when we consider either the sublime contemplation of St. John the Evangelist concerning the Word, in the Prologue of his Gospel, or that of St. Paul, the doctor of the Gentiles, who says: "I know a man in Christ above fourteen years ago (whether in the body I know not, or out of the body, I know not, God knoweth), such a one caught up to the third heaven.[76] And I know such a man, whether in the body or out of the body, I know not, God knoweth, that he was caught up into paradise, and heard secret word which it is not granted to man to utter." [77] But if St. Paul, that he might be the doctor of the Gentiles, and might always have more, by his preaching, in his mind and heart than in utterance, received such a gift of contemplation, so that his preaching came from the fullness of his contemplation, as St. Thomas says,[78] what must be thought of Christ's contemplation, so that He might fittingly be the supreme Doctor of all generations of men? Christ must have, however, what is most fitting for Him to have.

Moreover, it must be noted that St. Thomas, following St. Augustine, maintains that St. Paul, when in rapture, "saw the very essence of God and not a certain reflection of His clarity"; [79] and so he concludes: "Therefore it is more becoming to hold that he saw God in His essence." [80] St. Thomas considers this view the more probable one. But if such was the case, then a fortiori, Christ already in this life saw the Deity.[81]

St. Thomas, too, because of his sublime contemplation, toward the end of his life became incapable of dictating any more of his *Theological Summa,* which appeared to him as straw, and not wheat; yet Christ's contemplation was far more sublime. It certainly transcended Adam's contemplation in the state of innocence, concerning which St. Thomas says: "Adam did not see God in His essence. . . . The difference between the vision the blessed enjoy and that granted

[76] The Jews distinguished between three heavens: (1) the aerial or atmospheric heavens; (2) the astronomical or ethereal heaven; (3) the spiritual or empyrean heaven where God dwells and is seen by the angels.

[77] II Cor. 12:2 f.

[78] Cf. IIa IIae q. 188, a. 6.

[79] *Ibid.,* q. 175, a. 3.

[80] *Ibid.,* (about end). Cf. P. Sales, O.P., *Le lettere degli Apostoli,* II Cor. 12:4.

[81] See also P. B. Allo, O.P., *Commentaire sur la IIe Ep. aux Corinthiens,* 12:4. Allo says that St. Paul was raised to the highest form of contemplation, and he refers to the interpretation given by St. Augustine and St. Thomas, having nothing to say against it, merely remarking that it is not admitted by Estius and Cornelius a Lapide.

to the wayfarer does not consist in this, that the former sees more perfectly and the other less perfectly, but in this, that the former sees God and the latter does not see Him."[82] To believe is not to see, for faith is of things not seen. Adam's contemplation in the state of innocence remained within the order of faith, whereas Christ's contemplation in this life transcended this order.

Thus we understand how Christ's preaching is both most sublime and most simple and beyond all possibility of contradiction. Moreover, it is adapted to all minds, to most learned or simple minds; whereas, on the contrary, human teachers often speak in a terminology that is not accessible to all, because they do not sufficiently realize the relations that should exist between the doctrine to be explained and the more profound aspiration of the human heart. On this subject Bossuet remarks: "Who would not admire the condescension He shows in adapting the sublimity of His doctrine to His audience? It is milk for children and entirely bread for the strong. We see Him filled with God's secrets, but He is not astonished at this, as other mortals are to whom He communicates Himself. He speaks in a natural way of them, as though born to these secrets and this glory. What He has beyond measure,[83] this He imparts to others by degrees, so that our weakness may be able to bear it."[84]

He is the supreme Master, of unique and incomparable authority. Thus with the greatest simplicity He enlightens the mind, fills the heart with holy joy, and efficaciously moves the will to upright and holy action.[85] This preaching must come from the plenitude of most sublime contemplation.

Finally, this argument would find its corroboration by considering what such mystics as St. John of the Cross and St. Theresa have to say about most sublime mystic contemplation in this life, and the intellectual vision of the Most Holy Trinity by means of infused species. This vision, so far as God is not yet seen directly as He is in His essence, belongs to the order of faith.[86] There is not yet intrinsic evidence of the mystery of the Trinity, so that it is quite evident that God could

[82] *De veritate,* q. 18, a.1.

[83] John 3:34.

[84] *Discours sur l'histoire universelle,* Part II, chap. 19.

[85] It is in this way that apologetics develops the argument taken from the sublimity of Christ's doctrine and His manner of preaching. Cf. the author's work *De revelatione,* Bk. II, chap. 8.

[86] Cf. Ia, q. 12, a. 2: "The essence of God cannot be seen by any created likeness whatever."

not be God if He were not the triune God. But Christ already in this life certainly had a sublimer contemplation of the Trinity than that of the most sublime contemplative, even, as we shall see farther on, He was not without it when dying on the cross. Hence St. Paul says that in Christ Jesus "are hid all the treasures of wisdom and knowledge." [87]

This argument is derived from the end of the Incarnation. There are other arguments that have their foundation in the divine personality of Christ, and His consciousness of this personality.

Second argument. It rests on the consciousness Christ had of His divine nature and of His divine personality. He said, as we already remarked: "Although I give testimony of Myself, My testimony is true, for I know whence I came and whither I go." [88] And again: "I came out from God. I came forth from the Father and am come into the world." [89] From these texts it is clearly enough established that Christ was conscious of His divine nature, for He does not say "I believe," but "I know whence I came." There is also another text in which He says: "I speak that which I have seen with My Father." [90] He spoke as man, therefore He sees as man.

But this consciousness would not transcend the order of faith unless it were the direct vision of the Deity; for above the order of faith illuminated by the gifts of the Holy Ghost, such as we find in saints who are still wayfarers, there is only the beatific vision.[91] Therefore, if Christ did not have this beatific vision, then He only believed in His divine nature and divine personality, just as the saints believe in the indwelling of the most Holy Trinity in the souls of the just.

Objection. The saints who are still wayfarers have a quasi-experimental knowledge of this presence of the most Holy Trinity through the filial love God enkindles in their hearts, as St. Thomas says, for concerning the following text of St. Paul, "The Spirit Himself giveth

[87] Col. 2:3.

[88] John 8:14.

[89] *Ibid.,* 16:28 f. The expression "I came from the Father" can signify, indeed, the particular and eternal generation of the Word, but the following words, "I came into the world," signify the very incarnation of the Word. But Christ says: "I know whence I came"; therefore He does not believe but sees the mystery of the Incarnation and His own divine personality.

[90] *Ibid.,* 8:38.

[91] Even the most sublime prophetic illumination and the more exalted intellectual visions of the mystics do not go beyond the order of faith.

testimony to our spirit," [92] he remarks: "He gives testimony by means of the filial love He enkindles in our hearts." [93]

Reply. This quasi-experimental knowledge does not rise above the order of faith, for it is the result of faith illumined by the gifts of the Holy Ghost, especially the gift of wisdom, and so it is faith penetrating and tasting the mysteries of God in accordance with the text: "Taste and see that the Lord is sweet." [94] But these saints who are still wayfarers do not see the Trinity present in themselves, but they have a certain experimental knowledge and belief of this presence. On the contrary, Christ said: "I know whence I came." [95] "I speak that which I have seen with My Father." [96]

Third argument. It has its foundation in the influences of the hypostatic union. By the very fact of the hypostatic union, which in itself is more exalted than the beatific vision, Christ's soul was in the state of comprehensor. But this state of comprehensor pertains to the beatific vision. Therefore it was fitting for Christ to be both wayfarer and comprehensor, as all theologians commonly admit, especially after the twelfth century.

This argument is corroborated by considering the overflow from this grace of union. For the nearer any recipient is to an inflowing cause, the more it partakes of its influence, as already stated in discussing the fullness of habitual grace in Christ.[97] But Christ's human nature was united personally to the Word of God. Therefore it was supremely fitting for Christ as man, even in this life, to participate in this most perfect grace, which is the grace that is consummated by glory.

Fourth argument. It is founded on natural sonship. Christ as man, was predestined not to divine adoptive sonship, but to divine natural sonship, which surpasses even glory.[98] But divine natural filiation implies the right to divine heirship, even to the immediate attainment of this heirship, which consists in the intuitive vision of God. Therefore the beatific vision was befitting to Christ as man, even in this life.

[92] Rom. 8:16.
[93] *Com.* in Rom., 8:16.
[94] Ps. 33:9.
[95] John 8:14.
[96] *Ibid.,* 8:38. See St. Thomas, *De veritate,* q. 18, a. 1.
[97] Cf. IIIa., q. 7, a. 1, 9.
[98] *Ibid.,* q. 24.

As we have already stated, what was befitting to Christ must be attributed to Him, especially if this serves, as we have seen, the end of the redemptive Incarnation, so that Christ may be the ideal Master of all masters even to the end of the world.

It must be noted that this doctrine is also confirmed from what St. Thomas teaches concerning the knowledge of the apostles.[99]

The theologically certain conclusions to be deduced from all these arguments is that Christ already in this life had the beatific vision, and truly was, as commonly admitted by theologians since the twelfth century, both wayfarer and comprehensor. Thus Christ already in this life clearly saw the Trinity and all mysteries of grace, such as that efficacious grace is not only reconciled with free will, but is also the reason why the choice is free.

Doubt. Did Christ have the beatific vision from the first moment of His conception?

Reply. St. Thomas answers this question in the affirmative [100] because Christ's human nature from the first moment of its creation was assumed by the Word, and the beatific vision befitted Christ as man, inasmuch as, by virtue of the hypostatic union, He was the head of the Church. Hence all the preceding proofs apply with equal force for the first moment of conception. For this was in no way repugnant to the end of the Incarnation; it was even befitting to this end. Moreover, the Council of Constantinople condemned the proposition that Christ would have become better; but He would have become better if He had received the beatific vision in the course of the present life.[101]

Objection. It is more perfect to merit the glory of heaven than to

[99] Cf. *Tabula aurea,* under the word "Apostle." Here the holy doctor shows that the apostles were more perfect than the other saints, having all knowledge of things pertaining to faith and morals, inasmuch as this was expedient for the conversion of the world. The Holy Ghost taught the apostles all truth that was necessary for salvation, but not all future happenings. The words of the apostles are the result of intimate revelation received from the Holy Ghost and from Christ. Therefore they must be retained, because they belong to the canon of the Scripture, which forbids us to believe that it contains anything false. God gave the apostles knowledge of the scriptures and of divers tongues, which men can acquire by study or by accustoming themselves to speak the language, although they do not succeed in speaking it so perfectly. But if the apostles were so illumined concerning divine truth, Christ Himself must have been far more illumined concerning God's intimate life and more than all doctors and contemplatives after His time.

[100] Cf. IIIa, q. 34, a. 4.

[101] Denz., no. 224.

have it without merit, and Christ's merits were completed only by His death. In fact, Jesus said, as recorded in the Gospel: "Ought not Christ to have suffered these things, and so to enter into His glory?" [102] Therefore Christ entered into glory only after His death.

Reply. With St. Thomas, I distinguish the antecedent, namely, that it is also more perfect for Christ to have a thing by merit than without merit "unless it be of such a nature [for example, a gift] that its want would detract from Christ's dignity and perfection more than would accrue to Him by merit. Hence He merited neither grace nor knowledge, nor the beatitude of His soul, nor the Godhead . . . , the want of which would have diminished Christ's dignity more than His merits would have increased it. But the glory of the body and the like are less than the dignity of meriting which pertains to the virtue of charity." [103] Thus Christ merited the glory of His body, which is the sense of the text quoted above from St. Luke.[104]

Second objection. Utmost joy is incompatible with utmost sorrow. But Christ said in the Garden of Gethsemane: "My soul is sorrowful even unto death." [105] Therefore at this time He had neither this beatific joy, nor hence the beatific vision, to which this joy is the necessary sequel.

Reply. In answer to this, we say with St. Thomas: [106] that utmost joy is incompatible with utmost sorrow concerning absolutely the same object considered in the same aspect, I concede; otherwise, I subdistinguish; naturally incompatible, I concede; supernaturally so, I deny. But Christ was supernaturally both wayfarer, inasmuch as His human nature was passible, and comprehensor in the higher part of the mind. Nay, even as we showed in another work,[107] His utmost joy and His utmost sorrow were the result of this same plenitude of grace.

On the one hand, from the plenitude of consummated grace there

[102] Luke 24:26.

[103] Cf. IIIa, q. 19, a. 3.

[104] Luke 24:26.

[105] Matt. 26:38.

[106] Cf. IIIa, q. 46, a. 8, c. et ad 3; a. 6, ad 4; q. 84, a. 9, ad 2.

[107] Cf. *The Love of God and the Cross of Jesus,* I, 189–223. From this plenitude of grace there resulted in Christ, on the one hand, the light of glory and beatific charity, and on the other hand, utmost zeal for God's glory and the salvation of souls, by which He willed most perfectly to fulfill His redemptive mission by His holocaust on the cross offered with utmost grief of soul, as a better manifestation of His love for the human race.

resulted the light of glory, the beatific vision, the highest degree of love of God, and supreme joy. On the other hand, from this same plenitude of Christ's grace as wayfarer, and from His utmost love for God and for us, there resulted the utmost of supernatural grief for the sins of men, inasmuch as they are an offense against God and bring supernatural death to our souls. Moreover, because of His utmost love for God and for us, Christ willed as priest and voluntary victim to offer Himself as a most perfect holocaust; and for this reason, in virtue of His love, He most freely delivered Himself up to grief, by preventing the overflow of glory from the higher part of His mind into the lower parts and allowed Himself to be overwhelmed by all manner of grief in His sensitive nature. Herein is the miracle consequent upon the unique state of Christ as both wayfarer and comprehensor.

St. Thomas says: "Christ grieved not only over the loss of His own bodily life, but also over the sins of all others. And this grief in Christ surpassed all grief of every contrite heart, both because it flowed from a greater wisdom and charity, by which the pang of contrition is intensified, and because He grieved at the one time for all sins, according to Isaias 53:4: 'Surely He hath carried our sorrows.' "[108]

St. Thomas says likewise in another treatise about Christ's passion: "These same things about which [Christ] grieved according to the senses, imagination, and lower reason, in the higher [reason] were a source of joy, inasmuch as He referred them to the order of divine wisdom. . . . He allowed each of the lower powers to be moved by its own impulse,"[109] and He experienced sadness in the highest degree so that He might become a perfect holocaust. Thus He rejoiced in His passion inasmuch as it contributed to the redemption of the human race, and it made Him sad inasmuch as it was contrary to nature. Thus He most freely abandoned Himself to grief, limiting the beatific joy to the summit of His mind and preventing it from overflowing into the lower part of His mind and into His sensitive nature. Thus, by most freely abandoning Himself to grief, as a most generous and voluntary victim, He prevented the overflow of joy of the higher part of the mind into the lower. But this grief ceased when Christ was no longer a wayfarer. Hence Christ suffering in His hu-

[108] Cf. IIIa, q. 46, a. 6, ad 4.
[109] *Comp. theol.,* chap. 232.

man nature is like a mountain, the summit of which is poised in the clear sky, the base of which is made desolate by stormy weather.

THIRD ARTICLE

WHETHER CHRIST HAD IMPRINTED OR INFUSED KNOWLEDGE

State of the question. Besides the beatific vision, did Christ have knowledge infused by God, which is also called imprinted knowledge, inasmuch as it is given to the soul along with the nature as in the angels? The question concerns knowledge that is not only *per accidens* infused, but also *per se,* namely, that can be caused only by God, and cannot be acquired by one's own acts.

The difficulty is: (1) It seems that the beatific vision, since it is perfect knowledge, excludes that which is imperfect, and so it excludes faith; (2) it seems that infused knowledge is at least superfluous, just as the disposition for a form is superfluous, when it is already present; (3) finally, just as matter cannot receive simultaneously two forms, so also the intellect cannot simultaneously receive these two kinds of knowledge, the beatific and the infused.

Conclusion. It befitted Christ as man to have infused knowledge besides the beatific vision.

Scriptural proof. St. Paul says: "In Christ are hid all the treasures of wisdom and knowledge." [110] But included in these treasures is infused knowledge as found in the angels and in disembodied spirits, a knowledge which several of the saints also received in this life for the perfect exercise of their mission. Thus the apostles received the gift of tongues, but this knowledge of languages was in them only *per accidens* infused, because they could have learned these languages by their own efforts. Yet some saints also received knowledge that was at least *per se* infused concerning certain things, as mystic theologians show especially when they treat of intellectual visions that take place through the intermediary of infused species. St. Paul, too, who heard "the secret words of God" [111] received either the beatific vision as a transient act, which is the opinion of St. Augustine and St. Thomas, or else a sublime form of infused knowledge, transmitted by means of infused species. Therefore infused knowledge pertains to these

[110] Col. 2:3.
[111] II Cor. 12:4.

"treasures of wisdom and knowledge," [112] which St. Paul speaks of.

The Fathers often speak of Christ's imprinted knowledge, but they do not as yet explicitly distinguish it from beatific knowledge. But from the time of Peter Lombard, theologians commonly admit three kinds of knowledge in Christ, namely, beatific, infused, and acquired. This common consent of the theologians, however, would have for us the force of a certain argument from tradition if they were to assert that this doctrine is *de fide;* this, however, they do not assert. Hence it is only a theological conclusion that is commonly admitted by the Scholastics, which does not appear to be definable by the Church as doctrine that pertains to the faith, because it is the result of a strictly illative process of reasoning, and is not merely explicative. This consent of the theologians gives at least great probability to this opinion about the kinds of knowledge in Christ, as being a commonly accepted opinion.

Theological proof. It was fitting that the nature assumed by the Word should not be imperfect. But it would have been imperfect without infused knowledge. Therefore it was fitting that Christ as man should have infused knowledge.

Major. It expresses a certain moral necessity, which presupposes the hypostatic union, namely, that what is more worthy and more excellent and is not repugnant to the end of the Incarnation, must be granted to Christ. In other words, only corporal defects are to be attributed to Christ, such as passibility, death, thirst, and such defects that are necessary for our redemption by the sacrifice on the cross, as will be stated farther on.[113]

This moral necessity did not lessen, as some said, the divine liberty, because it depends on the most free decree of the redemptive Incarnation. But this decree being posited, then the great fitness of the Incarnation follows as a necessary consequence, and it was necessary because it was fitting. In other words, it was necessary to grant the Word of God incarnate what manifestly befits Him. Thus the conclusion is proved and is not merely a persuasive argument.

Minor. It is proved by the following syllogism. Everything in potentiality is imperfect unless it be reduced to act. But the possible human intellect is in potentiality to all intelligible things, and to know them not only in the Word by the beatific vision, or merely in them-

[112] Col. 2:3.
[113] Cf. IIIa, q. 15, a. 4.

selves by acquired knowledge, but in themselves by infused knowledge, as the angels and disembodied spirits know them. Therefore the soul of Christ had infused knowledge inasmuch as His possible human intellect was in potentiality to know intelligible things as the angels and disembodied spirits know them, which is by infused species.

This knowledge befitted Christ even in this life, before the separation of His soul from the body, because He was not only wayfarer but also comprehensor. Hence St. Thomas says: "Since Christ was both comprehensor and wayfarer, He had each way of considering things, one by which He was like the angels, inasmuch as He considered things without process of reasoning, the other by having recourse to phantasms." [114] Thus anyone who has the gift of tongues can actually make use of it without having to study the grammar of the language, but this can also be studied. Hence, as St. Thomas says: "Even as in the angels, according to Augustine (*Gen. ad lit.,* Bk. IV, chaps. 22, 24, 30), there is a double knowledge: one the morning knowledge, whereby they know things in the Word; the other the evening knowledge, whereby they know things in their proper natures by infused species, so also there was this twofold knowledge in Christ." [115] These species were imprinted on the minds of the angels by the Word of God, and it equally befitted the Word of God to perfect Christ's soul, which was personally united to the Word. Finally, Christ's soul would have been made more perfect if it had received these infused species only after its separation from the body. It was not fitting for Christ in this mortal life to be lacking in experimental knowledge of the mode of cognition pertaining to disembodied spirits, for whom He merited and grieved, and for whom He died. When in the parable of the wicked rich man He spoke of the state of the soul separated from the body, this shows that He had experimental knowledge of the mode of cognition of these souls.

This thesis finds its confirmation from the extraordinary events in the lives of the saints, for example, in the life of St. Catherine of Siena, for our Lord gave her infused knowledge concerning the hidden lives of several saints, and marvelous spiritual insight in doctrinal matters, a doctrine which she dictated when in ecstasy, and which is preserved for us in her *Dialogue;* she also learned to read and write not by her own efforts, but our Lord Himself was her teacher; even the secrets

[114] *De veritate,* q. 20, a. 3, ad 1.
[115] Cf. IIIa, q. 9, a. 3, c (end).

of hearts and distant events she often knew by infused knowledge.[116] Similar extraordinary knowledge was granted to other saints,[117] and a fortiori this was the prerogative of the most holy soul of Christ.

Doubt. Is this knowledge only *per accidens* infused, or is it *per se* infused?

Reply. It is *per accidens* infused so far as it concerns things that can be known by human efforts, and it is *per se* infused so far as it concerns things that cannot be acquired by human efforts and are therefore beyond the powers of our intellect. In fact, we must, in the same way, distinguish in Christ between two kinds of subordinated infused knowledge, just as in the just there are two kinds of prudence, one infused and of the supernatural order, specified by a supernatural object, the other acquired and of the natural order, specified by a natural object. Thus a musician has in a certain manner the art of music in the practical intellect, but the ability to play is in the hands. Indeed, Christ could by His infused knowledge of supernatural things know also by this eminent knowledge natural things in their relation to supernatural things, but it befitted Him also to know these things in another way, namely, by knowledge that is *per accidens* infused to which His intellect was in potentiality.[118] Thus Christ knew the supernatural secrets of hearts by knowledge that is *per se* infused, just as in our times He speaks in an exceptional way to certain saints, who are still wayfarers, in their own language or dialect.

Confirmation of this doctrine from the solution of the objections of this article.

Reply to first objection. The beatific vision excludes faith, which is of things not seen, but it does not exclude infused knowledge; for the same intellect can by two distinct means see things in two ways: first, in the Word, and secondly in themselves. Thus there are two ways, either by physics or by mathematics, whereby we can know the same conclusion, for example, the rotundity of the earth.

Reply to second objection. As he who knew some conclusion by a

[116] Thus the saints even in this life sometimes knew the secrets of hearts as if they saw another person not only exactly as in the flesh, but also had complete knowledge of the interior disposition of such a person, a quasi-photograph of the other person's soul, so that they could detect whether the acts of such a person were the result of true or false humility.

[117] St. Angela de Foligno saw her own soul, just as the angels see themselves.

[118] Several saints had knowledge that is per se infused concerning the secrets of hearts, and knowledge of languages that is *per accidens* infused.

probable argument, and afterward knows it by a demonstrative argument, can still consider the probable argument; although he no longer holds it as an opinion that he fears may be wrong, that is, he no longer wavers between uncertainty and certainty, so Christ can have simultaneously both beatific knowledge and infused knowledge.

Reply to third objection. The beatific vision does not render infused knowledge superfluous; for the ineffable knowledge of things in the Word does not make the knowledge of them in themselves superfluous. Moreover, these two acts can be simultaneous, provided that there is subordination, just as we can have knowledge of principle and conclusion. The Blessed Virgin Mary also had infused knowledge on this earth.

Fourth Article

WHETHER CHRIST HAD ANY ACQUIRED KNOWLEDGE

State of the question. This article concerns the habit of experimental knowledge acquired by the intellect through species abstracted from phantasms, or obtained gradually by individual acts.

The difficulty is: (1) If Christ had this knowledge, then He did not have it perfectly, because He never studied. (2) This acquired knowledge seems superfluous if Christ already had directly infused knowledge of created things, and especially if He already had accidentally infused knowledge of sensible things.

Conclusion. Christ had knowledge that is essentially capable of being acquired, and that was also actually acquired by Him.

Scriptural proof. St. Paul says: "Whereas, indeed, He was the Son of God, He learned obedience by the things which He suffered," [119] that is, by what He experienced. Farther on,[120] St. Thomas quotes the following Gospel text: "Jesus advanced in wisdom and age, and grace with God and men," [121] which He explains as resulting from an increase of acquired knowledge.

St. Thomas himself admits in the present article that he corrects what he wrote in an earlier work on this subject,[122] in which he taught that Christ had knowledge that is essentially acquirable, yet it was not acquired by His own acts, but was accidentally infused, as in the case

[119] Heb. 5:8.
[120] Cf. IIIa, q. 12, a. 2.
[121] Luke 2:52.
[122] Cf. *III Sent.*, q. 3, a. 3, quaestiuncula 5 a.

of Adam who was created completely developed. But now St. Thomas maintains that, as it was fitting for Christ's body to develop gradually, so also it was proper for His soul to advance gradually in the knowledge of natural things. Hence the Evangelist says: "Jesus advanced in wisdom and age." [123]

Theological proof. Nothing that God planted in our nature was wanting to the human nature of Christ, among which is the active intellect or the connatural active principle of intellectual knowledge.

But the active intellect would have been useless in Christ, lacking in its own and special operation, if He did not have knowledge acquired by His own acts by abstracting intelligible species from phantasms.

Therefore Christ had this knowledge.

Objection. Scotus maintains that the active intellect neither was useless in Adam, nor is it so in the blessed. The purpose of the active intellect is not only to abstract species, but it also serves the purpose of illustrating principles to be made use of in conclusions.

Reply. The Thomists point out that there is a difference between Christ and Adam, who was created not as a child, but as fully developed, as there is a difference between Christ and disembodied spirits that no longer have the connatural mode of understanding by turning to phantasms. If Christ had not acquired knowledge by repeated acts of the intellect, His active intellect would have been useless, not absolutely so, but as regards its connatural mode of operating; for it would be deprived of that act to which it is entitled in such a state and at such a time.

Moreover, it was no imperfection for Christ that as a child He was deprived of speech, or that He was unable as yet to acquire perfect knowledge of things. He already had by the beatific knowledge superabundant cognition for the perfect knowledge of divine things and of other things in the Word. Therefore Christ in a certain sense progressed intellectually, but not morally.

The solution of the objections of this article confirms the reply of St. Thomas.

Reply to first objection. "It was more fitting for Christ to possess a knowledge acquired by discovery than by being taught," hence He acquired acquirable knowledge not by learning, but rather by discovery, by a consideration of nature and men.

[123] Luke 2:52.

Reply to second objection. "It behooved Christ's intellect to be also perfected with regard to phantasms," although it was already perfected by infused knowledge. For this is a new and connatural mode of knowing. Someone may already have certainty of knowledge by the gift of prophecy that death will come on a certain day; in another way, however, there is experimental knowledge of the moment of death.

Reply to third objection. There was also a distinction between this acquired knowledge and infused knowledge concerning sensible things, for this second kind of knowledge, coming as it does from on high, is not proportioned to phantasms. Thus he who sings the melody of a musical composition solely from memory, not having studied music, can afterward in another way know this melody by distinguishing the various parts and notes of the musical score, reading it even to the least detail. Previously he knew the musical composition as some general melody, but now he knows its parts and the way these are distinctly related to the whole.

Thus, then, it is the common teaching of theologians since the time of Peter Lombard, that there were three kinds of knowledge in Christ: the beatific, infused, and acquired knowledge.

Each particular knowledge must now be considered briefly.

CHAPTER XII

QUESTION 10

The Beatific Knowledge of Christ's Soul

1) Was it comprehensive? (2) Though not comprehensive, did it extend to all things; if not to all possible things, at least to all things that God knows by the knowledge of vision, including even the Judgment Day? (3) Did Christ's soul know the infinite in the Word, at least those things that are in the potentiality of the creature, such as the thoughts and affections of immortal souls, which will never end? (4) Did Christ's soul see the Word clearer than any other creature did?

First Article

WHETHER THE SOUL OF CHRIST COMPREHENDED THE WORD

Reply. The answer is in the negative because "the infinite is not comprehended by the finite."

Reply to second objection. "Christ's soul sees the whole of God's essence, yet His soul does not see it totally," that is, "not as perfectly as it is knowable"; for it is infinitely knowable.

The contrary opinion was condemned in the Council of Basel, and this condemnation was approved by Nicholas V.

Second Article

WHETHER CHRIST'S SOUL KNEW ALL THINGS IN THE WORD

Reply. Christ's soul did not know in the Word all possible things, but it knew all present, past, and future things that will be.

Proof of negative part. If Christ's soul knew all possible things, this would mean that it comprehended all that God can do, which would mean that it comprehended the divine power, and consequently the divine essence.[1]

Proof of affirmative part. It may be presented in the following syllogistic form.

No beatified intellect fails to know in the Word whatever pertains to itself. But to Christ all things belong, inasmuch as all things are subject to Him, as the head of the Church, the end of the universe, the Lord of heaven and earth, the judge of the living and the dead. Therefore Christ's intellect knows in the Word all things that are subject to Him.

Evidently it belongs to the moral head to know his members and his influence for them; to one who has knowledge of the end to know the means by which it can be attained; to the judge to know all things that concern his tribunal, such as each and every thought of all men; the judge must also know whom to punish, and whom to reward.

In fact, Christ's soul seems to have not only habitual knowledge but also actual knowledge of all these things,[2] like a perfect theologian who not only could at will successively contemplate all theological conclusions, but who could simultaneously and actually contemplate all of them. The reason for this is that the beatific vision, objectively considered, is measured by eternity, which admits of neither succession nor change. Hence all the thoughts and actions of angels and men, known by Christ, although as regards their own duration they are successive, nevertheless are simultaneously present in the Word, according to the one now of eternity. It is like an intelligible panorama, just as in the sensible order the visible stars of the firmament are all seen in one glance. It must be observed that beatific love is likewise measured by participated eternity, as also Christ's adoration, thanks, and internal offering of Himself to His Father. Such enduring acts as these constitute, so to speak, the soul of the sacrifice of the Mass, whose principal priest is Christ as man.

The outstanding difficulty concerns the Judgment Day, inasmuch as we read in the Gospel that Christ says: "But of that day or hour no man knoweth, neither the angels of heaven, nor the Son, but the Father." [3]

Reply to first objection. St. Thomas says: (1) "Arius and Eunomius

[1] Cf. ad 2. The whole reply should be read.
[2] Cf. Ia, q. 12, a. 10.
[3] Mark 13:32.

understood this saying . . . of the divine knowledge of the Son, whom they held to be less than the Father. . . . But this will not stand, since all things were made by the Word of God" (John 1:3). Hence, especially inasmuch as Christ is God, He knew everything. (2) The Son knows also in the human nature the Day of Judgment, because, as Chrysostom argues (*hom.* 78 *in Matt.*); "If it is given to Christ as man to know how to judge which is greater, much more is it given to Him to know the less, namely, the time of Judgment." But "He is said not to know the day and the hour of the Judgment, because He does not make it known." Pope St. Gregory the Great spoke similarly against the Agnoetae.[4]

If some of the earlier Fathers spoke less accurately on this subject, this is because they were disputing with the Arians, to whom they replied: Christ did not know the Judgment Day, not indeed as God, as if they conceded that He did not know it as man.

The question of the knowledge given to Christ's soul had not yet arisen, and it had not yet occurred to anyone to distinguish between knowledge acquired naturally by human efforts, and knowledge not so acquired but received from a supernatural source, which is not meant to be made known to men.

Reply to second objection. "The soul of Christ knows all things that God knows in Himself by the knowledge of vision," yet not so clearly and distinctly.[5]

Third Article

WHETHER THE SOUL OF CHRIST CAN KNOW THE INFINITE IN THE WORD

The answer consists of two conclusions.

First conclusion. The soul of Christ does not know the actually infinite; that is, as is evident from the context, He does not know an actually infinite multitude of substances, because such a multitude was not created, which was proved in a previous article,[6] which

[4] Denz., no. 248. Moreover, as St. Augustine remarked, Christ as the best of teachers taught His disciples what was necessary and nothing more, because He said: "You cannot bear them now" (John 16:12).

In this we see pedagogy in its splendor. Thus it is said that younger professors seek to teach what they do not know; older professors seek to teach what they know; and teachers advanced in years what is useful to their disciples. This is what Christ did.

[5] Cf. ad 3.

[6] *Ibid.,* Ia, q. 7, a. 4.

stated: Multitude in nature is created, and everything created is comprehended under some clear intention. Nevertheless Christ's soul knows in the Word the thoughts and affections of angels and men, to which there will be no end, that is, they will go on for all eternity. But this multitude is not actually infinite, since all its parts do not constitute a simultaneous whole, and it is known, moreover, by Christ's soul inasmuch as it is represented in a certain unity, namely, in the infinitely perfect Word.

St. Thomas says: "But as material things can be received by the intellect immaterially, and many things unitedly, so can infinite things be received by the intellect, not after the manner of the infinite, but finitely." [7] But what is infinite, not materially but in perfection, can be known, although it cannot be comprehended by Christ's soul, which can actually and simultaneously know all our thoughts throughout eternity. St. Thomas, inquiring whether the name "Word" imports relation to creation, says: "Because God by one act understands Himself and all things, His one only Word is expressive not only of the Father, but of all creatures." [8]

Second conclusion. Christ's soul knows in the Word infinite things that are in the potentiality of the creature. Thus, as stated in the counterargument, "Christ's soul knows all its power and all it can do. It can cleanse, however, infinite sins."

Fourth Article

WHETHER CHRIST'S SOUL SEES THE WORD OR THE DIVINE ESSENCE MORE CLEARLY THAN DOES ANY OTHER CREATURE

Reply. The answer is in the affirmative. This conclusion is *de fide,* as His fullness of grace is.

Scriptural proof. St. Paul says: "God set Christ on His right hand in the heavenly places, above all Principality and Power and Virtue and Domination, and every name that is named, not only in this world, but also in that which is to come." [9] But this heavenly glory presupposes a more exalted knowledge of God.

Theological proof. The beatific vision is according to a participation of light that is derived from the Word of God. But Christ's soul,

[7] *Ibid.,* IIIa, q. 10, a. 3, ad 1.
[8] *Ibid.,* Ia, q. 34, a. 3.
[9] Eph. 1:20 f.

since it is united to the Word in person, is more closely associated with the Word than any other creature, even the angelic. Therefore Christ's soul received a greater influx of light, and thus sees the divine essence more perfectly.

Reply to second objection. Christ's soul sees the essence of God more clearly than even the highest of the angels, whose intellect is, nevertheless, naturally more powerful, because—and of this, Cajetan did not sufficiently take note—"the vision of the divine essence exceeds the natural power of any creature. And hence the degrees thereof depend rather on the order of grace, in which Christ is supreme, than on the order of nature, in which the angelic nature is placed before the human." [10] Thus, granted an equal degree of glory, St. Joseph's soul sees the divine essence just as clearly as the higher angels do. Hence the beatific vision that belongs to Christ's soul is in the highest degree, "although, absolutely speaking, there could be a higher and more sublime degree by the infinity of the divine power." [11] The highest possible degree of the light of glory cannot be conceived, because the divine nature is capable of infinite participation, and there is always an infinite difference between Christ's beatific vision and the uncreated and comprehensive vision, not as regards the object, but as regards the mode of cognition or penetration.

Cajetan seeks to explain the reply to the third objection of St. Thomas by saying: "If an angel were assumed by the Word of God in unity of person to an equal degree of glory, the angel would see God more perfectly than Christ's soul would, and the degree of the beatific vision would be more sublime, not because of the more sublime light or degree of light, but because of the more sublime intellect that is equally illumined." [12] Thus, in Cajetan's opinion, there can be a more sublime degree of the beatific vision in the angel, only because the angelic intellect is naturally more powerful than Christ's human intellect, and therefore transcends it in this order.

A considerable number of the other Thomists do not agree with Cajetan, especially Alvarez, and they say against Cajetan that St. Thomas in his reply to the third objection had spoken "of a possibly more sublime degree," not in the formal sense, but only materially, which is not his usual way of speaking. Moreover, they also remark

[10] Cf. Ia, q. 12, a. 4.
[11] Cf. IIIa, q. 10, a. 4, ad 3.
[12] *Com. in IIIam,* q. 10, a. 4, ad 3.

that Cajetan's view would conflict with the reply to the second objection in which St. Thomas said: "The essentially supernatural degrees of the vision depend rather on the order of grace . . . than on the order of nature." [13] Therefore, Christ's soul sees God's essence more clearly than the highest angels do. He received the light of glory in a degree that was in proportion to the plenitude of His grace, which is derived from the grace of union.[14]

[13] Cf. *supra,* q. 7, a. 11 f.
[14] *Ibid.,* a. 1, 9, 10, 11, 12.

CHAPTER XIII

QUESTION 11

The Infused Knowledge of Christ's Soul

It is the knowledge by which Christ's soul knows things outside the Word. This question considers (1) the object of this knowledge, (2) its acts (a. 2–4), (3) its habits (a. 5, 6).

First Article

WHETHER BY THIS KNOWLEDGE CHRIST KNOWS ALL THINGS

State of the question. The word "all" signifies not all possible things, but all things existing in any period of time, either natural or supernatural.

The difficulty is that it does not seem to pertain to the perfection of the human intellect to know things of which there are no phantasms. Therefore it does not seem that by this infused knowledge Christ knows angels as they are in themselves, or that He knows all singulars.

Reply. Nevertheless St. Thomas affirms that Christ by infused knowledge knew all things, both natural and supernatural, namely, all past, present, and future things; He did not, however, know the divine essence by this knowledge, since this is the proper object of the beatific vision.

St. Thomas, who is usually both conservative and prudent in his affirmations, does not fear to make this assertion, although not a few may look upon it as incredible.

Quasi-scriptural proof. The prophet says of Christ: "The Spirit of wisdom and understanding, of knowledge and counsel shall fill Him," [1] under which are included all knowable things, both in the speculative and the practical orders. And Christ had these gifts more

[1] Isa. 11:2.

perfectly than the angels, because they were in proportion to the fullness of His grace and charity, and hence evidently without limitation.

Theological proof. It was fitting that Christ's soul should be entirely perfect by having all its power reduced to act.

But there is a twofold power in Christ's soul: one is natural for knowing all natural things, not only by acquired species, but also by infused species;[2] the other is obediential for knowing all supernatural things, even by infused species, as often happens with the saints in this life. Therefore Christ knew all things by infused knowledge.[3]

If perfect works of human art are at times most beautiful, how beautiful must be those of divine art and how sublime must be the spiritual and supernatural operations of divine goodness, actually in the Blessed Virgin and especially in Christ Himself!

This article defines most accurately the natural and the obediential powers, either as regards a natural agent or a supernatural and free agent. Thus the obediential power is insatiable, that is, it cannot be satisfied, but in Christ it is reduced to perfect act according to the most fitting purpose of divine wisdom, as already stated.[4]

Reply to second objection. As separated souls see themselves and angels by their essence,[5] so Christ's soul already in this life saw itself and angels by His essence, because Christ was both wayfarer and comprehensor. This seems to us incredible, as if one born blind were told that we have seen by one glance innumerable stars in the heavens most distant from one another.

Reply to third objection. The knowledge of singulars pertains to the perfection of practical knowledge. But Christ had fullness of prudence and of the gift of counsel. This befitted Him, as already stated, because He is judge of the living and the dead, head of the Church and even of the angels, supreme Lord of the whole world. It is, indeed, true that He already knew these singulars because of the

[2] Because the normal method of knowing separated souls is by infused species, which is the same for comprehensors, and Christ already in this life was both wayfarer and comprehensor.

[3] He knew particulars, even the least of those that are recorded in the Old Testament, for example, in Deuteronomy or the books of Paralipomenon. If He had been questioned about them, He would not have shown Himself ignorant of anything, especially of even the least things that pertain to Sacred Scripture.

[4] Cf. *Summa theol.,* q. 7, a. 12, ad 2.

[5] *Ibid.,* Ia, q. 89, a. 1, 2.

beatific vision in the Word, but all comprehensors also know created things outside the Word.

Confirmation. The angels know all natural things even according to their individual conditions by means of infused species that are typified in or derived from the divine essence.[6] But Christ, by infused knowledge, knows natural things by means of infused species similarly typified in or derived from the divine essence, and His cognition is not inferior to angelic cognition. Thus one who knows a melody merely from memory knows all its notes, although each successive note has neither been learned nor read, and at times some cannot read the notes.

These infused species in Christ's soul, although not so universal as the angelic species since they are proportioned to the vigor of Christ's human intellect, are not, however, so restricted as those that are abstracted from sensible things, because they are likenesses derived from the divine essence. Moreover, the infused light of the gifts of wisdom, understanding, knowledge, and counsel is of a higher degree in Christ than in the angels, because it is proportioned to Christ's charity and the fullness of His habitual grace. But cognition is formally dependent more on light than on species, and thus the infused faith of angels as wayfarers was of the same species as ours, although the faith of the angels makes use of species that are infused and not acquired.

First doubt. How does Christ's infused knowledge include future contingent events and the secrets of hearts?

Reply. It includes these inasmuch as by this knowledge Christ knows the divine decrees in the terminative sense, not indeed as He knows them by the beatific knowledge, but through the intermediary of a certain species, which is a quasi-testimony of God revealing these future contingents and likewise the secrets of hearts.

Second doubt. Is this infused knowledge of future contingent events intuitive, just as by the beatific vision they are included in the Word and the now of eternity, in which futures are already present?

Reply. It is not intuitive. It is, however, called abstractive because it is measured by discrete time, which is not co-existent with the past

[6] *Ibid.,* Ia, q. 55, 56. These infused species are not abstract but concrete universals, for they represent even singulars that are contained under the universal; consequently each one is a quasi-intelligible but not sensible panorama. And the gifts of the Holy Ghost in Christ made use not only of acquired species, but also of infused species.

and future as eternity is, which is the measure of beatific knowledge.[7] Only eternity comprises all time, and in it future things are known not as future, but as present.[8]

Third doubt. Does Christ's soul by means of essentially infused knowledge have quiddative knowledge of created supernatural gifts, for example, of sanctifying grace? Expressed more briefly: Is it possible, apart from the beatific vision, to have quiddative knowledge or only analogical knowledge of sanctifying grace?

This question is of considerable importance, especially in its relation to the dignity of sanctifying grace.

Reply. The question is disputed among theologians, even among Thomists. Bannez,[9] Alvarez,[10] Lorca, and others deny that the knowledge is quiddative. They say that Christ's soul by inspired knowledge does not know sanctifying grace with objective evidence of it but with evidence that rests on divine testimony, which is objective evidence in the one who testifies. The reason is that sanctifying grace is intrinsically and essentially supernatural inasmuch as it is a formal participation of the divine nature as this nature actually is, and there can be no quiddative knowledge of the formal participation of any object, unless there is quiddative knowledge of the object in which there is participation. Thus it is impossible to have quiddative knowledge of the power of a seed unless there is quiddative knowledge of the fruit from the seed. The divine essence, however, can be known quiddatively only by the beatific vision and not by infused knowledge, because no created species can adequately represent this essence. A fortiori, as these theologians say, the light of glory cannot be known quiddatively by infused knowledge, because it transcends any other created light whatever. Therefore, as these theologians say, this light of glory can be known quiddatively only in the Word, and not outside the Word. Still more so, according to these theologians, it is impossible for the soul of Christ by infused knowledge to know quiddatively the hypostatic union, for this union transcends the order of grace. Thus it was only by the beatific vision that Christ could have quiddative knowledge of the hypostatic union. This first opinion, proposed

[7] Discrete time differs from continuous time, for instance, solar time, because it is not the measure of continuous time, but of a succession of thoughts, as in the case of the angels.

[8] Cf. Ia, q. 14, a. 13.

[9] *Com. in IIam IIae,* q. 5, a. 1.

[10] Disp. 61, 118 f.

by Bannez, Alvarez, and others, if not certain, merits a degree of probability, in fact, it is the far more probable opinion.

Other theologians, however, such as Suarez, and several Thomists, such as the Salmanticenses, Gonet, John of St. Thomas, and Billuart, maintain that it is possible for Christ's soul by means of essentially infused knowledge to have quiddative knowledge of essentially supernatural created gifts. They give as their reason that these gifts are of limited entity and therefore representable by a limited infused species, such as the infused species of the angels. This opinion seems to me not so probable as the first, which is evident from the following objection.

Objection. These gifts, such as habitual grace and the light of glory, although they are created and limited, nevertheless are essentially supernatural and essentially refer to God as He is in Himself. But God cannot, by infused knowledge, be quiddatively known as He is in Himself. Therefore these gifts cannot be quiddatively known by infused knowledge.

Reply. These theologians deny the consequence, saying that grace is not a universal participation, but an analogical participation of the divine nature, and it suffices to know the existence of the divine essence. This reason does not appear convincing. They say: "Because the hypostatic union, a property of which is infused knowledge, is the radical principle of cognition of Christ's infused knowledge, it suffices that this union be of the same degree of immateriality and perfection as the above-mentioned supernatural objects." This confirmation seems insufficient because the radical principle of infused knowledge does not change the nature of this knowledge, which is specified by its object, even though the infused light by which Christ's infused knowledge judges be substantially supernatural, as our faith is, which nevertheless does not give us quiddative knowledge of sanctifying grace. Hence it does not seem possible for infused knowledge, which makes use of created species, to have quiddative knowledge of sanctifying grace as it actually is. Thus the angels in the state of probation did not have quiddative knowledge of their grace, whereas on the contrary they already had quiddative knowledge of their angelic nature. This argument confirms us in saying that Christ already in this life had the beatific vision for the clear knowledge of His divine nature and personality.

Fourth doubt. Did Christ's soul by means of infused knowledge have evident cognition of the mystery of the Trinity as to its existence, it being supposed that only by the beatific vision is there quiddative knowledge of the Deity and the Trinity?

Reply. Alvarez and Lorca, as also Vasquez, answer in the negative, saying that the only way such knowledge is evident is from the evidence that is in the one testifying, inasmuch as the mystery of the Trinity was revealed to Christ's soul, yet it was not believed but seen by Him, by reason of the beatific vision He enjoyed, which is above infused knowledge, and this applies equally to the mystery of the Incarnation. This opinion, if not certain, is most probable.

But other Thomists, such as Gonet, John of St. Thomas, and Billuart, answer in the affirmative, because, so they say, by means of infused species Christ's soul outside the Word has knowledge of His beatific vision, the terminus of which is the Trinity. Thus He had by infused knowledge evidence concerning the existence of the Trinity, which is of a higher order that that enjoyed by the one who testifies to it.

It is difficult to prove the truth of this second opinion, since, as we saw in the solution of the preceding opinion, there is no certainty for its foundation, inasmuch as it is not certain and is even not probable, that by infused knowledge Christ's soul could have evident and quiddative knowledge of sanctifying grace and the light of glory. The possession of the beatific vision and a quiddative knowledge of the divine essence, of which grace is a formal participation, are indispensable for a quiddative knowledge of sanctifying grace, which is the seed of glory.

Second Article

WHETHER CHRIST COULD USE THIS KNOWLEDGE WITHOUT TURNING TO PHANTASMS

Reply. Christ could use this infused knowledge without having to turn to phantasms. The reason is (1) that by this knowledge He could know separate substances, such as angels, that cannot be known by means of phantasms; (2) that Christ was both wayfarer and comprehensor, and the condition of a comprehensor's soul is for it to be nowise subject to its body, or dependent on it, but completely to dominate it. Thus Christ could merit even during sleep.

Reply to third objection. "Although the soul of Christ could understand without turning to phantasms, yet it could also understand by turning to phantasms," also by means of infused knowledge. This means that Christ could, as He chose, use this knowledge either by not turning to phantasms or by turning to them, forming or not forming in the imagination pictures of the same object as is known by this infused knowledge. Thus in the sensible order one may be inspired to sing the melody of a musical composition, writing or not writing the score at one's choice. Similarly one is free to think in one language, and possibly express one's thoughts in another language.

Corollary. We must take care to distinguish between infused contemplation and essentially infused knowledge, for this normally functions without having recourse to the imagination, as in the case of angels and separated souls, as also by very special favor with certain wayfarers. But infused contemplation, which is the result of living faith illumined by the gifts of wisdom and understanding, normally functions with the concurrence of the imagination, which is the normal manner of sanctification, but it is not infused knowledge.

Third Article

WHETHER THIS KNOWLEDGE WAS COLLATIVE OR DISCURSIVE

St. Thomas replies that this knowledge was not collative or discursive in its acquisition, because it was divinely infused and not acquired by a process of reasoning. But Christ could use this knowledge in a discursive way, like wayfarers, though He was independent of this discursive process. This means that He could, like wayfarers, by divers acts of reasoning deduce conclusions from principles, effects from causes, properties from essences, as men at times who already know the effects conclude them from their causes, not that they may learn them anew, but wishing to use the knowledge they have; or as theologians who at times deduce from some revealed truth another which is otherwise revealed, and which prior to its deduction is already a certainty of faith. The reason given by St. Thomas as stated in this article,[11] is that the collative and discursive process is connatural to the rational soul, and also to the souls of the blessed, but not to the angels.

[11] Cf. c. et ad 3.

Fourth Article

WHETHER IN CHRIST THIS INFUSED KNOWLEDGE WAS GREATER THAN THAT OF THE ANGELS

St. Thomas replies that this knowledge in Christ was far more excellent because of its influencing cause, which is the Word; for the light divinely infused in the soul of Christ is much more excellent than the natural light of the angels. So this infused knowledge in Christ was absolutely more certain than was the infused knowledge of the angels, and extended to many more things, namely, to all things, even Judgment Day, including everything that pertains to the supreme judge of the living and the dead, and to the king of the angels.

Nevertheless, in a qualified sense Christ's infused knowledge was inferior to that of the angels, namely, on the part of the recipient, which is the rational soul, or as regards the mode of its reception, for, as we stated, Christ could use this knowledge by turning to phantasms and by having recourse to the discursive process of reasoning.

Moreover, as stated farther on [12] it was connatural for Christ's soul to receive species not so universal in scope as those of the angels. This means that the species are in proportion to the human intellect which is not so perfect as the angelic intellect. But if St. Thomas taught the contrary,[13] namely, that the infused species in Christ's soul were not so universal in scope as those of the angels, he clearly reversed his opinion in the sixth article of this question.

But although the infused knowledge of Christ as regards the mode of its reception is inferior to the angelic knowledge, this does not prevent it from being absolutely more exalted. Thus St. Thomas teaches that "faith is simply more certain than wisdom, the understanding of first principles, and knowledge; but these three, as denoting evidence, are more certain relatively, that is, for us." [14] Similarly it is certain that the faith of the Blessed Virgin Mary was simply more exalted than the faith of the angels as wayfarers although she made use of species not so universal in scope; for the perfection of knowledge depends more on the light than on the species since the light is the more formal principle.[15] For the light or the habit adapts itself

[12] Cf. IIIa, q. 11, a. 6.

[13] *Com. in III Sent.,* d. 14, q. 1, a. 3, *quaestiuncula* 4.

[14] *Summa theol.,* IIa IIae, q. 4, a. 8.

[15] *Ibid.,* q. 175, a. 2.

to the faculty in the exercise of its act and especially in passing judgment.

Fifth Article

WHETHER CHRIST'S INFUSED KNOWLEDGE WAS HABITUAL OR ACTUAL; THAT IS, WHETHER IT WAS ALWAYS IN ACT

The answer of St. Thomas: "The knowledge imprinted on the soul of Christ was habitual, for He could use it when He pleased." The reason is that this knowledge was in Him according to the connatural mode of the human soul, which is to receive knowledge as a habit that can be used at will. Thus Christ's infused knowledge was univocal to our knowledge, as stated in the argument and counterargument of this article, though it was not univocal in species but in the genus of knowledge.

Reply to first objection. This infused knowledge of Christ was inferior to that of the beatific vision, for this latter was always actual with respect to everything He knew in this way; nevertheless it seems that Christ's infused knowledge always actually knew certain objects even when He was asleep, during which times He could merit. Thus Christ's soul in this way always knew itself.

Sixth Article

WHETHER THIS INFUSED KNOWLEDGE OF CHRIST WAS DISTINGUISHED BY DIVERS HABITS

St. Thomas affirms that Christ's infused knowledge was distinguished by different habits, because He made use of species not so universal in scope as those of the angels, and thus His knowledge was distinguished according to the different kinds of knowable things.

CHAPTER XIV

QUESTION 12

The Acquired Knowledge of Christ's Soul

First Article

WHETHER CHRIST KNEW ALL THINGS BY THIS KNOWLEDGE

Reply. Christ did not know by this knowledge all things without exception, because all things cannot be known by species abstracted from the senses, and so by this knowledge He did not have quiddative knowledge of the angels, or also of all past, present, or future sensible singulars.[1] By this knowledge, however, He knew everything capable of being known by the abstractive faculty, because Christ's intellective power was most excellent.

Objection. But Christ did not have experimental knowledge of all these things.

Reply to first objection. But from those things of which Christ had experimental knowledge, He came to acquire knowledge of everything else in this order by means of this actual experimental knowledge, namely, by induction and deduction, understanding causes from effects, effects from causes, like from like, contraries from contraries, according to the power of His intellective faculty.

Reply to second objection. "Thus in seeing heavenly bodies Christ could comprehend their powers and the effects they have upon other things here below."

Wherefore Christ's soul by this acquired knowledge did not know the rate of acceleration of falling objects, and hence the universal law of gravitation. St. Thomas, long before Newton, in explaining the following text of St. Paul, "Comforting one another, and so much the more as you see the day approaching,"[2] wrote this most profound

[1] Cf. ad 3.
[2] Heb. 10:25.

comment: "One might say, why must we advance in faith? It is because natural motion, the more it approaches its terminus, the more it increases in intensity. It is the contrary with force. But grace inclines in a natural way. Therefore those in a state of grace, the nearer they approach their end, the more they must increase [in grace]" [3] in accordance with the scriptural text: "The path of the just, as a shining light, goeth forward and increaseth even to perfect day." [4]

If St. Thomas, considering natural motion, such as that of a falling stone, observes not only that natural motion is swifter toward the end, but also that the connatural motion of souls toward God, their ultimate end, must be for them swifter as they approach nearer to God and are attracted by Him. If St. Thomas sees this, formulating, as it were, the law of attraction not only for bodies but also for spirits that tend toward God, what must have been the knowledge of Christ's most sublime intellect, even by means of acquired knowledge!

This article presupposes the doctrine of inequality in human souls, notwithstanding their specific identity, as St. Thomas says: "The better the disposition of a body, the better the soul allotted to it." [5]

Hence, as St. Thomas says in another of his works: "We see real aptitude for vigorous thought in persons who are delicately constructed. . . . Likewise those in whom the imaginative, estimative, and memorative powers of the soul are better developed are better disposed for the act of understanding." [6] Providence eternally decreed in the case of Christ that this body of His should be better disposed for His soul.[7] Christ's body was formed miraculously in the womb of the Blessed Virgin Mary and destined for that most sublime soul united personally with the Word. Christ's intellect was far nobler than the intellects of Plato, Aristotle, Augustine, and others.

Second Article

WHETHER CHRIST ADVANCED IN THIS KNOWLEDGE

St. Thomas affirms that Christ did advance in this knowledge, both in the habit and in the act of knowledge. Thus the Evangelist says:

[3] *Com. in Heb.,* 10:25.
[4] Prov. 4:18.
[5] *Summa theol.,* Ia, q. 85, a. 7.
[6] *Com. on Aristotle's De anima,* Bk. II, lect. 94.
[7] *De veritate,* q. 12, a. 6, ad 4; q. 24, a. 8, ad 6.

"Jesus advanced in wisdom and age, . . . and grace with God and men," [8] which St. Ambrose understands of acquired knowledge.[9]

The reason given by St. Thomas is that Christ, after abstracting the first intelligible species from phantasms, could abstract others, and others again.

Thus St. Thomas retracts here what he wrote in an earlier work.[10]

On the contrary, Christ did not advance as regards the beatific vision and infused knowledge, but as He increased in age He performed greater works.

Reply to second objection. "This acquired knowledge was always perfect for the time being," which means that He always had every perfection of knowledge adapted to each age, so that He was never ignorant even by His acquired knowledge of those things that according to time and place befitted Him. Thus certain saints who died very young, at about the age of ten years, such as Blessed Imelda, practiced heroic virtues proportionate to this age. What is said of their relatively perfect virtues, must be said of Christ's acquired knowledge, but not of His holiness, since from the first moment of His conception He had not only the commencement of this plenitude of holiness, as the Blessed Virgin had, but also the consummation of this plenitude of habitual grace and charity, as already stated.[11]

Third Article

WHETHER CHRIST LEARNED ANYTHING FROM MAN

State of the question. It seems that Christ learned something from man, for the Evangelist says that Jesus was in the Temple asking the doctors questions.[12] But if He gradually acquired knowledge through the senses by the process of abstraction from phantasms, why not from men?

Nevertheless, St. Thomas denies that Christ learned anything from man. The reason is that, just as the first mover is not moved, the supreme teacher is not taught, but teaches. But Christ, even on this earth, was the supreme teacher of all men and even of angels. There-

[8] Luke 2:52.
[9] *De incarnatione Domini,* chap. 7.
[10] *Com. in III Sent.,* d. 14, q. 1, a. 3, quaestiuncula 5.
[11] Cf. IIIa, q. 7, a. 9, 11, 12.
[12] Luke 2:46.

fore "it did not befit His dignity that He should be taught by any man." [13]

Reply to first objection. As Origen says: "Our Lord asked questions not in order to learn anything, but in order to teach by questioning." [14] Thus Socrates made use of maieutics,[15] and thus he illumined and was not illumined.

Reply to second objection. To acquire knowledge from things by abstraction, is to be taught by God, the author of things, and it is more dignified to be taught by God than by man.

Fourth Article

WHETHER CHRIST RECEIVED KNOWLEDGE FROM THE ANGELS

Reply. It is denied that Christ received knowledge from the angels, because His soul was filled with knowledge and grace by reason of its immediate union with the Word of God.

Thus indeed the Evangelist says that in the garden of Gethsemane "an angel from heaven appeared to Christ, strengthening Him," [16] and this strengthening must be understood, as stated in this article,[17] for the purpose not of instructing Him, but of proving the truth of His human nature, as Venerable Bede explains.[18] Likewise St. Thomas remarks that Christ was strengthened by an angel by way of companionship and compassion, just as by the presence and conversation of a friend a man is naturally consoled in sadness, or also the angel strengthened the body of Christ, for instance, by wiping away the blood from His face.

This concludes the questions concerning the threefold knowledge of Christ. From what has been said, it is evident how sublime, even in this life, was Christ's contemplation, which continued on the cross, when He said, viewing all the fruits of the mystery of redemption: "It is consummated. . . . Father, into Thy hands I commend My spirit." [19]

[13] Cf. IIIa, q. 12, a. 3, c. (end).

[14] Hom. 19, *in Lucam.*

[15] This is known as the Socratic method in philosophy. It consisted in drawing the knowledge of the subject sought for gradually from the students by a series of easy questions; granted as implicitly known by them.

[16] Luke 22:43.

[17] Cf. ad 1.

[18] *Com. in Lucam,* 22:43.

[19] Luke 23:46; John 19:30. See also IIIa, q. 46, a. 7, 8.

Christ's doctrine, which St. Thomas discusses farther on,[20] is the complimentary of this question. He shows that it was fitting for this doctrine to be preached both by Christ Himself and by the apostles, first of all only to the Jews, to whom He was sent. It was also His duty publicly to refute the scribes and Pharisees for the preservation and salvation of souls. It was likewise fitting that He should teach all that pertains to the salvation of mankind not secretly but openly. Nevertheless He often proposed to the people spiritual matters disguised in the form of parables, and more explicitly to the apostles so that they could teach others. Finally, St. Thomas shows [21] that it was not fitting for Christ to commit His doctrine to writing, for the most excellent manner of teaching is for one to make his doctrine appeal immediately to the mind and hearts of his hearers. Moreover, Christ's sublime doctrine and all He accomplished in souls could not be understood in writing, and finally the new law was not first written, but it was first imprinted on the hearts by grace, as St. Paul says: "You are the epistle of Christ . . . written not with ink, but with the Spirit of the living God, not in tables of stone, but in the fleshly tables of the heart." [22]

[20] Cf. IIIa, q. 42.
[21] *Ibid.*, a. 4.
[22] II Cor. 3:3.

CHAPTER XV

QUESTION 13

The Power of Christ's Soul

If Christ had, as stated, knowledge of all things and even practical knowledge, why did He not have omnipotence? Certain Lutherans who are called Ubiquists because of their heresy, say that Christ's humanity as also His divinity is everywhere, and always omnipotent.

First Article

WHETHER THE SOUL OF CHRIST HAD OMNIPOTENCE IN THE ABSOLUTE SENSE

Conclusion. The soul of Christ could not have omnipotence in the absolute sense.

Scriptural proof. It is said of God: "Almighty is His name," [1] which means that omnipotence applies only to God.

Theological proof. In the hypostatic union the two natures remained distinct, each retaining its own properties. But omnipotence in the absolute sense is a property of the divine nature. Therefore omnipotence in the absolute sense cannot be attributed to Christ's human nature.

Thus, in created things, operation follows being, and only the divine nature, or the self-subsisting Being, has active omnipotence with respect to everything to which the term "being" can apply, or to which the notion of being is not repugnant. Hence Christ's human nature can neither create, nor produce whatever does not involve contradiction, nor cause itself.

Reply to first objection. Nevertheless, just as, on account of the unity of person in Christ, we can say: "This man, Jesus, is God," so we can

[1] Exod. 15:3.

say: "This man is omnipotent," not because of His human nature, but because there is one person in Christ, who is both God and man.[2]

Reply to second objection. Although the knowledge of Christ's soul extends to everything present, past, and future, it is not so with His active power, because infinite might is not required for the above-mentioned knowledge, whereas, on the contrary, it is required in creating,[3] for the most universal effect, namely, absolute being, can be produced only by the most universal cause.

Reply to third objection. "It is not necessary that Christ's soul should have practical knowledge of those things of which it has speculative knowledge." Thus Christ's soul has speculative knowledge of creation, since it knows how God creates, but it has not factual knowledge of creation.

Another objection. Nevertheless Christ said: "All things are delivered to Me by My Father,"[4] and "All power is given to Me in heaven and in earth."[5]

Reply. These words are true according to the predication of idioms, just as it is true to say, because of the one person in Christ, "this man is God." Moreover, the above-quoted texts can be understood of Christ as man concerning the power of excellence He had in commanding the preaching of the gospel. Hence Jesus says: "Going therefore teach ye all nations."[6]

But I insist. According to the teaching of St. Thomas,[7] there is only one being in Christ, namely, one divine existence, and even Christ's human nature is holy because of His substantial and uncreated holiness. Therefore, on similar grounds, He can be omnipotent.

Reply. The difference here is that omnipotence not only includes divine being, divine sanctity, and divine perfection, but it also implies the infinite mode in which this perfection is in God.

Hence absolute omnipotence is incommunicable. Moreover, divine being and divine holiness are said to be communicated to Christ's human nature because of the person, by means of the terminative but not informing union, for being follows person and where there

[2] Cf. IIIa, q. 16, on predication of idioms or properties.
[3] *Ibid.*, Ia, q. 45, a. 5.
[4] Matt. 11:27.
[5] *Ibid.*, 28:18.
[6] *Ibid.*, 28:19. See also IIIa, q. 13, a 2, ad 1.
[7] Cf. IIIa, q. 17, a. 2.

is one person there is one being. Similarly the human nature is sanctified by the grace of union, inasmuch as it is terminated and possessed by the Word. But omnipotence could not be communicated to the human nature solely in the terminative sense, but only by way of the informing form, that is, as the operative principle, and there is no divine perfection that can be communicated by way of informing form, but only as a terminus; for the informing form is less perfect than the whole of which it is a part. Finally, it is evident that Christ's human nature could not cause itself.

Second Article

WHETHER CHRIST'S SOUL HAD OMNIPOTENCE WITH REGARD TO THE TRANSMUTATION OF CREATURES

State of the Question. This article differs from the first article only in this, that the work of creation is included under omnipotence as discussed in the first article, whereas here we are concerned only with the miraculous transmutation of creatures.

It seems that Christ's soul would be endowed with this omnipotence, because He possessed most fully the grace of miracles which is mentioned among the graces gratis datae, and He also illumined the higher angels, inasmuch as they are ministers in the kingdom of heaven.

Conclusion. Nevertheless St. Thomas says that Christ's soul did not have omnipotence with regard to the transmutation of creatures.

1) General proof. It is taken from the counterargument of this article and may be expressed as follows: To transmute creatures miraculously belongs to Him who has the power to create and preserve them, as explained by St. Thomas.[8] The reason is that only the most universal cause, which can immediately produce and preserve any universal effect, whether this effect is embedded in material things or separated from matter, can immediately effect a change in it, because this immediate change presupposes the same universality in the cause as this latter immediate production. Thus God alone, who created and preserved things in being, can immediately change being as such by transubstantiation, prime matter by acting immediately on

[8] *Ibid.*, q. 13, a. 2, c. (end); see also Ia, q. 105, a. 1, 5, 6; q. 110, a. 2.

its obediential potency, also immediately change internally the intellect and the will that is ordained to universal good.[9]

Christ's soul did not have this same universality in causation as the divine nature, and so it cannot be the principal cause of miracles.

2) **Particular proof.** It is drawn more from the properties of Christ's soul, and is explained by three subordinated conclusions.

First conclusion. Christ's soul, by its own natural or gratuitous power, was able to produce those effects that are befitting to the soul, such as to rule the body, direct human acts and illumine by His plenitude of grace and knowledge even the angels. Nevertheless St. Thomas does not mean to say that Christ's soul is the physical and principal cause of grace, but that it is the moral cause by way of merit, and also, as he immediately remarks afterward, it is the physical and instrumental cause, by its effectiveness.

Second conclusion. Christ's soul, as it is the instrument of the Word, had instrumental power to effect all the miraculous transmutations ordainable to the end of the Incarnation, which is to restore all things either in heaven or on earth.[10] This is evident from the end of the Incarnation.

Third conclusion. Christ's soul, even as the instrument of the Word, has not the power to annihilate the creature, because annihilation corresponds to creation, which cannot be done by an instrument, because there is no presupposed subject that can be disposed for this action, as was shown above.[11]

Reply to third objection. Thus Christ had most excellently the grace of working miracles.

THE INSTRUMENTAL CAUSALITY OF CHRIST'S HUMAN NATURE

The question, whether Christ's human nature is the physical instrument of grace, miracles, and other supernatural effects, or merely the moral instrument, is one that is disputed in the schools of theology, and it finds its place here as an appendix to this article.[12]

[9] Cf. *De revelatione,* Bk. I, chap. 19, a. 3, *on the discernibility of the miracle,* where this subject has been fully treated by the author, in which it is shown that the most universal effects can be produced only by God, who is the most universal cause, and these are produced by Him as the principal cause.

[10] Eph. 1:10.

[11] Cf. Ia, q. 45, a. 5.

[12] In the expression "physically instrumental causality," the term "physical" is not

The Thomists maintain that Christ's human nature is a physical instrument, whereas the Scotists hold that it is a moral instrument. There is this same divergence of opinion as regards the causality of the sacraments, which are instruments of grace separated from the divine nature, whereas Christ's human nature is an instrument that is personally united with the divine nature.[13]

It is presupposed as certain (1) that Christ's human nature is not the principal physical cause of sanctifying grace, because St. Thomas makes it clear that "the gift of grace surpasses every capability of created nature, since it is nothing else than a certain participation in the divine nature. . . . And thus it is necessary that God alone should deify . . . just as it is impossible that anything but fire can enkindle." [14] (2) It is likewise certain that Christ's human nature is also the principal moral cause of grace and miracles, because He merited these by condign merit, and there is no other assignable meritorious cause above Christ.

Therefore the only question is whether Christ's human nature, after the accomplishment of the Incarnation, was not merely the moral cause, but also the physically instrumental cause of grace and miracles, and of other supernatural works that serve the end of the Incarnation.

It is a certainty that before the accomplishment of the Incarnation, Christ's human nature was not the physical cause, but only the moral cause of the grace bestowed on the patriarchs of the Old Testament, because physical operation follows physical being, or the existence of a physical cause. Therefore the question concerns only the influence exerted by Christ's human nature after the Incarnation.

The Thomists unanimously admit that after the completion of the Incarnation, Christ's human nature, either during His life on earth or as He is in heaven, was and is the physically instrumental cause of grace and miracles.

---

used in opposition to either metaphysical or spiritual and incorporeal, but to moral causality, by which the object proposed attracts the agent to act, or it is a causality that operates by way of merit, satisfaction, or prayer. The question concerns the instrumental production of some effect that is either corporeal, as in the case of physical miracles, or spiritual, as in the production of grace.

[13] Among those theologians who admit only a moral causality, we mention St. Bonaventure, Durandus, Scotus, Vasquez, Melchoir Cano, Franzelin. On the contrary, St. Thomas, the Thomists, Suarez, Billot, and several others admit also a physically instrumental causality.

[14] *Summa theol.,* Ia IIae, q. 112, a. 1.

1) This conclusion is at least implied in Sacred Scripture, for the Evangelist says of Christ: "Virtue went out from Him and healed all," [15] and Christ says of Himself: "I know that virtue is gone out from Me." [16] This can scarcely be interpreted as meaning moral power, such as the power of prayer, which, since it is a mental process, can be said only in a very improper sense to go forth from the body.

Likewise, according to the Sacred Scripture, Christ by breathing upon His apostles gave them the Holy Spirit, in a loud voice and commanding tone raised Lazarus to life. All such acts seem to imply a causality that is not moral but physical. Likewise, when Christ says: "The works [miraculous] that I do in the name of My Father, they give testimony of Me." [17] In other words, it was not only by means of prayer and merit that Jesus obtained the gift of miracles from His Father, but He actually performed them by His own power.

Similarly the First Council of Ephesus defined in its eleventh canon that "Christ's flesh has a vivifying power because of its union with the Word." [18] But Christ's flesh cannot have vivifying power morally by way of merit or prayer; therefore the power must be physical. Likewise, in the liturgy it is said of Christ's body in the Eucharist, that it is "a living and vital bread," [19] namely, a feeding and nourishing grace; therefore it produces graces not morally but physically.

But these quotations from Sacred Scripture and the councils are to be taken in their proper and obvious sense, according to the commonly accepted rule, unless anything unbefitting results therefrom. However, the words "healing power has gone forth from the body . . . , to do, to operate, to vivify," in their proper and obvious sense denote physically instrumental causality, and, as will at once be seen, nothing unbefitting results therefrom.

Authoritative proof from St. Thomas. In this second article he says: "If we speak of the soul of Christ as it is the instrument of the Word united to Him, it had an instrumental power to effect all the miraculous transmutations ordainable to the end of the Incarnation." Evidently it is a question here not of moral causality that operates by way of merit or prayer, but of physical causality. St. Thomas, in speaking

[15] Luke 6:19.
[16] *Ibid.,* 8:46.
[17] John 10:25.
[18] Denz., no. 123.
[19] *Lauda Sion,* liturgical hymn for Mass of Corpus Christi.

of Christ as head of the Church, taught that He causes grace both meritoriously and efficiently.[20]

To be sure, Christ's passion is now something of the past, but does it not virtually persist in the scars remaining from the wounds? Hence the physically instrumental cause is now Christ's human nature qualifiedly changed by His passion. Moreover, there remains in Christ's soul that willingness by which He offered Himself and by which "He is always living to make intercession for us," [21] in that, as the Council of Trent says in its treatise on the Sacrifice of the Mass, "the same victim is now offering by the ministry of His priests, who then offered Himself on the cross." [22]

Theological proof. To act not only morally but also physically is more perfect than merely moral action, so that a physical concurrence that truly produces its effect is more perfect than moral concurrence, by which the effect is obtained only by way of merit or prayer. But it must be admitted that Christ's human nature is more perfect if it proves to be compatible either in itself, or to the end of the Incarnation. Therefore, it must be conceded that Christ's human nature is the physically instrumental cause of supernatural effects that serve the end of the Incarnation.

Confirmation. According to the traditional terminology of the Fathers and theologians, Christ's human nature is the physical instrument of His divine nature in the production of grace and the working of miracles. It is not, however, the moral instrument, for Christ is the principal moral cause of the effects, inasmuch as there is no assignable meritorious cause above Him. Therefore Christ's human nature is the physical instrument, provided the distinction is drawn between physical and moral, to the exclusion of either metaphysical or spiritual.

Solution of objections.

First objection. An instrument must really contact the subject upon which it acts. But Christ's human nature, since it is now in heaven, does not really contact us in the production of our grace. Therefore Christ's human nature is not the instrument of our grace.

Reply. I distinguish the major: an instrument must really contact the subject upon which it acts, by virtual contact, this I concede; by

[20] Cf. IIIa, q. 8, a. 1, ad 1; see also IIIa, q. 48, a. 6; q. 49, a. 1; q. 50, a. 6; q. 62, a. 1; *De potentia,* q. 6, a. 4.

[21] Heb. 7:25.

[22] Denz., no. 940.

quantitative and personal contact, this I deny. Thus a trumpet is a physical instrument for the transmission of sound, yet it does not touch the ears of the hearers. So also the sun illumines and heats the earth from on high, and the magnet attracts iron to itself from a distance. I contradistinguish the minor; Christ's human nature as now existing in heaven does not really contact us, by His quantitative and personal contact, this I concede; by a virtual contact, that I deny.

There is no difficulty in this, especially for instruments made use of by divine power, in virtue of which all things that must be changed are made present to omnipresent omnipotence. Moreover, the superior part of Christ's soul is not itself located, and thus it is not locally distant from our souls. Finally, Christ's soul is united to God, and also our soul is united to God, although in a different way.[23]

Second objection. An instrument, that it be not purely a medium, must by its own action have a disposing influence in producing the effect of the principal agent. But Christ's human nature cannot thus be a disposing influence, by producing some disposition for grace or for a miraculous effect. We can in no way conceive what would be the nature of this previous disposition.

Reply. I distinguish the major: that an instrument must by its own action exert a disposing influence on the manner of operating of the principal agent, this I concede; thus a trumpet reinforces and directs the sound in the mode of its transmission; that an instrument always produces something objectively real that is the result of its action, this I deny; some instruments do so, such as a pen that deposits ink on the paper, but not all instruments, such as a trumpet, act in this manner.

Thus an instrument does not have to produce in the subject to be changed some prior effect or previous disposition. It suffices that the instrument operates by disposing the subject that must undergo a change. Thus Christ's human nature had and has its own action as regards miracles and grace, for instance, operating by means of words, signs, gestures, acts of the will, and other ways. Thus it is a disposing influence in the production of the divine effect at this particular time and place, for example, the healing of this particular man, of this particular disease in preference to some other disease.

Third objection. An instrument must receive its power from the

[23] Cf. E. Hugon, O.P., *La causalité instrumentale en théologie,* chap. 3, pp. 73–118; especially, pp. 101 f., 108, 111; see also *Summa theol.,* IIIa, q. 48, a. 6, ad 2.

principal cause, so as to be capable of producing the effect that surpasses its own power. But the power derived from the principal cause in Christ's human nature is either spiritual, and as such it cannot be received in Christ's flesh, or else it is corporeal, and consequently cannot produce grace. Therefore Christ's human nature cannot be the instrument of the principal cause in His operations.

Reply. I distinguish the major: that an instrument must receive transient power, or rather a transient motion from the principal cause, this I concede; a permanent motion, this I deny. I contradistinguish the minor: that this power is spiritual and cannot be in Christ's flesh as a permanent motion, let this pass without comment; as a transient motion, this I deny, because this transient motion is proportioned rather to the term of the action than to the subject of the action.

Explanation. This instrumental motion, however, as being something transient, differs completely from permanent power. For a permanent power is strictly for the benefit of the subject in which it inheres; hence it is proportioned to this subject. On the contrary, a transient motion, although it is in the instrument, since it is an accident, nevertheless, as it is formally transient, tending to produce the term of the action, must be proportioned preferably to the subject of inhesion. Thus, from the expression of a man's countenance, from the tone of his voice, and the manner of his utterance, something spiritual goes forth that is adapted to the hearer so that we say: a few words suffice to the wise.

In fact, this transient motion, also as a spiritual accident, is not received in Christ's body, inasmuch as Christ's body is formally something corporeal, but inasmuch as it is a being, for it is received in His body because of its obediential capacity, which applies to created things under the general notion of being and created substance. God makes use of bodies inasmuch as they are beings.

Finally, there seems to be nothing repugnant in the idea of a spiritual power being subjected to what is corporeal, inasmuch as the body is born to obey the spirit. Thus the rational soul, although it is spiritual, is dependent on the body, which it controls rather than being controlled by the body. Likewise the moral virtues of temperance and fortitude, although they are spiritual and infused virtues, are dependent on the sensitive faculties of the soul, which are intrinsically dependent on the animal organism.

Thus it befits Christ's human nature to be the physically instrumental cause of grace and miracles or of effects that serve the end of the Incarnation, as St. Thomas says in the present article. To exert one's influence on beings in both the moral and the physical orders shows greater perfection than to manifest it merely in the moral order, and therefore this greater perfection must be conceded to Christ as man.

This is a better way of illustrating what was said above concerning Christ's headship[24] and His influence on the members of His Church in the production of both habitual and actual grace.

Third Article

WHETHER CHRIST'S SOUL HAD OMNIPOTENCE WITH REGARD TO HIS OWN BODY

Reply. Christ's soul in its proper nature and power was incapable of changing the natural disposition of its body, so that it could not have the effect of exempting the body from the laws of gravitation or of the necessity of taking food, or of feeling the blows inflicted on it. The reason is that the soul of its own nature has a determinate relation to its own body. Christ's soul, although it was already beatified, had assumed a passible body, namely, a body that conformed to the conditions of passibility.[25]

Christ's soul, however, inasmuch as it was the instrument of the Word, could miraculously change the natural disposition of its body, so that the body was not subject to the laws of gravitation, or did not suffer from the blows and wounds inflicted on it. So also Christ miraculously preserved several martyrs from physical pain.

Fourth Article

WHETHER CHRIST'S SOUL HAD OMNIPOTENCE AS REGARDS THE EXECUTION OF HIS WILL

Reply. (1) Christ's soul was able by its own power to bring about absolutely whatever was willed for it; but Christ, in His wisdom, did not will absolutely that it should by its own power do what surpassed it, for there could have been no presumption in Christ.

2) Christ's soul, as the instrument of the Word, could do whatever

[24] Cf. IIIa, q. 8.
[25] *Ibid.*, q. 13, a. 3, ad 2; also q. 14, a. 1.

it absolutely willed was to be accomplished by divine power, such as the resurrection of its own body. But it could will in this way only what God had efficaciously decreed, and it knew these decrees.[26]

Was Christ's prayer always heard? The prayer He made according to His absolute will, was always heard, but not the prayer that was conditional, such as when He said: "If it be possible, let this chalice pass from Me." [27]

St. Thomas says farther on: "Christ willed nothing but what He knew God to will. Wherefore every absolute will of Christ, even human, was fulfilled, because it was in conformity with God." [28]

It is manifestly a sign of imprudence to will absolutely and efficaciously what certainly cannot come to pass. But Christ, as stated, certainly knew all future things by the beatific vision. Therefore He did not will absolutely and efficaciously what was not to be done either by His own power or by means of others.[29]

This concludes the question of Christ's power, and now we must consider antithetically the defects of Christ's human nature inasmuch as it was passible before the Resurrection.

[26] *Ibid.,* q. 13, a. 4, ad 3; also q. 18, a. 5; q. 21, a. 4.

[27] Matt. 26:39.

[28] *Summa theol.,* q. 21, a. 4.

[29] For this same reason Christ merited absolutely the efficacious graces bestowed or to be bestowed on men. Other graces that are not bestowed, these He merited in a qualified sense, namely, as offered, but not as bestowed. Thus, as will be stated farther on, His passion is of infinite value inasmuch as it sufficed for the salvation of all men, and it was efficacious to those to whom it is applied, namely, to the baptized children and to adults who place no obstacle in the way. But efficacious grace is included in the sufficient grace that is offered to the sinner, just as the fruit is included in the flower. Yet, if the sinner of his own accord refuses the sufficient grace, he deserves to be deprived of the efficacious grace.

CHAPTER XVI

QUESTION 14

The Bodily Defects Assumed by the Son of God

OUR first consideration must be about Christ's bodily defects inasmuch as He assumed a passible body; then in the following question the defects of soul must be discussed, namely, the passions or propassions such as sadness and fear, so as to explain what the Evangelist means by saying: "And Jesus began to fear and to be heavy." [1]

In this fourteenth question there are four articles about the bodily defects assumed by Christ.

1) Whether the Son of God ought to assume them.
2) Whether they were necessary or voluntary in Christ.
3) Whether He contracted these defects as we do.
4) Whether He assumed all bodily defects, such as sickness.

In these questions we see a marvelous progression in thought and methodical arrangement. They must be carefully considered, so as to avoid the confusion of ideas that not infrequently results concerning the death of Christ and that of the Blessed Virgin Mary.

First Article

WHETHER THE SON OF GOD IN HUMAN NATURE OUGHT TO HAVE ASSUMED DEFECTS OF BODY

State of the question. The question concerns bodily defects inasmuch as the body is passible or subject to pain, hunger, thirst, and death.

It seems that Christ ought not to have assumed these defects, because, just as His soul had every perfection both of grace and of truth,

[1] Mark 14:33.

why was not His body in every way perfect? Such perfection of body seems befitting for Christ, inasmuch as He was already in possession of the beatific vision and was likewise innocent, for punishment presupposes some fault. These bodily defects seem also to be an obstacle to the end of the Incarnation, which was destined to be a manifestation not only of God's goodness but also of His strength.

Conclusion. Nevertheless it was fitting for the body assumed by the Son of God to be subject to human infirmities and defects.

Scriptural proof. St. Paul says of Christ: "For in that, wherein He Himself hath suffered and been tempted, He is also able to succor them that are tempted." [2] There are likewise other texts that prove Christ was hungry and tired.

Traditional proof. It is also declared of Christ: "He suffered, was crucified, and died." [3] The Church also declared in the Council of Ephesus: "If anyone does not confess that the Word of God suffered in the flesh, was crucified in the flesh, and experienced death, . . . let him be anathema." [4]

Theological proof. It was fitting for Christ's body to be subject to defects, and this for three reasons.

1) So as to satisfy for us, by enduring for us the penalty for sin, namely, death, hunger, thirst, for "by sin death entered into the world." [5]

2) That He might establish the truth of His human nature, suffering truly as a man.

3) That He might give us a most heroic example of patience.

Reply to first objection. These sufferings are not contrary to the perfection of Christ's soul, for they are, as it were, the matter of satisfaction, whose meritorious principle was Christ's eminent charity. Thus in this reply St. Thomas draws a most admirable distinction between the matter of satisfaction and its principle or faculty. The principle of this satisfaction is Christ's love for God and for souls, and this love was of infinite value because of the divine personality of the Word incarnate.[6]

[2] Heb. 2:18.

[3] Apostle's Creed.

[4] Denz., no. 124.

[5] Rom. 5:12.

[6] The principle of merit is the same as the principle of satisfaction, for the meritorious act becomes satisfactory when it is of an afflictive nature, or when it is accompanied by a feeling of pain.

In fact, Christ willed to fear and be weary, so that His holocaust be perfect, whereas, on the contrary, He preserved certain martyrs from pain.

Reply to second objection. According to God's will, before Christ's resurrection the beatitude of His soul did not overflow into His body, except on the day of His transfiguration. Thus Damascene says: "It was by the consent of the divine will that the flesh was allowed to suffer and do what belonged to it," that is, what befitted a passible nature. His naturally passible flesh suffered under the blows inflicted on it.

Reply to third objection. Thus the absolutely innocent Christ was for us a voluntary victim.

Reply to fourth objection. "And although these infirmities concealed His Godhead, they made known His manhood, which is the way of coming to the Godhead." In this bodily infirmity, Christ showed heroic fortitude, by which He conquered the devil and healed our human and moral infirmity.

It does not follow, however, from these reasons, as Calvin would have it, that for Christ truly to satisfy for us, He had to undergo the punishment of hell deserved by sinners. Satisfaction for the sin of another does not require that the one who satisfies for the sin of another should undergo all the penalty that is due to the sin of another; it suffices that the satisfaction be equivalent, and Christ's satisfaction was more than this. As St. Thomas says: "He properly attones for an offense who offers something which the offended one loves equally, or even more than he detested the offense. But by suffering out of love and obedience, Christ gave more to God than was required to compensate for the offense of the whole human race"; [7] for the immense charity of the incarnate Son was more pleasing to God than all the sins of men were displeasing to Him, because this act of charity was a theandric act, inasmuch as it proceeded radically from the person of the Word.

Moreover, if Calvin's argument were valid, then it would follow that Christ ought to have suffered forever the punishments of hell, because sinners deserve eternal punishment. Calvin did not consider that the price of satisfaction, just as the value of merit, is the result of love. Merit and satisfaction have the same foundation, for the meritorious work is satisfactory when it is of an afflictive nature.

[7] *Summa theol.,* IIIa, q. 48, a. 2.

Second Article

WHETHER CHRIST WAS OF NECESSITY SUBJECT TO THESE DEFECTS

State of the question. It seems on the one hand that Christ was not, because He was a voluntary victim, and because His soul, united to His divine nature of which it was its instrument, could preserve His body from suffering, just as He did afterward to several martyrs. But, on the other hand, the Word assumed a passible body, which is under the natural necessity of dying and enduring other sufferings of a similar nature. Thus the saying that man is by nature mortal, and this necessity is physical. How then must this difficulty be solved?

Reply. St. Thomas says that as regards the assumed nature these defects were necessary, but as regards Christ's divine will and His deliberate human will these defects were objectively voluntary.

The *first part* of this conclusion is evident, namely, as regards the assumed nature, these defects were necessary, as it is necessary for a body composed of contraries to be dissolved. Thus every man is by nature mortal. And since the Word came in passible flesh for our salvation, He did not assume a body exempt from suffering, this exemption being a privilege bestowed upon Adam's body in the state of innocence. Hence St. Paul says: "God sent His own Son in the likeness of sinful flesh." [8] Hence Christ's death through the blows inflicted upon His body followed as a natural consequence, and was in no way, as in us, the consequence of original sin. Likewise in the Blessed Virgin Mary death followed as a natural consequence because she was conceived in passible flesh, and this death was not the result of original sin, from which she was preserved.

The *second part* of this conclusion is also apparent, namely, as regards Christ's divine will, and His deliberate human will, these sufferings were objectively voluntary. For indeed, by these two wills, He voluntarily accepted them, and He could have prevented them, if He had so willed, namely, if it had been the will of His Father. Thus the Blessed Virgin accepted her death in the natural order that she might be associated with the sacrifice of Christ for our salvation.

The reply of the following article completes this doctrine. What has been said shows clearly the most beautiful parallelism prevailing between Christ the Redeemer, and Mary the immaculate coredemptress.

[8] Rom. 8:3.

Third Article

WHETHER CHRIST CONTRACTED THESE BODILY DEFECTS

State of the question. In the title to this article the word "contracted" implies something more than "assumed" and "subjected to," for what is derived from some cause is said to be contracted, and so a disease or bad habit is said to be contracted. On the one hand, it seems that Christ contracted these defects, because together with His passible nature He derived them through His birth from His mother; for these infirmities are natural, resulting from the principles of nature, as stated in the preceding article, and Christ was like other men in His human nature, and they contracted these defects. On the other hand, however, St. Paul says. "By one man sin entered into this world, and by sin, death." [9]

But there was neither original sin nor actual sin in Christ, and the same must be said of the Blessed Virgin Mary.

Reply. Christ did not, like us, contract these defects as the result of original sin, but He voluntarily took them upon Himself.

First part of conclusion. It is proved by the following theological reasoning in syllogistic form.

That is said to be contracted which is derived of necessity together with its cause. Thus a person suffering from some congenital hereditary disease is said to have contracted it from birth. But the cause of death and suffering is sin,[10] which had absolutely no place in Christ. Therefore Christ did not contract these defects.[11]

Second part of conclusion. It is proved from the consideration that Christ willed for our salvation to assume a naturally passible body, which is composed of contraries.[12]

Reply to first objection. St. Thomas does not say: "the Virgin as a person was conceived in original sin," but "the flesh of the Virgin was conceived in original sin," and in accordance with this terminology of the thirteenth century, he distinguished between conception and subsequent animation when the rational soul comes that is created by God.

Nowadays we firmly believe, however, that the Blessed Virgin by a privilege was redeemed by preservative redemption. Thus she was

[9] *Ibid.*, 5:12.
[10] *Ibid.*
[11] Cf. ad 3.
[12] Cf. ad 1 et ad 2.

preserved from sin, which from her birth she ought to have contracted with all its consequences. Hence in the Blessed Virgin death was not the effect of sin, but the consequence of a passible nature, which she voluntarily accepted to be offered up in sacrifice in union with Christ. Hence the death of Christ and that of the Blessed Virgin are not the result of original sin, although they presuppose it in this sense, that the Incarnation in passible flesh presupposes the reparation of sin. On this point confusions frequently arise because not sufficient attention is paid to the distinctions so magnificently formulated by St. Thomas.

Fourth Article

WHETHER CHRIST OUGHT TO HAVE ASSUMED ALL THE BODILY DEFECTS OF MEN

State of the question. What is asked in this article is whether Christ ought to have assumed not only hunger, thirst, exhaustion, and death, but also other bodily defects, such as diseases, fever, leprosy.

Reply. Christ assumed only the defects that follow from the common sin of the whole human race, and that are not incompatible with the end of the Incarnation.

Christ assumed human defects precisely because He wished to satisfy for the sin of human nature. But satisfaction, which is penal, must correspond to the sin. Therefore, in reparation for the common sin, Christ voluntarily assumed common penalties, such as hunger, thirst, exhaustion, and death.

He did not assume, however, defects that are incompatible with the end of the Incarnation, such as difficulty in the performance of good works, proneness to evil. He did not either assume sicknesses and diseases that result from the actual sins of man, or from the defect in generative power. Christ was impeccable, and His body was most perfect in that it was miraculously conceived.

As regards the beauty of Christ's body, St. Thomas says: "Christ had beauty as it befitted His state and the reverence that is due to His condition"; [13] and in another work he says: "Christ was not imposing in aspect as it is said of Priam that his countenance befitted his imperial dignity." [14] In other words, the beauty of His countenance manifested especially the beauty of His most holy soul.

[13] *Com. in Ps. 44.*

[14] *Com. in Isa.,* chap. 53.

CHAPTER XVII

QUESTION 15

The Defects of Soul Assumed by Christ

IN this question St. Thomas asks: (1) whether there was sin in Christ, or at least the inclination to sin; (2) whether He had passions, such as sadness, fear, anger, at least holy anger.

First Article

WHETHER THERE WAS SIN IN CHRIST

State of the question. The particular purpose of this article is to inquire why Christ was sinless, in fact, why He was morally perfect.

Reply. Christ in no way assumed the defect of sin, either original or actual. This doctrine is of faith and manifestly has its foundation in Sacred Scripture.

Scriptural proof. That Christ was without original sin is evident from the following words of the Evangelist: "The Holy Ghost shall come upon thee, and the power of the Most High shall overshadow thee. And therefore also the Holy which shall be born of thee shall be called the Son of God." [1] This means that Christ did not descend from Adam by the natural process of seminal propagation. He was conceived miraculously by the Holy Ghost. Moreover, from the moment of His conception, as stated above, He was full of grace and enjoyed the beatific vision, both of which are incompatible with original sin.

As regards actual sin, there is the testimony of Christ Himself, when He said to His enemies: "Which of you shall convince Me of sin?" [2] Similarly St. John the Baptist says: "Behold the Lamb of God, behold

[1] Luke 1:35.
[2] John 8:46.

Him who taketh away the sin of the world." [3] Likewise St. Peter says: "Who did no sin." [4] St. Paul also says: "For it was fitting that we should have such a high priest, holy, innocent, undefiled, separated from sinners." [5]

There are several definitions of the Church that affirm the sinlessness of Christ.[6] Moreover, the Church has declared that Christ was impeccable (and not merely sinless) even before His resurrection,[7] and that He did not need purification.[8] This last declaration is directed against the Jansenists, who said that the Blessed Virgin Mary was in need of purification at the time of her purification, and that her Son contracted this stain from his mother, as the Mosaic law says.[9]

Theological proof. Christ assumed our defects that He might satisfy for us, and that He might prove the truth of His human nature, and be for us an example of virtue.[10] But sin instead of being conducive to this threefold end was a hindrance to it. Therefore Christ did not assume the defect of sin.

Sin is more of a hindrance to satisfaction, and it does not prove the truth of human nature, since it is contrary to reason; and it is not an example of virtue, since it is contrary to it. This proof receives its confirmation from the solution of the objections of this article.

Reply to first objection. St. Thomas explains how the words of the psalmist, "O God, my God, look upon me; why hast Thou forsaken me. Far from my salvation are the words of my sins," [11] are said of the person of Christ. He also shows with St. John Damascene and St. Augustine that certain things are said of Christ in our person, namely, those things that nowise befit Him, inasmuch as "Christ and His Church are taken as one person." [12] And in this sense Christ, speaking in the person of His members, says: "Far from my salvation are the words of my sins," [13] not that there were any sins in the Head.

[3] *Ibid.,* 1:29.

[4] I Pet. 2:22.

[5] Heb. 7:26. See also Isa. 53:12; II Cor. 5:21; I John 3:5.

[6] Denz., nos. 13, 65, 122, 148, 224 f., 251, 258, 286, 290, 711.

[7] *Ibid.,* no. 224.

[8] *Ibid.,* no. 1314.

[9] Lev. 12:6.

[10] Cf. q. 14, a. 1, 2.

[11] Ps. 21:1 f. According to the Hebraic text, the reading should be "my salvation is far from me," and not "far from my salvation are the words of my sins," which is the Septuagint and Vulgate version.

[12] Cf. ad 1.

[13] Ps. 21:2.

Such is the meaning of this particular Messianic psalm, the first words of which Christ uttered on the cross.

Reply to second objection. It explains how Christ was in Adam and how He is of the "seed of David." [14] Christ, says St. Augustine, was in Adam "according to bodily substance" [15] but not according to seminal virtue, that is, by way of natural generation. He did not receive the human nature actively from Adam but materially, and from the Holy Ghost actively. Thus He "was of the seed of David" [16] only materially, but not formally and actively. But if He accepted circumcision, which was a remedy for sin, He did so not as in need of it, but that He might give us an example of humility.[17]

Moreover, even though Christ had descended from Adam according to seminal propagation, He could not have contracted original sin, since this was incompatible with the grace of union and the fullness of inamissible habitual grace and by reason of the beatific vision, all of which adorned His soul from the moment of His conception. Thus the Blessed Virgin, although she descended from Adam according to seminal propagation, was preserved from original sin.

Reply to fourth objection. St. Thomas here explains the meaning of the words: "Him who knew no sin, God hath made sin for us"; [18] which means that God made Him a victim of sin, as the prophet says: "The Lord hath laid on Him the iniquity of us all." [19] Thus Christ willingly bore the punishment for sin.[20]

Calvin [21] objected that Christ in dying gave vent to feelings, if not of desperation, at least to words of such a nature when He said: "My God, My God, why hast Thou forsaken Me?" [22] and in the Garden He prayed inordinately, saying: "My Father, if it be possible, let this chalice pass from Me." [23]

Reply. Concerning these words uttered by our Lord in the Garden of Gethsemane it is generally agreed that they are an expression of His sensible will and are conditional, but that they are not an expres-

[14] Rom. 1:3.
[15] *Gen. ad lit.,* 10:20.
[16] Rom. 1:3.
[17] Denz., no. 1314, one of the condemned Jansenist errors.
[18] II Cor. 5:21.
[19] Isa. 53:6.
[20] Cf. *Summa theol.,* IIIa, q. 15, a. 1, ad 5.
[21] *Harmonia,* Matt. 27:46.
[22] Matt. 27:46.
[23] *Ibid.,* 26:39.

sion of His rational and absolute will. They manifest, as will be stated in the next question in treating of Christ's sadness, that He completely gave Himself up to grief, even extreme sadness, so as to make His sacrifice perfect and more meritorious.

The first quotation is not the utterance of one who is in despair, but it is the expression of one who experiences the greatest of grief. In fact, the words, "O God, My God, look upon Me; why hast Thou forsaken Me?" [24] constitute the first verse of one of the Messianic psalms. The end of this psalm, however, is a most beautiful expression of complete confidence in God, in spite of all adversities. Finally, immediately after these words, Christ says on the cross: "It is consummated. . . . Father, into Thy hands I commend My spirit." [25] These final words are an expression of perfect confidence and love. Last of all, certainly how can He despair who has already acquired the beatific vision and who by His sacrifice gives eternal life to others?

First doubt. Was Christ not only sinless but impeccable already before His resurrection?

Reply. The Second Council of Constantinople affirms and declares this against Theodore of Mopsuestia.[26] All theologians hold that at least according to the ordinary operation of divine law Christ was impeccable for three reasons; namely, because of the hypostatic union, the beatific vision, and the fullness of His inamissible habitual grace.[27]

The Scotists, however, admit that, if God by His absolute power were to take away from Christ His habitual grace and the beatific vision, then He would be peccable.

But the common opinion of Thomists and other theologians is that Christ as man, precisely by virtue of the grace of union, even independently of the fullness of habitual grace and the beatific vision, was absolutely incapable of sinning, whether such sin left the union intact or destroyed it. The principal reason is that otherwise sin would redound upon the Word itself, inasmuch as elicited actions are referred to the suppositum, because the principle that elicits the actions is the

[24] Ps. 21:1.

[25] Luke 23:46.

[26] Denz., no. 224.

[27] This fullness of grace and charity was inamissible inasmuch as it flowed from the grace of union as its quasi-property, and moreover, inasmuch as the fervor of this fullness of charity was itself inamissible, for it excluded venial sin, which does not intrinsically diminish charity, but its fervor.

suppositum. Thus, as will be more clearly explained farther on,[28] the meritorious actions of Christ are of intrinsically infinite value because of the suppositum or divine person of the Word, and they are theandric. Thus it is absolutely impossible for the Word incarnate to sin.[29]

The Thomists and other theologians generally assign three causes for Christ's absolute impeccability. These are: (1) the grace of union; (2) fullness of inamissible habitual grace by reason of its connection with the grace of union; (3) the beatific vision by which even the rest of the blessed are confirmed in good, and are no more capable of sinning, or turning away from God clearly seen, or ceasing from the act of loving God, because this act is indeed spontaneous; but it is not a free act, since it transcends liberty, inasmuch as concerning God clearly seen and to be loved above all things, there is no longer indifference either of judgment or of will, and concerning particular goods the blessed are free, to be sure, but they are incapable of sinning; in other words, they are free to do only what is good. St. Thomas says: "The will of him who sees the essence of God, of necessity loves whatever he loves in subordination to God." [30] Moreover, Christ always received efficacious grace by which *de facto* the will does not commit sin.[31]

We shall see farther on [32] that it is indeed extremely difficult to reconcile impeccability and free will in Christ, for without this freedom He would not have merited for us. We shall say here that Christ's

[28] Cf. q. 19.

[29] Objection. The Scotists say that the divine permission to sin is not evil, and thus God permits certain sins, even in the saints, as is evident in the life of St. Peter. Why could not the Word permit sin in the assumed nature?

Reply. The difference here is that, with respect to other men, God is related to them as the universal cause, the general foreseer, directing them in accordance with the laws of His general providence, to whom it pertains that what is defectible should fail at times, so that this should be the occasion of a greater good resulting therefrom. Thus God permitted Peter to deny Christ three times during His passion, so as to take away Peter's presumption and make him more humble.

On the contrary, as regards the actions of the assumed human nature, the Word stands in relation to these as the cause and particular foreseer, positing them as His own actions and as especially imputable to Him. These actions proceed from the Word, as the particular principle that operates, and it is incumbent upon Him so to govern the human nature that it does not sin.

[30] *Summa theol.,* Ia IIae, q. 4, a. 4. See also Ia IIae, q. 5, a. 4, and q. 10, a. 2.

[31] *Ibid.,* q. 10, a. 4, ad 3.

[32] *Ibid.,* q. 18, a. 4.

impeccable liberty is the most pure image of God's impeccable liberty, and that the command of dying for us, given by the Father to Christ, takes away moral liberty but not psychological liberty, since it is given, like every command, for the free fulfillment of the act; for a command that would destroy psychological freedom in the fulfillment of the act, would destroy the very nature of the command.

Second doubt. Could there have been moral imperfection in Christ, such as less fervent acts of charity, and less promptitude in the observance of God's counsels?

Reply. The answer is that there could have been no moral imperfection. This question has been the subject of special investigation by the Salmanticenses who, in their commentary on this article, distinguish between imperfection and venial sin.[33] For venial sin is absolutely an evil; although it is not a turning away from the final end, it is a morally evil deordination with reference to what pertains to the end. Moral imperfection, however, is not absolutely an evil, because it is not a privation of good that is strictly owing to one, for there is no obligation that we set before ourselves the greatest morally possible generosity as the ideal in our actions, except when anyone has made a vow to do what appears to be more perfect for such a person at the moment.

But imperfection is a lesser good. Thus a less fervent act of charity is not so great a good as a fervent act, but it is not an evil. In fact, in this less fervent act of charity, its diminished fervor or imperfection in the formal sense is indeed not a good thing, but it is not an evil, because it is not a privation of good that is strictly owing to anyone, because, as has been said, there is no obligation to set before ourselves the greatest morally possible generosity as the ideal in our actions each time we act. This imperfection is not good, it being a denial of greater perfection, rather than a privation in the strict sense. Thus, in some way, the fact that God does not preserve a creature in moral good, which means the permission by God to commit sin, is not a good thing, yet it is not an evil, not even an evil to which a punishment is attached. On the contrary, the refusal of efficacious grace by God is a punishment that presupposes sin or at least the beginning of the first sin.

[33] This question is sometimes directed solely against casuistry, according to which frequently and unjustifiably that is called an imperfection which truly is a venial sin. But this question must be examined in itself, and with reference to Christ and the Blessed Virgin, on a much higher plane than that of customary casuistic consideration.

Thus, even though moral imperfection is distinct from venial sin, there could have been no such imperfection in Christ because if we exclude God, no greater perfection could have been given to anyone than to Christ. Christ's acts of charity never diminished in fervor or were less in intensity or perfection as befitted the Word incarnate and He had the infused virtue of charity in the highest degree, according to the ordinary dispensation of God's power.

Expressed more briefly, there was never an occasion when Christ's human will was not so prompt in observing the divine counsels, in following the inspirations of grace given by way of counsel, and this is also commonly admitted concerning the Blessed Virgin Mary.

The Salmanticenses,[34] after proving that there could have been no transgression of the divine counsels in Christ, show clearly what is the foundation for the distinction between venial sin and imperfection. Concerning the distinction between a slight venial sin and imperfection, it must be observed that a few theologians do indeed call that an imperfection which is truly a venial sin, but these two are in themselves just as distinct as the difference between what is absolutely evil and that which is a less good. And this distinction is evident not only in the abstract but also in the concrete, especially in the lives of Christ and His Blessed Mother, who never were remiss in following the divine counsels.[35]

[34] *De incarnatione,* disp. 25, dub. 5.

[35] Cf. *Christian Perfection and Contemplation,* pp. 429–31; also *The Love of God and the Cross of Jesus,* I, 318 ff. in which we have discussed this question at length. Hence those who refuse to admit the distinction between imperfection and venial sin tend to confuse what is a less good with what is evil, which is against the first principle of ethics, namely, that there is a distinction between moral good and moral evil. Hence they ought to say that a less evil is good, and that a less evil is not only to be tolerated so as to avoid committing a greater evil, but that it is actually preferable as a good in itself.

Thus this confusion is accompanied by and is the cause of many other confusions. However, as there are venial sins that dispose a person to commit mortal sin, so there are certain imperfections that dispose a person to commit venial sin. And although the call to religious life does not in itself oblige anyone to enter this state, yet this way of life must be followed, as being an invitation to salvation especially if other ways seem to us more dangerous; Jesus saying to the young man: "If thou wilt be perfect . . . follow Me" (Matt. 19:21). Then if anyone, because of too great an attachment to the things of this world, refuses to enter the religious life, such a person sins, not because of the obligation of entering religion, but because of the aforesaid obligation of avoiding the too great attachment to the things of this world.

Second Article

WHETHER THERE WAS THE FOMES OF SIN IN CHRIST

State of the question. The "fomes" of sin implies the inclination of the sensual appetite to that which is contrary to right reason, as in the case of excessive pleasure. Thus, the "fomes" of sin is an inclination to sin, and when it actually inclines anyone to sin, it is called "fomes" in the second act.

St. Thomas does not even ask whether there was in Christ the "fomes" of sin in its second act, namely, an inordinate movement of the sensitive appetite.

Reply. The negative answer to this query is already sufficiently established from the first article. For the Word can and must prevent these irregular motions of the sensible nature, and He prevents them because He is under obligation to rule His assumed human nature, not only as it is rational, but as it is sensitive. These irregular motions of the sensitive nature not only were not in Christ, but could not have been in Him, because He was impeccable. The Second Council of Constantinople in canon ten declared: "If anyone defends the impious Theodore of Mopsuestia, who said that God the Word is different in person from Christ who suffered from the passions of the soul and the troublesome desires of the flesh, and who, gradually getting away from this inferior state, improved His condition by advancing in the performance of good works, . . . let him be anathema." [36]

If Christ was tempted, however, St. Thomas explains farther on,[37] He was tempted without having to endure sin and moral disgrace, consequences so derogatory to His sanctity.

Therefore, what theologians especially ask here, is whether the inclination to sin in its first act was in Christ.

St. Thomas answers this question in the negative, meaning that there neither was nor could have been such an inclination.

Scriptural proof. The angel said: "That which is conceived in her, is of the Holy Ghost." [38] But the Holy Ghost excludes both sin and the inclination to sin, which is what is meant by "fomes."

Theological proof. The moral virtues are in the sensitive appetite; and the more perfect they are, the more they subject it to reason.

[36] Denz. no. 224.
[37] Cf. IIIa, q. 41, a. 1, ad 3.
[38] Matt. 1:20.

But these virtues were most perfect in Christ. Therefore there was no fomes in Christ or inclination of the appetite to that which is contrary to reason.[39] This conclusion confirms the more common opinion of the Thomists, namely, that Christ possessed perfectly from the beginning not only the infused virtues, but also the acquirable moral virtues that make man absolutely good, and not merely good in a qualified sense, such as a good sculptor or carpenter.

Confirmation. The Word assumed all those human defects that can be ordained for the satisfaction of sins. The fomes of sin, however, cannot be ordained to this end, but, on the contrary, inclines to sin. Thus it was neither in Adam in the state of innocence, nor in the Blessed Virgin. But the grace of union is of a far higher order than the grace of original justice, which latter excluded the fomes of sin in Adam.

First objection. But if there was passibility of body in Christ and hence pain and death, why not the fomes of sin?

Reply to first objection. There is no parity of argument here, because the sensitive appetite must obey reason, whereas the vegetative powers of the souls do not obey it. Hence, among the principal consequences of original sin there are two that are deordinations, namely, error and concupiscence, and neither of these was in either Christ or the Blessed Virgin. There are two consequences, however, that imply no moral deordination, namely, grief and death, and these were both in Christ and in His Blessed Mother, not indeed as consequences of original sin, but as properties of nature, inasmuch as the Word assumed a passible flesh, and the Blessed Virgin was conceived without original sin but in passible flesh. But that the Word had to become incarnate in passible flesh, according to God's decree, this indeed presupposes God's permission of original sin, reparation for which was to be made by the redemptive Incarnation.

Third Article

WHETHER IN CHRIST THERE WAS IGNORANCE

St. Thomas answers that there was not, proving this from what He had already said about the fullness of grace and knowledge in Christ,[40] where the following words of the Evangelist are explained:

[39] See the replies to the second and third objections of this article.
[40] Cf. IIIa, q. 7, a. 9; q. 9, a. 1, 2.

"We saw His glory, the glory as it were of the only-begotten of the Father, full of grace and truth." [41]

There could not have been either error or ignorance in Him who said: "I am the way and the truth, and the life." [42] Ignorance is a privation of that which a person ought to have, and so it is opposed to simple nescience, or simple negation or absence of knowledge, as in a child who is not yet capable of knowing. Thus in Christ there was a certain nescience as regards His acquired knowledge, in which He made progress, as stated above.[43]

Fourth Article

WHETHER CHRIST'S SOUL WAS PASSIBLE

State of the question. It seems that Christ's soul was not passible, both because His soul was nobler than all creatures, and because the passions of the soul seem to be ailments of the soul as Tully says. Furthermore, the passions of the soul seem to be the same as the fomes of sin.

Reply. St. Thomas says, however, that in Christ there were both bodily passions and animal or psychological passions; yet they were otherwise in Christ than in us, and they are preferably called propassions.

Scriptural proof. The Psalmist says, speaking in the person of Christ: "My soul is filled with evils," [44] meaning that it is filled with pains and sadness. The Evangelist says that in the Garden of Gethsemane, "Jesus began to fear and to be heavy." [45]

Theological proof. First part. There are two kinds of passions in the soul: some are bodily passions, such as physical pain, by which the soul suffers when the body is hurt; others are called animal or psychological passions, because of some object that is presented to it, such as sensible sadness on foreseeing the details of a horrible death.

But Christ had a passible body and a sensitive appetite, both of which belong to the human nature, otherwise He would not have been truly man. Therefore Christ had both bodily passions, and animal or psychological passions.

[41] John 1:14.
[42] *Ibid.,* 14:6.
[43] Cf. IIIa, q. 12, a. 2.
[44] Ps. 87:4.
[45] Mark 14:33.

Second part. These passions were in Christ otherwise than in us. In us the passions often tend toward what is unlawful, often enough forestalling the judgment of reason, and sometimes they deflect the reason and obtain the consent of the will.

But in Christ the passions were able to produce none of these effects, because "in Christ all movements of the sensitive appetite sprang from the disposition of the reason," [46] and according to the consent of His will, as St. Augustine says.[47]

Hence, in Christ the passions never preceded the judgment of reason and the consent of the will, but followed them. Therefore they are preferably called propassions.

Therefore St. Jerome, commenting on the words, "He began to grow sorrowful and to be sad," [48] says: "Our Lord, in order to prove the reality of the assumed manhood, was sorrowful in very deed; yet lest a passion should hold sway over His soul, it is by a propassion that He is said to have begun to grow sorrowful." [49] Thus Christ's sensitive nature was most holy, and devotion to His most Sacred Heart is an expression of this sensibility.

Fifth Article

WHETHER THERE WAS SENSIBLE PAIN IN CHRIST

Reply. The answer is in the affirmative, for the prophet says: "Surely He hath borne our infirmities." [50] It is evident that Christ's passible body was hurt during His passion, and He felt that He was hurt, since Christ's soul was perfectly in possession of all natural powers. Thus His passible flesh naturally felt the pain of the blows inflicted on it.

Sixth Article

WHETHER THERE WAS SORROW IN CHRIST

Reply. The answer is that there was sorrow in Christ, for He said: "My soul is sorrowful even unto death." [51] Truly Christ's sorrow was natural at the thought of the horrible death He had to endure on the

[46] See argumentative part of this article.
[47] *De civitate Dei,* Bk. XIV, chap. 9.
[48] Matt. 26:37.
[49] *Com. in Matt.* 26:37.
[50] Isa. 53:4.
[51] Matt. 26:38.

cross; and there was spiritual sorrow because of the sin of His disciples and of those who would kill Him, and this sorrow arose from His love for God and for souls and hence it was supernatural. Thus in the exalted region of Christ's soul there was sorrow although not in the summit of His soul, because in the highest part of His intellect He enjoyed the beatific vision; but He most freely prevented its overflow into the inferior parts of the soul so that He might deliver Himself up fully to pain, and so be a perfect holocaust.

Seventh Article

WHETHER THERE WAS FEAR IN CHRIST

It is not a question here of the gift of fear, which has already been discussed,[52] but of fear inasmuch as it is a movement of the sensitive appetite.

Reply. The answer is that there was sensible fear in Christ, for the Evangelist says: "Jesus began to fear and to be heavy." [53] Truly, Jesus was able to perceive His death on the cross as an evil that cannot easily be avoided, which is the object of fear. There was natural fear in Christ, or the act of the soul naturally shrinking from evil and from contracting it. From another source Christ knew this evil as certainly to come, according to God's decree, and in the higher part of His soul He rejoiced at the thought of having accepted this pain for our salvation.

Eighth Article

WHETHER THERE WAS WONDER IN CHRIST

St. Thomas replies by saying that there was wonder in Christ as regards His experimental knowledge, but not as regards His divine knowledge, His beatific knowledge, and His infused knowledge. The reason is that wonder concerns the attention given by the faculties of the soul to what is new and unwonted, and this wonder was in Christ as regards only His experimental knowledge. Thus, "Jesus hearing the words of the centurion, marveled." [54]

[52] Cf. IIIa, q. 7, a. 6.
[53] Mark 14:33.
[54] Matt. 8:10.

Ninth Article

WHETHER THERE WAS ANGER IN CHRIST

Reply. There was holy anger or holy indignation in Christ against those buying and selling in the Temple, but in no way was there sinful anger in Him. This holy anger is called "the zeal of God's house." [55] It is a passion that follows an act of avenging justice, which inflicts punishment in accordance with right reason, how, when, and where it must be administered, and neither in excess nor defect.

Tenth Article

WHETHER CHRIST WAS AT THE SAME TIME WAYFARER AND COMPREHENSOR

Reply. The answer is that Christ was comprehensor, inasmuch as He enjoyed the beatific vision in the higher part of the soul. But He was also wayfarer, because concerning some things beatitude was wanting, for His soul was passible and His body passible and mortal.

Thus discussion ends concerning those things that pertain to what the Son of God assumed, along with His human nature, both as regards perfections, namely, His grace, knowledge, and power, and as regards defects, both of body and of soul.

[55] Ps. 68:10.

CHAPTER XVIII

QUESTION 16

THE CONSEQUENCES OF THE HYPOSTATIC UNION

AFTER considering the mode of the union in itself, as regards the person assuming, the nature assumed, and what was assumed with it, we come to discuss the consequences of the union.

There are three divisions to this part of the treatise on the Savior, inasmuch as the consequences of the union are considered, as to those things that belong to Christ:

1) In Himself as regards His being, will, and operation by which He merited for us.

2) In His relation to God the Father, for example, Christ's prayer, priesthood, predestination.

3) In His relation to us, namely, Christ as the object of our adoration, and His mediation on our behalf.

THE CONSEQUENCES OF THE UNION AS REGARDS THOSE THINGS THAT BELONG TO CHRIST IN HIMSELF

This question is about the terms employed in speaking of the mystery of the Incarnation.

We are concerned here with what is technically called the communication of idioms. "Idiom" is derived from the Greek and means the same as property in Latin. Hence communication of idioms is communication of properties. In other words, although the two natures in Christ are really distinct and inconfused, as defined against Eutyches, yet by reason of the hypostatic union the properties of the divine nature can be predicated of this man Jesus, and human attributes of God. Hence the communication of idioms is usually defined as the mutual predication and interchange in themselves of the two natures, the divine and the human, and their properties, by reason of the hypostatic union. The foundation for this communication of idioms in Christ is the hypostatic union itself, by reason of which one and the same suppositum has two natures, the divine nature and the human nature.

It must be observed concerning this communication that concrete names, such as God, man, in opposition to abstract names, such as Godhead, humanity, signify directly the suppositum, and indirectly the nature. For "God" signifies the suppositum that has the divinity, and "man" signifies the suppositum that has the humanity. If, therefore, the suppositum is the same for the two natures, then it is true to say: "God is man," although it is false to say: "The Godhead is the humanity." Thus we shall see [1] that the generally accepted rule, namely, concrete words of concrete subjects, both of natures and properties, generally speaking, can of themselves be predicated of either; but abstract words of abstract subjects cannot of themselves formally be predicated of either. Thus we shall see that we cannot say the Godhead is the humanity or that God is the humanity, or that the humanity is God.[2]

Therefore we must take great care to distinguish between abstract terms and concrete terms. The abstract term signifies the nature separated from the subject, for example, humanity. The concrete term signifies the nature as existing in the subject, for example, man. Hence this distinction between concrete and abstract term is of great importance in distinguishing between the nature and the suppositum, since the nature is an essential part of the suppositum. There is the same distinction between "being" as a noun and "being" as a participle, or between the reality and the real itself.

The principal definitions of the Church about the communication of idioms are to be found in the fourth and tenth canons of the Council of Ephesus,[3] and in the tenth and twelfth canons of the Second Council of Constantinople.[4]

[1] Cf. q. 16, a. 5.

[2] However, since God is His Godhead, in the material sense the following propositions are true: This man is the Godhead; the Godhead is this man. Taken in the material and identical sense the propositions are true because the subject of attribution is identical; but they are not strictly true in the formal sense, namely, in virtue of the difference of meaning in the terms. The meaning of the first proposition is: This man is God, who is His Godhead.

[3] Denz., nos. 116, 124.

[4] *Ibid.*, nos. 213, 215.

First Article

WHETHER THIS IS TRUE: GOD IS MAN

Reply. The proposition is affirmed to be true, and proper on account of the truth of the predication.

The reason is that in this proposition the concrete term "God" stands for the person of the Son. But the person of the Son is a man, although not the humanity, which is only a part of this suppositum. It is true to say: "Jesus is a man," as when it is said: "Peter is a man."

Hence to say: "God is a man" is to say: "God the Son is the same suppositum that is man." In every affirmative judgment, however, the verb "is" expresses real identity between subject and predicate. Hence this proposition is true in the formal sense.[5]

Doubt. Is the word "man" predicated univocally of God and human beings in this mystery?

Reply. The answer is in the affirmative.[6] For the word "man" signifies the suppositum that subsists in the human nature. But this nature is of the same species in Christ as in human beings. Therefore Christ is truly called a man.

Second Article

WHETHER THIS IS TRUE: MAN IS GOD

Reply. The answer is yes, because in this proposition the subject "man" can stand for whatever hypostasis of the human nature, and therefore for the person of the Son of God, who is truly God.

Third Article

WHETHER CHRIST CAN BE CALLED A LORDLY MAN

Reply. The answer is No, because "lordly" is said denominatively and by participation from Lord. But the name "Christ" stands for the person of the Son of God who is essentially the Lord, and not lordly by participation.

Hence it would be absolutely contrary to custom to conclude the liturgical orations by saying: "through Christ the lordly man," and not: "through Christ our Lord." Hence the expression that was in

[5] *Summa theol.* Ia, q. 13, a. 12.
[6] *Ibid.,* IIIa, q. 16, a. 5.

use among certain seventeenth-century authors in France is not entirely to be approved; namely, "Jesus is the perfect religious of His Father." It cannot properly and truly be said that He who is the very Lord is a lordly man.

Reply to third objection. Nevertheless we generally speak of the divine Word, the divine person, because the adjective "divine" is wont to be predicated of God's nature, which is called the divine nature and not merely as being a participation of this nature.

Fourth Article

WHETHER WHAT BELONGS TO THE SON OF MAN CAN BE ASSERTED OF THE SON OF GOD AND CONVERSELY

Reply. The answer to this question is in the affirmative.[7]

The reason for this is that, since there is one hypostasis of both natures, the same hypostasis is signified by the name of either nature. Thus it may be said that the Son of God suffered, was crucified; also it may be said that the Son of man is immortal, eternal, omnipotent, because the meaning is: this suppositum having the human nature is immortal, eternal, and possessing other divine attributes.

Fifth Article

WHETHER WHAT BELONGS TO THE SON OF MAN CAN BE PREDICATED OF THE DIVINE NATURE, AND WHAT BELONGS TO THE SON OF GOD OF THE HUMAN NATURE

Reply. The answer is in the negative. Thus it cannot be said that the Godhead suffered, or that Christ's human nature is omnipotent, because the two natures are entirely distinct, and abstract things, those that signify a nature and not the subject, cannot formally be predicated of abstract things (those that signify another nature), nor of concrete things. Hence, just as we cannot say the Godhead is the human nature, neither can we say that God is the human nature, or the human nature is God.

Only in the material sense and as expressing identity of person can it be said: "This man is the Godhead, the Godhead is this man," meaning that this man is God, who is His Godhead.

[7] Denz. nos. 116, 124. Council of Ephesus.

Sixth Article

WHETHER THIS IS TRUE: GOD WAS MADE MAN

Reply. The answer is in the affirmative. Thus, we can say: "And the Word was made flesh." For a thing is said to be made that which begins to be predicated of it for the first time.

However, the expression, "God becomes man," does not mean that God becomes so in the absolute sense of the term, for God became man without undergoing any change in Himself.

Seventh Article

WHETHER THIS IS TRUE: MAN WAS MADE GOD

Reply. The answer is in the negative, because in this proposition, since the subject "man" stands for the person of the Word, the meaning would be that the suppositum or person that is eternally God, became in time God, or that some pre-existing man became God, and each assertion is false.

For the same reason the expression, "man was assumed," cannot be admitted, but we must say: "the human nature was assumed," for the former statement would mean that some pre-existing man was assumed by the Word. Thus the Word would have assumed a human nature, and, if the human personality did not cease to exist at the moment of the assumption, there would be two persons, as the Nestorians maintained.[8]

Hence, although this proposition is true, "Man is God," the following proposition is false: "Man became God."

Eighth Article

WHETHER THIS IS TRUE: CHRIST IS A CREATURE

Reply. The answer is that the proposition is not true. The purpose is to avoid the suspicion of favoring the Arian heresy, and moreover, the assertion is false. But it can and must be said that Christ has a created nature, namely, a human nature. The reason why we cannot say that Christ is a creature, is that creation belongs to subsisting things, and to be created is consequent to person as the one that has being, but it is consequent to the nature as that by which something

[8] Cf. IIIa, q. 4, a. 2.

is such as it is. But as the person of Christ is uncreated and eternal, "creature" would apply not only to the created nature, but to the person of Christ, and this is false.

Ninth Article

WHETHER THIS IS TRUE: THIS MAN, POINTING TO CHRIST, "BEGAN TO BE"

Reply. The answer is that this assertion is not true, for Christ said of Himself: "Before Abraham was made, I am." [9] The aforesaid proposition must be avoided both because it sounds like Arianism, and also because it is false. Although the person of the Word for which Christ stands, began to be man, yet this person did not begin to be so in the absolute sense.

Tenth Article

WHETHER THIS IS TRUE: CHRIST AS MAN IS A CREATURE

Reply. The answer is that this proposition is more to be accepted than rejected, because the term covered by the reduplication signifies the nature rather than the suppositum.

Eleventh Article

WHETHER THIS IS TRUE: CHRIST AS MAN IS GOD

Reply. The answer is that this proposition is not true, because the term placed in the reduplication stands more for the nature, as stated above, than for the person.

Twelfth Article

WHETHER THIS IS TRUE: CHRIST AS MAN IS A HYPOSTASIS OR PERSON

Reply. This proposition must be avoided, because it favors Nestorianism and can be taken in a false sense. For if the word "man" taken exactly in its reduplicative sense, so that the particle as in its reduplicative sense, gives the formal reason why Christ is a person,

[9] John 8:58.

then this assertion is false, because it would signify that in Christ there would be a created person, as the Nestorians said.

However, this proposition could be accepted if interpreted in a good sense, if the term "man" were taken for the suppositum or for the specific nature, because it belongs to the human nature to be in a person. Hence this proposition is equivocal and as such must be avoided.

This terminates the question concerning the manner of speaking about Christ.

CHAPTER XIX

QUESTION 17

What Pertains Commonly to Christ's Unity of Being

THIS question concerns unity in common, but not unity in detail. It has already been determined (q. 9) that there is only one knowledge in Christ, and farther on (q. 35) it will be concluded that there are two births in Christ, the one eternal, the other temporal, but only one real filiation.

In treating of Christ's unity in common, we must consider His unity (1) of being, (2) of will, (3) of operation.

On unity of being there are two articles:

1) Whether Christ is one or two.
2) Whether there is only one being in Christ

First Article

WHETHER CHRIST IS ONE OR TWO

Reply. It is of faith that Christ is one (*unus*).

This conclusion is evident from the condemnation of Nestorianism, that admitted two persons in Christ; for the masculine form *"unus"* signifies a person. Hence, the Church has defined that "Christ is not two, but one." [1] And again: "I believe in one Lord Jesus Christ." [2] Likewise it can and must be said that Christ is one in the neuter form. The reason is that there is one person and one suppositum in Christ.

Some erroneously said, however, that there is one person but two supposita in Christ, and therefore they maintained Christ is one in

[1] Denz., no. 40. Athanasian Creed.

[2] *Ibid.*, no. 54; Council of Nicaea. See also Denz. nos. 118 f.; Council of Ephesus, can. 6.

person, but that He is not one being, because there are in Him two supposita. But it is false to assert that there are two supposita in Christ.[3] There is in Christ only one center of attribution, which is expressed by the personal pronoun I.[4]

Fifth objection. The three divine persons are declared one in being on account of their one nature; therefore there must be two beings in Christ because of the two natures.

Reply to fifth objection. I deny the consequence, for the difference here is that, since God is His Godhead, in the mystery of the most Holy Trinity the Godhead is predicated even in the abstract of the three persons; hence it may be said simply that the three persons are one. But in the mystery of the Incarnation, both natures are not predicated in the abstract of Christ. For Christ is not His humanity, this latter constituting a certain part of Him, and the part is not predicated of the whole. Therefore it follows that it cannot be said simply that Christ is two.

Doubt. Can it be said that Christ is both His divine nature and His human nature?

Reply. This proposition is not true in the strict and formal sense, because the term "Christ" includes more than is signified by both the divine and human natures, for it includes the note of person. But it must be said that Christ is a person that has both the divine nature and the human nature. Therefore Christ is one and He is also one being.

Second Article

WHETHER THERE IS ONLY ONE BEING IN CHRIST

State of the question. It seems that there are two beings in Christ, that is, two existences, for being follows the nature. Moreover, the being of the Son of God is the divine nature itself and is eternal, whereas the being of the man Christ is not the divine nature and is not eternal.

Likewise in the Trinity there is one being on account of the one nature. Therefore in Christ there are two beings just as there are two natures.

[3] Cf. IIIa, q. 2, a. 2, 3.

[4] This entire article I should be read.

Finally, in Christ the soul gives some being to the body, but it does not give the uncreated being. Therefore there are two beings in Christ.

There are three different opinions on this question.

1) The reply of St. Thomas is that there is one substantial being in Christ.

Thus the separated soul at the moment of the resurrection communicates its being to the re-assumed body. This thesis of St. Thomas is of sublime conception in that Christ's human nature enjoys not only the ecstasy of knowledge and love because of the beatific vision, but also the ecstasy of His very being, inasmuch as it exists by reason of the eternal being itself of the Word. Such is the opinion of all Thomists.

2) On the contrary, Scotus, the Scotists, Suarez, and generally those who deny a real distinction between created essence and existence, hold that there are two substantial existences in Christ, the divine existence, which is identical with His Godhead, and the human existence, which in their opinion is not really distinct from Christ's human nature.

3) Father Billot, however, defends the thesis that there is one substantial existence in Christ, but he identifies this unique existence with Christ's personality. According to his opinion, as stated above,[5] personality or subsistence is identical with existence. Against this opinion we stated above,[6] in challenging the major adduced by Father Billot to prove the real distinction between created essence and existence, by the following syllogism.

That which is not its own existence is really distinct from this existence. But Peter's person, even Peter's personality, is not his existence, which is predicated of it contingently. Therefore Peter's person, even Peter's personality, is really distinct from his existence.

Not even Peter's person is his humanity, because the humanity is only an essential part of his person. But the distinction is greater between Peter and his existence, than between him and his humanity, for he differs from his humanity as the whole from its essential part, whereas existence from which Peter differs is a contingent predicate of Peter, which nowise pertains to his essence. Therefore the denial

[5] See Father Billot's opinion, pp. 153–60 (*De Christo Salvatore*).

[6] *Ibid.*

of this conclusion would mean the destruction of the very foundation for the real distinction between created existence and created essence, a distinction that Father Billot always intended to maintain.

Moreover, if, in the opinion of St. Thomas, what formally constitutes personality were existence, being, then he would have spoken rather late of this formal constituent of personality in the present article, for he treated this subject *ex professo* concerning the mode of the union when discussing the union itself,[7] showing what is meant by a personal or hypostatic union, and that this union is not accidental but substantial, that is, subsistential. In the present question he is concerned only with the consequences of the union. It would be most surprising if now he were to take up the question of what formally constitutes the hypostatic union, after having treated in fourteen questions concerning the mode of the union on the part of the person assuming, and on the part of the nature assumed and those things assumed with it.

These things being posited, let us see how St. Thomas proves his opinion, namely, that there is one substantial being in Christ.

Everything is said to be a being inasmuch as it is one, for one and being are convertible. But Christ is one, not two. Therefore in Christ there is one being and not two beings. For "being" comes from "to be"; being is that whose act is to be. It is that which is.

In other words, if there were two substantial existences in Christ, there would be two beings. This conclusion rests on the following words of Christ: "Before Abraham was made, I am." [8]

This argument is valid against Suarez. It must be said in refutation of his view that Christ's human nature, if it had its own substantial being, would be entirely complete as a substance, with its ultimate actuality, and therefore complete as a suppositum, and hence its union with the Word could be only accidental, which is contrary to what was said above.[9] Thus in Christ there would be two supposita, or two things, or two beings. The substantial mode of Suarez, which accrues to being that already has its own existence, appears to be something entirely accidental, and so there is a certain danger of Nestorianism suggested in this doctrine.

[7] Cf. IIIa, q. 2.
[8] John 8:58.
[9] Cf. IIIa, q. 2, a. 6.

Second proof. It is founded on what properly belongs to the notions of substantial being, hypostasis, and nature, as declared in the argumentative part of this article.

Substantial being, which belongs to the notion of person as that which is, cannot be multiplied, since such multiplication is possible only of accidental being. Christ's human nature, however, does not accrue to the Son of God accidentally but personally, so that there is only one person in Christ.[10] Hence, there is only one substantial being in Christ.

Explanation of major. Substantial being belongs to the hypostasis as that which has being and to nature as that whereby anything has being. As St. Thomas says: "Being is consequent upon nature, not as upon that which has being, but as upon that whereby a thing is [such]; whereas it is consequent upon person or hypostasis, as upon that which has being. Hence it has unity from the unity of hypostasis, rather than duality from the duality of the nature."[11]

This denial of multiplicity in substantial being is well explained in the body of this article, by a comparison with accidental being, that can be multiplied.

In fact, the being of an accident is to inhere; thus, to be white is the being of Socrates, not as he is Socrates but inasmuch as he is white. And there is no reason why this being should not be multiplied in one hypostasis or person; for the being whereby Socrates is white is distinct from the being whereby he is a musician; but it is impossible that there should not be for one thing (or person) one (substantial) being. Being derives its name from "to be," because being is that which is or can be, and if there are two substantial beings, there are two beings, two supposita; and it is false to say that there are two such beings in Christ.

Explanation of minor. If, as Nestorius contends, the human nature of Christ were to accrue accidentally to the Word, as to be white or to be a musician accrues to Socrates, then there would be two substantial beings; but it accrues to him personally and substantially, just as when sight came to him who was born blind, this accrued to him as belonging to the constitution of his person. Hence there is only one substantial being in Christ, which is the eternal being of the Word

[10] *Ibid.,* q. 2, a. 2, 6.
[11] *Ibid.,* q. 17, a. 2, ad 1.

that is communicated to the assumed human nature, just as at the moment of the resurrection substantial being of the soul is communicated to the re-assumed body.

This argument can be presented in another form, as several Thomists have so presented it.

A thing that has acquired its ultimate actuality is incapable of being in potentiality for further determination. But existence is the ultimate actuality of a thing or person, whereby person is placed outside all its causes. Therefore a person having one substantial existence is incapable of further substantial existence. The idea is especially repugnant for the uncreated person of the Word that already has its own uncreated existence to exist by a created existence. Cajetan's interpretation concerning the formal constituent of person is completely in agreement with what is said in this article.[12]

Conclusion confirmed. There are four reasons advanced for this.

1) If Christ's human nature were to exist by its own created existence, it would also subsist by its own subsistence, because existence, since it is its ultimate actuality and presupposes subsistence, or personality, and there is only one personality in Christ, which is the divine personality.

2) If Christ's human nature were to exist by its own created existence, it could not be terminated by the subsistence of the Word; because what has its ultimate act, cannot be further determined.

3) If Christ's human nature were to exist by its own created existence, then it would not be one *per se* and substantial with the Word, because this supposition would postulate a double existence, one to which it would be in potentiality, and the other which would be its ultimate act. But also one created substantial existence, since it is the ultimate act, makes the human nature incapable of receiving another substantial existence.[13]

4) If Christ's human nature had its own created natural existence before it was assumed by the Word, then the Blessed Virgin Mary would not be the Mother of God. In fact, that Mary be truly the Mother of God, the term of her concurrence in the generation of the Son must be the God-man. But this could not be so if Christ's human

[12] This article must be read carefully, and Cajetan's commentary on it.

[13] It must be observed that Christ, although He has two distinct natures, is essentially one, not indeed in nature, but in suppositum or person, that per se subsists (in the third mode of per se predication). See Aristotle's *Post. Anal.,* Bk. I, chap. 4, lect. 10 of St. Thomas: On the four modes of per se (essential) predication.

nature had its own created existence, for the concurrence of whatsoever cause is considered totally terminated when the effect produced by it is existing, or has its ultimate actuality.

This conclusion of St. Thomas is also confirmed by the solution of the objections proposed in this article.

Reply to first objection. "Being is consequent upon person, as upon that which has being." Therefore, where there is only one person, there is likewise one being. It must be noted that St. Thomas says "being is consequent upon person"; he does not say: "being constitutes person." This text proves St. Thomas to be of the opinion that personality or subsistence is not the same as existence, which is a contingent predicate of a created person.

Reply to second objection. "The eternal being of the Son of God, which is the divine nature, becomes the being of man, inasmuch as the human nature is assumed by the Son of God, to unity of person." Thus the being of the separated soul will become, on the resurrection day, the being of the reanimated body.

Reply to third objection. "Because the divine person is the same as the nature, there is no distinction in the divine persons between the being of the person and the being of the nature." Hence in the Trinity there is one being because of the unity of the nature, between which and both the being and the persons there is no distinction; and in Christ there is one being, because of the unity of the person, which is really distinct from the human nature.[14]

It must be noted that this doctrine of St. Thomas, "the three divine persons have only one being," cannot be reconciled with Father Billot's opinion and with that of certain other theologians who say that personality is the same as existence; for there are in the Trinity three personalities and only one existence.

Reply to fourth objection. Soul and body constitute the human nature, whereby Christ is man, and independently of Christ's divine person they are not what is.[15]

Those who deny a real distinction between essence and being (existence) present the following objection.

Being that is produced is prior to being that is assumed. But the

[14] The person of the Word incarnate is really distinct from His human nature, just as there is a real distinction between the whole and its part; for before any consideration of our mind, the whole is not its part. This distinction is real and inadequate between created essence and being (existence).

[15] The entire answer to this fourth objection should be read.

production of anything terminates in its existence. Therefore Christ's human nature exists by its own existence before it is assumed by the Word.

In other words, it is assumed because it is; and it is, not because it is assumed.

Reply. I distinguish the major: that produced being exists by priority of reason, this I concede; that it exists by priority of time, this I deny. I subdistinguish the minor: that the production of anything terminates in its existence so that this thing always has this act of existence in the formal sense, please prove this; that it has this existence by something being, namely, by the being that assumes it, in a case that is absolutely miraculous, this I concede.

Hence, when it said, "Christ's human nature is therefore assumed because it exists," a distinction must be made in the expression, "because it exists"; by saying, because it is in the process of becoming to exist, in that it tends to exist, this I concede; because it exists in the sense that it is a complete and existing being, this I deny.

Hence at the very same moment, all these things take place, namely, Christ's soul is created, it is united with the body, and is assumed by the Word; therefore we must not seek for a created existence where the divine existence is communicated.

Similarly, prime matter, which, as St. Thomas teaches, cannot exist without a form, was created prior to the production of the whole composite by a priority of reason on the part of the material cause; but it was created instantaneously along with the form. Hence it is more correct to say, that is created along with its form that has priority as formal and final cause. Therefore prime matter has not its own existence, but it exists by the existence of the whole composite, or of the suppositum. Causes mutually interact. Thus the Word that terminates is prior as the terminating form, but the human nature is prior as material cause. The general rule is for essence to precede existence as a quasi-material cause, and for existence to precede essence as a quasi-formal cause. But in the Incarnation, existence is the eternal existence of the Word. Hence Christ said: "Before Abraham was made, I am." [16] He speaks as man, and hence implies that also His human nature exists by the eternal existence of the Word; but what is directly affirmed is the eternal pre-existence of Christ's one and only person.

[16] John 8:58.

But I insist. The Word did not assume a possible human nature, but a complete being. Therefore it previously existed.

Reply. I distinguish the antecedent: that the Word assumed a human nature that is a complete being existing by its own existence, this I deny; that it existed by the existence of the Word, which was communicated to it by the assumption, this I concede.

Another objection. The Thomistic thesis presupposes that subsistence precedes existence. But this is false, because subsistence is the very act itself of existence.

1) *Indirect reply.* The argument is reversed. If subsistence is the same as existence, then the Word assumed the human nature before it existed and subsisted, which is the heresy of Nestorius.

2) *Direct reply.* To subsist in the concrete includes both subsistence and existence; for subsistence is the abstract correlative name of what in the concrete is called suppositum, just as personality is the correlative of person; and to subsist is the existing of the suppositum.[17]

Hence there is a double correlative:

Abstract	subsistence personality	existence of substance
Concrete	suppositum person	to exist of the substance or to subsist

Hence even Suarez in a certain way distinguishes subsistence from existence, saying that subsistence is a mode of existence. But this presupposes the denial of a real distinction between created essence and being. Thus the truth of this particular judgment is not preserved intact, namely, Peter's human nature before any consideration of the mind *is not* his being.

Moreover, since existence is the ultimate actuality of a thing, the Suarezian mode of subsistence accrues only as an accident to the already existing nature. Thus the hypostatic union would be accidental.

Another objection. St. Thomas says: "The being of the human nature is not the divine being. Yet it must not be said simply that there

[17] Several are mistaken in thinking that subsistence is the abstract term that corresponds to what in the concrete subsists; whereas it corresponds to what in the concrete is the suppositum. Confusion is removed by substituting for "subsistence" the equivalent word "personality," because it is evident that *person* is the correlative concrete to it, and not to *subsist.*

are two beings in Christ; because the eternal suppositum does not refer equally to each being." [18]

Reply. Certain Thomists, such as Billuart, say that this passage is concerned with the being of the essence, and not with the being of existence.

Yet this answer does not remove all doubt from the mind, because generally when St. Thomas speaks of being, he means existence, and from a consideration of the context of this quotation it appears, as at least more probable, that St. Thomas is concerned with existence.

According to some modern critics, such as Mandonnet and Grabmann, this disputed question was written before the third part of the *Theological Summa,* and so it is not surprising to find the more perfect formula in the *Summa.* But several other more recent critics, Peltzer, Synave, Glorieux, are of the opinion that this disputed question had been written after the third part of the *Summa.* They acknowledge, however, that the *Compendium of Theology* is still later, and in it St. Thomas speaks as he did in the *Summa theologica.*[19]

Solution. This disputed question most probably concerns the distinction between the eternal existence of the Word and the same existence as communicated in time to Christ's human nature. Thus the existence of the separated soul at the moment of the resurrection is communicated to the body, and there is absolutely one existence, although it is true to say that now the human body again exists, but not before this reunion, because then there were only dust and ashes.

This interpretation of this particular disputed question has its foundation in the context, for in the body of this article it is said: "Existence properly and truly is predicated of the subsisting suppositum. . . . But Christ is absolutely one on account of the unity of the suppositum, and two in a qualified sense (*secundum quid*) because of the two natures; thus He has one existence on account of the one eternal existence of the eternal suppositum. But there is an-

[18] *Quaest. disp. de unione Verbi,* a. 4, ad. 1.

[19] Grabmann says the composition of this disputed question occurred between the years 1260–68; Mandonnet assigns it to the year 1268. Thus both maintain that it was written before the third part of the *Summa theologica* (1271–73). However, Father Peltzer, S.J., Father Synave, O.P. (*Bulletin Thomiste,* 1926), and Glorieux maintain that this disputed question was completed later. Yet the *Compendium of theology* appeared still later, and it contains the same doctrine as the *Commentary of St. Thomas on the Book of the Sentences,* and what is found in his *Summa theol.,* and he says nothing in these works about secondary being. Cf. Heris, O.P., *Le Verbe incarné,* 1931, pp. 291–93, 329.

other existence of this suppositum, not inasmuch as it is eternal, but inasmuch as in time this suppositum became man . . . , which is a secondary existence. But if there were two supposita in Christ, then each suppositum would have its own principal existence, and thus there would be absolutely two existences in Christ." [20]

The present article gives us the simpler and more perfect formula, for the argumentative part most splendidly says: "By the human nature there accrued to Christ no new personal being, but only a new relation of the pre-existing personal being to the human nature." [21]

Last difficulty. No divine perfection can actuate a created nature, for then this perfection would be limited since it would be received in a created nature, and would constitute with it a composite that is more perfect than its parts.

Reply. That no divine perfection can actuate a created nature by way of an intrinsically informing form, this I concede; by way of an intrinsically terminating term, this I deny. Thus, God's essence clearly seen terminates the act of the beatific vision. Thus the eternal existence of the Word is the ultimate act that terminates Christ's human nature, just as the apex of the pyramid terminates the new lines that are directed toward it.

Hence some appropriately said that in Christ there is not only ecstasy of contemplation and love, but also ecstasy of His existence, inasmuch as Christ's human nature exists by the eternal existence of the Word; being rapt as it were toward it, just as an ardent lover is attracted to the object loved.

Thus the doctrine of this article is fully in agreement with what was said above,[22] and Cajetan's interpretation concerning what constitutes personality plainly has its foundation in all these texts of St. Thomas and, moreover, is in conformity with natural reason, inasmuch as person is the intelligent and free subject or the ego, or the primary center of attribution to whom are attributed intellectual nature and existence. Thus, personality is distinct from both nature and existence.

This doctrine is the quasi-corollary of the real distinction between created essence and existence. Contrary to what Suarez says, however, this distinction most certainly follows from the fact that God alone is His existence, and, before any consideration of the mind, the crea-

[20] *Quaest. disp. de unioni Verbi,* a. 4, ad 1.
[21] Cf. IIIa, q. 17, a. 2.
[22] *Ibid.*, q. 2, a. 2, 6.

ture is not its existence. This will be most clearly evident when we shall see God as He is, and then we shall realize what an infinite difference there is between our essence and the divine essence. Moreover, if the divine person of the Word can take the place of the created personality, why could not the uncreated existence of the Word take the place of the created existence?

CHAPTER XX

QUESTION 18

What Pertains to the Unity of Christ as Regards His Will

THIS question concerns the human will of Christ as distinct from His divine will and as always freely in conformity with the divine good pleasure.

First Article

WHETHER THERE ARE TWO WILLS IN CHRIST

State of the question. Several heretics denied that there are two wills in Christ, and for various reasons. Thus Apollinaris and his disciples said that the Word in Christ took the place of His mind; hence they denied that Christ had a human will and a human intellect.

Eutyches and the Monophysites, deciding that there is only one nature in Christ, concluded that there is only one will.

The Nestorians, asserting that there was only an accidental union of love between Christ and the Word, also posited one will in Christ.

Finally, the Monothelites, namely, Sergius of Constantinople, Macharius of Antioch, Cyrus of Alexandria, asserting that there are two natures in the one person of Christ, thought that Christ's human nature was never moved by its own proper motion, but only as it was moved by the divine nature; and so they denied two wills and two volitions in Christ and admitted only the divine will.

Reply. There are two wills in Christ, namely, the divine will and the human will.

This conclusion is *de fide,* defined by the Church, against the Monothelites.[1]

[1] Denz., no. 251, Epistle of Pope Honorius I (634); see also no. 289, Third Council of Constantinople (680), in which it was defined that there are two wills in Christ; also no. 1465.

This defined truth is expressed in several texts of Holy Scripture. Thus we read: "Father, if Thou wilt, remove this chalice from Me, but yet not My will but Thine be done." [2] And again: "Not as I will, but as Thou wilt." [3] Also Jesus says: "I seek not My own will, but the will of Him that sent Me." [4]

Theological proof. The human will belongs to the perfection of the human nature, just as the divine will belongs to the perfection of the divine nature. But Christ is truly God and truly man, having two distinct natures. Therefore He likewise has two wills, namely, the divine will and the human will. Otherwise Christ could neither have obeyed nor have merited, for obedience and merit presuppose a created will that is subordinated to the divine will.

Reply to first objection. But Christ by His human will always followed the divine will. There was most perfect subordination of the human will to the divine will.[5]

Reply to second objection. Thus the human nature of Christ was the animated and free instrument of the divine nature.

Reply to third objection. Christ's human will, like ours, is inclined by its nature to something such as to happiness, or to good in general and to anything freely.

Second Article

WHETHER IN CHRIST THERE WAS A WILL OF SENSUALITY BESIDES THE WILL OF REASON

Reply. There was in Christ the sensitive appetite, which sometimes is called the sensual will, and this because the Word assumed a complete human nature.

Reply to second objection. In Christ there was no concupiscence (*fomes peccati*), and there was no indeliberate act in Him that in the sensitive part preceded reason.

[2] Luke 22:42.
[3] Matt. 26:39.
[4] John 5:30.
[5] Cf. *Summa theol.,* q. 18, a. 1, ad 4.

Third Article

WHETHER IN CHRIST THERE WERE TWO WILLS AS REGARDS THE REASON

Reply. In Christ there is one power or faculty of the human will; but if we consider the human will with reference to its acts, then there is a distinction between the *natural will* that is naturally inclined to good in itself, shrinking from what is harmful to nature, and the *rational will,* or free will, that is drawn to its object by comparison and deliberation.

Reply to second objection. Thus in the same intellective faculty there is a distinction between the intellect inasmuch as it is drawn toward principles as its object, and the discursive reason inasmuch as it is drawn toward conclusions as its object.

Fourth Article

WHETHER THERE WAS FREE WILL IN CHRIST

State of the question. The difficulty here is that the nature of free will is to be indifferent in its choice. But Christ's will was determined to be good, because He could not sin. Therefore it seems that there was not free will in Christ.

Reply. There was free will in Christ. This conclusion is of faith, just as it is of faith that Christ obeyed His Father and merited for us; for merit presupposes freedom not only from compulsion, but also from necessity.

Theological proof. The argument has its foundation in the previous article. Since there was in Christ not only the will as nature, but also the will as reason, we must say that He could choose, and consequently had free will, whose act is choice.

However, there was no doubt in Christ's deliberative judgment as to what must be chosen, because He had perfect knowledge of things.

Reply to third objection. St. Thomas answers the objection taken from Christ's impeccability by saying: "The will of Christ, though determined to good, is not determined to this or that good." Thus He was free to choose Peter in preference to John, as His vicar. "Hence it pertains to Christ, even as to the blessed, to choose with a free will confirmed in good." Thus God Himself cannot will evil, but most freely chooses this created good in preference to some other, this passible world in preference to some other.

In the above-quoted text, St. Thomas solves, indeed, the difficult problem of the compatibility of Christ's impeccability with His freedom. The words of the text were ever of penetrating clarity to him because he saw clearly that, just as God Himself is both impeccable and absolutely free, so also in due proportion is Christ as man, and it was a profound utterance when he said, "that it pertains to Christ, even as to the blessed, to choose with a free will confirmed in good," who remain free, not only in loving God clearly seen, but also concerning the possibility of choice as regards particular goods, and yet there is no fear of their changing their mind.

Nevertheless afterward, as the history of theology shows, this problem was very much disputed, especially concerning Christ's freedom as regards the commands of His Father, which He was not free to disobey. Therefore this question must be given special consideration so as to make it clear how Christ's will was free, though confirmed in good.

RECONCILIATION BETWEEN CHRIST'S FREEDOM OF WILL AND HIS IMPECCABILITY

State and difficulty of the question. It is certain that the soul of Christ was endowed with free will, which means not only freedom from internal compulsion, but also from external constraint. The Catholic Church defined against Calvin, Luther, and Jansenius, that free will implies these two kinds of freedom. The third condemned proposition of Jansenius reads: "For meriting and demeriting in the state of man's fallen nature, freedom from internal compulsion is not required; it is sufficient to be free from external constraint." [6] This means that the contradictory proposition is true, namely, for meriting and demeriting in the state of man's fallen nature, not only freedom from external constraint or spontaneity is required, which is found in the irrational animal, but also freedom from internal compulsion, or a dominating indifference of choice, under the direction of free judgment, as St. Thomas explains.[7] He also says: "The will of Christ, though determined to good, is not determined to this or that good.

[6] Denz., no. 1094.
[7] *De malo,* q. 6.

Hence it pertains to Christ, even as to the blessed, to choose with a free will confirmed in good." [8]

Where there is no command there is no difficulty, and so Christ freely chose Peter as His vicar in preference to John.

It is of faith that Christ had free will, because it was defined that there are two inconfused natures in Christ, and that each nature retains its own properties, faculties of understanding and willing, and each its own operations.[9]

The Catholic Church likewise defined that Christ freely merited and satisfied for us.[10] But, as already stated, against the Jansenists, free will is required for meriting, and freedom from internal compulsion.

All Catholic theologians are agreed on these declarations and they reject the teaching of Jansenius, who said that Christ was interiorly compelled to observe the command of His Father, since freedom from external constraint was, in the opinion of Jansenius, sufficient for meriting.

Likewise it is certain that there never was the stain of either original sin or actual sin in Christ, and this statement is of faith, as was shown above.[11] In fact, the Second Council of Constantinople declared that Christ was impeccable even before the Resurrection.[12]

All theologians maintain that Christ was thus impeccable at least by God's ordinary law, and this for three reasons, namely, because of the hypostatic union, the plenitude of inamissible habitual grace, and the beatific vision. In fact, as stated above,[13] the Thomists contend against the Scotists that, if God were to take away habitual grace and the beatific vision from Christ, He would still be impeccable and not merely sinless, because of the hypostatic union. In any other case, sin would be charged to the Word itself, since actions belong to the supposita or are elicited by the suppositum.

Thus Christ even in this life was absolutely impeccable, and this for three reasons: (1) because He had the grace of union; (2) because He had the fullness of inamissible habitual grace; (3) because He had

[8] Cf. IIIa, q. 18, a. 4.
[9] Denz., nos. 148, 288.
[10] *Ibid.*, nos. 122, 286, 319, 462, 794 f.
[11] Cf. IIIa, q. 15, a. 1.
[12] Denz., no. 224.
[13] Cf. *Summa theol.*, IIIa, q. 15, a. 1.

the beatific vision. He was also *de facto* sinless since He always received efficacious grace to do what is right, and this befitted Him as it did the Blessed Virgin Mary.

These facts being admitted, there arises the great difficulty about how we shall reconcile Christ's freedom from internal compulsion, in the acts commanded, with His absolute impeccability, which is more than sinlessness. For either Christ could refuse to perform the act commanded, and then He could sin, or He could not refuse, and then He was not free, with freedom from internal compulsion, and hence His act was not meritorious. It seems that Christ's impeccability and the freedom required in Him for meriting are irreconcilable. But our faith tells us that these two properties most certainly belonged to Christ even in this life. Christ's impeccability and His merits are underlying principles of all Christianity.

Scriptural proof. On the one hand, the Gospels and epistles state it to be an established fact that Christ's death was a truly free act. Thus Jesus says: "Therefore doth the Father love Me, because I lay down My life that I may take it again. No man taketh it away from Me; but I lay it down of Myself and I have power to lay it down and I have power to take it up again. This commandment I have received of My Father." [14] These words express Christ's liberty and the divine command. Christ reaffirms this in His discourse at the Last Supper: "The prince of this world cometh and in Me he hath not anything. But that the world may know that I love the Father, and as the Father hath given Me commandment, so do I." [15] It is also evident that Christ's death was truly meritorious.[16] On the other hand, it is certain that Christ was not only sinless but absolutely impeccable. Therefore He could not disobey. Then how was it possible for Him to obey or disobey as He chose?

VARIOUS OPINIONS PROPOSED FOR THE SOLUTION OF THIS DOUBT [17]

These may be reduced to the following three: (1) Some said that Jesus did not receive from the Father a true command to die. So said Lorca, who quotes Paludanus. Afterward Petavius and Franzelin held this view, and among more recent theologians was Father

[14] John 10:17 f.
[15] *Ibid.*, 14:30 f.
[16] Rom. 5:19; Phil. 2:8; I Pet. 2:21.
[17] *Dict. théol. cathol.*

Billot.[18] To these must be added, with some modification, Father de la Taille,[19] as we shall state farther on.

According to this opinion, Christ was not free in things that are commanded, either by the natural law or the positive law, because it is physically impossible for the comprehensor to will not to obey.

2) Others said that Christ received from the Father a command that determined only the substance of the death, but not circumstances of time, manner of death, and other conditions. Tournely said that Christ could have been dispensed by His Father from this command to die. Vasquez,[20] de Lugo,[21] and Lessius [22] held this view. This second opinion is eclectic and holds with the first opinion that Christ was not free in things commanded, though it maintains with the third opinion that Christ received the command to die. On seeking to reconcile the command with free will it restricts the command to the substance of the work.

3) There are those who say that Christ received a true and strict command to die, and it determined both the substance and the circumstances of His death. Nevertheless Christ offered Himself freely on the cross, because He was free not only from external constraint, but also from internal compulsion. This third opinion maintains, contrary to the two other opinions, that Christ was free even in things strictly commanded, both of the natural law and of the positive law. So say the Thomists; and also, with some qualification, St. Robert Bellarmine,[23] and Suarez; who explain their view by means of the *scientia media,* which the Thomists do not admit. The Thomists maintain that Christ's impeccable freedom of will is like God's freedom, whose will is both absolutely free and absolutely impeccable, inasmuch as God loves His own good, but He most freely loves it as the reason for loving creatures.[24] But there can be no command for God.

The secondary subject of dispute among Thomists, however, concerns the regulation of Christ's free choice, as to whether it was also

[18] *De incarnatione,* theses 29, 30.
[19] *Mysterium fidei, elucid.,* 7, 8; pp. 89, 95, 99.
[20] *De incarnatione,* disp. 74, chap. 5.
[21] *Ibid.,* disp. 26, sect. 7, no. 82; sect. 8, no. 102.
[22] *De Summo Bono,* Bk. II, no. 185.
[23] *De justificatione,* Bk. V, chap. II.
[24] *Summa theol.,* Ia, q. 19, a. 2, 3.

possibly regulated by the beatific vision, or only by the infused knowledge. This will be examined afterward.

Thus the fundamental difference between these opinions is clearly seen, inasmuch as the first two opinions assert that Christ was not free in things commanded, whereas the third opinion declares that He was free.

Various Opinions

reconciliation between Christ's freedom of will and the divine command to die on the cross.

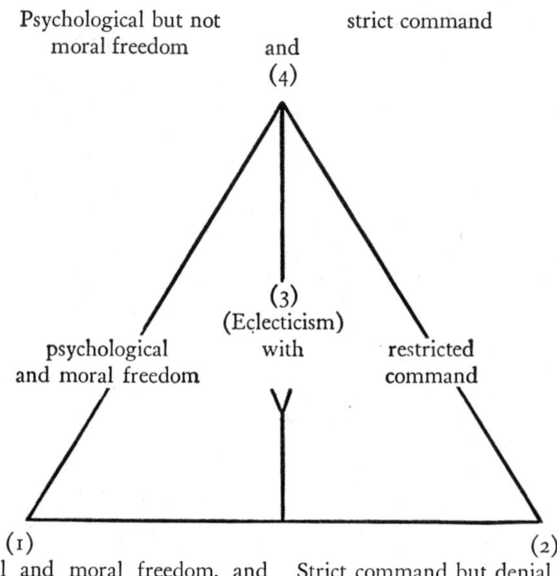

(1) Psychological and moral freedom, and no command

(2) Strict command but denial of moral and psychological freedom

(1) Franzelin
Billot (special view)

(2) Jansenius and
Jansenists

(3) Two classes:
a) Gregory of Valentia
Vasquez
Lessius
Theoph. Raynaud
Ysambert
b) Cabrera
De Lugo
Tournely

(4) All Thomists
St. Robert Bellarmine

Importance of this discussion. Thomists believe that it is a grave matter to deny Christ's freedom of will in things commanded, because Christ is the exemplar of all virtues, and especially in the conformity of His will with the divine will that commands. The denial of this freedom appears to them to be an entirely rash statement and somewhat of an insult to Christ. They are generally chary of detracting from the sublimity of mysteries in seeking for apparent clarity, which, instead of disposing a person for the contemplation of divine things, has rather the opposite effect. First of all, we must bear in mind that faith is of things *not seen,* and so too is contemplation that proceeds from living faith, illumined by the gifts of the Holy Ghost.

Hence, concerning the method to be followed by the theologian in these things, it must be noted first of all that most certain truths must not be either denied or minimized, as in the present question Christ's impeccability and His freedom from internal compulsion. This freedom of Christ must not be restricted, because it is the exemplar for our life and undoubtedly the most sublime image of God's freedom, which is both supreme and impeccable.

But no wonder that there must be for us obscurity in the intimate reconciliation of these most certain truths. It is not obscurity of the lower order, namely, of incompatibility or absurdity, but it is the higher obscurity of the mystery itself which is the object of faith and contemplation. Thus in the question of predestination, on the one hand it is certain that God does not command the impossible, and He makes salvation really possible for all. On the other hand, it is certain that, although God's love is the cause of goodness in things, nobody would be better than another unless that person were loved more by God, as St. Thomas shows.[25] But the intimate reconciliation of these two truths is hidden from us, because it is the reconciliation of supreme mercy, supreme justice, and supreme freedom in the Godhead. This intimate reconciliation can be seen only by seeing God Himself through the beatific vision.

Thomism does not fear either logic or mystery, for logic leads us to the most sublime of God's mysteries. Thus the beauty of the chiaroscuro in these mysteries is apparent.

The first two opinions that declare Christ was not free in things commanded must now be examined.

[25] *Ibid.,* Ia, q. 20, a. 3, 4.

WAS CHRIST TRULY UNDER OBLIGATION TO DIE FOR US, BECAUSE OF THE COMMAND IMPOSED UPON HIM BY THE FATHER?

State of the question. That Christ had to die for us was denied by Lorca, Petavius, Franzelin, Billot, and de la Taille because, so they say, in such a case, He would not have been free, for, inasmuch as He was impeccable, He could not disobey this command. Hence they held that God, apart from the command by which Christ was compelled to die, in His foreknowledge disposed and decreed that order in which He knew that the Jews, through their own malice, would kill Christ, and that Christ, by conformity of His will with the divine good pleasure, which was not obligatory, freely would embrace death on the cross. Father de la Taille [26] concedes to the Thomists that Christ was under a real moral obligation of dying for us, but in his opinion this obligation did not arise from the Father's command, for Christ contracted this obligation at the Last Supper by offering Himself to the Father to be put to death for us. Thus God inspires certain generous souls by way of counsel, but not of obligation, to offer themselves in holocaust along with Christ for the salvation of sinners, and they contract this obligation only after having freely accepted this divine inspiration, for example, by vowing to be a victim.

Reply. With the Thomists we say that Christ was really under obligation to die because of the command of His Father.

Scriptural proof. Sacred Scriptures speaks in various places of commands imposed upon Christ, especially of the command to die.

According to the general rule laid down by St. Augustine and commonly admitted by theologians, the words of Sacred Scripture are to be accepted in their literal sense when there is no incongruity.

We read in the Gospel that Jesus says: "Therefore doth the Father love Me, because I lay down My life, that I may take it up again. No man taketh it away from Me, but I lay it down of Myself, and I have power to lay it down and have power to take it up again. This commandment I have received of My Father." [27] The words used by Jesus to express His Father's command,[28] are always technical terms in the

[26] *Mysterium fidei, elucidationes* 7, 8, pp. 89–93.

[27] John 10:17 f.

[28] *Ibid.,* 1:18; 14:31. St. John, who wrote his Gospel in Greek, used the words ’εντέλλω, ’εντολή, which always mean a strict command. (Tr.)

New Testament, that signify divine commands in the strict sense.[29] There is no reason for saying here that this is a command improperly so called; otherwise it could always be said, when the word "command" occurs in the Scripture, that this word is not to be taken in the strict sense. Moreover, these words are said by Christ before He offers Himself at the Last Supper to the Father to die for us. Therefore Christ did not contract the obligation of dying for us from a later oblation of Himself, but from the command of the Father. In things that are partly clear and partly obscure, what is clear must not be denied, otherwise the mystery undergoes a change if the inferior obscurity of incoherence and contradiction is substituted for the higher obscurity.

Jesus also says after the Last Supper: "The prince of this world cometh, and in Me he hath not anything. But that the world may know that I love the Father, and as the Father hath given Me a command so do I." [30] This text is concerned strictly with the command of dying for our salvation.

Again Jesus says: "If you keep My commandment, you shall abide in My love; as I also have kept My Father's commandments, and do abide in His love." [31] In this text Christ gives the same meaning to the word "commandments" as imposed upon Him by His Father, and those He imposed on His apostles. But these were commandments in the strict sense, therefore those imposed upon Him by the Father were likewise strict commandments. Thus Christ was the exemplar of perfect obedience. Moreover, this text is concerned not only with the commandment to die, but with all the commandments of the Father observed by Christ, and He observed them indeed freely and meritoriously for us. It seems impossible to reconcile this text with the thesis that affirms Christ was not free in things commanded. But several of these commandments, those that are of the natural order, precede Christ's spontaneous oblation.

Likewise Jesus says: "And the Son of man indeed goeth according to that which is determined." [32] Again Jesus says in the Garden of Olives: "Father, if Thou wilt, remove this chalice from Me; but yet not My will, but Thine be done." [33] The Apostle declares that Christ

[29] Matt. 5:19; 22:36.
[30] John 14:30 f.
[31] *Ibid.*, 15:10.
[32] Luke 22:22.
[33] *Ibid.*, 22:42.

says, when He cometh into the world: "Sacrifice and oblation Thou wouldest not, but a body Thou hast fitted for Me; holocausts for sin did not please Thee. Then I said: Behold I come; in the head of the book it is written of Me that I should do Thy will, O God." [34] These texts concern Christ's will in the strict sense, and are not merely a simple counsel given to the Son to make an oblation of Himself for our salvation.

Hence it seems impossible to exclude the notion of a divine command from these texts of Sacred Scripture.

Confirmation. There are other texts of Sacred Scripture that refer to Christ's obedience. St. Paul says: "He humbled Himself, becoming obedient unto death, even to the death of the cross." [35]

Again he says: "For as by the disobedience of one man, many were made sinners; so also by the obedience of one, many shall be made just." [36] There is no reason to deny that these texts refer to both obedience and disobedience in the true and strict sense of these terms. But the formal object of obedience in the strict sense of the term consists in the absolute command given by the superior; for counsel is not of itself binding, nor does it distinguish the superior as such from inferiors; for equals and inferiors can also give advice as superiors can.

Finally, in the last quoted text (Rom. 5:19), Christ's obedience is placed in opposition to Adam's disobedience, which consisted in not complying with a strict command. Therefore the text refers to obedience in the strict sense, which consisted in complying with a strict command.

Furthermore it must be said that an appeal to God's counsel does not help in upholding Christ's freedom; for it is also repugnant to Christ's supreme holiness for Him to have been able to omit or neglect the counsels of God the Father, especially the counsel that is dependent on the eternal decree, and is that ordained for the salvation of mankind and for the greater glory of God. Even apart from any command,[37] it remains true that Christ's death with all its circumstances was decreed before all time, and Christ also knew the will of His

[34] Heb. 10:5 f. Also Acts 4:28; Ps. 39:8.

[35] Phil. 2:8.

[36] Rom. 5:19.

[37] Acts 4:28. If God had only permitted the crime of the Jews against Jesus, as He permitted the persecution against the martyrs, Christ's death would also infallibly have come to pass and He would have had to accept this consequence of the divine permission.

Father, and it was no less repugnant for Him not to be in conformity with it as to sin.

Two theological reasons are given which show clearly that the command to die cannot be denied.

First theological reason. It is a direct proof and it starts from the definition of command and it shows that a command does not take away psychological liberty.

Every command is given for the free fulfillment of the act. Thus it would be useless and foolish for fire to be commanded to burn, for the heart to be commanded to beat. Hence the command that would destroy psychological freedom in the person obeying, would destroy the essential meaning of command.

But the command to die for us, as a command, did not lose its essential meaning from the fact that Christ was impeccable. Therefore this command to die did not take away psychological freedom from Christ, or His free will as regards the act to which He was inclined.

Major. It is absolutely certain, for a command does indeed take away moral liberty inasmuch as it makes the opposite act illicit, but it does not take away psychological liberty, for it even requires this liberty in that it demands the free fulfillment of what is commanded.

Minor. It is likewise certain. Thus the command given by God to the good angels to perform some ministerial work for Him, does not lose its nature as a command because they cannot sin. And they freely comply with this command, inasmuch as its object is not in every respect good so that it necessitates their will. Thus the object of this command differs from God clearly seen.

Second theological reason. If the strict command to die for us had destroyed Christ's freedom and power to merit, the result would have been the same with natural commands and thus Christ would neither have been free nor merited in the observance of all commands of the natural law.

But to affirm this is to restrict Christ's freedom and merit without any reason, and it would be an excessive restriction, even, so it seems, derogatory to Christ's honor because He would no longer be the model of all virtues.

Christ's merit must in no way be restricted; on the contrary, it is beyond our power of conception. Hence, too, His freedom must not be restricted, for it is the perfect image of God's supreme and impeccable freedom. Hence the idea of a command must be admitted.

WHAT WAS THE SCOPE OF THIS COMMAND TO DIE FOR US?

Did it concern only the substance of the death, or did it include also circumstances of time, place, manner of death, and similar conditions?

As we remarked, Vasquez, de Lugo, and Lessius say that the scope of this command was only the substance of the death. Thus, in the opinion of these theologians, Christ was free only concerning the circumstances of His death, and it was not precisely because He died that He merited, but only because He died in such a place, such a time, and such a manner.

For these theologians, the command eliminates freedom in the impeccable Christ.

The Thomists give the following proofs of the contrary opinion.

Scriptural proof. St. Paul says of Christ: "He humbled Himself, becoming obedient unto death, even to the death of the cross for which cause God also hath exalted Him." [38] Therefore the scope of Christ's obedience included even this mode of death, namely, death on the cross. Also, concerning the other circumstances, after Christ was apprehended by the Jews on the night of His passion, the Evangelist says: "Now all this was done that the scriptures of the prophets might be fulfilled." [39] Even the time is included: "Before the festival day of the Pasch, Jesus knowing that His hour was come, that He should pass out of this world to the Father, having loved His own who were in the world, He loved them unto the end." [40]

Doctrine of the Church. The councils of the Catholic Church always affirmed that Christ merited our salvation by His passion and death and not only by the circumstances of His death. There are many texts in Sacred Scripture, even in the Old Testament, that confirm this assertion. Thus the prophet says: "If He shall lay down His life for sin, He shall see a long-lived seed." [41] The Council of Trent says that Christ "merited justification for us by His most holy passion on the wood of the cross." [42] All the faithful, in all centuries, attributed our redemption to Christ's death, and not only to its circumstances.

Theological proof. It must again be said that a command, which

[38] Phil. 2:8.
[39] Matt. 26:56.
[40] John 13:1.
[41] Isa. 53:10.
[42] Denz., nos. 799 f.

would take away psychological freedom, would destroy its own nature as a command, since it is given for the free fulfillment of the act. It would likewise follow that there was no merit in Christ's obedience, because He would not have been free concerning the thing commanded, inasmuch as it was commanded, and He would not have been free concerning the commands of the natural law.

It cannot be said that the command to die was imposed upon Christ conditionally, so that whenever He wished He could be dispensed from it, which is the contention of Tournely. Thus there would be absolutely no merit in Christ's obedience, or at least hardly any at all; for there is scarcely any obedience in a subordinate who is given freedom of choice so as to be able at any time to obtain a dispensation. Moreover, the work of our redemption would be attributed more to Christ's human will than to the divine will, which is an unbefitting condition.

Finally, the precepts of the natural law do not depend on Christ's acceptance of them, nor do they allow of a dispensation, and yet He observed them freely and meritoriously, saying: "If you keep My commandments you shall abide in My love; as I also have kept My Father's commandments." [43]

Hence the first two above-mentioned opinions: (1) have no basis in the Sacred Scriptures but, on the contrary, are rather in opposition to the testimony of Scripture; (2) they are false in presupposing a command that destroys psychological liberty whereas, on the contrary, the command presupposes this liberty; (3) they are useless as a means of reconciliation between Christ's freedom and His impeccability concerning the precepts of the natural law; (4) they unduly restrict the freedom and merit of Christ, who no longer would be the model of all virtues, and especially of perfect obedience. Thus they do not solve the difficulty but seek to escape from it. They do not ascend to a certain understanding of the mystery in this problem, but rather descend to merely human concepts of this mystery. Thus truth is sought, not so much by a penetration of the principles involved, but rather by a quasi-mechanical translocation of the element of the problem.

PRINCIPAL QUESTION

Positing the precepts of the natural law, and the strict command to die, how could Christ, who was impeccable, and free not only from

[43] John 15:10.

internal compulsion but also from external constraint, perform a free and meritorious act in obeying?

The fact that Christ's freedom is compatible with His impeccability, notwithstanding the command, is expressed in the very words our Lord uttered, as recorded in the Gospel: "I lay down My life, that I may take it again. No man taketh it away from Me, but I lay it down of Myself, and I have power [freedom] to lay it down and I have power to take it up again." [44]

The difficulty in explaining the compatibility of Christ's freedom with His impeccability is, as we already said,[45] that He could either disobey the command, and so could commit sin, or He could not disobey, and so He was not free, and His obedience was not meritorious.

Prerequisites. In the solution of this difficulty, there being a real command, several requirements are to be noted.

1) Liberty of exercise alone suffices to preserve intact the essence of free will, because by it man is sufficiently master of his act, which he can do or not do: the essence of free will does not require liberty of specification [46] either of contraries, as in the case of loving and hating, or of disparities, choosing for the end this means or another.

2) The power and freedom to commit sin is not required for real freedom of will; it is rather a sign of freedom, as a disease is a sign of life. This freedom to sin pertains to the defectibility of our nature and is therefore an imperfection in freedom. It is nowise found either in God or in the blessed. God is both supremely free and absolutely impeccable. But Christ's human freedom must be the most perfect image of divine freedom. This calls for most special consideration,[47] namely, that the impeccable God possesses this freedom only for what is good, but He created most freely. There is a certain fitness in His act of creating, inasmuch as good is self-diffusive; but He is most free in creating, so that neither His goodness nor His wisdom would

[44] *Ibid.*, 10:17 f.

[45] See pp. 324 f.

[46] See *God, His Existence*, II, 293 f. (Tr.)

[47] Hence St. Thomas defines liberty as the faculty of choosing the means, "keeping the order of the end in view," but "it comes of the defect of liberty for it to choose anything by turning away from the order of the end, and this is to sin . . . just as it belongs to the power of the intellect to be able to proceed to different conclusions, according to different principles; but for it to proceed to some conclusion, by passing out of the order of principles, comes of its own defect" (Ia, q. 62, a. 8, ad 3). See also Ia, q. 83, a. 4, c.

have been less if He had not created. He is not better because He created the universe and because He sent us His only-begotten Son.

3) Not to obey can be taken either as a privation or as merely a negation. As a privation it signifies the omission of obedience that is of obligation, or a sin of disobedience, and this is therefore strictly to disobey rather than to obey. But taken in the negative sense, it signifies simply the absence of obedience, as when a person performs an act that is not commanded, as in the case of sleeping; and this is rather not to obey than to disobey; not to obey in the sense of a privation is to combine the omission of obedience with the command. Whereas not to obey in the negative sense is not to perform the act, prescinding from the idea of a command.[48]

Thus that God does not preserve a creature in doing what is good and permits the beginning of the first sin is something that is not good, but it is not the evil of punishment. On the contrary, the divine denial of efficacious grace is a punishment that presupposes guilt, at least the beginning of the first sin.[49] In all these most difficult questions, we must carefully distinguish between negation and privation. But as evil is the privation of a good that one ought to have, so the denial of a good that is not due to a person is not an evil; for example, that God does not preserve a certain creature in the performance of good at this very moment and in the present circumstances. For He is not bound to preserve every creature in the performance of good, otherwise He could not permit sin since this would be impossible and what is liable to fail would never fail.

Hence it must be said of Christ, who was impeccable, that He was incapable of not obeying in the privative sense, because in such a case He would have been able to sin; He was not only sinless but absolutely impeccable, just as He not only never erred, but He was infallible.

It remains for us to examine whether He could not obey in the negative sense, prescinding from the idea of a command, carefully bearing in mind the distinction between privation and negation.

4) It is presupposed that death on the cross for our salvation has intrinsically no necessary connection, at the moment and in the pres-

[48] The French word *"désobéir"* means more than *"ne pas obéir."*

[49] This distinction is of great importance, and in omitting it there is danger of saying that a person can be punished before that person has begun to be guilty, whereas punishment can be inflicted only on account of guilt. Such a doctrine would lead to Calvinism.

ent circumstances, with Christ's will, or with His enjoyment of the beatific vision. The present object differs from others that necessarily move the will as regards their specification, such as being, living, and understanding, if considered in themselves, without any adnexed incongruity.

5) It is presupposed that a command is merely extrinsic to the will and nowise interiorly changes it, so that the will which before the command is presupposed to be psychologically free, after the giving of the command remains psychologically free, since a command cannot be given about necessary things. In fact, it is presupposed that God, in commanding His Son to die, at the same time willed that He should submit to death by obeying freely and thus meriting. For a command is given for the free fulfillment of the act; if it were to destroy this freedom, as stated above, it would destroy the very nature of a command. The distinction between psychological freedom and moral freedom is a common sense distinction which all understand; for a command that is a moral obligation is morally binding so that the act that is opposed to it is illicit or forbidden; but the command does not take away psychological freedom either as regards the exercise of the act or as regards its specification, and this psychological freedom or free will remains either in sin freely committed against the command, or in the free fulfillment of the command.

6) The common distinction of Thomists in the matter of helps in general are presupposed, such as necessity of consequence or hypothetical necessity and necessity of consequent or absolute necessity, as also the divided and composite senses, distinctions given by St. Thomas elsewhere,[50] in which he shows that if I see Peter running, he must necessarily run, by a necessity of consequence but not of consequent, for he runs freely; but it is necessary for him to run as long as he is running and while I see him running, because as Aristotle says: "Everything that is, while it is, must be." [51]

Likewise Peter must sit while he is sitting, that is, he cannot combine sitting with standing, or both sit and not sit in the composite sense; but while sitting he is able to stand, in the divided sense, that is, while sitting he retains the real power of standing, but not the act of standing; likewise, while sleeping he retains the real power of seeing and is not blind.

[50] *Summa theol.,* Ia, q. 14, a. 13, ad 2, 3.

[51] *Perihermeneias,* Bk. I, chap. 9 (lect. 15 of St. Thomas).

It remains, therefore, for us to see whether Christ's impeccability enabled Him not to obey in the negative or divided sense; so that, when He obeyed, His act of obedience was necessary by a necessity of consequence or hypothetical necessity, but not by a necessity of consequent or absolute necessity.

With these prerequisites, it must be shown in what the freedom of Christ's impeccability consists: (1) in its relation to God's impeccable freedom, of which it is the most pure created image; and (2) in its relation to command, especially the command to die for our salvation.

CHRIST'S IMPECCABLE FREEDOM INASMUCH AS IT IS THE MOST PURE IMAGE OF THE UNCREATED IMPECCABLE FREEDOM

It is evident that God nowise is free to sin, that is, He cannot turn away from Himself, from His infinite goodness which He necessarily loves. Nevertheless He is supremely free in what pertains to good, as regards His goodness inasmuch as it is the reason of His love for creatures, or the reason for the communication, diffusion, and manifestation of His goodness. These assertions are of faith as defined by the Vatican Council.[52]

There is indeed a mystery in this, namely, although it was truly fitting that God create the world, inasmuch as good and especially the supreme good is self-diffusive, yet God created with such absolute freedom that He could have most properly not created; it would not have been improper if He had not created. Whatever Leibnitz may say, God would not have been deficient either in wisdom or goodness if He had not created.[53] God is neither greater nor better for having created the universe.

Likewise, although it was truly fitting for God to have raised the human race and the angels to the life of grace, yet He could have not so raised them. Also, although it was truly fitting that God sent His Son into the world for our redemption, it was in His power not to have willed the redemptive Incarnation.

St. Thomas explains elsewhere the two aspects of this mystery of uncreated freedom.[54]

The fittingness of creation, as also the fittingness of the Incarnation,

[52] Denz., no. 1783.

[53] This point has been explained at length in *God, His Existence,* II, 342–54.

[54] *Summa theol.,* Ia, q. 19, a. 2, 3.

is apparent from the fact that good is self-diffusive. As St. Thomas says: "If natural things, so far as they are perfect, communicate their good to others, much more does it appertain to the divine will to communicate by likeness its own good to others, as much as possible." [55]

The fitness of creation that has its foundation in the aforesaid principle appears of such importance that Leibnitz, and several philosophers before him, said: "If God had not created, He would have been neither infinitely good nor infinitely wise." [56]

Nevertheless the Vatican Council defined it to be of faith that "God with absolute freedom of counsel created." [57] St. Thomas explains this assertion as follows: "The divine will has a necessary relation to the divine goodness, which is its proper object. Hence God wills His own goodness necessarily. . . . But God wills things apart from Himself so far as they are ordered to His own goodness, as their end. . . . Hence, since the goodness of God is perfect and can exist without other things, inasmuch as no perfection can accrue to Him from them, it follows that His willing things apart from Himself is not absolutely necessary." [58]

Hence we can present the argument in the following syllogistic form.

God is free, not to love His goodness in itself, but inasmuch as it is the reason for His loving creatures, which have no right to being. And although God is infinitely good and wise, He does not become better from the fact that He willed most freely to create. Thus, He enjoys supreme freedom as well as impeccability, namely, supreme freedom in what appertains only to good.

But the human will of Christ is the most pure reflection of the uncreated will, inasmuch as it is the human will of the incarnate Son of God. Therefore the human will of Christ must be likewise both impeccable and most free, not indeed in its relation to the divine goodness considered in itself and clearly seen, but in its relation to the divine goodness inasmuch as it is the reason for His loving creatures. There is no reason for surprise that there is a mystery in this, just as there is a mystery in uncreated freedom.

[55] *Ibid.,* Ia, q. 19, a. 2. See also IIIa, q. 1, a. 1, in which the same reason is given for the manifestation of the possibility and fitness of the Incarnation.

[56] *Œuvres de Leibnitz* (Erdmann ed.), 563 a.

[57] Denz., no. 1783.

[58] *Summa theol.,* Ia, q. 19, a. 3. See also ad 5; and *Contra Gentes,* Bk. I, chaps. 76, 82.

In other words, Christ as man, was not free to sin, for this results from a certain defectibility in our nature. He was truly not only sinless, but absolutely impeccable, and this for three reasons: (1) because of the hypostatic union; (2) because of the inamissible fulness of grace; (3) because of His having the beatific vision.

Strictly speaking, on account of the beatific vision, Christ necessarily loved the divine goodness clearly seen as it is in itself, and this act of love was indeed spontaneous, though it transcended freedom; but, like God, He freely loved the divine goodness, inasmuch as it is the reason for God's love of creatures. The mystery, indeed, is that for God to create is so fitting that not to create would be unfitting, and there is a similar mystery in Christ's human will.

However, there is a special difficulty to be explained. For God, though it is fitting for Him to create, there is no command. On the contrary, Christ was bound to obey the commands of His Father, even the command to die for our salvation. It is, indeed, easy to understand that, just as God most freely chose whom He wills for eternal salvation, Christ freely chose and called certain fishermen in preference to others for the grace of the apostolate. But it is very difficult to understand how He was free in the observance of His Father's commands. The whole difficulty, as we say, concerns the command; for if Christ could refrain from performing the act commanded, He could sin, for He was perhaps sinless but not impeccable. But if He could not refrain from performing the act commanded, then He was not free, and therefore He could not merit for us. This dilemma is the Thermopylae of theology, just as is the difficulty of defending the reconciliation of God's foreknowledge with free will, especially with true culpability in the sinner.

SOLUTION

Christ, though impeccable, was free as regards the commands of His Father, especially concerning the command to die for our salvation.

The argument for reconciling freedom with the commands imposed upon the impeccable Christ may be reduced to the following syllogism.

A command in the strict sense does not indeed leave the will morally free, in that it imposes an obligation, but it does leave it psychologically free; in fact, of itself the command is given for the free fulfillment of the act, and, if it were to destroy this psychological freedom, it would destroy its very nature as a command.

But before the command, Christ has psychological and impeccable freedom of will, a freedom, as was stated, that is the most pure reflection of the uncreated freedom concerning those things that are not necessarily and intrinsically connected, *hic et nunc,* with beatitude.

Therefore this psychological freedom is not destroyed by the commands of the Father, otherwise these commands would lose their very nature as such.

The major is evident from what has been said.

Explanation of minor. Indeed Christ's love for God clearly seen, as the ultimate end, and the means that are intrinsically and necessarily connected *hic et nunc* with this end, such as being, life, understanding, are not a free act but a necessary one; yet He freely loves the means that are only accidentally connected with the ultimate end because of an extrinsic command. There is, indeed, a speculative-practical judgment arising from the command, namely, this must be done;[59] but the practico-practical judgment, namely, death on the cross here and now is simply to be loved, remains undetermined because of the indifferent merits of the object; for the object commanded is not universally good, but is good in a certain sense as being useful for the salvation of man, and as being commanded; and in another sense it is not good, on account of the horrible pain it involves.

For the formation of this practico-practical judgment, namely, death on the cross is here and now simply to be loved, there must be an actual preference for the offering of this holocaust, or there must be an intervention of the free will. But there is befitting intervention of Christ's will, because the will of Christ, who is impeccable, is absolutely upright. Hence this ultimate practical judgment and the subsequent choice are necessary only by a necessity of consequence or of infallibility, but not by a necessity of consequent. There remains, therefore, liberty of exercise between willing to obey and not willing

[59] There is a distinction between the speculative-practical judgment and the practico-practical judgment as in the common saying: I see and approve of the better (speculative-practical judgment), but I choose the worse (ultimate practico-practical judgment and choice). The ultimate practico-practical judgment that immediately directs the choice, is not always in conformity with the speculative-practical judgment, and this already presupposes an actual affection for the object to be chosen. In the absence of this actual affection the practico-practical judgment, as is evident in the above-mentioned saying and in any sin, is not in conformity with the speculative-practical judgment, from which there arises in the intellect advertence to sin.

to obey in the negative sense, or refusing death in itself, but not between willing to obey and not willing to obey, in the privative sense, or refusing death as a command. Experience itself makes sufficiently clear the distinction between not obeying in the negative sense and not obeying in the privative sense. For if a superior were to command a most obedient religious something truly difficult, for example, not to go on a long journey to give the last absolution to his most beloved spiritual son, whom another priest will be able to assist in this case, then this obedient religious is right in feeling sad because it would be most sweet for him to assist his spiritual son who is dying and clamoring for him. Nevertheless, because he is obedient, he is not even inclined to do so against the command of his superior, that is, not to obey in the privative sense. On the contrary, another less obedient religious in this case, not only would be right in feeling sad, but would be inclined not to obey in the privative sense, and perhaps would not sufficiently resist the temptation.

A good religious would wish to perform this ministerial act in itself, but not inasmuch as it is forbidden. Likewise Christ could refuse death in itself, and it made Him sad; but He could not refuse death inasmuch as it was commanded, nor did it make Him sad inasmuch as it was commanded. Therefore this distinction is not merely a subtle play upon words, but has its manifest foundation in something psychological.

This problem is made clear for us in two most exalted examples of obedience: Abraham's obedience and that of the Blessed Virgin Mary on Calvary.

When Abraham had to prepare to sacrifice his son, he did not even think of the possibility of not obeying; he immediately was disposed to obey. Nevertheless he saw very clearly that the object of this act was in one aspect good, and in another aspect not good, even repugnant to natural paternal love. Therefore in the formation of the ultimate and determinate practical judgment, namely, this is for me here and now good, not only relatively but absolutely, and to be done, although it is most difficult, in the formation of this ultimate practical judgment, which directs the choice, Abraham's free will had to intervene, so that the former aspect of the object might prevail over the latter; but Abraham's will, moved by efficacious grace, befittingly intervened, freely indeed, and heroically. He could obey and not obey in the negative sense; in fact, because he was not impeccable, he could disobey in the privative sense by an act of disobedience or at least by a sin of omission, but he did not even think of this. So immediate, holy, and most meritorious was his obedience that he became for all posterity an example of both heroic obedience and perfect faith.

In this example we find verified what is said about free will in the twenty-four Thomistic theses proposed by the Sacred Congregation of Studies. The twenty-first reads: "The will that is free in its choice follows the judgment of reason, but that this judgment be the last and that another in opposition to it be not subsumed, this is effected by the free will, in accepting or not accepting this intellectual direction."

The Blessed Virgin Mary on Calvary gave us another example of heroic obedience. When she had to give her consent to the immolation of her Son, she did not even think of the possibility of disobedience or of deliberately praying that it may not happen.

Yet she most clearly saw that the object of this act of obedience was in one aspect good for our salvation, and in another aspect it was a very great affliction to her maternal heart. To form the ultimate practical judgment which directs the choice, the free will of the Blessed Virgin Mary must intervene, so that one aspect of the object may predominate over the other. But under the influence of efficacious grace and the special assistance of the Holy Ghost, by which she was preserved from even the least stain of sin, the will of the Blessed Virgin intervened most befittingly, freely indeed and heroically, so that she became forever the Queen of martyrs.

In these two examples, we have a clarification of the problem concerning Christ's impeccable freedom which is increasingly seen to be the most perfect reflection of God's impeccable freedom. It is freedom for good and not for evil, namely, free will confirmed in good,[60] as St. Thomas with the greatest of wisdom and brevity had said in the present article.

Confirmation. If this were not true, the blessed would not retain their freedom concerning those things that are not necessarily and intrinsically connected with beatitude. It is the common opinion among theologians, however, that the blessed, for example, St. Dominic, by necessarily loving God's goodness clearly seen, freely loves this son of his living on this earth and freely prays to obtain for him this or

[60] Cf. a. 4, ad 3.

that grace. Even though God were to command St. Dominic to pray for this religious, he would still freely pray for him, because the command that is given for the free fulfillment of the act cannot destroy the psychological freedom of this act, for then the very nature of the command would be destroyed. Thus all the blessed are impeccable and yet they retain their freedom concerning certain things, but for good and not for evil. Such was the case for Christ here below. But the saints no longer merit because they are no longer wayfarers.

SOLUTION OF OBJECTIONS

If we posit the certainty of command to die for us, we say that Christ, who was impeccable, did not obey freely. Therefore the thesis is false. I prove it.

First objection. Anyone freely wills anything when he is able not to will it. But, posited the certainty to die for us, Christ, who was impeccable, had to will to die for us. Therefore, posited the certainty to die for us, Christ, who was impeccable, did not obey freely.

Reply. I distinguish the major: that anyone freely wills anything when he is able at least in one aspect of the object not to will it, this I concede; that anyone must be able not to will anything in every aspect of the object, I deny. I contradistinguish the minor: Christ had to will death as commanded, I concede; death in itself, that I deny; for this the object was not universally good, and the fact that it was also commanded did not change the nature of this object, and, through taking away moral liberty by imposing this obligation, nevertheless the command left the will free.

I insist. But Christ, posited the certainty of the command, was incapable of not willing death in itself. Therefore the difficulty remains.

Proof. Christ, who was impeccable, could not disobey. But if, the certainty of the command to die being posited, He had not willed death in itself, then He would have disobeyed. Therefore, posited the certainty of this command, He had to will death in itself.

Reply. I distinguish the major: Christ, who was impeccable, had to obey in the privative sense, this I concede; in the negative sense, that I deny. I contradistinguish the minor. So that He would have disobeyed in the negative sense, this I concede; in the privative sense, that I deny.

Explanation. Inasmuch as Christ was indeed impeccable, He did not have the power to sin, not even by omission; but this freedom as regards specification of the object that is a contrary to either good or evil, is not required for free will. But He was capable of not obeying in the negative sense, because the supervening command, as stated, being quasi-extrinsic to the will, did not change the will psychologically and is given for the free fulfillment of the act. Not even Christ could sin *in sensu diviso* (as we can), but He was capable of not obeying in the negative sense.

Again I insist. But Christ was also incapable of disobeying in the negative sense, though this was not disobedience in the privative sense. Therefore the difficulty remains.

Proof. Not to obey in the negative sense is to separate the refusal to die from the command to die for us. But Christ, who was impeccable, could not separate the refusal to die from this command, or rid Himself of the command. Therefore Christ, who was impeccable, was incapable of not obeying in the negative sense, though this was not disobedience in the privative sense.

Reply. I distinguish the major. That not to obey in the negative sense is a positive separation, a quasi-separation of the refusal of death from the command to die, this I deny; that it is a precise separation of the refusal to die from the command to die, this I concede. I contradistinguish the minor in the same way.

I explain the distinction. In a true and good object, the intellect in attaining to truth does not separate it from the good, for there is only a distinction of reason between them, but it prescinds from the good; there is nothing more possible to prescind from than the formal object of a faculty. Likewise we cannot separate essence from existence, but we consider existence to be a contingent predicate of whatsoever creature, and that before the consideration of our mind, a creature is not its existence, and that its essence is really distinct from it. Therefore the notion of existence can be prescinded from that of essence without separating them.

Moreover, it sufficed for Christ's freedom that He could posit the refusal to die considered in itself, prescinding from the command, because the act was specified by an object that does not infallibly abstract the will, and the superadded command did not change the nature either of the specificative object or of the specified act; but the nominalists do not understand this, for they consider solely the concrete act but not its nature that is specified by the object. Moreover, it would follow from the denial of what has been said that the angels would not comply freely with God's commands; that the angel Gabriel did not come freely to the Blessed Virgin on the day of the Annunciation.

Hence Christ obeyed freely, not in this sense, that He could go against the command, but in this sense, that He had the power not to do what, because of another only, was commanded. Thus Christ freely obeyed the command to die for us by liberty of exercise.

Moreover, it must be noted that these objections presuppose the Molinist definition of psychological freedom; namely, a faculty that, presupposed all things required as prerequisite for acting, it can still act and not act.

The Thomists in their treatises on free choice[61] most wisely distinguish by saying that psychological freedom is a faculty that, presupposed what is required by a priority of time for acting, can still act or not act, even *in sensu composito;* but, presupposed all that is required only by a priority of nature, such as the divine efficacious motion and the ultimate practical judgment, it can still act or not act only *in sensu diviso,* that is, under the divine efficacious motion to act there remains only the power not to act.[62]

Finally, it must be noted that liberty of equilibrium is of rare occurrence, and it is not at all required for free will. Liberty of equilibrium is that which exists between two goods that are equally eligible, so that there is no reason why one is more to be preferred than the other. This is the very ideal of freedom, as when a workman constructs a wall of absolutely equal stones, he most freely takes one stone for the highest part of the wall and another for the lowest. Thus God could have chosen and predestined Judas in preference to Peter in accordance with His most free good pleasure.[63]

But generally freedom is found without this perfect equilibrium as to choice, as when a man chooses honest good in preference to delectable and dishonest good. Honest good is absolutely good and qualifiedly not good, and the converse is true for merely apparent good.

[61] Cf. Billuart, *Com. in Iam IIae,* q. 13.

[62] See *God, His Existence,* II, 296 f. The aforesaid Molinist definition does not sufficiently consider the object from which freedom receives its specification; but the faculty must be defined with reference to its specificative object; that is, freedom is the dominating indifference of judgment and will concerning an object that is not universally good. The determinate act also remains intrinsically free because of the object.

[63] *Summa theol.* Ia, q. 23, a. 5, ad 3.

Hence freedom is defined [64] as the dominating indifference of the will concerning an object that is not universally good. St. Thomas does not say, concerning an object that is equally good under one aspect and not good under another; even though the object may appear far more lovable than what is lacking in some good, as God not yet clearly seen, freedom remains intact.

Moreover, our mind does not pass from the speculative-practical judgment, namely, to see the better things and approve of them, to the practico-practical judgment, but I follow the worse, judging practically here and now that they must be chosen, unless our will already begins to be attracted actually by the object which *de facto* is chosen, and which thus appears to me here and now as absolutely good, although to be sure, if it concerns a sinful object, it is good only in a qualified sense.

Hence it is false to say that anyone is said freely to will anything for which the will already has an actual affection, when the will has the power not to will it even though this incipient actual affection of the will for this same object remains. This actual incipient affection must be repressed so that here and now this object be repudiated. Thus anger must be repressed for correct judgment.

The adulterer never gives up the sin of adultery unless the actual affection for it is given up and yet, though this affection for it remains, the sin is freely committed.

Similarly, in the present case, Christ refrained from obeying only when there was no command and yet, posited this command, He obeyed freely. Hence He freely willed death as commanded, although He was obliged to will it inasmuch as it was commanded, that is, although He could not commit sin. Thus He could obey in the negative sense, but not in the privative sense.

This distinction, however, is not understood by the nominalists because they consider only the fact, for example, either of obeying or of disobeying, and not the very nature of the fact, in our case the very nature of the free act that is specified by an object that is not in every respect good. There is a very great difference between their mental attitude concerning this problem and that of the truly speculative theologian. Their approach turns the mind away from the contemplation of divine things rather than disposing for it.

The distinction remains intact between disobeying in the privative

[64] *Ibid.*, Ia IIae, q. 10, a. 2.

sense and disobeying in the negative sense, which was explained analogically by examples taken from the lives of Abraham and the Blessed Virgin Mary.

Other objections concern the commandment of loving God, and other natural commandments of the Decalogue, especially negative commandments. In such cases the problem presents greater difficulty.

Objection. The blessed must love God clearly seen, even as regards the exercise of the act. But Christ already on earth enjoyed the beatific vision. Therefore He was not free concerning the command to love God.

The Thomists reply in two ways to this objection.

1) Capreolus, Francis Sylvester (Ferrariensis), Medina, and Soto say that the love of God in Christ, inasmuch as it was regulated by the beatific knowledge, was a necessary act, this I concede; that the love of God as regulated by the infused knowledge was a necessary act, this I deny. Thus there are two acts, or two kinds of love, which are specifically distinct, not substantially, but modally, on account of the twofold regulation, although they proceed from the same infused virtue of charity, concerning the same object, but taken in a different sense.

But this modal distinction suffices so that these two acts may be both present, one as a necessary act, the other as a free act.

Thus it is at least probable that Christ merited, not only by loving creatures for God's sake, but by loving God in Himself and for His own sake as known, not by the beatific vision, but by the infused knowledge.

However, even though this probable solution were not true, there would be this second solution, that must immediately be explained.

2) John of St. Thomas, who thinks both solutions are probable, and Alvarez and Gonet say that in the same act of love that is regulated by the beatific vision, there is a double termination: the first terminates in the divine goodness considered in itself, inasmuch as it is the reason for loving God and His necessary perfections; the second terminates in the divine goodness, inasmuch as it is the reason for loving creatures or the means not essentially and intrinsically necessary for the preservation of happiness.

Proof. Thus, according to the teaching of St. Thomas,[65] God's uncreated love is necessary as regards His own goodness, and free as

[65] *Ibid.*, Ia, q. 19, a. 3.

regards this same goodness, in that it is the reason for His loving creatures, inasmuch as "God's goodness, which is infinite in perfection, can exist without other things" [66] But this twofold termination is not incompatible with Christ's created love as regulated by the beatific vision; for even as regards this created love, creatures are not necessarily and intrinsically connected with the possession of God clearly seen. John of St. Thomas says: "It is befitting for the same act to be free and necessary, but from different points of view, as is evident in the act of beatific love, which, as it refers to God, is necessary, but as it refers to creatures is free." [67] Thus the saints in heaven, whereas they necessarily love God clearly seen, freely pray for this or that wayfarer, requesting for such a person this or that grace.

In fact, this free act that is regulated by the beatific vision could have been meritorious as long as Christ was both wayfarer and comprehensor; because the subject in question was still a wayfarer, this act was not only free, but meritorious.[68] This second solution appears to us to be more probable.

Therefore Christ's impeccability is compatible with His freedom even in things commanded. Therefore His freedom and His merit must not be restricted. It suffices to bear in mind: (1) that Christ's will is the most pure reflection of God's will that is both absolutely impeccable and absolutely free as regards creatures; (2) that, although the command takes away moral freedom, it does not take away psychological freedom concerning the means that are not necessarily, intrinsically, and evidently connected here and now with beatitude. In fact, every command presupposes this psychological freedom, inasmuch as it is directed for the free fulfillment of the act, and if it were to take away this freedom, then it would destroy its own nature as a command.

These two truths are most commonly accepted.

Thus the mystery indeed remains, but contradiction is avoided, and Christ is the most perfect model of free and meritorious obedi-

[66] *Ibid.,* c. et ad 2.

[67] *De incarnatione,* disp. 17, a. 3, no. 14.

[68] Other Thomists, who appeal to Christ's infused knowledge, nevertheless say that this act as regulated by the beatific vision belonged to Christ not as wayfarer, but as comprehensor. Thus this act, although it was free, was not meritorious, for merit requires not only freedom, but the state of the wayfarer. To this we can reply by saying that this act belonged, however, to Christ, who at this particular time was still a wayfarer.

ence to the divine commands. On the contrary, the other explanations unduly restrict Christ's freedom and merit to those things that are not commanded. Thus they do not solve the question of Christ's freedom and merit, but either take it away or avoid it.

Corollary. But if Christ's freedom remains notwithstanding that there are three causes for His impeccability, namely, the hypostatic union, the fullness of inamissible grace, and the beatific vision, and notwithstanding the fact that He always received efficacious grace which is intrinsically efficacious, a fortiori our freedom remains intact under the influence of intrinsically efficacious grace; but we have the power to sin, which Christ did not have. Under the influence of this grace the free will has the power to refuse its consent if it so wills, but under this influence it never wishes to refuse its consent.

Fifth Article

WHETHER THE WILL OF CHRIST WAS ALTOGETHER CONFORMED TO THE DIVINE WILL IN THE THINGS WILLED

State of the question. This doubt arises because we read in the Gospel that Christ as man somehow did not will His own death, yet He evidently willed it by His divine will. Hence the following words of Christ: "not as I will, but as Thou wilt," [69] must be reconciled with the above-expounded principles, namely, that Christ's charity was most perfect, the result of which is that His will was most perfectly in conformity with the divine will. Christ was also comprehensor, but comprehensors will only what God wills, otherwise they would not be blessed.

Reply. The rational will in Christ, considered after the manner of reason, as the absolute and efficacious will in that it was free, always was in conformity with the divine will, even in material things willed; it was not so, however, with either the sensual will, or the will considered after the manner of nature.

This is also the view of St. Augustine, who is quoted in the counterargument.

Proof of first part. Our Lord Himself says: "Not as I will, but as Thou wilt." [70] Christ, indeed, by His will as reason, because of His

[69] Matt. 26:39.
[70] *Ibid.*

supreme charity that was illumined by the beatific vision, deliberately, absolutely, and efficaciously willed the divine will to be fulfilled, that is, He willed to die a violent death for our salvation.

Proof of second part. St. Thomas says: "Now it was said above (q. 14, a. 1, ad 2) that by a certain dispensation, the Son of God before His passion allowed His flesh to do and suffer what belonged to it. . . . But it is plain that the will of sensuality, which is called will by participation, naturally shrinks from sensible pains and bodily hurt. In like manner the will as nature turns from those things that are against nature," [71] which at times are chosen for a higher end.

Reply to third objection. Christ was still a wayfarer and was passible in the flesh, although He was enjoying God in the mind.

Doubt. Can it be admitted that in Christ's will as reason, there were certain inefficacious and imperfect acts not in conformity with the divine will in material things willed, for example, concerning death on the cross, yet so that such an act was not a voluntary imperfection?

Reply. Several Thomists, such as Billuart, see no repugnance in this: that Christ could by His will as reason, shrink inefficaciously from death, not precisely as harmful to nature, but inasmuch as it presupposed several sins of the Jews, and others that united result therefrom. Thus from supreme charity He inefficaciously willed the salvation of all men; in fact, these acts can be declared also to be in conformity with the divine will, that is, to the inefficacious will.

Thus Christ's efficacious human will was always in conformity with the divine efficacious will, and Christ's inefficacious human will was always in conformity with the inefficacious divine will.

Sixth Article

WHETHER THERE WAS CONTRARIETY OF WILLS IN CHRIST

State of the question. The purpose of this article is to explain that diversity of wills, which was discussed in the preceding article, was not such as to induce real contrariety, either between the divine will and the human will, or between the human will and the sensitive appetite; because the diverse movements of these wills, although they are sometimes concerned about the same thing, yet they are considered under different aspects.

Reply. There was no contrariety of wills in Christ. It is of faith,

[71] Cf. IIIa, q. 18, a. 5, c.

having been decided in the Third Council of Constantinople, and quoted in the counterargument of the article, the council declaring: "We confess two natural wills, not in opposition . . . , but following His human will, and neither withstanding nor striving against but rather being subject to His divine and omnipotent will." [72]

Theological proof. Contrariety is opposition in the same subject and for the same reason. But this opposition was not in Christ, for the sensual will and the natural will shrank from death as harmful to nature, whereas the divine will and the rational will, in that it was free, willed death as good for the human race.

Moreover, Christ by His divine will and His rational will willed that both His sensual will and His natural will be moved according to the inclination of each, yet so that there be no deordination in them.

[72] Denz., no. 291.

CHAPTER XXI

QUESTION 19

Christ's Operation and His Merits

After considering the two wills in Christ, which are principles of action, the four articles of this question discuss His diverse operations.

1) Whether in Christ there is only one or several operations of the Godhead and manhood.

2) Whether in Christ there are several operations of the human nature.

3) Whether Christ by His human operation merited anything for Himself.

4) Whether He merited anything for us by it.

First Article

WHETHER IN CHRIST THERE IS ONLY ONE OPERATION OF THE GODHEAD AND MANHOOD

The principal conclusion of this article is that there are two operations in Christ, one of the human nature, the other of the divine nature. It is of faith, decided in the Third Council of Constantinople, against Monothelitism as quoted in the body of this article.[1]

Theological proof. It is evident, for operations follow forms, which are principles of action. But in Christ there are two principles of action, namely, two distinct natures and two wills. Therefore in Christ there are diverse operations.

Confirmation. The Scripture says that Christ was obedient and merited. But He could neither obey nor merit by the divine will. Therefore He obeyed and merited by the human will that was in

[1] Denz., nos. 290–92.

conformity with the divine will. Manifestly obedience and merit presuppose subordination of the lower will to the higher will.

Second conclusion. Nevertheless the divine nature operates by means of the human nature, using it as an instrument. Thus Christ as man in His ministry worked miracles, and the principal cause of these can be only God.[2]

Reply to fifth objection. It is pointed out that the two operations concurred even in these miracles; there was, for example, in the healing of the leper the proper operation of Christ's human nature, namely, contact with the body of the leper, and the divine operation, namely, the miraculous healing of the leper.

Corollary. We distinguish between three kinds of operations in Christ. Some are merely divine, such as creation and conservation. Some are merely human, namely, those which Christ performed by the power of His own human nature, such as eating, drinking, weeping, deliberating. Some are mixed, namely, those to which each nature contributes, the divine as the principal cause, the human as the instrumental cause, such as the raising of Lazarus, sight given to the man born blind, and others of this nature. The strictly miraculous operation, for example, the raising of the dead to life, is indeed one operation, which depends on God as the principal cause and on the human nature of Christ as the instrument in conjunction with it. But even in such a case there is at the same time the operation that belongs properly to the instrument, which does not exceed its own power, such as shouting, touching, speaking. This operation disposes for the effect of the principal agent, either producing its own disposition to be accomplished in the subject, as the pen contributes the ink, or acting only in a dispositive way, as the trumpet transmits the sound in a certain direction rather than in another.

What is the theandric or God-man operation?

St. Thomas explains this term in his reply to the first objection where he says: "Dionysius places in Christ a theandric, that is a God-manlike or divino-human operation not by any confusion of the operations or powers of both natures, but inasmuch as His divine operation employs the human, and his human operation shares in the power of the divine as when He healed the leper with a touch." Then there are two subordinated operations, namely, the touch that need not be miraculous, and the actual miraculous healing, which

[2] *Summa theol.*, IIIa, q. 19, a. 1, ad 1, ad 2.

proceeds from God as the principal cause and from Christ's human nature as the instrumental cause. Yet it must furthermore be remarked that the very action alone of Christ's human will is usually called in another sense theandric on account of the infinite value it derives from the divine suppositum that is the agent which operates. Thus it is said that Christ's meritorious and satisfactory acts were theandric in this sense, that they proceeded both from His human will and from His divine personality. And herein consists the essence of the very mystery of Redemption, in that the infinite value of these theandric acts of Christ, which are called theandric because of the suppositum or divine person of the Word incarnate, who operates through Christ's most holy soul.

Second Article

WHETHER IN CHRIST THERE ARE SEVERAL HUMAN OPERATIONS

Reply. St. Thomas says: "Much more than in any other man whatsoever, there is one operation in Christ." The sense is that according to the human nature there is in Christ one principle of free operation, to which every action of Christ as man was attributed as to the subject and was subordinated. For "there was in Him no motion of the sensitive part which was not ordered by reason. Even the natural and bodily operations pertained in some respects to His will, inasmuch as it was His will that His flesh should do and suffer what belonged to it, as stated above," [3] but without any deordination.

Third Article

WHETHER THE HUMAN ACTION OF CHRIST COULD BE MERITORIOUS TO HIM

State of the question. St. Thomas presupposes that Christ could have merited,[4] and in the present article he teaches what He merited for Himself, and in the subsequent article what He merited for us.

Reply. The Council of Trent in its sixth session, the seventh chapter, defined it to be of faith that Christ truly and properly merited, and in the tenth canon of this session expressly stated that Christ was the meritorious cause of our justification.[5]

[3] *Ibid.*, q. 17, a. 5.

[4] For He was full of grace and charity, free and a wayfarer.

[5] Denz., nos. 799, 820.

Scriptural proof. The New Testament establishes clearly the fact that Christ merited something for Himself. St. Paul says that Christ's exaltation is the reward of His humility and obedience, as in the following text: "He humbled Himself, becoming obedient unto death . . . for which cause God also hath exalted Him." [6] Therefore He merited His exaltation by obeying, and so He merited something for Himself. Similarly St. Paul says: "We see Jesus . . . , for the suffering of death, crowned with glory and honor." [7] The Evangelist quotes Jesus as saying: "Ought not Christ to have suffered these things and so to enter into His glory?" [8] namely, glory of the body. At the Last Supper Jesus said: "I have finished the work . . . and now glorify Me, O Father." [9] From these texts it is evident that Christ merited for Himself glory of the body, exaltation of His name, His ascension, and the adoration of the faithful.

Theological proof. It is nobler to merit anything than not to merit it, when there is parity in other respects, namely, when it does not detract from the greater dignity of another. But Christ could merit glory of the body, and other extrinsic good things, for He did not have these from the beginning, and these do not seem at all to have detracted from His greater dignity.

Therefore Christ merited for Himself this glory of His body and other extrinsic good things. Calvin unwarrantedly denied this merit to Christ, so that he might praise more His love for us, as if Christ willed to merit only for us.

Contrary to this, Christ did not merit for Himself either grace, or knowledge, or beatitude of soul, or the divine nature, because, since merit regards only what is not yet possessed, it would be necessary that Christ should have been without these at some time; and to be without them would have diminished Christ's dignity more than His merit would have increased it.[10] Moreover, the principle of merit, namely, habitual grace, does not come under merit.[11] Consequently Christ did not merit for Himself the infused virtues and the seven gifts of the Holy Ghost, for these are quasi-properties of habitual grace.

[6] Phil. 2:8 f.
[7] Heb. 2:9.
[8] Luke 24:26.
[9] John 17:4 f.
[10] *Summa theol.,* IIIa, q. 19, a. 3, c.
[11] *Ibid.,* Ia IIae, q. 114, a. 5.

For the same reason Christ did not merit His incarnation, for this was in Him the principle of merit; for merit presupposes a constituted person who produces the meritorious act.

The principal conclusion of this article becomes more evident when we consider that the six conditions required for merit, as explained in the treatise on grace, were verified in Christ: (1) the acts of His will were free; (2) they were good on the part of the object and the circumstances; (3) they were the acts of a person who is just and pleasing to God; (4) they were ordered by the virtue of charity for the glory of God; (5) they were the acts of a wayfarer, for Christ was both wayfarer and comprehensor; (6) it was in accordance with the divine plan that they should be rewarded.

Objection. Christ was indeed a wayfarer as regards His passible and mortal body, but not as regards His soul that enjoyed the beatific vision; but it is the soul that must merit, not the body.

Reply. I distinguish the antecedent. That Christ was not a wayfarer as regards His soul considered in itself and as directed to God clearly seen, this I concede; considered as the form of the body, this I deny.

It suffices that the subject be still a wayfarer so that his acts, even those more sublime, be free and meritorious. Thus all Thomists maintain that Christ's acts of charity, which were regulated by His infused knowledge, were both free and meritorious, although the infused knowledge did not belong to the soul inasmuch as it is the form of the body. For the same reason it seems correct to say that Christ's acts of charity for the salvation of mankind, even as regulated by the beatific knowledge, were not only free but also meritorious, as stated above.[12]

Reply to first objection. Christ merited as a wayfarer and therefore by charity not inasmuch as it was the charity of the comprehensor, but of the wayfarer.

Here it must be noted that Christ's merit could not be regulated by faith, which He did not have, but it was regulated either by the beatific knowledge or the infused knowledge, this latter presupposing the beatific knowledge and following from it as a property.

Thus the truth is established that Christ could not merit for Himself essential glory, or the beatific vision, which was in Him the principle of His merits; but the principle of merit does not come under merit.

Corollary. Christ obtained the glory of the body on two grounds,

[12] See introduction to q. 18, a. 5, *supra*.

namely, that it was connatural to Him, and so it was already due to Him, as being a redundance of glory from the soul; it was also due to Him on the grounds of merit. Thus the king's son can possess the kingdom on two grounds, namely, of inheritance and of merit.[13]

SOLUTION OF OBJECTIONS

First objection. If Christ had merited anything for Himself, He would have died for Himself, which is condemned by the Council of Ephesus.[14]

Reply. The council condemned the proposition that Christ suffered for His own sins. It would be false to say that the primary purpose of Christ's sufferings was for Himself, for He came down from heaven for us men and for our salvation. Yet He could as a consequence of this and in a secondary sense merit something for Himself, and also for the angels, since He merited accidental graces for them, that they may be His servants in the kingdom of God.

Second objection. On the contrary, it is more perfect to merit glory of soul than not to merit it. But we must attribute to Christ what is more perfect. Therefore He merited glory of soul.

Reply. I distinguish the major: it is more perfect when glory is the terminus of merit, this I concede; but if glory is the principle of merit in anyone, then I deny it. In Christ, however, glory of soul is the principle of merit, for in Him the regulating principle of the meritorious act was not faith, but the beatific vision or infused knowledge which followed from the beatific vision as a property.

But I insist. There is no repugnance in the notion that Christ's merit be regulated by His infused knowledge and that He merited His beatific knowledge.

Reply. The notion is repugnant because Christ's infused knowledge was a quasi-property following from the beatific vision, just as habitual grace in some way followed from the grace of union; for infused grace was given to Christ on this earth as a consequence of the mystery of the Incarnation, for the perfection of the human nature assumed by the Word, and Christ enjoyed the beatific vision prior to this consequence of the grace of union. Thus we shall see farther on [15] that Christ was predestined first to be the natural Son of God, then to

[13] See St. Thomas, his *com. on Ep. to Heb.,* chap. 1.

[14] Denz., no. 122, can. 10.

[15] Cf. *Summa theol.,* IIIa, q. 24.

glory, namely, to the beatific vision which He at once received as a consequence of the grace of union, and then to the graces of His life as a wayfarer.

Fourth Article

WHETHER CHRIST COULD MERIT FOR OTHERS

State of the question. The article concerns condign merit. The difficulty is that other persons who are in the state of grace cannot merit condignly, but only congruously, grace for another, as shown in the treatise on grace.[16] Moreover, if Christ as the God-man and the head of the Church condignly merited salvation for all, then, as stated in the third objection to this article, Christ would be unjust not to save all, and thus all would be entitled to grace, and all would have to be saved.

The common statement, indeed, is that "Christ's passion is of infinite value as regards its sufficiency for the salvation of all mankind, but it is efficacious only for those to whom it is applied." [17] This must be carefully examined.

Reply. Christ's merit extends to others inasmuch as they are His members, says St. Thomas; and this refers to condign merit.

1) **Scriptural proof.** St. Paul says: "As by the offense of one, unto all men to condemnation, so also by the justice of one unto all men to justification of life," [18] which means: just as others became partakers of Adam's transgression, so much more did they become partakers of Christ's merit. Thus he also says: "Blessed be the God and the Father of our Lord Jesus Christ, who hath blessed us with spiritual blessings in heavenly places, in Christ." [19] So also Christ Himself said: "Without Me you can do nothing." [20] And the Evangelist says: "And of His fullness we have all received, and grace for grace." [21]

2) **The councils** of the Church affirmed this truth on several occasions. The Council of Milevum [22] against the Pelagians, and the Second Council of Orange [23] against the Semi-Pelagians equivalently

[16] *Ibid.*, Ia IIae, q. 114, a. 6.
[17] *Tabula aurea*, nos. 106, 115.
[18] Rom. 5:18.
[19] Eph. 1:3.
[20] John 15:5.
[21] *Ibid.*, 1:16.
[22] Denz., nos. 103 f.
[23] *Ibid.*, no. 197.

affirmed this truth under the metaphor of the vine and the branches. The truth is expressly declared in the Council of Trent, in which, discussing the causes of justification, it says: "The final cause indeed is the glory of God and of Jesus Christ, and life everlasting; while the efficient cause is a merciful God who washes . . . , but the meritorious cause is His most beloved only-begotten, our Lord Jesus Christ, who when we were enemies [24] for the exceeding charity wherewith He loved us,[25] merited justification for us by His most holy passion on the wood of the cross, and made satisfaction for us unto God the Father." [26] The Council says the same in the corresponding canon on justification.[27] In the strict sense, Christ as man is called the Savior, inasmuch as He merited our salvation.

Likewise the Church in all orations earnestly entreats graces of salvation, invoking the merits of Christ, when it says: Through our Lord Jesus Christ.

Theological proof. Merit is co-extensive with the divine plan and grace. But according to the divine plan, grace was in Christ not only as in an individual, but as in the head of the whole Church, to whom all are united as members to the head, who constitute one mystical person. Therefore Christ's merit extends to others as to His members. Thus this revealed proposition is explained by something previously and equally revealed.

Thus, analogically, in our organism the head and the members harmoniously combine in the processes of sense perception. The solution of the objections confirms this.

Reply to first objection. "Just as the sin of Adam, who was appointed by God to be the principle of the whole nature, is transmitted to others by carnal propagation, so, too, the merit of Christ . . . extends to all His members."

Reply to second objection. Other men have only a particular grace and so they cannot merit for another condignly.

Reply to third objection. Grace that is granted to us by baptism and any other way, although it is owing to Christ's merits, yet it is gratuitous with reference to us.

Moreover, Christ's merits, the validity of which is sufficient for the

[24] Rom. 5:10.
[25] Eph. 2:4.
[26] Denz., no. 799.
[27] *Ibid.*, no. 820.

salvation of all men, are efficacious for the salvation of those to whom they are applied and until the end of their lives; but several put an obstacle in the way.

This question receives but a brief comment here by St. Thomas because he discusses it farther on in this treatise, inquiring whether Christ's predestination is the cause of ours.

He answers that it is, and in this sense: "For God, by predestinating from eternity, so decreed our salvation that it should be achieved through Jesus Christ." [28]

With reference to Christ's merits several doubts demand an explanation.

First doubt. Did Christ merit all the effects in the predestination of the elect, namely, their calling, justification, and glorification?

Reply. The common teaching of the Thomists is that Christ did not merit our predestination on the part of God who predestines.[29] But He condignly merited all the effects of our predestination. And this is true only of Christ, not of the Blessed Virgin, who, nevertheless, congruously merited these effects.

Thus St. Paul says: "Blessed be the God and Father of our Lord Jesus Christ, who hath blessed us with spiritual blessings in heavenly places, in Christ," [30] which means through Christ or through Christ's merits; but the highest benediction given to man is his predestination. The Apostle also says: "God hath predestinated us unto the adoption of children through Jesus Christ." [31] This text also concerns predestination in the comparative sense, namely, of these in particular in preference to others in accordance with the Gospel text: "I have called you friends. . . . You have not chosen Me, but I have chosen you." [32] Thus St. Thomas, following St. Augustine, says: "It follows

[28] *Summa theol.,* IIIa, q. 24, a. 4.

[29] This means that Christ did not merit the uncreated act by which God predestined us, but He merited whatever was willed by this divine act, that is, He merited our predestination not on the part of God willing, but on the part of the object willed and eternally willed. Hence St. Thomas says: "God wills this to be as means to that; but He does not will this on account of that" (Ia, q. 19, a. 5, the end). For example, God wills the effects of our predestination to be on account of Christ's merits, but He does not will this, namely, the act of God willing our predestination. The fundamental reason is, as stated in Ia, q. 19, a. 5, that there is only one act of will in God, for which no cause can be assigned in the created order.

[30] Eph. 1:3.

[31] *Ibid.,* 1:4.

[32] John 15:15 f.

from this that our predestination is gratuitous as regards ourselves, but not as regards Christ." [33]

Nevertheless the truth remains that the predestination of these in preference to others depends on God's good pleasure; for Christ neither chose these and those in preference to others, nor petitioned and merited that they be chosen, unless He had been directed and moved to do so by the will of His Father. Hence Christ Himself says: "Thine they were, and to Me Thou hast given them"; [34] that is, "Thou hast given them to Me, moving My will by the offering of My merits to have these chosen in preference to others, and Thou hast given to Me in time those whom Thou hadst chosen from eternity in view of My merits." [35] St. Thomas, too, inquiring whether Christ's prayer was always heard, says that it certainly was when it was the result of His consequent will.[36]

Second doubt. Whether Christ's merits were predestined before God's consequent will of efficaciously saving these in preference to others for example, Peter in preference to Judas.

Reply. The answer is in the affirmative. Christ's merits were predestined or efficaciously willed by God, if not before His antecedent will of saving all men, at least before His consequent will of saving some and certain persons in preference to others, that is, before He chose and predestined the elect. Thus our predestination and salvation is the means ordained for the glory of Christ, the first predestined, which is the common teaching of the Thomists in their discussions on the motive of the Incarnation. Thus Christ evidently was predestined before Peter and Paul, for the latter apostle says: "He predestinated us to be made conformable to the image of His Son, that He might be the first-born among many brethren. And whom He predestinated, them He also called; and whom He called, them He also justified. And whom He justified, them He also glorified." [37]

Third doubt. Whether Christ merited eternal life for all men.

Reply. Yes, He did; but He merited only for the elect the attainment

[33] *Com. ad Eph.,* I, lect. 1. See also St. Thomas' *com. in Joan.,* 17:24; also Salmanticenses, *De incarnatione,* disp. 28, dub. 8, nos. 93, 98, 99, 102; dub. 9, no. 107, especially no. 109. Also John of St. Thomas, *Com. in Iam,* q. 23, a. 5.

[34] John 17:6.

[35] Such is the common teaching of the Thomists either in their commentaries on our predestination (cf. *in Iam,* q. 23, a. 5) or concerning Christ's predestination as the cause of ours (cf. *in IIIam,* q. 24, a. 4).

[36] Cf. IIIa, q. 21, a. 4; also ad 2.

[37] Rom. 8:29.

of eternal life.[38] Thus the just person who is not predestined while remaining just, by means of good works merits eternal life, but eventually these merits are lost and with them the attainment of eternal life. The Council of Trent declares: "If anyone shall say that the good works of one that is justified . . . do not truly merit increase of grace, eternal life, and the attainment of that eternal life, if so be, however, that he depart in grace and also an increase of glory, let him be anathema." [39] Christ indeed did not lose His merits, but He knew that God permitted the sin of those not predestined and He consented to this divine permission for a greater good, namely, the manifestation of God's attributes. He most deeply grieved at the loss of these souls, but already on this earth He most clearly saw the higher good for which God permits sins, even the sin of final impenitence, namely, to manifest the splendor of divine justice above diabolical and human malice.

Fourth doubt. How did Christ merit efficacious graces which *de facto* are not granted, such as would be the grace of a good death for Judas?

The Thomists answer that Christ merited these graces as offered to men in sufficient grace that is given, but not as here and now conferred or to be conferred. For God offers efficacious grace to us as contained in the sufficient grace, as the fruit is contained in the flower; but if the sufficient grace is refused, the efficacious grace is not conferred. So say Lemos, O.P.,[40] John of St. Thomas,[41] and the Salmanticenses.[42] The same distinction must be made concerning Christ's prayer, whether it was always heard. On this subject St. Thomas says: "Our Lord did not pray for all those who crucified Him, for all those who would believe in Him, but for those only who were predestinated to obtain eternal life through Him." [43]

First corollary. Christ merited for the redemption of man all actual graces that dispose one for justification, such as the grace itself of justification, infused virtues, gifts, actual graces, and glory itself, that

[38] Cf. IIIa, q. 21, a. 4, ad 2; q. 48, a. 1; q. 62, a. 5; *De veritate,* q. 29, a. 7, ad 8 et 13; also *Com. in Joan.,* 17:24.

[39] Denz., no. 842, also nos. 803, 809 f.

[40] *Panoplia gratiae,* Vol. II, tr. 5, c. 20, no. 215.

[41] *Com. in Iam,* q. 23, a. 5 (end).

[42] *Com. in IIIam,* disp. 28, dub. 9, no. 109; dub. 8, nos. 93, 102.

[43] *Summa theol.,* IIIa, q. 21, a. 4, ad 2. See also Billuart's *De incarnatione,* disp. 22, a. 2.

is, all the effects of predestination. Thus He could say: "Without Me you can do nothing" [44] that concerns salvation.

The reason is that Christ merited for us all graces necessary for salvation; for St. Paul says: "Where sin abounded grace did more abound," [45] and this properly belongs to the role of the perfect Savior and Redeemer as Christ was. As St. Luke says: "Neither is there salvation in any other." [46]

First objection. Grace and justification are absolutely gratuitous. Therefore they are not on account of merits.

Reply. That they are gratuitous on our part, I concede; on Christ's part, I deny.

Second objection. Merit must precede the reward, since it is the cause of the reward. But Christ did not precede the fathers of the Old Testament. Therefore He did not merit grace for them.

Reply. That merit must precede reward as foreknown by the person rewarding, I concede; that it must actually, I deny. Since merit is only a moral cause, that it is foreknown by God is sufficient, for a moral cause moves inasmuch as it is known as the regulation of the superior advising something to be done, and it can be known by God from all eternity as destined to exist in some future time.

Second corollary. Christ did not merit essential grace and glory for the angels, but only accidental graces by which they are His ministers.[47]

Third corollary. Christ did not merit the grace that our first parents had in the state of innocence,[48] because He was not their head for that state. But He merited all the effects of predestination for Adam converted after the sin or as redeemed.

OTHER SPECIAL DOUBTS

First doubt. Did Christ merit from the moment of His conception until the end of His life?

Reply. It is generally affirmed with St. Thomas [49] that He did.

This answer has its foundation in the following scriptural text:

[44] John 15:5.
[45] Rom. 5:20.
[46] Acts 4:12.
[47] Cf. IIIa, q. 8, a. 4.
[48] *Ibid.*
[49] *Ibid.*, q. 34, a. 3.

"Coming into the world, Christ says: Sacrifice and oblation Thou wouldest not, but a body Thou hast fitted to Me. . . . Then I said: Behold I come; in the head of the book it is written of Me, that I should do Thy will, O God." [50]

"Coming into the world" means from the moment of His conception, for afterward He had already come. But this oblation by which Christ offered Himself as victim was meritorious at this moment, for it had everything required for merit.

Theological proof. It explains this merit, for, although Christ did not have as yet acquired knowledge, He already had from the moment of His conception until the end of His life infused knowledge, which He could use independently of reverting to phantasms. Thus He could from the first moment of His life to the end uninterruptedly elicit meritorious acts. Thus certain saints had infused knowledge on various occasions so that they were able sometimes to merit even during sleep, and several theologians say that the Blessed Virgin Mary probably enjoyed this privilege.

Thus the very moment Christ's soul was created, He already began to merit; and so His soul as regards merit had priority of nature, but not of time. Thus Christ merited neither the Incarnation nor fullness of grace and glory, but other things He merited for Himself and for us.

Objection. If Christ had merited from the moment of His conception, already this merit would have been of infinite value. Therefore He could not have merited anything afterward.

Reply. If this argument proved anything, it would prove that Christ could merit only at the last moment of His life. As a matter of fact, however, it does not prove this. This first merit of Christ was, indeed, of infinite value, but not separated from the other merits ordained and accepted for a reward. In fact, already from the beginning Christ offered His whole life until His death.

Second doubt. Did Christ merit actually the moment of His death in fact?

Reply. St. Thomas denies this, saying: "Christ's death in the becoming was the cause of our salvation, considered as His passion, that is, by way of merit; but Christ's death in fact cannot be the cause of our salvation, by way of merit, but only by way of causality." [51] The

[50] Heb. 10:5.

[51] *Summa theol.,* IIIa, q. 50, a. 6. It is said to be by way of causality, as pointed

reason is that a wayfarer can merit, and the first moment of ceasing to be a wayfarer is the first moment of separation of the soul from the body, and already at this moment there is no longer a wayfarer, but a separated soul. Christ did not give any indication that He was exempt from this law, for He said: "I must work the works of Him that sent Me, whilst it is day; the night cometh when no man can work." [52] The Fathers of the Church understand by "day" the time of this life, and by "night" the moment of death.

Third doubt. Were all the free acts of Christ's human will meritorious?

Reply. The answer is that they were.[53] The reason is that, freedom in Christ's human actions as long as He was a wayfarer being presupposed, there was nothing that prevented them from being meritorious, as stated above.[54] They were the actions of a wayfarer, in every respect good, in fact theandric, and were ordained by Christ's charity to God's glory and were ordained by God to a reward.

First corollary. Christ merited by an act of love for God inasmuch as it was regulated by infused knowledge, for thus this act was the free act of a wayfarer. Even the act of love for God, inasmuch as it is the reason for loving creatures, was a free act in that it was regulated by the beatific vision; yet certain Thomists say that this act so regulated belonged to Christ as comprehensor but not as wayfarer, and so they said it was not meritorious.[55] That Christ merited by a free act of love for God, inasmuch as it is the reason for loving creatures is indicated by our Lord in these words: "That the world may know that I love the Father, and as the Father hath given Me commandment, so do I. Arise, let us go hence." [56]

Second corollary. Christ, while still a wayfarer, merited by all acts

---

out here: "inasmuch as the Godhead was not separated from Christ's flesh by death; and therefore, whatever befell Christ's flesh, even when the soul was separated from the body, was conducive to salvation in virtue of the Godhead united to it."

[52] John 9:4.

[53] See St. Thomas' *Com. in III Sent.,* d. 18, a. 5.

[54] Cf. IIIa, q. 19, a. 4.

[55] This reason is not cogent, because for a meritorious act it suffices that the subject of this free act be still a wayfarer. But Christ was still a wayfarer in that His soul was still the form of His passible body; but neither did infused knowledge belong to His soul inasmuch as it was the form of His passible body. Therefore, if He could merit by a free act regulated by infused knowledge, so also He could merit by a free act regulated by the beatific vision.

[56] John 14:31.

elicited or commanded by charity, and by all acts of all virtues, for in these acts He was free.

Third corollary. Christ merited by all acts, even of His sensitive and vegetative faculties, inasmuch as these were under the dominion of His will. Thus He merited not only by acts of seeing, hearing, walking, groaning, and crying, but also by the beating of the heart, in His sleep, and when He was thirsty.[57] They note that, although these actions, especially those that pertain to the vegetative life, are not in themselves formally free, they were nevertheless subjected to Christ's will, because of the control He exercised over His body and His faculties. Hence, inasmuch as they were permitted for good ends, there was a certain moral goodness in these actions. Thus he was able not to suffer and not to die under the blows inflicted upon Him, because He could have miraculously prevented the suffering, as He did for divers martyrs; but, on the contrary, He freely and fully delivered Himself up to suffering.[58]

[57] On this subject cf. Billuart and other commentators of St. Thomas.

[58] *Summa theol.,* IIIa, q. 47, a. 1. St. Thomas says in this passage: "Christ could have prevented His passion and death. First, by holding His enemies in check, so that they would not have been eager to slay Him, or would have been powerless to do so. Secondly, because His spirit had the power of preserving His fleshly nature from the infliction of any injury, and Christ's soul had this power, because it was united in unity of person with the divine Word, as Augustine says (*De Trin.,* IV, chap. 13). Therefore, since Christ's soul did not repel the injury inflicted on His body, but willed His corporeal nature to succumb to such injury, He is said to have laid down His life, or to have died voluntarily." See also ad 1, 2, 3. Concerning the absolutely infinite value of Christ's merits, see q. 48.

CHAPTER XXII

CHRIST'S RELATION TO THE FATHER

Question 20

CHRIST'S SUBJECTION TO THE FATHER

First Article

WHETHER CHRIST IS SUBJECT TO THE FATHER

IT seems that Christ is not, because He is not a creature and because He is called Lord. But on the other hand, it is said that "He took the form of a servant,"[1] and "was obedient even to the death of the cross."[2] How shall we reconcile these seemingly apparent contradictions?

Reply. Christ as man is truly subject to the Father, and this for three reasons: (1) because His human nature only participates in the divine goodness; (2) because it is subject to the divine power; (3) because Christ's human will must obey the divine commands. Hence it must be said that Christ is subject to the Father by reason of His human nature.

Reply to first objection. Nevertheless, on account of the uncreated person of the Word, it cannot be said that Christ is a creature, although He has a created nature.

Likewise, because Christ is a person, He is called Lord; in fact, Christ as man on account of the hypostatic union is King of kings, Lord of lords.[3]

[1] Phil. 2:7.
[2] *Ibid.*, 2:8.
[3] See Billuart's *De incarnatione, Com. in q.* 20.

Second Article

WHETHER IT CAN BE SAID THAT CHRIST IS SUBJECT TO HIMSELF

Reply. This can be said of Christ, because of the diversity of natures in the same person. But this diversity must not be understood in the sense that there are two persons in Christ, one of which would be subject to the other, for this would be the heresy of Nestorius.

CHAPTER XXIII

QUESTION 21

CHRIST'S PRAYER

First Article

WHETHER IT IS BECOMING FOR CHRIST TO PRAY

Reply. The Gospel records that Christ prayed, and to pray befitted Him as man, because His human will was incapable of doing all things, and Christ knew that it was in accordance with His Father's divine plan that He should receive certain things only by prayer. He also prayed so that He might give us an example of having recourse to God.

Doubt. Does Christ now in heaven truly and in the strict sense pray for us. Medina, Vasquez, and certain others, such as Father de la Taille, say that Christ now in heaven prays for us only in the broad sense of the term, showing His human nature and His past merits to the Father.

The Thomists and many other theologians reply that Christ in heaven in the strict sense prays for us, interceding as our advocate so that at the favorable moment the fruits of His past merits and satisfaction may be applied to us.

Scriptural proof. St. Paul says: "Christ . . . who is at the right hand of God, who also maketh intercession for us." [1] Again he says of Christ: "Always living to make intercession for us." [2] This prayer of Christ in heaven has its own particular name, being called "intercession." Elsewhere it is said of Christ now in heaven that He is "our advocate," and that "we have an advocate with the Father." [3]

[1] Rom. 8:34.
[2] Heb. 7:25.
[3] I John 2:1.

Thus St. Ambrose, St. Augustine, St. Gregory the Great, and St. Thomas say that Christ also now in heaven prays for the Church. He can no more, indeed, either merit or satisfy for us, because He is no longer a wayfarer. But He can offer intercessory prayer for us; the saints pray for us in heaven, and the greater their charity is, the greater is their influence.[4]

But if in the litanies of the Blessed Virgin Mary we do not say "Christ, pray for us," but "Christ, hear us," this is because Christ, as God, hears our prayers, and we also say "Christ, hear us" to avoid the error of Nestorianism. Finally, it is a more perfect act to hear a prayer than to pray.[5]

Second Article

WHETHER IT PERTAINS TO CHRIST TO PRAY ACCORDING TO HIS SENSUALITY

In other words, what did Christ mean when He said in the Garden of Gethsemane: "Let this chalice pass from Me"? [6]

Reply. It means that then His prayer expressed to God the affection of His sensible nature, and in this His prayer was for our instruction in three things: (1) to show that He assumed a truly human nature with all its natural affections: (2) to show that we are permitted in accordance with our natural affection to request something conditionally from God; (3) to show that a man ought to subject his own affections to the divine will. Hence He said: "Nevertheless, not as I will, but as Thou wilt." [7]

Third Article

WHETHER CHRIST PRAYED FOR HIMSELF

Reply. Christ prayed for Himself in two ways: (1) by expressing to God the desire of His sensual nature and of His will, considered as a nature, as when He said: "Let this chalice pass from Me"; [8] (2) by expressing the desire of His deliberate will, which is regarded

[4] Cf. IIa IIae, q. 83, a. 11.

[5] Concerning this doubt, cf. St. Thomas, *Com. in Ep. ad Rom.* 8:34; also *ad Heb.*, and the Salmanticenses in their commentaries.

[6] Matt. 26:39.

[7] *Ibid.*

[8] *Ibid.*

as reason, as when He asked for the glory of His resurrection, saying: "Father . . . glorify Thy Son." [9] Thus He showed us that the Father is the author of all the good that He possesses in the human nature.

Fourth Article

WHETHER CHRIST'S PRAYER WAS ALWAYS HEARD

Reply. A distinction must be made: Christ's prayer in the strict sense, namely, that which proceeded from His absolute will as the result of deliberate reason, was always heard, because His will was always in conformity with the divine will, so that by this prayer He willed or sought only what He knew God wills. The words that Martha addressed to our Lord are to be understood in this sense when she said: "I know that whatsoever Thou wilt ask of God, God will give it Thee." [10] Also, when our Lord says: "And I knew that Thou hearest Me always." [11] And St. Paul says of Christ: "He was heard for His reverence." [12]

Christ's conditional prayer expressing the desire of His sensitive nature or of His will considered as nature, was not always heard, which is evident from His prayer in the Garden.

Second objection. Christ prayed that the sin of those who crucified Him might be forgiven.[13] Yet not all were pardoned this sin, since the Jews were punished on account thereof.

Reply to second objection. St. Thomas says: "Our Lord did not pray for all those who crucified Him, nor for all those who would believe in Him, but for those only who were predestinated to obtain eternal life through Him." [14]

[9] *John* 17:1.

[10] *Ibid.*, 11:24.

[11] *Ibid.*, 11:42

[12] Heb. 5:7.

[13] Luke 23:34.

[14] Certain professors of the Duacene theological faculty reviled this reply of St. Thomas as Jansenistic in their censure of August 22, 1722, which censure was condemned by Rome on June 18, 1726. These professors did not understand that St. Thomas in this reply to the second objection has in mind only efficacious prayer that is the result of what is simply willed; he is not speaking of conditional prayer that is in conformity with God's conditional will to save all.

CHAPTER XXIV

QUESTION 22

THE PRIESTHOOD OF CHRIST [1]

FIRST ARTICLE

WHETHER IT IS FITTING THAT CHRIST SHOULD BE A PRIEST

State of the question. It seems that it is not fitting: (1) because a priest is less than an angel; (2) because Christ was not descended from the priests of the Old Law, but from the tribe of Juda; (3) because Christ is a legislator and in the Old Testament, which is a figure of the New Testament, legislator and priest are distinct.

Reply. Nevertheless the affirmative answer is of faith, for St. Paul says: "Having, therefore, a great high priest that hath passed into the heavens, Jesus the Son of God." [2] The councils of Ephesus [3] and Trent [4] and the encyclical of Pius XI [5] concerning Christ's kingship, confirm this truth.

Theological proof. The office proper to a priest is to be a mediator between God and the people, inasmuch as He bestows sacred things on the people, and offers to God the prayers of the people and sacrifice for them. But this is most befitting to Christ, for St. Peter says: "He hath given us most great and precious promises, that by these you may be made partakers of the divine nature." [6]

[1] See St. Paul's *Epistle to the Hebrews,* chaps. 1, 2, 4, 7, 9, in which he states that Christ as priest is more excellent than the angels, Moses, and the priests of the Old Testament. Also Garrigou-Lagrange, *Le Sauveur,* pp. 282–93; J. M. Vosté, *Studia paulina,* sec. 6: also for Christ the priest, see St. Paul's *Epistle to the Hebrews,* chaps. 5–8, for Christ the victim.

[2] Heb. 4:14.

[3] Denz., nos. 122 f.

[4] *Ibid.,* nos. 938 f.

[5] *Ibid.,* no. 2195.

[6] II Pet. 1:4.

And St. Paul says: "In Him [Christ] it hath well pleased the Father that all fullness should dwell. And through Him to reconcile all things." [7] From these texts it is evident that Christ as man is a priest.

Reply to first objection. Christ the priest, as regards the passibility of His flesh, is inferior to the angels, but also as man He is superior to them because of the hypostatic union and His fullness of grace and glory.

Reply to second objection. Christ did not wish to be born of the stock of the figural priests, that He might make it clear that the true priesthood is not quite the same as the figural priesthood.

Reply to third objection. Christ, inasmuch as He is the head of all men, has the perfection of all graces and so He is eminently and formally legislator, priest, and king, as announced by the prophet.[8]

Second Article

WHETHER CHRIST WAS HIMSELF BOTH PRIEST AND VICTIM

State of the question. It seems that He was not: (1) because it is the duty of the priest to kill the victim or offer it in sacrifice, and Christ did not kill Himself; (2) because in the Old Testament, which is a figure of the New Testament, a man was never offered in sacrifice; (3) because every victim that is offered to God is consecrated to Him, but Christ's humanity from the beginning was consecrated to God.

Reply. Yet the answer is that Christ was both priest and victim. It is also of faith, for St. Paul says: "Christ also hath loved us, and hath delivered Himself for us, an oblation and a sacrifice to God for an odor of sweetness." [9] It was also defined by the Council of Trent in its canons concerning the institution of the Sacrifice of the Mass and the priesthood of the New Law established by Christ.[10]

Theological proof. St. Thomas shows that Christ was not only a victim, but a most perfect victim.

A man is in need of sacrifice for three reasons: first, for the remission of sins, for which the victim for sin was offered in the Old Testament; secondly, that man may be preserved in the state of grace, for which the sacrifice of peace-offering was offered under the Old

[7] Col. 1:19 f.
[8] Isa. 33:22.
[9] Eph. 5:2.
[10] Denz., nos. 938–40.

Law; thirdly, that the spirit of man be perfectly united to God, which will be most perfectly realized in glory. Hence in the Old Law the holocaust was offered as symbolizing the state of the perfect, in which the victim was entirely burnt in God's honor. But Christ was a most perfect victim, being at the same time victim for sin, victim for a peace-offering, and a holocaust, as clearly established from the scriptural texts quoted in the argumentative part of this article.

Reply to first objection. Christ did not kill Himself, but He willingly exposed Himself to death, willingly offered Himself, inasmuch as He willingly endured the blows of those killing Him, whom He could easily have repelled, as shown in the Garden of Gethsemane, when He answered those that came to apprehend Him with such authority that they fell to the ground. Hence He had said: "No man taketh it [My life] away from Me, but I lay it down of Myself." [11] It was the fire of love coming from heaven that burnt the victim, says St. Thomas elsewhere.[12]

The difference between Christ's death and the death of the martyrs consists in this, that theirs is not a sacrifice in the strict sense, although it is voluntary. Granted that the wound was mortal, the martyrs, unlike Christ, were not free to preserve their life or give it up, whereas Christ, unless the Father had given Him the command to die for us, miraculously had it in His power not to die under the blows inflicted upon Him. Hence Christ offered Himself as holocaust.[13]

Corollary. The priesthood of Christ cannot be more perfect, because the priest cannot be more united to God, the victim, and the people.[14] Christ is God, moreover, Christ is both priest and victim, and finally Christ is the head of His mystical body and of all mankind.[15]

Third Article

WHETHER THE EFFECT OF CHRIST'S PRIESTHOOD IS THE EXPIATION OF SINS

Reply. It is affirmed on the authority of St. Paul's texts quoted in this article.[16]

[11] John 10–18.
[12] *Com. in Lev.* chap. 1.
[13] Cf. ad 2, ad 3.
[14] Cf. Garrigou-Lagrange, *Le Sauveur,* pp. 284 f.
[15] *Summa theol.,* IIIa, q. 22, a. 3, ad 3; q. 48, a. 3.
[16] Rom. 3:24; Heb. 9:14.

Theological proof. St. Thomas shows that Christ by His death merited grace for us whereby sin is blotted out, and He fully satisfied for the punishments that are due to sin. Hence the effect of Christ's priesthood is the expiation of sins as regards both guilt and punishment. "He hath borne our infirmities and carried our sorrows." [17]

Reply to second objection. "The sacrifice which is offered every day in the Church is not distinct from that which Christ Himself offered, but is a commemoration thereof." It is substantially the same sacrifice, inasmuch as it is the one identical victim, the one identical principal priest; but the manner of offering is different; for now Christ's sacrifice is not bloody, but unbloody and sacramental. Moreover, Christ does not now either merit or sorrowfully satisfy for us, but the fruits of His past merits and satisfactions are applied to us.[18]

Reply to third objection. The paschal lamb was one of the principal figurative victims of the Old Testament; hence St. John the Baptist said of Christ: "Behold the Lamb of God, behold Him who taketh away the sin of the world." [19]

Fourth Article

WHETHER THE EFFECT OF THE PRIESTHOOD OF CHRIST PERTAINED NOT ONLY TO OTHERS BUT ALSO TO HIMSELF

Reply. The Council of Ephesus denies that the effect of the priesthood pertains to Christ.[20] The reason is that Christ as man was already most holy, full of grace, impeccable, and the fountainhead of the entire priesthood. Thus the sun illumines but is not illumined. This is clearly expressed by St. Paul, for he says: "Who [Christ] is innocent, needeth not daily, as the other priests, to offer sacrifices first for His own sins." [21]

[17] Isa. 53:4.
[18] Denz., nos. 938–40.
[19] John 1:29.
[20] Denz., no. 122.
[21] Heb. 9:26 f.

Fifth Article

WHETHER THE PRIESTHOOD OF CHRIST ENDURES FOREVER

Reply. The answer is in the affirmative, for the Psalmist says: "Thou art a priest forever." [22] Likewise St. Paul declares: "[Christ is] always living to make intercession for us." [23]

Nevertheless the difficulty is that the priesthood does not endure unless there is sacrifice in the strict sense, or a visible sacrifice, and this will cease after the celebration of the last Mass at the end of the world; for in heaven the blessed see God face to face, and no more need sensible signs.

Therefore St. Thomas answers the question of this article more precisely by saying that the priesthood of Christ is said to be eternal, not because of the sacrifice that is offered, but because of its consummation, namely, because of the perpetual union of men redeemed with God clearly seen, for this is the eternal fruit of the Savior's sacrifice.

Wherefore St. Paul says: "But Christ, being come a high priest of the good things to come . . . by His own blood entered once into the holies, having obtained eternal redemption." [24] Hence, after the celebration of the last Mass there will be no more sacrifice in the strict sense, nor reparation, nor prayer of petition; but there will always be the cultus of adoration and thanksgiving.[25]

Hence Christ's priesthood is said to be eternal: (1) because its effect is the eternal salvation of men, (2) because He had no successor in this respect; (3) because He continually intercedes for us and will offer sacrifice by His ministers until the end of time; (4) because He is anointed as High Priest.

Several Thomists, such as Billuart, say that Christ's priesthood is said to be eternal because of His imperishable anointing, which is nothing else but the hypostatic union itself. If there were in heaven a sacrifice in the strict sense, then it would be a more exalted sacrifice than the sacrifice on the cross, which would not be subordinated to this latter sacrifice, but would be coordinated with it also as more exalted, and therefore the words of Christ dying on the cross, "it is

[22] Ps. 109:4.
[23] Heb. 7:25.
[24] The whole article should be read.
[25] Cf. ad 1, ad 2.

consummated," [26] would be meaningless. On the contrary, the sacrifice of the Last Supper is directed to the sacrifice on the cross, and the sacrifice of the Mass is subordinated to the sacrifice of the cross, of which it is the application.

First doubt. What formally constitutes Christ's priesthood? [27]

It is a disputed question among Thomists. The Salmanticenses and certain other theologians maintain that the grace of headship is what constitutes Christ's priesthood so far as this grace presupposes or connotes the grace of union. Thus Christ would be a priest by the same created habitual grace by which He is the head of the Church.

Several other Thomist theologians, such as Gonet and Hugon, are of the opinion, which is now becoming more generally admitted, that the substantial grace of union is what formally constitutes Christ's priesthood, whereby Christ as man is primarily holy by a holiness that is not only innate, but also substantial and uncreated. By this same grace Christ is holy and the sanctifier. Hence Pius XI says in one of his sacred discourses: "It is solely because it is the Homoousion of Nicaea who became incarnate . . . who gives Himself lavishly, inexhaustible and infinite in Jesus Christ, what the theologians call substantial victim, which consecrated Him a priest." [28]

Scriptural proof. Christ as man is a priest inasmuch as He is anointed by God.[29] But His primary anointing is by the grace of union. Therefore Christ is a priest by the grace of union.

Theological proof. Christ is a priest who must offer sacrifice that is of infinite value for the redemption of men. But it was only by the grace of union that His sacrifice was of infinite value; for the offering of Himself is a theandric act.

It is not enough for Christ to be the head of the human nature, for Adam was the head of the human nature raised to the supernatural order, and yet he was incapable of offering a sacrifice of infinite value.

It does not suffice to say with the Salmanticenses that what formally constitutes Christ's priesthood is habitual grace inasmuch as it connotes the grace of union, because Christ's priesthood, in what formally constitutes it as such, must be capable of offering a sacrifice that is of

[26] John 19:30
[27] See Garrigou-Lagrange, *Le Sauveur,* pp. 289 f.
[28] *Civilta cattolica,* 1926, p. 182.
[29] Ps. 44:8; 9:24.

intrinsically infinite value; and this formally depends on the grace of union.

This seems to be the opinion of St. Thomas; for, speaking about Christ's human nature, he says: "It acquired then the actual holiness of a victim, [on the cross] from the charity it had from the beginning and from the grace of union sanctifying it absolutely." [30] Likewise it is evident from another text of St. Thomas that Christ was predestined to natural divine sonship before He was predestined to glory and habitual grace; for it was only because Christ had to be the Son of God that He was predestined to the highest degree of glory.[31]

Also, in the opinion of St. Thomas it is especially by the grace of union that Christ is the mediator.[32] This opinion is also admitted by Bossuet.[33]

Second doubt. Which title is greater in Christ, Savior or Priest forever?

Reply. Savior is the greater title, for the name "Jesus" signifies Savior. Hence the title generally used in the treatise on the Word incarnate and the Redeemer is, as in the *Theological Summa* of St. Thomas, the Savior, in preference to Christ the priest.

Moreover, the Savior must be a priest capable of offering a sacrifice of infinite value. But not every priest is strictly speaking a savior. The idea of savior includes more than the idea of priest.

Finally, the principal act of a priest is the act that belongs to the virtue of religion, namely, to offer sacrifice for the people; whereas the principal act of the Savior is the act of a higher virtue, namely, of charity, which commands the virtue of religion. Thus the principal act of Christ the Savior is the act of love, whereby on the cross He showed His supreme love for His Father and for souls to be saved.

Sixth Article

WHETHER THE PRIESTHOOD OF CHRIST WAS ACCORDING TO THE ORDER OF MELCHISEDECH

Reply. The answer is in the affirmative, for the prophet says: "Thou are a priest forever according to the order of Melchisedech." [34]

[30] *Summa theol.,* IIIa, q. 22, a. 2, ad 3. But this text is perhaps spurious. See Leonine edition.

[31] *Ibid.,* q. 24, a. 1, ad 2.

[32] *Ibid.,* q. 26, a. 2; q. 58, a. 3.

[33] *Elévations sur les mystères,* élévations 1 and 6.

[34] Ps. 109:4. See also Heb. 5:6, 10; 6:20; 7:1, 10, 11, 15, 17.

The meaning is that the priest Melchisedech typified, far more than the other priests of the Old Law, Christ the priest: and there are four reasons given for this.

1) Because Melchisedech offered bread and wine,[35] and not sheep and oxen, as Aaron did. But Christ at the Last Supper offered His body and His blood under the appearance of bread and wine.

2) Because Melchisedech is presented to us in Sacred Scripture as "without father, without mother, without genealogy, having neither beginning of days nor end of life," [36] that is, contrary to the custom of Sacred Scripture, no mention is made of his parents. In this he represents Christ's eternal priesthood, who had neither earthly father nor heavenly mother.

3) Because Melchisedech, having received tithes from Abraham as the superior of the latter, blessed Him and the lawful priests of the Old Law; and thus he typified the superiority of Christ's priesthood over that of the Law.

4) Melchisedech means the same as king of justice and of peace; But Christ was king of justice and of peace.

What has been said suffices for Christ's priesthood. It must be remembered that there cannot be a more perfect priesthood because no other priest can be more united to God, the victim, and the people.[37]

[35] Gen. 14:18.
[36] Heb. 7:3.
[37] Cf. IIIa, q. 48, a. 3; also q. 83.

CHAPTER XXV

QUESTION 23

The Adoption of Christ

THE purpose of this question is to refute the heresy of the Adoptionists who, following in the wake of Nestorianism, said in the eighth century that Christ as man is the adoptive son of God.

The Church has defined that the man Christ is the only and natural Son of God,[1] and nowise the adoptive son.[2] The Church also declared that it is only allegorically on account of Christ's obedience to His Father that He is called a servant.[3] He is not the Son of the Holy Spirit,[4] but truly the Son of the Virgin Mary.[5] In fact, He has two births, His eternal birth as God, and His temporal birth as man,[6] but not two sonships, neither adoptive sonship as regards God the Father, nor a real relation of sonship as regards the Blessed Virgin Mary.

The principal definitions of the Church against the errors of the Adoptionists are to be found in the Enchiridion.[7] The assertion that Christ as man is the adoptive son of the Father is rejected as heretical in both the Council of Frankfort and the Council of Frejus.[8] This assertion was again condemned in the Second Council of Lyons.[9]

This error gives St. Thomas the opportunity to explain here more fully what is the nature of divine adoption than in the treatise on

[1] Denz., nos. 2, 143, 1460.
[2] *Ibid.*, nos. 299, 309 f., 344, 462, 3007.
[3] *Ibid.*, nos. 310, 313.
[4] *Ibid.*, no. 282.
[5] *Ibid.*, nos. 20, 422.
[6] *Ibid.*, nos. 257, 290, 344.
[7] *Ibid.*, nos. 309–14.
[8] *Ibid.*, no. 3007.
[9] *Ibid.*, no. 462.

grace, although the fundamentals of the doctrine concerning divine adoption are explained in the treatise on grace.

First Article

WHETHER IT IS FITTING THAT GOD SHOULD ADOPT SONS

State of the question. It seems that it is not fitting, because only strangers are adopted, and nobody is a stranger to God.

Reply. Yet the answer is in the affirmative, for the Apostle says: "Who hath predestinated us unto the adoption of children." [10]

Theological proof. To adopt is to admit someone to share in another's inheritance. Thus a rich man adopts a poor man's son. But it is fitting that God of His infinite goodness admit His intellectual creatures to share in His inheritance, which is the enjoyment of Himself. For God is rich and happy in Himself, that is to say, in the enjoyment of Himself. Therefore it is indeed fitting for God to adopt sons.

It must be noted that reason alone cannot apodictically prove the possibility of this adoption; for this would be to prove the possibility of grace, which is essentially supernatural in that it is a participation of the divine nature of God's intimate life which therefore transcends the scope of truths that can be proved by reason alone.

But posited the revelation of this truth, God's infinite goodness makes it clear that it befits Him to adopt. Its possibility can neither be proved nor disproved, but we are persuaded of it and it is firmly held by faith alone.

First doubt. What is the difference between divine adoption and human adoption? [11]

Reply. The difference is that a man in adopting someone, for example, a poor man's son, does not make this son worthy to inherit from him, but in adopting such a person presupposes as worthy him whom he chooses. On the contrary, God makes the man whom He adopts worthy by the gift of His grace to receive the heavenly inheritance. Hence divine adoption is far superior to human adoption and much more real; for it elevates one to the higher order of the divine life and proceeds from uncreated love which is effective and productive of grace. It regenerates the soul so that the adoptive son is said to

[10] Eph. 1:5.
[11] Cf. IIIa, q. 23, a. 1, c. (end).

be "born . . . of God," [12] not indeed by nature as the only-begotten Son, but by grace, that is, regenerated spiritually by infused grace.

Second doubt. What is the difference between adoptive sonship and natural sonship?

Natural sonship is the relation that befits anyone inasmuch as by virtue of birth such a person receives from the generator either the numerically identical nature as in the case of the divine person or specifically the same nature as in created beings. Hence taken in the strict sense it is defined as "the origin of a living being from a living principle in the likeness of nature." [13] Thus the foundation of natural sonship is passive generation.

Adoptive sonship is a qualified imitation of natural sonship inasmuch as the adopted does not receive the adopter's nature, but a right to the inheritance as if he were the true son. Hence adoption among jurists and theologians is generally defined as being the gratuitous and free assumption of a stranger to the inheritance of the adopter.

The solution of the objections of this article confirms the reply.

Reply to first objection. "Considered in his nature, man is not a stranger in respect to God as to the natural gifts bestowed on him; but he is as to the gifts of grace and glory," because he has these not by nature, but only by adoption.

Reply to second objection. Adoptive sonship is a participation in the resemblance of divine natural sonship, hence the Apostle says: "He predestinated us to be made conformable to the image of His Son." [14] In other words, just as the only-begotten Son received from all eternity the whole divine nature from His Father, so the adoptive son receives in time a participation of the divine nature.

Reply to third objection. "Spiritual goods can be possessed by many at the same time, not so material goods. Wherefore none can receive a material inheritance except the successor of a deceased being; whereas all receive the spiritual inheritance at the same time in its entirety without detriment to the ever-living Father."

[12] John 1:13.
[13] Cf. Ia, q. 27, a. 2.
[14] Rom. 8:29.

Second Article

WHETHER IT IS FITTING THAT THE WHOLE TRINITY SHOULD ADOPT

State of the question. The difficulty is that, on the one hand, men are made by adoption brethren of Christ rather than His sons, for the Apostle says: "That He might be the first-born among many brethren." [15] On the other hand, when in the Lord's Prayer we say, "Our Father," this refers to the entire Trinity, equally with "Thy kingdom come," and "Thy will be done."

Reply. To adopt is an act that belongs to the whole Trinity.

Authoritative proof. When in the Lord's Prayer we say "Our Father," the word "Father" connotes the essence and not the person.[16] The same is to be said of "Thy kingdom come, Thy will be done."

Theological proof. Every divine free action *ad extra* is befitting to the whole Trinity, because it proceeds from omnipotence, which, like the divine nature, is common to the three persons. But to adopt is a divine free action *ad extra,* for it is the bestowal of grace. Therefore to adopt is befitting to the whole Trinity.

In other words, whereas the natural Son of God is "begotten not made," [17] the adoptive son is made, for the Evangelist says: "He gave them power to be made the sons of God." [18] Nevertheless the adoptive son is said to be "born of God," [19] on account of the spiritual regeneration that is gratuitous and not natural.

Reply to second question. "By adoption we are made the brethren of Christ, as having with Him the same Father who, nevertheless, is His Father in one way and ours in another. Whence, pointedly our Lord says, separately: 'My Father, and your Father.' [20] For He is Christ's Father by natural generation, and this is proper to Him; whereas He is our Father by a voluntary operation, which is common to the three persons." Hence, when we say, "Our Father," the word "Father" refers to the essence and not to the person. It is the opposite when Christ says, "My Father," for Christ is not the Son of the Trinity, as we are. Father Lebreton, S.J., in his recent work on the

[15] *Ibid.*
[16] Cf. Ia, q. 33, a. 3; q. 39, a. 7.
[17] Nicene Creed.
[18] John 1:12.
[19] *Ibid.,* 1:13.
[20] *Ibid.,* 20:17.

Trinity, insists exegetically very much on this point. This observation is referred to in its proper terms by St. Thomas in the present article, which is seldom quoted.[21]

Doubt. Is adoption, although common to the whole Trinity, appropriated to the Father?

Reply to third objection. "It is appropriated to the Father as its author, to the Son as its exemplar, to the Holy Ghost as imprinting on us the likeness of this exemplar."

Adoption is here taken in the active sense, and not in the passive sense, which is called "a participated likeness of eternal sonship,"[22] in a quasi-passive sense.

The reason is that appropriation is a manifestation of the divine persons by means of essential attributes which enter more closely into what constitutes this or that person. Thus to the Father, inasmuch as He is the principle from no principle, omnipotence is appropriated; to the Son, inasmuch as He is the Word, wisdom is appropriated; to the Holy Ghost, inasmuch as He is personal love, is appropriated goodness, sanctification, which is the special effect of infused charity.[23]

Third Article

WHETHER IT IS PROPER TO THE RATIONAL NATURE TO BE ADOPTED

Reply. Every intellectual creature, and only such, can be adopted, for only such a creature is capable of grace on which adoption rests, and of happiness in which inheritance consists.

Therefore the angels are adoptive sons of God; likewise our first parents in the state of innocence; the just of the Old Testament; also all who are in the state of grace, as long as they remain so, even though they are not predestined.

Objection. St. Paul introduces a state of opposition between the Christians and the just of the Old Testament,[24] inasmuch as the latter received the spirit of bondage in fear, whereas the Christians received the spirit of the adoption of sons.

Reply. St. Paul does not introduce opposition between them because

[21] Cf. IIIa, q. 23, a. 2, ad 3.
[22] *Ibid.*, ad 3.
[23] *Ibid.*, Ia., q. 39, a. 7, 8; q. 45, a. 6, ad 2.
[24] Gal., chap. 4; Rom., chap. 8.

of personal justice, but by reason of the difference of state and law in which each class lived; for the Old Law was the law of fear in itself, and of itself it did not have the power to justify; whereas the New Law is the law of grace previously imprinted on the hearts and having the power to justify.[25] Thus it is sufficient for salvation, although not all the just are actually saved, for some fall away from grace.

Fourth Article

WHETHER CHRIST AS MAN IS THE ADOPTED SON OF GOD

State of the question. About the end of the eighth century Archbishop Elipandus of Toledo, and Bishop Felix of Urgel, Adoptionists, taught that Christ as man is the adopted son of God. And more probably, whatever Vasquez says, they defended this thesis in the Nestorian sense, namely, by positing two persons in Christ. They were condemned as heretics in the Council of Frankfort (794) under Pope Hadrian I.[26]

But Durandus and Scotus were unaware of the acts of the Frankfort council, which for a long time remained unknown because of the astuteness of the heretics. These theologians said: The unity of the person being preserved intact, Christ as man is the adopted Son of God, inasmuch as He received habitual grace by which we are adopted sons.

Is this opinion of Scotus and Durandus already condemned by the Council of Frankfort, the acts of which were unknown to these theologians? The answer is that the Council of Frankfort excludes even this opinion, for it says: "Adopted, if indeed this means that Jesus Christ is not the natural Son of God." This council also says: "The unity of person eliminates the insult of adoption." St. Thomas in the counterargument to this article also quotes St. Ambrose as against this opinion.

Theological proof. The argumentative part of this article refutes the adoptive sonship of Christ as follows:

Sonship properly belongs not to the nature, but to the person, and He who is already the natural Son cannot be called the adopted son, because He is not a stranger to His Father according to His nature. Thus a man cannot adopt a boy who is already his son. But Christ is

[25] Cf. Ia IIae, q. 106, a. 1.

[26] Denz., nos. 309–14. See also Billuart's *De incarnatione*.

the natural Son of God. Therefore Christ cannot be called the adopted son.

In explanation of this proof, it must be observed that: (1) Adoption cannot apply to the humanity of Christ, both because the humanity is not a person, and only a person can be adopted, and because, on account of the hypostatic union, it already is entitled to the inheritance of God, which is the beatific vision.

2) It must be noted that Christ as man is already in the formal sense the natural Son of God, inasmuch as the Word who subsists in the human nature is the natural Son of God, for by assuming the human nature Christ did not lose His divine natural sonship.

The solution of the objections confirms this answer.

Reply to first objection. If it is said that "carnal humility was adopted by the Word"; the expression is metaphorical for "was assumed"; for adoption properly belongs only to the person, not to the nature, or to a part of the nature.

Reply to second objection. "Christ, by the grace of union, is the natural Son, whereas a Christian by habitual grace is an adopted son. Habitual grace in Christ does not make one who was not a son to be an adopted son, but is a certain effect of filiation in the soul of Christ."

Adopted sonship is not the formal and primary effect of habitual grace, but only the secondary effect; hence habitual grace can be in the soul without the former. It is present in Christ's soul as a participation of the divine nature rendering Christ more pleasing to God, and it enables Him in a special manner to merit continually by infused charity and the other virtues, of which habitual grace is the source.

Reply to third objection. We may say that Christ according to His human nature is a creature, and is subject to God; but we cannot say that He is the adopted Son of God, because sonship is not said of the nature but only of the person; for we do not say the humanity of Christ is the Son of God.

Corollary. The Blessed Virgin Mary is the first adopted daughter of God.

CHAPTER XXVI

QUESTION 24

The Predestination of Christ

IMPORTANCE OF THIS QUESTION

THIS most famous question evidently belongs to the relations prevailing between Christ and His Father.

Scotus engages in a lengthy discussion on Christ's predestination, and in his theological summa he explains his own view about the motive of the Incarnation, seeking to rest it on the principle that Christ is the first of all the predestined, and therefore the first intended by God, even before Adam. To this the Thomists reply that Christ is the first intended by God in the genus of final cause; but because He was willed by God as the Savior or Redeemer, the permission of Adam's sin to be repaired is first in the genus of material cause. Thus God wills the soul prior to the body in the genus of final and formal cause, but He first wills the body in the genus of material cause to be perfected, and if the embryonic body were not disposed for the reception of the rational soul, this soul would not be created. Likewise, in virtue of the present decree, if Adam had not sinned, the Word would not have become incarnate. St. Thomas realized the importance of the predestination of Christ, who is the first of all the predestined.

St. Thomas says indeed, as we shall immediately see, that Christ was not predestined first to glory, as Scotus contends, but to divine and natural sonship, which is more exalted, and he shows that Christ's gratuitous predestination is the exemplar and cause of our predestination, inasmuch as Christ condignly merited all the effects of our predestination.

There are four articles to this question.

1) Whether Christ is predestinated.
2) Whether He is predestinated as man.
3) Whether His predestination is the exemplar of ours.
4) Whether it is the cause of ours.

First Article

WHETHER IT IS BEFITTING THAT CHRIST SHOULD BE PREDESTINATED

State of the question. It would seem unfitting: (1) because Christ is not the adopted Son of God, for St. Paul says: "God hath predestinated us unto the adoption of children"; [1] (2) because the person of Christ is uncreated and therefore not predestinated, but predestining, and it cannot be said that Christ is predestined by reason of His human nature, for only persons are predestined, for example, Peter, Paul; (3) Christ was always God and the Son of God; therefore He was not predestined to be the natural Son of God.

Reply. Nevertheless the answer is in the affirmative.

Scriptural and authoritative proof. St. Paul says of the Son of God: "Who was made to Him of the seed of David according to the flesh who was predestinated the Son of God in power." [2] But this text presents a difficulty.[3]

St. Augustine understands the Greek word to mean "predestined," [4] because in Sacred Scripture, to destine, to define, to appoint, to declare, are the same in meaning. Thus divine knowledge is the same as foreknowledge.

Hence St. Augustine says: "Jesus was predestined, so that He who was to be the son of David according to the flesh would yet be in power the Son of God." [5]

The interpretation given by the Greeks seems to be more literal. But as regards the doctrine and the application of the notion implied in

[1] Eph. 1:5.

[2] Rom. 1:3 f.

[3] The Vulgate has "praedestinatus," as if the Greek reading were *προοριсθέντος*; in the Greek we find *ὁρισθέντος*, which has more the meaning of *declaratus est*," that is, "He was declared the Son of God, in power, according to the spirit of sanctification, from the resurrection of the dead." This last interpretation is the one proposed by St. John Chrysostom, Theophylactus, and others, as well as by many exegetes.

[4] *De praed. sanct.*, chap. 15.

[5] *Ibid.*, no. 31.

predestination, there is no difficulty, as will at once be evident from the argument as expounded in the body of this article.

Theological proof. Predestination, in its proper sense, is a certain divine preordination from eternity of those things which are to be done in time by the grace of God.[6] But it was done in time by God, through the grace of union, that the man Jesus should be God. Therefore the union of natures in the person of Christ falls under eternal predestination, and because of this union Christ is truly said to be predestinated.

Reply to first objection. Christ is not predestined, however, as we are, to be the adopted son of God, but to be the natural Son of God.

Reply to second objection. Predestination is attributed to the person of Christ, not indeed in itself, but inasmuch as the person subsists in the human nature; for by the grace of union it befits Christ, in His human nature, to be the Son of God.

Reply to the third objection. The antecedence implied in eternal predestination is not to be referred to the person of the Word in Himself but to Him by reason of the nature.

Second Article

WHETHER THIS PROPOSITION IS FALSE: CHRIST AS MAN WAS PREDESTINED TO BE THE SON OF GOD

Reply. The proposition is not false, because predestination is attributed to Christ only on account of His human nature, which means as man.

Reply to first objection. The meaning is that Christ as man was predestinated the Son of God, inasmuch as His human nature received the grace of union.

Reply to second objection. It is false to say that, just as Christ is visible by reason of His human nature, so it would be natural for Him to be the Son of God; but it is so inasmuch as His human nature is hypostatically united to the Word of God. Hence it is said that Christ as man was predestined the natural Son of God, but not the adopted son.

Doubt. Was Christ, as man, predestined primarily and principally to be the natural Son of God, and only secondarily to the beatific vision and other supernatural gifts bestowed on Him?

[6] *Summa theol.,* Ia, q. 23, a. 1, 5.

Reply. The Thomists affirm, against Scotus, that Christ was so predestined. They say that what was intended first and principally in the decree of predestination is to be the natural Son of God, or the hypostatic union, because it is greater to be God than to enjoy Him as the other blessed do. This decree of Christ's predestination to be the natural Son of God is nothing else but the decree of the Incarnation. It is only in consequence of this decree that Christ was predestined to glory, as to something secondary, resulting from the grace of union.

Likewise, in the treatise on Mariology, St. Thomas and very many theologians, such as Suarez and several others, say that by the decree of the Incarnation the Blessed Virgin Mary was first predestined to be the Mother of God, and only as a consequence of this to fullness of grace and glory "so that she might be fittingly and worthily the Mother of God." [7]

Objection. But Christ is made more perfect by the light of glory and the beatific vision. Therefore these are more perfect than the hypostatic union.

Reply. I deny the consequence, because the hypostatic union is not related to the light of glory, as a disposition to a more perfect form, but rather as an eminent cause to what results from it. In fact, the hypostatic union formally constitutes the hypostatic order, which infinitely transcends the order of grace and glory. Even the divine maternity belongs, because of that in which it terminates, to the hypostatic order, and it transcends the plenitude of grace in Mary although this plenitude is, indeed, a derived and most fitting perfection so that the Blessed Virgin Mary may be worthy to be the Mother of God.

Thus the rational soul, inasmuch as it pertains to the substantial order, is more perfect than the intellectual faculty and intellection, which pertain to the order of accidents and properties, though they perfect the substance.

Moreover, it must be noted that the common saying, namely, that everything is for its operation, does not mean that substance is for accident, for this would be false. The meaning of this axiomatic statement is, as Cajetan observes, that everything operates for its own sake. And the thing with its operation is a greater perfection than the thing apart from its operation, just as a tree and its fruit are more perfect than the tree alone. But it is better to give the tree than to give only the

[7] *Ibid.,* IIIa, q. 27, a. 5, c. et ad 2.

fruit or the usufruct. Wherefore, St. Thomas says: "He who vows something and does it, subjects himself to God more than he who only does it; for he subjects himself to God not only as to the act, but also as to the power, since in future he cannot do something else. Even so he gives more who gives the tree with its fruit than he who gives the fruit only, as Anselm says." [8] Operation follows being, and operation is for the perfection of the substance.

Hence Christ certainly was predestined to be the natural Son of God prior to His predestination to glory, and the Blessed Virgin Mary, by the same decree of the Incarnation, was predestined to be the Mother of God prior to her predestination to plenitude of grace and glory.

Corollary. Evidently both the predestination of Christ and that of the Blessed Virgin Mary are absolutely gratuitous. Neither Christ nor the Blessed Virgin Mary could merit the Incarnation, and the merits of Christ and of the Blessed Virgin Mary are the effects, and not the cause of their predestination; just as the merits of the elect are the effects and not cause of their predestination, as St. Thomas shows.[9] St. Paul says: "What hast thou that thou hast not received?" [10] And again: "God chose us before the foundation of the world, that we should be holy and unspotted in His sight in charity," [11] not because He foresaw our future holiness. God is not only the spectator, but the author of salvation.

Third Article

WHETHER CHRIST'S PREDESTINATION IS THE EXEMPLAR OF OURS

The answer is in the affirmative.

Authoritative proof. St. Augustine, in one of his works,[12] explains in his own admirable way, how Christ's predestination to be the natural Son of God, which is the result of no foreseen merits, is the exemplar of our predestination to salvation or to adoptive sonship of glory, which likewise is not because of our foreseen merits, since the merits of the elect are the effects and not the cause of their predestination.

[8] *Ibid.*, IIa IIae, q. 88, a. 6.
[9] *Ibid.*, Ia, q. 23, a. 5.
[10] I Cor. 4:7.
[11] Eph. 1:4.
[12] *De praed. sanct.*, chap. 15.

Theological proof. It is explained in the body of this article as follows:

Christ's predestination is the exemplar of ours not on the part of God willing, but on the part of the object willed.

It is not the exemplar because of God willing, for in God there are not several acts of intellect and will; hence St. Thomas says: "God wills this to be as means to that (on the part of things willed), but He does not on account of this (first intended) will that (by a consequent act)." [13] In this God differs from us, who are moved by the end to choose the means.

On the part of the objects willed, however, Christ's predestination is the exemplar of ours in two ways.

a) As regards the good to which we are predestinated; for Christ was predestinated to be the natural Son of God, whereas we are predestinated to be the adopted sons of God, which is a participated likeness of natural sonship, for St. Paul says: "He predestinated us to be made conformable to the image of His Son." [14]

b) As to the manner of obtaining this good, which is by grace, our preceding merits are not the cause but the effect of our predestination by God. Under this aspect, Christ's predestination is the exemplar of ours, because St. Thomas, following St. Augustine, says that "this is most manifest in Christ, because human nature in Him, without any preceding merits, was united to the Son of God"; [15] and the Evangelist says: "of His fullness we have all received." [16]

Reply to third objection. "The exemplate need not be conformed to the exemplar in all respects; it is sufficient that it imitate it in some." Our predestination, as we shall at once see, is because of Christ's merits, whereas Christ did not merit His predestination.

Fourth Article

WHETHER CHRIST'S PREDESTINATION IS THE CAUSE OF OURS

State of the question. The meaning is whether Christ's predestination is not merely exemplar, but also the final and efficient moral cause of ours, inasmuch as Christ merited the effects of our predestination.

[13] *Summa theol.,* Ia, q. 19, a. 5.

[14] Rom. 8:29.

[15] *Summa theol.,* IIIa, q. 24, a. 3, c.

[16] John 1:16.

St. Thomas answers the first part of this question as in the preceding article by stating that, on the part of God who predestines, Christ's predestination is not the cause of ours, because by one and the same eternal act God predestined both Christ and us.

On the part of the things willed, however, Christ's predestination is the final and efficient moral cause of ours.

a) It is the final cause, indeed, because St. Paul says: "All are yours, and you are Christ's; and Christ is God's." [17] And again: "He predestinated us to be made conformable to the image of His Son, that He might be the first-born among many brethren." [18]

b) It is also the efficient moral cause, inasmuch as Christ condignly merited all the effects of our predestination, namely, calling, justification, glorification.

St. Paul says: "God hath blessed us with spiritual blessings in heavenly places, in Christ . . . ,[19] who hath predestinated us unto the adoption of children through Jesus Christ unto Himself . . . unto the praise of the glory of His grace, in which He hath graced us in His beloved Son, in whom we have redemption through His blood, the remission of sins, according to the richness of His grace, which hath superabounded in us. . . . [God willed] to restore all things in Christ . . . in whom we also are called by lot, being predestinated according to His purpose." [20] Hence in the argumentative part of this article, St. Thomas says: "For God, by predestinating from eternity, so decreed our salvation that it should be achieved through Jesus Christ. For eternal predestination covers not only that which is to be accomplished in time, but also the mode and order in which it is to be accomplished in time." [21]

Confirmation. Christ's merits were foreseen and predestined by God before He gave any sign that men were to be predestined.

It is not only a question here of the predestination of some undetermined number of persons but of a particular number of persons individually in preference to others.

Christ indeed said: "You have not chosen Me, but I have chosen

[17] I Cor. 3:23.

[18] Rom. 8:29.

[19] Predestination is man's choicest benediction.

[20] Eph. 1:3 f.

[21] Cf. the Salmanticenses, Gonet, and John of St. Thomas in their commentaries on Ia, q. 23, a. 5. Also Billuart in his commentary on the present article. See also what we said above on Christ's merit.

you."[22] St. Augustine[23] and St. Thomas[24] interpret this text as referring not only to the grace of the apostolate, but also to glory, to salvation, or to the eternal kingdom. Just before the above-quoted text, Jesus said, and this applies to all the just: "I will not now call you servants . . . , but friends."[25] And to whatsoever Christian the Apostle says: "What hast thou that thou hast not received?"[26] and not only from God but from the merits of Christ, because "of His fullness we have all received."[27] Hence Christ merited all the effects of our predestination taken together.

Doubt. How then did Christ merit the efficacious graces that *de facto* are not granted, such as the grace of a happy death for Judas?

We already have answered this question in discussing Christ's merits.[28] He merited them not as conferred or to be conferred, but as offered to man in the sufficient grace; for the efficacious grace is offered to us in the sufficient as the fruit in the flower, but if one resists the sufficient grace, that person deserves to be deprived of the efficacious grace.

Hence Christ merited differently the grace of a happy death both for Peter and for Judas. The most holy soul of Christ was moved by God predestining to merit for Peter the grace of a happy death to be conferred and for Judas to be offered in the sufficient grace.

The mystery of predestination always remains a secret.

Objection. What is absolutely gratuitous does not depend on foreseen merits. But our predestination is purely gratuitous. Therefore it does not depend on any merits.

Reply. I distinguish the major: that it does not depend on our merits, I concede; on Christ's merits, I deny. I contradistinguish the minor: our predestination is said to be gratuitous as regards ourselves, but not as regards Christ.

Likewise the Blessed Virgin Mary merited *de congruo* all the effects of our predestination.

Hence God chose the elect from all eternity in view of Christ's merits, just as He willed from all eternity to preserve the Blessed

[22] John 15:16.
[23] *De praed. sanct.*, chap. 19; *De corrept. et gratia*, chap. 7.
[24] *Com. in Joan.*, chap. 15; also *Ep. ad Eph.*
[25] John 15:15.
[26] I Cor. 4:7.
[27] John 1:16.
[28] See p. 482.

Virgin Mary from original sin on account of Christ's future merits, as declared by Pius IX.[29]

But I insist. It seems that Christ's merits are the means whereby we are predestined; in fact, whereby we are saved, which is first intended by God. Therefore the solution is false.

Reply. I deny the antecedent, for the means is subordinate to the end; whereas Christ's predestination and His merits are of a higher order than our salvation. Hence it is rather our salvation that is the means, ordained by God for the glory of Christ, who is first predestined. St. Paul says: "For all are yours. And you are Christ's; and Christ is God's." [30] Therefore Christ is the first of all the predestined and was by God, who predestines, first willed in the genus of final cause; whereas the permission of Adam's sin to be repaired preceded in the genus of material cause to be perfected, as stated in our treatise on the motive of the Incarnation.

[29] Bull *Ineffabilis Deus.*
[30] I Cor. 3:22 f.

CHAPTER XXVII

QUESTION 25

The Adoration of Christ

We have considered Christ in His relation to the Father, and now we must consider His relation to us. There are two questions: (1) the adoration of Christ; (2) His mediation inasmuch as He is our mediator.

Concerning the adoration of Christ there are six articles.

1) Whether Christ's humanity and Godhead are to be adored with one and the same adoration.

2) Whether His flesh is to be adored with the adoration of latria.

3) Whether the adoration of latria is to be given to the images of Christ.

4) Whether the cross of Christ is to be adored with the adoration of latria.

5) Whether His mother is to be adored.

6) Concerning the adoration of the relics of saints.[1]

PREFATORY REMARKS

St. Thomas has three articles on adoration in his treatise on religion.[2] In the first he shows that adoration is an act of latria, or religion. It is directed to reverence Him who is adored, and it belongs properly to the virtue of religion, or latria, to show reverence to God, on account of His supreme excellence as Creator and Lord of all creatures. Hence to the devil, who tempted Christ in the desert, saying: "All these I will give Thee if, falling down, Thou wilt adore me," [3] Jesus answered: "Begone, Satan, for it is written: 'the Lord thy God thou

[1] Consult Father Hugon's *Tract. theol.*

[2] *Summa theol.,* IIa IIae, q. 84.

[3] Matt. 6:13.

shalt adore, and Him only thou shalt serve.' "[4] Adoration is an act of honor, but not every act of honor is adoration; for equals, even inferiors, are honored, but only the superior is adored. Adoration in the broad sense is not an act of latria, but of dulia. Thus the Scripture records that Nathan adored David,[5] bowing down to the ground, and that Abraham adored the angels, bowing down before them to show his veneration.[6] But the angels and the apostles refused to accept the adoration of latria. It would be idolatry as in paganism.

2) St. Thomas remarks that adoration is first an interior act, which is the cause of a bodily act that expresses our submission, such as genuflection, prostration, inclination.[7] But the principal act is the interior act of the mind, whereby, acknowledging God's excellence, by a profound interior inclination before Him, He is acknowledged as the most excellent Creator and Lord. Wherefore Jesus said: "The true adorers shall adore the Father in spirit and in truth."[8] St. Thomas says: "We prostrate ourselves, professing that we are nothing of ourselves."[9]

3) It is in accordance with what is fitting that adoration requires a definite place, namely, a temple, which is the house of God, as being a place that is set apart, so to speak, from worldly affairs.

First Article

WHETHER CHRIST'S HUMANITY AND GODHEAD ARE TO BE ADORED WITH THE SAME ADORATION

State of the question. It seems not: (1) because Christ's human nature is not, like the divine nature, common to the three divine persons that must be adored; (2) there is not the same excellence in the acts of Christ's human nature as in those of the divine nature; (3) if the soul of Christ were not united to the Word, then it would have to be venerated with the cultus of dulia, and it lost none of its dignity through the hypostatic union.

Reply. Nevertheless the answer is in the affirmative, and it is of

[4] Deut. 6:13.
[5] III Kings 1:23.
[6] Gen. 18:2.
[7] *Summa theol.,* IIa IIae, q. 84, a. 2.
[8] John 4:23.
[9] *Summa theol., loc. cit.,* ad 2.

faith. St. Thomas in the counterargument of this article quotes the Second Council of Constantinople.

On several occasions in the councils this truth has been declared, namely, that Christ's human nature is to be adored,[10] and indeed directly inasmuch as it is united with the divine nature [11] with only one kind of adoration,[12] and it is also to be loved by the perfect as defined against Michael de Molinos.[13] This cultus of latria also befits especially the Eucharistic Christ,[14] and the most sacred Heart of Jesus.[15]

The definition against the Nestorians must be remembered, in which the Church declared: "Christ must be adored by one adoration, by which we must adore God the Word incarnate together with His own flesh, which was the tradition in the Church of God from the beginning." [16]

Theological proof. Strictly speaking, honor is given to the person, and to the hands or feet only inasmuch as they belong to the person. But there is only one person in Christ to whom the two natures belong. Therefore by one and the same adoration the human and divine natures of Christ are to be adored.

Confirmation. A person of distinction is honored because of the qualities indeed of the soul, namely, wisdom and virtues, yet not only the soul is honored, but the whole composite, the body also. Likewise Christ is to be adored on account of His divine personality, but the whole person is to be adored, which includes His human nature.

We grant, however, to those who object, that there are two reasons for the adoration of Christ; for His divine nature of itself alone is to be adored, and His human nature in that it is hypostatically united to the Word. Yet it remains true that there is one honor of adoration on the part of the person who is adored.

[10] Denz., nos. 120, 221; Council of Ephesus and Second Council of Constantinople.

[11] *Ibid.,* nos. 224, 1561.

[12] *Ibid.,* no. 221.

[13] *Ibid.,* no. 1255.

[14] *Ibid.,* nos. 478, 878, 888; Councils of Vienne and Trent.

[15] *Ibid.,* no. 1563; errors of Pistoia.

[16] *Ibid.,* nos. 120, 221; Council of Ephesus and Second Council of Constantinople. Concerning the patristic doctrine, cf. Rouet de Journel.

Second Article

WHETHER CHRIST'S HUMANITY SHOULD BE ADORED WITH THE ADORATION OF LATRIA

State of the question. It seems not, because Christ's humanity is a creature. And Christ as man is less than the Father.

Reply. Authoritative proof. St. Thomas in the counterargument quotes the authority of St. John Damascene and of St. Augustine.

Theological proof. The honor of adoration properly belongs to the person. But the person to whom Christ's humanity belongs is divine, and the honor of latria is due to this person. Hence this adoration is not given to Christ's humanity because of itself, but because of the divinity to which it is united.

Corollary. We say that Christ's humanity must be adored, not by a relative adoration, as the image of Christ must be adored, but by adoration in the strict and absolute sense; because the person is adored whose humanity is a nature. However, first and primarily the person of the Word incarnate is adored, which is the terminus of the adoration.

DEVOTION TO THE SACRED HEART OF JESUS

The nature of this devotion is made manifest from its object and end. It is the physical heart of Christ, as united hypostatically to the divine person,[17] and inasmuch as it is the symbol of Christ's love for us, which constitutes the object of this cult of adoration, Christ's love is the love that comes from His most holy soul and also from the uncreated Word. The motive of this devotion is the infinite dignity of the Word to whom the heart of Christ is hypostatically united, and it is simultaneously the manifestation of both His uncreated and created love for us.

The terminus of this devotion is the very person of Christ inasmuch as it is by the heart that He manifests His love for us.

The end of this devotion is that our hearts may be inflamed with love for Christ, and as a consequence the reparation of injuries inflicted upon Him.

Our love for Christ must be both affective and effective, and it must manifest itself by imitating those virtues of which the most sacred heart of Jesus is the symbol, namely, charity, humility, and meekness,

[17] *Ibid.*, nos. 1562 f. against the Jansenists.

for He said: "Learn of me, because I am meek, and humble of heart." [18]

This devotion, repeatedly approved by the Church, whatever the Jansenists, unbelievers, and rationalists may have said, is most certainly lawful and holy. Discarding the physiological question, whether the material heart is the organ of love or not, it is certainly the organ that manifests emotional love, and hence it is the symbol of love. Therefore the heart of Christ is the symbol of the love whereby Christ "loved us and delivered Himself up for us." [19] All the graces we receive come from this love.

Thus there is a special reason for the adoration of this part of Christ's body. Finally, this devotion arose in a most opportune time, that of Jansenism, for the practical refutation of this heresy, which denied that Christ died for all men, and which caused many of the faithful to abstain from frequent Communion.

Devotion to the Eucharistic Heart of Jesus is likewise a true, holy, and opportune cult, for it refers to the Heart of Jesus inasmuch as this Heart moved Jesus to give us the Eucharist as the daily sacrifice and the most perfect of all the sacraments. As Leo XIII said: "This devotion reminds us of that act of supreme love by which our Redeemer, lavishing upon us all the riches of His Heart, so that on leaving this world, He might remain with us until the end of time, instituted the adorable sacrament of the Eucharist." [20] We owe a debt of deep gratitude for the institution of this devotion.

Third Article

WHETHER THE IMAGE OF CHRIST SHOULD BE ADORED WITH THE ADORATION OF LATRIA

Reply. Relative but not absolute adoration of latria must be given to the image of Christ.

Authoritative proof. St. John Damascene quotes St. Basil as saying: "The honor given to an image reaches to the prototype." [21] There are several declarations of the Church concerning the relative cult of images. The Second Council of Nicaea says: "The honor paid to an

[18] Matt. 11:29.

[19] Eph. 5:2.

[20] Epistle on the occasion of the establishment of the Archconfraternity of the Eucharistic Heart in the Church of St. Joachim at Rome, February 16, 1903.

[21] *De fide orthod.,* IV, 16.

image is transferred to the original, and whoever adores the image, adores the subsistence (or person) depicted in the image." [22]

Theological proof. There is a twofold movement of the mind toward an image; the first is toward the image itself as a certain thing; the second is toward the image so far as it is the image of something else. Moreover, as St. Thomas says in the body of this article: "the movement that is toward an image as an image, is one and the same as that which is toward the thing that is represented."

Hence no reverence is shown to the image of Christ inasmuch as it is a certain thing of gold or silver; but inasmuch as it is an image of Christ, the same reverence is shown to it as to Christ Himself, but as referring to Christ.

Fourth Article

WHETHER CHRIST'S CROSS SHOULD BE WORSHIPED WITH THE ADORATION OF LATRIA

Reply. The answer is in the affirmative, in accordance with the following chant of the Church: "Hail, O Cross, our only hope, during this Passiontide: give to the just increase of grace, grant to each contrite sinner pardon." [23]

St. Thomas gives two conclusions.

First conclusion. The true cross of Christ on which Christ was crucified is to be adored with the cult of latria both inasmuch as it represents to us the figure of Christ extended thereon, and because of its contact with the members of Christ, and of its being saturated with His blood.

Second conclusion. The effigy of Christ's cross in any other material is to be adored with the adoration of relative latria, as being the image of Christ.

Reply to first objection. Thus in the cross is considered not Christ's shame, but its divine power whereby it triumphed over its enemies.

Reply to second objection. Thus the true nails of the passion, and the true crown of thorns are adored, inasmuch as they came in contact with the members of Christ, and were likewise saturated with His blood.

[22] Denz., no. 302. See also nos. 304, 337, 679, and the Council of Trent, nos. 985 f., 998.

[23] Hymn, *Vexilla Regis.*

Fifth Article

WHETHER THE MOTHER OF GOD SHOULD BE ADORED WITH THE ADORATION OF LATRIA

Reply. The answer is in the negative; but the cult of hyperdulia must be given to her. The Collyridians were condemned because they said that the Blessed Virgin Mary is to be adored with the cult of latria.[24] The reason is that the Mother of God is a mere creature and the adoration of latria is to be given to God alone, and to no creature.

The cult of dulia or veneration must be given to the rational creature, however, on account of its excellence. Thus, even in the civil order, the generals of the army, kings, and great philosophers are venerated; and in the order of grace, the cult of supernatural dulia is given to the saints. The cult of hyperdulia must be given to the Blessed Virgin Mary, which more probably differs specifically from the cult of dulia, because the eminent dignity of divine motherhood belongs, by reason of its terminus, to the hypostatic order, which specifically transcends the order of grace and glory.[25] Billuart inclines to this view in his commentary on this article.

Thus, for example, munificence is a virtue that is specifically distinct from liberality, and St. Thomas says that virginity is also a specifically distinct virtue from even the perfect chastity of a widow.[26]

Objection. If the images of Christ and the cross are to be adored, each with the adoration of latria, then this adoration applies likewise to the Blessed Virgin Mary, because the Mother is related to the Son.

Reply. There is no comparison in that the images of Christ and the cross are not in themselves objects of veneration, but refer solely to Christ. On the contrary, the Blessed Virgin Mary and the saints are rational creatures, having an excellence of their own, and in themselves are objects of veneration. "Consequently, if the adoration of latria were shown to the rational creatures in which this image is, there might be an occasion of error,"[27] namely, because not a few might conclude that these persons are to be adored in themselves with the adoration not of relative, but of absolute latria. In other words, such adoration might afford anyone the occasion of judging that it

[24] See St. Epiphanius in his *Adv. haereses,* no. 79.

[25] Cf. Father Merkelbach's *Mariology,* last chapter.

[26] *Summa theol.,* IIa IIae, q. 152, a. 5.

[27] This quotation refers to the image of God imprinted on the soul. (Tr.)

should be attributed to this person because of his or her own excellence.

Doubt. Is the cult of hyperdulia for its own sake greater and nobler than the adoration of relative latria?

Reply. The answer is in the affirmative with Billuart and several other theologians, because, although latria is a species of cult more perfect than hyperdulia, nevertheless it can be that the act of hyperdulia is worthier than the act of latria in some individual; just as, although justice is a virtue specifically more perfect than temperance, nevertheless it is possible that the noblest act of temperance, for example, of virginity, is more perfect in some individual than the least act of justice, such as the payment of a debt in some business transaction.

This terminates the question of Christ's adoration.

Sixth Article

WHETHER ANY KIND OF WORSHIP IS DUE TO THE RELICS OF THE SAINTS

In this article St. Thomas shows that the relics of the saints must be venerated with the cult of dulia, because the saints excelled in the practice of all the virtues.

He says: "The bodies of the saints were temples and organs of the Holy Ghost dwelling and operating in them, and are destined to be likened to the body of Christ by the glory of the resurrection. Hence God Himself fittingly honors such relics, by working miracles in their presence." [28]

This argument is valid in refuting the error of Protestants who contend that the saints must not be venerated.

[28] *Summa theol., loc. cit.*, a. 6, c.

CHAPTER XXVIII

QUESTION 26

Christ the Mediator

First Article

WHETHER IT IS PROPER TO CHRIST TO BE THE MEDIATOR OF GOD AND MAN

State of the question. It seems not to be proper to Christ, because this is also fitting to prophets, priests, and angels.

Reply. The answer is that Christ alone is the perfect mediator between God and men; but there are other mediators in a qualified sense, or secondary and subordinate mediators, inasmuch as dispositively or ministerially they cooperate to unite men with God.

There are two parts to this conclusion.

Authoritative proof of first part. St. Paul says: "There is one mediator of God and men, the man Christ Jesus, who gave Himself a redemption for all." [1] He also declares that Jesus is called the mediator of the New Testament, because He reconciled us to God by the shedding of His blood that speaks more eloquently than the blood of Abel.[2]

Theological proof of first part. It belongs properly to the office of a mediator to unite those between whom he mediates. But to unite men perfectively to God belongs to Christ, who reconciled men to God, inasmuch as He condignly satisfied for them, and condignly merited for them the graces necessary for salvation and eternal life. St. Paul says: "God was in Christ reconciling the world to Himself," [3] and again: "Christ gave Himself a redemption for all." [4]

[1] I Tim. 2:5 f.

[2] Cf. Heb. 8:6; 9:15; 12:24.

[3] II Cor. 5:19.

[4] I Tim. 2:6.

Explanation of second part. There are other subordinate mediators inasmuch as they cooperate in uniting men to God, either dispositively, such as the prophets and priests of the Old Testament, or ministerially, such as the priests of the New Testament, who are strictly speaking Christ's ministers in the bestowal of grace.

Even the prophets and priests of the Old Testament ministerially cooperated in uniting men to God inasmuch as they foretold and prefigured the true and perfect mediator.[5]

In this sense the Blessed Virgin is called the universal mediatrix, subordinated to Christ, inasmuch as she merited strictly *de congruo* with Him what He merited *de condigno* for us, inasmuch as she also satisfied with Him *de congruo*. Now, too, she is also the mediatrix inasmuch as she intercedes for us along with Christ "always living to make intercession for us,"[6] and finally inasmuch as she is the distributor of all our graces.[7]

Reply to second objection. The good angels are also mediators ministerially and dispositively, inasmuch as they are Christ's ministers in the kingdom of God.

Reply to third objection. The Holy Ghost is not a mediator although it is said of Him that "He asks for us with unspeakable groanings,"[8] because He makes us ask by special inspiration.

Second Article

WHETHER CHRIST AS MAN IS THE MEDIATOR OF GOD AND MEN

State of the question. It seems that He is mediator inasmuch as He is both God and man. Moreover, He is mediator inasmuch as He reconciled us to God by taking away sin, but this He did as God.

Reply. Nevertheless Christ as man is mediator.

Authoritative proof. St. Augustine expressly says: "Christ, as man, is mediator."[9] So, likewise, we said that Christ, as man, is a priest, for as priest He prayed, merited, and satisfied for us.[10] But these acts

[5] Cf. IIIa, q. 26, a. 1, ad 1.
[6] Heb. 7:25.
[7] Denz., nos. 3033 and 3034 note.
[8] Rom. 8:26.
[9] *De civ. Dei,* Bk. IX, chap. 15.
[10] Cf. IIIa, q. 22, a. 1.

belong to Christ, as man, for they imply the subordination of His human will to the divine will.

Theological proof. There are two things to be considered in a mediator, namely, that such a person acts as a man, and unites others. But neither of these applies to Christ as God, but only as man. Therefore it applies to Christ as man to be mediator.

The major is self-evident.

Proof of minor.

a) It is the nature of a mean to be distant from each extreme. But Christ as God does not differ from the Father and the Holy Ghost either in nature or power of dominion. Hence He is not distant from them.

On the contrary, Christ as man is distant from God in nature and from men in dignity, grace, and glory, especially by the grace of union.

b) The mediator, however, unites God and men, by communicating the precepts and gifts of God to men, and by satisfying and appealing to God for men. But this Christ does, not indeed as God, but as man, because to satisfy and appeal presupposes subordination of the created will to the divine will. Hence Christ as man is mediator.

Reply to third objection. "Although it belongs to Christ as God to take away sin authoritatively, yet it belongs to Him as man to satisfy for the sin of the human race, and in this sense He is called the mediator of God and men."

Doubt. Is Christ as man mediator because of the fullness of habitual grace, inasmuch as this presupposes the grace of union, or is He more so formally because of the grace of union from which results the fullness of habitual grace?

The question is almost the same as the one about what formally constitutes Christ's priesthood. It is a disputed question even among Thomists. We have already seen that the Salmanticenses maintain that what formally constitutes Christ's priesthood is the grace of headship inasmuch as it connotes the grace of union.[11]

Others, such as Gonet, and in more recent times Father Hugon and many modern theologians, say that Christ is formally constituted priest and universal mediator by the grace of union, from which the fullness of habitual grace results. For He is priest and mediator

[11] See pp. 1012 f. (manuscript).

as anointed by God,[12] and He is anointed by God first by the grace of union. Moreover, as priest and mediator He must offer redemptive sacrifice or adequate satisfaction that is of infinite value. But the infinite value of Christ's merits and satisfaction depend not only presupposedly but also formally on the grace of union, or on Christ's divine personality.

This second opinion, which in our days is gradually gaining favor, seems to be the more correct one. We may quote in favor of this opinion what Pius XI teaches in his encyclical on Christ the king in which he states that Christ as man is the universal king of all creatures even of angels, inasmuch as by the grace of union His human nature is personally or hypostatically united to the Word. He says: "His kingship rests on that wondrous union which they call hypostatic. Hence it follows, not only that God is to be adored in Christ by angels and men, but also that angels and men are obedient and subject to His imperial sway as man, namely, that it is not only because of the hypostatic union that Christ has power over all creatures. . . . Moreover, Christ by the right of having redeemed us can command us." [13]

St. Thomas spoke in the same way about Jesus, in that He is the judge of the living and the dead. Jesus is judge even as man. "Judiciary power," says St. Thomas, "belongs to the man Christ on account of both His divine personality, and the dignity of His headship, and the fullness of His habitual grace." [14]

This judiciary power belongs to Christ with respect to all human affairs because "Christ's soul, which is filled with the truth of the Word of God, passes judgment upon all things." [15]

Christ's judiciary power, even as man, extends to the angels; "first of all from the closeness of His assumed nature to God." [16] Therefore it likewise seems that Christ as man is the universal mediator: (1) because of the grace of union; (2) because of the grace of headship. Thus He can have theandric acts of infinite value in meriting and satisfying for us, that is, in reconciling us to God, which is properly the office of the universal mediator.

[12] This sacerdotal unction is the very consecration of the priest. But Christ's humanity is consecrated to God, first and formally by the uncreated grace of union.

[13] Denz., no. 2194.

[14] *Summa theol.*, IIIa, q. 59, a. 3, c.

[15] *Ibid.*, a. 4, c.

[16] *Ibid.*, a. 6, c.

This terminates the first part of this treatise on the Incarnation, namely, on the union of the Word incarnate, on the consequences of the union, as regards Christ in Himself, as also in His relation to the Father and to us. We now pass on to consider what Christ did and suffered for us.

PART II

THE REDEMPTION

CHAPTER XXIX

PREFATORY REMARKS

THE second part of this treatise on the Incarnation by St. Thomas concerns "what Christ did and suffered." [1] It is explained from question twenty-seven to question fifty-nine, but it is too long a treatise for each question and its articles to be explained. We shall have to discuss what is more important. Thus we shall discuss the mystery of Redemption, and afterward there will be a compendium on Mariology.[2]

The student must read carefully what St. Thomas wrote about Christ's conception, about the mother who conceived, the mode of conception, the perfection of the offspring concerned, the birth of Christ, His manifestation, circumcision, and baptism, as also His manner of conversing with others, His temptations in the desert, His doctrine and miracles.[3] Those questions must especially be read in which it is shown that the three persons of the Trinity cooperated in the conception of Christ's body, though it is attributed by appropriation to the Holy Ghost.[4] But nowise must Christ be called the Son of

[1] Prologue to q. 29.

[2] Cf. Denzinger's *Enchiridion,* Index systematicus, VIII, h. on what the Church has defined and declared about the mysteries of Christ's life.

Concerning this part of St. Thomas' treatise, cf. such commentators as Cajetan and Bartholomew de Medina; Suarez, St. Robert Bellarmine, Petavius, L. Billot, L. Janssens, E. Hugon. Th. Pègues must also be noted. Father Vosté, O.P., has recently published a Commentary on the *Theological Summa* of St. Thomas, entitled *"De mysteriis vitae Christi"* (IIIa, q. 27–59), and another work, *De passione et morte Jesu Christi,* Rome, 1937.

On the history of the theology of redemption, cf. J. Rivière, "Le dogme de la Redemption," *Etude théologique; Le dogme de la rédemption chez S. Augustin; Le dogme de la rédemption après S. Augustin; Le dogme de la rédemption au début du Moyen-age.*

[3] Cf. IIIa, q. 27–45.

[4] *Ibid.,* q. 32–35.

the Holy Ghost, or even of the entire Trinity. At the first moment of conception, Christ's body was animated by a rational soul and was assumed by the Word. Likewise at the first moment of conception Christ was sanctified by grace, had the use of free will, and merited; in fact, from the first moment He was a perfect comprehensor. Birth is properly attributed to the person, as to the subject, and not to the nature, and so the Blessed Virgin Mary is the Mother of God. In Christ there are two births, one is eternal, the other is temporal, but there are not two real sonships. In Christ there is only one real sonship, namely, His eternal sonship from the Father, the other is a logical and temporal relation as regards the Mother, for every relation that is predicated of God in time, is only a logical relation. However, there is a real relation of the Mother to Him, who is really the Son of Mary.[5]

State of the question on Redemption. We already discussed in the first part of this treatise the necessity of Redemption,[6] and we said that redemption by a divine person who became incarnate is hypothetically necessary, after original sin, posited that God freely willed to exact adequate reparation whereas He could have freely condoned the offense or even accepted inadequate reparation.

We must now consider the nature of Redemption, in what it consists, how it was accomplished by Christ's passion, and the ways by which our Lord's passion caused our salvation.

The adequate concept of redemption. As Father E. Hugon observes: "Sometimes redemption is taken in the strict sense for liberation from the slavery of sin and the devil; but sometimes it refers to the entire supernatural economy whereby Christ, our Head, taking our place, offers to God adequate reparation for the offense and at the same time a perfect sacrifice; He liberates us from the captivity of sin and He renews in us the supernatural blessings, lost by the Fall, giving them back to us. Redemption essentially implies . . . the payment of the price required for the adequate reparation of the offense, which is called satisfaction. Wherefore satisfaction is the primary and fundamental concept in the dogma of redemption. But Christ acts in our name, and hence His satisfaction is called vicarious, inasmuch as He not only suffers for our sins, but takes our place. In other respects this satisfaction is made in a certain laborious manner, by means of a true

[5] *Ibid.*, q. 35, a. 5.
[6] See Part I, q. 1, a. 2.

immolation, which is most pleasing to God, and for this reason it is also a sacrifice. Moreover, there is reparation for the offense, and God is satisfied, in consequence of this, and placated by the sacrifice offered to Him, so that we are made free, and supernatural blessings are restored to us or we are reinstated in grace. Therefore the following divers notions concur in the adequate analysis of redemption, namely, satisfaction which presupposes merit and sacrifice, that may be considered the constituent elements; then liberation and restoration, which may be called the consequences or effects." [7]

That this was actually the concept of redemption held by St. Thomas is evident from what he wrote,[8] when discussing the various aspects of this mystery.

But some in reading this forty-eighth question understand satisfaction in a quasi-univocal sense, as being a juridical payment of debt, which among men can be without any love of charity toward the other, and hence they say that this depreciates the sublimity of this mystery of redemption, which is essentially a mystery of love.

But if we answer by saying that in the order of grace, and especially in the hypostatic order, the payment of the debt must be understood not univocally but analogically in the metaphorical sense, then they understand by this, analogically in the metaphorical sense, as when we say by figure of speech that God is angry. Thus the payment of the debt is no longer retained in the strict sense of the term.

On the contrary, St. Thomas understands satisfaction in the analogical though strict sense of the term, and not merely in the metaphorical sense, as when being, life, liberty, love, mercy, even vindictive justice but not anger, are attributed to God analogically and in the strict sense. Among men there may indeed be a legal payment of a debt that is true satisfaction, without the love of charity toward the other. But if we speak of the satisfaction offered by Christ for us, then we speak analogically, but still in the strict sense of satisfaction by the payment of the price offered because of His supreme love of charity toward God and toward us even because of His theandric love that is of infinite value.

Wherefore St. Thomas thus defines satisfaction: "He properly

[7] *Tractactus dogmatici de Verbo incarnato,* p. 667. This liberation and reparation of the human race is called *objective redemption* to which Jesus the Redeemer has condign right; the application of this liberation and reparation to such an individual, as Peter or Paul, is called *subjective redemption.*

[8] Cf. IIIa, q. 48.

atones for an offense who offers something which the offended one loves equally or even more than he detested the offense." [9] But Christ offered for us His most precious blood by a theandric act of love, which God loves more than He hates all sins and crimes taken together. We shall see that the essence of redemption, inasmuch as it is properly a mystery of love, consists in this theandric love, which is both meritorious and satisfactory. Other aspects of this mystery are subordinated to this supreme love, just as the virtues of religion, penance, justice, obedience, and fortitude are subordinated to the virtue of charity.[10] It is, indeed, true to say with St. Paul: "You are bought with a great price," [11] but this price is the infinite value of the love of Christ suffering for us.

Hence St. Thomas,[12] starting from this theandric love, speaks of merit, which belongs to charity, namely, of Christ's merit as our head, before he discusses satisfaction, which presupposes merit.[13]

Since redemption is the work of the Word incarnate, in its explanation we must proceed in the descending order from the Word incarnate to the remission of sin, rather than in the ascending order from sin to our liberation and justification. Here we must observe what St. Thomas says in his treatise on justification, where he writes: "Because the infusion of grace and the remission of sin regard God who justifies, hence in the order of nature the infusion of grace is prior to the freeing from sin. But if we look at what is on the part of the man justified, it is the other way about, since in the order of nature the being freed from sin is prior to the obtaining of justifying grace." [14]

What predominates in the mystery of redemption as in the conversion of St. Mary Magdalen or of St. Paul, is the Redeemer's love. Hence the conception of this mystery must be rather spiritual than juridical, even when it is strictly a question of satisfaction. Similarly in the general concept of merit with reference to God, it must be noted that the notion of merit is analogical, that is, it is called analogical in divine things in comparison with merit in human things. There-

[9] Cf. IIIa, q. 48, a. 2.

[10] Merit primarily belongs to charity, sacrifice to religion, satisfaction to justice, but in us it is a part of penance, which was not in Christ, who was impeccable, and martyrdom is an act of fortitude.

[11] I Cor. 6:20.

[12] Cf. q. 48, a. 1.

[13] Cf. *infra,* q. 48 of St. Thomas, for division and arrangement of this question.

[14] *Summa theol.,* Ia IIae, q. 113, a. 8, ad 1.

fore we must not stress too much the right to a reward, but we must insist more on either the condignness or the congruity and fittingness as regards the divine rewards, inasmuch as merit proceeds from infused charity, and this results from God's uncreated charity. Thus we preserve intact the sublimity of divine things and especially of this mystery.

Errors. In this matter, as frequently happens, there were errors by defect as well as by excess.

In the first centuries, the Subordinationists, the Arians, the Nestorians, from the very fact that they denied the divinity of Christ, also rejected the infinite value of redemption. The Docetae denied the reality of the Passion. The Pelagians, who do not admit the reality of original sin, consequently perverted the concept of redemption.

On the contrary, the Protestants of earlier times said that Christ, taking upon Himself our sins, was hateful to God the Father, cursed by Him and, as a real sinner, truly suffered the torments of the damned.

Finally, in opposition to the above heretics, in the sixteenth century, the Socinians, just as before them Abelard had said, contended that Christ redeemed us only in the broad sense of the term and metaphorically, namely, by preaching and example, not at all by paying the penalty that is due to our sins; but He submitted to death so as to give us an example of fortitude. If that were so, then Christ would neither have satisfied for our sins nor merited for us grace and glory. This concept of redemption scarcely differs from rationalism, which denies the order of grace and glory, and therefore the hypostatic order. So say the liberal Protestants [15] and the Modernists,[16] who admitted only a moral redemption, declaring that the doctrine of Christ's sacrificial death is not Evangelical, but originated with St. Paul.[17]

Doctrine of the Church. The Church never *ex professo* solemnly defined what is the revealed teaching on redemption. The schema of its definition was prepared in the Vatican Council, as we shall at once declare. It was equivalently contained beforehand: (1) in the Nicene Creed, which says: "Who for us men and for our salvation

[15] Such as Kant, Schleiermacher, Ritsch, A. Harnack, A. Sabatier. Cf. A. Sabatier, *La doctrine de l'expiation et son évolution historique,* pp. 38 f. See also Rivière, *Le dogme de la rédemption,* chap. 2, pp. 15 f.

[16] Denz., no. 2038. Cf. Rivière, *op. cit.,* p. 16.

[17] Cf. *infra,* chap. 33, on the stand taken by liberal Protestants (q. 48, a. 2, of St. Thomas).

came down from heaven. . . . And became man. . . . He was crucified for us under Pontius Pilate"; [18] (2) in the Council of Ephesus, which states that Christ "offered . . . Himself an oblation for us"; [19] (3) in the Council of Toledo, which declares that Christ "alone was made sin for us, that is, sacrifice for our sins"; [20] (4) also in the Fourth Lateran Council; [21] (5) and in the Council of Florence; [22] (6) in the Council of Trent, where we read: "Who [Christ], when we were enemies, for the exceeding charity by which He loved us merited justification for us by His most holy passion on the wood of the cross, and made satisfaction for us unto God the Father." [23]

Moreover, the Church condemned Abelard as a heretic, because he denied that "Christ assumed flesh so that He might free us from the devil's yoke." [24] The Socinians, too, were condemned as heretics, because they denied that "Christ endured a most bitter death on the cross so that He might redeem us from sin and eternal death and reconcile us with the Father by restoring to us the right to eternal life." [25] Finally, Pius X rejected this proposition of the Modernists, that "the doctrine of Christ's sacrificial death is not Evangelical, but merely the teaching of St. Paul." [26]

The Vatican Council intended to define this question and had already formulated this canon: "If anyone does not confess that God the Word suffering and dying in the flesh, could have satisfied for our sins or truly and properly did satisfy for them, let him be anathema."

In fact, from the various documents on this subject, Denzinger deduces the following proposition: "Christ, the Redeemer, satisfied for the sins of the whole world, and this satisfaction is of infinite value and superabundant." [27]

The various aspects of redemption. Were there different theories among Catholics concerning the mystery of redemption? In recent times certain persons distinguish between: (1) the theory of expiation,

[18] Denz., no. 86.
[19] *Ibid.*, no. 112.
[20] *Ibid.*, no. 286.
[21] *Ibid.*, no. 429.
[22] *Ibid.*, no. 711.
[23] *Ibid.*, no. 799.
[24] *Ibid.*, no. 371.
[25] *Ibid.*, no. 943.
[26] *Ibid.*, no. 2038.
[27] See Denzinger, nos. 794 f., 799, 319, 552, 1019, 3051.

or of substitution, which speaks especially of the guilt of undergoing punishment, and they bring forward many texts from the Old Testament; its over emphasis leads to the theory of the earlier Protestants concerning penal compensation; (2) the theory of satisfaction, which is more sublime and richer, especially as explained by St. Thomas; (3) the theory of reparation, which seeks to perfect the preceding theory, insisting more on this, that it is "not the death, but the will of the person dying that placated [the Father]," as St. Bernard says; [28] (4) finally, others stress more the Father's love for us ("God so loved the world, as to give His only-begotten Son") [29] and Christ's love "even unto death." [30]

Truly, these four theories are more the different aspects of the mystery of redemption, and we shall see that St. Thomas admitted these different aspects, subordinating the first three to the last, in that the mystery of redemption is especially a mystery of love. Many times he says that Christ suffered for us; [31] he speaks of satisfaction,[32] of reparation,[33] but he always affirms that the foundation of their validity is in Christ's theandric love, which is the source of all His merits. St. Thomas says: "But by suffering out of love and obedience, Christ gave more to God than was required to compensate for the offense of the whole human race." [34]

Finally, at the beginning of this question on redemption, we must recall what St. Thomas had already taught when he said: "Mercy and truth are necessarily found in all God's works. . . . Now the work of divine justice always presupposes the work of mercy, and is founded thereon. . . . We must come to something that depends only on the goodness of the divine will. . . . So in every work of God, viewed at its primary source, there appears mercy. In all that follows, the power of mercy remains and works indeed with even greater force." [35] Thus God purely of His goodness created us, elevated us to the order of grace which is the seed of glory, and gave us the Redeemer.

[28] *Epist.,* 190
[29] John 3:16.
[30] *Ibid.,* 13:2.
[31] Cf. IIIa., q. 46, a. 1.
[32] *Ibid.,* q. 48, a. 2.
[33] *Ibid.,* q. 1, a. 2.
[34] *Ibid.,* q. 48, a. 2.
[35] *Ibid.,* Ia, q. 21, a. 4.

It is from the uncreated love of divine goodness that mercy proceeds, inasmuch as good is self-diffusive, and then comes justice by reason of which the supreme Good has a right to be loved above all things. But first of all, the divine good is self-diffusive in creation, in raising us to the supernatural order, and finally in God's free decree to restore this order to us by means of the Word incarnate.

So as to proceed methodically in this second part, we shall see what Scripture and tradition have to say on this subject, and we shall also consult the teaching of St. Thomas as expounded in questions 46 to 48.

CHAPTER XXX

TESTIMONY OF SACRED SCRIPTURE AND TRADITION

First Article

TESTIMONY OF CHRIST AND THE APOSTLES

THIS testimony concerns the redemption by way of merit, satisfaction, and sacrifice, if not as to the actual meaning of these words, at least as to what is signified by them.

It must be observed that Christ only gradually manifested His divine sonship so far as the people were able to assimilate this doctrine, so that He announced His sorrowful passion to His apostles only after Peter's confession of faith on their way to Caesarea Philippi, when he said: "Thou are Christ, the Son of the living God." [1] It was more difficult, however, for the people to accept this revelation of Christ's passion and impending death on the cross, especially for those who still awaited the coming of the Messias as a temporal king, who would restore the kingdom to Israel, as the apostles said even on the day of the Ascension.[2]

Synoptic Gospels. Hence Jesus at the beginning of His preaching manifests Himself as the Savior, not asserting as yet by what manner of sacrifice and satisfaction He had to save men. So He began by saying: "The Spirit of the Lord is upon Me, wherefore He hath anointed Me to preach the gospel to the poor . . . to heal the contrite of heart." [3] "I am not come to call the just, but sinners." [4] When, after Peter's confession, "Thou are Christ, the Son of the living God," [5] Jesus announces His passion for the first time, "Peter, taking Him,

[1] Matt. 16:21.
[2] Acts 1:6.
[3] Luke 4:18; Mark 10:45.
[4] Matt. 9:13; Mark 2:17.
[5] Matt., 16:16.

began to rebuke Him saying: Lord be it far from Thee, this shall not be unto Thee. Who turning, said to Peter: Go behind Me Satan, thou art a scandal unto Me because thou savorest not the things that are of God, but the things that are of men." [6] Peter unknowingly spoke against the mystery of redemption that had to be accomplished according to God's most sublime decrees. From this moment Jesus speaks more clearly of His sacrifice that must be offered for the salvation of men. He says: "For the Son of man is come to save that which was lost." [7] "The Son of man is not come to be ministered unto, but to minister, and to give His life a redemption for many." [8] This text of the Synoptics is of great importance in establishing against the Modernists and liberal Protestants that the doctrine of the sacrificial death of Christ is not merely of Pauline origin, but is also Evangelical.

Jesus likewise on several occasions announces His passion to His disciples, saying: "The Son of man shall be betrayed to the chief priests and the scribes, and they shall condemn Him to death . . . and they shall deliver Him to the Gentiles to be mocked and scourged and crucified, and the third day He shall rise again. . . . Can you drink the chalice that I shall drink?" [9] But the apostles did not yet understand this most sublime mystery.

Before His passion, in instituting the Holy Eucharist, Jesus said more clearly: "This is My body, which is given for you. Do this for a commemoration of Me. . . . This is the chalice, the new testament in My blood, which shall be shed for you." [10] Thus He explicitly enunciates the mystery of redemption both as sacrifice and as satisfaction, or as a propitiatory sacrifice.

Gospel of St. John. Here again this same truth is several times enunciated so that it becomes increasingly apparent that the value of Christ's satisfaction or of His propitiatory sacrifice is the result of His exceeding love for God and for souls that are to be saved. Penal satisfaction is indeed expressed, but the price to be paid is to be attributed more to Christ's love. This love is especially proclaimed in the parable of the Good Shepherd, where He says: "I am the good shep-

[6] *Ibid.,* 16:22 f.
[7] *Ibid.,* 18:14; Luke 9:56.
[8] *Ibid.,* 20:28; Mark 10:45.
[9] *Ibid.,* 20:18 f.; Mark 10:34; Luke 18:32.
[10] Luke 22:19 f.; Matt. 26:28; Mark 14:24.

herd. The good shepherd giveth His life for his sheep. . . . Therefore doth the Father love Me, because I lay down My life, that I may take it again. No man taketh it away from Me; but I lay it down of Myself, and I have power to lay it down, and I have power to take it up again. This commandment I have received of My Father." [11] Thus Christ enunciates the sacrifice of satisfaction to be offered because of His exceeding love for God and souls.

Somewhat later, Jesus says: "My sheep hear My voice, and I know them, and they follow Me. And I give them eternal life, and they shall not perish forever and no man shall pluck them out of My hand." [12] This is the fruit of sacrifice; therefore it is not only a moral example of self-denial, such as the example given by Socrates.

Afterward His sorrowful satisfaction is expressed in these words: "Amen, amen I say to you, unless the grain of wheat falling into the ground die, itself remaineth alone. But if it die, it bringeth forth much fruit. . . . Now is My soul troubled. And what shall I say? Father, save Me from this hour." [13] He means, deliver Me, if it be possible, as He had said in the Garden of Gethsemane. Then Jesus continues to say: " 'But for this cause I came into this hour. Father, glorify Thy name. . . . Now is the judgment of the world; now shall the prince of this world be cast out. And I, if I be lifted up from this world, will draw all things to Myself.' Now this He said signifying what death He should die." [14] Truly this concerns the sorrowful mystery of redemption. Christ came to offer Himself in sacrifice on the cross; of this hour, predetermined by the Father, Jesus several times says: "The hour is come." [15]

Likewise, before the passion, He said: "Greater love than this no man hath, that a man lay down his life for his friends." [16] Therefore clearly and publicly Christ taught the dogma of redemption,[17] and it is absolutely false to say with the Modernists that "the doctrine of Christ's sacrificial death is not evangelical, but only of Pauline origin." [18]

[11] John 10:11 f.
[12] *Ibid.,* 10:27 f.
[13] *Ibid.,* 12:24 f.
[14] *Ibid.,* 12:27 f.
[15] *Ibid.,* 12:23; 13:1; 16:32; 17:1.
[16] *Ibid.,* 15:13.
[17] Cf. Rivière, *Le dogme de la rédemption,* pp. 68–99.
[18] Denz., no. 2038.

Acts of the Apostles. St. Peter likewise says to the Jews: "Jesus of Nazareth . . . by the determinate counsel and foreknowledge of God, you by the hands of wicked men have crucified and slain. Whom God hath raised up." [19] And again he says: "But the Author of life you killed, whom God hath raised from the dead, of which we are witnesses." [20] Also: "But those things which God before had showed by the mouth of all the prophets, that His Christ should suffer, He hath so fulfilled." [21] Finally, he says of Jesus: "This is the stone which was rejected by you the builders, which is become the head of the corner. Neither is there salvation in any other. For there is no other name under heaven given to men, whereby we must be saved." [22] Thus Christ's sacrifice is evident, as foretold by the prophets, in accordance with God's eternal decree, and it is simultaneously the fount of salvation.

St. Paul. He explained, however, the evangelical teaching concerning the value of Christ's death, especially as it referred to the removal of original sin. On this subject he says: "For all have sinned and do need the glory of God. Being justified freely by His grace, through the redemption, that is in Christ Jesus, whom God hath proposed to be a propitiation through faith in His blood." [23] He afterward explains these texts, saying: "For as by the disobedience of one man [Adam] many were made sinners: so also by the obedience of one, many shall be made just," [24] which means, inasmuch as "Christ became obedient unto death, even to the death of the cross." [25] The time eternally predetermined for this propitiatory sacrifice is also proclaimed in these words: "God spared not even His own Son, but delivered Him up for us all." [26]

Finally, He says: "Christ hath loved us, and hath delivered Himself for us, an oblation and a sacrifice to God for an odor of sweetness." [27] This doctrine is developed throughout the Epistle to the Hebrews, which strictly concerns the offering of propitiatory sacrifice for the redemption of man. St. John also says: "He is the propitia-

[19] Acts 2:22 f.
[20] *Ibid.,* 3:15.
[21] *Ibid.,* 3:18.
[22] *Ibid.,* 4:11 f.
[23] Rom. 3:23 f.
[24] *Ibid.,* 5:19.
[25] Phil. 2:8.
[26] Rom. 8:32.
[27] Eph. 5:2.

tion for our sins, and not for ours only, but also for those of the whole world." [28]

Moreover, this revealed doctrine on the sacrifice of the cross is confirmed from what is said in the New Testament about the sacrifice of the Mass, whereby the fruits of the Passion are applied to us, according to our Lord's words at the time of its institution, who said: "Do this for a commemoration of Me." [29]

Second Article

TESTIMONY OF TRADITION

This doctrine is often explained by both the Latin and the Greek Fathers.[30] Christ accomplished our redemption, they say, by way of a true sacrifice, which He offered to God on the cross, as priest and victim, and by a true vicarious atonement He paid the debt owing to God, but not to the devil. This satisfaction is superabundant and universal. In the above-mentioned work, precisely as regards vicarious satisfaction in the strict sense, we find the testimonies of St. Ignatius of Antioch, St. Justin, Origen, St. Cyprian, Eusebius of Caesarea, St. Athanasius, St. Ambrose, St. Jerome, St. Augustine, St. Prosper, and St. Gregory the Great.[31]

The prominent texts are the following.

St. Clement of Rome says: "Christ gave His blood for us." [32] He also says: "Because of His love for us, our Lord Jesus Christ, by God's will, gave His blood for us, His flesh for our flesh, and His soul for our souls." [33]

St. Ignatius of Antioch says: "Christ died for us, that through faith in His death, we might escape death." [34] In another epistle he says: "The Eucharist is the flesh of our Savior Jesus Christ, which suffered for our sins." [35]

St. Polycarp says: "Jesus Christ, 'who bore our sins in His own body

[28] I John 2:2.

[29] Luke 22:19; I Cor. 11:24 f.

[30] Cf. Rouet de Journel, *Enchiridion patristicum,* Index theologicus, nos. 416–21, for their principal testimonies.

[31] Cf. J. Rivière, *Dict. théol. cath.,* art. "Rédemption," cols. 1932–42. Columns 1941 f. contain the best conclusion of this entire historical compilation.

[32] *Ep. ad Cor.,* 21:6.

[33] *Ibid.,* 49:6; Journel, no. 26.

[34] *To the Trallians,* 2:1.

[35] *To the Smyrnaeans,* 7:1; Journel, 75.

on the tree,'[36] but for our sake that we might live in Him, He endured all things."[37]

St. Justin says: "The Father willed that His Christ take upon Himself the maledictions of the whole human race, and the Father also willed Him to suffer these things, namely, crucifixion and death, so that by His bruises the human race might be healed."[38]

St. Cyprian says: "He alone can pardon sins committed against Him, who took upon Himself our sins, who suffered for us, whom God delivered up for our sins."[39]

St. Athanasius says: Christ "in the body that He took to Himself, or in offering it as sacrifice and immaculate victim for death, immediately averted death from all alike, by offering it for others."[40]

St. Hilary says: "Therefore He offered Himself in sacrifice to death for those under the curse of the law, that it might be removed, willingly offering Himself as victim to God the Father, so that, by His becoming a voluntary victim, the curse . . . might be taken away."[41]

St. Basil says: "It was necessary for the Lord to experience death for all, and so justify all in His blood by having become a propitiation for the human race."[42]

St. Gregory of Nazianzus says: "By Christ's suffering on the cross, . . . we have been renewed, . . . by the celestial Adam we are again saved."[43]

St. John Chrysostom says: "Although we were subject to the sentence of condemnation, Christ freed us."[44]

St. Ambrose says: "The Lord Jesus offered His death for the death of all men; He shed His blood for the blood of the whole human race."[45]

St. Jerome says: Christ "was wounded for our iniquities . . . so that, having become a curse for us, He might free us from the curse."[46]

[36] I Pet. 2:24.
[37] *To the Philippians,* 8:1; Journel, 75.
[38] *Dial. cum Tryph.,* 95; Journel, 140.
[39] *De lapsis,* 17; Journel, 552.
[40] *Oratio de incar. Verbi,* chap. 9; Journel, 751.
[41] *Com. in Ps. 53,* no. 13; Journel, 889.
[42] *Epist.* 260, 9; Journel, 927.
[43] *Oratio,* 33, 9; Journel, 998.
[44] *In Epist. ad Gal.,* chaps. 2, 8; Journel, 1201.
[45] *Epist.* 41, chap. 7; Journel, 1252; see also 1275, 1313.
[46] *Com. in Isa.,* 53:5; Journel, 1401.

St. Augustine says: "Christ, though innocent, took upon Himself our punishment, so that thereby He might atone for our guilt and also put an end to our punishment." [47] In another work, he says: "By His death, indeed, by the one true sacrifice offered for us, whatsoever sins . . . He purged, abolished, extinguished." [48]

Therefore it can be said concerning the reality and effects of redemption, that the Fathers are unanimous in attributing this redemption not only to Christ's example, but also to His merits, satisfaction, and sacrifice on the cross. They do not either disagree among themselves as witnesses of tradition, although in their explanations some, such as the Greek Fathers, insist on the sanctifying power of the Incarnation, whereas others, especially the Latin Fathers, stress the passion and death of Christ. Sometimes Origen declares that the price of our redemption was paid to the devil.[49] But elsewhere he professes the true doctrine.[50] The same is to be said of St. Gregory of Nyssa. This theory of payment to the devil was already refuted at the end of the third century and condemned as blasphemous. The common teaching is that sin is strictly committed only against God; hence the price of liberation from sin must be paid to God alone. Nevertheless it remains true that by redemption man is freed from the slavery of the devil.[51]

From the eleventh to the thirteenth centuries, the theological thesis on the redemption gradually took shape under the doctrinal direction of St. Anselm and St. Thomas. According to St. Anselm,[52] our redemption was accomplished through the satisfaction whereby Christ freely paid our debts by repairing the wrong done to God, and through His merits whereby He restored the good things we lost. This doctrine manifestly has its foundation in Sacred Scripture, and therefore was generally admitted. But St. Anselm exaggerated the necessity of adequate redemption after sin, not sufficiently acknowledging that God could have freely condoned the offense, or even have accepted imperfect satisfaction.

This exaggerated view was gradually corrected by Hugo of St.

[47] *Contra Faustum,* Bk. XIV, chap. 17.

[48] *De Trinit.,* Bk. IV, chap. 17.

[49] *Com. in Rom.,* 2:13; 4:11; 5:3.

[50] *Ibid.,* Bk. III, no. 8; *Contra Celsum,* Bk. VII, chap. 17; Journel, 498, 533.

[51] Journel, *op. cit.,* Index theol., no. 420. J. Rivière, *Le dogme de la rédemption, Essai historique,* pp. 374–446. *Dict. théol. cath.,* art. "Rédemption."

[52] Cf. *Cur Deus Homo.*

Victor, Peter Lombard, Alexander of Hales, and St. Bonaventure, who prepared the way for St. Thomas to elaborate the complete and sound synthesis that was afterward commonly accepted. It is this synthesis that must now be explained.

CHAPTER XXXI

QUESTION 46

Christ's Passion

THE synthesis of St. Thomas contains especially the following three doctrinal points.

1) Redemption by the Word incarnate, posited the sin of our first parents, was not necessary, but fitting. For God could have either condoned the offense or accepted inadequate reparation; but the Incarnation as also the passion of God's son were fitting, and in all this we have the greatest manifestation of God's love for us.[1]

2) The Word incarnate, as the moral head of the whole human race, redeemed us or caused our salvation in five ways: (1) by meriting it for us; (2) by satisfying for us; (3) by offering Himself in sacrifice; (4) by liberating us; (5) by being the efficient cause. In these ways Christ's love prevails, which is the principle of merit, satisfaction, and sacrifice.

3) Christ's redemption is of infinite value, in virtue of the hypostatic union, inasmuch as it is a theandric act of love for His Father and for all men. This makes it apparent that this mystery is especially a mystery of love.

In the explanation of this thesis, St. Thomas discusses: (1) the Passion itself; (2) its efficient cause, on the part of Christ, the Father, and those that killed Christ; (3) how Christ's passion was effective, that is, how it caused our salvation; (4) the effects of the Passion.

This forty-sixth question, which concerns Christ's passion, treats especially of its fitness and its extreme sufferings. The predominating elements of the Passion must be noted.

[1] Cf. IIIa, q. 1, a. 1, 2.

The Fittingness of the Passion

First Article

WHETHER IT WAS NECESSARY FOR CHRIST TO SUFFER FOR THE DELIVERANCE OF THE HUMAN RACE

Reply. Christ's passion was not absolutely necessary, nor did He suffer because He was compelled to suffer; but, presupposing the end to be attained, it was necessary for Christ to suffer: (1) because we were freed by His passion;[2] (2) because Christ, by the humiliation of His passion, merited the glory of His exaltation;[3] (3) because God's decree, concerning Christ's passion, as foretold in the Scripture, had to be fulfilled.

Reply to third objection. "And this came of more copious mercy than if He had forgiven sins without satisfaction," because God gave us the Redeemer.

Second Article

WHETHER THERE WAS ANY OTHER POSSIBLE WAY OF HUMAN DELIVERANCE BESIDES THE PASSION OF CHRIST

Reply. Speaking simply and absolutely, it was possible for God to deliver mankind otherwise than by Christ's passion, even without any satisfaction; for this would not have been contrary to justice, because God, who is infinitely above a simple judge, since He has no superior, decreed that His Son must die and can also forgive the offense committed against Him, without requiring satisfaction; and then He acts mercifully and not unjustly. But, supposing God's foreknowledge and preordination concerning Christ's passion, then man's liberation from sin was not otherwise possible. The first part in the argument of this article and the reply to the third objection correct St. Anselm's extreme view.

[2] John 3:14.
[3] Luke 24:26.

Third Article

WHETHER THERE WAS ANY MORE SUITABLE WAY OF DELIVERING THE HUMAN RACE THAN BY CHRIST'S PASSION

Reply. The answer is that there was no other way more suitable; (1) because by Christ's passion man knows how much God loves him and is thereby incited to love Him in return;[4] (2) because thereby Christ gave us an example of obedience, humility, constancy, justice, and the other virtues;[5] (3) because Christ by His passion not only delivered man from sin, but also merited grace and glory for him; (4) because thereby man is all the more bound to refrain from sin;[6] (5) because in this way, it was in Christ that as man by dying, He conquered the devil and vanquished death.[7]

Fourth Article

WHETHER CHRIST OUGHT TO HAVE SUFFERED ON THE CROSS

Reply. The answer is that it was the most fitting for Christ to have suffered on the cross; (1) because Christ gave us an example of virtue, so that no kind of death ought to be feared by an upright man; (2) "so that whence death came [from the tree], thence life might arise, and that He who overcame by the tree, might also by the tree be overcome";[8] (3) and (4) that dying on a high rood, He might purify the air and prepare our ascent into heaven; (5) the fact that Christ died with outstretched hands signifies the universality of redemption; (6) because, as St. Augustine says, "The tree on which were fixed the members of Him dying was even the chair of the Master teaching";[9] (7) because there were very many figures in the Old Testament of this death on the cross.

First objection. In this kind of death the fire pertaining to holocausts is wanting. St. Thomas replies by saying that, "instead of ma-

[4] Rom. 5:8.
[5] I Pet. 2:21.
[6] I Cor. 6:20.
[7] *Ibid.*, 15:57.
[8] Preface of Passiontide.
[9] *Com. in Joan.*, tract. 109.

terial fire, there was the spiritual fire of charity in Christ's holocaust." [10]

Second objection. Death on the cross is most ignominious. St. Thomas replies to this by quoting St. Paul: "He endured the cross, despising the shame," [11] so that by His humility, He made reparation for our sins of pride.

Third objection. Death on the cross is a death of malediction. St. Thomas again quotes the following text from St. Paul: "Christ hath redeemed us from the curse of the law, being made a curse for us," [12] that is, He took upon Himself the penalty of sin.

All these remarks clearly manifest the fittingness of the Passion, and they better illustrate both God the Father's love and Christ's love for us. As the Evangelist says: "For God so loved the world, as to give His only-begotten Son." [13] As St. Paul says: "He that spared not even His own Son but delivered Him up for us all." [14] Therefore our redemption is predominantly a mystery of love.

The Extreme Sufferings of the Passion

Fifth Article

WHETHER CHRIST ENDURED ALL SUFFERINGS

Reply. Christ did not endure all sufferings specifically, because many of them are mutually exclusive, such as burning and drowning. It did not become Him to suffer interior bodily sicknesses, for, as St. John Chrysostom says: "It did not befit Him who healed the infirmities of others to have His own body afflicted with the same." [15]

But Christ endured every human suffering, because: (1) He suffered something from Jews and Gentiles, from the chief priests and their servants, from the mob, even from friends and acquaintances; (2) He suffered from His friends who abandoned Him, in His reputation, His honor, in His soul from sadness and weariness, in His body from wounds and scourgings; (3) He suffered in all His bodily members, from head to foot, and in all His senses.

Reply to second objection. "As Christ was uplifted above others in

[10] Cf. IIIa, q. 46, a. 4, ad 1.
[11] Heb. 12:2.
[12] Gal. 3:13.
[13] John 3:16.
[14] Rom. 8:32.
[15] Cf. IIIa, q. 46, a. 3, ad 2.

gifts of graces, so He was lowered beneath others by the ignominy of His sufferings."

Reply to third objection. "The very least one of Christ's sufferings was sufficient of itself to redeem the human race from all sins." However, because of His great love for us, He willed to offer Himself as a most perfect holocaust for us, and generically endure all sufferings.

Sixth Article

WHETHER THE PAIN OF CHRIST'S PASSION WAS GREATER THAN ALL OTHER PAINS

Reply. Christ experienced both sensible pain and interior pain, both of which were the greatest of pains in this present life. There are four reasons for this: (1) from the causes of this pain, because the death of the crucified is most bitter, and because He felt interior pain for all the sins of the human race, which He ascribed, so to speak, to Himself; (2) because of the susceptibility of His body that was endowed with a most perfect constitution, and because the interior faculties of His soul most efficaciously apprehended all the causes of sadness; (3) because Christ from His great love for us, in offering Himself as a perfect holocaust, refused to mitigate His pains and sadness by the overflow of contemplative joy through the higher part of His soul; (4) because "He embraced the amount of pain proportionate to the magnitude of the fruit which resulted therefrom," namely, that He might most perfectly accomplish His mission as the Redeemer of men.

Reply to second objection. Christ, that He might atone for the sins of all mankind, accepted indeed the greatest of sadness in absolute quantity, yet not exceeding the rule of reason.

Reply to fourth objection. "Christ grieved over the sins of all men, and this grief in Christ surpassed all grief of every contrite heart both because it flowed from a greater wisdom and charity, by which the pang of contrition is intensified, and because He grieved simultaneously for all sins, as the prophet says: 'Surely He hath carried our sorrows.' " [16]

Reply to sixth objection. In answer to the objection that the least of Christ's pains would have sufficed for man's salvation, St. Thomas says: "Christ willed to deliver the human race from sins not merely by His power, but also according to justice. And therefore He did not simply weigh what great virtue His suffering would have from

[16] Isa. 53:4.

union with the Godhead, but also how much, according to His human nature, His pain would avail for so great a satisfaction."

Seventh Article

WHETHER CHRIST SUFFERED IN HIS WHOLE SOUL

It seems that Christ did not, because He did not suffer in the summit of His soul, in the higher faculties, namely, of reason and will.

Reply. In answer to this, St. Thomas says in the body of this article: "So, then, we say that if the soul be considered with respect to its essence, it is evident that Christ's whole soul suffered. For the soul's whole essence is allied with the body, so that it is entire in the whole body and in its every part. Consequently, when the body suffered and was disposed to separate from the soul, the entire soul suffered. But if we consider the whole soul, according to its faculties, speaking thus of the proper passions of the faculties, He suffered indeed as to all His lower powers . . . whose operations are but temporal. But Christ's higher reason, since it considers only the eternal and not the temporal, did not suffer thereby on the part of its object, which is God, who was the cause not of grief, but rather of delight and joy, to the soul of Christ," for He continued in possession of the beatific vision and its resultant joy in the summit of His soul.

To understand the reply to the second objection, consult the eighth article and the footnote to the third objection of this article.

Reply to third objection. "Grief in the sensitive part of Christ's soul did not extend to reason so as to deflect it from the rectitude of its act." [17]

Eighth Article

WHETHER CHRIST'S ENTIRE SOUL ENJOYED BLESSED FRUITION DURING THE PASSION

It seems that Christ's entire soul did not, because simultaneous sadness and joy are impossibilities; in fact, vehement sadness checks every delight, and the converse is true.

Reply. Nevertheless, as St. John Damascene says in the counter-

[17] This proposition was condemned: "The inferior part of Christ's soul on the cross did not communicate to the higher part its involuntary emotions" (Denz., no. 1339); but this proposition was condemned because of the word "involuntary." Christ willed to permit these emotions.

argument of this article: "Christ's Godhead permitted His flesh to do and to suffer what was proper to it. In like fashion . . . His passion did not impede fruition [of mind]." St. Thomas explains this in the body of the article as follows: "If it be understood according to its essence, then His whole soul did enjoy fruition, inasmuch as it is the subject of the higher part of the soul to which it belongs to enjoy the Godhead. . . . But if we take the whole soul as comprising all its faculties, thus His entire soul did not enjoy fruition . . . because, since Christ was still upon earth, there was no overflowing of glory from the higher part into the lower, nor from the soul into the body. But since, on the contrary, the soul's higher part was not hindered in its proper acts by the lower, it follows that the higher part of His soul enjoyed fruition perfectly while Christ was suffering."

Reply to first objection. It is indeed impossible to be sad and glad simultaneously about the same object; but in Christ sadness and fruition were not about the same object. Thus, though Christ was in a way crushed by grief, He rejoices in His sorrow.[18]

In the next three articles of this forty-sixth question, St. Thomas considers the fitness of the Passion as regards time, the place between two thieves, of whom the one on the right was converted, but the one on the left died impenitent, just as on the Judgment Day a

[18] Cf. *De veritate,* q. 26, a. 9, 10. As we shall see farther on, in chapter 32, a. 2, concerning the union in Christ of extreme grief and supreme happiness, although Christ's sadness and joy were not about the same object, and hence they were not strictly contraries, nevertheless their union was a miracle; for, because of the different ways in which joy tends toward its object, if the joy is most perfect, then it naturally is incompatible with sadness.

As the commentators observe, to understand what St. Thomas says in his reply to the second objection of article 7 of this question, the higher reason and the lower reason are one faculty, it being called higher, inasmuch as it considers divine and eternal things (cf. Ia, q. 79, a. 9). For example, if sin is considered according to lower and human reason, then sorrow arises in the inferior parts of the will. But if sin is considered according to higher and divine reason, inasmuch as it is an offense against God, then there is sadness in the higher part of the will.

But Christ was sorry for our sins inasmuch as they are an offense against God; hence He felt sad, not only in the sensitive faculty, but in the lower reason inasmuch as it was ruled by the higher reason, as Cajetan maintains (*Com. in art. 7,* no. 6), because sin is something temporal, which is then considered in its eternal aspects. Others, such as Sylvius, say that Christ, grieving over the offense against God, was sad also in the higher reason or in the higher part of the will, but not from its primary object, which is God. So Sylvius interprets the words of St. Thomas in his reply to the second objection of the seventh article of this question, who says: "On the part of the proper object, Christ's higher reason did not suffer." See below, chap. 32.

distinction will be made among all human beings, inasmuch as the elect will be on Christ's right hand, and the reprobates on His left. In the last article of this question it is shown that Christ's passion is not to be attributed to His divine nature, which is incapable of suffering, but it is to be attributed to the person of the Word incarnate, because of His human nature.

CHAPTER XXXII

QUESTION 47

The Efficient Cause of Christ's Passion

THE efficient cause of Christ's passion must now be considered. (1) Was Christ an efficient cause? (2) Was the Father? (3) Were those who killed Him?

First Article

WHETHER CHRIST WAS SLAIN BY ANOTHER OR BY HIMSELF

It seems that Christ was not slain by another, for He said: "No man taketh My life from Me." [1] But, on the other hand, He declared of Himself: "And after they have scourged Him, they will put Him to death." [2]

Reply. There are two parts to this answer.

1) Christ was not the direct cause of His death, for He did not kill Himself, but His persecutors killed Him, as He Himself declared: "they will put Him to death." [3]

2) But Christ was the indirect cause of His passion and death, because He did not prevent it when He could have done so.[4] "This He was able to do: (1) by holding His enemies in check so that they

[1] John 10:18.

[2] Luke 18:33.

[3] *Ibid.*

[4] St. Thomas is not here speaking of the strictly moral indirect cause, but of the accidental cause in the physical sense. That anyone be called the moral and indirect cause of any effect, it is not enough that such a person can prevent the effect and does not do so; but it is also necessary that such person is bound to do so; otherwise the effect is neither imputed to such person, nor considered a morally voluntary act. But Christ was not bound to resist His persecutors in the protection of His life, but He could expose Himself to death for the redemption of mankind. Such is the opinion of Suarez.

would not have been eager to slay Him, or would have been powerless to do so; (2) because His spirit had the power of preserving His fleshly nature from the infliction of any injury. . . . Thus He is said to have laid down His life, or to have died voluntarily." [5]

Similarly Christ could say: No man taketh away life from Me, that is, against My will, and this He manifested for "He preserved the strength of His bodily nature so that at the last moment He was able to cry out with a loud voice, and hence His death should be computed among His other miracles." [6]

Second Article

WHETHER CHRIST DIED OUT OF OBEDIENCE

Reply. It is affirmed that out of obedience Christ gave Himself up to suffer.[7] Hence the Apostle says: "He became obedient unto death." [8] But this was most fitting: (1) because it was in keeping with divine justice that, "as by the disobedience of one man, many were made sinners, so also by the obedience of one, many shall be made just"; [9] (2) so that Christ's passion and death should be the result of obedience; (3) so that Christ should be victorious over death and the disobedience of the devil, as the Scripture says: "An obedient man shall speak of victory." [10]

Reply to first objection. Christ received a command from the Father to suffer. And so by dying He fulfilled all the precepts of the Old Law. He fulfilled all the moral precepts, for these are the result of His supreme charity and obedience; by the supreme sacrifice of Himself, all the ceremonial precepts; all the judicial precepts, by satisfying completely for so great a punishment. Thus Christ fulfilled all justice, and was obedient out of love for His Father, who commanded Him. In this we clearly see His supreme love both for God the Father,[11] and for His neighbor, as St. Paul says: "He loved me, and delivered Himself up for me." [12]

[5] Cf. IIIa, q. 47, a. 1, c.
[6] *Ibid.,* ad 2.
[7] *Ibid.*
[8] Phil. 2:8.
[9] Rom. 5:19.
[10] Prov. 21:28.
[11] John 14:31; 10:10.
[12] Gal. 2:21.

Third Article

WHETHER GOD THE FATHER DELIVERED UP CHRIST TO THE PASSION

The doctrine of this article, which is examined by St. Thomas, must be carefully considered. The holy Doctor begins by presenting three difficulties: (1) It seems wicked and cruel to hand over an innocent man to suffering and death. This objection is again brought up in these days by the liberal Protestants. (2) Christ delivered Himself to death; [13] therefore it was not God the Father who did it. (3) Judas is accounted guilty for having delivered up Christ to the Jews. Therefore it seems that God the Father did not deliver up Christ to His passion.

Reply. Nevertheless the reply is in the affirmative, the Apostle saying: "He that spared not even His own Son but delivered Him up for us all." [14] The following explanation is given.

Christ suffered voluntarily and out of obedience to the Father. Hence in three respects, God the Father delivered up Christ to the Passion: (1) because God eternally preordained Christ's passion for the liberation of the human race from sin; [15] (2) inasmuch as God inspired Him with the will to suffer; [16] (3) by not protecting Him from the Passion, but abandoning Him to His persecutors; hence Christ on the cross said: "My God, My God, why hast Thou forsaken Me?" [17] because, as St. Augustine says,[18] He had abandoned His Son to the power of His persecutors.

The earlier Protestants adulterated this doctrine when they said that the Father delivered up Christ by inspiring the Jews to put Him to death and urging them to it.

What is said in the article has its foundation in what St. Thomas teaches about the efficacy of the decrees of God's will.[19] This divine will does not make our acts necessary, because God wills them to be accomplished freely, and He does not destroy but actualizes human freedom. Thus Christ freely and meritoriously suffered.

Reply to first objection. It would be cruel to hand over an innocent

[13] Isa. 53:12.
[14] Rom. 8:32.
[15] Isa. 53:6 f.
[16] *Ibid.*, 53:7.
[17] Matt. 27:46.
[18] *Epist.* 140 (120 in some editions).
[19] Cf. Ia, q. 19, a. 8.

man to suffering and death against his will. "Yet God the Father did not so deliver up Christ, but inspired Him with the will to suffer for us. God's severity is thereby shown, for He would not remit sin without penalty . . . and His goodness in that . . . He gave us a satisfier." Wherefore the Apostle says: "God spared not even His own Son, but delivered Him up for us all." [20]

Reply to second objection. "Christ as man gave Himself up by a will inspired of the Father." So also it is with victim souls, and for this reason it is imprudent to vow to become a victim soul except under special inspiration, or presupposing this as a condition.

Reply to third objection. "The Father delivered up Christ, and Christ surrendered Himself, from charity; but Judas betrayed Christ from greed, the Jews from envy, and Pilate from worldly fear." All these things make it increasingly clear for St. Thomas as for all posterity that the mystery of redemption is especially a mystery of love.

Fourth Article

WHETHER IT WAS FITTING FOR CHRIST TO SUFFER AT THE HANDS OF THE GENTILES

In the last three articles of this forty-seventh question, St. Thomas inquires how Christ's persecutors were the cause of His passion, and first whether it was fitting for Him to suffer from the Gentiles.

Christ declared of Himself: "The Son of man shall be betrayed to the chief priests and the scribes, and they shall condemn Him to death, and shall deliver Him to the Gentiles to be mocked, and scourged, and crucified, and the third day He shall rise again." [21] But it was fitting that in this way the effects of Christ's passion should be prefigured in what He suffered. The effect of Christ's passion was that many Jews were baptized [22] and by the preaching of these Jews, the effects of Christ's passion were transmitted to Gentiles. Therefore it was fitting that Christ begin His suffering from the Jews and afterward, the Jews betraying Him, that His passion be accomplished by means of the Gentiles. In other words, the wicked Jews betrayed Him to the Gentiles to be scourged, and afterward the good and converted

[20] Rom. 8:32.
[21] Matt. 20:19.
[22] Acts, chaps. 2 and 3.

Jews, by their preaching, transmitted the effects of the Passion to the Gentiles.

Reply to first objection. Christ upon the cross prayed for His persecutors. Therefore Christ willed to suffer from both, so that the fruits of His petition might benefit both Jews and Gentiles.

Reply to second objection. Christ's passion on His part was the offering of a sacrifice out of supreme love for the human race; but on the part of His persecutors it was a most grievous sin.

Reply to third objection. "The Jews, who were subjects of the Romans, did not have the power to sentence anyone to death." What is meant here is the "power of the sword." [23]

Fifth Article

WHETHER CHRIST'S PERSECUTORS KNEW WHO HE WAS

In this article St. Thomas has in mind to reconcile the various texts of Sacred Scripture. On the one hand, Christ said: "Now they have both seen and hated both Me and My Father," [24] and in the parable of the wicked husbandmen, these said: "This is the heir, come let us kill him." [25] St. Matthew makes the additional comment farther on: "And when the chief priests and Pharisees had heard His parables they knew that He spoke of them." [26] On the other hand, Christ said: "Father, forgive them, for they know not what they do." [27] St. Paul, too, remarks: "If they had known it, they would never have crucified the Lord of glory," [28] and St. Peter, likewise, says to the Jews: "I know that you did it through ignorance, as did also your rulers." [29]

St. Thomas solves the difficulty by distinguishing between the elders and the common people, and also for the elders by distinguishing between Christ's Messiahship and His Godhead. He says: "According to St. Augustine [30] the elders, who were called rulers, knew, as did also the devils, that He was the Christ promised in the Law: for they saw all the signs in Him, which the prophets said would come to pass;

[23] Cf. Vosté, *Com. in IIIam,* q. 48, a. 4.
[24] John 15:24.
[25] Matt. 22:38.
[26] *Ibid.,* 22:45.
[27] Luke 23:34; I Cor. 23:34.
[28] I Cor. 2:8.
[29] Acts 3:17.
[30] Questions of New and Old Testaments.

but they did not know the mystery of His Godhead. Consequently the Apostle says that, if they had known it, they would never have crucified the Lord of glory. It must, however, be understood that their ignorance did not excuse them from crime, because it was, as it were, affected ignorance. For they saw manifest signs of His Godhead, yet they perverted them out of hatred and envy of Christ, and they would not believe His words, whereby He avowed that He was the Son of God." [31]

St. Thomas, however, goes on to remark: "But those of lesser degree, namely, the common folk, who had not grasped the mysteries of the Scriptures, did not fully comprehend that He was the Christ or the Son of God. For although some of them believed in Him, the multitude did not; and if they were inclined to believe sometimes that He was the Christ, on account of the manifold signs and force of His teaching,[32] nevertheless they were deceived afterward by their rulers so that they did not believe Him to be the Son of God or the Christ." [33] This article seems to be the expression of most sublime wisdom and penetration.

The replies to the first, second, and third objections confirm what is said in the body of this article.

Reply to the third objection. It says: "Affected ignorance does not excuse from guilt, but seems rather to aggravate it; for it shows that a man is so strongly attached to sin that he wishes to incur ignorance lest he avoid sinning. The Jews therefore sinned not only as crucifiers of the man Christ, but also as crucifiers of God."

Sixth Article

WHETHER THE SIN OF THOSE WHO CRUCIFIED CHRIST WAS MOST GRIEVOUS

Here, too, the question is how to reconcile these words of Christ, namely, "Father, forgive them for they know not what they do," [34] with the following text: "Fill ye up then the measure of your fathers." [35]

There are three conclusions. (1) "The rulers of the Jews knew that

[31] Cf. IIIa, q. 47, a. 5, c. See also John 15:22.
[32] John 7:31, 41.
[33] IIIa, q. 47, a. 5, c. See also Cajetan's commentary on this article.
[34] Luke 23:34.
[35] Matt. 33:32.

He was the Christ, and if there was any ignorance in them, it was affected ignorance, which could not excuse them. Therefore their sin was most grievous, on account of the kind of sin, as well as from the malice of their will. (2) The Jews also of the common class sinned most grievously as to the kind of their sin; yet in one respect their crime was lessened by reason of their ignorance. (3) But the sin of the Gentiles, by whose hands He was crucified, was much more excusable, since they had no knowledge of the Law."

Reply to first objection. "The excuse made by our Lord: 'they know not what they do,' [36] is not to be referred to the rulers among the Jews, but to the common people."

Concerning the reply to the second objection, Cajetan says: "It is a matter of dispute here whether Judas sinned more grievously or the rulers of the Jews, . . . and we must say that Judas sinned more grievously. For he was raised above them, inasmuch as he was an apostle. And he not only had seen Christ's miracles, but had also worked miracles in Christ's name, having received this power from Christ, just as the other apostles had.[37] And he confessed Jesus to be the Christ,[38] approving of Peter's answer who, in the name of all the disciples, said: 'Thou art Christ'; [39] and, in short, above the malice that he shared in common with the rulers, his ingratitude was the greatest, and he added to this kind of sin the baseness of betrayal." [40]

Thus we have sufficiently examined the causes of Christ's passion.

[36] Luke 23:34.
[37] Matt. 10:1.
[38] *Ibid.*, 16:17.
[39] *Ibid.*, 16:16.
[40] *Com. in IIIam,* q. 47, a. 6, ad 2.

CHAPTER XXXIII

QUESTION 48

The Efficiency of Christ's Passion

THIS question of St. Thomas must be carefully considered, and all its articles must be explained, because it is of great importance. He answers that Christ's passion caused our salvation by way of merit, satisfaction, sacrifice, redemption or liberation, and that it was the efficient cause.

Division and orderly arrangement of this question. Certain recent historians seem to think that St. Thomas placed in quasi-juxtaposition the notions of merit, satisfaction, sacrifice, and redemption, not subordinating them. They also find that this question is too complex, as if the holy Doctor did not know how to preserve the unity of the mystery by showing how it predominantly illustrates Christ's love for the Father and for us.

Truly it would be contrary to St. Thomas' method of procedure, not to subordinate these various notions, for it is the mark of the wise man to do so. If, on the contrary, this question is carefully examined, its wonderful order becomes quite clear.

1) The holy Doctor finds these different notions in Sacred Scripture and tradition, and he had therefore to explain them all as to their theological significance in due order.

2) These notions are of themselves subordinated as in the present enumeration beginning from the more universal and ascending to the less universal, and they all presuppose Christ's charity, which holds the first place. For Christ's act of charity is primarily meritorious, but it is strictly satisfactory only if it is laborious and difficult; for every satisfactory act is meritorious, but not vice versa. Then an act that is both meritorious and satisfactory is not always in the strict sense a sacrifice, whereas, on the contrary, a perfect sacrifice, such as

a holocaust, is both meritorious and satisfactory. Moreover, in the enumeration, redemption is taken in the restricted sense of liberation from the slavery of sin and the devil, but not in the complete sense, whereby Christ is said to be the cause or the author of our salvation. Wherefore several authors explain this question of St. Thomas, as we shall, by considering the different ways of redemption in the adequate sense, that is, by way of merit, satisfaction, sacrifice, liberation, and effectiveness. But in this enumeration, as E. Hugon observes, merit, satisfaction, and sacrifice belong to redemption as constitutive elements, but our liberation and the efficiency of our salvation in the application of the merits and satisfaction of the Passion, belong to it as consecutive elements or effects. Thus the orderly arrangement of these articles and the beautiful structure of this question become increasingly apparent. But the liberation and restoration of the human race is called objective redemption, and to this Jesus has condign right, the Blessed Virgin Mary, however, a congruent title. The application of this liberation and restoration to this particular person, such as to Peter or Paul, is called subjective redemption.

3) Finally, Christ the Savior in redeeming us practiced different subordinated virtues. First of all, He practiced charity, to which merit strictly belongs, for the other virtues are meritorious only as they are commanded by charity. Secondly, He practiced justice, of which satisfaction is a part. Thirdly, He practiced religion, to which sacrifice belongs. But these three elements, as stated, constitute the work of redemption from which our liberation and restoration follow, by the effective application of the merits and satisfaction of the Passion. Thus St. Thomas succeeded very well in the orderly arrangement of this question. It is no wonder that this question is rather complex, because the higher and more universal is the cause, the more it includes several modes of causality; but in this complexity shines forth the splendor of its unity, inasmuch as all these elements manifest Christ's love for the Father and for us.

This orderly arrangement is seen to be all the more profound when we take note of the fact that Christ, the head of the human race, as generally admitted, could have redeemed us by whatever meritorious act without painful satisfaction and sacrifice in the strict sense.

First Article

ON REDEMPTION BY WAY OF MERIT

State of the question. At the beginning of this first article St. Thomas presents three difficulties. It seems that Christ's passion was not the meritorious cause of our salvation: (1) because suffering, as such, is not meritorious; (2) He did not even merit our salvation as an interior offering of Himself, because Christ from the beginning of His conception, merited for us in fact by merit that is of infinite value. Therefore it would be superfluous for Him to merit again what He had already merited; (3) because charity is the foundation of merit, and this charity did not increase in Christ by His passion. Therefore He did not merit our salvation more by His passion than He had merited it before.

Reply. Nevertheless the answer is that Christ by His passion merited salvation for all His members.

This conclusion is of faith, for the Council of Trent says: "Our Lord Jesus Christ,[1] when we were enemies, for the exceeding charity whereby He loved us,[2] merited justification for us by His most holy passion on the wood of the cross." [3] The Council also says: "If anyone shall say that men are justified without Christ's justice, whereby He merited for us; let him be anathema." [4]

Scriptural proof. St. Paul says: "For as by the disobedience of one man, many were made sinners; so also by the obedience of one, many shall be made just." [5] In other words, just as by Adam's demerit we lost grace, so by the merit of Christ's grace we receive grace. Again he says: "Being justified freely by His grace through the redemption that is in Christ Jesus." [6] In another epistle, he says: "God hath predestinated us unto the adoption of children through Jesus Christ . . . unto the praise of the glory of His grace, in which He hath graced us in His beloved Son, in whom we have redemption through His blood, the remission of sins according to the richness of His grace." [7] Jesus Himself said: "The Son of man must be lifted up, that

[1] Rom. 5:10.
[2] Eph. 2:4.
[3] Denz., no. 799.
[4] *Ibid.*, no. 820.
[5] Rom. 5:19.
[6] *Ibid.*, 3:24.
[7] Eph. 1:5 f.

whosoever believeth in Him may not perish, but may have life everlasting." [8] By His passion He merited exaltation for Himself,[9] and for us sanctification, for Jesus said: "And for them do I sanctify [or sacrifice] Myself, that they also may be sanctified in truth." [10]

Theological proof. St. Thomas gives the fundamental argument as follows: Grace was given to Christ, not only as an individual, but inasmuch as He is the head of the Church, and therefore Christ's works are referred to Himself and to His members, just as the works of another man in a state of grace are referred to himself. But it is evident that whoever suffers for justice' sake, provided he is in the state of grace, merits his salvation thereby. Consequently Christ by His passion merited not only His exaltation but also salvation for all His members.

We are concerned here with condign merit, whereby Christ the head, by His theandric supernatural love that is of infinite value, merited for us in justice, the supernatural goods lost by sin, namely, grace and eternal life, as explained above.[11] All the conditions required for merit are eminently verified in this great act of charity, namely, grace and eternal life; for Christ was still a wayfarer, and God by appointing Him mediator and Head, had ordained His works for the salvation of His members.

Reply to first objection. Christ's suffering was meritorious not inasmuch as it was suffering, but inasmuch as Christ bore it willingly.

Reply to second objection. "From the beginning of His conception Christ merited our eternal salvation; but on our side there were some obstacles, whereby we were hindered from securing the effect of His preceding merits." Thus the souls of the just were awaiting Him in limbo,[12] for by His descent into limbo He delivered the holy fathers detained there. As St. Thomas says: "The holy fathers while yet living were delivered from original as well as actual sin through faith in Christ; also from the penalty of actual sins; but not from the penalty of original sin, whereby they were excluded from glory since the price of man's redemption was not yet paid." [13] Farther on, St. Thomas remarks: "Original sin spread in this way, that at first the

[8] John 3:14 f.
[9] Phil. 2:9.
[10] John 17:19.
[11] Cf. IIIa, q. 19, a. 4.
[12] *Ibid.,* q. 52, a. 5.
[13] *Ibid.,* ad 2.

person infected the nature, and afterward the nature infected the person. Whereas Christ in reverse order at first repairs what regards the person and afterward will simultaneously repair what pertains to the nature in all men. . . . But the penalties of the present life, such as death, hunger, and thirst, will not be taken away until the ultimate restoration of nature through the glorious resurrection." [14]

Reply to third objection. "Christ's passion has a special effect, which His preceding merits did not possess, not on account of greater charity, but because of the nature of the work, which was suitable for such an effect." [15] This means that the other preceding merits of Christ had indeed already a personal and infinite value, but the merits of the Passion had a greater objective value on account of the dignity of the object itself most arduous, namely, the sacrifice on the cross or the supreme holocaust. Right from the beginning, Christ offered up to His Father all His future merits, even those of the Passion, for St. Paul says: "When He cometh into the world, He saith, . . . 'Behold I come.' " [16] Christ's oblation and merit continued throughout His life until He completed the work of redemption, by saying: "It is consummated." [17]

WHAT CHRIST MERITED FOR US BY HIS PASSION

He merited for us all we had lost in Adam.[18] Thus the Evangelist says: "And of His fullness we have all received, and grace for grace," [19] from the first grace to the last grace.

Hence He merited for us sanctifying grace, the infused virtues, and the seven gifts, likewise all actual graces whereby we are prepared for justification, by means of which we perform meritorious acts and persevere. He likewise merited for us eternal life, or salvation, and also final resurrection or the preternatural gifts that we lost through Adam, namely, immunity from death, pain, concupiscence, and error.

But Christ's passion is a universal cause that produces its effect only if the fruits of Christ's merits are applied to us through the instrumentality of the sacraments or without them, and frequently

[14] *Ibid.,* q. 69, a. 3, ad 3.
[15] *Ibid.,* q. 46, a. 3, 4.
[16] Heb. 10:5 f.
[17] John 19:30.
[18] Rom. 5:15 f.
[19] John 1:16.

men, because of concupiscence or pride, place obstacles in the way of their application. Wherefore we said above [20] in treating of Christ's merit, that the efficacious graces which *de facto* are not granted, such as the grace of a good death for Judas, these Christ merited as offered to men in the sufficient grace, but not as here and now bestowed or to be conferred. For God offers us the efficacious grace in the sufficient grace, as the fruit is contained in the flower, but if a person resists the sufficient grace, then the efficacious grace is not conferred. For we must cooperate in our salvation, wherefore St. Paul says: "And if sons, heirs also; heirs indeed of God, and joint-heirs with Christ; yet so if we suffer with Him that we may be also glorified with Him." [21] But Christ merited for the elect by His passion all the effects of their predestination, namely, their calling, justification, perseverance, and glorification.[22]

Second Article

WHETHER CHRIST'S PASSION BROUGHT ABOUT OUR SALVATION BY WAY OF ATONEMENT

State of the question. St. Thomas asks in this second article whether Christ's passion caused our salvation by way of satisfaction. In his accustomed way, he most wisely set forth the state of the question in the three difficulties he presented. But because this question is again raised by the Socinians, the liberal Protestants, and the Modernists, we must inquire: (1) what the liberal Protestants and Modernists denied about this mystery of redemption and what was their conception of it; (2) what Sacred Scripture and tradition have to say about it; (3) whether Christ truly and strictly, or only improperly, satisfied for us; (4) whether Christ's operations were intrinsically of infinite value as regards both merit and satisfaction; (5) whether Christ's satisfaction was not only intrinsically condign, but also superabundant, and to what kind of justice it belongs?

THE STAND TAKEN BY THE EARLIER PROTESTANTS AND THE OPPOSITE OPINION OF THE LIBERAL PROTESTANTS

The general observation is that, as regards the dogma of redemption, the earlier Protestants erred by excess, whereas the Socinians

[20] Cf. IIIa, q. 19, a. 4.
[21] Rom. 8:17.
[22] Cf. IIIa, q. 24, a. 4.

and liberal Protestants deviated from the truth by defect, because of their excessive reaction against the Reformers. For in Luther's opinion and still more in Calvin's, Christ took upon Himself our sins as to become hateful to God and was cursed by Him, and on the cross, or in His descent into hell, He suffered the torments of the damned, so that He went so far as to be guilty of the sin of despair in saying: "My God, My God, why hast Thou forsaken Me?"[23] whereas, on the contrary, these words are a quotation from one of the psalms of the Old Testament, the concluding words of which express great confidence in God.[24] The Reformers concluded from this teaching of theirs, that there is nothing left for us to do or suffer, for we are saved by faith alone in Christ's merits.

Going to the other extreme, however, the Socinians and liberal Protestants fell into the opposite defect, and said that Christ redeemed us only in a moral sense, in that He saves only by His doctrine and example, in the same way as the prophets and martyrs did, although in a higher degree.

Thus the Socinians said that Christ satisfied for us only in the broad sense and metaphorically, by His heroic preaching and example, dying like the martyrs, that is, by affixing the seal to His preaching by the shedding of His blood. Thus His death moves us morally to perform penitential acts whereby our sins are forgiven; but, as they say, Christ did not, strictly speaking, die for us, that is, in our place, by paying the penalty incurred by our sins. Consequently they deny vicarious satisfaction in the strict sense.

No wonder the Socinians ended in this heresy; for they denied Christ's divinity. The denial of the mystery of the Incarnation results in the denial of the mystery of redemption. Pope Paul IV condemned them, for they: "asserted that there are not three persons in the omnipotent God . . . , that our Lord Jesus Christ is not truly God . . . and did not undergo a most bitter death on the cross that He might redeem us from sins and eternal death and reconcile us with the Father for eternal life."[25]

This Socinian error stems from another, namely, that, although they acknowledge that God punishes obstinate sinners, yet they want Him freely to forgive those that fall again, without demanding any

[23] Matt. 27:46.
[24] Ps. 21:2.
[25] Denz., no. 993.

satisfaction from them, otherwise, so they say, this would not be a manifestation of His mercy.

Liberal Protestants in our times and Modernists assent to this concept of redemption, as is evident from the Modernist propositions condemned by Pius X, one of which reads: "The doctrine of the sacrificial death of Christ is not evangelical, but originated with St. Paul." [26]

Scriptural proof. Sacred Scripture testifies that Christ redeemed us by paying the price, namely, by shedding His blood. But this means to satisfy in the strict sense and not merely metaphorically, namely, by preaching, giving us advice and example, as the apostles did. In the strict sense He died for us by paying the penalty that is due for our sins. This is already evident from the above-quoted scriptural texts [27] concerning the mystery of redemption considered in a general way. To these must be added the following texts: "Behold the Lamb of God, behold Him who taketh away the sin of the world." [28] "Even as the Son of man is not come to be ministered unto, but to minister, and to give His life a redemption for many." [29] "This is My blood of the new testament, which shall be shed for many unto remission of sins." [30] "For you are bought with a great price. Glorify and bear God in your body." [31] "You are bought with a price; be not made the bondslaves of men." [32] "Knowing that you were not redeemed with corruptible things as gold or silver . . . , but with the precious blood of Christ, as of a lamb unspotted and undefiled." [33] "He is the propitiation for our sins, and not for ours only, but also for those of the whole world." [34] In a word, as St. Paul says: "Christ died for our sins." [35]

Proof from tradition. We have already given the testimony of the Fathers, and the following patristic texts deserve special mention. Thus St. John Chrysostom says: "Christ died indeed for all that He might keep His promise to all in what concerns Him . . . for He

[26] *Ibid.,* no. 2038.
[27] Cf. chap. 1.
[28] John 1:29.
[29] Matt. 20:28.
[30] *Ibid.,* 26:28.
[31] I Cor. 6:20.
[32] *Ibid.,* 7:20.
[33] I Pet. 1:18 f.
[34] I John 2:2.
[35] I Cor. 15:3. See also Rom. 3:24 f.; Eph. 1:7; 5:2; I Tim. 2:6; 4:10; Apoc. 1:5; 5:9. Cf. Prat's *Theology of St. Paul,* II, 311 f.

took away the sins of men and offered them to the Father . . . that He might forgive them." [36] St. Augustine says: "In the remission of our sins the innocent blood of Christ was shed. . . . In this redemption, Christ's blood is given for us as the price. . . . Christ undertook, though innocent, our punishment, that thereby He might free us from guilt and also put an end to our punishment." [37]

Definitions of the Church. The councils have frequently declared that Christ died so that the nature lost by Adam might be repaired by Him; [38] that He satisfied for the sins of the whole world; [39] that the satisfaction is infinite [40] and superabundant.[41] Christ, by His death on the cross, redeemed us from sins and reconciled us with the Father,[42] and this He did because of His love for the human race, and not through fate.[43] Hence He is the Redeemer, the Savior, the Mediator between God and men.[44]

THEOLOGICAL PROOF THAT CHRIST TRULY AND STRICTLY SATISFIED FOR US

The Socinians maintain that the above-mentioned texts from Sacred Scripture must be understood of satisfaction and redemption improperly so called, as we read in various passages of the Old Testament that God is said to have redeemed His people,[45] or when Moses is said to have been sent as redeemer,[46] although in these cases there was no real redemption.

Therefore the texts from Sacred Scripture must be examined by the light of revealed principles as enunciated in Scripture. In this

[36] *Com. in Gal.,* chap. 2, no. 8.

[37] *De Trinitate,* Bk. XIII, chap. 14, no. 18; chap. XV, no. 19. Cf. Rouet de Journel, Index patrist., Index theol., no. 419.

[38] Denz., no. 194 (Council of Orange); nos. 794, 800 (Council of Trent).

[39] *Ibid.,* nos. 122 f., 286, 319, 323, 462, 794 f., 799, 809, 820, 1096, 1294 f., 1409. Christ accomplished our redemption by way of true vicarious satisfaction. Cf. also J. Rivière, *Le dogme de la rédemption; La rédemption chez les Pères Grecs,* pp. 101–210. *La rédemption chez les Pères Latins,* pp. 211–78. *Le dogme de la rédemption chez St. Augustin; Le dogme de la rédemption, étude théologique;* and *Dict. théol. cath.,* art. "Rédemption," cols. 1932–42.

[40] *Ibid.,* nos. 319, 552, 1019.

[41] *Ibid.,* no. 3051.

[42] Denz., nos. 286, 993 f.

[43] *Ibid.,* no. 3051.

[44] *Ibid.,* nos. 711, 790, 794, 796.

[45] Deut. 13:5; 9:26; 21:8.

[46] Acts 7:35.

way the subordination of revealed truths will be made manifest. It is thus that sacred theology proves from revealed principles conclusions otherwise revealed, and gives us a certain and indeed most fruitful understanding of these truths.[47]

It is presupposed that a meritorious action becomes strictly satisfactory when it is of an afflictive nature and is offered in reparation for the offense. Wherefore St. Thomas proposes the argument in the following manner, saying: "He properly atones for an offense who offers something which the offended one loves equally, or even more than he detested the offense. But by suffering out of love and obedience, Christ gave more to God than was required to compensate for the offense of the whole human race. First of all, because of the exceeding charity (theandric) from which He suffered; secondly, on account of the dignity of His life, which He laid down in atonement, for it was the life of one who was God and man; thirdly, on account of the extent of the Passion, and the greatness of the grief endured, as stated above.[48] And therefore Christ's passion was not only a sufficient but a superabundant atonement for the sins of the human race." [49]

St. Thomas here soars above the purely juridical consideration of the offense to most sublime spiritual things, namely, to the infinite value of the theandric act of charity in Christ the Redeemer. What he affirms with such prudent judgment most beautifully expresses the very essence of the mystery of redemption, namely, the infinite value of Christ's theandric act of love in meriting and satisfying. This satisfaction must be meritorious, and we shall immediately remark in the next article that it is also a most sublime sacrifice. This sacrifice pleases God more than all the sins and crimes of men and devils included displease Him, because Christ's love in the order of good transcends the enormity of malice in the sins and the magnitude of the offense.

If the objection is raised, however, that nobody can be contrite and confess for another, and therefore neither satisfy for another, St. Thomas replies in his answer to the first objection: "The head and the members are as one mystic person; and therefore Christ's satisfaction belongs to all the faithful as being His members. Also, so far

[47] Denz., no. 1796.
[48] Cf. IIIa, q. 46, a. 6.
[49] I John 2:2. See also IIIa, q. 48, a. 1, c.

as any two men are one in charity, the one can atone for the other, as will be shown later. But the same reason does not hold good of contrition and confession, because atonement consists of an outward action, for which helps may be used, among which friends are to be computed." [50] Contrition requires that the sinner's bad disposition be removed by his own act, and nobody can receive a sacrament for another.

Satisfaction is not indeed merely an external act, but it must be measured externally, that is, the satisfaction must be equal to the reparation of the offense, whereas contrition must directly remove the sinner's bad interior disposition.[51]

Hence Christ, as head of the human race, could both merit and satisfy *de condigno* for us, whereas the Blessed Virgin Mary, who had neither the grace of union nor the grace of headship, merited *de congruo* for us what Christ merited *de condigno,* and she likewise satisfied *de congruo,* as explained in Mariology. Satisfaction corresponds to merit and is proportionate to it.

Reply to second objection. St. Thomas observes: "Christ's love was greater than His slayer's malice, and therefore the value of His passion in atoning surpassed the murderous guilt of those who crucified Him; so much so that Christ's suffering was sufficient and superabundant atonement for His murderer's crime." This means that God the Father loved more Christ's act of love in suffering for us than the malice and offense of deicide displeased Him.

Reply to third objection. "The dignity of Christ's flesh is not to be estimated solely from the nature of the flesh, but also from the person assuming it, namely, inasmuch as it was God's flesh, the result of which was that it was of infinite worth." It is likewise with Christ's act of charity in offering Himself, for it was a theandric act. This constitutes essentially the mystery of the redemption. Thus Christ strictly satisfied for us.[52]

[50] *Supplement,* q. 13, a. 2.

[51] Consult Cajetan's commentary on this article.

[52] Redemption, inasmuch as it is willed by God, is indeed by way of merit, satisfaction, and sacrifice, but absolutely speaking redemption can be conceived, so it seems, by way of a theandric act, without pain, satisfaction, and sacrifice each in the strict sense; because the theandric act of love even of itself is more pleasing to God than all sins are displeasing to Him. But we human beings acknowledge the generosity of love only if it be manifested by a generous acceptance of suffering. Thus it is commonly said that sacrifice is a real manifestation or proof of true love.

SOLUTION OF OBJECTIONS

First objection. To make atonement belongs to the one who commits the sin. But Christ did not sin. Therefore it was not for Him to make satisfaction.

Reply. I distinguish the major: that it belongs to the one who commits the sin to atone for it, when the sinner or the representative are as one mystic person, this I concede; when the head of the human race is excluded, then I deny the major. But Christ is the head of the human race.

Second objection. There is no atonement by committing a greater offense. But in Christ's passion the greatest of all offenses was perpetrated. Therefore no atonement was made by committing a greater offense.

Reply. St. Thomas answers the second objection to this article by saying that "Christ's love was greater in His passion than the murderous guilt of those who crucified Him; so much so that Christ's suffering was sufficient and abundant atonement for His murderers' crime."

Third objection. Atonement implies equality with the trespass. But there is no equality in this case, because Christ did not suffer in His Godhead that was offended by sin, but in His flesh. Therefore Christ by suffering in the flesh did not establish equality of atonement.

Reply. I distinguish the major: that atonement implies material equality, this I deny; that it implies formal equality, that is, in accordance with the value of the price paid, this I concede. I distinguish the minor: that Christ suffered merely materially in the flesh, this I deny; in the flesh that was assumed by the Word, and offered to God by a theandric act of charity, this I concede; and I deny the consequent and consequence.

Fourth objection. If Christ died in our place, then why do we die and endure the other penalties of sin?

Reply. It is because the principal reason why Christ died is to free us from eternal death, but not immediately from temporal death and the other penalties of this life but afterward "in the ultimate restoration of nature through the glorious resurrection . . . ; for Christ first repairs what regards the person, and afterward will repair what pertains to the nature in all men." [53]

[53] Cf. IIIa, q. 69, a. 3, ad 3.

Fifth objection. For perfect atonement Christ ought to have submitted to the punishment of sin, namely, eternal death.

Reply. If the atonement concerned merely penal and material compensation, then I concede the antecedent; but I deny it if it is a question of formal atonement whose principal value is estimated from the love of the person who offers, because of His theandric act of charity. Moreover, Christ's voluntary and temporal death was of infinite value in that by it He offered to God the life of the Word incarnate.

Sixth objection. God is infinitely merciful. But to exact so great an atonement is repugnant to infinite mercy. Therefore God did not exact so great an atonement.

Reply. That God's infinite mercy excludes His infinite justice, this I deny; that it implies infinite justice conjoined with it, this I concede. Similarly I distinguish the minor.

God could have indeed pardoned the offense out of His pure mercy, but He willed to unite it with His justice, and so He mercifully gave us the Savior, who was able to offer adequate satisfaction to divine justice. "For God so loved the world as to give His only-begotten Son." [54] "Mercy and truth have met each other; justice and peace have kissed." [55] Hence in this mystery there is nowise a diminution of mercy, but its manifestation in the highest degree.

Seventh objection. God freely remits the sins of those who fall again into sin. Therefore He does not exact atonement from them.

Reply. I distinguish the antecedent: that God freely remits them as regards sinners, this I concede; as regards Christ the Redeemer, this I deny.

Eighth objection. God exhorts us to be benign, merciful, so that we do not become revengeful. Therefore in this way God pardons our offenses.

Reply. I distinguish the antecedent: if it is solely a question of our own subordinated right, then I concede the antecedent; if it also concerns higher rights, for example, the common good of one's country, then I deny it. Just as the judge must, for the common good of one's country, exact satisfaction from anyone who has done harm to or betrayed it, so the supreme Judge must proclaim the right of the supreme Good to be loved above all things. Moreover, the divine

[54] John 3:16.
[55] Ps. 84:11.

Judge, who is also merciful, gave us the Savior. So sometimes the general of an army for the safety of one's native land sends his most beloved son to death by placing him in command of a heroic legion, and his son freely accepts this glorious mission for the safety of the fatherland; in fact, he thanks his father for putting such a trust in him, and both are united in the same heroic love of their native land. Thus God the Father and Christ the Savior are united in the same love of the supreme goodness and the diffusion thereof for the salvation of souls. Thus Christ became the glorious conqueror over sin, the devil, and death.

Hence St. Thomas very well says: "God loves Christ not only more than He loves the whole human race, but more than He loves the entire created universe; because He willed for Him the greater good in giving Him a name that is above all names, so far as He was true God. Nor did anything of His excellence diminish when God delivered Him up to death for the salvation of the human race; He rather became thereby a glorious conqueror: the government was placed upon His shoulder, according to Isaias 9:6." [56]

Ninth objection. The remission of sins was not gratuitous if Christ completely paid the debt. But the remission of sins is gratuitous. Therefore Christ did not completely pay the debt.

Reply. I distinguish the major: that it was not gratuitous as regards Christ, this I concede; that it was not for us, this I deny.

Tenth objection. It is inhuman for the innocent and just to be punished for the guilty one. But it would have been so in this case.

Reply. I distinguish the antecedent: that it is inhuman, if the innocent person is not a voluntary victim, this I concede: otherwise, I deny it. Here the voluntary victim, however, has the supreme love of God and His neighbor at heart, and His vocation is the most sublime of all vocations.[57]

Eleventh objection. Then our satisfactions would be superfluous, which is unbefitting. Therefore Christ did not fully pay the debt.

Reply. That they are superfluous in the sense that they would again

[56] Cf. Ia, q. 20, a. 4, ad 1.

[57] St. Thomas explained above (q. 47, a. 3) in what sense "God the Father spared not even His own Son, but delivered Him up for us all" (Rom. 8:32). He delivered Him up: (1) by eternally preordaining Christ's passion for the liberation of the human race; (2) by inspiring Him with the will to suffer for us and by infusing charity in Him; (3) by not shielding Him from the Passion, but exposing Him to His persecutors.

be meritorious for reconciling the human race with God, this I concede; for the application of this reconciliation, this I deny.

Thus St. Paul says: "I fill up those things that are wanting of the sufferings of Christ, in my flesh, for His body which is the Church." [58] This means that I fill up not what is wanting in the price paid for redemption but as to its application; for this application is effected only by good works, for St. Paul says: "We are joint-heirs with Christ, yet so if we suffer with Him, that we may also be glorified with Him." [59] Just as the first cause does not nullify the effect of the secondary cause, but endows it with the dignity of causality, so Christ's satisfaction does not nullify our satisfactions, but enkindles them and attributes validity to them. Thus Christ enkindles victim souls and assigns to them a share of His victory over sin and the devil.[60]

Thus we conclude that Christ truly and in the proper sense redeemed us, by satisfaction strictly so called and a propitiatory sacrifice, both of which were the result of His supreme love for God His Father and for souls that must be saved. Thus God's love and mercy in a certain way transcend His justice, as already explained,[61] because redemption is principally a work of love and mercy of both God the Father and Christ toward men to be redeemed.

Conclusion. The solution of these objections sets the mind at rest as far as discursive reasoning is concerned, but we must rise above discursive reasoning to the act of faith and also the simple intuition of contemplation, which proceeds from lively faith illumined by the gifts of the Holy Ghost. Thus we attain to "a certain and most fruitful understanding" [62] of this mystery, as the Vatican Council declares. We must firmly believe that Jesus is the Savior and Redeemer in the strict sense of these words, with no attenuation of their meaning. In fact, the divine reality of this mystery far surpasses our conception of it, which means that Christ is ever so much more profoundly and sublimely the Redeemer than we think Him to be, when we attribute satisfaction in the true and strict sense to Him. In this, not only is theology free from all exaggeration, but it also cannot sufficiently express the surpassing reality of this mystery. There is more in God and in Christ than in the whole of our theology.

[58] Col. 1:24.

[59] Rom. 8:17.

[60] *Summa theol.,* IIIa, q. 49, a. 1, ad 4, and a. 3.

[61] *Ibid.,* Ia, q. 21, a. 4.

[62] Denz., no. 1796.

THE INFINITE VALUE OF CHRIST'S SATISFACTION

Were Christ's operations intrinsically of absolutely infinite value both for meriting and satisfaction?

State of the question. Certain theologians such as Durandus, Scotus, G. Biel, Lychetus, and others teach that Christ's satisfaction is only extrinsically condign, superabundant, and of infinite value, namely, because of God's gracious acceptance.[63] Yet these theologians acknowledge that Christ's works had, because of the divine person of the Word, the greatest of value, that was not capable of being equaled by a mere creature, and for this reason it was fitting that they should be accepted by God for infinite value.

On the contrary, almost all other theologians hold that Christ's works were intrinsically, because of the divine suppositum, of absolutely infinite value for both meriting and satisfying. So say William of Paris, Alexander of Hales, St. Thomas, and all Thomists, St. Bonaventure, and many others.[64]

It must be observed that these same principles apply equally to both merit and satisfaction, for it is the meritorious act that becomes satisfactory, when it is of an afflictive nature, and when this affliction is accepted by God and offered to Him in reparation for the offense.

However, before we prove this more common opinion, it must be noted that there is a difference between merit and satisfaction. Merit concerns the reward to be obtained by the rewarded and it therefore concerns either the good of the person meriting or of another, for whom the person merits. But satisfaction refers to the reparation that must be made for the injustice done to another's right. But merit and satisfaction both enter into Christ's works.

Moreover, it must be observed that there is a real and intrinsic relation of Christ's theandric operations both to the object by which they are specified and to the principle by which they are elicited. In Christ the principle that elicits these acts is the divine suppositum or the divine person of the Word, and the principle whereby these acts

[63] Cf. Durandus, *Com. in III Sent.,* d. 20, q. 2; Scotus, *Com. in III Sent.,* d. 19, q. un., no. 7; G. Biel, *Com. in III Sent.,* d. 19, q. un.; Lychetus, *Com. ad Scotum in III Sent.,* d. 19, q. un., nos. 9–11.

Cf. M. J. Scheeben, *Dogmatik,* Bk. IV, no. 415, his judgment on the insufficiency of Scotus' doctrine concerning the Incarnation.

[64] Cf. Gulielmus Paris., *Cur Deus Homo* (before middle); Alensis, Part III, q. 1, no. 4; St. Thomas, IIIa, q. 1, a. 2, ad 2; q. 46, a. 6, ad 6; St. Bonaventure, III Sent., d. 20, a. 1, 2, 3–5.

are elicited is the human nature, that operates by means of the faculties and habits or the virtues and gifts.

These operative principles, by which the suppositum operates, are physically finite, and so in Christ's works as man there is no such thing as physical infinity. But as regards their moral value, this can be estimated either from the more or less exalted nature of the object, and thus Christ's dolorous passion is objectively more meritorious than His other operations, or they can be estimated from the subject eliciting these acts, that is intrinsically and morally infinite, namely, because of the suppositum, although these operations of Christ come in contact with their object in a finite way. Thus there is a distinction between the personal value of all Christ's acts of charity, and their more or less exalted objective value.[65]

First authoritative proof. Pope Clement VI in explaining the words of St. Paul [66] and St. Peter [67] regarding the oblation of Christ, says: "The innocent Christ, who was immolated on the altar of the cross, shed not a little drop of blood, though this would have sufficed for the redemption of the entire human race, because of the union with the Word, but streams of it, like unto a river, so that 'from the sole of the foot unto the top of the head, there is no soundness in Him.' [68] Thus it is an infinite treasure for men, whereby those who use it may share in God's friendship. There is not the least fear that this treasure will suffer any loss by its use, both on account of Christ's infinite merits, as already stated, and for this reason, that the more many are drawn by the application of these merits to holiness of life, all the more there is an increase in the accumulation of their individual merits." [69]

Clement VI says that Christ's merits are of infinite value, not because of their extrinsic acceptation by God, but "on account of the union of Christ's human nature with the Word." [70] The Supreme

[65] It must be noted that for Thomists, in the order of grace and glory, several of these operations are of intrinsic value, such as intrinsically efficacious grace, happiness of heaven which is intrinsically impossible to lose; whereas, on the contrary, in the opinion of certain theologians, these have only an extrinsic value. The reason for this difference of opinion is that in these questions the Thomists consider, not only the fact itself, but the nature of this fact or act, or divine gift.

[66] Heb. 9:12.

[67] I Pet. 1:18.

[68] Isa. 1:6.

[69] Denz., nos. 550–52. Bull *Unigenitus Dei Filius.*

[70] *Ibid.,* no. 550.

Pontiff speaks as St. Thomas does, whom we shall immediately quote. It is evident that the hypostatic union with the Word is not something of extrinsic denomination, as, for example, a bank note is, whose value is by some law decreed to represent a determinate sum of money. This constitutes the outstanding difference between paper money and gold or silver.

Second authoritative proof. St. Thomas says: "Sin committed against God has a kind of infinity from the infinity of the divine majesty, because the greater the person we offend, the more grievous the offense. Hence for condign satisfaction it was necessary that the act of the one satisfying should have an infinite efficiency, as being of God and man." [71] Again, he says: "Christ willed to deliver the human race from sins not merely by His power, but also according to justice. And therefore He did not simply weigh what great virtue His suffering would have from union with the Godhead, but also how much, according to His human nature, His pain would avail for so great a satisfaction." [72] Such is the reply given by St. Thomas to his corresponding objection, which is as follows: "The slightest pain would have sufficed to secure man's salvation, because from His divine person it would have had infinite virtue. Therefore it would have been superfluous to choose the greatest of all pains." [73] In this article he says: "The dignity of Christ's flesh (and likewise of His human nature) is not to be estimated solely from the nature of flesh, inasmuch as it was God's flesh, the result of which was that it was of infinite worth." [74] If this is said of Christ's flesh, a fortiori this applies to charity. St. Thomas speaks in like manner in several other passages.

Theological proof. Both the meritorious and the satisfactory value of actions is derived not only from the object or from the principle whereby they are elicited, but also, and especially, from the dignity of the person who operates, and the greater the dignity of the person who operates, the more this increases the value of the operation. But Christ's person is infinitely worthy.

Therefore although Christ's operations, from the principle and the finite mode whereby they attain their object, are of infinite value, yet because the infinite dignity of the person from whom they pro-

[71] *Summa theol.,* IIIa, q. 1, a. 2, ad 2.
[72] *Ibid.,* q. 46, a. 6, ad 6.
[73] *Ibid.,* 6th obj.
[74] *Ibid.,* ad 3.

ceed, they have both meritorious and satisfactory values that are infinite; or the possibility of estimating their value is morally infinite.

The minor is certain, since Christ's person is the person of the Word.

First proof of major. Actions generally belong to the supposita, and moral immanent actions come from the person, as from the principle that formally and freely elicits them.

Second proof. In a special manner satisfactory and meritorious actions formally include the offerer, who by these actions submits and offers himself to the one to whom he avows his obedience. Thus in the notion of meriting and satisfying, the relation is not between merit and the person meriting, between satisfaction and the person satisfying; but the person is related to these actions by way of a moral form; for these actions are intrinsically related to the person who elicits them and who freely offers himself, the more what is offered to God belongs more intimately to the person, the more precious it is, for example, the immolation of the body or personal pain.

Wherefore we generally estimate of greater value a gift offered to us by a person of great merit than an equally valuable gift offered to us by a person of lower dignity. Thus it is said of God: "The Lord had respect to Abel and to his offerings,"[75] in that He considered more the person offering than the gift offered. Therefore, a fortiori, God looks upon the person of His Son offering Himself on the cross. More briefly, Christ's operations are intrinsically and morally of infinite value because they are theandric.

Confirmation. The common saying is: the greater the dignity of the person offended, the greater the offense, in that the greater the dignity of the person who honors and satisfies, the greater the dignity of the conferring honor and satisfactory work.

Another proof. There is a moral value in Christ's works of meriting always greater graces and of satisfying for an ever greater number of sinners. From this we clearly see that they are of infinite value.

SOLUTION OF THE OBJECTIONS

First objection. Every created work is intrinsically finite. But every meritorious work of Christ is human and hence created. Therefore every meritorious work of Christ is intrinsically finite.

Reply. I distinguish the major: that every created work is intrinsically and physically finite, this I concede; that it is so morally, this I

[75] Gen. 4:14.

deny; if the principle that elicits the act is of infinite dignity. I concede the minor. I distinguish the conclusion in the same way as I do the major. Christ's meritorious acts bear an intrinsic relation to the divine person of the Word.

But I insist. Even the oblation that the Blessed Virgin Mary made of Christ in the temple was intrinsically related to the person of the Word incarnate who was offered. And yet this action of the Blessed Virgin Mary was neither intrinsically of infinite value, nor sufficient for the redemption of the human race.

Reply. I distinguish the antecedent; that this oblation indicated an intrinsic order to the infinite person of Christ merely objectively considered, this I concede; that it indicates relation to Christ as to the principle, and subject which attributes a personal and infinite value to the action, this I deny. More briefly, this oblation of the Blessed Virgin Mary was objectively of infinite value, because she offered an infinitely worthy object, namely, the Word incarnate; but the oblation was not personally of infinite value.

Thus, in some manner, the act of charity whereby the Blessed Virgin Mary loved God was indeed infinite objectively considered, but subjectively or personally, it was of finite value, just as the act of charity is of any pure creature whatever; although the merits of the Blessed Virgin Mary were in their order of inestimable value because of the fullness of her charity.

Another objection. There is nothing greater than infinity. But the act of Christ's divine will is greater than the act of His human will. Therefore this second act is not of infinite value.

Reply. I distinguish the major: that there is nothing greater than absolute infinity in the order of being, namely, than God who is infinite, this I concede; nothing greater than infinity of a certain kind, for example, the moral value of acts, this I deny. I concede the minor because the act of Christ's divine will is infinite, not only morally, but also physically. I distinguish the conclusion: that Christ's meritorious act is not absolutely infinite even physically, this I concede; that it is not morally of infinite value, this I deny.

Still I insist. But in this order of moral value it is false to say that all Christ's merits are of infinite value, for His act of charity in offering Himself on the cross was of greater value than any other of His meritorious acts, for example, those of preaching to the people or conversing with His disciples.

Reply. I distinguish the proof: that this act of Christ in offering Himself on the cross was of greater value than the others, objectively, this I concede; personally, I deny. This personal value was of equal worth in all His meritorious acts, but their objective value depends on the dignity of the object.[76]

Again I insist. Two acts of charity of equal intensity are equal in value although one of them is elicited by a holier person. Therefore acts do not derive their greater validity from the dignity of the person.

Reply. Let the antecedent pass without comment; but the argument does not equally apply to Christ, for the greater holiness of some individual, such as Paul, does not impart a greater value to all his acts, even those that are less fervent. On the contrary, the divine person of the Word always exerted a moral influence on all His meritorious and satisfactory acts, and there never was any diminution of fervor in Christ's acts of charity.

OTHER OBJECTIONS

First difficulty. If this thesis were true, then Christ would have acquired just as much merit by shedding one tear as by His crucifixion.

Reply. I distinguish: that Christ would have gained just as much merit personally, this I concede; objectively, this I deny. There was equality of personal value in all Christ's works, but there was inequality as regards their objective value, because this depends on the more or less sublime nature of the object, the greater or less difficulty involved in attaining to it, and the accompanying circumstances. But Christ directed not only the personal value but also the objective value of His works, so that they might be meritorious and satisfactory.

Second difficulty. If Christ's first act on coming into this world would have been of infinite value, then His other works would have been useless.

Reply. It has already been said that Christ did not offer this first act separately, but in conjunction with all future acts until His death, as constituting the whole price of our redemption; and His oblation was a continuous act, which was not elicited just once and then not

[76] Thus it is generally said that it is objectively more meritorious to teach theology from love for God, than equally from love for God to perform some manual work; but personally it is more meritorious to do manual work with great love for God, than to teach theology with very little love for God.

continued. So it ought to be with Christians, and especially religious.

Third difficulty. Then our satisfaction would be superfluous.

Reply. As was said in replying to the second difficulty: they are superfluous in reconciling the human race with God, this I concede; that they are so in the application of this reconciliation, this I deny. In fact, it pertains to the abundance of Christ's satisfaction not only that He Himself satisfy, but that also He cause others to satisfy, just as it belongs to the perfection of the first cause to give the dignity of causality to others.

Fourth difficulty. Christ, however, in this way would have been entitled to a greater reward of merit than God could have given Him, for an infinite reward is a contradiction in terms.

Reply. Merit of infinite value does not demand an actually infinite reward, just as divine omnipotence is made manifest not because it produces something that is actually infinite, for this is an impossibility; but because of all things made by God, He can always make a better thing than He has made. Thus Christ merited the salvation of human beings without any limit to their number and although this would prolong the end of the world beyond the truly appointed time, human beings would always find in Christ's merits a sufficient source of salvation. Moreover, Christ merited something infinite in this sense, that He merited the Eucharist which is a sacrifice of infinite value, whereby the sacrifice of the cross is perpetuated until the end of time and whereby the merits of the Passion are continually applied to our souls. Likewise He merited the beatific vision for the elect and their love of God, which they cannot lose, and these are infinite on the part of the object seen and loved.

Finally, the infinite value of Christ's satisfaction is made manifested in the adequate reparation made for the offense against God, for this reparation demands an act that is morally infinite in value, not only potentially but actually.

Hence this thesis is certain chiefly on account of the proof given above.

First doubt. Was Christ's satisfaction not only intrinsically condign, but also intrinsically superabundant?

Reply. It is of faith that Christ satisfied for us condignly, for St. Paul says: "Christ Jesus who gave Himself a redemption for all"; [77] and the Council of Trent declares: "Our Lord . . . made satisfac-

[77] I Tim. 2:5 f.

tion to God the Father for us." [78] It concerns condign satisfaction, or the voluntary and equal payment of the debt, namely, of the sins that offended God.

But from what has been said, it also follows that Christ's satisfaction was intrinsically superabundant. And this is the more common opinion.

Scriptural proof. St. Paul says: "Where sin abounded, grace did more abound," [79] and this was especially so in the Savior.

The Fathers, too, in the explanation of this text affirm the superabundance of Christ's merits. Thus St. John Chrysostom says: "For Christ paid for more than we owed." [80]

Theological proof. The principal one is that given by St. Thomas, which is as follows: "He properly atones for an offense, who offers something which the offended one loves equally, or even more than he detested the offense. But by suffering out of love and obedience, Christ gave more to God than was required to compensate for the offense of the whole human race. First of all, because of the exceeding charity (theandric) from which He suffered; secondly, on account of the dignity of His life which He laid down in atonement, for it was the life of one who was God and man; thirdly, on account of the extent of the Passion, and on account of the greatness of the grief endured." [81]

Several theologians give an additional reason, namely, that the satisfaction was superabundant because by sin God, who is offended, is made morally subject indeed to a creature; but by His passion and crucifixion the Word incarnate because of His exceeding love subjects Himself even physically and really to penalties and sufferings. This reason is cogent if we consider that Christ's acts of charity and humility in suffering on the cross were theandric acts of intrinsically infinite value. Hence the reply to the present doubt is a corollary to the preceding thesis.

As regards the extent of this satisfaction, it is universal, inasmuch as it is sufficient for the salvation of all men without exception.

Sacred Scripture declares it to be so in the following text: "He

[78] Denz., no. 799.

[79] Rom. 5:20.

[80] *Com. in Rom., Hom.* 10. Cf. Rouet de Journel, *Enchiridion patristicum,* nos. 421 f., for testimony of several other Fathers.

[81] Cf. IIIa, q. 48, a. 2, c.

[Christ] is the propitiation for our sins, and not for ours only, but also for those of the whole world." [82]

Second doubt. Was Christ's satisfaction for men according to strict justice and as absolute right demands.

State of the question. Satisfaction is said to be according to strict justice when it is perfect according to the nature of justice,[83] that is, it must be made: (1) to another; (2) from the debtor's own means to which the creditor is not entitled on some other grounds; (3) the creditor must be under obligation to accept the satisfaction. The difficulty is that Christ Himself as God was offended, and that He could not, so it seems, satisfy to Himself; for justice concerns another.

The question so presented is disputed. Vasquez, Molina, Lugo, Billot and others deny that Christ's satisfaction was according to strict justice.[84]

It is generally admitted by the Thomists, especially by Capreolus, Cajetan, Salmanticenses, Billuart, and others, who quote various texts of St. Thomas. St. Bonaventure also forms the affirmative opinion.[85] Suarez [86] and, among more recent theologians, Franzelin, Pesch, Paquet, Janssens, and others take the affirmative view.

Proof of thesis. Strict satisfaction must be that which is made: (1) to another; (2) from the debtor's own means to which the creditor is not entitled on some other grounds; (3) the creditor must be under obligation to accept the satisfaction. But such was the nature of Christ's satisfaction. Therefore it was according to strict justice.

Proof of minor.

1) It was made to another, inasmuch as the divine person, who exists in both the divine nature and the human nature, satisfied to Himself, who exists in the divine nature. It is not necessary that satis-

[82] I John 2:2. Cf. Denz., no. 795.

[83] "Ex parte formae" here means those elements that constitute justice truly as such, just as body and rational soul truly constitute the nature of man. (Tr.)

[84] Vasquez, *in IIIam,* disp. 3, c. 1 f. Molina, *in Iam,* q. 21, a. 1; Lugo, *De mysterio incarnationis,* disp. 3, sect. 1, no. 4; L. Billot, *De Verbo incarnato,* thesis 53.

[85] Cf. Cajetan, *in IIIam,* q. 1, a. 2. Salmanticenses, *De incarnatione,* disp. 1, no. 214. See also Capreolus, Ferrariensis, Alvarez, John of St. Thomas, and others in their commentaries on St. Thomas. Among texts from St. Thomas, cf. IIIa, q. 1, a. 2, ad 2; q. 48, a. 2. Also St. Bonaventure, *in III Sent.,* disp. 20, q. 5.

[86] Suarez (disp., IV, sect. 3, no. 11) says about this opinion of the Thomists: "I consider it so certain that the contrary opinion seems neither probable nor pious nor sufficiently consistent with the faith."

faction be made to another suppositum, for it suffices that it be made to another by reason of the nature, because the distinction between the natures is the foundation for the distinction between rights and correlative duties. Thus Christ merited not as God, but as man. If Aristotle says: "Justice concerns another," [87] namely, another person, the reason is that he is speaking about human things.[88]

2) This satisfaction must be made out of one's own means, namely, from what belongs to the divine person in the human nature, and to which the creditor is not entitled, because God the creditor was not strictly entitled to Christ's meritorious and satisfactory works inasmuch as He was man, but they belonged properly to Christ as man, inasmuch as He was free; and they belonged only in a general way to God. But general ownership does not do away with particular ownership, just as the universal cause does not do away with the particular cause, just as a citizen pays to the state something that belongs to him as his own, although the state has the title of general domain over it.

3) God is not absolutely bound to accept this satisfaction, but only hypothetically, on the supposition that God constituted Christ our surety and Redeemer, whom He inspired to make this satisfaction to Him.

Confirmation. Strict satisfaction is that which is equal to the offense; but Christ's satisfaction was superabundant, for as St. Thomas says: "He properly atones for an offense who offers something which the offended one loves equally, or even more than he detested the offense. But by suffering out of theandric love and obedience, Christ gave more to God than was required to compensate for the offense of the whole human race." [89] Therefore this satisfaction was more than equivalent, more than according to strict justice, but truly and properly superabundant. We must always have recourse to this celebrated text of St. Thomas, which more clearly solves these doubts than anything that has been written on this subject after his time.

Third doubt. Was Christ's satisfaction an act of commutative justice?

State of the question. Justice is a virtue that attributes to each one his own. It is divided into general and particular. General justice,

[87] *Ethics,* V, 2.
[88] Cf. IIIa, q. 20, a. 2.
[89] *Ibid.,* q. 48, a. 2, c.

which is also called legal, immediately concerns the common good, just as equity or epikeia does. Particular justice is divided into distributive, whereby the superior gives to the subjects what is due to them in proportion to their merits or their needs, and commutative, whereby one person gives to another not in proportion to the needs of the other, but pays according to equity the debt and the price owing to the other. To the question as thus presented, the more common answer is in the affirmative.

Scriptural proof. St. Paul says: "You are bought with a great price." [90] Therefore it was the payment of the price that is strictly required for redemption, as above stated.

Theological proof. Two things are required and suffice for an act of commutative justice, namely, a strict obligation to pay the debt and absolute equality between the price and the debt. But it was so with Christ's satisfaction, which was not only equal, but superabundant, and Christ was bound to make this satisfaction because He was constituted as surety and Redeemer of men. Therefore this satisfaction perfectly complies with all that is required for commutative justice.

It must be noted, however, that, although Christ's satisfaction is especially and formally an act of commutative justice, it was commanded by charity toward God and men, and by the virtue of religion, so that it was a latreutic act. In fact, it reflects many other virtues, such as magnanimity and magnificence inasmuch as it was superabundant, mercy toward sinners, humility, meekness, and other virtues.

It must also be observed that Christ's commutative justice differs specifically from ours, because of its formal object. For its formal object is not a debt to man adjustable by a human method of reasoning in accordance with equality, but it is a debt owing to God adjustable in accordance with equality that transcends every human rule and measure. Wherefore we say that this satisfaction perfectly complies with all that is required for commutative justice.

The question here would be the universality of Christ's satisfaction, inasmuch as Christ died for all men without exception. But this subject is now frequently discussed in the treatise on the One God, in connection with the question of God's universal will to save, and we therefore refer the student to that treatise. However, we shall take up the principal points farther on.[91]

[90] I Cor. 6:20.

[91] See *infra,* chap. 34.

Reply. The answer is evidently in the affirmative, inasmuch as the value of redemption as to its sufficiency is infinite and thus it includes all men without exception, inasmuch as it is God's will to save all.

An example of the sublime genius of St. Thomas in comparison with all his commentators is apparent from the fact that he solves all these doubts about satisfaction in accordance with strict and even commutative justice, and this most briefly and clearly by means of this exalted principle, when he says: "He properly atones for an offense who offers something which the offended one loves equally [namely, satisfaction according to strict commutative justice] or even more [namely, superabundant satisfaction] than he detested the offense. But by suffering out of theandric love and obedience, Christ gave more to God than was required to compensate for the offense of the whole human race." [92] In fact, what Christ offered was more pleasing to God than He detested the offense of the devils, although Christ did not redeem them, because they are incapable of redemption. The mystery of redemption consists essentially in this statement of St. Thomas.

Third Article

ON REDEMPTION BY WAY OF SACRIFICE

State of the question. In this third article St. Thomas asks whether Christ's passion operated by way of sacrifice. He begins by presenting three difficulties. It seems that it did not: (1) because the truth must correspond with the figure; but in the sacrifices of the Old Law, which were figures of Christ, human flesh was never offered; nay, such sacrifices were considered impious; (2) sacrifice is a sacred sign; but Christ's passion is not a sign, but the thing signified by other signs; (3) those who killed Christ did not perform any sacred act or offer sacrifice, but rather did a great wrong.

Several heretics *de facto* denied that Christ's passion was a true sacrifice. (1) Pelagius, Abelard, and Hermes considered it to be evidence of great love and the most sublime example of heroism, such as martyrdom. (2) The Socinians said that Christ was a priest only on Ascension Day and then He offered sacrifice only in heaven, interceding with the Father for us. (3) The liberal Protestants and Modernists deny Christ's priesthood, and they see in His death only a most

[92] Cf. IIIa, q. 48, a. 2, c.

noble example of fortitude of soul, as in martyrdom.[93] But martyrdom is not in itself strictly speaking a sacrifice, for it is not an elicited act of latria, but of fortitude, and not all martyrs are priests.

Catholic doctrine. It is of faith that Christ is a priest and that He offered Himself on the altar of the cross, a sacrifice in the true and strict sense. The Council of Ephesus teaches that Christ is "our High Priest and Apostle, who offered Himself for us as an odor of sweetness to God." [94] Likewise the Council of Trent declares that Christ "offered Himself once on the altar of the cross to God the Father by means of His death, there to operate for them [men] an eternal redemption." [95]

Scriptural proof. It is explicitly revealed that Christ offered a true sacrifice on the cross. Already in the Old Testament the prophet says of the innocent and just servant of Jahve: "Surely He hath borne our infirmities and carried our sorrows. . . . He was wounded for our iniquities; He was bruised for our sins." [96] He was therefore a victim for us; but He was also a priest offering Himself for us to reconcile us with God, for it is said: "If He shall lay down His life for sin, He shall see a long-lived seed, and the will of the Lord shall be prosperous in His hand . . . and He shall see and be filled." [97]

In the New Testament we read: "Christ hath loved us, and hath delivered Himself for us an oblation and a sacrifice to God for an odor of sweetness." [98] "Christ our Pasch is sacrificed." [99] "Him, who knew no sin yet He hath made sin for us [victim for sin], that we might be made the justice of God in Him." [100] "Whom God hath proposed to be a propitiation, through faith in His blood," [101] which means a propitiatory victim. Again the Apostle says: "Being now justified by His blood." [102] And also: "Christ gave Himself for us, that He might redeem us from all iniquity, and might cleanse to Himself a people acceptable." [103]

[93] So says A. Sabatier, *La doctrine de l'expiation et son évolution historique,* pp. 37, 97 f. So also Loisy, *L'évangile et l'Eglise,* chaps. 3 and 4.

[94] Denz., no. 122; Eph. 5:2.

[95] *Ibid.,* no. 938. On the priesthood of Christ, cf. IIIa, q. 22.

[96] Isa. 53:4 f.

[97] *Ibid.,* 53:10.

[98] Eph. 5:2.

[99] I Cor. 5:7.

[100] II Cor. 5:21.

[101] Rom. 3:25.

[102] *Ibid.,* 5:9.

[103] Titus 2:14.

St. Paul treats especially of Christ's priesthood in the following texts: "Having therefore a great high priest that hath passed into the heavens, Jesus, the Son of God." [104] "For every high priest taken from among men is ordained for men . . . that he may offer up gifts and sacrifices for sins." [105] "But Christ . . . neither by the blood of goats, nor of calves, but by His own blood, entered once into the holies, having obtained eternal redemption. For if the blood of goats . . . sanctifies such as are defiled, to the cleansing of the flesh, how much more shall the blood of Christ, who by the Holy Ghost offered Himself unspotted unto God, cleanse our conscience from dead works to serve the living God?" [106] "Christ was offered once to exhaust the sins of many." [107] "For by one oblation He hath perfected forever them that are sanctified." [108]

Testimony of tradition. Both the Greek and Latin Fathers have commented on the above-mentioned texts from Scripture, such as St. Clement of Rome, St. Ignatius, Origen, St. Cyprian, St. Gregory of Nazianzus, St. Gregory of Nyssa, St. John Chrysostom, St. Cyril of Alexandria, St. Ambrose, and St. Augustine.[109] Two famous testimonies of St. Augustine are quoted by St. Thomas in the present article.

Theological proof. St. Thomas shows that Christ's voluntary death was truly a sacrifice and the most perfect of all sacrifices. He proves this by saying: "A sacrifice properly so called is something done for that honor which is properly due to God, in order to appease Him. But Christ offered Himself up for us in the Passion,[110] and this voluntary enduring of the Passion was most acceptable to God, as coming from charity. Therefore it is manifest that Christ's passion was a true sacrifice." [111]

In this proof we find verified the definition of sacrifice as already explained by St. Thomas,[112] in that it is, strictly speaking, the offering of a sensible thing by a priest made to God by means of a real,

[104] Heb. 4:14.
[105] *Ibid.,* 5:1.
[106] *Ibid.,* 9:11 f.
[107] *Ibid.,* 9:28.
[108] *Ibid.,* 10:14.
[109] See Rouet de Journel's *Enchir. patrist.,* nos. 416–18.
[110] Eph. 5:2.
[111] Cf. IIIa, q. 48, a. 3, c.
[112] *Ibid.,* IIa IIae, q. 85.

or in some way, change of the thing offered in testimony of God's supreme dominion, and our subjection to Him.

Thus Christ truly offered Himself to death by not repelling His killers, and after He was struck, by not preventing death, which He could have done.[113]

Therefore His voluntary death differs from simple martyrdom, as Father Vosté observes, who says: "The martyrs differ from Christ because, as a general rule, they were neither priests nor, strictly speaking, sacrificed themselves, for they were not free either to die or not to die, nor underwent death by some sacred rite, and their death was not an elicited act of religion, but an act of fortitude whereby they chose in preference to lose their life rather than deny the faith." [114]

In fact St. Thomas, referring to St. Augustine,[115] shows that the sacrifice of the cross, which was prefigured by the sacrifices of the Old Testament, was the most perfect of all sacrifices. For a sacrifice is more perfect, the more the priest is united with God to whom he offers it, with the victim which he offers, with the people for whom he offers it. But Christ, who is priest as man, cannot be more united with God, for He is God; nor with the victim, for He offers Himself; nor with men, who are His members. For St. Augustine says: "That the same one true Mediator reconciling us with God through the peace-sacrifice might continue to be one with Him to whom He offered it, might be one with them for whom He offered it, and might Himself be the offerer and what He offered." [116]

The sacrifice of the cross is offered on account of four ends, namely, adoration, petition for graces to be obtained, reparation for offenses, and thanksgiving. So it is also with the Sacrifice of the Mass, whereby the fruits of the sacrifice of the cross are applied to us.

Reply to first objection. St. Thomas shows beautifully how the sacrifice of the cross surpasses all the sacrifices of the Old Testament which prefigured it, and he quotes St. Augustine's wonderful text.

Reply to second objection. The sacrifice of the cross, typified by the ancient sacrifices of the Old Testament, signifies Christ's immense love for us, and also the necessity for us to mortify the flesh and refrain from sin.[117]

[113] *Ibid.*, IIIa, q. 47, a. 1, 2.
[114] *Com. in IIIam,* p. 367.
[115] *De Trinit.*, Bk. IV, chap. 14.
[116] *Ibid.*
[117] Cf. I Pet. 6:1 f.

Reply to third objection. Christ's passion on the part of His killers was a crime and a deicide; on Christ's part suffering willingly out of love, it was the most perfect of all sacrifices. Hence the very slaying of Christ does not have to be renewed sacramentally in the Sacrifice of the Mass, but in the Mass "the victim is one and the same, the same now offering by the ministry of priests, who then offered Himself on the cross." [118]

Particular opinion. In recent times Father Maurice de la Taille [119] conceived the notion that the Last Supper and the voluntary death of Christ on the cross are two component parts of the same sacrifice. At the Last Supper, Christ as priest offered Himself to be immolated on the cross, and on the cross, however, He was actually immolated and forever retains His state as victim.

However, if it were so, then Christ's voluntary death on the cross would not be a sacrifice in the strict sense, but only a part of the sacrifice. But this seems to be contrary to the traditional teaching, which, even irrespective of the Last Supper, considers the passion and death of our Lord as a most perfect sacrifice, and as such is explained by St. Thomas in the present article and elsewhere without any reference to the Last Supper.[120]

Truly Christ's oblation not only continues throughout the Passion, but is expressed sensibly by these words of Christ: "Father, into Thy hands I commend My Spirit. And saying this, He gave up the Ghost." [121] These are, so to speak, the words consecrating the sacrifice on the cross. This sacrifice is eminently a ritual, since as it is the thing signified in all ritualistic sacrifices, and inasmuch as it is the perfect fulfillment according to God's eternal preordination of the entire cultus of the Old Testament, a fulfillment that will ever afterward be commemorated by the Sacrifice of the Mass until the end of the world.

Hence this new theory does not seem to be in harmony with what the Council of Trent says about the Last Supper and the cross not being two complementary parts of one and the same sacrifice, but two sacrifices. The Council says: "Our Lord, though He was about

[118] Denz., no. 940.

[119] *Mysterium fidei,* pp. 101–6; also *Esquisse du mystère de la foi,* pp. 9, 13.

[120] Cf. E. Hugon, *Revue thomiste,* July–September, 1922. See refutation of Father de la Taille's theory in Lepin's *L'idée du sacrifice de la Messe,* pp. 688–90; also A. Michel, *Dict de théol. cath.,* art. "Messe," cols. 1245 f.

[121] Luke 23:46.

to offer Himself on the altar of the cross unto God the Father . . . by means of His death . . . , in the Last Supper, on the night in which He was betrayed, that He might leave to His own beloved spouse the Church, a visible sacrifice, whereby that bloody sacrifice, once to be accomplished on the cross, might be represented . . . , He offered up to God the Father His own body and blood under the species of bread and wine." [122] This text distinguishes between "offered" and "about to offer," and the sacrifice of the Last Supper is called "unbloody," whereas the sacrifice of the cross is called "bloody."

Hence the traditional teaching must be retained whereby, even irrespective of the Last Supper, Christ's voluntary death on the cross was not only a part of the sacrifice, but a true and even most perfect sacrifice, and solely of itself fully sufficed. The Resurrection and Ascension strictly speaking add nothing to the redemptive value of the cross, but are a visible manifestation that the sacrifice on Calvary was ratified and accepted by the Father for our redemption.

Fourth Article

REDEMPTION BY WAY OF LIBERATION

In this fourth article St. Thomas asks whether Christ's passion brought about our salvation by way of redemption. In this article redemption is not taken in the general sense of the term as when Christ is said to be "cause of our salvation," but in a restricted sense as meaning, "liberation from the bondage of sin, from the debt of punishment and the bondage of the devil." Thus a distinction is made between this mode of redemption and the others previously considered. It is not now a question of what constitutes the mode of redemptive work, but of its effect, as also is the case in the sixth article.

St. Thomas begins by presenting three difficulties: (1) Men never ceased to belong to God; therefore they are not redeemed; (2) nor are they to be redeemed from the bondage of the devil, because the devil has no right over them; (3) because Christ did not pay the price of redemption to the devil.

Reply. Nevertheless the answer is that Christ's passion liberated us from the bondage of sin, the devil, and the debt of punishment.

Scriptural proof. It is of faith, for at the time of the Annunciation, the angel of the Lord said to Joseph: "Thou shalt call His name

[122] Denz., no. 938.

Jesus. For He shall save His people from their sins." [123] The Precursor says of Him: "Behold the Lamb of God, behold Him who taketh away the sin of the world." [124] Jesus says of Himself: "The Son of man is come . . . to give His life a redemption for many." [125] Before His passion He says: "Now shall the prince of this world be cast out. And I, if I be lifted up from the earth, will draw all things to Myself." [126]

St. Paul says: "Giving thanks to God . . . who hath delivered us from the power of darkness and hath translated us into the kingdom of the Son of His love, in whom we have redemption through His blood, the remission of sins." [127] Farther on he says: "And you, when you were dead in your sins . . . He hath quickened together with Him [Christ], forgiving you all offenses, blotting out the handwriting of the decree which was contrary to us. And He hath taken the same out of the way, fastening it to the cross; and despoiling the principalities and powers, He hath exposed them confidently in open show, triumphing over them in Himself." [128]

And again he says: "That through death He might destroy him who had taken the empire of death, that is to say, the devil." [129]

In other words, Christ by His passion regained the victory over the devil and sin, and already virtually over death, which is "the wages of sin," [130] as is afterward made manifest by His resurrection, which is the forerunner of ours.

Testimony from tradition. Our liberation is likewise made clear from this source. Rouet de Journel [131] has collected many passages from the Latin and Greek Fathers, who explicitly taught that Christ redeemed us from sin and the bondage of the devil, by paying the price of our redemption, not to the devil but to God.

Theological proof. St. Thomas proves this truth from other revealed texts as follows:

Man was held captive on account of sin in two ways: First of all, by the bondage of sin, because "whosoever committeth sin is the serv-

[123] Matt. 1:21.
[124] John 1:29.
[125] Mark 10:45.
[126] John 12:31.
[127] Col. 1:13 f.
[128] *Ibid.,* 2:13 f.
[129] Heb. 2:14.
[130] Rom. 6:23.
[131] Rouet de Journel, *Enchiridion patrist.,* nos. 413, 420.

ant of sin,"[132] and "by whom a man is overcome of the same also He is the slave."[133] Since, then, the devil had overcome man by inducing him to sin, man was subject to the devil's bondage. Secondly, as to the debt of punishment, to the payment of which man was held fast by God's justice.

"Since, then, Christ's passion was a sufficient and a superabundant atonement for the sin and the debt of the human race, it was as a price at the cost of which we were freed from both obligations."[134] This is the effect of the satisfaction; it is not a constitutive element, but a consequence of this satisfaction.

More briefly: Sin brings about a twofold bondage, namely, of sin and debt of punishment. But Christ's passion was a superabundant satisfaction both for sin and the debt of punishment. Therefore it liberated us from both kinds of bondage. The Council of Trent retains this proof.[135]

Reply to first objection. Men never ceased to belong to God, in that they were always under His power; but by sin they ceased to belong to God as regards union with Him by charity. And men liberated from sin by Christ suffering for them are said to have been redeemed by His passion.

Reply to second objection. "Man by sin had offended God and, by consenting to the devil, had become his subject. And therefore justice required man's redemption with regard to God, but not with regard to the devil."

Reply to third objection. "The price of our redemption had to be paid not to the devil, but to God"; but the price being paid to God, by the reparation of the offense, men were liberated from the bondage of sin, and consequently from the bondage of the devil. Thus we have a most excellent correction of certain exaggerations of Origen and St. Gregory of Nyssa, who seem to affirm that the devil has certain rights over us. The devil has no right over us, and these same Fathers elsewhere give the true teaching. Christ paid the price of our redemption by repairing the offense committed against God. Therefore He paid this price, not to the devil, but to God; and it follows from this that men are freed from the devil's bondage.[136]

[132] John 8:34.
[133] II Pet. 2:19.
[134] Cf. IIIa., q. 48, a. 4, c.
[135] Denz., no. 799.
[136] Cf. Rouet de Journel, *op. cit.*, no. 420.

Fifth Article

WHETHER IT IS PROPER TO CHRIST TO BE THE REDEEMER

State of the question. It seems that also God the Father redeemed us, because He gave His Son in redemption for our sins. Moreover, the sufferings of other saints were also conducive to our salvation, for the Apostle says: "I rejoice in my sufferings for you, and fill up those things that are wanting of the sufferings of Christ in my flesh for His body, which is the Church." [137] Therefore it seems that not only Christ ought to be called the Redeemer.

Reply. Nevertheless the answer is that to be the Redeemer immediately belongs properly to Christ, inasmuch as He is man, although the redemption may be ascribed to the whole Trinity as its first cause.

This article concerns the redemption of the whole human race, which, as stated in the preceding article, is the effect of Christ's passion.

Scriptural proof. St. Luke records that St. Peter says: "There is not salvation in any other. For there is no other name under heaven given to men, whereby we must be saved." [138]

The Apostle declares that Christ is the Savior of all men, without exception, saying: "For all have sinned, and do need the glory of God, being justified freely by His grace, through the redemption that is in Christ Jesus." [139] He also says: "For it became Him . . . who had brought many children into glory, to perfect the author of their salvation, by His passion." [140]

Hence, too, the Blessed Virgin Mary was redeemed by Her Son, by the merits of her Son suffering, but by a preservative and most perfect redemption. Thus Christ merited *de condigno* for His mother also the first and last graces, but not the divine maternity, because thus He would have merited the Incarnation and Himself.

Theological proof. It is as follows: For someone to redeem, two things are required, namely, the act of paying and the price paid, which is his own. But the price of our redemption is Christ's blood, or His bodily life, which is what Christ paid. Hence each of these belongs immediately to Christ as man; but to the whole Trinity, as

[137] Col. 2:24.
[138] Acts 4:12.
[139] Rom. 3:23; cf. *ibid.,* 5:12, 19; see also Gal. 3:13, 22; II Cor. 5:14; I Tim. 2:6.
[140] Heb. 2:10.

to the first cause, to whom Christ's life belonged, and from whom He received the inspiration to suffer for us.

Reply to first objection. Thus the redemption belongs immediately to the man Christ, but principally to God.[141]

Reply to third objection. As Cajetan observes, a doubt arises concerning this reply, because the holy Doctor says elsewhere [142] that the treasury of the Church, from which indulgences derive their efficacy, contains the sufferings of the saints. Pope Clement VI expressly says the same.[143] But it is an evident fact that the sufferings applied to us through indulgences by way of satisfaction and by this way of redemption, are of benefit to the Church.[144]

Cajetan justly replies to this difficulty, by saying: "The author has in mind, however, the sufferings of the saints absolutely considered. Thus between Christ's sufferings and those of the saints there are many points of difference. The first is in the word 'sufferings.' For Christ's sufferings absolutely redeem the Church; whereas the sufferings of the saints do not do so absolutely, but satisfy for us only by way of superfluity, as stated by St. Thomas, here and as contained in the bull of Clement VI. The second difference is in the word 'redemption'; for Christ's passion redeems us absolutely, because it liberates us from guilt and punishment; but the sufferings of the saints redeem us only in a relative sense, namely, from a certain punishment, the temporal punishment that is due to actual sin. The third is in the word 'beneficial.' It is because Christ's passion is of benefit to the Church by way of redemption, even if there is no key of the Church that unlocks the door for us; but the sufferings of the saints are satisfactory on my behalf only if by means of the authoritative power of the keys they be applied to me.

"Therefore so many conditions are required so as to verify the fact that the sufferings of the saints benefit the Church by way of redemption, and for this reason the affirmative answer is only relatively true; we could simply and unconditionally deny the assertion without any prejudice to the truth, and say that the sufferings of the saints do not benefit the Church by way of redemption. And along with the truth

[141] Cf. ad 2.

[142] *Com. in IV Sent.,* d. 20, a. 1, *quaestiuncula prima.*

[143] Denz., nos. 552, 757, 1471, 3051.

[144] Thus the just person can merit *de congruo* (fittingly), the conversion of a sinner, as St. Monica merited the conversion of St. Augustine. See also Ia IIae, q. 114, a. 6.

of this negative conclusion it is already evident that the same must be said of the doctrine concerning the efficacy of indulgences from the merits of the saints." [145] Such is Cajetan's conclusion. More briefly, it is only Christ who frees us from guilt and eternal punishment, the merits of the saints free us from temporal punishment, and this only on the previous understanding that "our redemption was accomplished by Christ alone . . . inasmuch as He is the Head of the Church, and the Author of human salvation, as the Scripture says, and the saints can merit the first grace for another only congruously." [146]

Moreover, St. Thomas makes known more explicitly his mind on this subject concerning the words of the Apostle: "I fill up those things that are wanting of the sufferings of Christ." [147] He says: "These words, taken literally, could be interpreted in a wrong sense, as meaning that Christ's passion was not sufficient for our redemption, but that the sufferings of the saints were added as complementary. But this view is heretical, because Christ's blood is sufficient for the redemption even of many worlds. . . . These words, however, must be understood as meaning that Christ and the Church constitute one mystical person, whose head is Christ, and all the just are the body; any just person is, so to speak, a member of this head. . . . However, God ordained and predestined how much merit there must be in the whole Church both in the head and in the members, just as He predestined the number of the elect. Among these merits the sufferings of the holy martyrs are especially included. The merits of Christ, the Head, are infinite; but each saint contributes proportionately his or her share of merits. . . . Thus also all the saints suffer for the Church, which is fortified by their example." [148]

Hence Christ alone is the Redeemer. Nevertheless the Blessed Virgin Mary, as explained in Mariology, can truly be called the coredemptress, though subordinate to Christ. As Pius X said: "The Blessed Virgin Mary was admitted with Christ and by Christ to cooperate in the salvation of the human race, congruously as they say, to merit for us, what Christ condignly merited." [149] Likewise, along

[145] *Com. in IV Sent.*, d. 20, a. 1, quaestiuncula 1a. See also Cajetan's *Com. in Ep. ad Gal.*, 120, and his treatise *De fide et moribus contra Lutherum*, chap. 9, translated by Em. Mersch, S.J., in his *"Le corps mystique," Etude de théol. historique*, II, 275.

[146] Cf. Ia IIae, q. 114, a. 6, c.; Heb. 2:10.

[147] Col. 1:24.

[148] *Com. in. Ep. ad Col.*

[149] Denz., no. 3034.

with Him, she satisfied congruously, for Benedict XV says: "As she suffered with her Son in His passion and, so to speak, shared in His death, so she abdicated her maternal rights over her Son for the salvation of men and, as far as it was in her power, sacrificed her Son for the appeasement of divine justice, so that it can properly be said, that along with Christ she redeemed the human race." [150]

In this sense the Blessed Virgin Mary cooperated in the acquisition of graces that flow from the sacrifice on the cross. The other saints, however, do not cooperate in the acquisition, but in the application of the fruits of the Passion.[151] Finally, since the merits of Christ are infinite and those of the saints are finite, it can be said that the sufferings of the saints add something that is not intensively, but only extensively finite, as when we say that God and the creature do not make more of being than God alone, for after creation there are more beings, but only extensively more of being. Therefore only Christ is absolutely the Redeemer of the human race.

Sixth Article

REDEMPTION BY WAY OF EFFICIENCY

State of the question. St. Thomas inquires in this article whether Christ's passion brought about our salvation by way of efficiency. The query is not concerned with what constitutes the work of redemption, but with what follows from it as a part of the effect to be produced. It does not pertain to the faith as the preceding queries do, but belongs properly to theology.

It concerns not only moral causality, as being the causality of merit awaiting the effect from another, but also efficient and physical causality, which produces the effect. We have already seen [152] that Christ's soul, inasmuch as it is the instrument united with the Word, had and has instrumental power to produce supernatural effects.[153]

[150] *Ibid.,* note 4.

[151] The Blessed Virgin Mary congruously merited the liberation and the reparation of the human race, whereas the other saints congruously merited the application of this liberation and reparation to this particular person, as St. Monica to St. Augustine. Thus it is said that the Blessed Virgin Mary congruously merited the objective redemption of the human race, not indeed redemption taken in the active sense, for this is a theandric act of Christ the Redeemer, but the effect of this redemption. Christ had a condign right to this effect, and the Blessed Virgin Mary a congruous right to the same. The application of objective redemption to Peter or to Paul is called subjective redemption, namely, of this particular man or the other.

[152] Cf. IIIa, q. 13, a. 2.

[153] *Ibid.,* q. 8, a. 1, ad 1; q. 43, a. 2; *De veritate,* q. 27, a. 3.

Yet there remains a special difficulty for Christ's passion, which could not be the case with any man; for no corporeal agent acts except by actual contact. Moreover, Christ's passion is no more, and therefore it cannot operate efficiently; for that which no longer exists, no longer operates physically.

Reply. Yet the answer is that Christ's passion efficiently causes our salvation, not indeed as principal cause, but as instrumental cause.

Theological proof. Christ's humanity is the instrument of His Godhead, with which it is united. Therefore, as a consequence of this, all Christ's actions and sufferings operate instrumentally in virtue of His Godhead for the salvation of men.

Reply to first objection. It explains the words of the Apostle: "The weakness of God is stronger than men." [154]

Reply to second objection. "Christ's passion although corporeal, has yet a spiritual effect from the Godhead united, and therefore it secures its efficacy by spiritual contact." Corporeal contact is not required, but virtual or dynamic contact suffices. We find this to be true of several instruments used by man, as in the use of a trumpet to transmit a sound in a certain direction; for this instrument does not actually touch the ears of the hearers. A fortiori, God makes use of similar instruments to produce spiritual effects.

The objection that Christ's passion no longer is in action, and therefore cannot operate efficiently, is of no value; for it is a question of Christ's humanity, as formerly subject to suffering and now persists in His glorified wounds. Such is the explanation given by the holy doctor.[155]

Reply to third objection. It is a recapitulation of this subject about Christ's sufferings, for it says: "Christ's passion, according as it is compared with His Godhead, operates in an efficient manner, but so far as it is compared with the will of Christ's soul it acts in a meritorious manner, considered as being within Christ's very flesh, it acts by way of satisfaction, inasmuch as we are liberated by it from the debt of punishment; while inasmuch as we are freed from the servitude of guilt, it acts by way of redemption; but so far as we are reconciled with God it acts by way of sacrifice."

[154] I Cor. 1:25.

[155] Cf. IIIa, q. 49, a. 1 (end).

CHAPTER XXXIV

QUESTION 49

The Effects of Christ's Passion and the Universality of Redemption

IN this question St. Thomas shows the six effects of Christ's passion, which are His merits and satisfaction. Since these six articles present no difficulty, it suffices to give a brief recapitulation of the doctrine contained in them, so that we may pass on to discuss the universality of redemption. All the conclusions of this question must be understood as meaning that Christ's passion is the universal and sufficient cause for the production of these effects; however, that His passion actually produces these effects, it must be applied to us by means of the sacraments and good works.

As regards the definitions of the Church, it has been especially defined in the Second Council of Orange,[1] and in the Council of Trent, that Christ so redeemed us that "the nature lost by Adam was repaired by Him." [2] Christ by His death on the cross redeemed us from sins and reconciled us with the Father.[3] He satisfied for the sins of the whole world.[4] Thus He suffered for all,[5] even for the damned.[6]

First Article

WHETHER WE WERE DELIVERED FROM SIN THROUGH CHRIST'S PASSION

By Christ's passion we have been delivered from sin, in that Christ inasmuch as He is our head, by His passion which He endured for us

[1] Denz., no. 194.
[2] *Ibid.*, nos. 794, 800.
[3] *Ibid.*, nos. 286, 993 f.
[4] *Ibid.*, nos. 122 f., 286, 319, 323, 462, 794, 799, 809, 820, 1096, 1294 f., 1409.
[5] *Ibid.*, nos. 319, 462, 480, 551.
[6] *Ibid.*, no. 323.

out of love and obedience, as by the price of His passion, redeemed us as His members from sins. He redeemed us in the same way as if a man by the good industry of his hands were to redeem himself from a sin committed with his feet. We are here concerned with the sufficiency of the Passion as regards all past, present, and future sins,[7] but the fruits of the Passion must be applied to us by means of the sacraments, or at least by implicit living faith in Christ.

Second Article

WHETHER WE WERE DELIVERED FROM THE DEVIL'S POWER THROUGH CHRIST'S PASSION

Conclusion. By Christ's passion we are freed from the devil's power, under whose slavery we had fallen through sin.

Reply to second and third objections. "God so permitting it, the devil can still tempt men's souls and harass their bodies; yet there is still a remedy provided for man through Christ's passion . . . , namely, a remedy for defending themselves against the wicked snares of the demons, even in Antichrist's time. But if any man neglect to make use of this remedy, it detracts nothing from the efficacy of Christ's passion."

Third Article

WHETHER MEN WERE FREED FROM THE PUNISHMENT OF SIN THROUGH CHRIST'S PASSION

Conclusion. Sin having been taken away, we are freed from eternal punishment that is due to it.

Reply to second objection. "Hence no punishment of satisfaction is imposed upon men at their baptism, since they are fully delivered by Christ's satisfaction."

Fourth Article

WHETHER WE WERE RECONCILED TO GOD THROUGH CHRIST'S PASSION

Conclusion. By Christ's passion we are reconciled to God, in that the cause of enmity against God, which was sin, has been taken away.

[7] Cf. ad 3.

Reply to second objection. The general sense of this reply is that God is said to be placated by a change that is effected not in Him, but in us.

Fifth Article

WHETHER CHRIST OPENED THE GATE OF HEAVEN TO US BY HIS PASSION

Conclusion. Christ opened the gate of heaven to us by His passion, in that He removed the obstacle to its entrance, which is sin.

Reply to first objection. Before Christ's passion no one could enter the kingdom of heaven, because living faith, which sufficed in the Old Testament for the cleansing of the individual, did not suffice for removing the barrier arising from the guilt of the whole human race because of original sin.

Reply to second objection. Elias and Enoch are believed to be living in the earthly paradise until the coming of Antichrist.

Sixth Article

WHETHER BY HIS PASSION CHRIST MERITED TO BE EXALTED

Conclusion. Christ by His passion merited to be exalted [8] as regards His glorious resurrection, His ascension, His sitting at the right hand of the Father, and His judiciary power.

THE UNIVERSALITY OF REDEMPTION

From what has been said, it follows that Christ's redemption is universal, inasmuch as, concerning its sufficiency, it included: (1) all men; (2) all sins; and (3) all good things lost by sin.

1) Redemption included all men, or Christ died for all men. This doctrine on redemption and God's universal will to save are about equivalent in meaning. Luther, Calvin, and the Jansenists, in denying that God wills to save all men, consequently denied that Christ, who came into the world to do His Father's will, died for all men, and so they said that Christ died only for the predestined.

This proposition of Jansenius was condemned, namely: "It is a Semi-Pelagian heresy to say that Christ died or shed His blood for all men without exception." [9] This proposition, understood in this sense,

[8] Phil. 2:8.

[9] Denz., no. 1096.

that Christ died for the salvation only of the predestined, was condemned as heretical.

Moreover, that redemption includes all the faithful seems also to be *de fide,* for the Church declares of Christ: "Who for us men and for our salvation came down from heaven, and was also crucified for us." [10] All the faithful are bound to recite this symbol of the faith.

Finally, Alexander VIII condemned the following proposition of the Jansenists: "Christ gave Himself for us as an oblation to God, not for the elect only, but for all the faithful, and for the faithful alone." [11]

The Council of Trent says: "But, though He died for all,[12] yet all do not receive the benefit of His death, but those only unto whom the merit of His passion is communicated." [13] Hence theologians generally maintain that it is certain, proximate to the faith, that Christ also died at least for all adult infidels. It is even commonly held against Vasquez that Christ died for all men without exception, even for infants who die without being baptized, inasmuch as Christ merited for them the grace of baptism; yet this was made dependent on secondary causes that sometimes prevent the conferring of baptism. There is no passage in Scripture that excludes infants from the benefit of redemption, but it asserts in a general way that Christ died for all.

Scriptural proof. There are no limitations. Thus St. Paul says: "Therefore as by the offense of one man, unto all men to condemnation, so also by the justice of one, unto all men to justification of life." [14] "Christ died for all, that they also who live, may not now live to themselves, but unto Him who died for them, and rose again." [15] "God will have all men to be saved, and to come to the knowledge of the truth. For there is one God, and one mediator of God and men, the man Christ Jesus, who gave Himself a redemption for all." [16] "We see Jesus . . . crowned with glory and honor that through the grace of God He might taste death for all." [17] In one of the epistles we read that "Jesus is the propitiation for our sins, and not for ours only, but also for those of the whole world." [18]

[10] Nicene Creed.
[11] Denz., no. 1294.
[12] II Cor. 4:15.
[13] Denz., no. 795.
[14] Rom. 5:18.
[15] II Cor. 5:15.
[16] I Tim. 2:4 f.
[17] Heb. 2:9.
[18] I John 2:2.

Patristic testimony. The Fathers unanimously assert and explain this doctrine on redemption as shown from the texts quoted by Rouet de Journel.[19] St. Augustine, too, says of infants: "Are not infants also men, so as not to belong to those of whom it is said that God wills all to be saved?" [20] He also says: "God does not command what is impossible, but in commanding advises you to do what you can, and to ask for what you cannot do." [21] It is impossible, however, for adults to observe God's commands without Christ's grace. Therefore the Council of Quierzy declared against the predestinarians: "Just as there neither is, was, nor will be any man whose nature was not assumed by Christ Jesus our Lord, so there neither is, was, nor will be a man for whom Christ did not suffer, although not all are redeemed by the mystery of His passion . . . , because the goblet of Christ's blood for the salvation of men, which was prepared . . . has indeed in itself the power to benefit all; but no one is healed except those who drink from this goblet." [22] Hence Christ's redemption is universal as regards men, because all are included.

2) Christ's redemption includes all sins. In other words, Christ truly satisfied for all sins, both original sin and the actual sins of all human beings. The Council of Trent says: "Him [Christ] God hath proposed as a propitiator, through faith in His blood, for our sins,[23] and not for our sins only, but also for those of the whole world." [24]

This second point, namely, that redemption includes all sins, is *de fide,* for the sins of the faithful, certain for the sins of infidels, commonly admitted doctrine for original sin of infants, as proportionately stated for the first point. Otherwise Christ would not have died absolutely for all men.

Moreover, since Christ's satisfaction is superabundant and of infinite value, it follows that He freed us not only from guilt, but also from eternal and temporal punishment. But we are *de facto* freed from punishment only if Christ's satisfactions are applied to us both by the sacraments, the Sacrifice of the Mass, and by living faith, "which operates by charity." [25]

[19] *Enchiridion patristicum,* no. 422. See especially texts from St. Basil, St. Gregory Nazianzen, St. Ambrose, St. John Chrysostom, St. Augustine.

[20] *Contra Julianum,* chap. 4, nos. 8, 24.

[21] *De natura et gratia,* chap. 43, no. 50.

[22] Denz., no. 319.

[23] Rom. 3:25.

[24] Denz., no. 794; I John 2:2.

[25] Cf. IIIa, q. 49, a. 1.

Christ's satisfaction is not applied to adults without their cooperation, for our Lord says: "If any man will come after Me, let him deny himself, and take up his cross and follow Me." [26] The Prince of the Apostles also teaches that Christ left us "an example that we should follow His steps." [27] Christ the Savior moves us to act and gives us grace, not that our will remain inactive, but that we act by means of the virtues to keep His precepts.

3) Christ's redemption also includes all good things lost by sin, so that we may be restored to our former state, a work begun in this life and completed in the next.

For, as St. Thomas says,[28] by Christ's passion we are freed from sin, punishment, the power of the devil, reconciled to God, and by it the gate of heaven is opened to us. Thus Christ sufficiently merited for all men habitual grace, actual graces that prepare for or follow justification, and also eternal life. He also merited for us natural good things, inasmuch as these are conducive to salvation. He did not indeed merit that the preternatural gifts of immunity from death, suffering, concupiscence, and error should be restored to us in this life. As St. Thomas explains: "A Christian receives grace in baptism as to his soul; but he retains a passible body, so that he may suffer for Christ therein, . . . and this is suitable for our spiritual training, namely, in order that, by fighting against concupiscence and other defects to which he is subject, man may receive the crown of victory." [29] Yet Christ merited that these defects should not gain the mastery over us in this life,[30] and that they be completely eliminated in the next.

Thus Christ's passion is the sufficient cause of salvation for all, and it is efficacious for those to whom it is applied either by the sacraments, or by living faith, and to those who do not resist sufficient grace. But those who resist it deserve to be deprived of efficacious grace.[31] Thus

[26] Matt. 16:24.

[27] I Pet. 2:21. Cf. II Cor. 4:10; Gal. 5:24; Heb. 5:1; Rom. 8:17; II Pet. 1:10.

[28] Cf. IIIa, q. 49, a. 1–5.

[29] *Ibid.,* q. 69, a. 3.

[30] Rom. 5:3 f.; II Cor. 4:17.

[31] So St. Thomas has spoken in several places. See the *Tabula aurea* of his works, under the heading "satisfaction," no. 36, where he says that Christ satisfied sufficiently for the whole human race, but not efficaciously. Cf. IIIa, q. 79, a. 7, ad 2, where he says: "Christ's passion benefits all, for the forgiveness of sin and the attaining of grace and glory, whereas it produces no effect except in those who are united with Christ's passion through faith and charity." In the *Contra Gentes,* Bk. IV, chap. 55, ad 7, we read: "There is sufficient power in the divine Incarnation for the salvation of all

Christ merited all the effects of predestination for the elect, namely, calling, justification, glorification, and also all the efficacious graces that *de facto* are and will be conferred. As regards the efficacious graces, however, which will not be conferred because of the resistance to sufficient grace, He merited these as offered in the sufficient grace, but not as conferred or to be conferred. God offers the efficacious grace to us in the sufficient grace, as the fruit is contained in the flower; but when the sufficient grace is resisted, then the efficacious grace is not conferred.[32]

Therefore Christ's redemption is universal including all men, all sins, and all natural good things that were lost by sin. This is a corollary resulting from the superabundant and infinite value of Christ's atonement.

---

men; but that not all are saved thereby happens because of their disposition, in that they refuse to receive in themselves the fruit of the Incarnation, by not abiding in the incarnate God by faith and charity." Likewise in *De veritate,* q. 29, a. 7, ad 4, he remarks: "Christ's merit was sufficient for the salvation of all men, but it was not efficacious for all, partly because of free will, partly because of divine choice, by which the effect of Christ's merits is conferred mercifully on some, but on others it is withdrawn by God's just judgment." We find the same formula in his *Com. on St. Matthew,* chap. 20 (end); also in his *Com. on I Tim.,* chap. 2, lect. 1 (end), where he says: "[Christ merited] efficaciously for some, but sufficiently for all, because the price of His blood is sufficient for the salvation of all, but it is efficacious only for the elect, because of the obstacle."

[32] Cf. IIIa, q. 19, a. 4; q. 21, a. 4.

CHAPTER XXXV

THE SUBLIME MYSTERY OF REDEMPTION INASMUCH AS IT IS A MYSTERY OF LOVE

BY way of combining synthetically what St. Thomas has said,[1] that we may see more clearly the sublimity of the mystery of redemption inasmuch as it is a mystery of love, two questions remain to be considered: (1) Why Christ suffered so much for us, when the least of His theandric acts of love already superabundantly satisfied for the redemption of all men. (2) How shall we reconcile in Christ crucified the union of supreme suffering with perfect peace and happiness resulting from the beatific vision?

First Article

WHY CHRIST SUFFERED SO MUCH WHEN THE LEAST OF HIS ACTS OF LOVE SUPERABUNDANTLY SUFFICED FOR THE SALVATION OF ALL MEN

State of the question. When we meditate on Christ's passion, this question often arises: why Christ endured so many humiliations, so many physical and moral sufferings for our salvation, if even by the least act of theandric love He could have merited eternal life for all of us, if the least suffering, joined with theandric love and accepted by God, could have superabundantly redeemed and satisfied for the sins of a thousand worlds, as is commonly taught even in catechisms. It is certain, as was shown above, that the least of Christ's theandric acts of love has an infinite personal value for meriting and satisfying, because it pleases God the Father more than all crimes displease Him. St. Thomas says: "The very least one of Christ's sufferings was suffi-

[1] *Summa theol.*, IIIa, q. 46–49.

cient of itself to redeem the human race from all sins." [2] St. Thomas also says:

> "O loving Pelican! O Jesu Lord!
> Unclean I am, but cleanse me in Thy blood!
> Of which a single drop for sinners spilt,
> Can purge the entire world from all its guilt." [3]

Clement VI likewise says: "The innocent Christ who was immolated on the altar of the cross shed not merely a little drop of blood, though this would have sufficed for the redemption of the entire human race, because of the union with the Word, but streams of it, like unto a river." [4] Wherefore, then, such great humiliations? Christ was forcibly stripped of His garments, scourged, struck in the face, spit upon by the soldiers, crowned with thorns, a reed in derision was placed in His hand; His entire body was made a victim of suffering, and even in His heart He suffered, being abandoned by His own nation, even by His disciples, and He was opposed by the priests of the synagogue, who preferred Barabbas to Him; He was a victim even in His soul, saying in the Garden of Gethsemane: "My soul is sorrowful even unto death," [5] and on the cross He cried aloud those words of the Messianic psalm: "My God, My God, why hast Thou forsaken Me?" [6]

Why all these physical and moral sufferings, when the pain endured from theandric love and accepted by God sufficed superabundantly for the redemption of all men?

St. Thomas answers this question by giving three reasons subordinated to one another in an ascending order for this supreme grief, and founded on revelation. They are: (1) on our part; [7] (2) on the part of Christ crucified; [8] (3) on the part of the Father, who did not spare His Son, but delivered Him up to suffer for us.[9]

All these reasons are expressed, more or less explicitly, in the Messianic prophecies, which Christ explained to the two disciples going

[2] *Ibid.,* q. 46, a. 5, ad 3.
[3] Liturgical hymn *Adoro Te.*
[4] Denz., no. 550.
[5] Matt. 26:38.
[6] *Ibid.,* 27:46; Mark 15:34.
[7] Cf. IIIa, q. 46, a. 3, 4.
[8] *Ibid.,* q. 47, a. 2.
[9] *Ibid.,* a. 3.

to the town of Emmaus, to whom He finally said: "Ought not Christ to have suffered these things, and so to enter into His glory?" [10]

These three principal reasons must be separately explained; each consists of several subdivisions.

1) As regards ourselves, it was fitting for Christ to suffer in so many ways and to the utmost, so that He might give us the supreme example of love.

"The proof of love," as St. Gregory says, "is shown in act," [11] and especially in painful sacrifice. Hence Christ Himself said: "Greater love than this no man hath, that a man lay down his life for his friends." [12] But Christ also gave His life for His enemies, and for His executioners for whom He prayed.

St. Thomas says the same in the following words: "Man knows thereby how much God loves him, and is thereby stirred to love Him in return, and herein lies the perfection of human salvation. Hence the Apostle says: God commendeth His charity toward us, for whereas yet we were sinners . . . Christ died for us." [13]

On our part, there are other subordinated reasons why Christ suffered for us, reasons which are mentioned here, namely: Because thereby Christ set us an example not only of supreme charity, but also of such subordinated virtues as obedience, humility, constancy, justice, and the other virtues displayed in the Passion, which are requisite for man's salvation. Hence it is written: "Christ suffered for us, leaving you an example that you should follow His steps." [14] In fact, Christ in His passion gave us an example of practicing virtues that are at such extremes from one another that they appear to be contraries, and yet they are intimately and perfectly united in most perfect sanctity, such as supreme fortitude and absolute meekness. St. Thomas, declaring that Christ willed to suffer for us, quotes St. Augustine, who says: "No kind of death should trouble an upright man . . . because among all kinds of death, none was more execrable, more fear-inspiring than this." [15]

Consequently, as intimated,[16] Christ's passion vividly manifests

[10] Luke 24:26.
[11] *Com. in Joan.*, 15.
[12] John 15:13.
[13] Cf. IIIa, q. 46, a. 3; Rom. 5:8.
[14] *Ibid.;* I Pet. 2:21.
[15] *Summa theol.*, IIIa, q. 46, a. 4.
[16] *Ibid.*, a. 3.

the gravity of sin, inasmuch as reparation is made for the sin of pride by great humiliations, sins of impurity by such intense sufferings, sins arising from concupiscence of the eyes by such want and deprivation, sins of disobedience by obedience even unto death on the cross.

Likewise Christ's passion most sublimely makes clear to us the value of both the supernatural life of grace and eternal life, which is obtained for us by so much self-denial, in despising all the joys and honors of this life; so that He appears to be completely conquered, stripped of all temporal goods, whereas He truly is the Savior of all these things. This constitutes the chiaroscuro of our Lord's passion considered as it concerns us.[17] These reasons that refer to us are capable of different modes of development, according as they apply in various ways to us.

Finally, under this aspect it must be said with St. Thomas: "As man was overcome and deceived by the devil, so also it should be by a man becoming humble and perfectly obedient that the devil should be overthrown; and as man deserved death, so a man by dying should vanquish death. Hence it is written: 'Thanks be to God, who hath given us the victory through our Lord, Jesus Christ.'" [18] Sinful men need this greatest proof of love for their conversion.

2) As regards Christ the Savior, it befitted Him to suffer in many ways and in the highest degree, so that He might most perfectly accomplish His glorious mission as Savior of the whole human race.[19]

Christ truly fulfilled His mission by heroic obedience even to death on the cross, which was also a most perfect holocaust that was offered from supreme love. St. Thomas says: "Instead of material fire, there was the spiritual fire of charity in Christ's holocaust." [20]

Thus the words of St. Paul are verified: "For as by the disobedience of one man, many were made sinners; so also by the obedience of one, many shall be made just." [21]

Moreover, Christ as priest could not offer any victim worthier than His own self. Hence it is said: "He hath delivered Himself for us, an oblation and a sacrifice to God for an odor of sweetness," [22] and it is a most perfect holocaust in which the whole victim is consumed in

[17] *Ibid.*, q. 47, a. 2.
[18] *Ibid.*, q. 46, a. 3; I Cor. 15:57.
[19] *Ibid.*, q. 47, a. 2.
[20] *Ibid.*, q. 46, a. 4, ad 1.
[21] Rom. 5:19.
[22] Eph. 5:2.

God's honor and for the reparation of sin. As we said above,[23] the more perfect the sacrifice is, the more the priest who offers it is united with God to whom he offers it, the more he is united with the people for whom he offers it, and finally with the victim, which is an external expression of adoration and of interior reparation. Hence Christ was most fittingly both priest and hostage, and hostage or victim not only in the body, by enduring physical pain, but also in the heart and soul by submitting to the most intense of moral suffering. Thus among the three apostolates of doctrine and prayer and suffering or sacrifice, the last is the more fruitful; Christ saved more by His death on the cross than by His preaching on the Mount of the Beatitudes, and He preached nowhere better and more sublimely than on the cross.

Thus it was fitting that the most perfect Redeemer should accomplish His mission in a most perfect manner, by a heroic sacrifice of supreme love, offered out of supreme love for God's glory and the salvation of souls. Hence in this way Christ not only merited, but He merited in the highest degree the exaltation of His name, and what He was already entitled to because of His divine sonship, this He acquired because He had supremely merited it. But if anything can be the object of merit, it is better to have it from merit than without merit.[24]

Moreover, as will be said in the following question, while Christ was still both wayfarer and comprehensor, He could not have fullness of grace, and love for God and souls without experiencing the greatest of grief for mortal sin, since it is an offense against God and the death of souls that leads to eternal misery. On this point St. Thomas says: "This grief in Christ surpassed all grief of every contrite heart, both because it flowed from a greater wisdom and charity, and because He grieved at the same time for all sins, as the prophet says, Surely He hath carried our sorrows." [25]

Finally, it must be observed that very great holiness arouses men of bad disposition neither to admiration nor indifference, but to hatred which results in fierce persecution. The Evangelist says: "Men loved darkness rather than the light." [26] Hence Christ said of the Pharisees: "Now they have hated both Me and My Father." [27] The old man

[23] St. Augustine's *De Trinitate,* Bk. IV, chap. 14.
[24] Cf. IIIa, q. 19, a. 3.
[25] *Ibid.,* q. 46, a. 6, ad 4; Isa. 53:4.
[26] John 3:19.
[27] *Ibid.,* 15:24.

Simeon had said of Jesus in His early childhood: "Behold this child is set for a sign which shall be contradicted . . . that out of many hearts thoughts may be revealed." [28]

3) As regards God the Father, it was fitting that the Father should deliver up His Son to the greatest of suffering, so that Christ by this sorrowful way might attain to the greatest of all glory, namely, victory over sin, the devil, and death. It is in this way that in the case of certain great servants of God, such as St. Paul of the Cross, their life is made illustrious.[29] The holy Doctor, St. Thomas, presents the following objection on this subject: "It seems that God does not always love more the better things. For it is manifest that Christ is better than the whole human race, being God and man. But God loved the human race more than He loved Christ; for it is said: 'He spared not His own Son, but delivered Him up for us all.' Therefore He does not always love more the better things." [30]

St. Thomas replies by saying: "God loves Christ not only more than He loves the whole human race, but more than He loves the entire created universe; because He willed for Him the greater good in giving Him a name that is above all names, so far as He was true God. Nor did anything of His excellence diminish when God delivered Him up to death for the salvation of the human race; rather did He become thereby a glorious conqueror. The government was placed upon His shoulder, as the prophet says." [31] In other words, Christ became conqueror of sin and the devil by offering Himself in sacrifice on the cross, and the conqueror of death by His resurrection inasmuch as "the wages of sin is death," [32] and it is destroyed after sin is destroyed.

Thus sometimes in human affairs, the general of the army in time of war must sacrifice several of his soldiers for the safety of his country; then he often chooses the better soldiers. The example is quoted of the magnanimous general who chose his son to lead the soldiers who were to die fighting for the safety of their country. In such a case, the son thus chosen fulfills perfectly his military calling, thanks his father for this glorious mission, and in this we see clearly the heroic love of the father for his son, and of the son for his father

[28] Luke 2:34.
[29] Cf. Ia, q. 20, a. 4, ad 1.
[30] *Ibid.,* 1st obj.; Rom. 8:32.
[31] *Summa theol., loc. cit.;* Isa. 9:6.
[32] Rom. 6:23.

and the safety of the fatherland. This is a remote comparison with the sacrifice on the cross; for God the Father truly "delivered up His Son for us" [33] and gave Him a strict command to die for us on the cross.

St. Thomas beautifully explains this in commenting on these words of our Lord: "I lay down My life, that I may take it again. No man taketh it away from Me, but I lay it down of Myself, and I have power to lay it down of Myself and I have power to take it up again. This commandment I have received of My Father." [34] He considers that this text concerns a command in the strict sense, and says: "The fulfillment of a command is a proof of love for the person who commands." [35] St. Thomas in another article shows [36] that, although this command is dour, yet it results from the supreme love of the Father for the Son.

At the beginning of the above-mentioned article, St. Thomas puts this objection to himself: "It is a wicked and cruel act to hand over an innocent man to torment and death; but the Apostle says: He spared not even His own Son, but delivered Him up for us all." [37]

We quoted the following reply of the holy Doctor: "In three respects God the Father did deliver up Christ to the Passion. In the first way, because by His eternal will He preordained Christ's passion for the deliverance of the human race,[38] according to the words of the prophet: 'The Lord hath laid on Him the iniquities of us all,' [39] and again: 'The Lord was pleased to bruise Him in infirmity.' [40] Secondly, inasmuch as, by the infusion of charity, He inspired Him with the will to suffer for us. Hence we read in the same passage: 'He was offered because it was His own will.' [41] Thirdly, by not shielding Him from the Passion, but abandoning Him to His persecutors. Hence we read that Christ, while hanging upon the cross cried out: 'My God,

[33] *Ibid.*, 8:32.

[34] John 10:17 f.

[35] *Com. in Joan.*, 10:17. See also his *Com. in Epist. ad Rom.* 8:32; also *in Epist. ad Phil.* 2:8.

[36] Cf. IIIa, q. 47, a. 3.

[37] *Ibid.;* Rom. 8:32.

[38] Evidently here we have the predominating decree, independently of the *scientia media* or the conditionally free future merits of Christ; for Christ's merits are the effect and not the cause of His predestination. Cf. Ia, q. 23, a. 5.

[39] Isa. 53:6.

[40] *Ibid.*, 53:10.

[41] *Ibid.*, 53:7. At Least in Vulgate.

My God, why hast Thou forsaken Me?' [42] because to wit, He left Him to the power of His persecutors, as Augustine says." [43]

There was not any cruelty in this on the part of the Father, because "God the Father did not deliver up Christ against His will, but inspired Him with the will to suffer for us. God's severity is thereby shown, for He would not remit sin without penalty . . . and His goodness shines forth, since by no penalty endured could man pay Him enough satisfaction." [44]

Reply to third objection. "The Father delivered up Christ, and Christ surrendered Himself from charity, and consequently we give praise to both. But Judas betrayed Christ from greed, the Jews from envy, and Pilate from worldly fear, for he stood in fear of Caesar. And these accordingly are held guilty." Thus on the part of God the Father inspiring and commanding and on the part of Christ offering Himself, His death was a sacrifice, whereas for the Jews it was a sacrifice and a crime.

But the divine decree concerning the command Christ received to die for us, can be illustrated by divers subordinated motives with respect to the glory which God the Father willed eternally for His Son.

1) The greatest degree of glory is acquired in accepting with great love the more profound humiliations. Thus Christ Himself said: "Everyone that exalteth himself shall be humbled, and he that humbleth himself shall be exalted." [45] The parable of the Pharisee and the publican is likewise an example.[46] This truth is often mentioned in the Old Testament, and it is clearly illustrated in the lives of Job, the prophet Joseph, who was sold by his brothers but was afterward exalted, as also in the life of Isaac, who was a figure of Christ, inasmuch as he was bound on the altar by his father to be sacrificed, and afterward he was blessed with an innumerable progeny. This law of the supernatural order finds its supreme verification in Christ. Because of His divine sonship, indeed, by reason of His birth and heredity, He already had the right to the greatest glory, namely, to sit at the right hand of the Father; but it was also most fitting that He should obtain this greatest of glory on grounds of supreme merit.

[42] Matt. 27:46.
[43] Cf. IIIa, q. 47, a. 3, c. Also *Epist.* 120, no. 6, of St. Augustine.
[44] *Ibid.,* ad 1.
[45] Luke 14:11.
[46] *Ibid.,* 18:14.

Thus also we find verified these words which the prophet said of our Lord: "Behold My Servant, My elect; My soul delighteth in Him . . . The bruised reed He shall not break, and smoking flax He shall not quench; He shall bring forth judgment unto truth. . . . I, the Lord, this is My name. I will not give My glory to another." [47] But God wills from all eternity to give this supreme glory to the incarnate Word, that He sit at the right hand of His Father forever, as supreme Judge of all, as King of kings, Lord of lords; but this highest glory is deservedly obtained by the more profound humiliations of the Passion accepted with great love. This explains clearly our Lord's words to the disciples on their way to Emmaus: "Ought not Christ to have suffered these things, and so to enter into His glory?" [48]

2) The greatest victory over sin whereby charity is lost, was deservedly obtained by that supreme act of charity, whereby Christ heroically gave His life for us. Thus we have in this the most eminent verification of these classic words of St. Augustine: "And so the two loves made two cities; the love of self that resulted in contempt of God constituting the worldly city, and the love of God that resulted in contempt of self, constituting the heavenly city." [49] This contempt of self resulted in the perfect sacrifice of the present life, and of all humiliations; it ended in the ignominy or opprobrium of dying on the cross between two thieves.

3) The greatest victory over the demon of pride and disobedience was deservedly obtained also by humble "obedience unto death, even to the death on the cross." [50] Hence God the Father, eternally willing for His incarnate Son this most exalted victory, decreed that He become obedient even to the death on the cross. This follows from the supreme love of the Father for His Son and for us in His Son. St. Thomas quotes St. Augustine as saying: "It was fitting means of overthrowing the pride of the devil . . . that Christ should liberate us by the lowliness of the Passion." [51]

4) The greatest victory over death, which is the "wages of sin," [52] justly so is obtained by the resurrection. But this glorious resurrection

[47] Isa. 42:1 f.
[48] Luke 24:26.
[49] *De civitate Dei,* chap. 28.
[50] Phil. 2:8.
[51] Cf. IIIa, q. 46, a. 4, ad 3.
[52] Rom. 6:23.

presupposes death, and death that is accepted through love for the victory over sin, which is the cause of death.[53]

St. Thomas quotes St. Chrysostom as saying: "How could Christ's victory over death be apparent unless He endured it in the sight of all men, and so proved that death was extinguished by the incorruption of His body?"[54] St. Thomas likewise says: "Christ's obedience unto death befitted His victory, whereby He triumphed over death and its author."[55] Thus we chant in the liturgy: "O great work of mercy! Death then died when Life died on the tree. Alleluia."[56]

Because of these subordinated motives, God the Father willing this glory and threefold victory of Christ over sin, the devil, and death, decreed to deliver Him up to sufferings, and the greatest humiliations of the Passion.

St. Paul enunciates all these victories in the following sublime combination: "Christ humbled Himself, becoming obedient unto death, even to the death of the cross. For which cause God also hath exalted Him, and hath given Him a name which is above all names. That in the name of Jesus every knee should bow, of those that are in heaven, on earth, and under the earth. And that every tongue should confess that the Lord Jesus Christ is in the glory of God the Father."[57]

All these victories appear the more sublime when we consider that the gratuitous predestination of Christ was eternal as regards: (1) His divine natural sonship; (2) His supreme degree of glory; (3) His fullness of habitual grace and charity, whereby Christ was to merit the glory previously intended by God.[58]

[53] Cf. IIIa, q. 46, a. 3.

[54] *Ibid.*, ad 2.

[55] *Ibid.*, q. 47, a. 2.

[56] Feast of Finding of the Holy Cross. First antiphon of Lauds.

[57] Phil. 2:8. St. Thomas (*Com. in Epist. ad Phil.* 2:8) quotes this text from Job 22:29; "He that hath been humbled shall be in glory." He also quotes this text from St. Paul (Eph. 1:21): "God set Him on His right hand in the heavenly places, above all."

[58] This doctrine is confirmed by the Scripture; for the Gospel says: "On the last and great day of the festivity, Jesus stood and cried, saying: If any man thirst, let him come to Me and drink. He that believeth in Me, as the Scripture saith: From within Him shall flow rivers of living water. Now this He said of the Spirit which they should receive, who believed in Him; for as yet the Spirit was not given, because Jesus was not yet glorified" (John 8:37 f.). St. Thomas (*Com. in Joan.* 8:38) says: "These words 'the Spirit was not yet given' must be understood of that abundant bestowal, and by visible signs, such as was given to the apostles after the resurrection

These are the reasons for the supreme humiliation and sufferings of Christ, whose least act of love fully and superabundantly sufficed for the redemption of the whole human race.

These reasons must be sought partly in ourselves, partly in Christ, and partly in God the Father, for men needed this supreme manifestation of love; Christ had to accomplish His mission in the most perfect manner; and God the Father, in this way, willed to give His Son supreme victory.

Which of these is the more exalted? The more exalted reason is that of God the Father who predestines, as St. Paul says: "For all are yours; and you are Christ's, and Christ is God's." [59] Hence the ultimate end of both the Incarnation and the Passion is the manifestation of God's goodness, especially by way of mercy. Thus in the liturgy we say: "O God, who dost manifest Thine almighty power above all in showing pardon and pity," [60] for thus God not only makes something from nothing, as in creation, but from evil, even from the profound and universal evil of the fallen human race, He brings out the greatest good. Hence the Apostle says: "Where sin abounded, grace did more abound" [61] for us, and it was at the same time a definite manifestation of Christ's victory over sin, the devil, and death, as also of God's goodness and mercy.

These are the reasons for the humiliations and most intense sufferings of Christ our Redeemer, who appears far more glorious as the Redeemer of the fallen human race and subjected to the various miseries of life than if He had come, in virtue of another decree of Providence, as the Head, the King, and the Teacher of the human race in the state of innocence.

Then Christ would not have come in passible flesh and as a victim; He would not have had the sufferings and humiliations of the Passion, and He would not have merited His future and supreme glory for all eternity in heaven. Hence the complete answer to this question

and ascension in the form of fiery tongues. . . . And the reason assigned why Christ willed to be glorified before He would give the Holy Spirit, is that the Holy Spirit is given for the purpose of weaning our hearts from attachment to worldly things so that they be centered on our spiritual resurrection and hasten with all our supernatural powers toward God." Moreover, the Holy Spirit is Christ's supreme gift, namely, the uncreated gift, which is ultimately granted on the culmination of His mission and glorification, that is, after the humiliations of His passion.

[59] I Cor. 3:22 f.

[60] Collect for Tenth Sunday after Pentecost.

[61] Rom. 5:20.

is found in these words of St. Paul: "He humbled Himself, becoming obedient unto death, even to the death of the cross. For which cause God also hath exalted Him, and hath given Him a name which is above all names," [62] since God exalted Him to the highest of glory in that He sits at the right hand of the Father, as God equal to the Father, and as man glorifying the Father.

But the victory of the cross over the devil and sin far surpasses the victory over death on the Resurrection day. The Resurrection, indeed, is a resplendent miracle, but it is only the result of Christ's victory over sin, in that the "wages of sin is death." [63]

This glory of the cross is wondrously expressed in the following lines of the sacred liturgy:

Resplendent is the mystery of the Cross,
On which Life itself died,
And by death our life restored.
Most royally empurpled o'er,
How beauteously thy stem doth shine,
How glorious was its lot to touch
Those limbs so holy and divine.
Hail Cross, thou only hope of man,
Now in this joyous paschal time
Justice in godly souls increase
And free the guilty from their crime.[64]

Likewise in the following sequence:

Let me, to my latest breath
In my body bear the death
Of that dying Son of Thine.
Wounded with His every wound,
Steep my soul till it hath swooned
In His very blood away.
Christ, when Thou shalt call me hence,
Be Thy Mother my defense
Be Thy Cross my victory.[65]

[62] Phil. 2:8 f.
[63] Rom. 6:23.
[64] Hymn *Vexilla Regis*.
[65] Hymn *Stabat Mater*.

Second Article

ON THE UNION IN CHRIST THE SAVIOR OF THE GREATEST SUFFERING AND THE BEATIFIC VISION

After the discussion of the problem concerning the motive for the humiliations and very great sufferings of Christ the Redeemer, another very secret aspect of the Passion must be considered, namely, how Christ endured the greatest sufferings, even in the moral order, and at the same time retained the joy of supreme happiness in the beatific vision.

This problem is examined by St. Thomas in four articles,[66] wherein he asks: Whether Christ endured all sufferings; whether the pain of His passion was the greatest; whether He suffered in His whole soul; whether His entire soul enjoyed blessed fruition during the Passion. We have already discussed these articles, but now the doctrine contained in them must be considered more profoundly, and from a more exalted point of view.

PRELIMINARY REMARKS

What makes this whole question so famous is the fact that Christ as man received from the first moment of His conception fullness of grace and charity together with the beatific vision, and hence He always had an ardent desire of most perfectly accomplishing His mission as Redeemer, by offering Himself as a supreme holocaust.

Hence we shall see: (1) that He often expressed this desire during His life; (2) that He endured all kinds of sufferings and the greatest of pain;[67] (3) that He always had, however, the greatest of peace and happiness;[68] (4) that the greatest of sadness and the greatest of happiness were compatibly united in Him. Concerning this last inquiry, there are three theories which, as we shall declare, are insufficient. They are: (1) that Christ suffered only in the sensitive part of His soul, which is a grave error; (2) that Christ during His passion refused the joy of the beatific vision; (3) that the greatest of happiness and the greatest of sadness are strictly contraries, and yet they are miraculously united. We shall declare that they are not strictly contraries, but their union is, nevertheless, both a miracle and a mystery, and be-

[66] Cf. IIIa, q. 46, a. 5–8.
[67] *Ibid.,* a. 5, 6.
[68] *Ibid.,* a. 7, 8.

cause of this mystery it followed that Christ was both a wayfarer and a comprehensor.

This whole question must be clarified by the aid of the principle that Christ from the beginning of His human life had absolute fullness of grace from which there resulted on the one hand the light of glory, the beatific vision, and supreme joy, and on the other hand supreme charity, the greatest of zeal for God's glory and the salvation of souls, together with a most ardent desire of most perfectly accomplishing His redemptive mission by the supreme sacrifice of His life through the most perfect immolation of Himself. Hence these two effects that differ in the highest degree, namely, the greatest of joy and the greatest of suffering, originate from the same source, that is, the fullness of grace, and thus they must be intimately reconciled. In fact, we shall see that Christ's most intense suffering was concerned with sin and was in accordance with the intensity of His charity or love for God who is offended, and for souls of sinners; for it was Christ's love for souls that made Him utterly sad at the sin and loss of many souls. St. Thomas says that Christ grieved exceedingly at the sin of the Jews killing Him (cf. IIIa, q. 15, a. 6; q. 46, a. 6). In this most exalted principle, we already clearly see the intimate reconciliation of those things that differ in the highest degree, and that are naturally incompatible.

1) The plenitude of Christ's charity is the cause of His ardent desire for the sacrifice of the cross.

It is a generally accepted principle in theology that, when God immediately entrusts anyone with a very special mission of a divine nature, He demands proportionate sanctity in His legate. For God's works are perfect, especially His own immediate and exclusive operations; in these works there cannot be any deordination or lack of proportion. This principle, especially as it applies to Christ, is a revealed truth, for the Apostle says: "In the dispensation of the fullness of times [God] proposed to re-establish all things in Christ." [69] The importance of this most certain principle is still more clearly seen if by contrast we examine carefully what more often happens in the regulation of human affairs. Frequently incapable and imprudent persons are placed in very high positions to the detriment of those over whom they must rule. But nothing like this happens to those who, immediately chosen and prepared by God for this special ministry of the supernatural order, are called by Him. To these God gives

[69] Eph. 1:10.

proportionate grace, so that they may perfectly fulfill their mission, as is clearly seen in the lives of those saints who were founders of religious orders, and in the lives of the apostles. But we find this truth most of all verified in Christ the Savior.

For, as stated above,[70] Christ had received both in intensity and in extent absolute plenitude of habitual grace and charity, and therefore in accordance with this fullness of charity He ardently desired from the beginning of His earthly life most perfectly to accomplish His mission by the sacrifice on the cross, willed by God for our salvation.

If Daniel the prophet was a "man of desires," [71] if to all Christians our Lord said, "Blessed are they that hunger and thirst after justice, for they shall have their fill," [72] then certainly Christ Himself had on earth an ardent desire of accomplishing His redemptive mission, no matter what obstacles and persecution He had to encounter, so that even these persecutions might serve the purpose of His mission, which is to be both priest and victim.

Christ's mission is already clearly proclaimed by St. John the Baptist, who says: "Behold the Lamb of God, behold Him who taketh away the sin of the world." [73]

But this ardent desire of most perfectly completing this sacrifice of Himself on the cross, is expressed by Christ Himself in various ways.

Thus St. Paul, who in one of his epistles speaks of Christ the great high priest and victim, points out the inadequacy of the sacrifices of the Old Law, and says: "For it is impossible that with the blood of oxen and goats sin should be taken away. Wherefore when He cometh into the world He saith: Sacrifice and oblation Thou wouldest not, but a body Thou hast fitted to Me. Holocausts for sin did not please Thee. Then I said: Behold I come. In the head of the book it is written of Me that I should do Thy will, O God. . . . Then I said: Behold I come to do Thy will, O God." [74] St. Paul at once adds: "In the which will, we are sanctified by the oblation of the body of Jesus Christ once." [75] He says "once," because Christ's bloody sacrifice was accomplished once on the cross, and because the interior oblation of

[70] Cf. IIIa, q. 7, a. 9-13.
[71] Dan. 9:23; 10:11.
[72] Matt. 5:6.
[73] John 1:29.
[74] Heb. 10:4 f.
[75] *Ibid.*, 10:10.

Himself thus made from the beginning continued without interruption, and this offering did not have to be renewed because it was never interrupted. If a perfect religious, after taking vows for life, lives always, so to speak, in a state of actual oblation, a fortiori this is so with Christ Himself.

Truly this oblation never ceased in Christ's soul, and He expressed it in equivalent words in the Garden of Gethsemane, saying: "Not as I will, but as Thou wilt." [76]

But Christ, between the beginning and the end of His life on earth, clearly expressed this desire of suffering for us; for the Evangelist records Him as saying: "I am come to cast fire on the earth, and what will I but that it be kindled? And I have a baptism wherewith I am to be baptized, and how am I straitened until it be accomplished." [77] It concerns the baptism of blood, which is the most perfect of all, as St. Thomas shows,[78] for it is at the same time a sacrifice.

Likewise the desire of the Passion or of the cross is most beautifully expressed in the parable of the good shepherd: "I am the good shepherd. The good shepherd giveth his life for his sheep. But the hireling . . . seeth the wolf coming . . . and flieth. . . . I am the good shepherd . . . and I lay down My life for My sheep. . . . No man taketh it away from Me, but I lay it down of Myself. . . . This commandment I have received of My Father." [79] Therefore this interior oblation continues without interruption in Christ's will.

Similarly, after Jesus had foretold His sorrowful passion to His apostles, Peter "began to rebuke Him, saying: 'Lord, be it far from Thee, this shall not be unto Thee.' Who turning, said to Peter: 'Go behind Me, Satan, thou are a scandal unto Me, because thou savorest not the things that are of God, but the things that are of men.' " [80] Unknowingly Peter spoke against the whole economy of salvation, against the infallible disposition of Providence concerning the sacrifice of the cross for the salvation of the human race. Christ again affirms His mission and perfectly wills its accomplishment, notwithstanding the extreme pain of the crucifixion.

In like manner He speaks of taking up the cross in these words: "He that findeth his life [that is, in loving too much the joys of this

[76] Matt. 26:39; Luke 22:42; Mark 14:36.
[77] Luke 12:49 f.
[78] Cf. IIIa, q. 46, a. 12.
[79] John 10:11 f.
[80] Matt. 16:22 f.

world] will lose it; and he that shall lose his life [or sacrifice his life for God] shall find it." [81] To the sons of Zebedee, "Jesus answering said: 'You know not what you ask. Can you drink the chalice that I shall drink? or be baptized with the baptism wherewith I am baptized?' They say to Him: 'We can.' Jesus saith to them: 'You shall indeed drink of the chalice.' " [82]

Again, after His triumphant entry into Jerusalem, Christ speaks of His glorification by means of the cross, when He says: "The hour is come that the Son of man should be glorified. Amen, amen, I say to you, unless the grain of wheat falling into the ground die, itself remaineth alone; but if it die, it bringeth forth much fruit." "A voice therefore came from heaven. 'I have both glorified it, and will glorify it again.' . . . Jesus said to the multitude: 'This voice came not because of Me, but for your sakes. Now is the judgment of the world, now shall the prince of this world be cast out. And I, if I be lifted up from the earth, will draw all things to Myself.' " [83] This is a beautiful expression of Christ's ardent desire for the passion. The Evangelist at once adds: "Now this He said signifying what death He should die." [84]

Finally, this ardent desire for the sacrifice of the cross is most clearly expressed on the day before He suffered, when Christ instituted the Sacrifice of the Mass, which is substantially the same as the sacrifice of the cross. As the Evangelist narrates, He said to the apostles: "With desire I have desired to eat this pasch with you, before I suffer." [85] In other words, I have desired most earnestly to eat this pasch with you, that is, as Eusebius observes, the pasch of the New Testament, which is the Eucharist in which Christ is as a victim; hence He at once afterward said: "I say to you, that from this time I will not eat it, till it be fulfilled in the kingdom of God." "And taking bread, He gave thanks and broke, and gave to them saying: 'This is My body, which is given for you. Do this for a commemoration of Me.' In like manner the chalice also, after He had supped, saying: 'This is the chalice, the new testament in My blood, which shall be shed for you.' " [86]

[81] *Ibid.,* 10:39. See also Mark 8:34; 10:35.
[82] Matt. 20:20; Mark 10:38.
[83] John 12:23 f.
[84] *Ibid.,* 12:33.
[85] Luke 22:15.
[86] *Ibid.,* 22:16 f.

Immediately after the supper, on His way to the Garden of Gethsemane, Jesus expresses this same desire, saying: "For the prince of this world cometh and in Me He hath not anything. But that the world may know that I love the Father, and as the Father hath given Me commandment, so do I." [87]

He also says: "Greater love than this no man hath, that a man lay down his life for his friends." [88] "Sanctify them [the apostles] in truth. . . . And for them I sanctify Myself, that they also may be sanctified in truth." In other words, I sacrifice Myself.[89]

From these different texts it is evident that Christ continually desired the perfect fulfillment of His mission by the sacrifice of the cross. These various passages are also clarified from the teaching on the plenitude of grace and charity in the Savior, as stated above.[90] This fullness of grace disposed Christ so that He most perfectly desired and efficaciously willed to accomplish His mission of Redeemer and victim by offering Himself as a perfect holocaust, suffering for us all the physical and moral pains of the Passion and crucifixion.[91] This explains why He willed to suffer sadness unto death for us,[92] and why "He began to fear and to be heavy," [93] in that He willed to suffer this extreme anxiety, so that His sacrifice might be a perfect holocaust, in which the victim is completely destroyed and consumed in God's honor for the remission of sins.[94]

2) Did Christ endure all kinds of suffering, and even the greatest?

St. Thomas in examining this question shows that "it was not necessary for Christ to endure every kind of suffering, since many are mutually exclusive, as burning, and drowning," [95] and it did not become Him to suffer bodily sicknesses.[96] But He endured all kinds of

[87] John 14:31.

[88] *Ibid.,* 15:13.

[89] *Ibid.,* 17:17, 20.

[90] Cf. IIIa, q. 7, a. 9-13.

[91] Christ willed that certain martyrs at the moment of their martyrdom should experience the greatest joy that would lessen the pain, as in the case of St. Lawrence, St. Ignatius of Antioch, and St. Andrew: but Christ Himself willed to experience "sorrow even unto death" (Matt. 26:38) so that His sacrifice might be more perfect and meritorious.

[92] Matt. 26:38.

[93] Mark 14:33.

[94] Cf. Louis Chardon, O.P., *La Croix de Jésus,* chap. 5, wherein he says: "The plenitude of grace that belongs properly to Jesus, as head of His mystical body, causes in His soul a desire for the cross" (pp. 46-52).

[95] Cf. IIIa, q. 46, a. 5, 6.

[96] *Ibid.,* q. 14, a. 4.

sufferings, in that: (1) on the part of men, He suffered from all classes, namely, from the Gentiles, the Jews, the rulers, the people, His apostles, as is evident from Judas who betrayed Him, and Peter who denied Him; (2) on the part of those things whereby man can suffer, He suffered from His friends deserting Him, from hunger, by contempts and blasphemies against His honor, in His body, in His soul through extreme sadness and weariness; (3) then He suffered in all parts of His body, from the feet nailed to the cross to the head crowned with thorns.

But was the pain of Christ's passion greater than all other pains? St. Thomas replies that the pain of Christ's passion was the greatest of all pains in the present life, and this for four reasons: (1) from the quasi-efficient causes of this pain; (2) from the susceptibility of the sufferer; (3) because of the lack of any mitigation of the pain taken in the formal sense; (4) from the end in view, because the pain willed by Christ was to be proportionate for the liberation of the human race, in that the sacrifice of Himself must be a most perfect holocaust.

St. Thomas develops this subject here,[97] and thus explains the words of the prophet: "Attend and see if there be any sorrow like to my sorrow." [98]

1) The cause indeed of the sensible pain was most bitter, in that the crucifixion affected His whole body, especially the most sensible parts, which are the hands and the feet. Also the cause of the interior pain could not be a greater evil, for it was first the sins of the human race, for which Christ satisfied by suffering, which he ascribes to Himself, and secondly, His being abandoned by His people and His disciples.

2) There could not have been greater sensibility in the sufferer, both as to soul and body, for "Christ's body was endowed with a most perfect constitution, since it was fashioned miraculously, and His sensitiveness of touch was most acute, which is the reason for our feeling pain. His soul, likewise, from its interior powers, apprehended most vehemently all the causes of sadness." [99]

3) Christ's suffering was not mitigated, as in other sufferers, from some consideration of reason, by some derivation of joy from the

[97] *Ibid.*, q. 46, a. 6.
[98] Lam. 1:12.
[99] Cf. IIIa, q. 46, a. 6, first reason.

higher powers into the lower, for as Damascene says: "He permitted each one of His powers to exercise its proper function,"[100] by not lessening the pain from some higher consideration, which He could have done. Thus He most freely and fully delivered Himself up to pain.

4) Because Christ willed to suffer pain that was in proportion to the liberation of men from sin. St. Thomas expresses it as follows: "Fourthly, the magnitude of the pain of Christ's suffering can be reckoned by this, that the pain and sorrow were accepted voluntarily, to the end of men's deliverance from sin; and consequently He embraced the amount of pain proportionate to the magnitude of the fruit which resulted therefrom."[101]

Reply to second objection. "And so to atone for the sins of all men, Christ accepted sadness, the greatest in absolute quantity, yet not exceeding the rule of reason," that is, not preventing the use of reason. But, as it was said above, He delivered Himself up fully and most freely to pain for our salvation.

Reply to fourth objection. Christ grieved not only over the loss of His own bodily life, but also over the sins of all others. And this grief in Christ surpassed all grief of every contrite heart, both because it flowed from a greater wisdom and charity, by which the pang of contrition is intensified, and because He grieved at one time for all sins, according to the prophet who said: "Surely He hath carried our sorrows."[102]

This last text could be developed at length. For Christ grieved not only in the sensitive part of His soul, but in His will motivated by charity. This finds its confirmation in the lives of the saints who offered themselves as victims for certain sinners only, and grieved very intensively for their sins. Thus it was, for example, with St. Catherine of Siena. But Christ not only grieved for the sins of certain sinners, but for those of all men of whatever generation and nation, and for all sins taken together. The chalice about which He said in the Garden of Gethsemane: "Let this chalice pass from Me,"[103] was the chalice of all human iniquities. He accepted this chalice, so that He might give us another chalice, to wit, the chalice of His most precious blood.

[100] *Ibid.*, second reason.
[101] *Ibid.*, fourth reason.
[102] Isa. 53:4.
[103] Luke 22:42.

These two chalices represent the whole history of the human race, all the abundance of evil and all the superabundance of good.

Moreover, as St. Thomas says in the above-mentioned text, Christ grieved for all sins taken together, so that His grief might exceed the grief of any contrite person whatever, because it was a supernatural detestation not only of certain sins, but of all sins, and moreover because it was the result of greater wisdom and charity. This reason is most evident. St. Thomas says [104] that contrition is grief of the intellective part of the soul, namely, a displeasure of the will about sin, and is always accompanied by grace and charity; for the soul grieves about sin because of God who is infinitely lovable and loved above all things. There was, indeed, neither contrition nor penance in Christ, because He had never sinned; in fact, He was absolutely impeccable. But there was supreme detestation of sin in the higher part of His soul, and as long as He was both wayfarer and comprehensor, He grieved to the utmost spiritually for the sins of men.

This point is clarified by the following principles.

The just person grieves all the more for sin, the more that person knows its gravity; but nobody knew better than Christ the Savior the quasi-infinite gravity of mortal sin, which practically denies God His dignity of being the ultimate end. If St. Catherine of Siena saw the interior state of souls as regards certain prelates of her time, so as to feel nauseated, then what effect must Christ's knowledge have had upon Him!

Likewise the greater the degree of love which the just person has for God who is offended by sin, the greater is the grief for sin. Sermons are preached about this on the feast day of the Blessed Virgin Mary of Compassion to show how great was her grief for sin. A fortiori, much more did Christ grieve for all sins because of the fullness of His love for God the Father, who is offended by sin, and for souls that through sin lose eternal life. In other words, the fullness of Christ's charity increased in Him to the utmost extent His capacity of suffering for the greatest of evils, which is sin. On the contrary, egotism prevents this holy grief, for the egotist, who lives only a superficial life of soul, grieves only superficially over evils that wound his sensuality or pride.

What has been said establishes how much Christ willed to suffer for us, as the following texts prove: "Surely He hath borne our iniquities

[104] Cf. IIIa, q. 84, a. 9; q. 85, a. 1.

and carried our sorrows"; [105] "Who His own self bore our sins in His body upon the tree, that we, being dead to sins, should live to justice"; [106] "He appeared to take away our sins." [107] Therefore most certainly, as our faith teaches, Christ most vehemently desired to suffer for our salvation even to the death of the cross.

This ardent desire of the cross and supreme happiness of the suffering Christ constitute, as stated, the two principal effects of His fullness of grace to which all other effects can be reduced. They are the two extremes of His interior life.

For Christ's supreme happiness, which consists in the beatific vision, is the nobler element in His human intellect, just as the love of God and peace of mind resulting from this beatific vision constitute what is nobler in His human will. But the ardent desire of Christ for the cross is another aspect of which Christ's life seems to be contrary to what has been said, but it most evidently corresponds to His primary mission of Savior and victim. Thus we have, as L. Chardon says, a beautiful combination of the whole of Christ's interior life.

We must now consider how these two principal effects of Christ's plenitude of grace, although apparently contraries, could simultaneously be present in the Passion.

All these statements pertain more to the teaching of faith than to theology. They transcend it. Yet theology is most useful in showing the subordination of these statements in the body of doctrine. In fact, the principal part of sacred theology is not the deduction of theological conclusions through the medium of a natural premise, but it is the explanation of the truths of the faith and their logical subordination. In the manifestation of this subordination, theology in some manner hides itself; somehow as St. John the Baptist says of Christ: "He must increase, but I must decrease." [108] This means that sacred theology no longer uses strictly technical terms, but speaks in the words of Sacred Scripture, which are like precious stones logically arranged by it, so that in their subordinate and doctrinal setting they may interact as searchlights. This most exalted part of theology proposes the object of faith in a doctrinal manner, that is, in logical order, and thus it is

[105] Isa. 53:4.
[106] I Pet. 2:24.
[107] I John 3:5.
[108] John 3:30.

of great service to contemplation, because thus it prepares for us a general synthesis of the truths wherein we have a view of the whole doctrine of faith, as also a complete and intelligent grasp of it.

3) Christ always retained His supreme happiness even when hanging on the cross.[109]

We have seen,[110] that Christ already in this life enjoyed the beatific vision. He says of Himself: "We speak what we know, and we testify what we have seen." [111] "He that cometh from above is above all. . . . And what He hath seen and heard, that He testifieth." [112] But Christ speaks of Himself as man, therefore He sees God as man. This vision is the direct source of His testimony. He has not only faith in His own divinity and personality, but something more than faith, namely, beatific vision or knowledge.

Likewise He says: "No man hath ascended into heaven, but He that descendeth from heaven, the Son of man who is in heaven." [113] This is the same as saying that the Son of man, still living on earth as man, is already in heaven, or is both wayfarer and comprehensor, as tradition asserts.

Similarly, a short time before His passion, He says: "Father, I will that where I am, they also whom Thou hast given Me may be with Me, that they may see My glory which Thou hast given Me." [114] The phrase, "where I am," signifies the termination of this life, or glory.

This is also quite clear from the Transfiguration, which was the sign of Christ's hidden glory in the soul, which He then allowed to have its repercussion on the body, according to the common teaching of the Fathers.

Hence the Holy Office declared (June 7, 1918) that the following proposition cannot safely be taught. "There is no evidence that Christ when on earth had the knowledge of which the blessed or comprehensors have." [115] To say that this proposition can be safely taught would be an error.

In fact, we have seen [116] that, if Christ's soul did not have from the beginning the beatific vision but received it later on, then His charity

[109] Cf. IIIa, q. 46, a. 7, 8.
[110] *Ibid.*, q. 9, a. 2.
[111] John 3:11.
[112] *Ibid.*, 3:31 f.
[113] *Ibid.*, 3:13.
[114] *Ibid.*, 17:24.
[115] Denz., no. 2183.
[116] Cf. IIIa, q. 9, a. 2; q. 10.

was capable of increase, which is contrary to the teaching of the Second Council of Constantinople, which says: "Christ was not made better by advancing in perfection."[117] From the first moment of His conception His soul was raised to the highest degree of being, namely, to the being of the Word, and consequently to the highest of all operations, that is, to the beatific vision, which was permanent in Christ continuing during sleep, just as His plenitude of grace was, which resulted from the uncreated grace of union. Thus because of the beatific vision He already enjoyed the utmost happiness.

But there is no reason why the beatific vision should have been interrupted at the moment of His passion and crucifixion. On the contrary, of its nature the beatific vision cannot be lost, and it is measured by participated eternity.

Even the theological reason that St. Thomas advances,[118] shows that the sublime fitness of the beatific vision in Christ still a wayfarer, especially applies to the moment of His passion and crucifixion. The reason is this, that Christ already in this life had to be the Teacher of all teachers, namely, of the apostles and doctors of the Church, so as to lead the human race to eternal life, which is the vision of God. But what is in potentiality is reduced to act by what is already in act. Therefore it was most of all fitting that Christ, the Teacher of all teachers, in those things that pertain to eternal life, should already have in this life the immediate vision of God or eternal life to which He was to lead men.

But now it must furthermore be said that Christ, during His passion and on the cross, also teaches in a more sublime manner than before, in uttering the following last words of His: "Father, forgive them, for they know not what they do";[119] "This day thou shalt be with Me in paradise";[120] "Woman, behold thy son. . . . Behold thy mother";[121] "My God, My God, why hast Thou forsaken Me?"[122] "I thirst";[123] "It is consummated";[124] "Father, into Thy hands I commend My Spirit."[125]

[117] Denz., no. 224.
[118] Cf. IIIa, q. 9, a. 3.
[119] Luke 23:34.
[120] *Ibid.*, 23:43.
[121] John 19:36 f.
[122] Matt. 27:46.
[123] John 19:28.
[124] *Ibid.*, 19:30.
[125] Luke 23:46.

During these last moments, Jesus most sublimely teaches all men, more so than all the apostles, doctors, and saints. He teaches mercy toward those who err, promises the joys of paradise in the near future to those who invoke Him, teaches that the Blessed Virgin Mary is the spiritual mother of all men, and also by His sufferings satisfies the demands of divine justice. In fact, by the words, "It is consummated," [126] He teaches that the mystery of redemption is accomplished by the victory of charity gained over sin and the devil.

Therefore, if the beatific vision befitted Christ, inasmuch as already on this earth He was the Teacher of all teachers, it especially befitted Him on the cross, because He never spoke so sublimely as the Teacher and Savior of all as at that time. Thus the martyrs receive special illumination at the time of their martyrdom, as St. Stephen did who "saw the glory of God and Jesus standing on the right hand of God." [127] Hence no theologian of any importance is quoted as teaching that Christ's beatific vision was interrupted during His passion and crucifixion.

However, some such as Cano, Valentia, Salmeron, and Maldonatus said that Christ had the beatific vision at the time of His death, but renounced beatific joy, so as to suffer sadness for the purpose of man's redemption.

But, as Gonet shows,[128] this opinion displeases other theologians, and rightly so. The beatific vision and beatific joy are inseparable, because it is impossible for the will to have supreme good presented to it, namely, God clearly seen, and not find joy and complete satisfaction in this. Granted the beatific vision, the created rational being finds complete satisfaction in its love for God, the uncreated Being, and it is not a free act either on the part of the object which specifies it or on the part of the act itself, for it is an absolutely spontaneous act, though it transcends liberty. As St. Thomas teaches: "If the will be offered an object which is good universally, and from every point of view, the will tends to it of necessity, if it wills anything at all." [129]

Hence St. Thomas,[130] in the solution of his objection concerning

[126] John 19:30.

[127] Acts 7:55.

[128] *Clypeus theol., de Incarn.,* disp. XVI, a. 1, solv. obj., no. 14.

[129] *Summa theol.,* Ia IIae, q. 10, a. 2; see also *ibid.,* q. 5, a. 4.

[130] *Ibid.,* IIIa, q. 46, a. 8 ad 1.

the incompatibility of supreme happiness with supreme sorrow in Christ during His passion, did not deny beatific joy to Him in the summit of His soul, but affirmed it.

It is also clearly evident from the foregoing that Christ often spoke of the utmost peace of mind which He had and which was the normal effect of His fullness of grace. Thus He says: "Peace I leave with you, My peace I give unto you; not as the world giveth, do I give unto you." [131] Before the Passion He says: "These things I have spoken to you, that in Me you may have peace." [132] Peace is the effect of charity, and it consists in the tranquillity of order of all the affections subordinated to the love of God; it is the union of the powers of the soul subject to God, who is loved above all things. Likewise holy joy is the effect of charity.[133] Hence in Christ it was in accordance with the fullness of His grace and charity, which He always had.

4) The intimate union prevailing between supreme peace and supreme sadness in Christ's passion.

This union belongs to the very mystery of redemption. It is, as we shall see, a miracle and also an essentially supernatural miracle, being like two united extremes. Hence this intimate union cannot be explained in a natural way. But, as the Vatican Council says, "Reason enlightened by faith, when it seeks earnestly, piously, and calmly, attains by a gift of God some and that a very fruitful, understanding of mysteries." [134] It attains especially an understanding or contemplation of the above-mentioned union and connection between the virtues in Christ's passion that is most fruitful for the spiritual life of which the Savior is the exemplar.

Our starting point must be the fact affirmed in the Gospel, that although Christ said, "My soul is sorrowful even unto death," [135] yet He maintained the utmost peace of mind in the midst of the greatest physical and moral sufferings of the Passion, complete mastery over Himself, and absolute conformity of His will with His Father's will. This is so from the very words uttered by our Lord in the Garden of Gethsemane and during His passion, particularly these last words: "It is consummated," [136] and "Father, into Thy hands I commend

[131] John 14:27.
[132] *Ibid.* 16:33.
[133] Cf. IIa, IIae, q. 28, 29.
[134] Denz., no. 1796.
[135] Matt. 26:38.
[136] John 19:30.

My spirit." [137] These last words are a quasi-consecration of the sacrifice on the cross, which therefore would be a true sacrifice even though there had not been a previous Eucharistic oblation at the Last Supper, as commonly taught. It was Calvin, indeed, who chose to see an expression of desperation in the words, "My God, My God, why hast Thou forsaken Me?" [138] But these words are manifestly nothing else but the holy and inspired words of the Messianic psalm, wherein we read, on the contrary: "In Thee our fathers have hoped, they have hoped, and Thou hast delivered them. . . . But I am a worm and no man, the reproach of men and the outcast of the people. . . . They have dug my hands and my feet. They have numbered all my bones. . . . But Thou, O Lord, remove not Thy help to a distance from me. . . . Save me from the lion's mouth. . . . I will declare Thy name to my brethren, and in the midst of the Church I will praise Thee. You that fear the Lord, praise Him . . . because He hath not slighted, nor despised the supplication of the poor man. . . . For the kingdom is the Lord's and He shall have dominion over the nations." [139] There is no expression of desperation in this Messianic psalm, in which the details of the Passion are most completely given. There is nothing of despair, but it starts with an expression of greatest grief on the part of Christ suffering for the sins of the whole human race, which bring down God's malediction, in accordance with the following words of St. Paul: "Christ hath redeemed us from the curse of the law, being made a curse for us, for it is written: Cursed is every one that hangeth on a tree." [140] Therefore they are the words of a victim who suffers to the utmost under the curse that is due to sin. But Christ wishes so to suffer because of His utmost charity, and He at the same moment also adores and loves God's infinite justice. Hence almost immediately afterward He says: "It is consummated," [141] that is, the holocaust is completed; and then: "Father, into Thy hands I commend My spirit." [142] These last words evidently are not the words of a despairing and conquered person, but, as stated,[143] they are the words of consecration in the sacrifice of the cross. They are the words of the

[137] Luke 23:46.
[138] Matt. 27:46.
[139] Ps. 21:5 f.
[140] Gal. 3:13.
[141] John 19:30.
[142] Luke 23:46.
[143] See p. 0785.

conqueror over sin and the devil, who very soon will be, on the Resurrection Day, the conqueror over death that is the result of sin. "It is consummated" [144] is the expression of peace that has been restored, which is tranquillity of order. Christ could say: "I have overcome the world." [145]

Hence it is thus that St. Thomas and St. Augustine explain these words: "My God, My God, why hast Thou forsaken Me?" [146] because God left Him to the power of His persecutors.[147] Thus St. Paul says: "He that spared not even His own Son, but delivered Him up for us all." [148] And the prophet declares that: "The Lord hath laid on Him the iniquity of us all. . . . And was pleased to bruise Him in infirmity." [149]

Hence there is no doubt about the union prevailing between utmost peace and utmost grief during the time of Christ's passion.

EXPLANATION OF THIS FACT

But how can these two apparently contrary extremes be united in the same soul and at the same moment?

This aspect of the mystery of the redemption was often the object of speculation among theologians and of infused contemplation for mystics. It must be noted, as the Salmanticenses and Gonet report, in commenting on the beatific knowledge of Christ, that some not knowing how to explain this union, devised three insufficient theories that are generally rejected by theologians.

First theory. It is that of Aureolus and those who, as Capreolus reports,[150] said that Christ suffered only in the sensitive part of His soul; but, as the Salmanticenses observe,[151] this view is contrary to the common opinion of the Fathers, who said that Christ grieved for the sins of all men, and this grief is evidently in the will, just as contrition is in our will. This is evident, as the Salmanticenses state, from the epistle of Pope St. Agatho to which the Sixth General Council, the Third of Constantinople, referred against the Monothelites, wherein

[144] John 19:30.
[145] *Ibid.*, 16:33.
[146] Luke 23:46.
[147] Cf. IIIa, q. 47, a. 3.
[148] Rom. 8:32.
[149] Isa. 53:6, 10.
[150] *Com. in IIIam,* d. 16, q. 1, a. 2.
[151] *Loc. cit.*

a distinction is drawn between Christ's human spiritual will and His divine will. Hence this theory seems heretical or at least proximately heretical, it being contrary to the general doctrine, in accordance with Scripture and tradition, of the ordinary magisterial teaching of the Church. Aureolus was a nominalist, and the forerunner of William of Occam.

Second theory. It is the view taken by Melchior Cano, Valentia, Salmeron, and Maldonatus. They say that Christ during His passion gave up His beatific joy, which is the normal consequence of the beatific vision. But this opinion, which is contrary to the teaching of St. Thomas,[152] seems to involve a contradiction, as Gonet says,[153] for it seems impossible for the will to have the supreme good presented to it, namely, God clearly seen, and not find delight therein, because, granted this immediate vision of God's essence and goodness, as already stated,[154] the human will as regards this object no longer has either liberty of specification or liberty of exercise.

Third theory. It was proposed by Theophile Raynaud, who said that by God's absolute power, supreme happiness and supreme sadness can miraculously be present at the same time in the same subject, even though these are contraries. But as Gonet says,[155] this theory does not seem to be reasonable, because this contrariety includes contradiction, if it be of the same object concerning which the will would experience both joy and sorrow. But not even God by His absolute power can cause contradictories to be present at the same time. Almost all theologians admit that this union of utmost grief and utmost joy was miraculous or the result of a miracle by which Christ was both comprehensor and wayfarer, having prevented the overflow of glory into the inferior part of the soul; but a miracle cannot involve a contradiction.

Let us see what St. Thomas says. He has discussed this problem in various articles.[156] He has most admirably presented the difficulty to be solved, by remarking that "it is impossible to be sad and glad at the same time, as the Philosopher says." [157] This first objection reads:

[152] Cf. IIIa, q. 46, a. 8.

[153] *Com. in IIIam,* q. 46, a. 8.

[154] See p. 0783.

[155] *Clypeus theol.,* disp. 16, a. 1, no. 14.

[156] Cf. IIIa, q. 46, a. 7; also q. 9, a. 2. See also Salmanticenses, Gonet, and Cajetan in their commentaries on these articles.

[157] Cf. IIIa, q. 46, a. 8, 1st obj. See also Aristotle's *Ethics,* Bk. XIV, chap. 4.

"It is not possible to be sad and glad at the same time, since sadness and gladness are contraries. But Christ's whole soul suffered grief during the Passion, and His grief was the greatest." [158] Therefore He could not have at the same time utmost joy.

St. Thomas answers this objection by quoting St. John Damascene, who says: "Christ's Godhead permitted His flesh to do and to suffer what was proper to it." [159] He explains this assertion as follows: "The whole soul can be understood both according to its essence, which is entirely present in each part of the body and in each of its faculties, or according to all its faculties. If it be understood according to its essence, then His whole soul did enjoy fruition, inasmuch as it is the subject of the higher part of the soul to which it belongs to enjoy the Godhead." [160] So also as St. Thomas says in the preceding article, Christ's whole soul suffered in the body that suffered, for it is entirely present in the whole body that suffers, and entirely present in each part of the body. "But if we consider the whole soul, as comprising all its faculties, thus His entire soul did not enjoy fruition . . . because, since Christ was still upon earth, there was no overflowing of glory from the higher part into the lower, nor from the soul into the body. But since, on the contrary, the soul's higher part was not hindered in its proper acts by the lower, it follows that the higher part of His soul enjoyed fruition perfectly while Christ was suffering." [161] The first part of St. Thomas' explanation is ontological, and the second part is psychological.

Objection. A superficial reading of this text of St. Thomas makes it appear that Christ suffered only in the lower faculties of His soul, or in His sensitive nature, as the nominalist Aureolus thought according to what Capreolus says. But this opinion of Aureolus is contrary to the teaching of the ordinary magisterial authority of the Church, since it declares that Christ grieved even morally for our sins.

Reply. Most certainly this is not what St. Thomas means, for just previously he had said: "Christ grieved . . . over the sins of all others [men]. And this grief in Christ surpassed all grief of every contrite heart, because it flowed from a greater wisdom and charity." [162] He grieved also for man's perdition.

[158] 1st obj.
[159] *De fide orthod.*, Bk. III, chap. 15.
[160] Cf. IIIa, q. 46, a. 8.
[161] *Ibid.*, a. 8, c.
[162] *Ibid.*, a. 6, ad 4.

It is manifest that this grief does not belong to the sensitive appetite but to the will. In fact, it seems to pertain to the exalted part of the will that is regulated by greater wisdom and deified by charity.

Instance. But then it seems, as Scotus and Suarez contend, that Christ grieved also in the higher reason for the sins of all men, inasmuch as these are contrary to the eternal law which is the object of the higher reason. Likewise, so it seems, He grieved for the eternal perdition of a number of men, according to the higher reason. So say Scotus and Suarez. But St. Thomas teaches in various passages of his works that Christ did not grieve in the higher reason.[163] These two difficulties, namely, that Christ grieved to the utmost for the sins of all men, but not in His rational will, find their mode of reconciliation in the doctrine of St. Thomas.

Reply. Certainly, as St. Thomas says, "Christ's higher reason did not suffer on the part of its proper object, which is God clearly

[163] Cf. *De veritate,* q. 26, a. 9, ad 7; *Compend. theol.,* chap. 232. He had said in *De veritate,* q. 26, a. 9, ad 7: "The rational will regarded Christ's passion only as it concerned eternal truths, and according to these the will rejoiced in the Passion inasmuch as it was pleasing to God." See also *Quodl.* VII, a. 5, and *III Sent.,* d. 15, q. 2, a. 1; q. 3, a. 3, q. 2. Also in *Compend. theol.,* chap. 232, he said: "Christ's soul enjoyed the perfect vision of God. Therefore in the rational will of Christ's soul, whose particular function . . . is to contemplate and take counsel concerning eternal truths, there was nothing adverse or repugnant therein, which would give rise to any suffering detrimental to it. . . . Christ suffered sadness inasmuch as He knew there was imminent danger of guilt or punishment for those whom He loved because of His charity. Hence He grieved not only for Himself, but also for others. And because the love of one's neighbor belongs in a certain way to the higher reason, inasmuch as one's neighbor from charity is loved for God's sake, yet Christ's higher reason could not feel sad about the defects of His neighbors as it is possible for us to be sad. Because Christ's higher reason fully enjoyed the beatific vision, and so He apprehended that whatever pertains to the defects of others, inasmuch as this is included in divine wisdom, is fittingly ordained for some purpose, and inasmuch as anyone is permitted to sin and will be punished for the sin. Therefore neither Christ's soul, nor the souls of any of the blessed, who see God, can feel sad about the defects of others here on earth. But such is not the case with wayfarers, who as yet do not see the purpose of divine wisdom. These also according to the rational will are saddened at the defects of others, when they think that it belongs to God's honor and the exaltation of the faith, that some be saved, who nevertheless will be lost. Thus, therefore, such a person grieves according to the senses, imagination, and sensitive will for those who will be lost, but rejoices according to the rational will, inasmuch as these defects are referred to the ordering of divine wisdom. Therefore it could happen that Christ's sensitive will shrank from something that His rational will desired; yet there was no contrariety of appetites in Him, or rebellion of the flesh against the spirit . . . , but Christ permitted each of His lower faculties to be moved in its own way, as was becoming to Him."

seen." [164] But it also appears certain, as Cajetan remarks, that, according to St. Thomas, Christ simply did not grieve in His higher will in what is concerned with eternal truths. The reason is, as Cajetan says,[165] that Christ's higher reason already in this life was in full possession of the beatific vision, and the blessed do not grieve over sin; although it displeases them, this displeasure is not sadness, because sadness brings on depression and worry, as St. Thomas says.[166] The angels in heaven do not grieve over sin. How then did Christ grieve to the utmost over the sins of men, yet not in His higher reason? Cajetan replies: "Grief over sin belongs to the lower reason, since the object of such an act is something temporal, namely, an offense against God. Nothing prevents this sadness from being present even when eternal truths are being considered, because the lower reason is regulated by the higher and receives its principles from the higher. According to the nature of their objects, either temporal or eternal, a distinction is drawn between the higher reason and the lower, as St. Thomas says (Ia, q. 79)." [167]

Cajetan's explanation does not conflict with the teaching of St. Thomas in the above-mentioned texts.[168] Hence, at least Christ grieved not only in His sensitive nature, but also in His lower reason inasmuch as this was regulated by the higher, that is, He grieved over the sins of all men in that according to His higher reason He realized, better than we do, their infinite grievousness.

Therefore the higher reason, in which Christ did not grieve for sin, is the culmination of the human intellect and will, the summit of the mind. In this summit Christ enjoyed the beatific vision, and thus He saw the most sublime reason why God permits sins, which is the purpose of a greater good, namely, to manifest God's mercy and the splendor of His justice. This He saw most evidently, as the blessed see it, who no longer grieve over sin, for they see the victory of God's mercy and the splendor of His justice,[169] since they are no more wayfarers.

[164] *Summa theol.,* IIIa, q. 46, a. 7, c. and ad 2.

[165] *Com. in IIIam,* q. 46, a. 7, no. 6.

[166] *Summa theol.,* Ia, q. 113, a. 7.

[167] *Com. in IIIam, loc. cit.*

[168] *De veritate,* q. 26, a. 9, ad 7; *Compend. theol.,* chap. 232.

[169] St. Thomas says: "Angels do not grieve, either for sin or for the pains inflicted on men. For grief and sorrow, according to St. Augustine, are for those things which occur against our will. But nothing happens in the world contrary to the will of the

Christ in this life still grieved for sin, and to the utmost, because He was both wayfarer and comprehensor, and He voluntarily prevented the connatural overflow of glory into the lower reason so that He might abandon Himself to grief.

Doubt. Was this intimate union of utmost joy and utmost grief in Christ a miracle?

As the Salmanticenses observe, this was a miracle, just as when Christ voluntarily and suddenly put an end to the storm on the lake; for in accordance with the natural laws connected with the life of the soul, joy in the higher part of the soul overflows into the lower part, and conversely it is natural for grief in the lower part of the soul to affect the higher. This deprivation of overflow was both voluntary and miraculous, or it was voluntary because of the miracle inasmuch as Christ was both wayfarer and comprehensor. It was both a miracle and a mystery, that is, it was something essentially supernatural and also extraordinary even in the supernatural order, and it pertains to the hypostatic order as a consequence of the Incarnation; for even according to the laws of the supernatural order, permanence of the beatific vision is not given in this life, but only in the next life. If the beatific vision as a transient act, which was probably granted to St. Paul on this earth, was miraculous, a fortiori the permanence of the beatific vision in Christ here on earth was miraculous. This was the consequence of the miracle and mystery of the Incarnation, while Christ was still in some way a wayfarer according to the lower part of His soul before His resurrection and ascension, He was also a com-

---

angels and the other blessed, because their will cleaves entirely to the ordering of divine justice; while nothing happens in the world except what is effected or permitted by divine justice. Therefore, simply speaking, nothing occurs in the world against the will of the blessed. . . . Therefore, universally and absolutely speaking, the angels do not will sin and the pains inflicted on its account; but they do will the fulfillment of the ordering of divine justice in this matter, in respect to which some are subjected to pains and are allowed to fall into sin." To quote Cajetan again (*Com. in IIIam,* q. 46, a. 7, no. 6): "Sin displeases the blessed, but this displeasure is not sadness, because this sadness adds to the displeasure, depression, and worry that afflict the nature." See note 163 concerning what St. Thomas says in his *Compend. theol.,* chap. 232: "Christ's higher reason fully enjoyed the beatific vision, and so He apprehended whatever pertains to the defects of others, inasmuch as this is included in divine wisdom, is fittingly ordained for some purpose, and inasmuch as anyone is permitted to sin and will be punished for the sin."

Cf. *Xenia thomistica,* II, 349–491, by Fr. Sadoc Szabo, O.P. *De scientia beata Christi,* especially the part that treats of the compatibility of the simultaneous presence in Christ of utmost joy and utmost grief, pp. 432–48.

prehensor or at the end of His earthly life as regards the higher part of His soul. Thus Father Monsabré says that Christ, during His passion, was like a mountain peak that is brilliantly illumined by the rays of the sun and remains most perfectly calm, whereas its lower part is very much disturbed by the storm.[170]

St. Thomas, as the Salmanticenses remark,[171] admits this miracle in replying to the following objection: "The Philosopher says (*Ethics,* VII, chap. 14) that, if sadness be vehement, it not only checks the contrary delight, but every delight; and conversely. But the grief of Christ's passion was the greatest as shown above (a. 6); and likewise the enjoyment of fruition is the greatest." [172]

Reply to second objection. "The Philosopher's contention is true because of the overflow which takes place naturally from one faculty of the soul into another; but it was not so with Christ, as was said above in the body of the article."

In other words, beyond the natural laws connected with the life of the soul, or the miraculous, Christ the wayfarer voluntarily and most freely prevented the overflow of glory from the higher part of the soul to the lower, so that He might abandon Himself more completely to suffering as a voluntary victim offered in holocaust.

Yet I insist. But it seems that there is contrariety and contradiction inasmuch as in the same faculty Christ grieved to the utmost and greatly rejoiced in the same object, namely, His passion, inasmuch as it was fruitful for salvation and the effect of crime. Likewise in the same faculty He grieved to the utmost for the sins of men and rejoiced in the higher good for which sin was permitted.

Reply. This grief and joy were not about the same object considered under the same aspect. Christ grieved for His passion in that it was contrary to His nature, and the effect of the crime of those who killed Him. At the same time, in accordance with the eternal truths in the higher reason, "He rejoiced in this passion, inasmuch as it was, according to God's good pleasure, conducive to God's glory and the

[170] Cf. Salmanticenses, *De incarnatione,* disp. XVII, dub. 4, no. 47, who say: "The prevention of the overflow of joy (in the higher reason) was against the connatural consent of these parts (of the soul) and was a miracle. Hence the union of utmost joy and utmost sadness in Christ is miraculous, at least according to our previous supposition; just as proportionately is the case with the union of the state of comprehensor and wayfarer in the same Christ."

[171] *Ibid.*

[172] *Summa theol.,* IIIa, q. 46, a. 8, 2nd obj.

salvation of men." [173] St. Thomas well explains this when the question arises about how the penitent is saddened for his sins and rejoices in his sorrow. In his reply to this objection, he says: "Of sorrow and joy we may speak in two ways: first, as being passions of the sensitive appetite, and thus they can nowise be together since they are altogether contrary to each other, either on the part of the object (as when they have the same object) or at least on the part of the movement, for joy is with expansion of the heart, whereas sorrow is with contraction; and it is in this sense that the Philosopher speaks in *Ethics,* Bk. IX, chap. 4. Secondly, we may speak of joy and sorrow as being simple acts of the will, to which something is pleasing or displeasing. Accordingly they cannot be contrary to each other, except on the part of the object as when they concern the same object in the same respect, in which way joy and sorrow cannot be simultaneous, because the same thing in the same respect cannot be pleasing and displeasing. [Theophile Raynaud saw the necessity of adverting to this.] If, on the other hand, joy and sorrow, understood thus, be not of the same object in the same respect, but either of different objects, or of the same object in different respects, in that case joy and sorrow are not contrary to each other, so that nothing hinders a man from being joyful and sorrowful at the same time; for instance, if we see a good man suffer, we both rejoice at his goodness and at the same time grieve for his suffering. In this way a man may be displeased at having sinned, and be pleased at his displeasure together with his hope for pardon, so that his very sorrow is a matter of joy. Hence St. Augustine says in *De poenitentia,* chap. 13: The penitent should ever grieve and rejoice at his grief." [174]

Thus Christ in His higher reason rejoiced in His passion, inasmuch as it was pleasing to God for the redemption of the human race, as St. Thomas says.[175] Thus, following our Lord's example, "the apostles went from the presence of the council, rejoicing that they were accounted worthy to suffer reproach for the name of Jesus." [176] So St. Ignatius of Antioch rejoiced, when writing to his faithful followers and ardently desiring martyrdom; he said: "By the death of wild beasts, I am to be ground that I may prove Christ's pure

[173] Cf. *Compend. theol.,* chap. 232.
[174] Cf. IIIa, q. 84, a. 9, ad 2.
[175] *Compend. theol.,* chap. 232.
[176] Acts 5:41.

bread."[177] If the desire of martyrdom in St. Ignatius and in many martyrs was so ardent, then what must it have been in Christ, although it was His wish to experience the utmost grief in the Garden of Gethsemane so that He might be more perfectly a holocaust!

So likewise Christ grieved to the utmost for the sins of all men at one time, for "His grief surpassed all grief of every contrite heart, because it flowed from a greater wisdom and charity."[178] Thus He grieved in His lower reason which was under the direction of His higher reason, whereby God's infinite dignity is known, who is offended by sin. And yet, at the same time, Christ in His higher reason did not grieve over the divine permission of sin, but He rejoiced at the sight of a greater good, for which God permitted the sins of men, that is, He rejoiced in the victory of God's mercy and in the splendor of His justice, or in the supreme victory of the supreme good over sin, the devil, and death.

Thus there is no contradiction in this mystery, which is also a miracle just as the Incarnation is.

As the Salmanticenses say: "Christ's supreme joy was not only that He saw God, but it was also that He realized that the fittingness of His death contributed to the glory of God and the exaltation of His own name. But His utmost sadness concerned the unfitness of His death as regards His human nature considered in itself, and the sins of men inasmuch as these are contrary to God's glory and their redemption. Hence there was no contradiction."[179] So also says St. Thomas.[180]

CONCLUSION

From all that has been said, it is clear that the plenitude of Christ's created grace is the cause of these two apparently contrary effects, which are the two extremes of His interior life. These are, on the one hand, utmost happiness and, on the other, an ardent desire to suffer for us, even to suffer sadness unto death, so that His sacrifice might be complete, a perfect holocaust, and an efficacious manifestation of His love for God the Father for us, because peace, which is tranquillity of order, is the effect of charity, whereby God is loved above

[177] Ignatius to Romans, no. 4.
[178] Cf. IIIa, q. 46, a. 6, ad 4.
[179] Cf. *De incarnat.*, disp. XXII, dub. 4, no. 47.
[180] Cf. IIIa, q. 15, a. 6, ad 3. See also Cajetan, Gonet, Billuart, S. Szabo, *loc. cit.*

all things and all things are subordinated to Him. At the same time this love of God in Christ was the principle of His ardent desire to make reparation for the offense, and it was the reason why He grieved to the utmost for sins.

Hence these two effects, namely, peace and utmost sadness, were the result of His love for God the Father.

These effects were likewise the result of His love for us. For Christ's very great love for our souls was certainly the principle of great joy since it prompted Him to say on the cross: "It is consummated," [181] namely, the work of the redemption of souls is consummated, the tranquillity of order is restored by the victory over sin and the devil, so that Christ could say: "Have confidence, I have overcome the world." [182]

But on the other hand, this utmost love of Christ for us was the cause of His utmost grief, for our Savior's grief for our sins was proportionate to His love for our souls that are troubled by sin. Hence there is no contradiction in this, but supreme harmony, as when it is said that human liberty remains under the influence of efficacious grace, which does not destroy liberty, but on the contrary actualizes it. In this consists the synthesis of the interior life of Christ the Savior as proposed by Father Louis Chardon, O.P., in his beautiful book.[183]

Great saints in this life experience to a certain extent this intimate union between utmost grief and joy, especially those who are called to a life of reparation, such as St. Paul of the Cross, founder of the Passionists, who at about the age of thirty-five, after He had attained to the state of transforming union, remained nevertheless for forty-five years in a condition of very great aridity and perplexity of spirit for the salvation of souls, and yet in the midst of this perplexity he maintained a sublime peace, which he imparted to his brethren.[184]

[181] John 19:30.

[182] *Ibid.*, 16:33.

[183] Cf. *La Croix de Jesus* (ed. 1937).

[184] Cf. *Oraison et ascension mystique de Saint Paul de la Croix,* by Father Cajetan of the Name of Mary, C.P.

CHAPTER XXXVI

CHRIST'S THREEFOLD VICTORY

PRELIMINARY REMARKS

CHRIST said to His disciples: "In the world you shall have distress; but have confidence, I have overcome the world."[1] St. Thomas says in explanation of this text: "Christ overcame the world first of all by taking away its weapons of attack; for these are its objects of concupiscence. The Evangelist says: 'All that is in the world is the concupiscence of the flesh and the concupiscence of the eyes and the pride of life' (I John 2:16). But Christ overcomes riches by poverty, for the Psalmist says: 'I am needy and poor' (Ps. 85:1). And the Evangelist: 'The Son of man hath not where to lay His head' (Luke 9:58). He overcame honor by humility, for Christ says: 'Learn of Me, because I am meek and humble of heart' (Matt. 11:29). He overcame pleasures by suffering and hardship, for the Apostle says of Him: 'He humbled Himself, becoming obedient unto death even to the death of the cross' " (Phil. 2:8).[2] This is the victory over sin gained principally by Christ on the cross.

"Secondly," says St. Thomas, "Christ overcame the world by excluding the prince of this world, for He said: 'Now shall the prince of this world be cast out' (John 12:31); and St. Paul says: 'Despoiling the principalities and powers, He hath exposed them confidently in open show, triumphing over them in Himself' (Col. 2:15). From this He showed us how the devil must be overcome by us . . . , so that after His passion young maidens and boys, followers of Christ, deride the devil."[3]

This twofold victory of Christ, namely, over sin and the devil, was made manifest by the conversion of many pagans, and thus the fol-

[1] John 16:33.
[2] *Com. in Joan.* 2:16.
[3] *Ibid.*

lowing words of Christ were verified: "and I, if I be lifted up from the earth, will draw all things to Myself." [4]

Christ's final and third victory is over death, which is the result of sin; and this victory was clearly seen in His glorious resurrection and ascension, and it will ultimately be manifested on the Judgment Day by the resurrection of all the dead.

CHRIST'S VICTORY OVER SIN

First of all, there is Christ's victory over original sin, for the Apostle says: "As by the offense of one, unto all men to condemnation; so also by the justice of one, unto all men to justification of life. For as by the disobedience of one man, many were made sinners; so also by the obedience of one man, many shall be made just. . . . Where sin abounded, grace did more abound; that as sin hath reigned to death, so also grace might reign by justice unto life everlasting, through Jesus Christ our Lord." [5]

But the holy Doctor explains: "Original sin spread in this way, that at first the person [Adam] infected the nature, and afterward the nature infected the person [of Adam's posterity]. Whereas Christ in reverse order at first repairs what regards the person (by baptism of water or by baptism of desire), and afterward will simultaneously repair what pertains to the nature in all men. Consequently by baptism He takes away from man forthwith the guilt of original sin and the punishment of being deprived of the heavenly vision. But the penalties of the present life, such as death, hunger, thirst, and the like, pertain to the nature, from the principles of which they arise, inasmuch as it is deprived of original justice. Therefore these defects will not be taken away until the ultimate restoration of nature through the glorious resurrection." [6]

St. Thomas explains: "A Christian retains a passible body so that 'if we suffer with Christ, we may be also glorified with Him' (Rom. 8:11), and this is suitable for our spiritual training, so that, by fighting against concupiscence and other defects, we may receive the crown of victory." [7]

Christ's victory over original sin fulfills the prophecy of St. John

[4] John 12:32.
[5] Rom. 5:18 f. See also St. Thomas' *Com. on Romans.*
[6] Cf. IIIa, q. 69, a. 3, ad 3.
[7] *Ibid.,* c.

the Baptist, who said: "Behold the Lamb of God, behold Him who taketh away the sin of the world." [8]

The Scripture records that, after St. Peter's first sermon to the Jews on the day of Pentecost, three thousand were converted and baptized: "And there were added in that day about three thousand souls." [9] St. Peter had said to them: "Do penance, and be baptized every one of you in the name of Jesus Christ, for the remission of your sins, and you shall receive the gift of the Holy Ghost." [10]

But during twenty centuries a vast number of infants and adults have been freed from the stain of original sin through baptism by water, or baptism of desire.

Likewise Christ's victory over actual sin is many times affirmed in Sacred Scripture. Thus St. Paul says: "But God, who is rich in mercy, for His exceeding charity wherewith He loved us, even when we were dead in our sins, hath quickened us together in Christ (by whose grace you are saved) and hath raised us up together, and hath made us sit together in the heavenly places through Christ Jesus." [11] Again he says: "And you, when you were dead in your sins . . . , He hath quickened together with Him, forgiving you all offenses." [12]

Thus it is that very many persons rise again spiritually by means of sacramental absolution or without the sacrament by the grace of contrition. And every day the most abundant fruits of the sacrifice on the cross are applied to us through the Sacrifice of the Mass.

In fact, the victory over the spirit of the world, that is, over the concupiscence of the flesh, the eyes, and the pride of life, is clearly seen from the foundation of the Church, since many Christians actually observe the evangelical counsels of poverty, perfect chastity, and obedience, or at least by self-denial retain the spirit of the counsels, so that they may increasingly advance in the observance of the greatest commandment, which is "Thou shalt love the Lord thy God with thy whole heart and with thy whole soul and with all thy strength, and thy neighbor as thyself." [13]

Sometimes this victory over sin is strikingly illustrated in martyrdom, as happened in the first three centuries in the life of the Church

[8] John 1:29.
[9] Acts 2:41.
[10] *Ibid.*, 2:38.
[11] Eph. 2:38.
[12] Col. 2:13.
[13] Luke 10:27.

amid incessant persecutions, and as happened in our times; for instance, during the revolution in Spain, when so much blood was shed that 6,000 priests were killed. Thus the words of the Evangelist are verified: "For whatsoever is born of God, overcometh the world; and this is the victory which overcometh the world, our faith. Who is he that overcometh the world but he that believeth that Jesus is the Son of God . . . ? He that believeth in the Son of God, hath the testimony of God in himself. . . . And this is the testimony that God hath given to us, eternal life. And this life is in His Son." [14]

Thus amid the miseries of the present life, the holiness of the Church shines conspicuously in the lives of many servants of God who are truly His friends, and who lead others to Him.

CHRIST'S VICTORY OVER THE DEVIL

The Savior Himself announced this second victory, when He said shortly before His passion: " 'Now is the judgment of the world; now shall the prince of this world be cast out. And I, if I be lifted up from the earth, will draw all things to Myself.' (Now this He said, signifying what death He should die.)" [15] Immediately before, when Christ asked His Father to glorify His name, a voice from heaven was heard to say: "I have both glorified it, and will glorify it again," [16] which means, I will again glorify My Son in His passion whereby He will triumph over the devil, in His resurrection and ascension, and in the conversion of the whole world.[17] The devil no longer controls the wills of men who are free from sin; he still tempts them, but does not reign over them.

Likewise the Evangelist says: "He that committeth sin is of the devil, for the devil sinneth from the beginning. For this purpose the Son of God appeared, that He might destroy the works of the devil. In this the children of God are manifest, and the children of the devil." [18]

And St. Paul says: "God . . . hath quickened [you] together with Him [Christ], forgiving you all offenses; blotting out the handwriting of the decree that was contrary to us, and He hath taken the same

[14] I John 5:4 f.
[15] John 12:31 f.
[16] *Ibid.,* 13:27.
[17] *Com. S. Thomae in Joan.* 12:21.
[18] I John 3:8.

out of the way, fastening it to the cross, and despoiling the principalities and powers, He hath exposed them confidently in open show, triumphing over them in Himself." [19] This means that Christ by His passion has freed us from sin, the punishment of sin, and the slavery of the devil. In former times almost the whole world served idols; now the devil no longer thus reigns; and although he still attacks the just, we have a most powerful help in Christ. Hence the Apostle says: "Finally, brethren, be strengthened in the Lord and in the might of His power. Put you on the armor of God, that you may be able to stand against the deceits of the devil." [20]

St. John announces the persecution of the dragon against the woman, and of Antichrist against the Church; [21] but the triumph of the good and the condemnation of the wicked is foretold.[22] Finally, from the seventh chapter there is a description of God's last judgment, the fall of Babylon, the jubilation in heaven, the triumph of Christ over Antichrist and Satan.[23] On the garment of the Word of God is written: "King of kings, and Lord of lords." [24] Satan is definitely conquered, the dead rise again and are judged; there is a new Jerusalem, and Christ renders to everyone according to his works, saying: "I am Alpha and Omega, the first and the last, the beginning and the end. Blessed are they that wash their robes in the blood of the Lamb, that they may have a right to the tree of life, and may enter in by the gates into the city." [25]

Long ago the prophet had seen an immense and splendid statue whose feet of clay were destroyed "by a stone cut out of the mountains without hands . . . but the stone that struck the statue became a great mountain and filled the whole earth," [26] says the prophet. He explains this vision, by saying that this statue represents various kingdoms, "but in the days of those kingdoms, the God of heaven will set up a kingdom that shall never be destroyed . . . and it shall stand forever." [27]

Christ is declared "the stone which the builders rejected, the same

[19] Col. 2:13 ff.
[20] Eph. 6:10.
[21] Apoc. 12:1 f.
[22] *Ibid.*, 14:1 f.
[23] *Ibid.*, 19:11—22:9.
[24] *Ibid.*, 19:16.
[25] *Ibid.*, 22:13.
[26] Dan. 2:34 f.
[27] *Ibid.*, 2:44.

is made the head of the corner." [28] By His humility and passion He overcame the pride of the devils. Hence St. Paul says: "But we preach Christ crucified, unto the Jews indeed a stumbling block and unto the Gentiles foolishness. But unto them that are called, both Jews and Greeks, Christ the power of God, and the wisdom of God. For the foolishness of God is wiser than men, and the weakness of God is stronger than men." [29] Again he says: "Christ humbled Himself, becoming obedient unto death, even to the death of the cross. For which cause God hath exalted Him, and hath given Him a name which is above all names. That in the name of Jesus every knee should bow, of those that are in heaven, on earth, and under the earth. And that every tongue should confess that the Lord Jesus Christ is in the glory of God the Father." [30] This victory of Christ over the devil is sometimes sensibly and vividly manifested in exorcism, especially where these words are said: "Christ, the eternal Word of God made flesh, who for our salvation, which was lost by thy envy, humbled Himself, becoming obedient unto death, commands thee, unclean spirit." [31]

In the language of theology, however, Christ's victory over the devil implies victory over sin as previously established, and the consequence of this, namely, victory over death, immediately to be discussed. From what has been said, it is already certain, as St. Thomas said, that "Christ's passion frees us from sin, inasmuch as it causes forgiveness of sins by way of redemption," [32] and "by Christ's passion man was delivered from the devil's power so far as Christ's passion is the cause of the forgiveness of sins . . . inasmuch as it reconciled us with God." [33]

CHRIST'S VICTORY OVER DEATH

Christ gained victory over death first of all by His glorious resurrection, and He announced the resurrection of the body, which will take place on Judgment Day.

He had chosen and announced His resurrection to be the sign in

[28] I Pet. 2:7; Ps. 117:22; Isa. 8:14.
[29] I Cor. 1:23 f.
[30] Phil. 2:8 f.
[31] Exorcismus, *Rit. Rom.*, Titulus XI, chap. 3.
[32] *Summa theol.*, IIIa, q. 49, a. 1.
[33] *Ibid.*, a. 2.

proof of His miracles and the indisputable argument of His divine mission.[34] This is developed at length in apologetics. We wish here only to show the connection between Christ's victory over sin and His victory over death.

The apostles particularly appeal to the miracle of Christ's resurrection to confirm the truth of their preaching.[35] In fact, St. Paul twice declares: "If Christ be not risen again, your faith is vain." [36]

St. Paul does not mean that other miracles are insufficient motives of credibility, but he intends to say and expressly affirms: "If Christ be not risen again, then is our preaching vain. . . . Yea, and we are found false witnesses of God"; [37] that is, our preaching is false that rests on this fact attested to by all the apostles. Moreover, he explains himself by saying: "And if Christ be not risen again, your faith is vain for you are yet in your sins." [38] This means that if Christ did not rise again, then faith in Christ risen, which is the root of justification,[39] is false, and does not cleanse us from sins. In fact, as St. John Chrysostom, Theophylactus, and Oecumenius say, Christ's death proved inefficacious for the remission of sins, if Christ remained dead, and was conquered by it. For if Christ by His resurrection was unable to conquer death, then He did not conquer sin, for to conquer sin is more important and more difficult than to conquer death. Therefore sin is not destroyed unless its effect, namely, death, is destroyed.

St. John Chrysostom says: "If the dead cannot rise again, then neither sin is destroyed, nor death is overcome, nor the curse is taken away." [40] Theophylactus is of the same opinion.[41] Oecumenius likewise says: "If Christ Himself was also detained by death . . . then neither was sin destroyed by Christ's death; for if sin had been destroyed, then certainly death also which was caused by sin, would have been abolished." [42] Cornelius a Lapide, quoting the above-mentioned authors, offers the same interpretation. In recent times, similar

[34] Matt. 12:39 f.; 16:21; 17:22; 20:19; Luke 11:29; 18:33; Mark 8:31; 9:30; 10:34; 14:28; John 2:19.

[35] Acts 2:32 f.; 17:31; I Cor. 15:5 f.

[36] I Cor. 15:13 f.

[37] *Ibid.*, 15:14 f.

[38] *Ibid.*, 15:17.

[39] Rom. 4:25.

[40] *P.G.*, LXI, 335.

[41] *P.G.*, CXXIV, 759.

[42] *Ibid.*, CXVIII, 867.

views are expressed by Father Ladeuze [43] and Father J. M. Vosté.[44]

In the foregoing we truly see the intimate connection between Christ's resurrection and the other mysteries of Christianity. This connection may be expressed by saying that, if Christ did not overcome sin by rising again, then we are not certain that He overcame sin on the cross and that our redemption was accepted by God. Why so? Because as explained at length in the Old Testament and also by St. Paul: "As by one man sin entered into this world and by sin death; and so death passed upon all men in whom all have sinned." [45] And again: "The wages of sin is death. But the grace of God, life everlasting in Christ Jesus our Lord." [46] He also says: "And if Christ be in you, the body indeed is dead, because of sin, but the spirit liveth, because of justification." [47] Therefore He who invisibly takes away sin, must visibly take away death, or the effect of sin, so that we may have a most certain sign of His victory over sin and of our redemption.[48] Christ on the cross does not appear visibly as conqueror but rather as conquered; through the Resurrection, on the contrary, He shows Himself as the master of death, and so we understand how He could say to His disciples: "In the world you shall have distress, but have confidence, I have overcome the world." [49] Hence Christ's resurrection is the greatest motive of credibility, inasmuch as, according to divine providence, it is a most splendid sign of Christ's victory over sin and the devil; it is also the fulfillment of several of Christ's prophecies and the pledge of our future resurrection.

St. Thomas says about the same in the following passage: "Because it was shown above, that through Christ we have been freed from those things which we incurred through the sin of the first man; because the first man sinned, not only sin was transmitted to us, but also

[43] "La resurrection du Christ devant la critique contemporaine," *Science et foi,* pp. 1–6.

[44] *Studia Paulina,* p. 62. Father Vosté gives a good explanation of St. Pauls's words: "If Christ be not risen again, your faith is vain" (I Cor. 15:14); "vain" (Greek κενὴ) not only means without foundation, but it also signifies "empty," which means that there is no purpose to our faith in Christ the Savior.

[45] Rom. 5:12.

[46] *Ibid.,* 6:23.

[47] *Ibid.,* 8:10.

[48] St. Peter says: "Whom God hath raised up, having loosed the sorrows of hell, as it was impossible that He should be holden by it" (Acts 2:24). This means that it was impossible for Christ to be held in the bonds of death, for then He would have been conquered by death, instead of being its conqueror.

[49] John 16:33.

death, which is the penalty of sin (Rom. 5:12); it is necessary for Christ to free us from both, that is, from sin and from death." Hence the Apostle says: "For if by one man's offense death reigned through one, much more they who receive abundance of grace, and of justice, shall reign in life through one, Jesus Christ. Therefore, that He might prove both to us, He willed to die and to rise again. He willed to die, indeed, that He might cleanse us from sin. . . . He willed to rise again, however, that He might deliver us from death." [50]

Therefore Christ's victory over death, by His own glorious resurrection, is the result and sign of His victory over sin and the devil. And because the Blessed Virgin Mary was associated with Christ's perfect victory over the devil and sin, it was most fitting that she be associated with His perfect victory over death, and for this to be perfect her resurrection had to be anticipated as also her assumption. It was impossible for Christ to be detained in the bonds of death, for then He would have been conquered by death and not be its conqueror. The same must be said with due reservations for the Blessed Virgin Mary.[51]

Finally, Christ's victory over death will be made manifest on Judgment Day, when all will rise again. He Himself announced this, saying: "This is the will of My Father that sent Me; that everyone who seeth the Son, and believeth in Him, may have life everlasting, and I will raise Him up in the last day. . . . No man can come to Me, except the Father who hath sent Me, draw Him, and I will raise him up on the last day. . . . He that eateth My flesh and drinketh My blood, hath everlasting life, and I will raise him up on the last day." [52] St. Paul reaffirms this: "And as in Adam all die, so also in Christ all shall be made alive. . . . And the enemy death shall be destroyed last; for He hath put all things under His feet. . . . And when this mortal hath put on immortality, then shall come to pass the saying that is written: Death is swallowed up in victory. O death, where is thy victory? O death, where is thy sting? Now the sting of death is sin. . . . But thanks be to God, who hath given us the victory through our Lord Jesus Christ." [53] On this question, St. Thomas says: "The necessity of dying is a defect in human nature resulting from sin. But Christ by the merit of His passion repaired the defects of nature,

[50] *Contra Gentes,* Bk. IV, chap. 79; Rom. 5:17.
[51] See Appendix: The definability of the Blessed Virgin Mary's Assumption.
[52] John 6:40, 44, 55.
[53] I Cor. 15:22, 26, 54, 57.

which were visited upon Him because of the sin of man; for as the Apostle says: 'But not as the offense, so also the gift. For if by the offense of one, many died; much more the grace of God, and the gift, by the grace of one man, Jesus Christ, hath abounded unto many' (Rom. 5:15). From this we see that Christ's merit is more efficacious in taking away death, than Adam's sin was in bringing it about. Therefore those who rise again through Christ's merit, are freed from death, and no longer will suffer from the penalty of death." [54] Hence St. John says: "Death shall be no more, nor mourning nor crying nor sorrow shall be any more, for the former things are passed away." [55]

From this it becomes apparent what already has been said, namely, Christ's perfect victory over the devil implies perfect victory over sin as presupposed and its consequence, perfect victory over death by an anticipated resurrection. The same must be said, with due reservations, of the Blessed Virgin Mary, inasmuch as, in that she is the Mother of the Savior, particularly on Calvary, she is most closely associated with Christ's perfect victory over the devil and sin. Hence she is also associated with His perfect victory over death, as the ancient and venerated prayer for the feast of the Assumption states, which says: "The Holy Mother of God underwent temporal death, yet could not be held down by the bonds of death, who of herself begot Thy incarnate Son our Lord." [56]

[54] *Contra Gentes,* Bk. IV, chap. 82.

[55] Apoc. 21:4.

[56] Oration "Veneranda," for Assumption, now abrogated.

CHAPTER XXXVII

CHRIST'S DEATH AND DESCENT INTO HELL

WE shall consider briefly the question of Christ's death and resurrection, which already have been discussed at length in their apologetic aspect in the treatise on revelation. The principal points in these questions of St. Thomas must be recapitulated,[1] treating in order Christ's death and descent into hell, His resurrection and ascension, Christ the king, judge, and head of the blessed.

QUESTION 50

CHRIST'S DEATH

FIRST ARTICLE

It was fitting for Christ to die: (1) so as to satisfy for us, who were sentenced to death because of sin; (2) to show that He truly assumed a human nature; for if, after conversing with men, He had suddenly disappeared without dying, then all would have looked upon Him as a phantom; (3) that by dying He might take away from us the fear of death; (4) that He might give us the example of dying spiritually to sin; (5) that by rising from the dead He might show His power whereby He overcame death, and instill into us the hope of rising again.

SECOND ARTICLE

In Christ's death the divine nature was not separated from His body. St. Thomas gives and explains the answer of tradition, namely, that the divine nature remained hypostatically united with Christ's body. What is bestowed through God's grace as something that is by nature destined to be permanent, is never taken away without sin, for

[1] *Summa theol.*, IIIa, q. 50-59.

"God's gifts are without repentance." [2] Such is the grace of adoption in the just person. But the grace of the hypostatic union is much greater and more permanent in itself than the grace of adoption, and Christ was absolutely impeccable.

Thus it is said of the Son of God that "He died and was buried," [3] which befitted Him on the part of His body before and after death. Not only His body was buried, but the Son of God was buried, for, during the three days of His death, His divine person was not separated from His dead body, nor even from His blood, all of which was shed.

Third Article

In Christ's death the divine nature was not separated from His soul. The reason is that the soul is united with the Word of God more immediately and more primarily than the body is. But in Christ's death the divine nature was not separated from the body. Therefore, a fortiori, it was not separated from the soul. Hence it is predicated of the Son of God that His soul descended into hell.

Fourth Article

It is erroneous to assert that Christ during the three days of death was a man, because His soul was separated from His body and the human nature ceased as such through the separation of the soul from the body.

Fifth Article

Christ's body, living or dead, was absolutely and identically the same, because anything is said to be absolutely and identically the same which is the same in its suppositum. But Christ's body, either living or dead, was the same in its suppositum, as is evident from what was said. It was not, however, absolutely and totally the same identical body, because the life that was lost by death belongs to the essence of a living body. It is more probable that Christ's body during the three days of death had its substantial form, but it had the form of a human corpse, for matter cannot naturally be without a form.

[2] Rom. 11:29.
[3] Nicene Creed.

Sixth Article

Christ's death in becoming (*in fieri*), or His passion, was the meritorious cause of our salvation. But Christ's death in fact nowise caused our salvation by way of merit, because Christ, who was then dead, was beyond the condition of meriting, for He was no longer a wayfarer. However, Christ's dead flesh remained the instrument of His divine nature with which it was united, and thus it could be the efficient cause of our salvation.

Question 51

Christ's Burial

First Article

It was fitting for Christ to be buried, because it proves the truth of His death and because by His rising again from the grave we are given hope of rising again through His resurrection.

Second Article

Christ was buried in a becoming manner as the Evangelists record.[4] His body was anointed with aromatic spices of myrrh and aloes, according to the custom of the Jews, so as to preserve it longer from corruption. It was buried in a clean shroud, according to the dictates of becoming propriety, and in another's tomb, because He was the exemplar of poverty; in a new tomb in which no one had been buried before Him, lest by the burial of another there it might be pretended and believed that this other had risen again. It was buried in a monument hewn out of a rock, and thus according to the plan of divine providence, lest it might be said afterward that His disciples dug up the earth and stole His body. Finally, Joseph of Arimathea and Nicodemus rolled a great stone against the opening of the sepulcher,[5] so that the stone could be rolled away from the monument only by the help of many hands. Thus Providence forestalled the calumnies of the Jews.

[4] Matt. 27:1 f.; John 19:1 f.
[5] Matt. 27:60.

Third Article

Christ's body remained incorrupt in the tomb so that divine power should be manifested and so that nobody might believe His death resulted from the weakness of nature, and was not voluntary.

Fourth Article

Christ's body was fittingly one day and two nights in the tomb, because that was the required and sufficient time to prove the truth of Christ's death, otherwise there would have been no true resurrection. The Evangelist says: "The Son of man will be in the heart of the earth three days and three nights," [6] by way of synecdoche, taking the part for the whole. Thus then, the first day and first night are computed from the end of Good Friday, the day of Christ's death and burial, until midnight on Holy Saturday; the second day and second night, from midnight Saturday until midnight Sunday; the third night and the third day, from midnight Sunday to daybreak of the same day on which Christ rose again. This was the method of computing time among the Jews; for them, one day and one night signified a civil day of twenty-four hours, either complete or incomplete.

Question 52

Christ's Descent into Hell

It is of faith and is expressed in the Apostles' Creed according to the *Ordo Romanus,*[7] that Christ descended into hell, and it is afterward declared that His soul descended there,[8] but He did not abolish hell.[9]

This mystery is expressed in St. Peter's sermon on Pentecost Day, in which he quotes the words of the Psalmist as referring to Christ, namely, "Thou wilt not leave My soul in hell," [10] and he says: "The prophet . . . foreseeing this, spoke of the resurrection of Christ, for neither was He left in hell, neither did His flesh see corruption." [11]

St. Paul also says of Christ: "Ascending on high, He led captivity

[6] *Ibid.,* 12:40.
[7] Denz., nos. 3, 6, 40, 462.
[8] *Ibid.,* nos. 385, 429.
[9] *Ibid.,* no. 532.
[10] Ps. 15:10.
[11] Acts 2:31.

captive; He gave gifts to men. Now that He ascended, what is it, but because He also descended into the lower parts of the earth? He that descended is the same also that ascended above all the heavens, that He might fill all things." [12]

Did Christ's soul really and substantially descend into hell and not merely effectively; and then was this descent fitting; and what hell was this, and whom did He deliver? St. Thomas gives and exemplifies the answers of tradition.[13]

First Article

Christ's soul really and substantially descended into hell and not merely effectively. The Apostles' Creed says: "He descended into hell," [14] which obviously and naturally means a real and substantial descent. Similarly St. Paul says: "He also descended first into the lower parts of the earth. He that descended is the same also that ascended above all the heavens, that He might fill all things." [15] Likewise St. Peter says, quoting the Psalmist: "Because Thou wilt not leave My soul in hell, nor suffer Thy holy one to see corruption." [16] The Fathers thus understood this text, especially St. Ignatius, St. Gregory Nazianzen, and St. Augustine.[17]

St. Thomas explains that Christ's soul did not descend into hell by that kind of motion whereby bodies are moved, but as the angels are moved. And Christ's separated soul was not inoperative in hell, for it operated as the instrument of the divine nature, expelling exterior darkness and illuminating this place.

Second Article

IT WAS FITTING FOR CHRIST TO DESCEND INTO HELL

There are three reasons for this.

1) Because man by sin had incurred not only death of the body, but also descent into hell. Therefore it was fitting for Christ to die

[12] Eph. 4:8 f.

[13] See *Catechism of the Council of Trent;* also *Dict. théol. cath.,* art. "Descente aux enfers."

[14] Denz., nos. 3, 6, 40, 462, Christ descended into hell; nos. 385, 429, His soul descended; no. 532, but He did not abolish hell.

[15] Eph. 4:9.

[16] Acts 2:27.

[17] Journel, *Enchiridion patrist.,* no. 426.

and descend into hell, so that He might deliver us from the necessity of permanent death (because we shall rise again) and from descent into hell. In this sense Christ is said to have power over death and in dying to have conquered it, according to the prophet, who says: "O death, I will be thy death." [18]

2) It was fitting for the devil to be overthrown by Christ's passion, so that He should deliver the captives detained in hell.[19]

3) As He showed forth His power on earth by living and dying, so also it was fitting for Him to manifest it in hell, by visiting it and enlightening it; and so at the name of Jesus every knee should bow, not only of them that are in heaven, but likewise of them that are in hell.[20]

Third Article

Christ did not actually descend into the hell of the lost; because, as the Fathers teach, He descended into hell to console and liberate those who were detained there. But nobody is consoled and liberated in the hell of the lost, as will at once be stated. Moreover, the hell of the lost is not a fitting place for Christ. Therefore He descended into the hell of the lost only effectively, arguing with them and convincing them of their infidelity and malice; and this He did by speaking to them or manifesting His will by signs, because local distance is no impediment for spirits.[21]

Fourth Article

Christ's soul remained in hell, namely, in the limbo of the holy fathers, until the moment of His resurrection. Hence the Church in the blessing of the paschal candle, sings: "This is the night wherein Christ ascended victorious from hell." [22] Such is the opinion of St. Irenaeus, St. Gregory of Nyssa, and Tertullian.

Fifth Article

Christ, descending into hell, delivered the holy fathers. He delivered them from the penalty of original sin, namely, from the penalty

[18] Osee 13:14.
[19] Zach. 9:11.
[20] Phil. 2:10.
[21] Cf. IIIa, q. 52, a. 2, for the solution of objections taken from certain passages of Sacred Scripture. He delivered them from the penalty that was due to them.
[22] *Exultet* of Holy Saturday.

whereby they were excluded from the life of glory, of whom the prophet says: "Thou also, by the blood of Thy testament, hast sent forth Thy prisoners out of the pit wherein is no water." [23] And St. Paul says: "Despoiling the principalities and powers," [24] namely, the infernal ones, by taking away the just, He brought them from this place of darkness to heaven, that is, to the beatific vision. Such is the opinion of the Fathers, especially St. Augustine [25] and St. Gregory the Great [26] and St. Jerome.[27]

Thus Christ's descent into hell was the cause of exceeding joy to those souls already purified, such as the souls of Abraham, Isaac, Jacob, Moses, the prophets, as also many just and holy women of the Old Testament.

Thus we clearly see that the whole of the Old Testament was not an immediate preparation for eternal life, but for the coming of the Redeemer, who after having suffered and died, had to open the gates of heaven, so that we might enter into eternal life. The first and most abundant fruits of the sacrifice on the cross are also made manifest. Then, too, the fathers of the Old Testament fully understood that the passion of Jesus was the source of all graces, and that without it they could neither have been justified nor have merited an increase of grace, nor obtained eternal life. Therefore they were most sincerely thankful to the Savior whose coming they awaited for many centuries, who is called "the desire of the eternal hills, the joy of the angels, the King of patriarchs, the Crown of all the saints." [28]

By the mystery of the holy Incarnation, by the labors of Jesus, by His agony and passion, by His infirmities, and by His death they were liberated. In all these things they saw the most perfect fulfillment of what had been announced and the truth that the mystery of the redemptive Incarnation far transcends all figures, all sacrifices of the Old Law, all prophecies. Christ's descent into hell truly meant for them, "it is consummated." [29] All these things proclaim the glory of the cross.

[23] Zach. 9:11.
[24] Col. 2:15.
[25] *Hom. 57 in Evang.*
[26] *Hom. 22 in Evang.*
[27] *Com. in cap. IIum Jonae.*
[28] Litany of the Sacred Heart.
[29] John 19:30.

Sixth Article

Christ did not deliver any of the lost by His descent into hell; because, since Christ's descent into hell operated in virtue of His passion, He liberated only those whom He found united to His passion by means of faith that is actuated by charity. But the lost did not believe in Christ's passion and they were not finally united with Christ by charity, and after death there is no possibility of conversion, because the lost are confirmed in evil, as the just are in good.

Seventh Article

For the same reason, the children who died in original sin were not liberated by Christ. Baptism is administered to men in this life, wherein man can be changed from sin to grace. But Christ's descent into hell was granted to the souls after this life, when they are no longer capable of this aforesaid change.

Eighth Article

Christ did not deliver all the souls in purgatory by His descent into hell. For Christ's passion did not have greater power then than now. But now it does not free all souls in purgatory, but only those that are sufficiently cleansed, or to whom Christ's passion is applied by the Sacrifice of the Mass. Christ's descent into hell was not satisfactory; it operated, however, in virtue of the Passion; thus He did not free all those who, when still living united with their bodies, had merited by their faith and devotion toward Christ's death, that by His descent there, they should be freed from the temporal punishment of purgatory, as St. Thomas says.[30]

Some theologians, however, said that Christ's descent, although it did not of itself free all souls from purgatory, there was then granted to them the favor of a quasi-plenary indulgence, which is a probable opinion. Yet the commentators of St. Thomas follow his view, and furthermore say that the souls in purgatory that were not then liberated, were consoled and also rejoiced at the thought of the glory they will at once receive after their purgation.

[30] Cf. IIIa, q. 52, a. 8, ad 1, ad 2.

CHAPTER XXXVIII

CHRIST'S RESURRECTION AND ASCENSION

ST. THOMAS has discussed at length Christ's resurrection, the quality, manifestation, and causality of His resurrection, as also His ascension.[1] The more important things will be recapitulated.[2]

Question 53

Christ's Resurrection

It is of faith that Christ rose again from the dead on the third day, as declared in the Gospel, the Epistles of the apostles, and in the Apostles' Creed.[3] In fact, it was declared that He rose again by His own power;[4] that it was a true resurrection of the body,[5] that the soul was reunited to the body,[6] and that He afterward truly did eat, though He did not have to.[7]

First Article

WHETHER IT WAS NECESSARY FOR CHRIST TO RISE AGAIN

Christ's resurrection was not absolutely necessary, but it was necessary if we take into consideration the divine plan, the prophecies, the merits of Christ, and our benefit.

St. Thomas gives five reasons for asserting this necessity, all of which have their foundation in Sacred Scripture.

The resurrection was necessary:

[1] See IIIa, q. 53-58.
[2] *Dict. théol. cath.*, art. "Jésus-Christ," *La résurrection*, col. 1213-24.
[3] Denz., nos. 2 f., 13, 16, 20, 40, 54, 86, 255, 994, 2036, 2084.
[4] *Ibid.*, no. 286.
[5] *Ibid.*, nos. 344, 422.
[6] *Ibid.*, nos. 422, 462.
[7] *Ibid.*, nos. 344, 422.

1) For the commendation of divine justice, to which it belongs to exalt the humble. For Christ by His charity and obedience humbled Himself even to death on the cross; hence it behooved Him to be exalted by God to a glorious resurrection.[8]

2) For our instruction in the faith; because by Christ's resurrection our belief in His divinity is confirmed.[9]

3) For the raising of our hope, because in seeing Christ, who is our head, rise again, we hope that we, too, shall rise again.[10]

4) To set in order the lives of the faithful, so that we also may walk in newness of life.[11]

5) To complete the work of our salvation, because Christ was thus glorified in rising again, so that He might advance us to good things.[12] For it was so ordained by God, that only after the resurrection would the Holy Spirit be given, or the apostles be sent to preach.[13]

Second Article

IT WAS FITTING FOR CHRIST TO RISE AGAIN THE THIRD DAY

To confirm our belief in the truth of Christ's divinity, it was necessary for Him to rise soon, and that His resurrection be not delayed until the end of the world. But to confirm our belief in the truth of His humanity and death it was necessary that there be some delay between His death and resurrection. That the truth of His death be made manifest, however, it sufficed that His resurrection be deferred until the third day.

The third day, on which Christ rose again, was the first of the week, which is our Sunday; it was daybreak or about dawn. In other words, the night following the Sabbath, "when it began to dawn toward the first day of the week." [14]

Third Article

Christ was the first to rise again, His resurrection being perfect, in that He never died again. Some rose again before Him, but their

[8] Cf. Ps. 138:1; Luke 24:26.
[9] I Cor. 15:12.
[10] *Ibid.*
[11] Rom. 6:4.
[12] *Ibid.*, 4:25.
[13] Luke 24:47; John 7:39.
[14] Matt. 28:1. See Mark 16:1; Luke 24:1; John 20:1. Cf. St. Thomas, *Summa theol.*, IIIa, q. 53, a. 2, ad 3.

resurrection was imperfect, for they were rescued from actual death, but not from the necessity and possibility of dying. Thus, like Lazarus, they returned to life, merely to die again.

St. Thomas says: "There are two opinions regarding those who rose with Christ. Some hold that they rose to life so as to die no more. . . . But Augustine seems to think that they rose to die again . . . and his reasons seem to be more cogent." [15] The common opinion of the faithful is that nobody ascended bodily into heaven before Christ and the Blessed Virgin.

But some saints rose again with Christ though the Scripture does not give their names. It is very probable, according to the more common opinion, that these referred in a special manner to Christ, and were His more illustrious types, such as Abraham, Isaac, Jacob, Moses, David, Melchisedech, and such as these, as also some of those who died later on, such as Zacharias, John the Baptist, Simeon, and others of this kind.

Fourth Article

Christ according to His divine nature was the principal efficient cause of His resurrection, but His soul and body were instruments of His divine nature, and "they mutually took back each other." [16] Moreover, Christ by His passion was the meritorious cause of His resurrection.[17]

Question 54

First Article

Christ rose again with the same true body, otherwise His resurrection would not have been true; for that is said to rise again, which has fallen.[18]

Second Article

Christ's body rose again entire, because it was of the same nature after His resurrection as it was before death, although glorified. Christ

[15] *Ibid.*, a. 3, ad 2. On this subject cf. Billuart, who refutes Sylvius, and defends the second opinion.
[16] *Ibid.*, a. 4.
[17] *Ibid.*, q. 53, a. 4.
[18] *Ibid.*, q. 54, a. 1.

also took again all His blood, morally speaking, all that is necessary for the integrity of the body.

Third Article

Christ arose with a glorified body; for, the mystery of the redemption being completed by Christ's passion and death, in the resurrection His soul at once communicated its glory to its reunited body.[19]

Fourth Article

It was most fitting for Christ to rise again with scars,[20] as permanent marks of His victory, so as to convince His disciples that the same crucified body rose again; that when He pleads for us with the Father, He may always show what manner of death He endured for us; that on the Judgment Day, He may manifest these scars to all that are to be judged, to the just, indeed, as a motive for their love and gratitude, but to the reprobates for their reproof and shame.

Question 55

First Article

Christ ought not to have immediately manifested Himself to all after His resurrection, but to some, who were as witnesses to make known His resurrection to others. For such things as concern future glory are beyond the common knowledge of mankind. Hence St. Thomas says: "Christ appeared first to the women . . . because the women, whose love for our Lord was more persistent, so much so that when even the disciples withdrew from the sepulcher they did not depart, were the first to see Him rising in glory." [21] And again he says: "A woman is not to be allowed to teach publicly in church; but she may be permitted to give familiar instruction to some privately." [22] Therefore, as St. Ambrose says: "A woman is sent to them who are of her household, but not to the people to bear witness to the Resurrection." [23] It is a pious and probable opinion that Christ first appeared to the Blessed Virgin His Mother; the affection of the Son for His most loving mother is the reason for this assertion. Such is the

[19] *Ibid.,* a. 3.
[20] John 20:27; cf. St. Thomas, *Summa theol.,* IIIa, q. 54, a. 3.
[21] Cf. IIIa, q. 55, a. 1, ad 3.
[22] *Ibid.,* c.
[23] *Com. in Lucam* 24:22.

teaching of Abbot Rupert, St. Albert the Great, St. Bonaventure, and several more recent commentators.[24]

Second Article

Christ's actual resurrection should not have been seen by His disciples, because the divinely established order is that those things above men's knowledge be revealed to them by angels, or at least it is the accustomed way for these to be proclaimed by angels.

Second objection of St. Thomas. "In order to have certainty of faith, the disciples saw Christ ascend into heaven.[25] Therefore it seems for the same reason that Christ ought to have been seen to rise again by the disciples."

Reply to second objection. "Christ's ascension as to its term, wherefrom, was not above men's common knowledge, but only as to its term whereunto. . . . Thus the disciples did not see how Christ raised from the earth was received into heaven." [26]

Third Article

Christ ought not to have lived continually with His disciples after His resurrection because, for the manifestation of the glory of Him who rose, this was not befitting, lest it might seem He rose to the same life as before. "But it is unknown," says St. Thomas, "in what places He was bodily present in the meantime, since Scripture is silent and His dominion is in every place." [27]

St. Thomas observes [28] that there were apparitions not mentioned in the Gospels; for St. Paul records the appearance to five hundred brethren at once,[29] afterward to James,[30] and yet these are not mentioned by the Evangelists.

Hence several authors think that between the times of the ten apparitions recorded in the Gospels, it is very probable that Christ was for some time with His most beloved Mother.

[24] If the objection is raised that "Christ appeared first to Mary Magdalen" (Mark 16:9), we reply to this that the appearance was the first reported by the Evangelists, and that she preceded the disciples, the witnesses and the messengers, in this respect.

[25] Acts 1:10.

[26] Read the entire answer.

[27] *Summa theol.*, IIIa, q. 53, a. 3, ad 2.

[28] *Ibid.*, ad 3.

[29] I Cor. 15:6.

[30] *Ibid.*, 15:7.

What is the meaning of these words of Christ to Magdalen: "Do not touch Me, for I am not yet ascended to My Father"? [31] St. Thomas gives the following explanation: "If you say that Christ wished to be touched by the disciples, but not by the women, this cannot be; for it is said of Magdalen and the other women that they came up and took hold of His feet, and adored Him." [32] But St. John Chrysostom is of the opinion that Christ first said to Magdalen, "Do not touch Me," as if to say: "Do not think that I am still mortal and living with you the same way as before." [33]

Fourth Article

Christ appeared in His own shape to some who were well disposed to believe; but in another shape to those who already seemed to be getting tepid in their faith. Such is the view of St. Gregory the Great.[34]

Fifth and Sixth Articles

Christ by various testimonies and signs sufficiently proved the truth of His resurrection. The first testimony is given by Christ to the disciples on their way to Emmaus, as recorded in the Gospel.[35] The second testimony is when the angels [36] announced the Resurrection to the women. The third is when He appeared bodily present to the eyes of His disciples, in His own shape, conversing with them, eating, drinking with them, allowing them to touch Him, and showing them His scars.[37] The fourth is where He asserted that it is He Himself, confirming this assertion by miracles, by passing through closed doors,[38] on the occasion of the catch of the vast number of fishes,[39] and when He ascended into heaven.[40]

The objection is raised that even the angels appeared in human form and spoke, and yet they were not truly human.

St. Thomas replies to this objection by saying that the angels who

[31] John 20:17.
[32] Matt. 28:9.
[33] *Com. in Joan.* 20:17.
[34] Cf. IIIa, q. 55, a. 4.
[35] Luke 24:27.
[36] Matt. 28:5 f.
[37] Luke 24:39 f.
[38] John 20:19.
[39] *Ibid.*, 21:6.
[40] Acts 1:9 f.

appeared in human form did not assert that they were truly men, and they did not work miracles in confirmation of this assertion. Hence all the above-mentioned arguments and signs "taken collectively perfectly manifest Christ's resurrection, especially owing to the testimonies of the Scriptures, the saying of the angels, and even Christ's own assertion supported by miracles." [41]

Moreover, in the treatise on revelation, it is shown apologetically that the testimony of the apostles invincibly proves the truth of Christ's resurrection. This argument is ably set forth by Billuart in his treatise on Christ's resurrection.

Question 56

Christ's resurrection is the exemplar and efficient instrumental cause of the resurrection of our bodies and souls.[42] It is called an efficient instrumental cause, not inasmuch as it is an act that is immediately transient, but inasmuch as the humanity, according to which Christ rose, is the instrument of the divinity united with it to raise our bodies and sanctify our souls. St. Thomas says: "Christ's resurrection is the efficient cause of ours, through the divine power whose office it is to quicken the dead; and this power by its presence is in touch with all places and times; and such virtual contact suffices for its efficiency." Its contact is not quantitative, but virtual or dynamic.[43]

Question 57

Christ's Ascension

It is of faith that Christ ascended into heaven, as stated in the Apostles' Creed; [44] that He ascended body and soul; [45] that He sits at the right hand of the Father,[46] according to the natural mode of existing; [47] that His kingdom is eternal; [48] and that He will judge the living and the dead,[49] coming in His body.[50]

[41] *Summa theol.,* IIIa, q. 55, a. 6, ad 1.
[42] *Ibid.,* q. 56, a. 1, ad 3.
[43] *Ibid.,* a. 2, ad 2.
[44] Denz., nos. 2 f., 13, 20, 54, 86.
[45] *Ibid.,* nos. 13, 344, 429, 462.
[46] *Ibid.,* nos. 2 f., 13, 16, 86.
[47] *Ibid.,* no. 874.
[48] *Ibid.,* nos. 9, 13, 16, 86.
[49] *Ibid.,* nos. 2 f., 13, 40, 54, 86, 287, 344, 422, 427, 429, 462, 994, 3028.
[50] *Ibid.,* nos. 13, 225.

The principal passages from Sacred Scripture in testimony of the Ascension are: "And the Lord Jesus, after He had spoken to them, was taken up into heaven, and sitteth on the right hand of God"; [51] "And it came to pass whilst He blessed them, He departed from them and was carried up to heaven"; [52] "And when He had said these things, while they looked on, He was raised up, and a cloud received Him out of their sight. And while they were beholding Him going up to heaven, behold two men stood by them in white garments, who also said: 'Ye men of Galilee, why stand you looking up to heaven? This Jesus who is taken up from you into heaven, shall so come as you have seen Him going into heaven.' " [53]

St. Thomas, having presupposed faith in Christ's ascension, in this question makes several inquiries about the fittingness, manner, and effects of Christ's ascension.

First Article

It was fitting for Christ to ascend into heaven because after the resurrection Christ's body was incorruptible, and heaven is a place of incorruption. Moreover, this was a better way of manifesting Christ's victory over death. Finally, it befitted Christ to ascend, since this increased our faith, which is of things unseen; it advanced us in hope, because thus Christ, our head, gave us hope of reaching heaven, for He said: "I go to prepare a place for you." [54] This mystery also increases love in us, for St. Paul says: "Seek the things that are above, where Christ is sitting at the right hand of God." [55]

Christ fittingly ascended into heaven forty days after His resurrection,[56] so as to prove more efficaciously the truth of the Resurrection; and also as the Scripture says: "For forty days appearing to them, and speaking of the kingdom of God," [57] in order to instruct them in those matters that pertain to the faith.

[51] Mark 16:19.

[52] Luke 24:51.

[53] Acts 1:9 f. Cf. Eph. 4:8; Col. 3:1 f. Also testimony of the Fathers; *Enchir. patrist.*, nos. 427, 428. On this mystery, see *Catechism of Council of Trent*, chap. 7, Apostle's Creed.

[54] John 14:2.

[55] Col. 3:1.

[56] Cf. IIIa, q. 57, a. 1, ad 4.

[57] Acts 1:3.

Second Article

Christ ascended into heaven as man, but by the power of the divine nature.

Third Article

Christ ascended into heaven by His own power, first of all by His divine power, and secondly by the power of His glorified soul moving His body at will, "inasmuch as His glorified body was endowed with the gift of agility." [58] Although Christ did ascend into heaven by His own power, yet "He was raised up and taken up into heaven by the Father, since the Father's power is the same as the Son's." [59]

Fourth Article

"Christ ascended above all the heavens," [60] and this was most fitting because of His dignity. Hence St. Paul says: "For it was fitting that we should have such a high priest, holy, innocent, . . . and made higher than the heavens." [61] "God's seat is said to be in heaven, not as though heaven contained Him, but rather because it is contained by Him." [62]

Fifth Article

Christ's body ascended above every spiritual creature on account of the dignity of the hypostatic union, for St. Paul says: "He set Him above all principality and power, and virtue, and dominion, and every name that is named not only in this world, but also in that which is to come." [63]

Sixth Article

Christ's ascension is the cause of our salvation. (1) On our part, because by it faith which is of things unseen, is increased, there is an advancement in hope, an enkindling of charity, and greater reverence for Christ is thereby fostered. (2) On His part, for by thus ascending

[58] Cf. *Suppl.,* q. 84, a. 1.
[59] Cf. IIIa, q. 57, a. 3, ad 1.
[60] Eph. 4:10.
[61] Heb. 7:26.
[62] Cf. IIIa, q. 57, a. 4, ad 1.
[63] Eph. 1:20.

into heaven He prepared the way for us, as our Head.[64] In sign whereof He took to heaven the souls of the saints delivered from hell, as the Scripture says: "Ascending on high He led captivity captive." [65] So also Christ "entered into heaven to make intercession for us," [66] and "that He might fill all things." [67]

Reply to first objection. Christ's ascension is the cause of our salvation, by way not of merit, but of efficiency, as His resurrection was.

Reply to third objection. "Christ . . . from some special dispensation sometimes comes down in body to earth, either in order to show Himself to the whole world, as at the judgment; or else to show Himself particularly to some individual, as to St. Paul.[68] And lest any man may think that Christ was not bodily present, but in some way, when this occurred the contrary is shown from what the Apostle says to confirm faith in the Resurrection: 'Last of all He was seen also by Me, as by one born out of due time.' " [69]

This vision would not prove, of course, the truth of the Resurrection, unless he had seen Christ's true body.

St. Thomas does not here discuss the mission of the Holy Ghost, because He had already spoken about this mystery at the end of the treatise on the Trinity,[70] concerning the mission of the divine persons.

It suffices to note that the effects produced in the apostles by the mission of the Holy Ghost on the day of Pentecost were a great increase of sanctifying grace and charity, to confirm them in grace, a proportionate increase of the seven gifts of the Holy Ghost, and the twelve fruits resulting from these gifts,[71] and the *gratiae gratis datae* enumerated by St. Paul.[72] Thus the gift of tongues was bestowed upon each of the apostles so that they might speak in the languages of the various nations, and also they sometimes spoke in one language so that the people of various nations understood them. Thus it is said: "They began to speak with divers tongues, according as the

[64] John 14:2.
[65] Eph. 4:8; Ps. 67:19.
[66] Heb. 7:25; 9:24.
[67] Eph. 4:10.
[68] Acts 9:5.
[69] I Cor. 15:8.
[70] Cf. Ia, q. 43.
[71] Gal. 5:22.
[72] I Cor. 12:8 f.

Holy Ghost gave them to speak";[73] "They shall speak with new tongues";[74] "I thank my God I speak with all your tongues."[75]

The virtual catholicity of the Church was in this way manifested, which had to become increasingly an actual fact by the preaching of the gospel throughout the world.

[73] Acts 2:4.
[74] Mark 16:17.
[75] I Cor. 14:18.

CHAPTER XXXIX

CHRIST THE KING, JUDGE, AND HEAD OF THE BLESSED

First Article

CHRIST THE KING

THERE are three parts: (1) The principal testimonies of the Old and New Testaments concerning Christ's universal kingship. (2) Whether and by what titles Christ even as man is the king of all, both spiritually and temporally. (3) Christ's universal influence as king over all men in the social order.

It is of faith that Christ after His ascension sits at the right hand of the omnipotent Father and reigns forever. The various symbols of the faith express this.[1]

TESTIMONY OF SCRIPTURE

1) In the time of the patriarchs, the Messias is announced as the Savior of the world, during the time of the kings He is described as king, Son of God, and priest; in fact, His passion or sacrifice are foretold. His royal dignity and universal power are proclaimed in the following text: "In His days shall justice spring up, and abundance of peace, till the moon be taken away. And He shall rule from sea to sea, and from the river unto the ends of the earth. Before Him the Ethiopians shall fall down . . . the kings of the Arabians and of Saba shall bring gifts. And all kings of the earth shall adore Him, and all nations shall serve Him. For He shall deliver the poor from the mighty, and the needy that had no helper. . . . And He shall save the souls of the poor. . . . For Him they shall always adore.

[1] Denz., nos. 2 f., 9, 13, 16, 86, 874. Cf. IIIa, q. 58, Christ sitting at the right hand of the Father.

. . . And in Him shall all the tribes of the earth be blessed; all nations shall magnify Him." [2]

Likewise it is said: "The kings of the earth stood up, and the princes met together, against the Lord and against His Christ. . . . He that dwelleth in heaven shall laugh at them . . . and trouble them in His rage. But I am appointed king by Him over Sion, His holy mountain, preaching His commandment. The Lord hath said: 'Thou art My Son, this day I have begotten Thee. Ask of Me, and I will give Thee the Gentiles for Thy inheritance.' " [3]

Also the prophet announces the Messias as king in this text: "For a child is born to us, and a son is given to us, and the government is upon His shoulder, and His name shall be called Wonderful, Counsellor, God the Mighty, the Father of the world to come, the Prince of Peace." [4]

And similarly another prophet speaks of a stone that struck the statue, and the stone became a great mountain and filled the whole earth, which is a symbolical announcement that Christ's kingdom is to replace all other kingdoms and be preferred to them.[5]

One of the minor prophets describes also the powers of this king, saying: "Rejoice greatly, O daughter of Sion. . . . Behold, thy King will come to thee, the just and Savior, He is poor and riding upon an ass and upon a colt, the foal of an ass." [6] This prophecy is quoted by the Evangelist: "Behold thy king cometh to thee sitting upon an ass." [7]

New Testament. Here Christ's universal kingdom is more clearly affirmed. It is, indeed, first of all declared by the angel announcing Christ's birth to the Blessed Virgin, and saying: "The Lord God shall give unto Him the throne of David His father and He shall reign in the house of Jacob forever." [8] Christ Himself says: "All power is given to Me in heaven and in earth," [9] which means right over all nations, so that nations are under obligation to hear His teaching, for He says: "Teach all nations," [10] and they must observe His laws, to which they

[2] Ps. 71:7 f.
[3] *Ibid.*, 2:2 f.
[4] Isa. 9:6.
[5] Dan. 2:34 f.
[6] Zach. 9:9.
[7] Matt. 21:5; see also John 12:15.
[8] Luke 1:32.
[9] Matt. 28:18.
[10] *Ibid.*, 28:19.

are subject after having been baptized, for He says: "Baptizing them in the name of the Father and of the Son and of the Holy Ghost, teaching them to observe all things whatsoever I have commanded you." [11]

This universal power of Christ includes both angels and the elect, for He says: "He shall send His angels, and shall gather together His elect." [12] This universal power extends to demons, whom Christ rejects by His power, and it also includes all created beings, inasmuch as miracles were worked over all creatures, which absolutely obey Him.

The Fourth Gospel frequently refers to Christ's kingdom, especially in this text, when "Pilate said to Jesus: 'Art Thou the King of the Jews?' Jesus answered: 'My kingdom is not of this world. If My kingdom were of this world, My servants would certainly strive that I should not be delivered to the Jews; but now My kingdom is not from hence.' Pilate therefore said to Him: 'Art Thou a king then?' Jesus answered: 'Thou sayest that I am a king. . . . Everyone that is of the truth heareth My voice.' " [13] Therefore His kingdom is of a higher and universal order. Likewise Pilate orders the title to be inscribed on the cross, "King of the Jews," in three languages: Hebrew, Greek and Latin; [14] that is, as Bossuet says, in the language of God's people, in the language of philosophers, and in the language of imperial power, jurists, and statesmen.

Finally, St. John the Evangelist particularly exalts Christ the King, whom He calls: "beginning and the end, King of kings, and Lord of lords, the supreme Judge, who renders to each according to His works, the Prince of the kings of the earth." [15]

St. Paul in one of his epistles also often speaks of Christ's universal reign; in fact, he even points out why Christ is the universal king, because He is: (1) the natural Son and heir of God; (2) the Redeemer. As for the first reason, he says: "In these days, [God] hath spoken to us by His Son, whom He hath appointed heir of all things . . . who sitteth at the right hand of the majesty on high." [16] The second reason is given as follows: "Who is He that shall condemn Christ Jesus that died, yea, that is risen also again; who is at the right hand of God, who

[11] *Ibid.*
[12] Mark 13:27; see also Matt. 13:41; 24:31.
[13] John 18:33 f.
[14] *Ibid.*, 19:20.
[15] Apoc. 1:5 f., 19:16, 22:13.
[16] Heb. 1:2.

also maketh intercession for us?"[17] And again he says: "For He must reign. All things are put under Him."[18]

The liturgy often recalls the title of King as in the hymn, "Thou art the King of glory, Christ,"[19] and the antiphon, "O King of nations,"[20] and in the invocation, "Christ the King, Ruler of nations, let us adore."[21] In the liturgy, Christ is called King of angels, of apostles, of martyrs; moreover, Christ conquers, Christ reigns, Christ commands. In the symbol of faith, we chant: "Whose reign will never end."[22] That Christ is King is therefore of faith.[23]

BY WHAT TITLES IS CHRIST ALSO AS MAN KING OF ALL CREATED THINGS?

His claim to kingship rests on three titles: (1) the hypostatic union; (2) plenitude of created grace, and these titles He claims by natural right; (3) His redemption of us, which is not a natural right, but one that is acquired by His sacrifice on the cross.

1) The hypostatic union. Because of this title, Christ, as man, transcends all creatures, even the higher choirs of angels, who must adore and obey Him as we do. Moreover, because of this union His acts are theandric and of infinite value.

This doctrine is clearly expressed by Pope Pius XI in the following words: "His kingship is founded upon that wonderful union which is called hypostatic. Hence it follows that Christ is to be adored by angels and men as God, and also that to Him as man, angels and men are subject and must recognize His empire, since, solely because of the hypostatic union, Christ has power over all creatures."[24]

2) His claim to plenitude of grace, virtues, and gifts. Because of this title Christ excels all creatures, and is the head of the Church. The Evangelist says: "Of His fullness we all have received."[25] For this reason He also has the highest degree of the light of glory and charity. This plenitude of grace He also has by natural right.

[17] Rom. 8:34; see also Exod. 1:20.
[18] I Cor. 15:25 f.
[19] Te Deum.
[20] Antiphon before Christmas.
[21] Invitatory for Corpus Christi.
[22] Nicene Creed.
[23] Denz., no. 2195; Encycl. *Quas primas.*
[24] Denz., no. 2194; *Quas primas.*
[25] John 1:16.

3) He is entitled to be King because He has redeemed us. Since all Christ's acts are theandric, they are meritorious and satisfactory, and of infinite value. Under this aspect, He transcends the angels who are His ministers and who must assist the redeemed in attaining their end. Therefore Pope Pius XI says: "But a thought that must give us even greater joy and consolation is this, that Christ is asking for us by acquired right as well as by natural right, because He has redeemed us. Would that they who forget what they have cost our Savior might recall the words: 'You were not redeemed with corruptible things as gold or silver . . . but with the precious blood of Christ as of a lamb unspotted and undefiled.' [26] For we are no longer our own property since Christ bought us with a great price,[27] and our bodies are the members of Christ." [28]

St. Thomas expresses this doctrine clearly saying: "To sit on the right hand of the Father is nothing else than to share in the glory of the Godhead with the Father, and to possess beatitude and judiciary power, and that unchangeably and royally." [29] Again he says: "Christ as man is exalted to divine honor, and this is signified in the aforesaid sitting." [30]

He also asks whether it belongs to Christ as man to sit at the right hand of the Father. His reply is: "To sit at the right hand of the Father belongs to Christ first of all as the Son of God . . . , because He has the same nature as the Father. . . . Secondly, according to the grace of union. . . . According to this, Christ as man is the Son of God, and consequently sits at the Father's right hand; yet so that the expression 'as' does not denote condition of nature, but unity of suppositum, as explained above (q. 16, a. 10, 11). Thirdly, the said approach can be understood according to habitual grace, which is more fully in Christ than in all other creatures, so much so that human nature in Christ is more blessed than in all other creatures, and possesses over all other creatures royal and judiciary power." [31]

St. Thomas goes on to say: "If 'as' denote unity of person, thus again as man He sits at the Father's right hand as to equality of power, since we venerate the Son of God with the same honor as we do His as-

[26] I Pet. 1:18 f.
[27] I Cor. 6:20.
[28] *Ibid.,* 6:15; Denz., no. 2194.
[29] Cf. IIIa, q. 58, a. 2.
[30] *Ibid.,* ad 2.
[31] *Ibid.,* a. 3.

sumed nature, as was said above (q. 25, a. 1) concerning the adoration of Christ's humanity inasmuch as it is personally united to the Word."[32] Afterward he says: "Judiciary power goes with royal dignity."[33]

Again he says: "It belongs to no one else, angel or man, but to Christ alone to sit at the right hand of the Father."[34] Thus He alone is the King of all. The holy Doctor also frequently speaks about Christ's title of Redeemer. In fact, he says: "Judiciary power belongs to the man Christ on account of His divine personality and the dignity of His headship and the fullness of His habitual grace; and yet He obtained it also from merit."[35]

To understand these assertions, we must properly define with St. Thomas the meaning of "king."

The word *"rex"* comes from *"regere,"* which means to rule, to govern, and universal government belongs to the king, ordering things to a good end. Thus the king is in his kingdom as God is in the world, and as the soul is in the body.[36]

Hence St. Thomas says: "To direct belongs more to the king," wherefore "prudence and justice belong most properly to a king,"[37] especially legal justice and equity.

To direct and to govern are defined by St. Thomas as follows: "To govern the world is to bring the things of the world to their end,"[38] and "the best government is government by one. The reason of this is that government is nothing but the directing of the things governed to the end; which consists in some good. But unity belongs to the idea of goodness. . . . Now the proper cause of unity is one. . . . From this it follows that the government of the world, to be the best, must be by one."[39]

Thus the supreme and intelligent designer, who directs all things, corresponds to the ultimate end.

But the spiritual king directs his subjects to a spiritual end; the temporal king, however, to a temporal end, to the common good

[32] *Ibid.*, a. 3; see also ad 1.
[33] *Ibid.*, q. 59, a. 4, ad 1.
[34] *Ibid.*, q. 58, a. 4; q. 59, a. 2, c., ad 2.
[35] *Ibid.*, q. 59, a. 3; see also a. 6.
[36] *Opusc.* 20, no. 12.
[37] *Summa theol.*, IIa IIae, q. 50, a. 1, ad 1.
[38] *Ibid.*, Ia, q. 103, a. 1.
[39] *Ibid.*, a. 3.

of society, which is not only a useful good, but a moral good, and which is subordinated to the ultimate supernatural end.

Is Christ as man, both the spiritual and temporal king of the universe, and was He the king of all kings and kingdoms in the whole world? Let us first see the three assertions on which all theologians are agreed.

1) All theologians always held that Christ as God rules as Lord and King of all, both spiritually and temporally, because "in Him were all things created in heaven and on earth, visible and invisible." [40]

2) All theologians also maintain that Christ, as man, is spiritual king of all men and societies, even of angels, as is evident from the above-quoted scriptural texts, for example: "King of kings, Lord of lords." [41] Thus civil governments must accept Christian revelation, and legislate, for example, as regards indissolubility of marriage, in accordance with this revelation.

3) Theologians are also all in agreement that Christ did not exercise this power as temporal king of the whole world. In fact, as the Evangelist says: "Jesus, therefore, when He knew that they would come to take Him by force and make Him king, fled again into the mountain Himself alone." [42]

But the theologians disagreed whether Christ as man, had, if not the exercise of the power, at least the power of temporal king of the world.

St. Robert Bellarmine, Toletus, Sylvius, Billuart,[43] and others reply in the negative. On the other hand, St. Antoninus, the Salmanticenses,[44] and others replied in the affirmative, quoting several texts of St. Thomas,[45] and this opinion afterward becomes the more generally accepted one, and is finally approved by Pius XI in his encyclical.[46] The summary of his declaration is that Christ as man is king by legislative jurisdiction, coercion, and administration, and has this right over members of His spiritual kingdom, over all men,[47] all civil affairs; [48] hence laicism must be condemned.[49]

[40] Col. 1:16.
[41] Apoc. 17:14.
[42] John 6:15.
[43] *De justitia,* diss. III, a. 6.
[44] *De incarn.,* disp. 32, dub. 2.
[45] Cf. IIIa, q. 59, a. 4, ad 1; q. 58, a. 2.
[46] Denz., no. 2194.
[47] *Ibid.*
[48] *Ibid.,* no. 2196.
[49] *Ibid.,* no. 2197.

Proof of affirmative opinion. St. Thomas says: "Christ, although established king by God, did not wish while living on earth to govern temporarily an earthly kingdom, because He came to raise men to divine things." [50]

Objection. But the pope has only indirect power over temporal things. Therefore Christ also.

Reply. The Salmanticenses are right in saying that, although the pope may have only indirect power in temporal affairs, Christ could have direct and immediate power, by reason of the hypostatic union. Not all power that Christ had was granted to the Roman Pontiff even in spiritual things. Thus the pope cannot institute new sacraments.

In our days, after the pope's encyclical,[51] there is no more disagreement among theologians on this point. Pope Pius XI says in this encyclical: "This kind of kingdom is especially of a spiritual nature and concerns spiritual things. . . . It would be a grave error, on the other hand, to say that Christ has no authority whatever in civil affairs, since by virtue of the absolute empire over all creatures committed to Him by the Father, all things are in His power. Nevertheless, during His life on earth, He entirely refrained from the exercise of such authority." [52]

Does this kingship of Christ consist of certain powers? The Pope's encyclical replies by saying that it consists of a threefold power, namely, legislative, judicial, and executive, "which, if it be deprived of these renders this kingship scarcely intelligible. This becomes sufficiently clear from the scriptural testimony already adduced concerning the universal dominion of our Redeemer, and moreover it is a dogma of faith that Jesus Christ was given to man, not only as our Redeemer, but also as a lawgiver, to whom obedience is due (C. Trid., Sess. VI, can. 21). Not only do the Gospels tell us that He made laws, but they present Him to us in the act of making them. Those who keep them show their love for their divine Master, and He promises that they shall remain in His love (John 14:15; 15:10). He claimed judicial power as received from His Father, when the Jews accused Him of breaking the Sabbath by the miraculous cure of a sick man. 'For neither does the Father judge any man, but all judgment He has given to the Son' (John 5:22). In this power is included the right of

[50] Cf. IIIa, q. 59, a. 4, ad 1.
[51] Denz., nos. 2195 f.; *Quas primas.*
[52] *Ibid.,* nos. 2195 f.

rewarding and punishing all men living, for this right is inseparable from that of judging. Executive power, too, belongs to Christ, for all must obey His command; none can escape the sanctions imposed by Him. Nevertheless this kingdom is in a special manner of a spiritual nature and concerns spiritual things." [53]

The universal extent of Christ's influence as king is the same as His influence as head of the Church. Thus His influence is universal, bestowing upon the just grace and charity, upon sinners in the Church the supernatural virtues of faith and hope, upon schismatics, heretics, Jews, and pagans, actual graces of illumination and inspiration, which can dispose them for salvation.[54] Christ died for all men, and is king and lord of all.

Christ also, as king of the angels, exerts at least accidental influence of grace and glory upon them, inasmuch as they are His ministers in the heavenly kingdom. He also reigns as judge by exercising His justice over demons whom He cast out of creatures during His life on earth.

Christ the King, as explained in the encyclical, reigns in the whole of man, in our souls which He deifies, in our intellects so that they may always think of Him, in our wills so that they may be subject to Him, in the affections so that Christ may be loved above all things, in our bodies so that our members may serve "as instruments of justice unto God" for His honor and glory.[55]

This kingdom also includes civil society, for as Leo XIII remarks,[56] civil society no less than the individual is dependent on God as its author, for "there is no power but from God," [57] and without Christ's help man cannot observe even the whole natural law, provide for sound morality, pass good laws, for, as St. Thomas says: "In the state of corrupted nature man cannot fulfill all the divine commandments without healing grace," [58] nor the whole natural law.

Hence Pope Pius XI declares against laicism, "that by the rejection of Christ's universal kingdom, it gradually comes about that no distinction is made between the true religion and false religions, and then all religion, even natural religion, is abolished, and thus the

[53] *Ibid.*, no. 2195.
[54] *Ibid.*, no. 1295.
[55] Rom. 6:13; *Quas primas.*
[56] *Immortale.* See Denz., no. 1866.
[57] Rom. 13:1.
[58] Cf. Ia IIae, q. 109, a. 4.

reign of impiety and immorality is established," [59] so that the words of our Lord are verified: "He that is not with Me is against Me." [60]

In our times, because of the institution of this feast of Christ the King, some have taken occasion to object to the Thomistic doctrine concerning the motive of the Incarnation. They have said that Christ as man is King of all creatures, even of angels, independently of our redemption from sin. But in virtue of the present decree, Christ came as King. Therefore in virtue of the present decree, He came also independently of sin.

We concede that this could be so in virtue of another decree, but not in virtue of the present decree. And we reply: Let the major pass without comment, because for Christ to be King of all creatures, formally as such, does not depend upon redemption from sin.

I distinguish the minor: in virtue of the present decree that Christ came primarily as King, this I deny; that He came so secondarily, I concede; for He came primarily as Savior, priest, and victim, although He is also King of all creatures. I distinguish the conclusion in like manner. Therefore, in virtue of the present decree, He came independently of sin if He came only as King, this I concede; if He also came, even primarily, as Savior of men, then I deny that He came so as king.

For the present decree, since it is efficacious and most prudent, concerns not only the substance of the Incarnation, but also all its circumstances, and therefore it is about the redemptive Incarnation, that is, it is about Christ who is to come in passible flesh. Hence, in virtue of the present decree, Christ nowise would have come unless man had sinned. This means that He would not have come in passible flesh, or in any other way, either as Savior or as King. But *de facto,* after the sin of the first man, He came principally as the Savior of man and as the King of all creatures. As we said, God, perceiving by His knowledge of simple intelligence the possibility of the fall of man and the redemption, by one decree willed the creation of the natural order, the elevation of the human race and of the angels to the order of grace, and at the same time, in permitting original sin, willed the redemptive Incarnation and therefore by the same sole decree ordered all created things for the incarnate Word and Redeemer, or for the conqueror of sin, the devil, and death, as also for Him as King.

[59] Denz., no. 2197; *Quas primas.*

[60] Matt. 12:30.

This is also clearly seen in the Mass of Christ the King, in which the title of King is intimately connected with that of Savior, and this not only once a year in the Mass of this feast, but daily in every Mass that is celebrated throughout the year.

The Introit of this Mass reads: "Worthy is the Lamb who was slain, to receive power and honor. To Him be glory and empire forever and ever." The oration says: "Almighty and eternal God, who has willed to restore all things in Thy beloved Son, who is King of all things, mercifully grant that all the nations of the earth, freed from sin, may be subject to His sweet rule."

The Epistle thanks God "who hath delivered us from the power of darkness and hath translated us into the kingdom of the Son of His love, in whom we have redemption through His blood, the remission of sins . . . because in Him it hath well pleased the Father that all fullness should dwell, and through Him to reconcile all things unto Himself." [61] The Gospel of this Mass recalls that Christ affirmed His kingship during His passion and intimately connected this royal dignity with redemption. The same is said in the Secret prayer. Also the Preface, in which Jesus is declared Priest before He is called King, says: "Thou who didst anoint with the oil of exaltation Thine only-begotten Son Jesus Christ eternal Priest and King of all: so that offering Himself . . . on the altar of the cross, He might accomplish the mysteries of human redemption, and having subjected all creatures to His empire, might deliver an eternal and universal kingdom to Thy immense Majesty. . . ."

Therefore the title of "King of kings" is nowise in opposition to the teaching of St. Thomas concerning the motive of the Incarnation. Christ is first of all the Savior.[62]

Second Article (Q. 59)

CHRIST THE JUDGE

It is of faith that Christ will judge the living and the dead, coming corporeally.[63]

1) Judiciary power befits Christ for three reasons: (1) because of

[61] Col. 1:12 f.

[62] The title of Savior or Priest and victim thus transcends the title of King.

[63] Denz., nos. 2 f., 13, 40, 54, 86, 255, 287, 422, 427, 429, 462, 994, 3028. See Acts 10:42; Rom. 14:9 f.

the hypostatic union; (2) because of His fullness of grace and dignity of headship; (3) because of His infinite merits.[64] Thus the Scripture says: "It is He who was appointed by God to be judge of the living and of the dead." [65] It was most fitting that He who fought for God's justice and conquered, having been unjustly condemned, should be, even as man, judge of all in accordance with God's justice.[66]

2) Judiciary power befits Christ as regards all human affairs, according to both natures.[67] Thus the Evangelist says: "The Father hath given all judgment to the Son." [68] And St. Paul says: "For this end Christ died and rose again, that He might be Lord both of the dead and of the living. . . . For we shall all stand before the judgment seat of God." [69]

3) Christ's judgment is twofold, that is, particular at death for every individual, namely, for each particular person; and it is also universal, inasmuch as each individual is a part of the universe, and this will be at the end of the world. Thus St. Paul says: "It is appointed unto men once to die, and after this the judgment," [70] that is, the particular judgment. And the Evangelist says: "The word that I have spoken, the same shall judge him in the last day." [71] The sentence delivered on the Judgment Day means the separation of all the good from the bad. It is more probable that the sentence and all that pertains to the general judgment is done mentally and not vocally. [72]

There will be in the last days a world-wide persecution by the wicked against the good; therefore the wicked will feel secure, and the good will fear.[73] But on the day of the Last Judgment the just will deride the condemned for three things, namely, their pride, their trust in themselves, and the passing glory of this world.[74]

4) Christ according to His human nature exerts judiciary power over all the angels, as regards the dispensation of graces granted through them and their accidental rewards; but He gives essential

[64] Cf. IIIa, q. 59, a. 1-3.
[65] Acts 10:42.
[66] Cf. IIIa, q. 59, a. 3.
[67] *Ibid.*, a. 4.
[68] John 5:22.
[69] Rom. 14:9 f.
[70] Heb. 9:27.
[71] John 12:48.
[72] *Com. in IV Sent.*, d. 47, q. 1, a. 1, q. 2.
[73] *Ibid.*, d. 48, q. 1, a. 4, q. 1, 6.
[74] *Com. St. Thomae in Ps.* 50.

reward only in accordance with His divine nature. On this point St. Thomas says: "As to the essential reward of the good angels, which is everlasting bliss, and as to the essential punishment of the wicked angels, which is everlasting damnation, this was done by Christ from the beginning of the world, inasmuch as He is the Word of God." [75]

Nevertheless, as St. Thomas says: "The angels are subjects of Christ's judiciary power even as regards His human nature: (1) from the closeness of His assumed nature to God, namely, by reason of the hypostatic union; (2) because by the lowliness of His passion, the human nature in Christ merited to be exalted above the angels, so that as is said: 'In the name of Jesus every knee should bow, of those that are in heaven, on earth, and under the earth.' [76] And therefore Christ has judiciary power also over all the angels both good and bad. In testimony of this the Scripture says: 'All the angels stood round about the throne.' " [77]

5) Will Christ come to judge the whole world in His human nature? [78] The answer is in the affirmative. The Evangelist says: "The Father hath given Him power to do judgment, because He is the Son of man." [79] Christ truly judges inasmuch as He is Lord, and Lord not only as Creator, but as Redeemer, which means according to His human nature. Hence St. Paul says: "For to this end Christ died and rose again, that He might be Lord both of the dead and of the living." [80]

Third Article

CHRIST THE HEAD OF THE BLESSED

1) It is said that "Christ sitteth on the right hand of God," [81] and according to both natures.[82] By reason of His divine nature He is equal to the Father, and in His human nature He excels all other creatures in the possession of divine good things. And both claims befit only Christ.

[75] *Summa theol.,* q. 59, a. 6, c.
[76] *Ibid.;* cf. *Phil.* 2:10.
[77] Apoc. 7:11.
[78] Suppl., q. 90.
[79] John 5:27.
[80] Rom. 14:9.
[81] Mark 16:19.
[82] Cf. IIIa, q. 58, a. 1-4.

2) Christ as God preserves all the blessed in being and in the consummation of grace. He preserves the light of glory and unfailing charity in them, and moves these powers to their respective acts. Christ as man illumines the blessed, rules them, gives them joy in accordance with the scriptural saying: "The Lord God Almighty is the temple thereof [of the new city], and the Lamb. And the city hath no need of the sun nor of the moon to shine in it; for the glory of God hath enlightened it, and the Lamb is the lamp thereof." [83]

3) Christ glorious as man adores the Father, thanks and offers Him His whole mystical body; and until the end of the world intercedes for wayfarers. St. Paul says: "Christ, being come a high priest of the good things to come," [84] concerning which St. Thomas says: "He sits next to the Father to intercede for us. He likewise sits there to help us." [85]

Likewise the Church chants in the Mass: "It is truly worthy and just . . . for us always and everywhere to thank Thee, O holy Lord, omnipotent Father, eternal God, through Christ our Lord, through whom the angels praise Thy majesty, the dominations adore Thy majesty." [86]

Likewise St. Augustine says [87] that all the blessed thank God through Christ for their predestination and for all its effects.

4) Christ glorious is adored by the blessed and He receives their thanks inasmuch as He is the Savior of all. The Church addresses Him in these words: "O Lord Jesus Christ, the only-begotten Son, O Lord God, Lamb of God, Son of the Father . . . Thou only art holy, Thou only art the Lord, Thou only, O Jesus Christ, together with the Holy Ghost, art most high in the glory of God the Father." [88] St. John says: "I heard all saying: To Him that sitteth on the throne, and to the Lamb, benediction and honor and glory and power, forever and ever." [89]

[83] Apoc. 21:23.
[84] Heb. 9:11.
[85] *Com. in Heb.* 9:11.
[86] Common Preface.
[87] *De praedest. sanct.,* chap. 3.
[88] *Gloria* of Mass.
[89] Apoc. 5:13; also 7:10.

IS THERE SACRIFICE IN HEAVEN?

This has been admitted by some and in recent times by Talhofer and Father Lepin [90] because Christ offers to God the Father His glorious scars and because the Scripture says: "I saw the Lamb standing as it were slain." [91]

There is a considerable difficulty here, because first of all sacrifice in the strict sense implies external immolation, at least sacramentally, and this does not continue in heaven any more than the sacraments do, because the blessed see God directly, without sensible signs.

Moreover, it seems that the sacrifice in heaven would not be subordinated, but coordinated with the sacrifice on the cross, whereby therefore the work of our redemption would not have been completed, and would be contrary to what our Lord said in dying: "It is consummated." [92] In fact, it seems that the sacrifice in heaven as such would be more perfect than the sacrifice on the cross, which latter would be subordinated to it as a disposition to its ultimate perfection.

Wherefore neither a new sacrifice in heaven in the strict sense must be admitted, nor a new and formal oblation of the sacrifice on the cross, but merely its consummation, which, St. Thomas says, "consists in this, that those for whom the sacrifice is offered, obtain the end of the sacrifice . . . according to Heb. 9:11, that Christ is a high priest of the good things to come, for which reason the priesthood of Christ is said to be eternal." [93]

Nevertheless, until the end of the world, Christ glorious appeals to the Father for us, as the fruits of the sacrifice on the cross are applied to us, and thus also He actually offers the Masses that are daily offered by His priests. After the end of the world, Christ as our High Priest along with the members of His mystical body, will offer to the Father the cult of praise, adoration, and thanksgiving, wherein the sacrifice on the cross will be consummated without a new sacrifice in the strict sense.[94]

[90] *L'idée du sacrifice de la Messe,* pp. 698 f., 745 f.

[91] Apoc. 5:6.

[92] John 19:40.

[93] *Summa theol.,* IIIa, q. 22, a. 5, c.

[94] Cf. Heb. 7:24 f.; 9:12 f., 24 f.; 10:12 f.; I Cor. 15:55 f.; Rom. 6:6 f.; Col. 2:14 f.; see Bossuet, *Sermon pour la fête de tous les saints;* Monsabré, *Exposition du dogme catholique, carême,* 1879. This same doctrine has also been well explained by J. Grimal, *Le sacerdoce et le sacrifice de N. S. J. Chr.,* pp. 189–228; A. Michel, *Dict. théol. cath.,* art. "Jésus-Christ," cols. 1340–42; J. M. Hervé, *Manual théol. dogm.,* II, 587 f.

The sacrifice of the cross, however, is not actually but virtually perpetuated in its consummation; for it is more perfect to reach consummation than to tend toward it, and the mystical body already glorified is more perfect than the mystical body not yet glorified. Likewise, generally speaking, merit is subordinated to the reward toward which it tends.

CHAPTER XL

COMPENDIUM OF MARIOLOGY

THESE questions have been discussed fully enough in a special book.[1] Therefore we shall give a very brief explanation of them in the present treatise, considering them in their speculative aspect, as they pertain to the body of theological doctrine.

First Article

THE EMINENT DIGNITY OF THE DIVINE MOTHERHOOD

The Blessed Virgin Mary is the Mother of Christ, and is therefore truly and properly the Mother of God, as defined by the Council of Ephesus.[2] St. Thomas says: "Conception and birth are attributed to the person and hypostasis in respect of that nature in which it is conceived and born. Since, therefore, the human nature was taken by the divine person (of the Word) in the very beginning of the conception, it follows that it can be truly said that God was conceived and born of the Virgin Mary." [3] Hence she is truly the Mother of God.

The Blessed Virgin Mary was first predestined to this divine motherhood and then as a consequence of this to fullness of glory and grace, so as to be worthy of being the Mother of God.[4] This is sufficiently clear from the bull of Pope Pius IX in which it is said: "The ineffable God from the beginning and from all eternity chose and ordained for His only-begotten Son, a mother from whom His Son

[1] *La Mère du Sauveur et notre vie intérieure.* See also Bittremieux, *De meditatione universali B. M. Virginis quoad gratias;* B. H. Merkelbach, O.P., *Mariologia;* Friethoff, O.P., *De Alma Socia Christi mediatoris; Dict. théol. cath.,* art. "Marie" (Duplanchy).

[2] Denz., no. 113; see also nos. 218, 290, 708, 993, 1462.

[3] *Summa theol.,* IIIa, q. 35, a. 4.

[4] *Ibid.,* q. 27, a. 5.

took flesh so as to be born in the blessed fullness of time, and pursued her with such great love above all creatures, so as to find the greatest of delight in her." [5] A little farther on it says: "By one and the same decree [He chose her] along with the Incarnation of divine wisdom." [6]

In other words, the eternal decree of the Incarnation is not directed toward the quasi-abstract Incarnation, but toward the Incarnation here and now to be brought into being or, so to speak, individualized; that is, it concerns the incarnation of God's Son from the Virgin Mary, as stated in the Nicene-Constantinopolitan symbol.[7]

Therefore by the same eternal decree Christ as man was predestined to be by nature the Son of God, and the Blessed Virgin Mary to be the Mother of God. But this decree is antecedent to the predestinating decree of men who are to be saved by Christ's merits, and of whatsoever other human persons to glory and grace. Therefore the Blessed Virgin Mary was predestined to be the Mother of God, as to what was principally intended, prior to being predestined to glory, just as Christ was predestined to be the Son of God by nature, as to what was principally intended, prior to being predestined to glory. That to which anyone is first predestined is called the end, and is nobler than any other things to which a person is afterward predestined. From this it is already apparent that divine motherhood is nobler than fullness of grace and glory, which is a consequence of the former and which accompanies it so as to render the Blessed Virgin worthy of being the Mother of God.

This superiority of divine motherhood is evident also for several other reasons. First, because the Blessed Virgin Mary could indeed merit eternal life, but she could not merit the Incarnation, which is the eminent principle of all Mary's merits, just as it is of all men after the Fall, and hence she could not merit the divine motherhood, which is closely connected with the Incarnation, and which, like the Incarnation, transcends the sphere of merit.[8] From what has been said it

[5] *Ineffabilis Deus.*

[6] *Ibid.*

[7] Denz., no. 86.

[8] The Blessed Virgin Mary did not even merit congruously in the strict sense the Incarnation and the divine motherhood, because the principle of merit does not come under merit, as Billuart well explains, *De incarnatione,* diss. V, a. 3; for the Incarnation and future merits of Christ are the foundation and principle of all the Blessed Virgin Mary's merits and not the effects. From this it would also follow that the Blessed Virgin Mary merited something better than Christ Himself merited; and

is also apparent that the Blessed Virgin Mary's predestination is entirely gratuitous.

Secondly, the divine motherhood is a dignity which by reason of its terminus whereunto, namely, the Word incarnate, belongs to the hypostatic order, which transcends the order of grace and glory.

Thirdly, the divine motherhood is the reason for all the graces bestowed upon the Blessed Virgin Mary. Thus it is their measure and end, and is therefore of a higher order than these. Such is the common teaching of the theologians.

Fourthly, the divine motherhood is the motive for the cultus of hyperdulia paid to Mary, to which she would not be entitled if she were only full of grace and the highest of all the saints, but not Mother of God.[9]

Fifthly, it follows from this that the divine motherhood is also considered in itself superior to the fullness of grace that was granted to Mary so as to render her worthy of being the Mother of God. So also in the natural order the spiritual soul, even considered in itself, because it belongs to the substantial order, is more perfect than its intellectual faculty, although it is perfected by this latter.[10]

Second Article

THE IMMACULATE CONCEPTION OF THE BLESSED VIRGIN MARY

The plenitude of grace in Mary was first made manifest through the privilege of the Immaculate Conception, which was more and more explicitly admitted in the Church, and was finally solemnly defined by Pope Pius IX on December 8, 1854.[11] Pius IX says in this definition: "We define the doctrine that holds the Blessed Virgin Mary in the first instant of her conception was by a singular grace and privilege of almighty God, in view of the merits of Jesus Christ the Savior of the human race, preserved exempt from all stain of original sin, and that this is a doctrine revealed by God and therefore must be believed firmly and constantly by all the faithful." [12]

so the Incarnation would not be a work of pure mercy, for congruous merit, strictly so called, implies an amicable right to a reward as a compensation.

But the Blessed Virgin Mary merited congruously in the broad sense the Incarnation and divine motherhood.

[9] See reply of Congregation of Rites, June 1, 1884.

[10] Cf. *La Mère du Sauveur,* pp. 24 f.

[11] Denz., no. 1641; see also, nos. 256, 734 f., 792, 1073, 1100, 3035.

[12] *Ibid.,* no. 1641.

This privilege, according to the bull of definition, is implicitly affirmed by the archangel Gabriel to Mary on the day of the Annunciation, who said: "Hail, full of grace, the Lord is with thee, blessed art thou among women"; [13] and St. Elizabeth uttered similar words.[14] The Blessed Virgin Mary would not have received this fullness of grace if her soul at any moment had been in a state of spiritual death because of original sin, that is, if at any moment she had been without sanctifying grace and charity, and therefore turned away from God the ultimate end, a daughter of wrath, whom the devil could have claimed as having once been his slave.

This is especially evident from tradition, as this same bull declares, for it quotes the testimonies of St. Justin, St. Irenaeus, Tertullian, St. Ephrem, St. Ambrose, and St. Augustine.[15] The feast of the Conception of the Blessed Virgin Mary has been celebrated especially in the Greek Church since the seventh century, and almost in the whole of Europe since the twelfth century.

The theological proof for this privilege completes by the notion of preservative redemption what St. Thomas had said for the sanctification of the Blessed Virgin Mary in the womb before her birth. He had said: "For it is reasonable to believe that she who brought forth the only-begotten of the Father, full of grace and truth, received greater privileges of grace than all others." [16]

Now it must be said to be fitting that the most excellent Redeemer most perfectly redeemed the person who was most closely connected with Him as Mother and associated with Him in the redemption of the human race. But most perfect redemption liberates not only from sin, but also preserves from sin. Therefore it was far more fitting that the most excellent Redeemer, by His merits, that were of infinite value, preserve His mother from original sin and also from actual sin, as tradition affirms.

This argument was proposed by Eadmer in the twelfth century, and was afterward more clearly explained by Scotus,[17] and is valid even regardless of the special opinion held by Scotus concerning the motive of the Incarnation.

[13] Luke 1:28.

[14] *Ibid.*, 1:42.

[15] Cf. P. Le Bachelet, *Dict. apol.*, art. "Marie," Immaculate Conception, cols. 210–75. Rouet de Journel, *Ench. patrist.*, no. 435.

[16] Cf. IIIa, q. 27, a. 1.

[17] *Com. in III Sent.*, d. 3, q. 1, et *Reportata*, Bk. III, d. 3, q. 1.

The bull of definition declares that it is not fitting for the most perfect Redeemer to have had a Mother conceived in sin.

The consequences of the particular privilege of the Immaculate Conception are that the Blessed Virgin Mary never had concupiscence, and never had any absolutely first deordinate movements arising in her sensitive nature, but that there was always perfect subordination of her sensitive nature to the intellect and will, which were fully in subjection to the divine good pleasure, as in the state of innocence. Thus the Blessed Virgin is inviolate and undefiled.

Her intellect was never exposed to either error or illusion, so that she was always correct in her judgments, and if she was not at any time enlightened about anything, then she suspended her judgment, avoiding all precipitation. Thus she is called Seat of Wisdom, Queen of Doctors, Virgin most Prudent, Mother of Good Counsel.

In what way was she subjected to pain and death? She submitted to it as Christ did, inasmuch as pain and death were in her not the result of original sin, but of human nature or of the body conceived in passible flesh. For human nature of itself, just like all animal nature, is subjected to pain and death, and man is by nature mortal. The human body in the state of innocence was endowed with the preternatural gift of immortality, but when this was taken away, then the laws of nature at once came into operation. But Jesus, that He might be our Redeemer by His passion and death, was conceived in passible flesh, and thus willingly accepted pain and death for our salvation. The Blessed Virgin Mary also accepted pain and death, so that she might be united with her Son in the sacrifice of redemption.

The privilege of the Immaculate Conception and the beginning of the fullness of grace very much increased in Mary her capacity of grieving for the greatest of all evils, which is sin. It is precisely because she was most pure, and loved God and her Son in the very highest degree, that she grieved to the utmost for our sins, whereby God is offended and for which Christ was crucified.

THE TEACHING OF ST. THOMAS ON THE IMMACULATE CONCEPTION

It seems that we must distinguish between three periods in the life of St. Thomas as to his teaching on this subject.

In the first period, which was from 1253 to 1254, he affirmed the privilege, for he wrote: "Such was the purity of the Blessed Virgin

Mary, who was exempt from both original and actual sin."[18]

In the second period, St. Thomas sees more clearly the difficulties of the problem, and, because some theologians said that Mary had no need of redemption, the holy Doctor affirms that, according to revelation,[19] Christ is the Redeemer of the human race, and that nobody is saved without him. But giving no thought to preservative redemption, St. Thomas seems to deny the privilege of the Immaculate Conception, saying: "It remains, therefore, that the Blessed Virgin was sanctified after animation."[20] St. Thomas fails to distinguish, as he often does in other questions, between posteriority of nature, which is compatible with the privilege, and posteriority of time, which is incompatible with it. He says: "The Blessed Virgin did indeed, contract original sin,"[21] not sufficiently distinguishing between the debt of incurring original sin and the fact of incurring it.

Concerning the question as to the precise moment when the Blessed Virgin was sanctified in the womb, St. Thomas does not come to any conclusion. He only says: "This sanctification took place immediately after her animation,"[22] and "it is not known when she was sanctified."[23]

It must be observed with Fathers del Prado, O.P.,[24] Mandonnet, O.P.,[25] and Hugon, O.P.,[26] that the principles invoked by St. Thomas do not contradict the privilege and remain intact if preservative redemption be admitted. But St. Thomas, at least in this second period of his life as teacher, does not seem to have thought of this most perfect mode of redemption. Moreover, it must be noticed that the feast of the Conception of the Blessed Virgin was not as yet celebrated in Rome;[27] but what is not done in Rome, does not appear to be in conformity with tradition.

In the last period of his life, however, from 1272 until 1273, St. Thomas wrote a work that is certainly authentic.[28] In a recent critical

[18] *Com. in I Sent.,* d. 44, q. 1, a. 3, ad 3.

[19] Rom. 3:23; 5:12, 19; Gal. 3:22; II Cor. 5:14; I Tim. 2:6.

[20] Cf. IIIa, q. 27, a. 2.

[21] *Ibid.,* ad 2.

[22] Quodl. VI, a. 7.

[23] Cf. IIIa, q. 27, a. 2, ad 3.

[24] Santo Tomas y la Immaculada.

[25] *Dict. théol. cath.,* art. "Frères-Prêcheurs," col. 899.

[26] *Tractatus dogmatici,* II, 749.

[27] Cf. IIIa, q. 27, a. 2, ad 3.

[28] This work is entitled *"Expositio super salutatione angelica."*

edition of this small work made by J. F. Rossi, C.M., we read: "For she [the Blessed Virgin] was most pure because she incurred the stain neither of original sin nor of mortal sin nor of venial sin." [29] If it be so, then St. Thomas at the end of his life, after mature reflection, and in accordance with his devotion toward the Blessed Virgin, again affirmed what he had said in the first period of his life.[30]

We must note other passages indicative of this happy return to his first opinion.[31]

A similar change of opinion is often enough to be found in great theologians concerning very difficult questions that belong to Mariology. First something of the privilege is affirmed in accordance with tradition and devotion; afterward difficulties become more apparent which give rise to doubts, and finally upon more mature reflection, enlightened by the gifts of the Holy Ghost, the theologian returns to his first opinion, considering that God's gifts are more fruitful than we think and there must be good reasons for restricting their scope. But the principles of St. Thomas, as we have observed, do not decide against the privilege, they even lead to it, at the same time as the mind is acquiring an explicit notion of preservative redemption.

Thus St. Thomas probably at the end of life reaffirmed the privilege of the Immaculate Conception. Father Mandonnet [32] and Father J. M. Vosté [33] thought so.

[29] Cf. *Divus Thomas,* pp. 445–79, and *Monografie del Collegio Alberoni.* Sixteen out of the nineteen codices have the words "nec originale"; hence Father Rossi concludes that the text is authentic.

[30] Cf. *Com. in I Sent.,* d. 44, q. 1, a. 3, ad 3.

[31] Cf. *Compendium theologiae,* chap. 224, wherein we read: "Not only was the Blessed Virgin Mary immune from actual sin, but also from original sin, being purified in a special manner." But it would not have been a special privilege if she had been purified as Jeremias and St. John the Baptist had been in the womb, some time after her animation. Likewise in the explanation of the Lord's Prayer, the fifth petition, St. Thomas says: "Full of grace, in whom there was no sin." Also in the *Com. in Ps.* 14:2, we read: "There was absolutely no stain of sin both in Christ and the Blessed Virgin Mary." Also *Com. in Ps.* 18:6, he writes: "There was no obscurity of sin in the Blessed Virgin."

[32] *Bulletin thomiste,* January to March, 1933, pp. 164–67.

[33] See his *Com. in Summam theol. S. Thomae.* De mysteriis vitae Christi; 18 f. In the explanation of the Hail Mary, St. Thomas still says: "The Blessed Virgin was conceived in original sin," but, as Father Vosté observes: "Unless we admit an intolerable contradiction in this same passage, it must evidently be understood . . . as referring to the stain that is to be instrumentally transmitted through the seed and the flesh, but not at all of formal original sin personally, contracted by the soul and person of Mary."

Third Article

THE BLESSED VIRGIN MARY WAS PRESERVED FROM ALL ACTUAL SIN, EVEN VENIAL SIN

The Council of Trent declares the belief of tradition in the following words: "If anyone shall say that a man once justified . . . is able, during his whole life, to avoid all sins, even those that are venial, except by a special privilege from God, as the Church holds concerning the Blessed Virgin, let him be anathema." [34]

St. Hippolytus, St. Irenaeus, St. Justin, Tertullian, and St. Ambrose are quoted as witnesses of tradition, who place opposition between Eve and Mary, and St. Augustine says: "About the holy Virgin Mary, on account of the Lord's honor, concerning sins, I will that no questions at all be raised." [35]

St. Thomas gives the theological proof in the following words: "God so prepares and endows those whom He chooses for some particular office, that they are rendered capable of fulfilling it, for St. Paul says: 'Who hath made us fit ministers of the New Testament.' [36] But she would not have been worthy to be the Mother of God if she had ever sinned. . . . So that what is written is fulfilled: 'Thou are all fair, O my love, and there is not a spot in thee.' " [37]

Mary was not only sinless but incapable of sinning, yet not absolutely so and in her own right as Christ was, but in virtue of the confirmation of grace that was granted her from the beginning and because of the special assistance of divine providence. This special assistance was the effect of the Blessed Virgin Mary's predestination, and under this particular help she retained her complete freedom in the performance of good, without deviating from the right path. This is a participation in the immortality and impeccability of God's supreme liberty.

It is the common teaching of theologians that the Blessed Virgin was also preserved from every imperfection, either directly or indirectly willed, which means that she was never less prompt in following the inspirations of grace given by way of counsel, and her acts of charity did not vary in intensity.

[34] Denz., no. 833.
[35] *De natura et gratia,* 36.
[36] II Cor. 3:6.
[37] Cf. IIIa, q. 27, a. 4; Cant. 4:7.

Fourth Article

THE BEGINNING OF PERFECTION IN THE BLESSED VIRGIN'S FULLNESS OF GRACE

Pius IX says: "The ineffable God . . . from the beginning and from all eternity chose and ordained for His only-begotten Son a mother from whom His Son took flesh, so as to be born in the blessed fullness of time, and pursued her with such great love above all creatures so as to find the greatest of delight in her. Wherefore, far excelling all the angelic spirits and the saints, He so enriched her with an abundance of all heavenly charismata drawn from the treasury of His divine nature, that always absolutely free from all stain of sin, and all beautiful and perfect as she is, He might present in her a fullness of innocence and sanctity, greater than which, after God, cannot at all be known and, after God, no one can be thought to attain." [38]

St. Thomas manifests the fitness of this privilege by this principle: "In every genus the nearer a thing is to the principle, the greater the part it has in the effect of that principle. . . . But Christ is the principle of grace, authoritatively as to His Godhead, instrumentally as to His humanity. But the Blessed Virgin Mary was nearest to Christ in His humanity, because He received His human nature from her. Therefore it was due to her to receive a greater fullness of grace than others." [39]

If this incipient fullness of grace in the Blessed Virgin is compared with the final grace of men and angels before their entrance into heaven, theologians commonly teach that this beginning of fullness already surpassed the final grace of any man or angel whatever. This is today considered certain and is expressed by Pius IX.[40]

The reason is that grace is the effect of God's active love, which makes us pleasing in His eyes, as His adopted sons. But the Blessed Virgin from the first moment of her conception, destined to be the Mother of God, was loved by Him more than any saint or angel whatever. Therefore the Blessed Virgin received greater grace than any of them. Moreover, this incipient fullness of grace was already a worthy preparation, although remote, for divine motherhood, which

[38] Bull *Ineffabilis Deus.*
[39] *Summa theol.,* IIIa, q. 27, a. 5.
[40] Bull *Ineffabilis Deus.*

transcends the order of grace inasmuch as terminatively it belongs to the hypostatic order.

In fact, the majority of theologians now teach as most probable, if not certain, that this incipient fullness of grace in the Blessed Virgin already transcended the final grace of all the saints and angels taken together.

Pius IX evidently favors this view, for he says: "God pursued her with such great love above all creatures, so as to find the greatest delight in her. Wherefore, far above all the angelic spirits and the saints, He so enriched her with grace . . . , and this fullness of grace is, after God, the greatest conceivable." [41]

But these expressions denote not only every one of the saints and angels, but all of them taken together. In fact, a little farther on in this papal bull, the Blessed Virgin is said to be "above all the choirs of angels," [42] that is, all the angels taken together.

This assertion is conceded by all concerning Mary as she is in heaven, but the degree of glory in heaven corresponds to the degree of merit at the moment of death, and this in the Blessed Virgin was in proportion to her dignity as Mother of God, for which the incipient fullness of grace already disposed her.

The theological proof of the aforesaid teaching, which is more generally accepted, is this. A person that is loved more by God than all creatures taken together, received greater grace. But God from all eternity loved Mary more than all creatures taken together, because He loved her as His future mother. Therefore He enriched her with a greater fullness of grace. And He considered her as His future mother from the first moment of her conception, in fact from all eternity, when He predestined her to divine motherhood.

Moreover, if this incipient fullness of grace surpasses the final grace of the highest saint or the highest angel, for this reason it surpasses the grace of all the saints taken together, for grace does not belong to the quantitative order, but to the qualitative order.

Thus the intelligence of an archangel surpasses the intelligence of all angels inferior to him. The intellectual vigor of St. Thomas exceeds that of all his commentators taken together. Likewise the power of the king not only surpasses the power of his prime minister, but of all his ministers taken together.

[41] *Ibid.*
[42] *Ibid.*

Hence the Blessed Virgin even in this life, without the cooperation of the saints and angels, could obtain more by her prayers and merits than all the saints and angels taken together could obtain without her.

The consequences of this beginning in the fullness of grace are that all the infused virtues, and the seven gifts of the Holy Ghost, which are connected with charity, were from the beginning in Mary in a proportionate degree.

Moreover, many theologians think that the Blessed Virgin more probably received, through infused knowledge, the use of reason and of free will from the first moment of her conception, for the purpose of offering herself to God and for the purpose that this beginning in the fullness of the graces of the virtues and gifts might produce fruit in her. It is also probable that she was not afterward deprived of this use of free will, because thus she would have become less perfect through no fault of her own.[43]

Fifth Article

THE BLESSED VIRGIN MARY'S INCREASE IN GRACE

Whereas Christ received in the first moment of His conception, absolute fullness of grace, for the Second Council of Constantinople says, "He never was made better in the advancement of good works," [44] the Blessed Virgin Mary always was made better until death, increasing in the grace of the virtues and the gifts. Just as a stone falls more swiftly as it approaches the ground, so, says St. Thomas, the just soul more promptly goes to God the more it approaches Him and is attracted and drawn by Him.[45] Thus there was always an increase of progress in the Blessed Virgin Mary.

This spiritual progress in the Blessed Virgin Mary was the fruit of merit and prayer.

It was especially on the day of the Annunciation at the moment

[43] This point has been more fully examined by us in *La Mère du Sauveur,* pp. 77 f., in which we quote authors who admit this opinion, especially St. Francis de Sales (Sermon 38) and St. Alphonsus (*Glories of Mary,* II, discourse 2, second point).

[44] Denz., no. 224.

[45] St. Thomas says (*Com. in Epist. ad Heb.* 10:25): "The natural motion (for example of a falling stone), the more swift it becomes, the more it approaches its destined end. . . . But grace inclines the will after the manner of nature. Therefore those who are in a state of grace must all the more increase in it, the more they approach their end . . . for the path of the just, as a shining light, goeth forwards and increaseth even to perfect day" (Prov. 4:18).

of the Incarnation that she received a great increase of grace. Then when the Word was made flesh, she received this Word with the greatest fervor, and the Incarnation by reason of the operation effected (*ex opere operato*) produced in her a great increase of grace more so than Eucharistic Communion does in a person very well disposed.

The spiritual joy of the Blessed Virgin Mary was made manifest on the day she uttered her canticle of praise, when visiting Elizabeth.[46]

The Church has defined [47] that the holy Mother of God was a virgin before her parturition, in her parturition, and after parturition, and always remained a virgin; wherefore she did not need to be purified.[48] The Fathers of the Church have often said this.[49] St. Thomas says: "The error of Helvidius, who dared to assert that Christ's Mother, after His birth, was carnally known by Joseph, and bore other children . . . is derogatory to Christ's perfection . . . , is an insult to the Holy Ghost . . . , and is derogatory to the dignity and holiness of God's Mother, for thus she would seem to be most ungrateful, were she not content with such a Son, and were she of her own accord, by carnal intercourse to forfeit that virginity which had been miraculously preserved in her." [50]

Then the grace of the virtues and the gifts was in a special manner increased in Mary on the day of our Lord's birth, on the day when Jesus was presented in the Temple, during His flight into Egypt, afterward when the holy family lived in Nazareth. But this grace was especially increased in her on Mount Calvary, when the mother of our Savior was intimately associated with the sacrifice of her Son, also on the day of Pentecost, and when she most fervently received Holy Communion from the hands of St. John the Evangelist.

Therefore the Blessed Virgin Mary had the greatest of faith, illumined by the gifts of understanding, wisdom, and knowledge, and hence her knowledge of Sacred Scripture was profound, especially as regards those things that are more closely related to the mysteries of the Incarnation and Redemption.

It is commonly held that she was exempt not only from error, but also from ignorance in the strict sense, which is a privation in a fit

[46] Luke 1:46 f.
[47] Denz., nos. 91, 256, 282, 993, 3029.
[48] *Ibid.*, no. 1314.
[49] Cf. Rouet de Journel's *Enchiridion patrist.*, no. 432.
[50] *Summa theol.*, IIIa, q. 28, a. 3.

subject. Certain things she did not know, but she was not ignorant of those things which it befitted her to know.

It is more probable that she had infused knowledge for the use of reason and free will from the first moment of her conception, and afterward was not deprived of this use, because she would have become less perfect through no fault of her own.

From her Canticle of the Magnificat it is evident that she had the gift of prophecy. Like many of the saints, she also received the gift of discernment of spirits, especially in giving counsel to those who appealed to her. Finally, perhaps toward the end of her life, she had the beatific vision in a transient manner, as St. Augustine and St. Thomas affirm that St. Paul probably had.

The principal virtues of the Blessed Virgin Mary were her most firm hope, especially her heroic charity on Mount Calvary, eminent prudence, enlightened by the gift of counsel, justice always tempered by the greatest mercy, the greatest of piety, invincible fortitude, most renowned virginity, exceeding meekness, and most profound humility. Thus she is the exemplar of the contemplative life in the hidden apostolate made most fruitful by prayer and sacrifice.

Sixth Article

THE FINAL PLENITUDE OF GRACE IN MARY

1) What was this plenitude at the moment of death? The immaculate Mother of God did not die on account of original sin; [51] her death, like that of Christ, as we have said, was not the result of sin but of nature, or of natural consequences, inasmuch as she was conceived in passible flesh, as Christ was, for man is by nature mortal.

In union with her Son on Calvary she offered the sacrifice of the cross and the sacrifice of her own life, and, as St. John Damascene,[52] St. Francis de Sales,[53] and Bossuet [54] testify and explain, she died not only in love, but from love for her divine Son, that is, from a strong desire of seeing God immediately and forever. In accordance with this final plenitude of grace and charity, her soul was ultimately disposed for the beatific vision.

2) The assumption of the Blessed Virgin Mary. According to

[51] Denz., no. 1073.
[52] *Homiliae duae de dormitione Virginis Mariae.*
[53] *Amour de Dieu,* Bk. VII, chaps. 13, 14.
[54] *Premier Sermon pour la fête de l'Assomption,* ler point.

documents of tradition the feast of the Assumption has been solemnly celebrated both in the Latin Church and in the Greek Church since the seventh century. But this solemn feast is the liturgical expression of the ordinary magisterial teaching of the whole Church, for the law of praying is the law of believing, and this presupposes that the privilege of the Assumption is certain and at least implicitly revealed. The Blessed Virgin Mary's entrance into heaven could not be naturally known with certainty; even though the apostles saw His body rise from the ground as to its term wherefrom, they did not see it as to its term whereunto as St. Thomas says of our Lord's ascension.[55] Therefore the certainty of the Assumption as expressed in the institution of this solemn feast can be the result only of at least implicit revelation.

That this privilege, however, was implicitly revealed, is evident from especially two traditionally alleged theological reasons. For the Blessed Virgin Mary according to the angelic salutation was "full of grace and blessed among women." [56] But this exceptional benediction excludes the malediction, "Unto dust thou shalt return." [57] Therefore the body of the Blessed Virgin Mary was under no obligation to suffer the corruption of the tomb.

Moreover, according to the words of Simeon, "And thy own soul a sword shall pierce," [58] the Blessed Virgin Mary was closely associated on Calvary with Christ's perfect victory over the devil and sin. Therefore she was associated with Christ's perfect victory over death, which is a part of the victory over the devil, and victory over sin follows, inasmuch as "death is the wages of sin." [59] But perfect victory over death requires that the Mother of God "could not have been held down by the bonds of death." [60] Therefore this victory requires an anticipated resurrection and assumption. Thus the privilege of the Assumption seems proximately definable as one hundred and ninety-seven Fathers of the Vatican Council postulated. Denzinger also points out: "Concerning the Assumption of the Blessed Virgin Mary, at the time of the Vatican Council two hundred and four bishops and theologians urged its dogmatic definition since, unless

[55] *Summa theol.,* IIIa, q. 55, a. 2, ad 2.
[56] Luke 1:28.
[57] Gen. 3:16 f.
[58] Luke 2:35.
[59] Rom. 6:23.
[60] Hymn *Veneranda* in Ambrosian and Dominican rites.

we wish to say that the most firm faith of the Church savors too much of slight credulity, which it is impious to think, without doubt it is of divine and apostolic tradition, that is, it must be most firmly held to have been revealed." [61]

3) The final plenitude of the Blessed Virgin Mary's grace received its confirmation in heaven for she was raised "above the choirs of angels" [62] as the liturgy says, to the highest degree of essential glory or of the beatific vision after Christ, as His worthy Mother, who was intimately associated with Him in the work of our salvation, and reached the highest degree of charity after Him. The degree of glory corresponds to the degree of merits acquired at the end of this life.

But the accidental beatitude of the Blessed Virgin Mary consists in the intimate knowledge of Christ's glorious human nature, in the functioning of her office as universal mediatrix and spiritual mother, and in the cult of hyperdulia that is owing to her as Mother of God. To her is attributed the threefold aureole of martyrs, confessors of the faith, and virgins.

Seventh Article

THE BLESSED VIRGIN MARY'S UNIVERSAL MEDIATION

The holy Mother of the Redeemer is often called by the Fathers "the new Eve" or the spiritual mother of all men.[63] Afterward, more and more explicitly her universal mediation was affirmed in the liturgy and in the works of theologians. In the Middle Ages St. Bernard says: "Mary is the procurer of grace, the mediator of salvation, the restorer of the ages." [64] St. Albert the Great calls Mary "the coadjutor and associate of Christ." [65] Finally, in most recent times, the Supreme Pontiffs expressly affirm that she is the mediatrix of all graces.

Leo XIII says: "It is God's will that nothing be bestowed on us ex-

[61] *Enchiridion,* no. 1641, note 1; see also *Coll. Lacensis,* VII, 868 f.; and Appendix: The definability of the Blessed Virgin Mary's Assumption.

[62] Responsory for Vespers of Assumption.

[63] Cf. Rouet de Journel, *Enchir. patrist.,* no. 433. St. Cyril of Jerusalem, St. Epiphanius, St. Jerome, St. John Chrysostom, and St. Ephrem are quoted, agreeing substantially in praying: "Hail, best mediatrix between God and men. Hail, most efficacious conciliatrix . . . and after the Mediator, the Mediatrix of the whole world." Cf. St. Ephrem, *Opera omnia,* Vol. III, col. 528.

[64] *Epist.* 174.

[65] *Mariali,* q. 42.

cept through Mary; so that, as nobody can reach the supreme Father except through the Son, so that almost nobody can approach Christ except through Mary."[66] Leo XIII also says: "She is the one from whom Jesus was born, His true Mother, and for this reason the worthy and most accepted Mediatrix to the Mediator."[67]

Pius X more explicitly declared: "But from the communion of griefs and purpose between Mary and Christ she merited, as Eadmer says, to become most worthily the reparatrix of a lost world, and therefore the dispenser of all the gifts which Jesus procured for us by His death and the shedding of His blood. . . . Since she excelled all others in sanctity and in her union with Christ and was summoned by Him in the human work of salvation, it was congruous, as they say, that she should merit for us what Christ condignly merited for us; and she is the principal minister in the dispensation of graces."[68]

Benedict XV likewise says: "As she suffered with her Son in His passion and, so to speak, shared in His death, so she abdicated her maternal rights over her Son for the salvation of men and, as far as it was in her power, sacrificed her Son for the appeasement of divine justice, so that it can truly be said, that along with Christ she redeemed the human race."[69]

Pius XI said in equivalent words: "The most sorrowful Mother participated in the work of redemption with Jesus Christ."[70]

Finally, a decree of the Sacred Congregation of the Holy Office praises the custom of attaching the name of Jesus to that of Mary: "His Mother, our coredemptress, the blessed Mary."[71] Therefore the title "Coredemptress of the human race" is approved.[72]

Theological proof. It shows the genuineness of this title, for in the strict sense this title of coredemptress and universal mediatrix befits the Mother of the Redeemer, if she is associated with Christ in the work of the redemption of the human race by way of merit and satisfaction. But she was truly so associated with Him by a perfect communion of will and suffering, inasmuch as she gave her consent to the mystery of the Incarnation. Thus she gave us the Redeemer, and

[66] Encyclical, *On the Rosary,* September 22, 1891.
[67] Encyclical *Fidentem,* September 20, 1896.
[68] Denz., no. 3034.
[69] *Litt. Apost.; "Inter sodalicia,"* March 22, 1918.
[70] *Litt. Apost.; "Explorata res,"* February 2, 1923.
[71] Section, *De indulgentiis,* decree "Sunt quos amor," June 26, 1913.
[72] Denz., no. 3034 note.

afterward, especially on Calvary, along with Christ congruously merited and satisfied for all of us; now finally in heaven she intercedes with Christ for us and distributes all graces we receive. Therefore the aforesaid title strictly befits her.

But this association with Christ the Redeemer is properly understood when we exclude what it is not. Certainly the Blessed Virgin Mary was not the principal and perfective cause of our redemption, for she could not condignly redeem us in justice. For this, Christ's theandric act of infinite value, as the head of the human race, was necessary. The Mother of the Savior could not elicit a theandric act of reparation, nor was she constituted the head of the human race. But, subordinated to Christ, she is really the secondary and dispositive cause of our redemption.

It is said "subordinated to Christ" not only in this sense, that she is inferior to Him, but that she concurs in our salvation, by the grace which comes from Christ's merits. Thus she operated in Him and through Him. Hence Christ is the supreme mediator of all, and the Blessed Virgin Mary was redeemed by Him by a most perfect redemption, not by being freed from sin, but by being preserved from it.

She is also the dispositive cause of our redemption, inasmuch as she disposes us to receive Christ's influence who, as the author of salvation, perfects the work of our redemption.

Some have raised the objection, that the principle of merit does not come under merit. But the Blessed Virgin Mary was redeemed by the sacrifice of the cross. Therefore she could not even congruously merit the attainment of graces for us.

Reply. I concede the major and minor, but the conclusion does not follow. All that follows is that she could not even congruously merit the attainment of all these graces for herself, this I concede. But she could merit these for us.

Christ merited condignly all the effects of the Blessed Virgin Mary's predestination, except the divine motherhood, because in such a case He would have merited the Incarnation and therefore Himself. Hence Christ merited the first grace and final perseverance for the Blessed Virgin Mary. But the Blessed Virgin Mary did not even congruously merit for herself either the first grace or final perseverance, because the principle of merit does not come under merit. But the Blessed Virgin Mary merited for us congruously what Christ merited for us condignly, namely, all the graces we receive, even the first grace and final perseverance. In this there is no contradiction, but great harmony.

Hence the Blessed Virgin Mary was indeed redeemed by Christ through the sacrifice of the cross in the preservative sense, and so she was immaculate; but as a consequence of this, she merited congruously with Christ for us, not only the distribution or application of graces, but the attainment of graces that flow from the sacrifice of the cross; for in the strict sense together with Christ she offered this sacrifice. Thus she merited with Him redemption in the objective sense, namely, our liberation from sin and our reinstatement in grace.

But I insist. The Blessed Virgin Mary merited congruously for us what, for example, St. Monica congruously merited and obtained for St. Augustine, namely, the grace of conversion. Therefore there is only a difference of degree between her and other saints who intercede for us, and it must not be said that she is the coredemptrix in the strict sense, but only in an improper sense, as the apostles are said to have labored for the salvation of souls.

Reply. The difference is that the Blessed Virgin Mary gave us the Redeemer, and with Him offered the sacrifice of the cross by meriting and satisfying. St. Monica and other saints, on the contrary, did not offer with Christ the sacrifice of the cross, and therefore did not merit congruously the attainment of graces that flow from this sacrifice but only the application of these, and therefore cannot be called coredeemers. They can be said only to labor in the salvation of souls. They did not merit congruously our redemption in the objective sense.

Hence St. Albert the Great could say that the Blessed Virgin Mary is not assumed into the ministry of our Lord, but as a consort and help, in accordance with the saying: "Let us make him a help like unto himself" (Gen. 2:18).[73] In this the Blessed Virgin is above the apostles and she alone can be properly called the mediatrix and coredemptrix of the human race.

THE WAY THE BLESSED VIRGIN MARY MERITED THE LIBERATION AND RESTORATION OF THE HUMAN RACE

In these times, as is known, in divers theological periodicals, especially in Belgium, and also in Italy, France, Spain, and Germany, there was and still is a controversy concerning the exact meaning of this doctrine that is commonly accepted among theologians and is sanctioned by Pius XI, namely, that what Christ merited *de condigno*

[73] *Mariale,* q. 42.

for us, the Blessed Virgin Mary merited *de congruo* for us as the mediatrix of the human race.

What is the exact meaning of saying that the Blessed Virgin Mary merited *de congruo* for us? Many theologians say that, although she did not merit condignly, yet she still merited in the proper sense, or strictly congruously, the liberation and restoration of the human race. The Blessed Virgin Mary properly merited for us *de congruo* also the first grace and also the last grace, namely, that of final perseverance, but under Christ, through Him and in Him, inasmuch as she was most closely and indissolubly united with Him in offering up the sacrifice of the cross.

Among these theologians, some, a few indeed, hint and sometimes say that merit in the strict sense is condign merit. Therefore the Blessed Virgin Mary, if she strictly merited for us the first grace, merited it also condignly, which is admitted by very few theologians.

Against this last conclusion several wrote that this would detract from the primacy of Christ the Redeemer, by whom the Blessed Virgin Mary was redeemed by preservative redemption, and they appealed to the common teaching as formulated by St. Thomas, who says: "No one can merit condignly for another the first grace, except Christ alone . . . inasmuch as He is the head of the Church, and the Author of human salvation." [74] In fact, some, but a few, replied that merit in the strict sense is condign merit; but the common teaching is that the Blessed Virgin Mary did not merit condignly for us. Therefore she did not merit properly but only improperly for us the first and the ultimate grace.

Therefore these last theologians wish to reduce the Blessed Mary's merit for us to merit improperly so called or to the impetratory power of prayer, which can be in the sinner without merit, and which continues now in the blessed with merit. They interpret the following words of Pius X in this sense: "Since she excelled all others in sanctity and in her union with Christ, and was summoned by Him to the work of human salvation, it was congruous, as they say, that she should merit for us what Christ condignly merited for us." [75] According to this interpretation Pius X, concerning the merit of the Blessed Virgin Mary for us, would have had in mind only merit improperly so called of intercession such as that which continues in

[74] Cf. Ia IIae, q. 114, a. 6.
[75] Denz., no. 3034.

heaven, which is not strictly merit, and which therefore does not refer to the attainment of graces, but only to their application, just as other saints intercede for us. This last opinion is admitted by very few.

Theologians generally hold that the Blessed Virgin Mary merited for us strictly speaking, but only congruously, the first and last grace.[76]

I do not now wish to enter into the particulars of this controversy, but I should like to make some preliminary observation, which has not been sufficiently noted, the necessity of which is clearly seen from the extremely opposite views on both sides. Both parties to the controversy hold that merit in the strict sense is condign merit; and one party to the controversy deduced therefore that the Blessed Virgin Mary merited condignly for us, which is contrary to the common teaching; the other party to the controversy deduces therefore that the Blessed Virgin Mary did not strictly merit for us, which is likewise against the common teaching, but in the opposite sense.

This controversy seems to result from an insufficient analysis of the notion of merit in general. On the one hand, the adversaries take a quasi-univocal view of merit, and therefore consider merit in the strict sense to be only condign merit. Wherefore either the Blessed Virgin Mary merited condignly for us, or did not strictly merit for us; and both parties depart from the common opinion.

But the first question to be asked is whether the notion of merit is univocal or analogical; and whether merit that has its foundation in an amicable right may be called analogically but still properly merit.

We often take univocally what must be understood analogically, and we do not sufficiently distinguish between what is said analogically and metaphorically, as when we say that God is angry, and what is said analogically and properly, as when we say that God is just.

Some, for example, seem to consider that cause in general is predicated univocally of the four causes, whereas it is predicated only analogically, or proportionately, but nevertheless it is still predicated properly of the final cause, the efficient cause, the formal cause, and the material cause. Others speak as if cognition would be predicated univocally of intellection and sensation, whereas it is predicated of them analogically, but still properly, for sensation is the lowest kind of cognition, but it is still cognition in the strict sense. Likewise love

[76] On this controversy, cf. B. H. Merchelbach, O.P., *Mariologia,* pp. 327–44, and C. Friethoff, O.P., *De Alma socia Christi mediatoris.* P. G. M. Roschini, O.S.M., *De Corredemptrice.*

is predicated analogically of spiritual love and of sensitive love, but this second kind is strictly love. Also, life is predicated analogically of divine life, of our intellectual life, our sensitive life, even of vegetative life, which still is life properly so called, distinct from life in the metaphorical sense, as when we speak of living water. Also, being is not predicated univocally but analogically of God, created substance, and accident; although accident is being in another, it is still properly something real; the quantity of bread, the wisdom of the doctor, are strictly something real and entirely distinct from a logical being, which is not strictly being. In all these examples analogy of proper and not merely metaphorical proportionality is verified.

Finally, according to the teaching of St. Thomas, sin is not predicated univocally but analogically of mortal sin and venial sin; nevertheless, venial sin is still sin in the strict sense, and thus is distinct from imperfection, for example, from less generosity or promptness in following the divine counsel. But if sin or demerit is predicated analogically, but still properly, of venial sin, likewise merit is not predicated univocally but analogically of condign merit and congruous merit; and why could it not still be properly predicated of merit that has its foundation in an amicable right?

What St. Thomas says of sin or of demerit is equally applicable to merit. He writes: "The division of sin into venial and mortal is not a division of a genus into a species, which have an equal share of the generic nature, but it is the division of an analogous term into its parts, of which it is predicated, of the one first, and of the other afterward, consequently the perfect notion of sin, which Augustine gives, applies to mortal sin. On the other hand, venial sin is called a sin in relation to mortal sin, even as an accident is called a being, in relation to substance, in reference to the imperfect notion of being." [77] Nevertheless, just as accident is still properly something real and not a logical being, so venial sin is still in the proper sense sin, but imperfectly so, just as vegetative life is very imperfect life, but it is still, however, properly called life.

Likewise merit, or the right to a reward analogically and not univocally is predicated of merit in the natural order, for example, in civil life or military life, and of supernatural merit. Likewise, in the supernatural order merit is predicated analogically: (1) of merit that has its foundation in strict justice in accordance with the absolute

[77] *Summa theol.,* Ia IIae, q. 88, a. 1, ad 1.

equality between the work performed and the reward, namely, Christ's theandric merit is of infinite value; (2) condign merit still has its foundation in justice, yet not so that the work performed is equal to the reward, but proportionately so and according to the divine ordination and promise; (3) congruous merit properly so called has its foundation in merit, or in an amicable right to a reward, presupposing the state of grace, and in the Blessed Virgin Mary fullness of grace. So far merit has been predicated analogically, indeed, but still in the proper sense, just as accident still is being, and just as vegetative life still is life properly so called; (4) merit is predicated improperly or metaphorically of congruous merit in the broad sense which has its foundation in God's liberality or mercy; then there is no more a right, not even an amicable right to a reward, because this last improperly called right does not suppose the state of grace, but a certain disposition for grace or prayer that the sinner offers, which has not a meritorious but an impetratory power.

St. Thomas, inquiring whether a man can merit the first grace for another, says: "No one can merit condignly for another his first grace; since each one of us is moved by God to reach life everlasting through the gift of grace; hence condign merit does not reach beyond this motion, but Christ's soul is moved by God through grace, not only so as to reach the glory of life everlasting, but so as to lead others to it, inasmuch as He is the head of the Church, and the author of human salvation. . . . But one may merit the first grace for another congruously; because a man in grace fulfills God's will, and it is congruous and in harmony with friendship that God should fulfill man's desire for the salvation of another." [78] Thus it is commonly held that St. Monica not only obtained by her prayers, but also merited fittingly, though not condignly, the conversion of St. Augustine; a fortiori, the Blessed Virgin Mary, full of grace, the Mother of God and the spiritual mother of all men, merited for us in a strictly congruous sense the first grace, in fact, all the graces we receive and for the elect the ultimate grace of final perseverance, which they cannot strictly merit for themselves, because thus the principle of merit or the state of grace lasting until the moment of death would come under merit.

This congruous merit has its foundation not only in God's liberality and mercy, like the impetratory power of a sinner's prayer, but has

[78] *Ibid.*, a. 6, c.; also ad 1.

its foundation in an amicable right or in the rights of friendship, and presupposing the state of grace, and in the Blessed Virgin Mary fullness of grace, is still merit properly so called.

Nevertheless the idea of merit is not absolutely the same in condign merit and in strictly congruous merit; this notion is simply different, but in a qualified manner the same, that is, in accordance with a proper proportionality and is not merely metaphorical.

Thus the notion of life is not simply the same in the divine life and in the vegetative life, they are only proportionately the same; nevertheless the vegetative life is still life properly so called, and is not so metaphorically as when we speak of "living water." Thus it remains true that the Blessed Virgin Mary properly merited for us the first grace and others, yet not condignly, but in a strictly congruous sense. Thus the Blessed Virgin Mary with Christ, through Him, and in Him congruously merited objective redemption, that is, the liberation and restoration of the human race, or the attainment of graces, which afterward are applied to individuals.

Thus the solution of the objections against the title "coredemptress" presents no difficulty.

Objection. Only Christ is the Redeemer.

Reply. That Christ alone is the Redeemer essentially, condignly, perfectively, this I concede; the Blessed Virgin Mary is coredemptress through Christ, congruously and imperfectly.

But I insist. The principle of merit does not come under merit. But Mary was redeemed by Christ. Therefore she cannot be the coredemptress.

Reply. That she cannot be her own coredemptress, this I concede; of others, I deny. Thus she could not even congruously merit for herself either the first grace or the immaculate conception, or the grace of final perseverance; for in such cases the principle of merit would fall under merit. But she could merit in a strictly congruous sense for us the first and last graces which Christ merited for us condignly. First of all the Blessed Virgin Mary was preserved from sin, and she was afterward the coredemptress.

Still I insist. Redemption is one and indivisible. Therefore, if the Blessed Virgin Mary is redeemed and hence is not her own coredemptress, she is also not the coredemptress of others.

Reply. Father Merkelbach distinguishes the antecedent as follows: That redemption is one and undivided according to the principal and perfective cause, and thus is a theandric act of Christ, this I concede; that redemption is one and undivided in its effects as a secondary and subordinated cause, this I deny. This presupposes the preservative redemption of the Virgin in her action as mediatrix and coredemptress for others. Thus the soul, which vivifies the head, through the mediation of the head moves the members. Thus Christ was predestined first of all before us.[79]

Thus Christ's primacy is absolutely maintained, for the Blessed Virgin Mary is mediatrix only, subordinately and in dependence on Christ. Only in virtue of her suffering and grace in union with Christ has she merited and satisfied congruously for us. It is only by Christ's grace that the Blessed Virgin gave her consent on the day of the Annunciation, and on Calvary said: "May the Father's will be done."

Final objection. The Blessed Virgin Mary could not immediately cooperate with the act of redemption, or offer the sacrifice of the cross, because she was not a priest.

Reply. That she could not immediately cooperate in the redemptive act, by eliciting a theandric act, or by exercising a truly sacerdotal and sacrificial action, this I concede: that she could not by suffering with Him, this I deny. It is in this sense that Benedict XV says: "As she suffered with her Son in His passion and, so to speak, shared in His death, so she abdicated her maternal rights over her Son for the salvation of men and, as far as it was in her power, sacrificed her Son . . .

[79] The present objection is similar to this: Christ Himself was predestined, therefore He could not merit our predestination. We reply with St. Thomas, IIIa, q. 24, a. 4: Christ was predestined by an eternal decree before us, and could not merit our predestination on the part of God predestining, that is, He could not merit the eternal act of our predestination, for, as St. Thomas says: "By one and the same act God predestined Him and us" (*ibid.*). But He merited our predestination on the part of the effects, that is, He merited all the effects of our predestination. Christ has a condign right to these effects, and this does not exclude a congruous right, in a subordinate sense, by the Blessed Virgin Mary to these effects. Christ vivifies us through the mediation of the Blessed Virgin Mary, just as the head through the medium of the neck moves the members. We never said that the Blessed Virgin Mary merited the theandric act of Christ the Redeemer, which is impossible, just as Christ did not merit the uncreated and eternal act of our predestination. These distinctions, which all should know, are classical ones.

Thus in an army, although the head of a legion is commanded by the general of the whole army, this latter commands the soldier, because between the two commanders there is not coordination but subordination. More briefly, although the Blessed Virgin Mary is redeemed by Christ, she is our coredemptrix, because between her and us there is not coordination but subordination, just as between Christ and Mary. Hence it is easy to see that she is the mediatrix to the Redeemer.

so that it can truly be said, that along with Christ she redeemed the human race."[80]

In this sense the Blessed Virgin Mary congruously merited in the strict sense the attainment of graces that flow to us from Christ's passion, whereas other saints can only congruously merit for us not the attainment but the application of graces that flow from the passion. And just as Christ condignly merited all the graces we receive, so the Blessed Virgin Mary merited them congruously; and just as Christ merited for the elect all the effects of predestination, namely, calling, justification, and glorification, so the Blessed Virgin Mary congruously merited these effects for the elect. Thus she is to us the mediatrix of all graces, and can and must be called the coredemptress as subordinated to Christ in the work of our salvation. This nowise detracts from Christ's primacy, but better affirms it, for just as God gave to creatures the dignity of causality, so Christ gave to His mother the dignity of causality, as regards meriting and satisfying for us.

Thus the unity of Mariology is preserved intact. There are not two quasi-equal principles, namely, Mary is the Mother of God, and Mary is the mediatrix of all. The supreme principle in Mariology is: Mary is the Mother of God the Redeemer, and hence she is intimately associated with Him in the work of redemption.

The mediation of the Blessed Virgin Mary as subordinated to Christ's mediation, is not necessary, but most useful and efficacious and is granted to us by God because of His mercy and our weakness. Truly the Blessed Virgin Mary congruously merited for us in the strict sense what Christ condignly merited. She also congruously satisfied for us, whereas Christ condignly satisfied for us.

Now in heaven the Mother of the Savior exercises her universal mediation by means of her all-powerful intercession, and by the distribution of all graces, congruously, since she already merited what she asks for. In this distribution, she is more probably, like Christ, not only the moral cause, but also the physical and instrumental cause of grace. Thus the parallelism with the Savior is preserved, as regards these four: namely, merit, satisfaction, intercession, distribution. There is no reason to deny this causality, which is found also in the priest absolving a penitent and in the wonderworker when he performs miracles. This causality is suggested in the liturgy when it

[80] Denz., no. 3034 note. Pius XI is also quoted in this note as saying: "The Virgin by her bitter sorrows shared with Jesus Christ in the work of redemption."

chants: "Make my heart burn with the love of God. . . . Make me bear in my body the death of Christ. . . . Grant that I may be wounded with His wounds. . . . Grant that I may be inebriated with the teaching of the Cross." [81]

On account of the aforesaid reasons the Blessed Virgin Mary's universal mediation seems to be proximately definable.

The Blessed Virgin Mary especially shows herself as Mother of mercy toward men, inasmuch as she is the health of the sick, the refuge of sinners, comforter of the afflicted, help of Christians, mother of holy joy.

Similarly, as Mother of the Savior, she is queen of all, queen of angels, of patriarchs, of apostles, of prophets, of martyrs, of confessors, of virgins. As Mother of God, she is entitled to the cult of hyperdulia.[82]

THE EXCELLENCE OF ST. JOSEPH OVER ALL OTHER SAINTS

Finally, something must be said of St. Joseph's predestination and of his eminent sanctity. The doctrine according to which St. Joseph among the saints in heaven is the highest after the Blessed Virgin Mary, is the quasi-commonly accepted teaching in the Church, especially from the sixteenth century.[83] It was approved by Leo XIII in proclaiming St. Joseph patron of the universal Church, who wrote: "Certainly the dignity of Mary as the Mother of God in heaven is so great that nothing greater can be attributed to her. But, because there intervened between St. Joseph and the most Blessed Virgin Mary a marital bond, there is no doubt that to the most distinguished dignity whereby the Mother of God very far surpasses all creatures, it came about that nobody is greater than St. Joseph. Marriage is a partnership and a necessity that is the greatest of all, which by its nature has added to it the mutual communication of goods. Wherefore, if God gave Joseph as spouse to the Virgin, He assuredly gave him not only as companion in life, as witness of her virginity, guardian of her virtue, but also as sharer by this conjugal bond in her high dignity." [84]

The Church invokes St. Joseph immediately after the Blessed Virgin

[81] Cf. *Hymns of the Breviary,* by Matthew Britt, O.S.B., though I preferred to depart slightly at times from his rendition. (Tr.)

[82] In what our true and perfect devotion toward her should consist is best explained in Blessed Louis Mary de Montfort's golden book entitled: *Le traité de la vraie devotion à la Sainte Vierge.*

[83] Cf. *Dict. de théol. cath.,* art. "Joseph."

[84] Encyclical *Quamquam pluries,* August 15, 1889.

Mary and before the apostles in the oration of the Mass.[85] She also addresses him with the following titles: "St. Joseph, light of patriarchs, spouse of the Mother of God, chaste guardian of the Virgin, foster father of the Son of God, diligent protector of Christ, head of the holy family . . . , glory of home life, guardian of virgins, pillar of families, solace of the wretched, hope of the sick, patron of the dying, terror of demons, protector of the holy Church, pray for us." [86]

No one is greater among the saints after the Mother of the Savior.

But what is the principle of this doctrine about the excellence of St. Joseph, admitted for the last five centuries? It is that proportionate sanctity is required for an exceptional divine mission, as in the case of Christ, His holy Mother, the apostles, founders of orders, and others who are immediately chosen by God.

But Joseph was predestined for an exceptional mission, one that is unique in the world and throughout all time, namely, that he should be the spouse of the Blessed Virgin Mary, the foster father of the Son of God, and that he should have in the guardianship of the Word incarnate the heart of a father, full of benevolence and love. There is nothing more exalted after the dignity of divine motherhood. Therefore St. Joseph received sanctity in proportion to this mission, and this sanctity increased until the end of his life. In fact, St. Joseph was probably predestined to his exceptional mission before he was predestined to glory, for there is no distinction between his predestination and the decree of the Incarnation, which is directed to the Incarnation not in a general way but as to something individualized, namely, as concerning the incarnation of the Word by the Virgin Mary "espoused to a man whose name was Joseph, of the house of David." [87] This decree includes both Christ's predestination to be the natural Son of God, predestination of Mary to be the Mother of God, predestination of Joseph to the protection of the Son incarnate and His Mother. Hence it can be said that just as Christ was predestined to be the natural Son of God before He was predestined to glory, and the Blessed Virgin to divine motherhood before glory, so it seems that St. Joseph was first predestined to his exceptional mission, on account of which he was afterward predestined to a very high degree of glory and grace. The reason for this conclusion is that Christ's predestina-

[85] *A cunctis.*
[86] Litany of St. Joseph.
[87] Luke 1:26 f.

tion as man to be the natural Son of God, precedes the predestination of any of the elect, because Christ is the first of all the predestined.[88] But Christ's predestination to be the natural Son of God is nothing but the decree of the Incarnation thus fulfilled here and now. But this decree implies Mary's predestination to divine motherhood and Joseph's predestination to the protection of the Son of God incarnate and of His Mother.

Monsignor G. Sinibaldi says: "The mystery of St. Joseph is in close relation with the order of the hypostatic union as so constituted. . . . The cooperation of St. Joseph is not equal to Mary's cooperation. Whereas Mary's cooperation is intrinsic, physical, immediate, St. Joseph's is extrinsic, moral, through Mary's mediation; but it is a true cooperation." [89]

It has recently been asked exactly in what sense St. Joseph is called father of Jesus, for example, when the Evangelist says: "The child Jesus remained in Jerusalem, and His parents knew it not. . . . And His mother said to Him: Son, why hast thou done so to us? Behold Thy father and I have sought Thee sorrowing." [90]

Reply. St. Joseph is not called father in the strict sense. Three things are required to be father in the strict sense, namely, that he produce of his own substance, one like himself in species, and principally, as St. Thomas shows in many places,[91] that the father gives to his son three things, namely, being, nourishment, and education. If he gives being, he is already father in the strict sense, even though his son be illegitimate; but to be father in the full sense he must give not only being, but nourishment, good education, and instruction. Father in the strict sense is attributed analogically to the eternal Father because of the eternal generation of His only-begotten Son, and to the earthly father because of his temporal generation.

But many times the term "father" is not attributed in the strict sense, as in the cases of adoptive father, spiritual father, foster father intellectual father. Among these paternities not taken in the strict sense, the most exalted is the paternity of St. Joseph toward Jesus. It is a paternity absolutely of its own kind, which transcends common adoptive paternity and foster paternity. St. Thomas says: "The child is not called the good of marriage only inasmuch as it is the result of

[88] Cf. IIIa, q. 24, a. 1-4.
[89] *La Grandezza di S. Giuseppe,* pp. 36 f.
[90] Luke 2:43, 48.
[91] Cf. *Tabula aurea,* under the words "Father," no. 3, and "Sonship," nos. 6, 11.

marriage, but inasmuch as it is received and educated in marriage. And so the good of the Blessed Virgin Mary's marriage was that child, not taken in the first sense; neither a child born in adultery nor an adopted son who is educated in matrimony is the good of marriage, because matrimony is not ordered to the education of those, as this marriage between Mary and Joseph was ordered especially to this, that the child be both received and educated in marriage." [92] Thus St. Joseph's paternity was absolutely of its own kind and therefore Joseph received from God, as Bossuet says, a paternal heart, so that with the greatest of affection, he might take care of the Word incarnate, the Son of God, who was truly and properly the Son of his consort, the Blessed Virgin Mary.[93]

[92] Cf. *Com. in IV Sent.,* d. 30, q. 2, a. 2, ad 4.

[93] This has been more fully explained by us in the *Angelicum* of October 1, 1945, under the title, "De paternitate Sancti Joseph," and in the book, *The Mother of the Savior,* pp. 342–61: "The predestination of St. Joseph and his eminent sanctity."

APPENDIX

The Definability of the Blessed Virgin Mary's Assumption

REVELATION declares that the Mother of the Savior is the vanquisher of and is not vanquished by the devil, sin, and death.

In recent times William Hentrich and Rudolf Gualtero de Moos published a work in two volumes, which contains the petitions addressed to the Holy See postulating the definition of the corporeal Assumption of the Blessed Virgin Mary into heaven. These petitions were proposed by various members of the hierarchy, starting with the highest and included the reasons of the more prominent dogmatic theologians, from various parts of the world, and were arranged in chronological order in manifestation of the consent of the Church.[1]

From the day when the Immaculate Conception of the Blessed Virgin Mary was proclaimed a dogma of our faith, many bishops throughout the Catholic world, very many priests, religious, and faithful postulated the definition of the Blessed Virgin Mary's Assumption as constituting the crowning doctrine of the Church concerning the privileges that stem from her divine maternity. From the time of Leo XIII these petitions have been placed on file by a special department of the Supreme Congregation of the Holy Office, but up to the present time these had not been published. The Most Reverend Fathers W. Hentrich and R. G. de Moos, S.J., qualifiers of the Holy Office, with the greatest of care prepared for publication a work containing all these petitions. For this all lovers of this cause of Mary's Assumption are most thankful, and especially theologians who study the questions about the definability of this privilege.

As explained in the introduction to the first part of this work, contained in the first volume and in the second volume up to page 658, these petitions are arranged in hierarchical order, beginning with the

[1] Typis polyglottis Vaticani, 1942.

cardinals, patriarchs, councils and synods, residential bishops, vicars capitular, coadjutors, bishops, auxiliary bishops, prefects apostolic, religious orders, universities, Catholic faculties, and congresses.

Moreover, for each diocese, there is a collection of all the petitions sent in by each of the successive ordinaries. There is an analysis attached to each petition, so that its doctrinal import may be more clearly seen.

In this documentary part, petitions are collected of 113 cardinals, 18 patriarchs, 2,505 archbishops and bishops, 383 vicars capitular, and a great number of other prelates, rectors of Catholic faculties, and also 32,000 petitions from the secular and regular clergy, 50,000 from nuns and sisters, and more than 8,000,000 petitions from the faithful.

In the second part, the possibility and opportunity of solemnly defining the dogma of the Assumption is methodically and clearly set forth. There is a special inquiry about what the teaching Church dispersed throughout the world, represented by more than 3,000 petitions of bishops, apostolic vicars, and others, teaches concerning this question, namely, whether the truth of Mary's Assumption is contained in the deposit of revelation.

With this end in view, the dogmatic, geographical, and historical nature of the aforesaid documents was written. These petitions were arranged in thirty-five sections, according to the various formulas made use of by the authors of the petitions. As Hentrich and de Moos reported in their work: "Many argue from the fact that the faith of the whole Church in the Assumption cannot be explained without formal divine revelation." [2] In this same work [3] the petitions are arranged according as they agree in their method of argumentation with this or that theological proof.

From all these inquiries it appears that almost all the petitions of the ordinaries [4] from the year 1869 to 1941 postulate the definition of the Assumption as a dogma of the faith. Moreover, it must be noted that the number of dioceses that were not vacant, whose bishops sent in these petitions, represent almost three fourths of all the dioceses in the Catholic Church.[5]

Then what results from this laborious compilation is that in the Eastern Church all the patriarchates, and three fourths of the dioceses

[2] The work by Hentrich and Gualtero, II, 740.

[3] *Ibid.*, p. 739.

[4] About 97 per cent.

[5] *Op. cit.*, I, xx, the proportion was 73 per cent.

with resident bishops in union with Rome, also postulate the dogmatic definition of the Assumption.[6]

The geographical location of all the dioceses from which these petitions came is set forth.[7]

Finally, the above-mentioned work records the history of this movement that postulates the dogmatic definition of the Blessed Virgin Mary's Assumption into heaven.[8]

The publication of this great work was most gratefully received by all the bishops of the Catholic Church, by all Catholic universities and seminaries, and by all who discuss theologically the definability of this truth and who pray that this privilege of the Blessed Virgin Mary may be solemnly defined as a dogma.

DIFFICULTY TO BE SOLVED

Some will say perhaps that it is not quite certain that these petitions of the bishops are postulating the definition of the Assumption as formally and implicitly revealed. Several perhaps think that it is only virtually revealed, and according to the majority of theologians, this is not enough so that any truth can be defined as a dogma of the faith formally to be believed on the authority of God revealing.

There are two ways of answering this objection.

1) The bishops of almost the whole Catholic Church do not speak as private theologians, using the precise terminology of Scholasticism; but they speak as witnesses of tradition and judges in matters of faith, and, as was said: "many argue from the fact that the faith of the whole Church in the Assumption cannot be explained without formal divine revelation." [9] This was already made clear by two hundred fathers of the Vatican Council, who said: "Most ancient and constant in both the Western Church and the Eastern Church, in the Church both teaching and taught, is the opinion about the corporeal assumption of the Mother of God. But this fact, namely, that a man's body be living in heaven before the Judgment Day, cannot be confirmed either by the senses or any human authority. . . . Therefore, unless we wish to say that the most firm faith of the Church regarding the corporeal assumption of the Blessed Virgin Mary savors of

[6] *Ibid.,* I, xxiii.

[7] *Ibid.,* II, 825.

[8] The movement began in 1863 and showed notable progress, excluding the period of Modernism, until 1940.

[9] *Op. cit.,* II, 740.

slight or excessive credulity, which is undoubtedly impious even to think of, it must be most firmly held that this opinion is of divine and apostolic tradition, namely, that it originates from revelation. We assert that this glorious event could have been revealed to the divine-like Evangelist St. John who died after the Blessed Virgin's repose." [10]

It must be observed that the fact of the Assumption is certain from tradition, inasmuch as the solemn feast of the Assumption is universally celebrated in the Latin and Greek Churches, at least from the seventh century. For the institution of this solemn and universally celebrated feast is an expression of the general tradition of the Church, even of her ordinary and universal magisterial authority, and expresses the consent of the Church both teaching and taught, which is confirmed by these recent and most numerous petitions, which strictly postulate the dogmatic definition. All these facts presuppose that the fact of the Assumption is a certainty in the Church.

But this fact of the Assumption cannot be certain without divine revelation, as regards the term whereunto of the Assumption, or as regards the entrance of the Blessed Virgin Mary body and soul into heaven. St. Thomas well explains this for our Lord's ascension, whose term whereunto transcended any natural knowledge of the witnesses.[11]

We already gather from the preceding that the certainty the Church has about the fact of the Assumption presupposes formal and at least implicit revelation. The history of this question was never concerned with any private revelation of the Assumption, which might have resulted, apart from any discussion, in the institution of this solemnity in both the Western and Eastern Churches.

Hence now, in our times, the bishops in almost all parts of the world speak, not as private theologians, but as witnesses and judges in the matters of faith, for whom the fact of the Assumption is certain because of the universal tradition, and it cannot be certain without formal and at least implicit revelation. Hence there is no need to inquire whether these bishops, as private theologians, maintain these two propositions, namely: for the definability of any truth it must be formally and implicitly revealed and not merely virtually, and that it is sufficiently proved theologically that the privilege of the Assumption is formally and implicitly revealed. This calls for a deep and

[10] *Ibid.*, I, 94.
[11] Cf. IIIa, q. 55, a. 2, ad 2.

complex study of the question, and it is no wonder that in this difficult question not all theologians are in agreement.

2) Moreover, these bishops are aware of the fact that the majority of theologians maintain that for any truth to be defined as a dogma of the faith, it must be at least formally and implicitly revealed, which seems to us to be absolutely true, and many of the aforesaid petitions clearly state this. For many of these petitions point out that it was gradually and formally revealed that the *Mother of the Savior* is *the vanquisher* of the *devil, sin, and death.*

For example, 144 of the petitioners argue from the special victory gained by Mary over the devil and sin or from the absolute opposition prevailing between the Virgin and the devil and his kingdom.[12] But this reason frequently proclaimed by the Fathers [13] was invoked by Pius IX in the definition of the Immaculate Conception; [14] it was proposed by 200 fathers of the Vatican Council, to show that the Assumption of the Blessed Virgin Mary is formally and implicitly revealed, that is, not only as the effect is contained in the cause but as the part is in the whole; whereas the cause can be without its actual effect that is virtually contained in it, the whole cannot be without its parts.

The postulation of 200 of the fathers of the Vatican Council begins by saying: "O most blessed Father, since in accordance with the doctrine of the Apostle, as given in Rom. V–VIII; I Cor. 15:24, 26, 54, 57; Heb., 2:12, 15, and in other passages, the threefold victory over sin, and the fruits thereof, concupiscence and death, constitute the quasi-integral parts of this triumph that Christ obtained over Satan, the ancient serpent; together with what is said in Gen. 3:15, the Mother of God is presented as singularly associated with her Son in this triumph; together with the unanimous consent of the holy Fathers, we do not doubt that in the above-mentioned oracle, the same blessed Virgin is presignified as illustrious in that threefold victory. Therefore, just as by her immaculate conception she conquered sin, and by her virginal maternity concupiscence, so also in

[12] *Op. cit.,* I, 740.

[13] This theological proof was invoked by St. Germanus Constant., *P.G.,* XCVIII, 345; by St. Anselm, *P.L.,* CLVIII, 966; by Peter Cell., *P.L.,* CCII, 850; by St. Bernardine of Siena, *De assumpt.,* a. 3, chap. 1.

[14] Bull *Ineffabilis Deus:* "[The holy Virgin Mary] united by a most close and indissoluble bond with Him [Christ] together with Him and through Him exerted everlasting enmity against the venomous serpent, and completely triumphing over him crushed his head with her immaculate foot."

this same scriptural text it was foretold that she will obtain a singular triumph over hostile death, like her Son, by an anticipated resurrection." [15]

This reason that associates the Blessed Virgin Mary with Christ's perfect victory over the devil and sin is a more proximate reason for the Assumption than the divine maternity, the fullness of grace and her divine blessedness among all women, all of which are likewise referred to by many of the petitioners. Hence it is no wonder that 144 of the petitions invoke this first reason, as well as 200 fathers of the Vatican Council.[16]

There are two revealed premises, however, in this argument, which would be already sufficient for its definability, and moreover it is not a strictly illative argument of a new truth, but an explanatory argument wherein the conclusion is contained in the premises, not only virtually as the effect is contained in the cause, but also formally and implicitly, as the part is contained in the whole; whereas the cause can be without the effect afterward to be produced, on the contrary, the whole cannot be without its actual parts.

This theological reason may be expressed by the following syllogism.

Christ gained a perfect victory over the devil, which contains as parts a perfect victory over sin, and consequently a perfect victory over death, manifested by His glorious resurrection and ascension. This major is formally revealed even explicitly in the texts of St. Paul quoted by 200 fathers of the Vatican Council in their postulation.[17]

But the Blessed Virgin Mary, as Mother of the Savior, who in all tradition is called the second Eve, is most closely associated with Christ's perfect victory over the devil and sin.[18]

Therefore the Blessed Virgin Mary, as Mother of the Savior and the new Eve, is also most closely associated with Christ's perfect victory over death, so that "she could not be held down or detained by

[15] *Op. cit.,* I, 97 f. See also *Acta Conc. Vat., Collectio Lacensis,* VII, 868 f.

[16] *Op. cit.,* II, 740.

[17] Rom. 5:9–21; 6:12–17; I Cor. 15:24–26, 54–57; Col. 2:15; Heb. 2:14 f.; John 12:31; 1:29; 6:40–44, 55; 10:25; Acts 27:31.

[18] The minor is likewise formally and progressively revealed in the following texts: Gen. 3:15; Luke 1:28, 42; 2:35, 51; John 19:25. These texts must be read by the guiding light of tradition, and this minor was proclaimed by Pius IX in his above-quoted dogmatic bull.

the bonds of death," as the liturgy says; [19] otherwise she would have been vanquished by death and would not have been the vanquisher, and her parallelism with Christ's resurrection and ascension, before the general resurrection of the dead, would be destroyed. Moreover, the exceptional benediction, "blessed art thou among women," [20] excludes the malediction "into dust thou shalt return." [21]

As we said, the major and minor of this argument are revealed, and this already suffices for the definability of the conclusion. Moreover, it is not a strictly illative argument resulting in a new truth, but an explanatory argument, whereby the parts contained in Christ's victory over the devil are shown, namely, victory over sin and consequently over death. But the whole cannot exist without its parts. Hence in this way its definability is certainly proved.

Moreover, 171 petitions argue from the Immaculate Conception,[22] showing in the same way that the Blessed Virgin Mary's victory over sin infers victory over death according to this revelation.

Likewise 196 petitioners argue almost the same way from the intimate union and consent prevailing between the Virgin and Christ, her Son.

Therefore the conclusion of the aforesaid traditional argument is not only virtually revealed, but is also formally and implicitly revealed. The denial of the Assumption means the denial of the major or minor, both of which are revealed; doubt about the Assumption means doubt about the major or minor. Therefore it was progressively and formally revealed that the Mother of the Savior, the new Eve, is the vanquisher of, and is not vanquished by, the devil, sin, and death.

Hence these very many petitions show the definability of this privilege of the Blessed Virgin Mary and with equal clarity they manifest the opportuneness of its dogmatic definition, as the crowning doctrine of the Church concerning the divers privileges that stem from the divine maternity. Thus also the existence of eternal life would again be solemnly affirmed, of which the present life, unless it be to no purpose, must be ordered as merit to reward, and as the precious commencement for the ultimate end.

[19] See the ancient oration "Veneranda," which was formerly recited in Rome before the procession on the feast of the Assumption, and which still remains in the Dominican rite and also in the Ambrosian rite.

[20] Luke 1:28, 42.

[21] Gen. 3:19.

[22] *Op. cit.*, II, 739.

INDEX

Abelard, errors of, 80, 535 f., 588
Abraham: and the angels, 517; Incarnation in the stock of, 223; obedience of, 461 f.
Acosmism, 118 note
Action: and faculty, 123; and passion, 182 and note, 245 and note
Actions of Christ, 342, 411, 577-82
Acts of the Apostles: date of, 17 note, 24; and the divinity of Christ, 24 f.
Adam
  Christ the head of, 320-26
  Christ's generation and, 222-24, 407, 409
  disobedience of, 450
  grace of, 320-26
  infused knowledge of, 367 f.
  predestination of, 323
  virtues of, 271
Adoption, divine, 500-506
Adoptionists, errors of, 110, 500, 505
Adoration: of Christ, 516-23; kinds of, 517
Adult, ecclesiastical meaning, 196 note
Affirmations and negations, 69 f., 72
Agatho, St. (pope): suffering of Christ, 635
Agnoetae, errors of, 344, 347, 372
Albert (the Great), St.: Christ's appearance to Mary, 666 f.; mediation of Mary, 704, 707; motive for the Incarnation, 76-78
Alexander VIII (pope), condemnation of Jansenism, 604
Alexander of Hales: motive for the Incarnation, 76-78; the redemption, 546; satisfaction of Christ, 577
Allo, P. B.: contemplation of St. Paul, 356 note
Alphonsus Tostatus (Abulensis), blood of Christ, 228
Alvarez
  beatific vision of the angels, 289
  Christ's beatific knowledge, 374
  Christ's love of God, 467
  grace of the angels, 330
  intensity of Christ's grace, 304
  knowledge of Christ, 379-81
Ambrose, St.: Christ's prayer for us, 490; knowledge of Christ, 386 f.; the redemption, 544; resurrection of Christ, 666; sinlessness of Mary, 697
Analogy of faith, 11
Andrew, St.: death of, 625 note
Angel of the Passion, 388
Angela de Foligno, St., 366 note
Angels, the
  adoptive sons of God, 504
  "adored" by Abraham, 517
  Christ the head of, 53, 288 f., 312, 321, 326-35
  Christ the king of, 676, 680, 682
  Christ's acquired knowledge and, 388
  Christ's judiciary power and, 685 f.
  compared to the Blessed Virgin, 698 f.
  faith of, 383
  fall of, 55, 331 f.
  grace of, 288-90, 322 f., 328-35
  in human form, 668 f.
  knowledge of, 38 f., 365: inferior to Christ's knowledge, 383; infused, 363, 365, 378
  Mary the queen of, 715
  mediators, 525
  nature and personality in, 217
  no grief in, 639 and note
  obedience of, 451
  perfection of, 51
  will of, 55, 216 and note
Anger in Christ, 419
Annunciation, the, 693, 700 f.
Anomoeans, errors of the, 110, 344

Anselm, St.: necessity of the Incarnation, 55; the redemption, 545, 548
Antichrist, 340, 649
Antoninus, St.: kingship of Christ, 680
Apollinarians, errors of the, 31, 109 f., 112, 239 f., 344, 439
Apocalypse and the divinity of Christ, 29 f.
Apostles: on the day of Pentecost, 672 f.; knowledge of, 360 note, 363; preaching of, 389
Apostles' Creed, the hypostatic union, 113, 120
Appelles, errors of, 110
Aristotle,
  happiness and sadness, 636, 641
  justice, 586
  meaning of "nature," 116 f.
  the suppositum, 124 note
  virtuous men, 134
  works of, 287
Arians, errors of the, 109-12, 230 f., 535
Ascension of Christ, 667, 669-73
Assumption of Christ's human nature, 183, 200-211, 424
Assumption of the Blessed Virgin, 653 f., 702-704, 719-25: feast of, 722
Athanasian Creed: hypostatic union, 113, 115 f., 118, 120; unity in Christ, 427
Athanasius, St.: knowledge of Christ, 350; motive for the Incarnation, 80; the Redemption, 544; reply to the Arians, 110, 112
Atonement; *see* Satisfaction
Augustine, St.
  adoration of Christ, 519
  assumption of Christ's soul, 235, 242
  authority of Christ, 59
  beatific vision of St. Paul, 273, 354, 702
  bishop of Hippo, 54
  charity, 62
  Christ the mediator, 66 f., 525
  Christ's descent into hell, 659, 661
  Christ's prayer for us, 490
  Christ's victory over pride, 616
  continence, 269
  death of Christ, 610
  freedom of the Incarnation, 56 f.
  grace of Adam, 320
  grace of Christ, 260, 281 f.
  headship of Christ, 311
Augustine, St. (*continued*)
  the Incarnation, 200 f.
  interpretation of Scripture, 448
  joy and sorrow, 642
  knowledge of Christ, 347, 372 note
  knowledge of the angels, 365
  love, 616
  merits for the Incarnation, 188
  motive for the Incarnation, 77, 81, 85, 98
  the passions in Christ, 417
  predestination of Christ, 508, 511 f., 514
  the redemption, 545, 549, 557, 570: universality of, 605
  reply to Volusianus, 52
  resurrection of the just, 665
  sacrifice of Christ, 591
  St. Monica and, 597 note, 599 note, 707, 711
  sanctity of Christ, 250 f.
  sinlessness of Christ, 408 f.
  sinlessness of Mary, 697
  will of Christ, 469
Aureolus, suffering and joy of Christ, 635-37
Autonomy of personality, 130-33, 143

Baius, 52, 140
Bannez: intensity of Christ's grace, 303 f.; knowledge of Christ, 379 f.
Baptism, 647: formula of, 23 f.
Barbado, order of conception, 241
Basel, Council of: beatific knowledge of Christ, 370
Basil, St.: beatific vision of Christ, 353; knowledge of Christ, 347; the redemption, 544; veneration of images, 520
Basilides, heresy of, 225
Beatific vision
  beatific joy and, 632, 636
  essence of God and, 41
  extent of, 371
  faith and, 273, 358 and note
  gratuitous gift, 52
  hypostatic union and, 359 f.
  impeccability and, 411
  infused knowledge and, 363 f., 366 f.
  merited by Christ, 583
  nature of, 371
  termination of, 182

Beatific vision of Christ, 273, 304 f. and note, 350-64, 370-75
beatific joy and, 632, 636
at the Crucifixion, 620, 631-33
extent of, 370-75
impeccability and, 410 f.
not merited, 476
during the Passion, 620 f., 629-40
sorrow and, 418, 620 ff., 629-40
tradition concerning, 353 f.
Beatitudes, the eight, 100 note
Being: assumed and produced, 433-35; operation and, 170; *see* Existence, Subsistence
Bellarmine, St. Robert: free will of Christ, 445 f.; kingship of Christ, 680; membership in the Church, 319
Benedict, St.: grace of, 289
Benedict XV (pope), Blessed Virgin, coredemptress, 66, 599, 705, 713 f.
Benedict Joseph Labre, St., 101
Benedictus, 194
Bergson, dynamic evolutionism of, 142 f.
Bernard, St.: grace of Christ, 260; grace of the angels, 330; mediation of Mary, 704; the redemption, 537; unity of the Trinity, 185
Biel, G.: satisfaction of Christ, 577
Billot
Cajetan and, 153 f.
Capreolus and, 154
free will of Christ, 444-46, 448
grace in Christ, 305 and note
reply to Scotus, 147 f., 150 note
satisfaction of Christ, 585
Suarez and, 153 f.
theory of personality, 145, 153-60, 429 f.
uncreated union in Christ, 180
Billuart, 9, 37
Christ the head of Adam, 325 f.
eternal priesthood of Christ, 496
freedom of the Incarnation, 56
grace of the angels, 330, 333 f.
habitual grace in Christ, 258 and note, 263
heretical popes, 319
inefficacious will of Christ, 470
intensity of Christ's grace, 303
kingship of Christ, 680
knowledge of Christ, 380 f.
motive of the Incarnation, 97, 322
Billuart (*continued*)
nature and subsistence, 129 f.
the Resurrection, 669
sanctity of Christ, 255
satisfaction of Christ, 585
uncreated union in Christ, 180
veneration of the Blessed Virgin, 522 f.
Blessed, the
compared to Mary, 698 f.
free will of, 442, 462 f.
love for God, 468
no grief in, 639 and note
prayers of, 490
predestination of, 511
Blessed Virgin
adopted daughter of God, 506
assumption of, 653 f., 702-704, 719-25: feast of the, 722
Christ's manifestation to, 666
Christ's presentation in the Temple, 581
conception of Christ, 226 f., 232-41
coredemptress, 66, 598 f., 705-707, 712-15
death of, 404-406, 702
devotion to, 715 note
divine maternity of, 223, 432, 532, 690-92, 714: declared at Ephesus, 120; errors concerning, 110-12
Eve and, 697, 704, 724 f.
faith of, 274 f. and note, 383, 701
fullness of grace, 287-89, 300, 510, 692 f., 698-704
grace of, 261
grief in, 415, 694
Immaculate Conception of, 240, 405 f., 415, 514 f., 692-96
increase of grace, 700-704
infused knowledge of, 367, 484, 700-702
joy of, 701
love of, 581
maternity of, 192, 197
Mediatrix, 339 note, 525, 704-15
merit of, 188 f. and note, 194-97, 339 note, 572, 598 f. and note, 691 f. and note, 705-15: and her predestination, 511, 691 f.; and our predestination, 514
and merits of Christ, 192, 596, 706
moral perfection of, 413

Blessed Virgin (*continued*)
Mother of God, 223, 432, 532, 690-92, 714: declared at Ephesus, 120; errors concerning, 110-12
obedience of, 462
predestination of, 510 f., 691 f.: and St. Joseph's predestination, 716 f.
queen of angels and saints, 715
queen of martyrs, 462
role in the Incarnation, 198 f.
St. Joseph and, 715-18
satisfaction of, 66, 572, 598 f., 714
sinlessness of, 694, 696 f.
suffering of, 694
titles of, 694, 705
veneration of, 522 f., 692, 704, 715
victory of, 653 f.: over death, 703, 719, 723-25
virginity of, 192, 701
virtue of faith, 274 f. and note
virtue of hope, 275
virtues of, 701 f.
Blood of Christ, 227-30
Body, relation to the soul, 236 f.
Body of Christ, 401-406
at the Ascension, 671
assumed by the Word, 225-30: order of assumption, 232 ff.
after his death, 655 f.
dignity of, 572
glory of, 476 f.
at the Resurrection, 665 f.
sensitiveness of, 626
in the tomb, 216, 224, 229 f., 241, 655 f.
united to the soul, 175
Bonaventure, St.
beatific vision and faith, 273
Christian life, 101 note
Christ's appearance to Mary, 666 f.
intensity of Christ's grace, 291
motive for the Incarnation, 76, 81, 94
the redemption, 546
satisfaction of Christ, 577, 585
Boethius: definition of personality, 119, 124 f.; meaning of "nature," 117
Bossuet: Christ as teacher, 357; death of the Blessed Virgin, 702; mediatorship of Christ, 498; St. Joseph, 718; the title on the cross, 676
Burial of Christ, 656-58
Cabrera, Christ's free will, 446
Caiphas, Christ before, 23
Cajetan
beatific knowledge of Christ, 374 f.
beatific vision of Christ, 304 f.
Billot and, 153 f.
the blessed in heaven, 640 note
blood of Christ, 228
the communication of divine life, 50
continence of Christ, 269
degrees of charity, 296 f.
dignity of passivity, 186 f.
explanation of the Incarnation, 165 ff.
grace of Christ, 338: intensity of, 291, 296-98, 301 f.
grace of union, 249
grief of Christ, 553 note, 639
heretical popes, 319
hypostatic union, 128 f.
Judas' sin, 561
membership in the Church, 318 f.
mercy, 94
motive of the Incarnation, 87-97
predestination, 87-93
principle of individuation, 125
satisfaction of Christ, 585
substantial union in Christ, 176 f.
sufferings of Christ and the saints, 597 f.
theory of personality, 145, 153 f., 158-72, 218 f., 432, 437
Calvin, errors of, 603: condemnation of, 442; despair of Christ, 409, 634; suffering of Christ, 403, 568
Cano, Melchior: Christ's beatific vision during the Passion, 632, 636; heretical popes, 319
Capreolus
Billot and, 154
blood of Christ, 228
Christ's love of God, 467
intensity of Christ's grace, 303 f.
satisfaction of Christ, 585
suffering of Christ, 635, 637
theory of personality, 145, 154, 159
Causes: interaction of, 91 f., 104; kinds of, 709
Casuistry, moral imperfections and venial sin, 412 note
Catherine of Siena, St., 136, 365, 627 f.
Ceuppens, J. F.: divinity of Christ, 30 f.; motive of the Incarnation, 79 note

Cerinthians, errors of the, 109 f.
Chalcedon, Council of: Christ's body, 225; the hypostatic union, 113, 115 f., 120
Chardon, Louis: Christ's desire for the Passion, 625 note; the interior life of Christ, 629, 644
Charity
  the Ascension and, 670 f.
  degrees of, 296 f., 305 f.
  enkindled by the Incarnation, 62 f.
  finite, 69
  hope and, 62
  motive of, 62
  natural qualities and, 297
  see also Love
Christ
  absence of faith in, 267, 269, 272-74
  absence of hope in, 267, 269, 274 f.
  absence of penance in, 267, 269, 275 f.
  actions of, 342, 411, 577-82
  adoration of, 516-23
  anger in, 419
  ascension of, 667, 669-73
  beatific vision of; *see* Beatific vision of Christ
  beauty of, 406
  births of, 532
  blood of, 227-30
  bodily defects of, 401-406
  body assumed by, 225-30: order of assumption, 232 ff.
  body of; *see* Body of Christ
  burial of, 656-58
  before Caiphas, 23
  cause of grace, 313, 318, 334 f. and note, 337, 393-99
  charity of, 563
  command to die, 444-67
  commutative justice of, 587
  composite person, 173-75
  comprehensor and wayfarer, 419
  conception of, 226 f., 232-41, 531 f., 690: beautific vision and, 273; sinless, 407, 409
  conformity to, 101 f.
  conqueror of sin, the devil, and death; *see* Victory
  contemplation of, 356-58
  cross of: adoration of the, 521: glory of the, 619
Christ (*continued*)
  death of, 404-406, 655-57: fittingness of, 655; foreseen, 417 f.; practical judgment and, 460; a sacrifice, 494; voluntary, 555-58
  defects in, 364: of the soul, 407-19
  descent into hell, 658-62
  desire for the cross, 620-25, 629
  despair in, 409, 634
  divine personality of, 200 f., 209 f.
  divinity of: denial of, 13, 17, 25; ecclesiastical definitions, 32 f.; errors concerning the, 31 f., 109 f.; proved from Scripture, 18-31; proved from tradition, 31-33
  eternity of person, 425
  exaltation of, 603
  example of, 402
  fear in, 418
  fullness of grace; *see* Grace of Christ
  the gifts of, 276 ff.: fear, 279 f.; not merited, 475; prophecy, 283
  glorified body of, 665 f., 671
  glory of, 615-19, 648, 650: at the Ascension, 670 f.; and His kingship, 678; at the Resurrection, 664
  grace of; *see* Grace of Christ, Grace of union
  grief of, 361-63, 409 f., 415, 551-53, 627-44: for sin, 612
  head of all men, 315-26
  head of our first parents, 320-26
  head of the angels, 53, 288 f., 312, 321, 326-35
  head of the blessed, 686 f.
  head of the Church, 310-20, 326-28, 335-39: by merit, 565
  holiness of, 243 f., 247-309, 391, 407-15
  human nature of: adoration of the, 517-20, 679; instrument of grace, 337 f., 393-99; and judiciary power, 685 f.; sanctity of, 243 f., 247-66
  humanity of: errors, 109-12; excellence of, 51; *see also* Human nature
  humiliations of, 615-19
  humility of, 95 f.
  ignorance of, 343 f.
  images of, 520 f.
  impeccability of, 253, 407 f., 410-12: causes for, 410 f., 443 f., 459, 469; and free will, 411 f., 441-69

Christ (*continued*)
imperfections in, 412 f.
Incarnation; *see* Incarnation
infallibility of, 344 ff.
intellect of, 231: at the moment of conception, 265
the judge, 684-86
judiciary power of, 527, 679, 681 f., 684-86
justice of, 563
king of the angels, 676, 680, 682
kingship of; *see* Kingship
knowledge of; *see* Knowledge of Christ
love of, 362: for creatures, 468 f.; for God, 467 f., 485; and merit, 562, 571 f., 608; and the Passion, 620 f.; and satisfaction, 533-35, 537, 540, 572 and note
the mediator, 66 f., 498, 524-27: and Mary's mediation, 706, 712-14
mercy of, 95
merits of; *see* Merits of Christ
Messiahship of, 13-17
mind of, 231
miracles of, 20, 392-95, 473
miraculous generation of, 407, 409
model of virtues, 610 f.
moral perfection of, 407-15: fomes of sin, 414 f., 440
motive of faith, 58, 60
mystical body of, 311-14, 332 f.: and Christ's satisfaction, 571 f.; membership in the, 315-20, 326-28; sufferings of the, 598; union of members in the, 184 f.
noblest of men, 7
obedience of, 448-67, 556 f.: and victory, 616 f., 646, 650
omnipotence of, 390-400
the only Redeemer, 596-99
operations in, 472-86, 577-82: kinds of, 473 f.; merited, 486
pain of, 417, 625-27
passibility of, 364, 401-406: and fomes of sin, 415; in His soul, 416
passion of; *see* Passion of Christ
passions in, 416 f.
personality of, 137-39
powers of, 390-400, 681 f.
prayer of, 400, 482, 489-91: in the Garden, 409 f., 490

Christ (*continued*)
preaching of, 389
predestination of, 321, 498, 507-15: and our predestination, 511-15; and St. Joseph's predestination, 716 f.
presentation in the Temple, 581
priest and victim, 611 f., 622
priesthood of, 492-99: eternal, 496-98; and kingship of Christ, 683 f.; and sacrifice, 589-93
relation to the Father, 487, 503 f., 556-58, 613-15; *see also* Sonship of Christ
after the Resurrection, 666-69
resurrection of; *see* Resurrection
sacrifice of; *see* Sacrifice of Christ
sadness of, 551-53, 627-44: and happiness, 620 f., 632-44
sanctity of, 243 f., 247-309, 391, 407-15
satisfaction of; *see* Satisfaction of Christ
the Savior, 96, 101, 498
sinlessness of, 407-15: fomes of sin, 414 f., 440
sonship of, 209 f., 252-54, 498: and beatific vision, 359; not adoptive, 500-502, 505 f.; and predestination, 509-12
sorrow of, 361-63, 417 f., 551: and joy, 361 f., 621, 632-44
soul of; *see* Soul of Christ
subject to Himself, 488
subject to the Father, 487
sufferings of, 486 and note, 608 ff.: and the beatific vision, 620 f., 629-40; extent of, 550 f., 625-27; intensity of, 551 f., 626 f.
the teacher, 19, 355 and note, 357, 387 f., 631 f.
temptation of, 414, 516
the Truth, 58, 345, 355
two natures in, 115-19
union of body and soul in, 175
union with, 101 f.
unity in, 427 ff.: His being, 427-38; His operations, 472-86; His will, 438-71
the victim, 493-95
victory of; *see* Victory
virtue of religion, 563
virtues of, 266 ff., 563, 610: and the gifts, 276 f.

Christ (*continued*)
the way, the truth, and the life, 345, 355
will of; *see* Will of Christ
wonder in, 418
wounds of, 666
zeal of, 361 note
Christ the King, Mass of, 684
Christian life, 101 and note
Christology, 8
Chrysostom (Father, O.F.M.), motive of the Incarnation, 81 f. note, 93
Church, the: catholicity of, 673; Christ the head of, 310-20, 326-28, 335-39, 565; holiness of, 648; membership in, 315-20, 326-28
Cipullus, grace of the angels, 325 f., 333 f.
Circumcision of Christ, blood shed at, 230
Circumstances of the Incarnation, 191-93
Clement VI (pope): blood of Christ, 228; indulgences, 597; infinite merits of Christ, 578 f., 609
Clement of Rome, St.: the redemption, 543
Collyridians, errors of the, 522
Command, nature of, 451, 456, 468
Communicability, idea of, 126 f., 204
Communication of divine life, 49 f.
Communication of idioms, 420-26
Complutenses Abbreviati, 155 f., 158, 165 ff.
Composition of Christ's person, 173-75
Compulsion, internal and external, 441 ff.
Conception, order of, 233 note, 238-41
Conception of Christ, 226 f., 232-41, 531 f., 690: beatific vision and, 273; sinless, 407, 409
Constantinople, First Council of: the hypostatic union, 113
Constantinople, Second Council of
adoration of Christ's humanity, 518
beatific vision of Christ, 353
composition of Christ's person, 173
grace in Christ, 299, 307 f., 631, 700
the hypostatic union, 116
impeccability of Christ, 410, 414, 443
virtues of Christ, 272
Constantinople, Third Council of: two wills in Christ, 342, 439 note, 471
Contemplation: of Christ, 356-58; infused, 382
Contenson, graces merited by Christ, 326, 333 f.
Contrition, 628: satisfaction and, 572
Counsel, gift of, 278 f., 378
Cornelius a Lapide, 651
Cum fundamento in re, 38 and note
Creation, free act of God, 48 and note, 454 f., 457 f.
Creatures, transmutation of, 392 f.
Cross, death on the: fitness of, 549 f.; shame of, 550
Cross of Christ: adoration of, 521; glory of, 619
Crucifixion and the beatific vision, 620, 631-33
Cyprian, St.: the redemption, 544
Cyril of Alexandria, St.
grace in Christ, 260
the hypostatic union, 114 f., 118 f.
knowledge of Christ, 350
motive for the Incarnation, 80
reply to the Nestorians, 111, 114 f., 118 f.
sanctity of Christ, 250
Cyrus of Alexandria (Monothelite), 439

Damned, the, 662
David: "adoration" of, 517; and Christ's generation, 409
Death: of the Blessed Virgin, 404-406, 702; necessity of, 404; victory over, 616 f., 646, 650-54
Death of Christ, 404-406, 655-57: fittingness of, 655; foreseen, 417 f.; practical judgment and, 460; a sacrifice, 494; voluntary, 555-58
Decrees: conditional, 97 f., 102-104; divine, 82, 97 f., 101 note, 308
Deity, communicability of, 204
Denzinger, Mary's Assumption, 703 f.
Descartes, theory of knowledge, 139
Devil: bondage of, 593-95, 602, 649; head of the wicked, 339; redemption and the, 545, 593-95; vanquished by Christ, 617 f., 645, 648-50, 683
Diodorus of Tarsus, 110
Dionysius: nature of goodness, 46; on passivity, 187
Dioscorus, errors of, 114
Docetae, errors of the, 31, 109, f., 535
Dominic, St.: grace of, 289

Dualists, errors of the, 31
Dulia, cult of, 517, 522 f.
Durandus
adoptive sonship of Christ, 505
blood of Christ, 228
faith and the beatific vision, 273
grace of union, 249
intensity of Christ's grace, 291
mode of union in Christ, 177
satisfaction of Christ, 577

Eadmer: the Immaculate Conception, 693; merits of Mary, 705
Earth, center of the universe, 45, 52-54
Ebionites, denial of Christ's divinity, 25, 109 f.
Economy, principle of, 3 note
Ecstasy of Christ's existence, 437
Elect, sins of the, 90
Elias, 603
Elipandus of Toledo (Adoptionist), 505
Embryo, animation of the, 233 note, 238-41
Enoch, 603
Ephesus, Council of
body of Christ, 225, 402
condemnation of Nestorianism, 113, 120
hypostatic union, 113, 120
Mary's divine maternity, 690
merit of Christ, 477
passibility of Christ, 402
power of Christ, 395
priesthood of Christ, 492, 495
the redemption, 536
sacrifice of Christ, 589
soul of Christ, 230
Epiphanius, St.: Creed of, 32
Equilibrium, liberty of, 465
Essence and existence, 122 f., 144-73, 218-20, 429 f., 433-38: of God, 144, 146; Scotus on, 149 f., 429; Suarez on, 429 f.
Essence and suppositum, 156
Essence of God, 38, 41
Eucharist, the: adoration of, 518; blood in, 228-30; hope strengthened by, 61 f.; instrument of grace, 395; merited by Christ, 583
Eucharistic Heart, devotion to, 520
Euclid, 154 note
Eusebius of Caeserea, 353: the Last Supper, 624
Eutyches, errors of, 111 f., 114 f., 439: refutation of, 114-19
Eutychians, errors of the, 32, 109, 111 f., 114 f., 439: refutation of, 114-19
Eve and Mary, 697, 704, 724 f.
Evil, overcome through the Incarnation, 63 f.
Evolutionism, theory of, 118 note, 142 f.
Existence
definition of, 123
essence and, 122 f., 144-73, 218-20, 429 f., 433-38: Scotus on, 149 f., 429; Suarez on, 429 f.
of God: known by reason, 38
personality and, 429-38
subsistence and, 156, 165-72, 432-37
suppositum and, 144-73, 218-20, 436 f.

Faculty: action and, 123; definition of, 123
Faith
analogy of, 11
of the angels, 383
and the Ascension, 670 f.
beatific vision and, 273, 358 and note
of the Blessed Virgin, 274 f. and note, 383, 701
grace *gratis data,* 281 f. and note
knowledge and, 358 f.
motive of, 57 f., 60
strengthened by the Incarnation, 57-60
wanting in Christ, 267, 269, 272-74
Fall of man, 55, 320 f., 331 f.: motive for the Incarnation, 323 f.
Father, meaning of the term, 717
Father, the: and adoptive sonship, 503 f.; and Christ's death, 556-58; and Christ's passion, 613-15; *see also* Sonship of Christ
Fatherhood of St. Joseph, 717 f.
Fear: in Christ, 418; gift of, 276 f., 279 f.
Felix of Urgel (Adoptionist), 505
Fire, nature of, 296 note
"Flesh," Scriptural meaning of the word, 35
Florence, Council of: the redemption, 536
Fomes of sin, 414 f., 440
Form and matter, 434

Fortitude: gift of, 276; virtue of, 398
Francis de Sales, St.: death of the Blessed Virgin, 702
Francis of Assisi, St., 136: Christian life, 101 note; grace of, 289
Frankfort, Council of: grace of Christ, 251 note; sonship of Christ, 500, 505
Franzelin: free will of Christ, 444-46, 448; satisfaction of Christ, 585; theory of personality, 151 note
Free will, 454-56, 459-66: of the blessed, 442; of Christ, 441 ff.; merit and, 442 f., 451-54
Freedom: definition of, 466; kinds of, 442; psychological and moral, 456, 459 f., 465
Frejus, Council of: sonship of Christ, 500
Froschammer, 36
Fulgentius, St.: Christ's beatific vision, 353 f.; the Incarnation, 200 f.

Gabriel, archangel, 328
Galtier, theory of personality, 151 note
Gebhardt, 27
Generationism, 141
Gentiles, persecutors of Christ, 558 f., 561
Gethsemane, Garden of: Christ's prayer in, 409 f., 490; Christ's sorrow in, 361 f., 409 f., 627
Gifts, the: definition of, 277; of Christ, 276 ff.
Glorieux, 436 and note
Gnostics, errors of the, 110
God
- Christ's love for, 467 f., 485
- decrees of, 82, 97 f., 101 and note, 308
- essence and existence of, 144, 146
- essence of, 38, 41
- foreknowledge of, 82 f., 87 f., 90-93, 97
- immutability of, 39 f.
- liberty of, 48 and note, 99 f., 102 f., 454 f., 457-59
- mercy and justice of, 128, 574, 576
- nature of, 46, 49
- visibility of, 40
- will of, 82 f., 87 f., 91

"God is man," 421 f.
Godet, F.: divinity of Christ, 13, 18
Godliness, gift of, 276 f.
Godoy: grace of Adam and the angels, 325 f.; grace of the angels, 329 f., 333 f.; habitual grace in Christ, 258 and note, 263; headship of Christ, 320; motive for the Incarnation, 97
Gonet
- beatific vision of Christ, 632, 636
- Christ's love of God, 467
- gifts of Christ, 276, 279
- grace of Christ, 248 f., 290, 303
- grace of the angels, 330, 333
- habitual grace in Christ, 258 and note, 263 f.
- headship of Christ, 320, 325 f.
- justification of adults, 265
- knowledge of Christ, 380 f.
- motive for the Incarnation, 84 note, 97, 322
- priesthood of Christ, 497, 526
- sanctity of Christ, 255

Good, incidental, 92 f.
Goodness: nature of, 46-48; nature of God, 46-49; and pantheism, 48; Plato on, 46; St. John Damascene on, 46
Gore, divinity of Christ, 18
Gotti, congruous merit, 196
Goudin, justification of adults, 266
Government, the best form of, 679
Grabmann, 436 and note
Grace
- cause of the hypostatic union, 243-45
- Christ the cause of, 313, 318, 337, 393-99
- divine adoption and, 500-506
- efficacious, 469, 576: denial of, 455 and note; merited by Christ, 482, 514, 606 f. and note
- of final perseverence, 99 note
- *gratia gratis data,* 280-82: and capital grace, 339; on Pentecost, 672 f.
- habitual, 297
- meaning of the term, 243
- sanctifying, 101 f.
- sufficient: merited by Christ, 606 f. and note

Grace of Christ, 247-339
- beatific vision; *see* Beatific vision of Christ
- division of graces, 247 f.
- efficacious grace, 411, 444, 469
- fullness of, 284-308, 410 and note: and Christ's kingship, 677 f.; during the Passion, 620-22, 625 and note, 643

Grace of Christ (*continued*)
gift of fear, 279 f.
gift of prophecy, 283
the gifts, 276 ff.: not merited, 475
grace of union; *see* Grace of union
gratia gratis data, 280-82: and capital grace, 339
habitual grace, 247, 251 f., 256-66, 268 and note, 288: and capital grace, 335-39; fullness of, 622; and the gifts, 277; and grace of union, 308 f.; impeccability and, 410 f.; not infinite, 291-308
as head of the Church, 294 f., 310-20, 326-28, 335-39: and habitual grace, 335-39
impeccability, 253, 407 f., 410-12: and free will, 411 f., 441-69
infinite, 291-308
infused virtues, 415: not merited, 475
kinds of, 336
moral perfection of Christ, 407-15: fomes of sin, 414 f., 440
moral virtues and 414 f.
not merited, 475
sonship of Christ and, 506
virtues in Christ, 266 ff.: and the gifts, 276 f.
Grace of union, 243 f., 247-58
capital grace and, 338
habitual grace and, 308 f.
impeccability and, 410 f.
infinite, 291 f.
insufficiency of, 258, 262 f.
priesthood of Christ and, 497 f., 526
sonship of Christ and, 506, 509 f.
Gratia gratis data, 280-82: and capital grace, 339; on Pentecost, 672 f.
Gravitation, law of, 385 f.
Gredt: the order of conception, 241; perfection of souls, 237
Gregory Nazianzen, St.
Christ's descent into hell, 659
the hypostatic union, 115, 119
knowledge of Christ, 350
motive for the Incarnation, 80
the redemption, 544
sanctity of Christ, 250, 255
Gregory of Nyssa, St.: Christ's descent into hell, 660; the redemption, 545, 595
Gregory of Valentia, 38 f.: Christ's free will, 446
Gregory the Great, St. (pope)
Christ's descent into hell, 661
Christ's prayer for us, 490
conception of Christ, 239 note
grace of the angels, 330
knowledge of Christ, 346 f., 372
love, 610
manifestation of Christ after the Resurrection, 668
Grief and joy, 361 f.
Grief of Christ, 361-63, 409 f., 415, 551-53, 627-44: for sin 612
Gunther, 139 note: knowledge of Christ, 344; theory of personality, 111, 130, 139-41

Habitual grace: and natural qualities, 297; *see also* Grace of Christ
Hadrian I (pope), condemnation of Adoptionism, 505
Happiness and sadness, 620 f., 636 f., 640 f.
Harnack: date of St. Paul's epistles, 25; date of the Acts of the Apostles, 17 note, 24; denial of Christ's divinity, 13, 17; Messiahship of Christ, 13, 17
Heaven: Jewish division of, 356 note; opened by Christ's passion, 603; sacrifice in, 688
Hell, Christ's descent into, 658-62
Helvidius, error of, 701
Hentrich, William: Assumption of Mary, 719 f.
Heresies concerning the Incarnation, 109-12
Heretics, membership in the Church, 318 f.
Hermes, errors of, 588
Hilary, St.: the redemption, 544
Hippolytus, St.: sinlessness of Mary, 697
History of dogma: the divinity of Christ, 31 f.; and positive theology, 11
Holiness of Christ, 243 f., 247-309, 391, 407-15
Holy Ghost: and Christ's glorification, 617 f. note; gifts of, 276 ff.; heart of the Church, 314; mission of, 672 f.

Holy Office: beatific vision of Christ, 630; knowledge of Christ, 348, 351
Holy Trinity; *see* Trinity
Holzmann, O.: Messiahship of Christ, 13
Hope
the Ascension and, 670 f.
of the Blessed Virgin, 275
charity and, 62
motive of, 62
strengthened by the Eucharist, 61 f.
strengthened by the Incarnation, 60-62
virtue of, 60
wanting in Christ, 267, 269, 274 f.
Hugo of St. Victor, the redemption, 545 f.
Hugon, E.: existence and suppositum, 172; meaning of redemption, 532 f.; order of redemption, 563; priesthood of Christ, 497, 526; reply to Scotus, 151 note
Human nature
as assumed by the Word, 212-31: body and soul, 225-31; in one individual, 222; not a person, 217-21; not abstract, 221 f.; order of assumption, 232-46; from the stock of Adam, 222-24
of Christ: adoration of, 517-20, 679; instrument of grace, 337 f., 393-99; judiciary power of, 685 f.; sanctity of 243 f., 247-66
dignity of, 63
fitness for the hypostatic union, 113-17
means of restoring, 56 f.
a microcosm, 214
need for redemption, 214 and note
the Word's assumption of, 183, 200-11, 424
Hume, empiric phenomenalism of, 142
Humiliation and glory, 615, 650
Hurtado, intensity of Christ's grace, 291
Hus, John: membership in the Church, 315-17
Hyperdulia, cult of, 522 f., 692, 704, 715
Hypostatic union
beatific vision and, 359 f.
body assumed, 225-30: order of assumption, 232 ff.
after Christ's death, 216, 224, 229 f., 241, 655 f.
communication of idioms, 420-26
consequences of, 420 ff.
Hypostatic union (*continued*)
created union, 179-83
decrees of the Church, 113 f., 120
divine nature assuming, 202-204, 424
errors concerning, 110-12
Fathers of the Church on, 122
through grace, 187, 243-45
greatness of, 184-87
Gunther's theory of, 140
human nature assumed by, 183, 212-31: order of assumption, 232-46; *see also* Human nature
kingship of Christ and, 677 f.
mode of, 108, 113 ff.
not a moral union, 114, 118, 121
not in the nature, 114-19, 127 f.
not merited, 187-97
in one person, 119-75, 222, 427-38
order of union, 434
in the person, 217-20, 424-26
the person assuming, 183, 200-211, 424
predestination of Christ, 509-11
in Sacred Scripture, 116, 120 f.
St. Cyril on, 114 f., 118 f.
Scotus on, 100
soul assumed, 230 f.: order of assumption, 232 ff.
substantial union, 175-79, 430
supernatural grace and, 198 f.
in the suppositum, 172 f., 425
terms used in defining, 115 and note, 117
Hypostasis: and person, 173; and suppositum, 425 f., 431; *see also* Person

Idioms, communication of, 420-26
Ignatius of Antioch, St.: death of, 625 note; desire for martyrdom, 642 f.; the redemption, 543
Ignorance: affected, 560; in Christ, 343 f.
Images: of Christ, 520; veneration of, 520-23
Imelda, Blessed, 387
Immaculate Conception, the, 692-96: feast of, 693, 695; merited by Christ, 192; and St. Thomas, 195 note
Immutability of God, 39 f.
Impeccability of Christ, 253, 407 f., 410-12: causes for, 410 f., 443 f., 459, 469; and free will, 411 f., 441-69

Imperfections, moral: in Christ, 412; and venial sin, 412 f. and notes
Incarnation, the
- announcement by the prophets, 106
- the Blessed Virgin and, 198 f.
- body assumed, 226-30: order of assumption, 232 ff.
- Cajetan's explanation of, 165 ff.
- charity enkindled by, 62 f.
- circumstances of, 191-93
- continuation of, 193 f.
- divine decree, 690 f.
- division of the treatise on, 8
- an example of virtues, 63
- the fact of, 10-33, 35
- faith strengthened by, 57-60
- fitness of, 43-54, 57-64, 137 f.: objections to, 45, 51 f.
- free act of God, 48-50, 54-57, 64, 99 f.
- greatest historical event, 8
- heresies concerning, 109-12
- hope strengthened by, 60-62
- human nature assumed, 183, 212-31: order of assumption, 232-46; *see also* Human nature
- an incidental good, 92 f.
- meaning of the term, 35
- for men on earth, 53
- mode of union, 108 ff.; *see* Hypostatic union
- motive for (man's sin), 76-98, 102-107, 322-26, 507, 618: and kingship of Christ, 683 f.
- the mystery of, 10, 35-39
- necessary for man's salvation, 54-75: errors concerning, 48 and note, 54
- not merited, 187-97, 476
- original sin removed by, 105 f. and note
- participation in divine life, 49
- the person assuming, 183, 200-211, 424
- possibility of, 34-43: beyond human reason, 35-39, 43; objections to, 39-43
- protection against evil, 63 f.
- redemption and, 93 f., 96 f.
- salvation for all, 607 f. note
- satisfaction rendered by, 64-76
- soul assumed, 230 f.: order of assumption, 232 ff.
- in the stock of Adam, 222-24
- supernatural character of, 36-39, 198 f.
- the time of, 106 f.

Inclination to sin, 414 f., 440
Independence of personality, 130-33, 143
Individuality and personality, 119 f., 125 f.
Indulgences, 597
Infallibility of Christ, 344 ff.
Infidels, 329: membership in the Church, 315 f.; redemption for, 604 f.
Inhabitants of other planets, 53
Insanity, 70
Instrumentality, kinds of, 393-98
Intellect, active, 368 f.
Intellectualism, 99 f.
Irenaeus, St.: Christ's body, 225 f.; Christ's descent into hell, 660; motive for the Incarnation, 80; sinlessness of Mary, 697
Isaac, figure of Christ, 615

Jansenists, errors of the, 408, 603 f.
Jansenius: Christ's free will, 446; merit and free will, 442 f.
Janssens, satisfaction of Christ, 585
Jerome, St.: Christ's descent into hell, 561; the passions in Christ, 417; the redemption, 544
Jerusalem, destruction foretold, 348 f.
Jews: persecutors of Christ, 558-61; predestination of, 223
John, St. (apostle), divinity of Christ, 28-30
John Chrysostom, St.
- Christ's appearance to Mary Magdalen, 668
- Christ's victory over death, 617, 650
- grace of Christ, 260
- knowledge of Christ, 372
- merits of Christ, 584
- motive for the Incarnation, 80
- the redemption, 544, 569 f.

John Damascene, St.
- adoration of Christ, 519 f.
- assumption of Christ's soul, 235, 238
- composition of Christ's person, 173
- death of Mary, 702
- fitness of the Incarnation, 46
- hypostatic union, 119
- knowledge of Christ, 347 f.
- passibility of Christ, 403
- the passion of Christ, 552 f., 637
- sanctity of Christ, 250, 408

John of St. Thomas, 9
- Christ's love of God, 467 f.
- efficacious grace, 482
- essence and existence, 152 f.
- grace of Christ, 306: habitual, 264; intensity of, 303 f.
- grace of the angels, 330
- knowledge of Christ, 342, 380 f.
- merit *de condigno,* 74
- motive for the Incarnation, 97
- reply to Scotus, 147 f.

John of the Cross, St., 357
Joseph, St., 328 f., 715-18
Joseph of Arimathea, 657
Joy and sorrow, 361 f., 642: in Christ, 621, 632-44
Judas: betrayal by, 615; sin of, 561
Judgment, practical, 460 and note, 466
Judiciary power of Christ, 527, 679, 681 f., 684-86
Julicher, date of St. Paul's epistles, 25
Justice
- of Christ, 563
- commutative, 74, 587: and Christ's satisfaction, 586-88
- distributive, 74
- kinds of, 586 f.
- mercy and, 574
- satisfaction and 585-88

Justification, 534: of adults, 265 f.; merited by Christ, 480-83, 513, 606 f.
Justin, St.: the redemption, 544; sinlessness of Mary, 697

Kant, autonomy of the will, 132
Kenotic theory, 112 note
King, meaning of the word, 679
Kingship of Christ, 674-84: extent of, 675-77, 682; powers of, 681 f.; and redemption, 678, 683 f.; testimony of Scripture, 674-77
Knowledge
- acquired, 367-69
- of the angels, 365: inferior to Christ's knowledge, 383; infused, 363, 365, 378
- of the apostles, 360 note
- experimental, 367-69
- gift of, 276, 278 f., 378
- infused, 363-67, 369

Knowledge (*continued*)
- intensive and extensive plenitude of, 286

Knowledge of Christ, 272, 341-88
- acquired knowledge, 367-69, 385-88: extent of, 385 f.
- beatific vision, 350-64, 370-75: and merit, 476 f.
- created knowledge, 343 ff.
- errors concerning, 342, 344, 348 ff.
- fullness of, 415 f.
- at His conception, 360 f.
- infused knowledge, 363-67, 369, 376-84: discursive, 382; extent of, 376-81; habitual, 384; and merit, 476 f., 484; and phantasms, 381 f.
- kinds of, 364
- merit and, 476 f., 484
- tradition concerning, 346-48, 353 f.

Labre, St. Benedict Joseph, 101
Ladeuze, death of Christ, 652
Laicism, condemnation of, 680, 682 f.
Lamentabili, propositions condemned in the decree, 13
Last Judgment, 649, 685
Last Supper and the sacrifice of the cross, 497, 592 f.
La Taille, de: Christ's free will, 444 f., 448; Christ's prayer for us, 489; created union in Christ, 180 and note; grace of the hypostatic union, 243; the Last Supper and Calvary, 592
Lateran Council: membership in the Church, 317; the redemption, 536
Latria, cult of, 516-23
Lawrence, St.: death of, 625 note
Lazarus, resurrection of, 664 f.
Lebreton, the Holy Trinity, 503 f.
Leibnitz, 140: necessity of the Incarnation, 48 note, 54, 99 f., 457 f.
Lemos, efficacious grace, 482
Leo I, St. (pope): Christ's divine mediatorship, 67; Christ's soul, 236
Leo XIII (pope): analogy of faith, 11; Christ the king, 682; devotion to the Eucharistic Heart, 520; mediation of Mary, 705; St. Joseph, 715
Lepin, sacrifice in heaven, 688
Lessius, Christ's free will, 445 f., 452

Libertism, 99 f.
Liberty: definition of, 454 note; of equilibrium, 465
Life, kinds of, 710
Locke, definition of person, 130
Loisy, Messiahship of Christ, 13
Lorca: free will of Christ, 444 f., 448; knowledge of Christ, 379, 381
Lord, meaning of the word, 25 note
Love
  of Christ; *see* Christ
  for the cross, 101 f.
  divine, 7: manifested by the Incarnation, 62 f.
  kinds of, 62, 709 f.
  motive of the Incarnation, 100
  proved by sacrifice, 572 note
  see also Charity
Lucifer, head of all the wicked, 339
Lugo, de: free will of Christ, 445 f., 452; grace of the angels, 330; necessity of the Incarnation, 55; satisfaction of Christ, 585
Luther, errors of, 603: condemnation of, 442; suffering of Christ in hell, 568
Lychetus, satisfaction of Christ, 577
Lyons, Council of: sonship of Christ, 500

Macharius of Antioch, 439
Macrobius on virtue, 269
Maieutics (Socratic method), 388 and note
Major, grace of Christ, 291
Maldonatus: beatific vision of Christ, 632, 636; intensity of Christ's grace, 291
Malebranche, necessity of the Incarnation, 48 note, 54, 99
Man, fall of, 55, 320 f., 331 f.: motive of the Incarnation, 323 f.
"Man is God," 421 f., 424
Mandonnet, 436 and note: the Immaculate Conception, 695 f.
Manichaeans, errors of the, 45, 110, 225
Marcion, errors of, 110
Marcionites, errors of the, 225
Mariology, 690-725
Marriage of Joseph and Mary, 715
Martyrdom: not a sacrifice, 589, 591; painless, 625 note; victory over sin, 647 f.
Martyrs, 591: death of, 494
Mary, mother of Christ; *see* Blessed Virgin
Mary Magdalen: Christ's appearance to, 667 note, 668; conversion of, 534
Mass, the; *see* Sacrifice of the Mass
Materialism, 126 note
Matter, 126 and note: and form, 434; principle of individuation, 122, 125 f., 149
Matuissi, G.: existence and suppositum, 157 f., 170
Medina: Christ's love of God, 467; Christ's prayer for us, 489; grace of the angels, 330; intensity of Christ's grace, 304; knowledge of Christ, 342
Melchesidech, priesthood of, 498 f.
Mercy: fitness of the Passion, 548; justice and, 574; motive of the Incarnation, 86, 94-98, 104, 618; motive of the redemption, 537 f.
Merit, 709-11
  of the Blessed Virgin, 188 f. and note, 194-97, 339 note, 572, 598 f. and note, 691 f. and note, 705-15: and her predestination, 511, 619 f.; and our predestination, 514
  condign, 188-91, 572: and congruous, 478, 708-15
  conditions required for, 476
  congruous, 189-91, 194-97: and condign, 478, 708-15
  definition of, 189
  divisions of, 189 f.
  free will and, 442 f., 451-54
  for the Incarnation, 187-97
  inequality of, 582 and note
  of the patriarchs, 188 f., 194-97
  satisfaction and, 74, 402 f. and note, 562 f., 571, 577
Merit of Christ, 188, 190-94, 196 f., 360 f., 474-86, 562-67
  application of, 566, 606 f. and note
  Blessed Virgin and, 192, 596, 706
  extent of, 400 note
  free will and, 442 f., 451-54, 468 f. and note, 472 f., 485
  for Himself, 474-78
  His exaltation, 603
  indulgences and, 597 f.
  infinite value of, 577-83

Merit of Christ (*continued*)
love and, 562, 571 f., 608
merits of the Blessed Virgin and, 339 note, 572, 598 f. and note, 706-708, 712-15
for others, 478-86
our justification and, 480-83, 513
our predestination and, 480-83, 511-15
satisfaction and, 533 f.
Merkelbach, 712 f.
Messias, meaning of the word, 14 note
Messiahship of Christ, proved from Scripture, 13-17
Milevum, Council of, merits of Christ, 478
Mill, empiric phenomenalism of, 142
Miracles of Christ, 20, 392-95, 473
Misery, reason for mercy, 95 f.
Modernists, errors of: concerning the hypostatic union, 111, 114; knowledge of Christ, 344, 348-50; concerning the redemption, 535 f., 567-69, 588 f.
Molina, satisfaction of Christ, 585
Molinists, definition of freedom, 465 and note
Molinos, Michael de, adoration of Christ, 518
Monica, St., 597 note, 599 note, 707, 711
Monophysites, errors of the, 109, 111 f., 114 f., 344, 439: refutation of, 114-19
Monothelites, errors of the, 112, 342, 344, 439
Monsabré, passion of Christ, 641
Montfort, Bl. Louis Mary de: devotion to Mary, 715 note
Moos, Rudolf Gualtero de, 719 f.
Mysteries, supernatural, 35-38
Mystical body of Christ, the, 311-14, 332 f.: and Christ's satisfaction, 571 f.; membership in, 315-20, 326-28; sufferings of, 598; union of members in, 184 f.

Nathan and David, 517
Nature: meaning of the term, 116 f.; and person, 122-29, 218-20, 424 f., 431-33: *see also* Personality
Nazarius, intensity of Christ's grace, 291
Necessity: kinds of, 456 f.; modes of, 55
Necessity of the Incarnation, 54-75: errors concerning, 48 and note, 54
Negations about God, 69-71
Nestorianism: and the Adoptionists, 500, 505; and Gunther, 141; refutation of, 175 f.; and Rosmini, 142; and Scotus, 150
Nestorians
condemned at Ephesus, 113, 120
errors of, 32, 109 f., 119, 344, 424-27, 439: refutation of, 119 ff., 175 f.; value of the redemption, 535
opposed by Eutyches, 111 f., 114
opposed by St. Cyril, 111, 114 f., 118 f.
Nestorius: condemned at Ephesus, 113, 120; errors of, 111 f., 127, 137, 217 f.; opposed by Eutyches, 111 f.
Nicaea, Council of: body of Christ, 225; divinity of Christ, 32 f.; hypostatic union, 113, 120; unity in Christ, 427; veneration of images, 520 ff.
Nicene Creed: hypostatic union, 113; Mary's divine maternity, 691; motive of the Incarnation, 80, 331; the redemption, 535 f.
Nicholas V (pope), beatific knowledge of Christ, 370
Nicodemus, 657
Nominalists, 466

Obediential power, 86, 213-15 and note, 306, 377
Oecumenius, death of Christ, 651
Offenses, gravity of, 67-72
Old Law, law of fear, 504 f.
Old Testament: and the divinity of Christ, 30 f.; sacrifices of, 588, 591
Omnipotence of Christ, 390-400
Operation and being, 170
Orange, Council of: merits of Christ, 478 f.; effects of the redemption, 601
Ordo Romanus, 658
Origen: error of, 232 f., 235, 238 and note; knowledge of Christ, 388; the redemption, 545, 595
Original sin: consequences of, 415; in the patriarchs, 565; removed by the Incarnation, 105 f. and note; vanquished by Christ, 646 f.
Ottley, divinity of Christ, 18
"Our Father," 503

Paludanus: free will of Christ, 444 f.; habitual grace in Christ, 257
Pantheism, 118 note: and the Incarnation, 45
Paquet, satisfaction of Christ, 585
Parable of the wicked husbandmen, 22
Parmenides, acosmism of, 118 note
Particular judgment, 685
Passibility of Christ, 364, 401-406: and fomes of sin, 415; in His soul, 416 f.
Passion and action, 182 and note, 245 and note
Passion of Christ
- for all men, 603-607
- effects of, 601-607
- efficiency of, 562-600
- the efficient cause of, 555-61
- extent of suffering, 550 f., 625-27
- fitness of, 547-50
- gravity of sin seen in, 610 f.
- His desire for, 620-25, 629
- intensity of pain, 551 f., 626 f.
- instrumental cause of salvation, 599 f.
- love and, 608 ff., 644
- merit and, 562-67
- necessity of, 547 f.
- the place, 553
- a sacrifice, 588-93
- satisfaction and, 562 f., 567-88
- suffering of the saints and, 597-99
- victory over death, 616 f., 646, 652-54
- victory over sin, 616-18, 645-50
- victory over the devil, 617 f., 645, 648-50
- by way of liberation, 601 f.

Passions, the: in Christ, 416 f.; kinds of, 416
Pascal, glory of the saints, 136
Paschal candle, blessing of, 660
Paschal lamb, 495
Patriarchs
- Christ as head of, 337
- delivery from hell, 660 f.
- grace of, 394
- members of the Church, 318
- merits of, 188 f., 194-97
- predestination of, 223

Patrology and Christ's divinity, 31 f.
Paul, St. (apostle): authority of Christ, 59; beatific vision of, 273, 354, 356, 672; the divinity of Christ, 25-27; on hope, 61; mystical body of Christ, 311-14
Paul IV (pope), condemnation of the Socinians, 568
Paul of Samosata, 110
Paul of the Cross, St., 644
Peace, 633: in Christ, 633 ff., 644
Pelagians, errors of, 535
Pelagius, errors of, 589
Peltzer, 436 and note
Penance, wanting in Christ, 267, 269, 275 f.
Pentecost, 672 f.
Per se predication, modes of, 176-78
Persecutors of Christ, 558-61: sin of the, 560 f., 573
Person
- attributes of, 123, 126
- composition of Christ's, 173-75
- definition of, 124, 126, 144 ff., 171
- hypostasis and, 173
- incommunicability of, 126 f., 204
- independence of, 130-33, 143
- meaning of the term, 119, 121 and note, 122-27, 130-33, 138
- moral aspect of, 130-44
- nature and, 122-29, 218-20, 424 f., 431-44; *see also* Personality
- ontological aspect of, 130 ff., 138, 143 ff.
- psychological aspect of, 130-36, 138-44
- suppositum and, 173, 425-28, 435 and note
- theories concerning, 130 f., 139 ff.
- *see also* Suppositum

Personality
- Billot's theory of, 145, 153-60, 429 f.
- Cajetan's theory of, 145, 153 f., 158-72, 432, 437
- Capreolus' theory of, 145, 154, 159
- of Christ, 137-39
- definitions of, 119, 121 and note, 144 ff., 164 f., 171: *see also* Person
- dependence on God, 134-37
- existence and, 429-38
- Gunther's theory of, 130, 139-41
- independence of, 130-33, 143
- individuality and, 119 f., 125 f.
- Rosmini's theory of, 130, 139, 141 f.
- scholastic theories concerning, 144-72

Personality (*continued*)
  Scotus' theory of, 144 f. and note, 147-51
  Suarez' theory of, 151-53
  theories concerning, 130 f., 139 ff.; *see also* Person and nature
  vicious, 133 f.
  virtuous, 134-37
Pesch, satisfaction of Christ, 585
Petavius, Christ's free will, 444 f., 448
Peter, St.: confession of Christ's divinity, 21; predestination of, 83 f., 87 f.
Peter Lombard: knowledge of Christ, 364, 369; the redemption, 545 f.
Phantasms and Christ's infused knowledge, 381 f.
Phenomenalism, 142 f.
Philosophy: and speculative theology, 10, 34; traditional, 143 ff.
Photinus, error of, 234, 238 and note
Pilate, condemnation of Christ, 615
Pius II (pope), blood of Christ, 228, 230
Pius IX (pope): divine mysteries, 36; Gunther condemned by, 140; the Immaculate Conception, 514 f., 692, 698; Mary's divine maternity, 690 f.; Mary's fullness of grace, 698 f.
Pius X (pope): condemnation of Modernism, 114, 536, 569; merits of the Blessed Virgin, 66, 598, 705, 708
Pius XI (pope): kingship of Christ, 527, 677 f., 680-82; Mary coredemptress, 705, 714 note; merit of Mary, 707 f.; necessity of Christ's incarnation, 67; priesthood of Christ, 492, 497
Pius XII (pope), 340 note
Plato: divine goodness, 46; on the ideal teacher, 355 note
Platonists, error of the, 221 f.
Plotinus, on virtue, 269
Polycarp, St.: the redemption, 543 f.
Pope, the: head of the Church, 328 f.; power of the, 681; secretly heretical, 319
Power, divine, 303 f.
Powers of Christ, 390-400, 681 f.: judiciary, 527, 679, 681 f., 684-86
Prado, Norbert del, 144
Prayer, merit of, 196 and note
Prayer of Christ, 400, 489-91: efficacy of, 482, 491; in the Garden, 409 f., 490;
Prayer of Christ (*continued*)
    in heaven, 489 f.; for Himself, 490 f.; for us, 482, 489 f.
Preaching, before the written word, 389
Predestination, 50, 86 f., 90-93, 243
  of the Blessed Virgin, 510 f.
  of Christ, 321, 498, 507-15: and our predestination, 511-15; and St. Joseph's predestination, 716 f.
  grace of, 324
  gratuitous, 514
  of the Incarnation, 86-93
  meaning of the term, 509
  and merits of Christ, 480-83, 512-15, 606 f., 713 f. and note
  a mystery, 447, 514
  of the patriarchs, 223
  of St. Joseph, 716 f.
Presumption, removed by the Incarnation, 64
Priam, beauty of, 406
Pride: removed by the Incarnation, 64; victory over, 616, 650
Priesthood of Christ, 492-99: eternal, 496-98; and kingship of Christ, 683 f.; and sacrifice, 589-93
Priests, mediators, 524 f.
Prime matter, 434
Principium quod, 155 f. and note
Propassions, in Christ, 416 f.
Prophecy, gift of, 283: in Mary, 702
Prophets, mediators, 524 f.
Protestants (early), the redemption, 535, 567 f.
Protestants (liberal): the redemption, 535, 567-69; sacrifice of Christ, 588 f.
Prudence: infused, 278; kinds of, 366; virtue of, 270
Purgatory, souls in, 662

Quesnal, membership in the Church, 315-17
Quierzy, Council of: universality of redemption, 605

Raynaud, Theophile: free will of Christ, 446; happiness and sadness of Christ, 636, 642
Reason, higher and lower, 553 and note 639 f.
Reconciliation to God, 602 f.

Redemption
 eauses of, 321
 doctrine of the Church, 535 f.
 efficiency of, 562-600
 errors concerning, 535 f.
 essence of, 474
 the Incarnation and, 93 f., 96 f.
 the kingship of Christ and, 678, 683 f.
 meaning of, 532 ff.
 motive of, 537
 mystery of love, 533-35, 537, 608 ff.
 necessity of, 532
 objective and subjective, 533 note, 563
 order of, 547, 562 f., 572 note, 600
 the Passion and, 547 ff.
 payment to the devil and, 545, 593, 595
 testimony of Scripture, 539-43, 569
 testimony of tradition, 543-46, 569 f.
 value of, 547
 various aspects of, 536 f.
 by way of efficiency, 547, 562 f., 572 note, 599 f.
 by way of liberation, 547, 562 f., 572 note, 593-95, 600
 by way of merit, 547, 562-67, 572 note, 600
 by way of sacrifice, 547, 562 f., 572 note, 588-93, 600
 by way of satisfaction, 547, 562 f., 567-88, 595, 600
 universality of, 603-607
Religious life, 647: obligation of embracing the, 413 note
Renan: denial of Christ's divinity, 13, 17; nobility of Christ, 7; virtues of Christ, 267
Renouvier, rational phenomenalism of, 142
Reparation, value of, 68, 71-74
Resurrection of Christ, the, 663-69
 fittingness of, 664
 His manifestations after, 666-69
 motive of credibility, 652 f.
 necessity of, 663 f.
 our resurrection and, 653 f., 669
 victory over death, 616 f., 650-54
Resurrection of the just: and Christ's resurrection, 653 f., 669; at Christ's resurrection, 665
Rex, 679
Ricardus, intensity of Christ's grace, 291
Richard, blood of Christ, 228 and note
Roschini, motive of the Incarnation, 102 f.
Rosmini: errors of, 111, 137; theory of personality, 130, 139, 141 f.
Rossi, J. F.: 696
Rupert, Abbot: Christ's appearance to Mary, 666 f.

Sacraments, the, 602, 655
Sacred Heart: adoration of, 518, 520; devotion to, 519 f.
Sacrifice: definition of, 590; and merit, 562 f.; necessity for, 493; proof of love, 572 note; satisfaction and, 562 f.
Sacrifice of Christ, 588-93
 applied in the Mass, 497, 543, 583, 591, 647
 errors concerning, 588
 four ends of, 591
 in heaven, 688
 His priesthood and, 589-92
 the Last Supper and, 592 f.
 love and, 610 ff.
Sacrifice of the Mass
 application of Calvary, 497, 543, 583, 591, 647
 Council of Trent on, 396, 493
 the end of the world and, 496
 institution of, 624
 merited by Christ, 583
 offered by Christ, 688
 blood sacrificed at, 227-30
 same as Calvary, 495, 592
Sacrifices of the Old Testament, 588, 591
Sadness: of Christ, 551-53, 627-44; and happiness, 620 f., 636 f., 640 f.
Saints
 compared to the Blessed Virgin, 698 f.
 contemplation of, 355-58
 faith and knowledge of, 358 f.
 infused knowledge of, 363, 365 f. and notes, 484
 joy and sorrow of, 644
 merits of, 597-99, 707
 personality of, 134-37
 relics of, 523
 sufferings of, 597-99
Salmanticenses
 circumstances of the Incarnation, 192
 efficacious grace, 482

Salmanticenses (*continued*)
the Fall, 320
grace of the angels, 330
habitual grace in Christ, 258 note, 263
kingship of Christ, 680 f.
knowledge of Christ, 380
moral imperfections and venial sin, 412 f. and notes
motive for the Incarnation, 97, 322-24
priesthood of Christ, 497, 526
satisfaction of Christ, 585
suffering of Christ, 635, 640 f. and note, 643
Salmeron, beatific vision of Christ, 632, 636
Salvation: the Incarnation as means of, 54-75, 93 f., 96 f.; other means of, 56 f.
Sanctity: of Christ, 243 f., 247-309, 391, 407-15; conditions for, 252 f.; definition of, 249 f.
Sanday, divinity of Christ, 13, 18
Satisfaction
of the Blessed Virgin, 66, 572, 598 f., 714
condign (perfect), 65-67, 71-75
contrition and, 572
justice and, 585-88
kinds of, 65-67
merit and, 74, 402 f. and note, 562 f., 571, 577
necessity of, 66
by the non-incarnate Word, 75
rendered by the Incarnation, 64-76
value of, 68, 71-74
for venial sin, 73
vicarious, 66
Satisfaction of Christ, 66, 402 f., 562 f., 567-88
application of, 606 f. and note
condign, 572, 583 f.
errors concerning, 567-69
infinite value of, 71 f., 577-88
justice and, 585-88
love and, 533-35, 537: St. John on, 540
our satisfaction and, 575 f., 583
in Scripture and tradition, 569 f.
superabundant, 583 f., 586-88, 595
universal, 584 f., 587 f.
vicarious, 532
Saturninus, heresy of, 225
Savior, title of Christ, 96, 101, 498
Schell, knowledge of Christ, 344
Scotists, motive for the Incarnation, 81-85, 93 f.
Scotus
the active intellect, 368
adoptive sonship of Christ, 505
Billot and, 153 f.
essence and existence, 149 f., 429
faith and the beatific vision, 273
grace of the angels, 329 f.
grief of Christ, 638
the Immaculate Conception, 693
intensity of Christ's grace, 291
the motive for the Incarnation, 76-78, 81 and note, 84 note, 88, 90-95, 507
necessity of the Incarnation, 99 f.
predestination, 88, 90-93: of Christ, 507
satisfaction of Christ, 577
Suarez and, 151
theory of personality, 144 f. and note, 147-51
two existences in Christ, 429
Scripture: divine inspiration of, 12; interpretation of, 11 f.
Sergius of Constantinople, 439
Sermon on the Mount, the Messiahship of Christ, 14
Serra, justification of adults, 265
Simeon, prophecy of, 60, 613
Simon Magus, heresy of, 225
Simon of Cyrene, 225
Sin
of Christ's persecutors, 560 f., 573
the condoning of, 74 f.
of the elect, 90 note
gravity of: shown by the Passion, 610 f.
kinds of, 710
liberation from, 593-95, 601 f.
mortal: infinite gravity of, 67-72
original, 338, 105 f. and note
permitted by God, 411 note, 412, 455
practical judgment and, 466
reason of the Incarnation, 76-98, 102-106, 322-26, 507, 618
removed by the Incarnation, 105 f. and note
venial: gravity of, 73; and moral imperfections, 412 f. and notes; satisfaction for, 73
victory over, 616-18, 645-50
Sinibaldi, G.: St. Joseph, 717

Sinners, membership in the Church, 315, 317
Socinians, errors of, 110, 535 f.: the redemption, 568, 570; sacrifice of Christ, 588
Socratic method, 388 note
Son, scriptural meaning of the word, 18
Sonship: adoptive, 209 f. and note, 252, 500-506; natural and adoptive, 502
Sonship of Christ, 209 f., 252-54, 498: and the beatific vision, 359; not adoptive, 500-502, 505 f.; and predestination, 509-12
Sophronius, knowledge of Christ, 347
Sorrow: of Christ, 361-63, 417 f., 551; and joy, 361 f., 642: in Christ, 621, 632-44
Soteriology, 8 f.
Soto, Christ's love of God, 467
Soul, relation to the body, 236 f.
Soul of Christ
  assumed by the Word, 230 f.: order of assumption, 232 ff.
  defects of, 407-19
  higher and lower parts of, 553, 637-43
  passibility of, 416 f.
  power of, 390-400
  St. Leo on, 236
  sublimity of, 236
  suffering of, 552 f., 627 f., 635-43
  united to the body, 175
Stabat Mater, 619
Stephen, St.: death of, 632
Stevens, divinity of Christ, 13, 18
Stuart, empiric phenomenalism of, 142
Suarez
  Billot and, 153 f.
  the cause of Christ's death, 555 note
  essence and existence, 429, 435
  free will of Christ, 445
  grace of the angels, 329 f.
  grief of Christ, 638
  habitual grace in Christ, 258 note
  headship of Christ, 320
  heretical popes, 319
  intensity of Christ's grace, 304
  merits of Christ, 190, 193
  motive for the Incarnation, 84 note
  necessity of the Incarnation, 55
  predestination of the Blessed Virgin, 510
  satisfaction of Christ, 585 and note
Suarez (*continued*)
  Scotus and 151
  theory of personality, 144 f., 151-53
  two existences in Christ, 429 f.
Subordinationists, errors of the, 535
Subsistence: and existence, 156, 165-72, 432-37; meaning of the term, 435 note; and suppositum, 156, 165-72, 435 and note; *see also* Suppositum
Suffering, means of salvation, 101
Supposita, incommunicability of, 126 f., 204
Suppositum
  attributes of, 123, 126
  definition of, 123
  essence and, 156
  existence and, 144-73, 218-20, 436 f.
  hypostatic union in the, 172 f., 425
  nature and, 122-29, 218-20, 430-32
  person and, 173, 425-28, 435 and note
  subsistence and, 156, 165-72, 435 and note
  see also Person
Sylvius, Francis: congruous merit, 196; grace in Christ, 259; grief of Christ, 553 note; kingship of Christ, 680
Synave, 436 and note

Taine, empiric phenomenalism of, 142
Talhofer, sacrifice in heaven, 688
Temperance, virtue of, 271, 398
Terms, abstract and concrete, 421
Tertullian: Christ's descent into hell, 660; nature of Christ, 31; sinlessness of Mary, 697
Themistius, errors of, 344
Theodore of Mopsuestia, 110, 410, 414
Theological Summa of St. Thomas, division of, 5-9
Theology
  divisions of, 5 f.
  method of, 629 f.
  moral and dogmatic, 5 f.
  positive: and the history of dogma, 11; and the Incarnation, 10 ff.
  speculative: and the Incarnation, 34 ff.; method of, 10, 34
  unity of, 6
Theophoron (title for Christ), 120
Theophylactus, death of Christ, 651
Theresa, St., 357

Thomas, St.: contemplation of, 356; grace of, 289; works of, 436 and note
Thomists, disagreement between, 96-98
Time: discrete and continuous, 378 f. and note; Jewish computation of, 658
Tiphanus, nature and person, 152 note
Tischendorf, 27
Toledo, Council of, 35 f.: the Incarnation of the Word, 203, 205; the redemption, 536
Toletus: kingship of Christ, 680; multiplication of supposita, 208 f.
Tongues, gift of, 282, 363, 365
Tournely: Christ's free will, 446, 453; God's freedom of pardoning, 56; necessity of the Incarnation, 55
Tradition: and Christ's divinity, 31-33; and interpretation of Scripture, 11 f.
Traducianism, 141
Transmutation of creatures, 392 f.
Trent, Council of
  blood of Christ, 228-30
  Christ the victim, 493
  death of Christ, 452
  effects of redemption, 601
  headship of Christ, 312 f.
  merit of Christ, 474, 479: and our justification, 564
  predestination, 482
  priesthood of Christ, 492
  the Real Presence, 313
  the redemption, 536
  sacrifice of Christ, 589: and the Last Supper, 592 f.
  satisfaction of Christ, 583 f.
  sinlessness of Mary, 697
  universality of redemption, 604 f.
  victim of the Mass, 396, 493
Trinity, the
  adoptive sonship, 503 f.
  Christ's infused knowledge of, 380 f.
  divine missions of, 205 f.
  first cause of redemption 596 f.
  Gunther's theory of, 139
  incommunicability of Deity, 204 and note
  internal operations of, 204
  operations *ad extra,* 205 f., 503
  persons and nature, 428, 433
  Rosmini's theory of, 141
Tully, the passions, 416

Ubiquists, 390
Unbaptized, the, 662
Understanding, gift of, 276, 279, 378
Union: grace of: *see* Grace of union; hypostatic: *see* Hypostatic union; meaning of the term, 179 f.; of body and soul, 178 f.: in Christ, 175
Unitarians, errors of the, 110

Valentia: beatific vision of Christ, 632, 636; grace of the angels, 329 f.; necessity of the Incarnation, 55
Valentinus, errors of, 109 f., 226
Vasquez
  Christ's prayer for us, 489
  free will of Christ, 445 f., 452
  grace of Christ, 336: intensity of, 304
  grace of the angels, 330
  grace of union, 338
  knowledge of Christ, 381
  satisfaction of Christ, 585
  universality of redemption, 604
Vatican Council
  condemnation of Kant, 132 f.
  divine mysteries, 36, 633
  freedom of creation, 48, 458
  interpretation of Scripture, 12
  Mary's assumption, 703, 721 f., 724
  the redemption, 535 f., 576
Vexilla Regis, 619
Victory of Christ, 616-18, 645-55, 683
  over death, 96, 98, 101, 616 f., 646: by the Ascension, 670; and His kingship, 683; by the Resurrection, 650-54
  over the devil, 617 f., 645, 648-50, 683
  Mary's assumption and, 703, 723-25
  over sin, 616-18, 645-50, 683
Victim souls, 576
Vigilius (pope), order of Christ's assumption of human nature, 232, 235
Vincent de Paul, St., 136
Vincent of Asturia, grace of the angels, 330
Virtues
  of Christ, 266 ff., 563, 610: and the gifts, 276 f.
  the gifts and, 276 f.
  infused and acquired, 270-72
  moral, 270: exemplified in the Incarnation, 63
  opposite, 268

Voluntarism, 99 f.
Volusianus, 45, 52
Vosté, J. M.: the Immaculate Conception, 696 and note; martyrdom and sacrifice, 591; resurrection of Christ, 652 and note

Weiss, B.: denial of Christ's divinity, 13, 17
Wellhausen, denial of Christ's Messiahship, 13, 17
Wendt, H.: denial of Christ's divinity, 13, 17
Will: freedom of, 442 f., 451-56, 459-66; natural and rational, 441, 469-71
Will of Christ, 231, 399 f., 438-71
  in conformity with God's will, 400
  Council of Constantinople on, 342
  errors concerning, 342
  freedom of, 441 ff.
  impeccability and, 411 f., 441-69
  inefficacious, 470
  merit and, 485
  no contrariety in, 470 f.
  sensitive, 440, 469-71
William of Occam, 636
William of Paris, satisfaction of Christ, 577
Wisdom, gift of, 276, 278, 378
Word, the: non-incarnate, 75; recipient of human nature, 40 f.
Wyclif, necessity of the Incarnation, 54

Ysambert, free will of Christ, 446

Zapletal, 11 f.